ECONOMIC
REPORT
OF THE
PRESIDENT

TRANSMITTED TO THE CONGRESS

FEBRUARY 2015

TOGETHER WITH
THE ANNUAL REPORT
OF THE
COUNCIL OF ECONOMIC ADVISERS

C O N T E N T S

---

*For a detailed table of contents of the Council's Report, see page 11.

ECONOMIC REPORT
OF THE
PRESIDENT

ECONOMIC REPORT OF THE PRESIDENT

As I send you this *Economic Report of the President*, the United States has just concluded a breakthrough year. In 2014, our economy added jobs at the fastest pace since the 1990s. The unemployment rate plunged to its lowest point in over 6 years, far faster than economists predicted. Ten million Americans gained the security of health coverage. And we continued to cut our dependence on foreign oil and invest in renewable energy, making us number one in the world in oil, gas, and wind power.

These achievements took place against a backdrop of longer-term economic strength. Since the crisis, we've seen our deficits cut by two-thirds, our stock market double, and health care inflation at its lowest rate in 50 years. The housing market is rebounding. Manufacturers are adding jobs. More Americans are finishing college than ever before.

Now America is poised for another good year, as long as Washington works to keep this progress going. But even as the economic recovery is touching more lives, we need to do more to restore the link between hard work and opportunity for every American. That's the idea behind middle-class economics—the simple fact that our country does best when everyone has a fair shot, does their fair share, and plays by the same set of rules.

Over the course of this year, I will continue to put forward ideas to make that fundamental value a reality—not just so that more Americans can share in their country's success, but so that more Americans can contribute to their country's success. At this moment when our economy is growing and creating jobs, we've got to work twice as hard, especially in Washington, to build on our momentum. And I will not let politics or partisanship roll back the progress we've achieved on so many fronts.

I want to work with the Congress to invest in middle-class economics in three key ways.

First, let's help working families achieve greater security in a world of constant change. That means giving Americans the peace of mind that comes with knowing they'll be able to afford childcare, college, health care, a home, and retirement.

At a time when having both parents work is an economic necessity for many families, high-quality, affordable childcare isn't a nice-to-have—it's a must-have. That's why I've proposed tripling the maximum child tax credit to $3,000 per child per year, and creating more slots in childcare programs nationwide.

Meanwhile, we're the only advanced country in the world that doesn't guarantee workers either paid sick leave or paid maternity leave. Let's help more States adopt paid leave laws and put it to a vote in Washington too, because no parent should ever have to choose between earning a paycheck and taking care of a sick child.

Of course, nothing helps families make ends meet like raising wages. We still need to pass a law that guarantees women equal pay for equal work. We still need to make sure employees get the overtime they've earned. We still have a minimum wage of $7.25 per hour. That means minimum-wage workers are actually earning 20 percent less than they were when President Reagan was in office. It's time to give some of America's hardest-working people a raise, because wages of $14,500 a year are simply not enough to support a family.

In a 21st century economy, we should lower taxes on working families and make mortgage premiums more affordable, so responsible families can own their own homes. And we should strengthen programs like Social Security, Medicare, and Medicaid that help workers save for retirement and protect them from the harshest adversities. These ideas will make a meaningful difference in the lives of millions of Americans, and I look forward to working with the Congress to get them done.

Second, middle-class economics means helping more Americans upgrade their skills so that they can earn higher wages down the road.

By the end of the decade, two in three jobs will require some higher education. Yet far too many young people are priced out of college. That can't stand in the 21st century, and that's why my Administration has announced a bold new plan to offer 2 free years of community college to responsible students. Let's work together to make college as free and universal as high school, because a modern economy requires a highly educated workforce.

While we strengthen the higher education system, my Administration is working to update our job training system and connect community colleges with local employers to train workers directly for existing, high-paying jobs. And I've encouraged more companies to offer educational benefits and paid apprenticeships so more workers have a chance to earn a higher-paying job even if they don't have a higher education.

Finally, as we better train our workers, we need to ensure that our economy keeps creating high-skilled, high-wage jobs for our workers to fill. That means building the most competitive economy anywhere, so that more businesses locate and hire in the United States.

Let's start by making sure that our businesses have 21st century infrastructure—modern ports, stronger bridges, better roads, clean water, clean energy, faster trains, and the fastest internet. A bipartisan infrastructure plan would create thousands of middle-class jobs and support economic growth for decades to come.

Investments in science, technology, and research and development can fuel new inventions and breakthroughs that will keep American businesses one step ahead of the competition. And protecting a free and open internet, and extending its reach to every classroom and community in America, will ensure that the next generation of digital innovators and entrepreneurs have the platform to keep reshaping our world.

At a time when 95 percent of the world's consumers live outside our borders, new trade agreements would help American businesses reach new markets and put stronger environmental and labor standards in place, to ensure that all countries are playing by the same, fair set of rules. The trade deals that my Administration is negotiating in the Atlantic and the Pacific regions would do just that.

And to make our economy more competitive, let's build a tax code that truly helps middle-class families get ahead. Let's reform our business tax system to close wasteful loopholes, lower the rate, and simplify the system so small business owners spend less time on accounting and more time running their businesses. And let's reform our broken immigration system, so the United States continues to be the number one destination for highly-skilled immigrants.

Over the past 6 years, America has risen from recession freer to write our own future than any other nation on Earth. A new foundation is laid. A new future is ready to be written. It's up to all of us—Democrats, Republicans, and Independents—to write it together.

THE WHITE HOUSE
FEBRUARY 2015

THE ANNUAL REPORT
OF THE
COUNCIL OF ECONOMIC ADVISERS

LETTER OF TRANSMITTAL

COUNCIL OF ECONOMIC ADVISERS
Washington, D.C., February 19, 2015

MR. PRESIDENT:

The Council of Economic Advisers herewith submits its 2015 Annual Report in accordance of the Employment Act of 1946 as amended by the Full Employment and Balanced Growth Act of 1978.

Sincerely yours,

Jason Furman
Chairman

Betsey Stevenson
Member

Maurice Obstfeld
Member

CONTENTS

APPENDIXES

FIGURES

TABLES

BOXES

C H A P T E R   1

MIDDLE-CLASS ECONOMICS: THE ROLE OF PRODUCTIVITY, INEQUALITY, AND PARTICIPATION

As the 2015 *Economic Report of the President* goes to press, the U.S. economic recovery continues to accelerate. The economy grew at an annual rate of 2.8 percent over the past two years, compared with 2.1 percent in the first three-and-one-half years of the recovery. The speedup is particularly clear in the U.S. labor market, where the pace of job gains has improved each year since President Obama took office. The American private sector has created 11.8 million new jobs over 59 straight months, the longest streak on record. 2014 was the best year for overall job growth since 1999, ushering in 3.1 million new jobs, and the unemployment rate fell 1.3 percentage points between 2013 and 2014, the largest decline in three decades. A reduction in long-term unemployment, one of the economy's major post-crisis challenges, accounts for most of the fall in the unemployment rate.

As the U.S. recovery has progressed, the economy has grown in a more sustainable way than before the global financial crisis began. In fact, the United States has improved several structural imbalances that jeopardized the economy's stability prior to the crisis. The domestic energy production boom has reduced U.S. dependence on foreign oil, helping to narrow the current account deficit and reduce U.S. dependence on foreign borrowing. Health-care prices have been growing at the lowest rate in nearly 50 years. The Federal Budget deficit has fallen at the fastest pace since the post-World War II demobilization, and households are spending less of their income servicing debts than they have in decades.

But one key benchmark of the economy goes beyond increases in national income accounts and decreases in financial deficits: the well-being of the middle class and those working to get into the middle class.

It is essential that a broad range of households share in the United States' resurgent growth. This year's *Report* views the recovery through the lens of the typical middle-class American family. It begins with a review of recent economic progress and provides historical and international context for the key factors impacting middle-class incomes: productivity growth, labor force participation, and income inequality. The President's approach to economic policies, what he terms "middle-class economics," is designed to improve these elements and ensure that Americans of all income levels share in the accelerating recovery.

The Progress of the U.S. Economic Recovery

After the global financial crisis, the United States and many other countries faced obstacles to recovery that were more challenging than those posed by a normal cyclical recession. Despite being hit particularly hard by the financial crisis, the United States has recovered faster than many of its developed-world counterparts. The recession began with a collapse in household wealth and global trade that initially exceeded the declines at the onset of the Great Depression, as shown in Figure 1-1a and Figure 1-1b. The headwinds to recovery included weak bank balance sheets that constrained credit supply, highly indebted consumers that constrained credit demand, and substantial investment overhang in key cyclical sectors such as housing.

Figure 1-1a
Global Trade Flows in the Great Depression and Great Recession

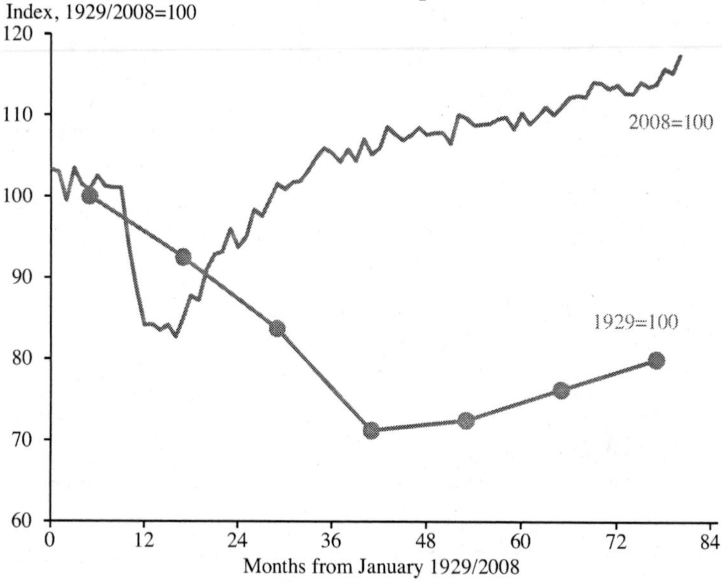

Note: Red markers represent annual averages.
Source: CPB World Trade Monitor; Statistical Office of the United Nations.

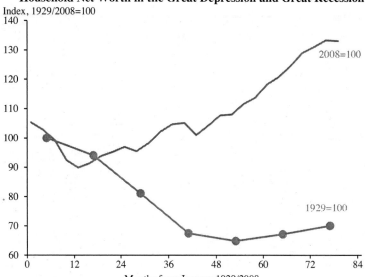

Figure 1-1b
Household Net Worth in the Great Depression and Great Recession

Months from January 1929/2008

Note: Red markers represent annual averages.
Source: Federal Reserve Board of Governors; Mishkin (1978).

Table 1-1

Components of U.S. Real GDP Growth,
Percent Change at an Annual Rate

	Start of Recovery (2009:Q2-2012:Q4)	2013 and 2014 (2012:Q4-2014:Q4)
Gross Domestic Product	**2.1**	**2.8**
Consumer Spending	2.0	2.8
Business Fixed Investment	5.2	5.1
Residential Investment	5.9	4.7
Exports	7.4	3.5
Imports	6.8	3.9
Federal Government	- 0.6	- 3.1
State & Local Government	- 2.2	1.1

Source: Bureau of Economic Analysis, National Income and Product Accounts.

Box 1-1: Macroeconomic Rebalancing

A broad set of economic structural imbalances that pre-dated the financial crisis have improved in the recovery. The United States has reduced its indebtedness on four levels: in international trade (as a net recipient of global capital flows), in gross national saving (as a result of reduced Budget deficits), in the household sector, and in the private-business sector. On top of recent acceleration in U.S. output and employment growth, these structural improvements lay the foundation for more sustainable growth beyond the current business cycle.

On the international side, the current account deficit as a share of GDP—a measure of U.S. net transactions with the rest of the world in goods, services, and income—increased steadily for nearly two decades, but fell in the Great Recession and has continued to drift down in the recovery. Recently, the deficit fell to the smallest share of GDP since the 1990s. Drivers of the recent decline include the domestic energy production boom and an increase in domestic saving that has reduced the U.S. need for foreign financing.

Domestically, gross saving has increased as a share of the economy, driven by the reduction in Federal dissaving amid the fastest pace of deficit reduction since the demobilization after World War II. The pace of discretionary spending reductions was faster than optimal, creating challenges for growth. However, when taken together with factors such

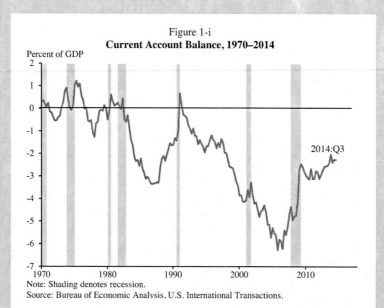

Figure 1-i
Current Account Balance, 1970–2014

Percent of GDP

2014:Q3

Note: Shading denotes recession.
Source: Bureau of Economic Analysis, U.S. International Transactions.

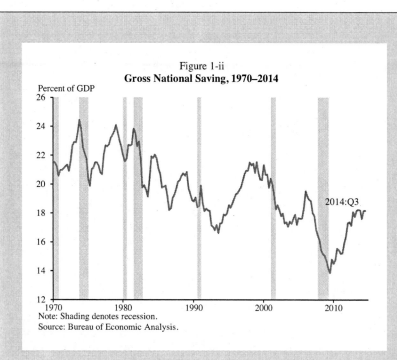

Figure 1-ii
Gross National Saving, 1970–2014

Percent of GDP

2014:Q3

Note: Shading denotes recession.
Source: Bureau of Economic Analysis.

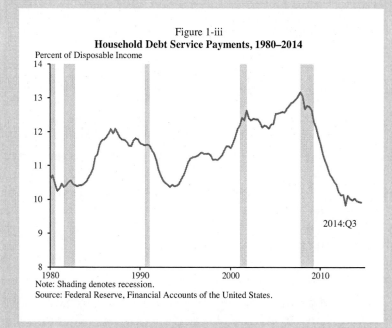

Figure 1-iii
Household Debt Service Payments, 1980–2014

Percent of Disposable Income

2014:Q3

Note: Shading denotes recession.
Source: Federal Reserve, Financial Accounts of the United States.

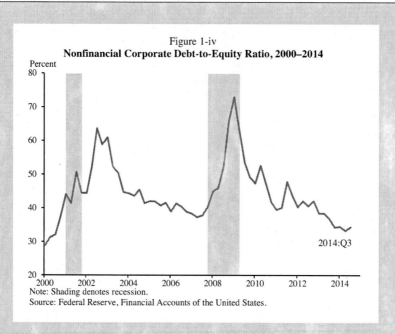

Figure 1-iv
Nonfinancial Corporate Debt-to-Equity Ratio, 2000–2014

Percent

2014:Q3

Note: Shading denotes recession.
Source: Federal Reserve, Financial Accounts of the United States.

as revenue increases from high-income households and slower health cost growth, the economy is in a more sustainable position today compared with a few years ago.

While many households still face challenges, the aggregate ratio of debt-to-disposable income in the household sector has decreased to a level last seen in 2002, as households have both increased their savings and reduced their borrowing. The combination of lower debt levels and lower interest rates has reduced the aggregate value of households' debt-service payments to 9.9 percent of disposable income, the lowest level since at least 1980. America's corporations have also partially shed their debt burdens. Corporate debt-to-equity ratios in the non-financial sector have retraced all of the increase that resulted from the crisis.

The recovery's challenges were compounded by unprecedented State and local government spending cuts that dragged on growth through the first few years of the recovery. A wide range of shocks and slowdowns in other countries have also restrained the U.S. recovery.

The Recovery in GDP and Labor Markets

Although there is more work to do, the U.S. economy has managed a lasting and growing recovery amid these challenges. Despite the steeper initial declines, both trade and wealth recovered faster after the Great Recession than during the Great Depression. In 2013 and 2014, the U.S. economy grew 0.7 percentage point faster per year than in the first three-and-one-half years of the recovery. A large increase in personal consumption growth and a shift from State and local contraction to expansion contributed to the pickup over this period. More recently, growth in 2014 was aided by a shift toward a more neutral stance for Federal fiscal policy, an important reminder of the need for policymakers to avoid returning to the harmful impact of sequestration and fiscal brinksmanship.

The recovery's strength has been particularly pronounced in the labor market. The pace of total job growth rose to 260,000 a month in 2014, up from 199,000 a month in 2013, as shown in Figure 1-2.

As recently as 2013, most forecasters expected that the unemployment rate would not fall to 5.6 percent until after 2017—but it did so in December 2014, as shown in Figure 1-3. The labor force participation rate has stabilized since fall 2013. Long-term unemployment and the number of workers employed part-time for economic reasons – while still elevated – have also declined.

These labor market improvements have begun to translate into wage gains for middle-class workers. Average earnings for production and non-supervisory workers, shown in Figure 1-4, function as a reasonable proxy

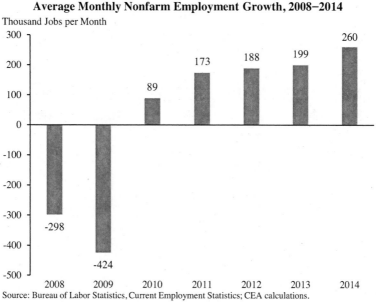

Figure 1-2
Average Monthly Nonfarm Employment Growth, 2008–2014

Source: Bureau of Labor Statistics, Current Employment Statistics; CEA calculations.

Figure 1-3
Unemployment Rate and Consensus Forecasts, 2008–2014

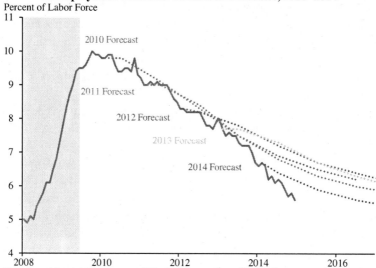

Percent of Labor Force

Note: Annual forecasts are current as of March of the stated year. Shading denotes recession.
Source: Blue Chip Economic Indicators; Bureau of Labor Statistics, Current Population Survey.

Figure 1-4
**Real Hourly Earnings,
Production & Nonsupervisory Workers, 2010–2014**

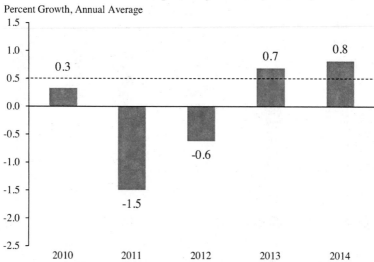

Percent Growth, Annual Average

Note: Dashed line represents 2001-2007 average.
Source: Bureau of Labor Statistics, Current Employment Statistics; CEA calculations.

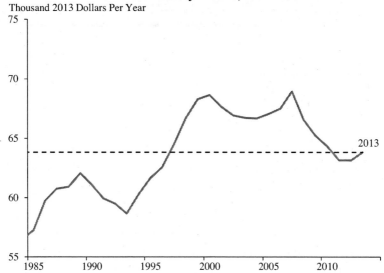

Figure 1-5
Real Median Family Income, 1985–2013

Thousand 2013 Dollars Per Year

Note: Dashed line traces the 2013 level of real median family income for comparison purposes.
Source: U.S. Census Bureau, Current Population Reports.

for median wages. Real hourly earnings for these workers rose 0.7 percent in 2013 and 0.8 percent in 2014.

This real wage growth, however, still falls well short of what is needed to make up for decades of sub-par growth. Real median family incomes were at mid-1990s levels in 2013, as shown in Figure 1-5. There is no denying the strength of the aggregate recovery, but its benefits have not yet been fully shared with middle-class families.

A Brief History of Middle-Class Incomes in the Postwar Period

The ultimate test of an economy's performance is the well-being of its middle class. This in turn has been shaped by three factors: how productivity has grown, how income is distributed, and how many people are participating in the labor force. Although many of these factors have evolved continuously, varying from year to year, it is instructive to divide the post-World War II years into three periods that capture major differences among the trends in these three variables. Specifically, these periods are: the Age of Shared Growth from 1948 to 1973, where movements in productivity, participation, and distribution aligned; the Age of Expanded Participation from 1973 to 1995, when women entered the labor force at a rapid pace but

Table 1-2

Table 1-2

Middle-Class Income Growth and its Determinants, 1948–2013

	Age of Shared Growth 1948-1973	Age of Expanded Participation 1973-1995	Age of Productivity Recovery 1995-2013
Real Middle-Class Income Growth			
Average Household Income for the Bottom 90 Percent *(World Top Incomes Database)*	2.8%	-0.4%	-0.2%
Median Household Income *(Census Bureau)*	N/A	0.2%	0.0%
Median Household Income with Benefits *(CBO, adj. for household size)*	N/A	0.4%	0.4%
Median Household Income with Gov't Transfers/Taxes *(CBO, adj. for household size)*	N/A	0.7%	1.3%
Productivity Growth (annual rates)			
Labor Productivity Growth	2.8%	1.4%	2.3%
Total Factor Productivity Growth	1.9%	0.4%	1.1%
Income Shares			
Top 1 Percent	11.3% → 7.7% -0.1 pp/yr	7.7% → 13.5% +0.3 pp/yr	13.5% → 17.5% +0.2 pp/yr
Bottom 90 Percent	66.3% → 68.1% +0.1 pp/yr	68.1% → 59.5% -0.4 pp/yr	59.5% → 53.0% -0.4 pp/yr
Labor Force Participation Rate			
Overall	59% → 61% +0.1 pp/yr	61% → 67% +0.3 pp/yr	67% → 63% -0.2 pp/yr
Prime Age Male (25-54)	97% → 95% -0.1 pp/yr	95% → 92% -0.2 pp/yr	92% → 88% -0.2 pp/yr
Prime Age Female (25-54)	35% → 52% +0.7 pp/yr	52% → 76% +1.1 pp/yr	76% → 74% -0.1 pp/yr

Note: Income levels from the World Top Incomes Database and the Census Bureau are deflated with the CPI-U-RS price index, and income levels from the Congressional Budget Office (CBO) are deflated with the personal consumption expenditures price index. Income shares are provided by the World Top Incomes Database, cited below, median household income is provided by the U.S. Census Bureau, and median household income including benefits, transfers, and taxes is provided by CBO. CBO median income is extended before 1979 and after 2010 with the growth rate of Census median income.
Source: World Top Incomes Database; Census Bureau; Congressional Budget Office; Bureau of Labor Statistics; Bureau of Economic Analysis; CEA calculations; Saez (2015).

productivity slowed and distribution worsened; and the Age of Productivity Recovery from 1995 through 2013, when productivity improved (at least until the run-up to the financial crisis) but participation declined and income inequality continued to worsen.

The Age of Shared Growth (1948-1973)

All three factors—productivity growth, distribution, and participation—aligned to benefit the middle class from 1948 to 1973. The United States enjoyed rapid labor productivity growth, averaging 2.8 percent annually. Income inequality fell, with the share of income going to the top 1 percent falling by nearly one-third, while the share of income going to the bottom 90 percent rose slightly. Household income growth was also fueled by the increased participation of women in the workforce. Prime-age (25 to 54) female labor force participation escalated from one-third in 1948 to one-half by 1973. The combination of these three factors increased the average income for the bottom 90 percent of households by 2.8 percent a year over this period. This measure functions as a decent proxy for the median household's income growth because it ignores the large, asymmetric changes in income for the top 10 percent of households. At this rate, incomes double every 25 years, or about once every generation.

While these levels of shared income growth and low income inequality worked to benefit the middle class, it is important to recognize that these factors do not capture the many non-economic dimensions (such as racial and gender discrimination) on which the United States has made considerable progress over the past half-century. Accordingly, while this period illustrates the combined power of productivity, income equality, and participation to benefit the middle class, it is not necessarily a model for other important aspects of domestic policy.

The Age of Expanded Participation (1973-1995)

Starting in 1973 and running through 1995, two of the three factors that had been driving middle-class incomes derailed. Labor productivity growth slowed dramatically to only 1.4 percent annually, in part due to the exhaustion of pent-up innovations from World War II, reduced public investment, dislocations associated with the breakup of the Bretton Woods international monetary system, and the oil shocks of the 1970s. Not only did the economy grow more slowly in these years, but these smaller gains were distributed increasingly unequally—the share of national income that went to the top 1 percent nearly doubled, while the share that went to the bottom 90 percent fell accordingly. As a result, productivity gains did not boost middle-class incomes and average income in the bottom 90 percent declined by 0.4 percent a year during these years. One important factor that prevented a larger fall in middle-class incomes was greater labor force participation. The share of dual-income households rose as women surged into the labor force even faster than in the Age of Shared Growth.

Some alternative and likely more accurate measures of middle-class income show slight increases during these years. Real median household income as measured by the Census Bureau rose by 0.2 percent a year from 1973 to 1995. And after including employer-paid health premiums and adjusting for changing family size, the Congressional Budget Office (CBO) estimates that median income climbed 0.4 percent a year, and 0.7 percent a year after taxes and transfers. But regardless of how it is measured, middle-class income growth clearly slowed dramatically over this period.

The Age of Productivity Recovery (1995-2013)

The third period is defined as lasting from 1995 through 2013, though it will take a longer perspective to understand whether and how the Great Recession and the current recovery fit into this period. Amid the worst recession since the Great Depression, the average real income for households in the bottom 90 percent declined at a 0.2 percent annual rate during these years. When including employer-paid health premiums and adjusting for family size, median income rose 0.4 percent a year according to CBO data, still considerably slower than in the Age of Shared Growth. Largely as a result of substantial tax cuts, post-tax and post-transfer incomes rose at a 1.3-percent average annual rate in this third period.

Labor productivity grew at a 2.3 percent annual rate over the period as a whole, near the rates achieved in the first era, fueled by a new economy that made unprecedented advances in the production and use of information technology. However, these gains did little to contribute to rising wages for the middle class as the trend of worsening inequality from the previous era continued into this period. The share of income going to the bottom 90 percent fell to 53 percent, well below the 68 percent earned by this group in 1973. Meanwhile, the labor force participation rate fell as women's entry into the workforce plateaued and even started to drift down, albeit at one-half the pace of the decline in prime-age male participation, a notable trend over the entire postwar era. After 2008, the retirement of the baby boomers added to the decline in participation.

While productivity growth was high on average from 1995 to 2013, it varied substantially within this period. It was higher from 1995 to 2005, declined prior to the start of the crisis, and then was adversely affected by the crisis itself. Understanding the degree to which the years 1995 through 2013 should be considered a single regime for the productivity growth rate, or one with an adverse break in the trend during or just before the crisis, will take many more years of data and analysis.

The Importance of Productivity, Inequality, and Participation

As productivity, the income distribution, and participation evolved over the past 65 years, middle-class incomes went from doubling once in a generation to showing almost no growth at all by some measures. But if these three factors had recently continued the strong trends observed in earlier periods, the outcome for typical families would be quite different. Four counterfactual thought experiments give a sense of the magnitudes involved in this dramatic change:

- *The impact of higher productivity growth.* What if productivity growth from 1973 to 2013 had continued at its pace from the previous 25 years? In this scenario, incomes would have been 58 percent higher in 2013. If these gains were distributed proportionately in 2013, then the median household would have had an additional $30,000 in income.

- *The impact of greater income equality.* What if inequality had not increased from 1973 to 2013, and instead the share of income going to the bottom 90 percent had remained the same? Even using the actual slow levels of productivity growth over that period, the 2013 income for the typical household would have been 18 percent, or about $9,000, higher.

- *The impact of expanded labor force participation.* What if female labor force participation had continued to grow from 1995 to 2013 at the same rate that it did from 1948 to 1995 until it reached parity with male participation? Assuming that the average earnings for working women were unchanged, and maintaining the actual histories of productivity and income distribution, the average household would have earned 6 percent more in 2013, or an additional $3,000.

- *The combined impact of all three factors.* Finally, if all three factors had aligned—if productivity had grown at its Age of Shared Growth rate, inequality had not increased, and participation had continued to rise—then these effects would have been compounded and the typical household would have seen a 98-percent increase in its income by 2013. That is an additional $51,000 a year.

In combination, these factors would have nearly doubled the typical household's income had they sustained their more favorable readings from earlier historical periods. Productivity, inequality, and participation constitute the fundamental challenges facing the future of middle-class incomes, and this year's *Report* addresses policies designed to strengthen all three. But first, this chapter situates the United States' recent progress in these dimensions in a global context.

Table 1-3

Counterfactual Scenarios for Productivity, Inequality, and Participation

Thought Experiment	Factor	Base Period	Percentage Impact on 2013 Average Income	Income Gain to Typical 2013 Household
Impact of Higher Growth	Total Factor Productivity Growth	Age of Shared Growth (1948-73)	58%	$30,000
Impact of Greater Equality	Share of Income Earned by Middle Quintile	1973	18%	$9,000
Impact of Labor Force Participation	Female Labor Force Participation Rate	Age of Shared Growth, Age of Expanded Participation (1948-95)	6%	$3,000
Combined Impact	**All of the Above**		**98%**	**$51,000**

Note: These thought experiments are intended to demonstrate the importance of these three factors for middle-class incomes. They do not consider second-order effects or interactive effects. The first thought experiment assumes that an increase in productivity is associated with an equal increase in the Census Bureau's mean household income. The second thought experiment uses the Census Bureau's mean income of the middle quintile as a proxy for median income. The third thought experiment assumes that newly-participating women will have the same average earnings as today's working women, and halts the growth of female labor force participation when it matches male participation. The first and third thought experiments assume that income gains are distributed proportionally such that mean and median incomes grow at the same rate. Dollar gains are calculated off a base of the Census Bureau's median household income in 2013. The fourth thought experiment compounds the effects of the first three.
Source: World Top Incomes Database; Census Bureau; Congressional Budget Office; Bureau of Labor Statistics, Current Population Survey; Bureau of Economic Analysis; CEA calculations.

THE DRIVERS OF MIDDLE-CLASS INCOMES: AN INTERNATIONAL COMPARISON

A wide range of advanced economies has faced similar challenges for middle-class incomes. Most of today's large advanced economies experienced rapid growth in the immediate post-World War II years followed by substantially slower growth and plateauing, as shown in Figure 1-6. That development took place relatively early in the United States (around 1973) and later in other countries (for example, around 1980 in France and Canada). In Japan, middle-class incomes slowed in the 1970s and have substantially declined over the past two decades.

Labor Productivity Growth

The first driver of incomes—labor productivity growth—underlies the progress of both potential GDP and family income. Over the past year, the

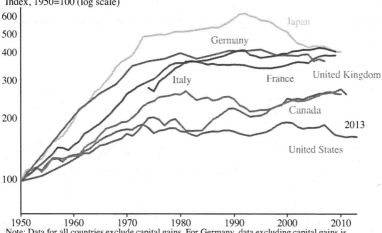

Figure 1-6
Growth in Real Average Income for the Bottom 90 Percent, 1950–2013
Index, 1950=100 (log scale)

Note: Data for all countries exclude capital gains. For Germany, data excluding capital gains is unavailable after 1998, so this chart displays data including capital gains adjusted for the historical relationship between capital-inclusive and capital-exclusive incomes. Italian data begins in 1974 and is indexed to the average of the other series at that point. Italian data is calculated by CEA from the income level and share of the top 10 percent as provided by the World Top Incomes Database.
Source: World Top Incomes Database; Saez (2015); CEA calculations.

Organisation for Economic Co-operation and Development (OECD) and the International Monetary Fund (IMF) reduced their productivity growth estimates for many high-income countries. In recent years, the United States has been somewhat better situated than many other advanced economies, in part because this country has been the center of much high-tech innovation. In fact, the United States has defied the trend in other high-income economies by experiencing a pickup in productivity growth over the last 20 years. In contrast, productivity growth has generally declined in most other high-income economies over the same period, as shown in Figure 1-7.

Income Inequality

The second important factor influencing the dynamics of middle-class incomes is inequality. This, too, is a global issue. In the United States, the top 1 percent has garnered a larger share of income than in any other G-7 country in each year since 1987 for which data are available, as shown in Figure 1-8. From 1990 to 2010, the top 1 percent's income share rose 0.22 percentage point a year in the United States versus 0.14 percentage point a year in the United Kingdom. While comparable international data are scarce after 2010, the gains of the top 1 percent continued since then in the United States, until a noticeable downtick in 2013.

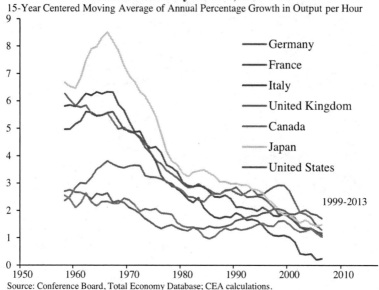

Figure 1-7
Labor Productivity Growth, 1951–2013
15-Year Centered Moving Average of Annual Percentage Growth in Output per Hour

Germany
France
Italy
United Kingdom
Canada
Japan
United States

1999-2013

Source: Conference Board, Total Economy Database; CEA calculations.

Labor Force Participation

The third driver of income growth is labor force participation, discussed in more detail in Chapter 3. Although the United States has enjoyed a strong labor market recovery amid surging employment, its labor force participation rate has fallen more than that of other high-income countries.

The recent decline in the labor force participation rate is largely the result of demographic changes. Since 2008, when the first of the baby boomers turned 62 and became eligible for Social Security, the baby boom has become a retirement boom. This loss of productive workers was compounded by the severe recession that hit around the same time. But even before either of these events, the economy already faced labor force participation challenges, including a long-running decline in male labor force participation and an end to the rapid increase in female participation.

Since the early 1990s, the United States has experienced a marked decline in labor force participation among males aged 25 to 54 ("prime age"), as shown in Figure 1-9. In this regard, the U.S. experience has been something of an outlier compared to many other high-income countries. Since the financial crisis, U.S. prime-age male participation has declined by about 2.5 percentage points, while the United Kingdom has seen a small uptick and most large European economies were generally stable. Of 24

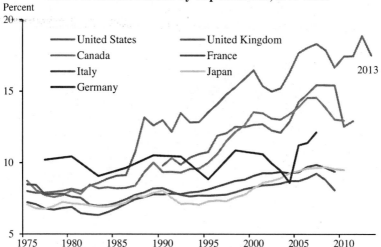

Figure 1-8
Share of Income Earned by Top 1 Percent, 1975–2013

Percent

Note: Data for all countries exclude capital gains. For Germany, data excluding capital gains is unavailable after 1998, so this chart displays data including capital gains adjusted for the historical relationship between the capital-inclusive and capital-exclusive ratios.
Source: World Top Incomes Database; Saez (2015).

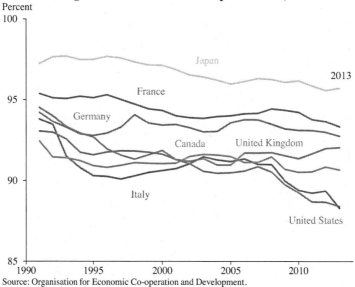

Figure 1-9
Prime-Age Male Labor Force Participation Rates, 1991–2013

Percent

Source: Organisation for Economic Co-operation and Development.

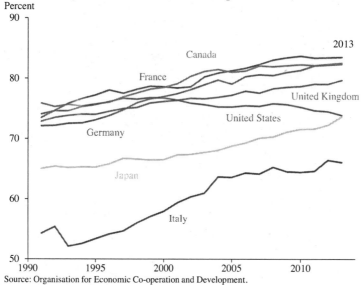

Figure 1-10
Prime-Age Female Labor Force Participation Rates, 1991–2013

Source: Organisation for Economic Co-operation and Development.

OECD countries that reported prime-age male participation data between 1990 and 2013, the United States fell from 16th to 22nd.

The story is somewhat similar among prime-age females. Historically, the United States showed leadership in bringing women into the workforce. In 1990, the United States ranked 7th out of 24 current OECD countries reporting prime-age female labor force participation, about 8 percentage points higher than the average of that sample. But since the late 1990s, women's labor force participation plateaued and even started to drift down in the United States while continuing to rise in other high-income countries, as shown in Figure 1-10. As a result, in 2013 the United States ranked 19th out of those same 24 countries, falling 6 percentage points behind the United Kingdom and 3 percentage points below the sample average. A recent study found that the relative expansion of family leave and part-time work programs in other OECD countries versus the United States explains nearly one-third of the United States' relative decline (Blau and Kahn 2013).

The challenges facing productivity growth, inequality, and labor force participation are all substantial. As this *Report* further details, the United States has important structural opportunities that can help address each of the challenges, though the degree to which we do so will also depend on the policies that we choose to adopt.

The 2015 Economic Report of the President

The well-being of the middle class and those working to get into the middle class is the ultimate test of an economy's performance. The best way to grow the economy on a sustainable and inclusive basis is to address squarely the three drivers of incomes: productivity growth, income inequality, and labor force participation. With these factors in mind, this year's *Report* reviews the progress the economy has made and identifies the areas where more work is needed.

Chapter 2 reviews the macroeconomic performance of the U.S. economy during 2014, including the growth of output and employment, the continued decline in the unemployment rate, the housing market, the growth of wealth over the year, and the improvement in the deficit as a fraction of GDP. The chapter also explains the economic assumptions about future growth that underlie the President's Fiscal Year 2016 Budget, including the economic benefits of the President's agenda.

Chapter 3 reviews the opportunities and challenges facing the U.S. labor market. Perhaps no recent economic development has been more surprising than the rapid fall in the unemployment rate, spurred by the pickup in the rate of job growth in 2014. But economic performance must be gauged by more than just the unemployment rate—a successful job market also encourages labor force participation, supports quality jobs, and facilitates effective job matching of workers and positions.

The American workforce and family lives have changed drastically over the last half-century. Women now represent almost one-half the workforce, married couples increasingly share child-care responsibilities, and people live—and work—longer than in the past. Chapter 4 examines these recent changes in American family life and their implications for labor markets. It also as analyzes Americans' access to paid leave and workplace flexibility policies and the economic evidence on how these policies can benefit workers, firms, and our economy. Both Chapter 3 and Chapter 4 address two factors affecting middle-class incomes: labor force participation and the income distribution.

Chapter 5 shifts the focus to productivity growth with an examination of business tax reform as well as a briefer discussion about the complementary issues in individual taxation. The chapter summarizes the international context for business tax reform, describes the President's approach to reform, and documents four channels through which reform can boost productivity and living standards: encouraging domestic investment, improving the quality of investment, reducing the inefficiencies of the international tax system, and investing in infrastructure.

Chapter 6 reviews the profound transformation of the U.S. energy sector. The United States is producing more oil and natural gas, generating more electricity from renewables such as wind and solar, and consuming less petroleum while consuming the same amount of electricity. To build on this progress, to foster economic growth, and to ensure that growth is sustainable for future generations, the President has set out an aggressive all-of-the-above clean energy strategy. This chapter lays out the key elements of the strategy: enhancing energy security and laying the foundation for a low-carbon future in ways that also support economic growth and job creation.

Finally, Chapter 7 situates the United States in the context of the global economy. The United States is more integrated with the rest of the world than ever before. This chapter examines the impact on the economy of increased global interdependence, through both international trade in goods and services and financial transactions in international capital markets. It presents empirical evidence on the economic effects and benefits to the middle class of enhanced U.S. trade, highlighting the United States' central position to take advantage of the growth in world trade in services. These issues are important for understanding both productivity growth and the distributional implications of globalization.

CONCLUSION

The 2015 *Economic Report of the President* considers the recovery and our economic future from the perspective of the typical American family. Although workers have begun to reap the benefits of our accelerating recovery, a skewed income distribution and subdued labor force participation have restrained the full benefit of U.S. growth from accruing to the middle class. As the economy continues to grow, President Obama's focus on middle-class economics is designed to foster productivity growth in a shared and sustainable way, so that the typical family participates fully in the Nation's resurgence. These are the values that should drive American economic policy in this next age for the middle class, and they are the values that animate this *Report*.

❧

C H A P T E R 2

THE YEAR IN REVIEW AND
THE YEARS AHEAD

The U.S. economy took another major step forward in 2014 as it continued to recover from the worst economic crisis since the Great Depression. Real gross domestic product (GDP) has grown at a solid 2.8-percent annual pace over the past two years, a pickup from the 2.0-percent pace seen during the 12 quarters of 2010 through 2012. The labor market firmed markedly during 2014, as reflected in the fastest pace of job gains since 1999 and nearly the fastest decline in the unemployment rate since 1983. Cumulatively, the private sector added 11.5 million jobs during 59 consecutive months (through December 2014) of positive job growth, the nation's longest streak of uninterrupted private-sector job growth on record. The unemployment rate declined 1.1 percentage points during the 12 months of 2014, or almost an average of 0.1 percentage point a month, falling to 5.6 percent by year end (see Figure 2-1). Real average hourly earnings of production and nonsupervisory workers rose 1.5 percent over the 12 months of the year, as nominal wage growth continued to run somewhat ahead of the subdued pace of consumer price inflation. While substantial progress has been made, the economic recovery remains incomplete, and more work remains to support growth, boost job creation, and lift wages.

The strengthening of the labor market occurred while real GDP grew 2.5 percent during the four quarters of 2014. The quarterly pace of economic growth was uneven as unusually cold and snowy weather contributed to a first-quarter drop in real GDP (at a 2.1-percent annual rate). The economy rebounded in the second and third quarters at a nearly 5.0-percent annual rate, followed by a slowing to 2.6 percent in the fourth quarter (advance estimate).

Growth in consumer spending, business fixed investment, and exports sustained average aggregate demand growth during the four quarters of 2014, albeit with substantial quarter-to-quarter fluctuations. Inventory investment proved uneven. The State and local sector bottomed out in 2012

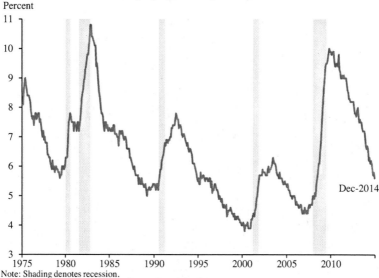

Figure 2-1
Unemployment Rate, 1975–2014

Percent

Dec-2014

Note: Shading denotes recession.
Source: Bureau of Labor Statistics, Current Population Survey.

and 2013, and provided a bit of support for the economy in 2014. Although slow growth among our international trading partners limited the growth of foreign demand, U.S. exports still grew 2 percent during the four quarters of the year. Manufacturing production also grew 4.5 percent during the four quarters as annual motor vehicle assemblies reached 11.7 million units in 2014, their highest level since 2005.

The price of imported petroleum, as measured by the spot price of European light crude oil from the North Sea (known as Brent), averaged $108 per barrel during the first eight months of the year but fell to $63 per barrel for the month of December. The price decline reflected both increased global supply, including U.S. production, and weak world consumption, and it lowered the Nation's net petroleum bill by roughly $70 billion at an annual rate and dampened headline inflation in the final months of the year.

Although fiscal restraint continued in fiscal year (FY) 2014 with the Federal Budget deficit falling 1.3 percentage points to 2.8 percent of GDP, the restraint was less severe than during the two preceding years and mostly reflected the effects of automatic stabilizers rather than changes in the structural deficit. The cumulative five-year (2009 to 2014) decline in the deficit-to-GDP ratio was the steepest five-year drop since the demobilization following WWII. Following the October 2013 government shutdown, the two-year Ryan-Murray budget agreement (in December 2013) helped provide fiscal-policy stability during FY 2014 and FY 2015. The Consolidated and Further Continuing Appropriations Act, signed into law in December 2014, will help to extend this more stable fiscal environment into 2015. By the fourth quarter of 2014, consumer sentiment, as measured by both the Reuters/University of Michigan index and the Conference Board index, reached its highest levels since 2007, which likely reflects the additional fiscal certainty, improving income and employment expectations, and declining gasoline prices.

KEY EVENTS OF 2014

Aggregate Output Growth during the Year

Growth during the year was volatile partly due to exceptionally severe weather in the first quarter and a puzzling first-quarter decline in reported health-care spending, followed by a surge in growth as the level of real output rebounded in subsequent quarters. Cold weather played a major role in depressing GDP in the first quarter; in fact, it was the third most unusually cold quarter in the past 60 years. Four snowstorms in the first quarter were severe enough to be rated on the Northeast Snowfall Impact Scale, an index produced by the National Oceanic and Atmospheric Administration that aims to capture the economic impact of snowstorms on populations. Prior to 2014, no quarter going back to 1956 had more than three such storms. The bad weather appears to have reduced many of the weather-sensitive components of GDP. Outright real spending declines occurred in inventory investment, equipment investment, residential investment (mostly reflecting a drop in real estate commissions), exports (especially to Canada), and State and local government spending (mostly through construction spending). Also, real consumer spending on goods registered below-trend growth. Weakness in these categories was only partially offset by higher consumer spending on services, which rose owing to a weather-related increase in electric and natural gas utility outlays.

Growth rebounded to 4.6- and 5.0-percent annual rates in the second and third quarters followed by a 2.6-percent rate in the fourth quarter. Over the four quarters of the year, real GDP grew 2.5 percent. Figure 2-2 shows the growth rate of real output, as represented by the average of the income-side and product-side measures.[1] Measured in this way, real output grew 2.5 percent during the first three quarters of 2014, up slightly from 2.3 percent

---

[1] Real output can be measured as the sum of the product-side components (known as gross domestic product, GDP) or by the sum of the income-side components (known as gross domestic income, GDI). In principle, these two quantities are the same, but these two measures will differ due to measurement error. Figure 2-2 plots both measures and their average.

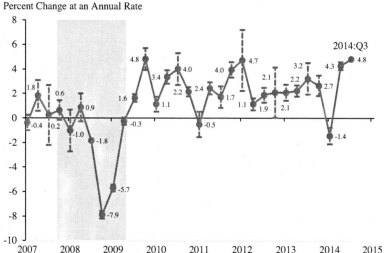

Figure 2-2
Mean GDP Growth, 2007–2014
Percent Change at an Annual Rate

Note: Mean real GDP growth is the average of the growth rates of real GDP and real gross domestic income (GDI). The bullets show mean GDP and the bars show the GDP and GDI growth in each quarter. Shading denotes recession.
Source: Bureau of Economic Analysis, National Income and Product Accounts; CEA calculations.

during the four quarters of 2013. Relative to this 2.5-percent pace, growth was fast in durable goods consumption and business fixed investment while growth was slow (but still positive) in consumer spending on nondurables and services, exports, Federal nondefense purchases, and State and local spending. Residential investment grew at about the same pace as overall GDP. Inventory investment (both farm and nonfarm) contributed a bit to GDP growth during 2014, and it played an important role in the quarter-to-quarter fluctuations. An aggregate of consumption and fixed investment, known as private domestic final purchases (PDFP), is an especially predictive indicator of future real GDP growth. Real PDFP grew 3.2 percent during the four quarters of 2014 (see Box 2-1).

Fiscal Policy

Federal fiscal policy was less restrictive during FY 2014—which ended on September 30, 2014—than a year earlier. It was also more predictable, since Congress had agreed in December 2013 on discretionary spending caps for the remainder of FY 2014 and all of FY 2015; and on appropriations bills for FY 2014 and FY 2015, enacted in January and December 2014, respectively.

The agreement to end the 16-day October 2013 shutdown (the Continuing Appropriations Act of 2014), together with subsequent

Box 2-1: Private Domestic Final Purchases as a Predictive Indicator of GDP

Real GDP, like many indicators, can be volatile from quarter-to-quarter for purely transitory reasons related to fluctuations or measurement issues that provide little information about the underlying state of the economy. As discussed in the text, 2014 provides an example with a sharp contraction in GDP in the first quarter of 2014 and a sharp expansion in the second quarter, suggesting a fluctuation around an underlying economic trend. One reason why GDP is so volatile is that subcomponents can have large transitory fluctuations, for example, the volatile inventory investment component of GDP, which subtracted from the first quarter of 2014 and added to it in the second quarter.

Table 2-i
Component Ability to Forecast One-Quarter-Ahead Real GDP Growth

Component (Real)	Predictive Power (Adjusted R^2) of GDP
Government	-0.02
Exports	0.02
Inventories	0.02
GDP	0.22
Final Sales of Dometic Product	0.23
Imports	0.28
Fixed Investment	0.29
Mean Output (GDP, GDI)	0.29
PCE	0.30
GDI	0.31
Final Sales to Domestic Purchasers	0.33
Final Sales to Private Domestic Purchasers (PDFP)	**0.36**

Note: Mean output refers to the average of GDP and GDI. The quarterly growth rate of real GDP is regressed on four lags of growth rates for the listed variables over 1984:Q1 to 2014:Q4, using revised data.
Source: Bureau of Economic Analysis, National Income and Product Accounts; CEA Calculations.

Do other national income concepts provide a better gauge of the underlying trend in economic activity? One way to assess this is to determine which factors provide the best prediction of one-quarter ahead real GDP growth, thereby capturing the more inertial component or components of GDP. Of the candidates, one might consider lags of overall real GDP itself, or the lagged values of individual spending-side components of real GDP (consumer spending, fixed investment, and government spending). One might also consider the income-side measure of real GDP, known as gross domestic income (GDI), which would be identical to GDP but for measurement error. The best predictor could be some combination of these components.

Table 2-i above shows how well lagged growth rates of these variables predict one-quarter ahead overall GDP growth, as measured by percent of the variance of GDP (known as R^2) explained by each of these candidates. On this scale, a perfect predictor would have an R^2 of 1, and a variable with no correlation would have an R^2 of 0. Among the possibilities shown in Table 2-i, consumer spending and fixed investment are good predictors of future GDP. The best-fitting predictor, however, is an aggregate of these two variables called private domestic final purchases (PDFP). This is likely attributable to the fact that PDFP excludes the volatile and possibly inaccurate measures of exports, imports, inventory investment, and government spending. It therefore equals the sum of consumption and fixed investment. As can be seen, PDFP predicts future GDP growth better than the lags of GDP itself, GDI, or a simple average of GDP and GDI. PDFP also predicts GDP better than final sales (GDP less inventory investment) and all the other components of GDP.

Figure 2-i below illustrates that real PDFP growth is much more stable than real GDP growth. Although PDFP growth was low in the first quarter of 2014 (because weather affected consumption and fixed investment), it was not negative because PDFP excludes volatile components like inventory investment. PDFP then rebounded in the second and third quarters but not by as much as GDP. In the second, third, and fourth quarters, growth of PDFP was stable at 3.8, 4.1, and 3.9 percent, respectively. In contrast, real GDP growth was more volatile, surging to

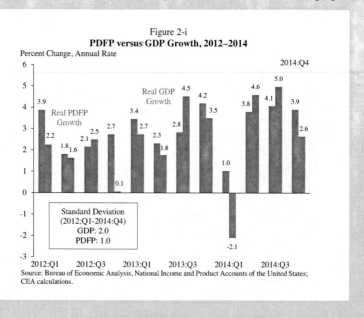

Figure 2-i
PDFP versus GDP Growth, 2012–2014

Source: Bureau of Economic Analysis, National Income and Product Accounts of the United States; CEA calculations.

5.0 percent in the third quarter boosted by defense and net exports, and then slowing to 2.6 percent in the fourth quarter when these components reversed direction. Overall, the growth rate of PDFP is more stable than GDP, allowing a reasonable quarter-by-quarter measure of the underlying growth rate of the economy.

agreements reached in December 2013 and the following January, suspended the debt ceiling through March 2015, provided partial relief from the automatic sequestration of discretionary spending in fiscal years 2014 and 2015, and resulted in appropriations bills that funded the Federal Government through the end of FY 2014. In September, Congress passed a continuing resolution to fund the government through December 11, 2014. Finally, in mid-December, the 113th Congress passed and the President signed an appropriations bill that funded most of the Federal Government through the end of FY 2015. This legislation provided positive support to a number of key initiatives, including the extension of the FY 2014 funding gains for early childhood education, investment in manufacturing innovation hubs around the country, and provision of additional funding for key financial watchdogs like the Commodity Futures Trading Commission and Securities and Exchange Commission.[2] In addition, Congress retroactively approved a variety of tax "extenders" that affected 2014 liabilities, including incentives for research and development and clean energy, and tax deductions for teacher expenses.

The five-year decline of 7.0 percentage points in the deficit-to-GDP ratio since FY 2009 has been the largest since the demobilization at the end of World War II. The Federal deficit-to-GDP ratio fell 1.3 percentage points to 2.8 percent in FY 2014. The year-to-year reduction in this ratio followed steeper declines of 1.7 and 2.7 percentage points in fiscal years 2012 and 2013, respectively (see Figure 2-3). The deficit-to-GDP ratio in FY 2009 was elevated by the steep recession as well as by fiscal measures deployed to combat that recession. Overall, fiscal support substantially raised the level of output and employment during and after 2009, as discussed in the 2014 *Economic Report of the President* (Chapter 3). But the reduction in the deficit has acted as a drag on growth rates, especially in 2013. One source of fiscal drag during 2012 and 2013 was the end of various countercyclical fiscal policies following the recession, the largest change being the expiration of the payroll tax cut at the end of 2012. The declining deficit in 2014 largely

---

[2] http://www.whitehouse.gov/blog/2014/12/17/
omb-director-shaun-donovan-passage-hr-83-consolidated-and-further-continuing-appropr

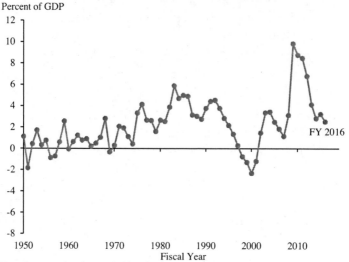

Figure 2-3
Federal Budget Deficit, 1950–2016

Percent of GDP

Fiscal Year

FY 2016

Note: Orange markers denote administration forecasts.
Source: Office of Management and Budget; Bureau of Economic Analysis, National Income and Product Accounts.

reflected an increase in tax collections resulting from growing incomes. With the deficit-to-GDP ratio projected to edge up in FY 2015, before it edges down in FY 2016, fiscal drag is likely to be negligible in the near term.

Monetary Policy

In 2014, the Federal Open Market Committee (FOMC) maintained a historically accommodative monetary policy stance. With its usual tool—the Federal funds rate—at its effective lower bound, the Committee continued to employ the unconventional policy tools it has introduced in the years since the global financial crisis. These tools included forward guidance for the future path of the Federal funds rate and additional purchases of longer-term U.S. Treasury securities and agency-guaranteed mortgage-backed securities.

As the U.S. economy increasingly showed evidence of strength, however, the Federal Reserve moved gradually to tighten monetary policy. At its December 2013 meeting, the FOMC announced a decision to reduce the monthly increase in its holdings of long-term securities by $10 billion a month to $75 billion a month. This tapering of asset purchases continued with further modest reductions in the monthly pace of purchases at each FOMC meeting through October 2014, when new purchases were discontinued entirely. As of February 2015, the Federal Reserve continues to purchase long-term debt securities, but only in amounts sufficient to replace maturing debt in its portfolio, such that the overall size of the Federal Reserve's holdings remains approximately constant. Plans for the taper were communicated to markets beforehand and markets experienced little volatility in response to the actual reductions in purchases when they started in December 2013. The yield on the 10-year Treasury note fell 69 basis points over the 12 months of the year.

The end of new Federal Reserve asset purchases does not mean the end of the effect of the Federal Reserve's asset holdings on the level of longer-term interest rates. On the contrary, the better measure of the effect of the Fed's portfolio policy on longer-term interest rates is thought to involve the size and expected duration of the Fed's holdings, not the pace at which those holdings are increased. Therefore, the stock of Federal Reserve asset holdings continues to influence the long-term interest rate even after the end of new purchases.[3]

At the start of 2014, interest-rate futures markets expected the initial increase (liftoff) in the Federal funds rate to occur during the second quarter of 2015, as shown in Figure 2-4. By the end of 2014, markets expected the liftoff to occur in the third quarter of 2015. The shift likely reflected the slowdown in global growth and the Committee's indication that it can be patient in beginning to normalize policy even after the end of the asset purchase program. The Committee has emphasized that future policy will remain dependent on incoming economic data.

Financial Markets

Developments in U.S. financial markets over the course of the year largely reflected the evolving global economic outlook and shifting monetary policy expectations. Longer-term interest rates, as measured by the yields on 10-year U.S. Treasury notes, declined from 2.9 percent in December 2013 to 2.2 percent in December 2014, as shown in Figure 2-5. The decline in interest rates came despite rapid improvement in the U.S. labor market and an end to the expansion of the Federal Reserve's balance sheet. The decline was likely driven in large part by the evolving expectation during 2014 for a later increase in the Federal funds rate that occurred, as depicted in Figure 2-4, along with continued low readings on inflation.

---

[3] Then-Chairman Bernanke has stated that "we do believe the primary effect of our purchases is through the stock that we hold, because that stock has been withdrawn from markets, and the prices of those assets have to adjust to balance supply and demand." Chairman Ben S. Bernanke, Press Conference, June 19, 2013, available at http://www.federalreserve.gov/mediacenter/files/FOMCpresconf20130619.pdf.

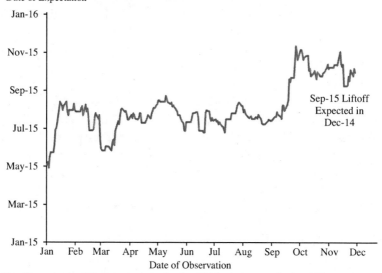

Figure 2-4
Market-Implied Date of Initial Federal Funds Rate Increase, 2014

Date of Expectation

Sep-15 Liftoff
Expected in
Dec-14

Date of Observation

Note: The market-implied expectation is the date for which futures contracts imply a 0.25 percent increase in the Federal funds effective rate.
Source: Bloomberg Professional Service; CEA calculations.

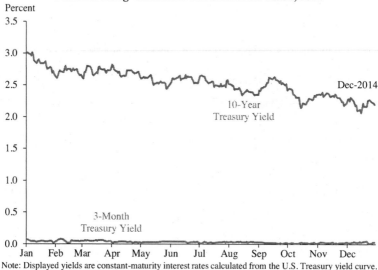

Figure 2-5
Nominal Long- and Short-Term Interest Rates, 2014

Percent

Dec-2014

10-Year
Treasury Yield

3-Month
Treasury Yield

Note: Displayed yields are constant-maturity interest rates calculated from the U.S. Treasury yield curve.
Source: Federal Reserve Board, H.15 Release.

Downward revisions to global growth projections have also been important contributors to the decline in interest rates. The move in U.S. interest rates coincided with decreasing long-term interest rates across the developed world, including in the United Kingdom, Japan, and the euro area. The general decline in interest rates among advanced economies likely reflects in part the environment of slowing global growth and weakening inflation: the one- and five-year ahead growth rates projected by the International Monetary Fund (IMF) for these countries were revised down during 2014, and again in January 2015.

Other interest rates also declined in 2014, as shown in Table 2-1. The average rate on a 30-year fixed rate mortgage has fallen 60 basis points over the 12 months of the year to 3.86 percent. Before the last several weeks of 2014, the average mortgage rate had not fallen below 4 percent since mid-2013. Similarly, corporate borrowing costs declined over the course of the year. Credit spreads—differences between corporate interest rates and U.S. Treasury yields that reflect the risk of default by corporate borrowers—were unchanged on balance during 2014. Short-term interest rates (such as the Federal funds rate, and the 91-day Treasury bill rate) were largely stable over the course of the year, as markets consistently expected the first Federal funds rate increase to occur more than three months into the future.

Reflecting the ongoing economic recovery, the stock market saw continued positive performance in 2014. The Standard and Poor's 500 index rose 11.4 percent for the year. That performance follows increases of 13 percent in 2012 and 30 percent in 2013 (the best year since 1997). In December, the Standard and Poor's index was 32 percent above its pre-financial-crisis monthly peak in 2007.

International Developments

Faced with weak global economic performance over 2014, the IMF reduced its forecast for year-over-year 2015 global real GDP growth from 4.0 percent in October 2013 to 3.5 percent in January 2015. Most economies experienced low rates of inflation in 2014 and low interest rates. The pace of recovery was uneven across countries, with country-specific factors playing an important role. In its World Economic Outlook assessments, the IMF pointed to the legacies of the crisis, including high levels of public and private debt and subdued investment, as impediments to growth.

Euro zone. There is considerable divergence in the pace of the recovery across Europe. The euro zone suffered a debilitating crisis from late 2009 to 2012, fast on the heels of the 2007 to 2009 global financial crisis. Germany, Sweden, and most countries in central and eastern Europe have recovered to their pre-crisis levels of real GDP relative to working-age population, while

Table 2-1

Selected Interest Rates, 2014

(Percent)	Dec-13	Dec-14	Difference
Federal Funds Effective	0.09	0.12	0.03
3-Month U.S. Treasury Yield	0.07	0.03	-0.04
2-Year U.S. Treasury Yield	0.34	0.64	0.30
5-Year U.S. Treasury Yield	1.58	1.64	0.06
10-Year U.S. Treasury	2.90	2.21	-0.69
10-Year BBB Corporate Bonds	4.83	4.18	-0.65
30-Year U.S. Treasury	3.89	2.83	-1.06
30-Year Fixed Mortgage Rate	4.46	3.86	-0.60

Note: All interest rates are averages of daily or weekly data throughout the given month. Treasury yields are constant-maturity yields estimated by the Federal Reserve Board. Corporate bond yields are option-adjusted yields estimated by Standard & Poor's Global Fixed Income Research. The mortgage rate is that reported in the Freddie Mac Primary Mortgage Survey.
Source: Board of Governors of the Federal Reserve System; Standard & Poor's; Freddie Mac; CEA calculations.

in the rest of the continent, notably the aggregate of the peripheral euro area economies (Greece, Ireland, Italy, Portugal, and Spain), real GDP remains 9 percent below the pre-recession peak. (For a detailed discussion of the dispersion in real GDP trajectories across countries, see Box 2-2 below.) For the euro area as a whole, real GDP growth in the third quarter of 2014 (the latest available as this *Report* goes to press) was weak. The growth rate of real GDP per working age population from the third quarter of 2013 to the third quarter of 2014 was a meager 0.8 percent for the euro area, 1.2 percent in Germany, 0.4 percent in France, while Italy dipped back into recession with a decline of 0.5 percent. The unemployment rate edged down during 2014 across the euro area, but inflation fell sharply as well, with Greece and Spain experiencing outright deflation (Figure 2-6).

At the height of the euro crisis in July 2012, European Central Bank (ECB) President Mario Draghi pledged "to do whatever it takes to preserve the euro."[4] A month later, in August 2012, the ECB announced it was pre-pared to use large-scale "outright monetary transactions" (OMT), if neces-sary, to offset the effects on sovereign yields of speculation that some mem-ber states might exit the euro. OMT would involve possibly massive ECB purchases of the sovereign debts of countries whose yields spiked upward because of fears they might abandon the euro in favor of a new national

---

[4] Mario Draghi, President of the European Central Bank, Global Investment Conference, July 26, 2012, available at http://www.ecb.europa.eu/press/key/date/2012/html/sp120726.en.html.

Figure 2-6
Falling Euro Area Inflation, 2011–2014

Percent, Year-over-Year

Germany

Europe Outside
Euro Area

Euro Area Minus
Germany and
Peripherals

Dec-2014

Peripherals

Note: Peripherals include Greece, Ireland, Italy, Portugal and Spain.
Source: Eurostat, Harmonized Index of Consumer Prices, Gross Domestic Product; CEA calculations.

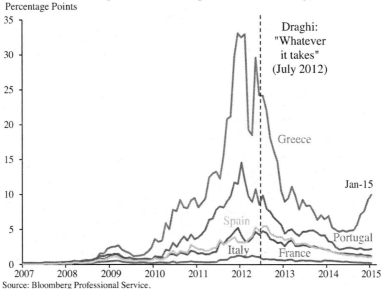

Figure 2-7
Euro Area Sovereign Interest Rate Spreads over Germany, 2007–2015

Percentage Points

Draghi:
"Whatever
it takes"
(July 2012)

Greece

Jan-15

Spain

Portugal

Italy

France

Source: Bloomberg Professional Service.

Box 2-2: International Comparison of Growth Performance

Nearly every advanced economy endured a recession amid the global financial crisis, but the experience since then has varied widely across economies. Figure 2-ii shows real GDP divided by working-age population since 2008 for most advanced economies. All of the economies represented in the Figure experienced a deep and almost synchronous decline ranging from 4 to 10 percent measured from peak to trough. Since then, the United States, the United Kingdom, Germany, and Japan have surpassed the levels of real GDP per working-age population they achieved before the crisis, while most of the euro area has not. The figures in parentheses show the recent annualized rate of growth in real GDP per working-age population as measured over the eight-quarter interval through the third quarter of 2014. The United States and the United Kingdom have experienced recent growth of 2.1 and 1.9 percent a year respectively, and have both exceeded their pre-crisis peaks. Germany has also surpassed its pre-crisis peak, but, in contrast to the United States and the United Kingdom, real GDP per working-age

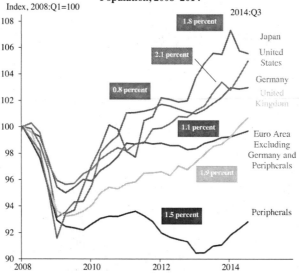

Figure 2-ii
Real Gross Domestic Product per Working-Age Population, 2008–2014

Note: Peripherals include Greece, Ireland, Italy, Portugal and Spain. Numbers in parentheses are the annualized eight-quarter percent changes in real GDP per working-age population ended in 2014:Q3. Working age population is 16-64 for the U.S. and 15-64 for all others.
Source: Eurostat; CEA calculations.

population has been almost flat since 2011, with annualized growth of 0.8 percent over the last eight quarters. Japan's annual growth rate was 1.8 percent, but this was driven largely by the decline in its working-age population. (Real GDP over the same interval has grown at only a 0.6 percent annualized rate.) The high-debt peripheral euro economies (Greece, Ireland, Italy, Portugal, and Spain), which were battered by the euro financial crisis between late 2009 and 2012, experienced a double-dip recession and as a group remain 9 percent below their 2008 GDP-per-worker level, though growth has picked up in the last year. The weak recovery is not confined to the high-debt peripheral economies. The rest of the euro area, excluding Germany and the high-debt peripheral countries, is close to attaining its pre-crisis peak with recent annualized growth of 0.9 percent in real GDP per worker.

The diverging paths within advanced economies can partly be attributed to different conditions prior to the crisis: differences in outstanding household debt, differences in public debt, the health of the financial sector, and whether the country is part of a crisis-afflicted monetary union. But much of the post-crisis difference must also be placed at the feet of government policy, which has failed to stimulate aggregate demand. A country's ability to tackle demand shortfalls through higher public spending or tax cuts may be limited if fiscal space is insufficient—either because government debt is already high or because markets doubt the government's ability to manage its budget sustainably over the longer term. Thus, governments must accumulate fiscal space through prudent

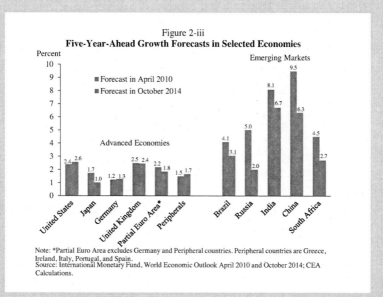

Figure 2-iii
Five-Year-Ahead Growth Forecasts in Selected Economies

Note: *Partial Euro Area excludes Germany and Peripheral countries. Peripheral countries are Greece, Ireland, Italy, Portugal, and Spain.
Source: International Monetary Fund, World Economic Outlook April 2010 and October 2014; CEA Calculations.

budgets during periods of stronger growth, as many emerging economies did during the 2000s.

At the same time, supply shortfalls have also played an important role in the slower pace of global growth. The IMF has marked down its medium-term growth projections for many of the world's major economies, as shown in the Figure 2-iii. The figure compares the five-year-ahead growth forecasts made in the April 2010 World Economic Outlook to the five-year-ahead growth forecasts made in the October 2014 World Economic Outlook, a rough proxy for revisions to the expectation of the growth of aggregate supply. While Japan and the euro area excluding Germany and peripherals have seen downward revisions to medium-term growth expectations, the striking aspect of this figure is the sharp downward revisions to prospects for the BRIC economies, which saw growth outlooks marked down by 1 to 3 percentage points. In fact, in the October 2014 World Economic Outlook, the IMF noted the BRIC economies have been responsible for one-half of the IMF's total growth forecast errors from 2011 to 2014 despite representing just over one-quarter of global GDP. The emerging market slowdown may be just a temporary response to the economic crisis and weak global demand. Another possibility is that it could represent the end of an unusual period in global economic history when the integration of China and India into the global economy led to a rapid period of catching up with the technological frontier. As these nations edge closer to the frontier, opportunities for growth are diminishing.

currency. President Draghi's announcement marked the start of a period of declining peripheral sovereign interest-rate spreads over the German bund. As a result, some commentators view the euro crisis as being in remission if not over (Ireland and Portugal have formally exited from their "troika" assistance programs administered by the IMF, EU, and ECB). The exception is Greece, which has so far been unable to meet its commitment to deficit reduction under the troika program despite government efforts to bring its budget under control. Spreads rose sharply in January 2015 as the anti-austerity party Syriza came to power, vowing to renegotiate the terms of Greece's sovereign debts (see Figure 2-7). Syriza and its coalition partner, the Independent Greeks, campaigned on platforms aggressively opposed to the deficit-reduction policies to which Greece must adhere under the terms of the troika assistance program.

Despite the generally low and falling spreads on sovereign debt, deflation in the peripheral countries has meant that real interest rates (nominal rates less inflation) are highest where unemployment is highest. Figure 2-8 shows the relationship between real interest rates and unemployment. The figure suggests that high real interest rates are suppressing recovery in precisely those countries with the greatest economic slack.

One reason that the United States has recovered more quickly than other advanced economies is its combination of accommodative monetary policy, quick action to recapitalize the financial sector, and aggressive demand management through countercyclical fiscal policy. The American Recovery and Reinvestment Act of 2009 was the largest countercyclical fiscal effort in U.S. history, and together with a dozen other fiscal-jobs measures and automatic stabilizers, fiscal support to the U.S. economy totaled 5.5 percent of GDP in 2010. But some euro area countries are constrained by fiscal rules from pursuing stronger countercyclical measures, while those that are unconstrained are largely unwilling to do so, or to allow much flexibility to the others. Because structural reform tends to work slowly, monetary policy must bear the immediate burden of resisting deflation and supporting demand. In contrast to the Federal Reserve's balance sheet, which increased through October 2014 but is being maintained at roughly a constant level for now, the ECB's balance sheet (as measured by the asset side) was allowed to contract between mid-2012 and mid-2014 from roughly €3 to €2 trillion, as euro area banks repaid ECB long-term loans taken out during the crisis. With the ECB's main refinancing interest rate effectively at the zero lower bound and its deposit rate negative since June 2014, President Draghi stated near the end of 2014 that the ECB "will do what we must to raise inflation and inflation expectations as fast as possible...."[5] In January 2015, Draghi announced an open-ended program of large-scale debt purchases, including sovereign debt, designed to increase the ECB's balance sheet more than €1 trillion by September 2016.

Other advanced economies. Japan continues to face longstanding economic challenges. The "three arrows" of Abenomics (fiscal stimulus, monetary easing, and structural reforms) that Prime Minister Shinzo Abe launched in December 2012 were greeted with optimism that they would end deflationary expectations and generate sustained growth. After two decades of anemic growth in Japan, the apparent initial success of the Abe agenda—initially driven mainly by aggressive monetary policy and yen depreciation—was a welcome development. Real GDP grew at a rate of about 1.6 percent (year over year) in both 2012 and 2013, and expected inflation rose. In April 2014, however, the government permanently increased the national consumption tax from 5 percent to 8 percent as a step toward

---

[5] Mario Draghi, President of the European Central Bank, Frankfurt European Banking Conference, November 21, 2014, available at http://www.ecb.europa.eu/press/key/date/2014/html/sp141121.en.html.

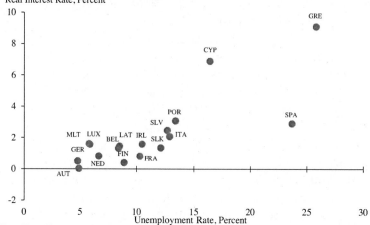

Figure 2-8
Euro Area Unemployment and Real Interest Rates, December 2014

Note: The real interest rate is equal to the nominal monthly average interest rate minus the 12-month inflation rate. Greek data are from October, and Slovakian data are from November.
Source: Eurostat, Harmonized Unemployment Rate; European Central Bank, Harmonized Long Term Interest Rates; National Sources.

reducing the large public debt (roughly 250 percent of GDP). This policy, a fiscal contraction equal to about 1.5 percent of GDP, was partly offset by temporary expansionary fiscal measures. Nonetheless, recent economic data from Japan raise troubling questions about the net effects of the consumption tax increase on growth. Real GDP surged 5.8 percent at an annual rate in the first quarter of 2014 as consumers raced to complete purchases before the tax hike, but then plunged 6.7 percent at an annual rate in the second quarter after it took effect, and another 1.9 percent in the third quarter, leaving real GDP below its level at the end of 2013. At the same time, inflation (excluding the effects of the consumption tax) remains far below the Bank of Japan's target of 2 percent a year. In response, the Bank of Japan expanded its program of quantitative and qualitative easing at the end of October. Slowing growth reflects weakness in consumer spending and business investment, which has led forecasters to revise down growth expectations for future quarters. Faced with these developments, Abe postponed by 18 months a second stage of the consumption tax increase (from 8 to 10 percent) planned for October 2015 and called a snap election that reaffirmed his parliamentary majority and extended by two years the horizon available for carrying out his policies.

As of the fourth quarter of 2014, real GDP in the United Kingdom was 3.4 percent above its pre-crisis peak, and unemployment stands at 5.8 percent for the September-to-November 2014 period. (See Box 3-2 for more details on the UK labor market and a comparison with the United States.)

Consumer price inflation was 0.5 percent over the 12 months of 2014, and the rate on the 10-year bond was 1.9 in December. Given the rapidly improving labor market, the Bank of England is anticipated to raise interest rates sometime in 2015 or 2016. On the downside, however, the strong economic linkages between the United Kingdom and continental Europe mean that troubles in the euro zone may dampen growth.

Emerging markets. China's economy grew 7.3 percent during the four quarters ended in the fourth quarter of 2014, down from an annualized rate of 9.2 percent in the eight quarters ended in the fourth quarter of 2011 (Figure 2-9). Both the IMF and the World Bank have downgraded their projections for Chinese growth in 2015 to a rate below 7.5 percent, which until recently was thought to be the Chinese authorities' target rate.

China may face stresses in adapting to a slower rate of expansion. In May, President Xi Jinping reportedly suggested that the Chinese "… must boost our confidence, adapt to the new normal condition based on the characteristics of China's economic growth in the current phase and stay cool-minded." One concern is the growth in credit to nonfinancial corporations and households, much of which has been channeled through the so-called shadow banking sector (which undertakes risky bank-like functions, but outside the government-regulated part of the financial sector). As shown in Figure 2-10, credit growth in China since 2008 has increased faster than in many developed countries. An initial surge in 2009 was seen as an aggressive response to the global financial crisis, in line with expansionary policies around the world. The renewed boom in credit since 2012, however, has raised worries about the rapid expansion of the unregulated shadow banking sector and a bubble in real estate prices. The government has responded with a number of policy measures to limit lending activities outside of the traditional banking sector. Property price gains have moderated, however, and prices began to fall in 2014, even in larger, wealthier cities where in the past demand has typically outstripped supply. There is growing concern about overbuilding because contraction in the construction sector would further depress aggregate growth and could cause financial instability.

A further economic slowdown in China would have ramifications for the global economy and, in particular, for low- and middle-income countries. Trade between China and other emerging BRICS economies (Brazil, Russia, India, and South Africa) has expanded since 2000. China is now the top export destination for 15 African countries, 13 Asian economies, and 3 Latin American countries. If demand in China slows, exports to China would decline, broadly dampening emerging-economy growth. Since mid-2011, the other BRICS countries have suffered declining terms of trade (the relative price of a country's exports compared with its imports). This decline

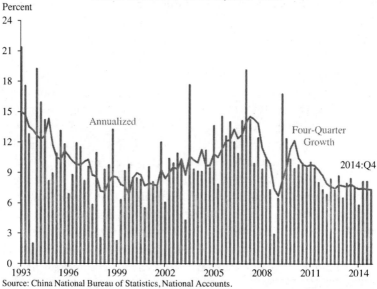

Figure 2-9
China: Real GDP Growth, 1993–2014

Percent

Annualized

Four-Quarter
Growth

2014:Q4

Source: China National Bureau of Statistics, National Accounts.

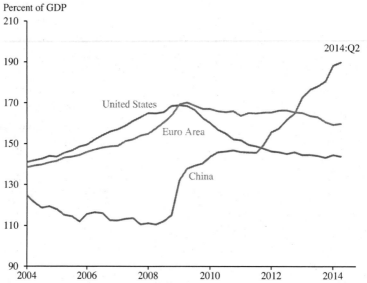

Figure 2-10
Credit to Nonfinancial Corporations and Households, 2004–2014

Percent of GDP

2014:Q2

United States

Euro Area

China

Source: Bank for International Settlements; People's Bank of China; Federal Reserve Board; National
Sources.

is accounted for in large part by falling prices of commodities and raw materials, to which China's slowdown is a major contributor. The price of oil has recently fallen much more sharply than prices of other commodities because the effects of low world demand for oil have been reinforced by exceptionally ample global supply. Emerging energy exporters, including Russia, Nigeria, and Venezuela and countries in the Middle East, have suffered most, while this development has been positive for energy importers including China and the big industrial economies (see Box 2-3).

An additional challenge facing emerging economies is the potential for capital flow reversals as the Federal Reserve moves toward positive interest rates and the demand for higher-yield assets in emerging economies subsides. That said, the stronger U.S. economy that motivates monetary policy normalization will benefit emerging market exporters. Vulnerabilities may have declined over the course of 2014 as foreign borrowing by several important emerging economies has fallen. Many analysts remain concerned, however, by the reportedly large stock of offshore dollar liabilities incurred by emerging-economy corporations.

Exchange rates, exports, and imports. Since the global financial crisis, the U.S. dollar has generally fluctuated in a lower range against foreign currencies relative to the early 2000s, but it took a particularly sharp upturn from September 2014 – a 7.2 percent appreciation against a broad index of trade partners through January 2015 (see Figure 2-11). Among the drivers of the recent appreciation is the strong performance of the U.S economy against a backdrop of relatively weak growth in the rest of the world, along with the implications of this growth pattern for countries' monetary policies. Federal Reserve policy is at a very different juncture than monetary policy in most foreign countries, though the United Kingdom is similarly situated. While indicators in the United States and the United Kingdom suggest that markets expect monetary tightening steps sometime in the 2015 to 2016 timeframe, the ECB and Bank of Japan remain fully engaged in battling below-target inflation and slow growth, with no near-term prospect of policy reversal.

Both the recent strength of the dollar and slowing demand in much of the world outside the United States will work to weaken U.S. export growth in the near term. The U.S. nominal trade deficit in goods and services edged up from 3.0 to 3.1 percent of GDP in 2014, as measured in the national income and product accounts. Against this downward pressure on exports, it will become especially important to open new markets to which the United States can sell goods and services. This is an important driver of the President's trade agenda, which is described more fully in Chapter 7.

Box 2-3: Imported Petroleum Prices and the Economy

Oil prices fell 43 percent during the 12 months of 2014 (as measured by the European, Brent, price of crude oil), the combined effect of a surge in U.S. crude oil production, a decrease in global oil demand, and OPEC's recent decision to maintain production levels despite the drop in prices (see Chapter 6 of this *Report*). Low oil prices benefit major segments of the U.S. economy. Lower fuel costs increase real household income and stimulate consumption both directly—mostly through lower prices of gasoline, which fell more than $1.00 per gallon in the last six months of 2014— and indirectly by reducing the production costs for oil-consuming businesses, which ultimately translates to lower prices for consumer goods and services. The drop in oil prices also hurts American oil producers, but because the United States is a net importer of crude oil, the overall benefit of falling oil prices to the United States exceeds the costs to domestic oil producers.

The net benefit to the economy is roughly proportional to the share of net oil imports in nominal GDP. In 2014, the United States, on net, imported about 1.9 billion barrels of petroleum and products, down more than 50 percent since 2008. Each $10 per barrel drop in the price of oil saves U.S. consumers and producers about $19 billion a year, or about 0.11 percent of GDP. As a result, the roughly $40 per barrel decline (roughly 40%) in the price of oil during the last four months of 2014 will save the U.S. economy about $70 billion a year, or 0.4 percent of GDP.

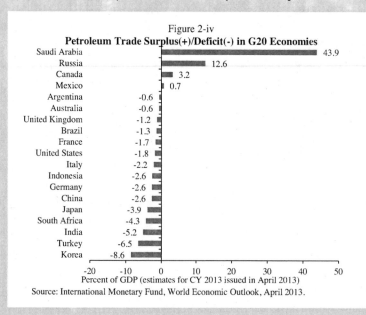

Figure 2-iv
Petroleum Trade Surplus(+)/Deficit(-) in G20 Economies

Source: International Monetary Fund, World Economic Outlook, April 2013.

Measured in dollars, the net import share of petroleum and petroleum products was 1.8 percent of nominal GDP in 2012, but fell to 1.1 percent during 2014. The situation is reversed for countries that are net crude oil exporters. Calculations by the IMF based on 2012 data suggest that Canada, for example, had a petroleum surplus equal to 3.2 percent of GDP, in contrast to the 2012 U.S. petroleum deficit of 1.8 percent of GDP. And so the same 40-percent oil-price decline reduces Canada's real income by 1.3 percent. Figure 2-iv shows the estimates by the IMF based on 2012 data of the petroleum trade balance as a percent of GDP for G-20 countries.

The back-of-the-envelope estimates described above, however, are far too simplistic to capture potential impacts for a large number of national economies, where policy and structural idiosyncrasies deliver different economic implications. In particular, countries like Iran, Russia, Venezuela, Nigeria, and Iraq will face challenges as low oil prices place their governments under extreme financial pressure. Analysts have made similarly rough estimates of the net effect of the oil price declines on global GDP. Largely because the world petroleum supply has increased, the IMF estimates that global real GDP could be around 0.5 percent higher in 2015 if the price decline persists for the entire year.

Aside from its positive implications for U.S. and global incomes, the decline in oil prices has also created fear of financial instability among energy companies. As oil prices have plunged, yields on oil

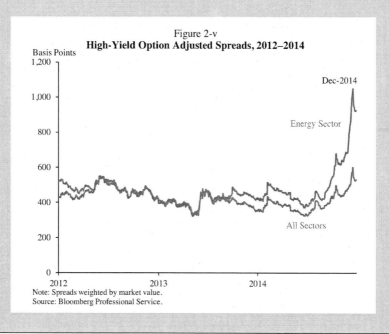

Figure 2-v
High-Yield Option Adjusted Spreads, 2012–2014

Note: Spreads weighted by market value.
Source: Bloomberg Professional Service.

company debt have skyrocketed in response to investor fears that companies will have a harder time paying creditors. In particular, Figure 2-v shows that, in just six months, the option-adjusted spread for high-yield energy debt (a measure of how risky a financial instrument is, relative to Treasury debt) has more than doubled from an average of under 400 basis points in June 2014, to over 920 basis points in December 2014. (The option adjustment corrects the spread for the value of rights to repay bonds before maturity.) By contrast, the option-adjusted spread for all sectors combined (including energy) has increased by less than one-half that amount over the same time period. As of December 2014, energy companies constitute almost 15 percent of the high-yield bond market, and there is growing concern that sustained, low prices will put investments in future oil projects at risk.

The net goods deficit was unchanged at 4.4 percent of GDP in 2014, while the services surplus edged down by 0.1 percentage point of GDP to 1.3 percent (see Figures 2-12 and 2-13, which show these concepts on the closely related balance of payments basis). Our services exports have consistently grown relative to merchandise exports since at least the beginning of the 1990s and the start of the digital revolution. If current trends continue,

Figure 2-11
Select Dollar Exchange Rates, 2000–2015

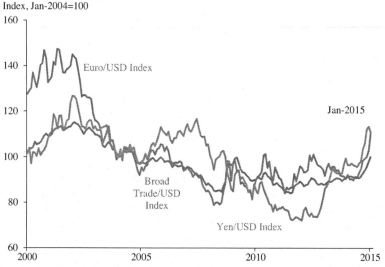

Note: The broad Trade Index is a weighted average of foreign exchange values of the U.S. dollar against major U.S. trading partners.
Source: Federal Reserve Board, Foreign Exchange Rates.

Figure 2-12
Trade in Goods, 2000–2014

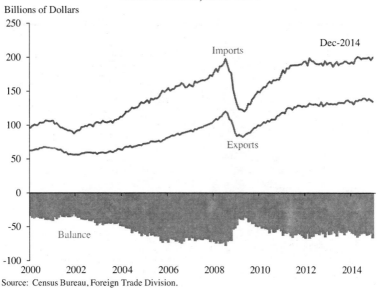

Billions of Dollars

Source: Census Bureau, Foreign Trade Division.

Figure 2-13
Trade in Services, 2000–2014

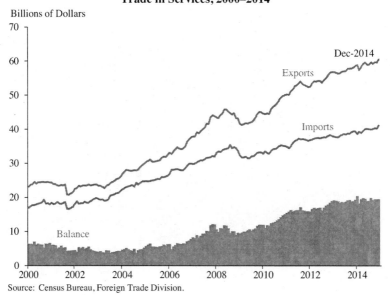

Billions of Dollars

Source: Census Bureau, Foreign Trade Division.

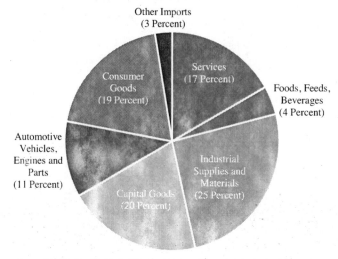

Figure 2-14a
Services and Goods Composition: Imports, 2013

Other Imports
(3 Percent)

Consumer
Goods
(19 Percent)

Services
(17 Percent)

Foods, Feeds,
Beverages
(4 Percent)

Automotive
Vehicles,
Engines and
Parts
(11 Percent)

Industrial
Supplies and
Materials
(25 Percent)

Capital Goods
(20 Percent)

Source: Census Bureau, Foreign Trade Division; Bureau of Economic Analysis, Balance
of Payments Division.

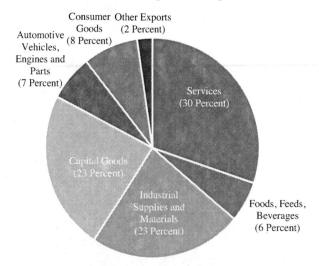

Figure 2-14b
Services and Goods Composition: Exports, 2013

Consumer Other Exports
Goods (2 Percent)
Automotive (8 Percent)
Vehicles,
Engines and
Parts
(7 Percent)

Services
(30 Percent)

Capital Goods
(23 Percent)

Industrial
Supplies and
Materials
(23 Percent)

Foods, Feeds,
Beverages
(6 Percent)

Source: Census Bureau, Foreign Trade Division;Bureau of Economic Analysis, Balance
of Payments Diviision.

services exports should remain an increasingly important component of overall U.S. export success.

In 2013, services accounted for over 30 percent of all U.S. exports, while services amounted to just 17 percent of all U.S. imports. On the import side, 19 percent of U.S. imports are consumer goods (see Figure 2-14). Overall trade in industrial supplies, which includes petroleum, accounts for between 23 and 26 percent of imports and exports, though the composition of exports and imports differs. Buying from our trading partners the goods and services at which they are relatively more efficient lowers prices and increases choice for U.S. consumers and businesses (see Chapter 7).

One ongoing trade trend that accelerated in late 2014 is the continuing decline in U.S. energy imports (see Chapter 6 for a detailed discussion). A major part of the decline is due to an expansion in U.S. production of unconventional oil and natural gas, while another element is growing U.S. energy efficiency and reliance on renewable energy sources. In addition, the world price of oil fell precipitously in the fourth quarter of 2014. Between 2011 and 2014, petroleum's share of the U.S. trade deficit in goods fell from 45 percent to 26 percent, according to data from the Census Bureau.

DEVELOPMENTS IN 2014 AND THE NEAR-TERM OUTLOOK

Consumer Spending

Real consumer spending grew 2.8 percent during the four quarters of 2014, the same as the year-earlier rate. This growth was accompanied by upward trends in consumer sentiment, encouraging reductions in household debt, and gains in household wealth over the course of 2013 and 2014.

Growth was strong for real household purchases of durable goods (8.4 percent), especially motor vehicles. Growth was moderate for nondurables (2.3 percent) and services (2.1 percent). Within nondurables, consumer spending on gasoline and other energy goods rose 2.9 percent during 2014, after falling at a 1.5-percent annual rate during the preceding seven years, a generally negative trend driven by increasingly fuel-efficient motor vehicles. Sharply lower nominal oil prices during the fourth quarter of 2014, which drove the price of gasoline to levels last seen in 2010, probably encouraged growth in real consumer energy spending.

Light motor vehicle sales rose to 16.4 million units in 2014, the fifth consecutive yearly increase, and the highest-selling pace since 2006. Sales of light motor vehicles averaged 16.4 million units during the decade through 2007. Sales trended up during the four quarters of the year, consistent with the emerging strength in labor markets and real incomes. Motor vehicle assemblies also increased from the first to the second half of the year and, at year end, inventory-to-sales ratios were near their long-term averages. Between 2007 and 2013, the average age of the fleet of private light motor vehicles has risen from 10.0 to 11.4 years, which may partly reflect an increase in quality but also suggests that households may have postponed new vehicle purchases during the period of elevated unemployment. If so, replacement demand is likely to support new vehicle sales during the next couple of years.

Consumer sentiment resumed its upward trend in 2014 after interruptions by the debt-limit crisis in the summer of 2011, the fiscal cliff in the winter of 2012, and the government shutdown in October 2013. By year end, the Reuters/University of Michigan Index of Consumer Sentiment had reached its highest level since 2007, and was in the top 30 percent of its historical range. Survey administrators cited rising wage and employment expectations as the principal contributors to improving sentiment, along with declining gasoline prices. The Conference Board index in the second half of 2014 was also at its highest level since 2007.

Meanwhile, U.S. households continued to pay down their debts. Figure 2-15 shows the dramatic rise in the household sector's liabilities-to-income and debt-service ratios in the run-up to the financial crisis, along with the reduction in these ratios (known as deleveraging) that followed. By 2013, the liabilities-to-income ratio was at its lowest level since 2002. Household debt service (the share of income allocated to making required payments on that debt) has fallen even more dramatically: not only has outstanding debt principal fallen relative to income, but interest rates are at historically low levels. By the second quarter of 2014, required payments on mortgage and consumer debt had fallen to 9.9 percent of disposable income, nearly the lowest level on record. During the deleveraging process, heightened foreclosure activity and lower borrowing for home purchases led to a large reduction in debt. In the eight quarters through the third quarter of 2014, this adjustment process appears to have tapered off, and debt has been stable relative to disposable income at levels that are near historic lows. At these lows, real consumer spending has a firmer foundation for growth than it did earlier in this expansion. However, these estimates are based on aggregate data, largely from the Financial Accounts of the United States (FAUS), that could mask higher debt-service burdens for some families; that is, the health of personal finances varies substantially across households.

In addition to the uptrend in sentiment and the progress in deleveraging, gains in real consumer spending have also been supported by gains in net worth (that is, household assets less liabilities, see Figure 2-16). Although the wealth-to-income ratio was little changed during 2014, it had increased

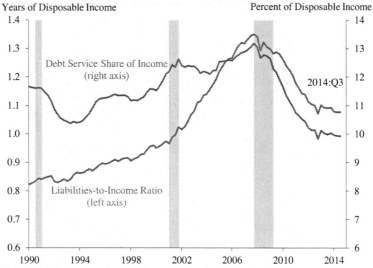

Figure 2-15
Household Deleveraging, 1990–2014

Years of Disposable Income

Percent of Disposable Income

Debt Service Share of Income
(right axis)

2014:Q3

Liabilities-to-Income Ratio
(left axis)

Note: Shading denotes recession.
Source: Federal Reserve Board, Financial Accounts of the United States.

Figure 2-16
**Consumption and Wealth Relative to Disposable
Personal Income (DPI), 1950–2014**

Consumption/DPI Ratio

Years of Disposable Income

2014:Q4

Total-Wealth-to-DPI Ratio
(right axis)

Consumption-to-DPI Ratio
(left axis)

Stock Market
Wealth-to-DPI Ratio
(right axis)

Net Housing
Wealth-to-DPI Ratio
(right axis)

Note: Values imputed for 2014:Q4 by CEA. Shading denotes recession.
Source: Bureau of Economic Analysis, National Income and Product Accounts; Federal Reserve
Board, Financial Accounts of the United States; CEA calculations.

Box 2-4: U.S. Household Wealth in the Wake of the Crisis and Implications for Wealth Inequality

Supported by rising home values and stock-market gains, real household net worth—the difference between the value of a household's assets and debts, adjusted for inflation—increased further in 2014 to about $700,000 per household according to the FAUS, just under its pre-recession peak. Because wealth is unevenly distributed and concentrated among a relatively small number of households, and because the FAUS includes holdings of nonprofit institutions in its definition of wealth, the recovery in mean household net worth does not necessarily reflect the experiences of most families.

The Federal Reserve Board's latest triennial Survey of Consumer Finances (SCF), conducted during 2013, does measure the evolution of wealth for households at different income levels. Broadly speaking, the SCF shows that the recovery in net worth has been uneven for households across the income distribution, as the top 10 percent of income earners have regained much more of their wealth through 2013, on average, than the bottom 90 percent of earners. Figure 2-vi shows how the wealth of different income groups changed between the 2007 and 2013 surveys. This differential recovery owes partially to disparities in the holdings of assets across the income distribution. The value of stock market wealth generally increases more than housing wealth as one

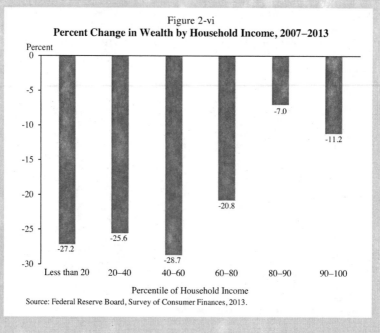

Figure 2-vi
Percent Change in Wealth by Household Income, 2007–2013

Source: Federal Reserve Board, Survey of Consumer Finances, 2013.

moves up the income distribution. For example, according to the SCF, the top 10 percent of income earners held nearly four times as much housing wealth as did the middle 20 percent in 2013 but almost 12 times as much stock-market wealth. The appreciation of equities during 2014, discussed earlier in this chapter, is likely to have benefited higher-income households disproportionately.

Such an uneven recovery implies that wealth inequality has continued to increase in recent years. Moreover, even among the highest 10 percent of earners, mean and median wealth diverged between 2007 and 2013, suggesting that wealth has become even more concentrated within a smaller share of households. Because the SCF excludes the wealthiest 400 households in the United States—and because the distribution of wealth becomes increasingly concentrated near the very top—the increasing concentration seen in the SCF likely understates the actual increase. However, the rise in inequality has been mitigated by the President's policies, including the Affordable Care Act and the restoration of a more progressive individual income tax code. The President's FY 2016 Budget proposes further policies to ensure the benefits of growth are more widely shared, including investments in early childhood and college education, new tax credits for low-income workers, and curbs to tax expenditures for high-income earners.

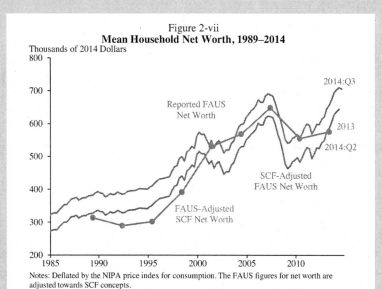

Figure 2-vii
Mean Household Net Worth, 1989–2014
Thousands of 2014 Dollars

Notes: Deflated by the NIPA price index for consumption. The FAUS figures for net worth are adjusted towards SCF concepts.
Source: Federal Reserve Board, Survey of Consumer Finances (private data), Financial Accounts of the United States; CEA calculations.

But the rise in wealth inequality is not a recent phenomenon; research shows that it is decades in the making. In a study spanning 100 years of U.S. tax records, Saez and Zucman (2014) find that wealth inequality has been increasing in recent decades, especially at the very top of the distribution. According to the Saez-Zucman data, the wealthiest 0.1 percent of households saw their share of U.S. wealth grow from 7 percent in 1979 to 22 percent in 2012. More broadly, the study finds that wealth concentration has been increasing since 1978, and is now approaching levels not seen since the period immediately before the Great Depression.

Because the most recent SCF survey was conducted over the course of 2013, it would not have picked up some of the wealth gains during the second half of 2013 and during 2014, as shown in Figure 2-vii. In addition, some of the divergences between the two measures of household wealth (the SCF and the one in the FAUS) can be accounted for by conceptual differences between the two surveys, such as: institutional endowments, assets of defined-benefit pension plans, and pension fund reserves. As can be seen, average household wealth was similar across the two surveys in 2007 and 2013, but the FAUS measure of wealth appears to have fallen further during the recession and risen faster during the recovery.

sharply during 2013, boosted by sizeable gains in stock-market and housing wealth. The year-end 2013 and year-end 2014 levels of wealth relative to income were up by more than one year of disposable income from the trough of the recession, reaching 6.25 years, a level surpassed only during the years 2005 to 2007. Adjusted for inflation and population growth, real household net worth finally overtook the 2007 level at the end of 2013 and made further gains during 2014. Changes in net worth have been spread unevenly across households, however, and these disparities may have implications for families and macroeconomic activity (see Box 2-4).

Housing Markets

With abnormally cold weather during the first quarter of 2014, housing market activity got off to a slow start but eventually increased above 2013 levels (see Figure 2-17). As the 30-year fixed mortgage interest rate fell 60 basis points during the 12 months of the year to 3.9 percent, housing starts and permits edged up to 1.0 million units, helping to support a 2.6-percent increase in residential investment during the four quarters of 2014. New and existing home sales also got off to a slow start in 2014 but recovered somewhat as the year unfolded.

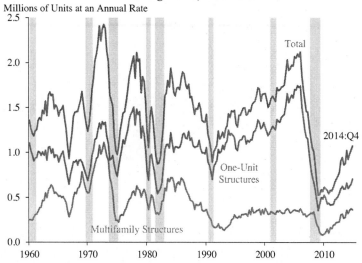

Figure 2-17
Housing Starts, 1960–2014

Millions of Units at an Annual Rate

Note: Shading denotes recession.
Source: Census Bureau, New Residential Construction.

Other housing market indicators suggested continued recovery in this sector in 2014. The stock of delinquencies and foreclosures as a share of all mortgages decreased to levels not seen since 2007, particularly in states where court appearances are unnecessary to begin a foreclosure process, while the rate of new mortgage delinquencies fell, on balance, to a level last seen in 2006. Accordingly, fewer households sold homes under distressed conditions and so the share of sales comprised by non-foreclosure properties rose. With fewer distressed sales, speculative investor activity receded as did the share of home purchases financed with cash.

Supported by improving labor markets, rising sales, and lower mortgage interest rates, house prices increased in 2014. Major house price indexes, shown in Figure 2-18, increased 5 to 7 percent during the 12 months through November 2014, helping to lift an additional 1.9 million borrowers out of negative equity (where they owed more than their homes were worth) in the first three quarters of the year.[6] Notably, owing in part to these house price gains, many more homeowners were able to sell their properties without realizing a loss and this contributed to a modest increase in the inventory of existing homes available for sale from the low levels seen in 2013. Although national house price indexes in November 2014 remained

---

[6] As of this writing, data for some of the major house price indexes were not yet available for December 2014, and data on underwater mortgages were not yet available for the fourth quarter of 2014.

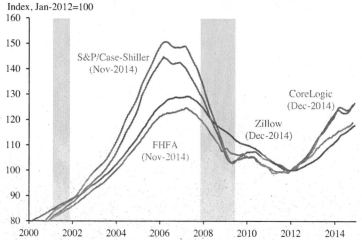

Figure 2-18
National House Price Indexes, 2000–2014

Index, Jan-2012=100

Note: The Standard & Poor's/Case-Shiller, Federal Housing Finance Agency, and CoreLogic indexes all adjust for the quality of homes sold but only cover homes that are bought or sold, whereas Zillow reflects prices for all homes on the market. Shading denotes recession.
Source: Zillow; CoreLogic; Federal Housing Finance Agency; Standard & Poor's/Case-Shiller.

4 to 13 percent below their pre-recession highs, they are now slightly above levels implied by their traditional relationship with the cost of renting (Figure 2-19). As a result, house price increases may moderate in the coming years, particularly in light of the expected increases in long-term interest rates discussed later in this chapter.

Residential investment, which increased 6.9 percent during the four quarters of 2013, stepped down to an annual growth rate of 2.6 percent during 2014. As defined in the national income and product accounts, residential investment includes permanent-site new home construction, real estate commissions, home improvements, and spending on manufactured homes. Permanent-site new home construction rose during each of the four quarters of the year, cumulating in an 8.5-percent increase over the four quarters of the year. In contrast to the gains in permanent-site construction, "other construction" (the aggregate of real estate commissions, manufactured homes, and home improvements) fell. Sales of new homes hovered only just above the lows seen during the Great Recession. Meanwhile, existing home sales dipped early in the year but recovered to a level that is 46 percent higher than its monthly trough in 2010.

Looking ahead, residential investment has the potential for strong gains as a large cohort of "millennials" (that is, 18-to-34-year olds) will soon participate in the housing market in greater numbers as renters and eventually as homeowners (Figure 2-20). Typically, homebuilding depends

Figure 2-19
Home Prices and Owners' Equivalent Rent, 1975–2014

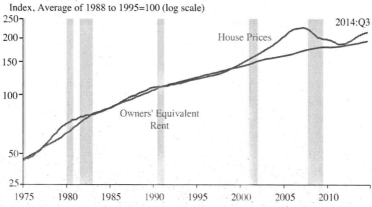

Index, Average of 1988 to 1995=100 (log scale)

2014:Q3

House Prices

Owners' Equivalent Rent

Note: Shading denotes recession. House prices are measured by the FHFA's price index (total index before 1991, purchase-only index after 1991). Owners' equivalent rent is measured by the Personal Consumption Expenditures price index for imputed rent of owner-occupied nonfarm housing (before 1983) and the Consumer Price Index for owners' equivalent rent of residence (1983-present).
Source: Federal Housing Finance Agency, House Price Index; Bureau of Economic Analysis, National Income and Product Accounts; Bureau of Labor Statistics, Consumer Price Index; CEA calculations.

Figure 2-20
U.S. Population Distribution by Age and Gender, 2013 Census

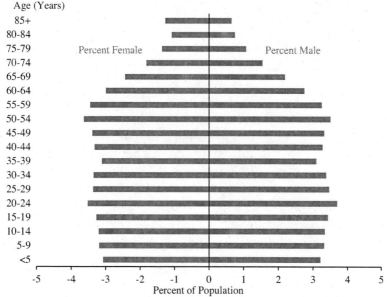

Age (Years)

Percent Female   Percent Male

Percent of Population

Source: Census Bureau, Population Division, 2013.

positively on household formation, reductions in vacancies, and demolitions. With much of the cyclical overhang in vacant housing having abated during the past several years, the outlook for homebuilding will depend, in large part, on the recovery in household formation, particularly among millennials. Since 2006, rates of household formation among millennials have been depressed, in part due to high unemployment and the rapid increase in cost of rental housing. However, improved labor market conditions in 2014 and a slight easing in rental prices provide favorable conditions to push up household formation and in turn boost residential investment activity.[7]

Expected further strengthening of the labor market could provide additional support to release the pent-up demand for housing due to demographic factors. According to a November 2014 Gallup survey, 30 percent of respondents believe that the current labor market provides a good environment for finding a quality job, up 4 percentage points from November 2013 and well above the low of 8 percent seen in 2011.[8] The Federal Reserve Board's 2014 Survey of Young Workers similarly finds that young adults are optimistic about future job stability, which also bodes well for household formation and thus housing demand.[9] Consistent with optimism about their prospects in the labor market, the share of households expecting an improvement in their finances edged up to 45 percent by December from 38 percent last year.[10] A National Association of Home Builders survey showed that the positive outlook also extended to homebuilders, as their sentiment on whether it is a good time to build increased in 2014 to its highest level since 2005 (Figure 2-21).

In the mortgage market, rates on a 30-year fixed rate mortgage decreased by 60 basis points during the 12 months of 2014, in line with the decrease in 10-year Treasury yields, and are 63 basis points lower than their recent high in 2013 (See Figure 2-22). In spite of this decline, mortgage applications for home purchases were flat, on balance, in 2014, consistent with slowing home sales and tight mortgage credit availability (see Figure 2-23). Refinancing activity was well below the highs seen in early 2013 and did not show much response to the drop in rates, in part because previous refinancing waves already lowered rates for many borrowers. The Government-Sponsored Enterprises (GSEs)—Fannie Mae and Freddie Mac—and the Federal Housing Administration (FHA), continued to support an outsized share (over 70 percent) of mortgage originations in 2014,

---

[7] See Council of Economic Advisers, "15 Economic Facts about Millennials," http://www. whitehouse.gov/sites/default/files/docs/millennials_report.pdf

[8] http://www.gallup.com/poll/179483/americans-perceptions-job-market-hold-steady.aspx

[9] http://www.federalreserve.gov/econresdata/2014-survey-young-workers-young-workers-outlook.htm

[10] http://www.fanniemae.com/portal/about-us/media/corporate-news/2014/6192.html

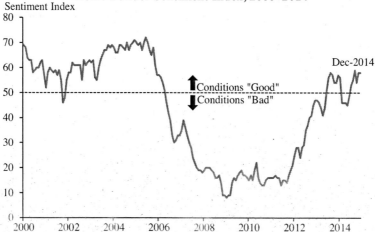

Figure 2-21
Home Builder Sentiment Index, 2000–2014

Note: The NAHB surveys builder perceptions of current single-family home sales, sales expectations for the next six months, and level of traffic of prospective home buyers. NAHB then uses builders' responses to calculate a seasonally adjusted index of sentiment.

Source: National Association of Home Builders, Builders Economic Council Survey.

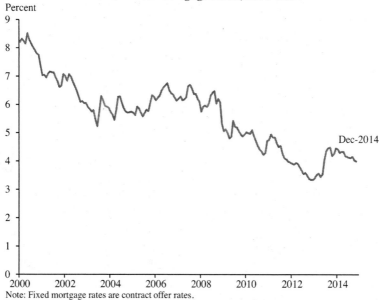

Figure 2-22
30-Year Fixed Mortgage Rates, 2000–2014

Note: Fixed mortgage rates are contract offer rates.
Source: Freddie Mac, Primary Mortgage Market Survey.

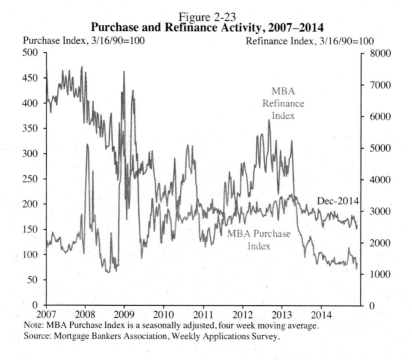

Figure 2-23
Purchase and Refinance Activity, 2007–2014

Purchase Index, 3/16/90=100   Refinance Index, 3/16/90=100

MBA
Refinance
Index

Dec-2014

MBA Purchase
Index

Note: MBA Purchase Index is a seasonally adjusted, four week moving average.
Source: Mortgage Bankers Association, Weekly Applications Survey.

with banks' portfolios supporting much of the rest. Since 2007, private-label securitization activity has been negligible, providing funds only to a tiny segment of extremely high credit quality borrowers with high-balance, "jumbo" mortgages.

One important headwind to continued normalization in the housing sector is low credit availability. Across a broad range of measures, mortgage underwriting standards remain tight, and the Federal Reserve's Senior Loan Officer Opinion Survey showed only modest signs of continued easing during 2014. Accordingly, mortgage purchase originations are low relative to the volume of home sales activity. The Federal Housing Finance Agency and the FHA took important steps in 2014 to clarify and mitigate the legal risks lenders face and the conditions under which housing agencies may force them to repurchase loans ("putback risk"). The Administration has also enacted other policies to improve credit access, including a reduction in FHA mortgage insurance premiums from 1.35 percent to 0.85 percent, which will help homebuyers borrow for less. Nonetheless, it may take some time before lenders can fully implement the necessary steps to improve access to credit prudently and before more borrowers, particularly borrowers with less-than-pristine credit histories, feel that credit conditions have eased enough to apply for mortgage loans.

Investment

Business Fixed Investment. Real business fixed investment grew 5.5 percent during the four quarters of 2014, up from a 4.7-percent increase during 2013. The rate of investment growth picked up in each of its three components: structures, equipment, and intellectual property.

Investment spending has grown more slowly than usual for a business-cycle expansion. One reason might be the general surplus of capital services relative to output that has persisted since the last recession (Figure 2-24). After output fell sharply during that recession and during the slow recovery, firms found themselves with more capital than they needed. But as the recovery has progressed, output has grown faster than capital services, so that firms have only recently had a general reason to increase their use of capital services. (In Figure 2-24, the blue line has only recently fallen below the orange line.) This shift argues for faster growth in investment spending during the next year than in the recent past.

Nonfinancial corporations spent a lower-than-average share of their internal funds (also known as cash flow) on investment during 2011 to 2013 (see Figure 2-25). Instead, these corporations used a good part of those funds to buy back shares from their stockholders. Share buybacks are similar to dividends insofar as they are a way for corporations to return value to shareholders. They differ, however, with regard to permanence: whereas dividend changes tend to persist, share buybacks are one-time events. (When firms raise investment funds by issuing new equity, the nonfinancial sector aggregate of share buybacks in the figures can be negative, as was common in the 1950s and 1960s.) The decline in the invested share of internal funds from 2011 to 2013, together with the rise in share buybacks, suggests that firms had more internal funds than they thought they could profitably invest. As can be seen in Figure 2-25, the investment outlook appears to have improved in 2014, and the investment share of internal funds has rebounded to near its historical average. Share buybacks, however, remain high.

Inventory Investment. Inventory investment contributed 0.3 percentage point to the 2.5-percent growth rate of real GDP during the four quarters of 2014, down from the preceding year when it accounted for 0.5 percentage point of growth. A substantial portion of the 2013 inventory contribution to growth was accounted for by agricultural inventory investment when a bumper year for farm production followed the 2012 drought. In 2014, in contrast, agricultural inventory investment was relatively steady. Inventory investment was an important part of the year's quarterly fluctuations, accounting for more than one-half of the reported 2.1-percent annual rate of decline in first-quarter real GDP. In the manufacturing and trade sector, the buildup of inventories through 2014 was no faster than sales; by November,

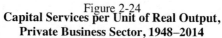

Figure 2-24
**Capital Services per Unit of Real Output,
Private Business Sector, 1948–2014**

Index, 2009=100

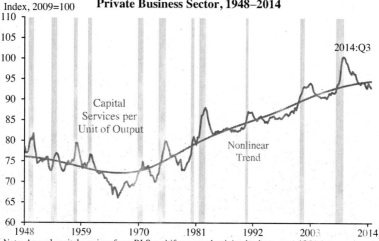

Note: Annual capital services from BLS multifactor productivity database, post-1964 data interpolated quarterly using Macroadvisers quarterly data; pre-1965 data interpolated by moving average. Nonlinear trend is a bi-weight filter using at 60-quarter window.
Source: Bureau of Labor Statistics, Labor Productivity and Costs; Macroeconomic Advisers; CEA calculations.

Figure 2-25
**Share Buy Backs vs. Investment,
Nonfinancial Corporate Business, 1952–2014**

Percent of U.S. Internal Funds, Four-Quarter Moving Average

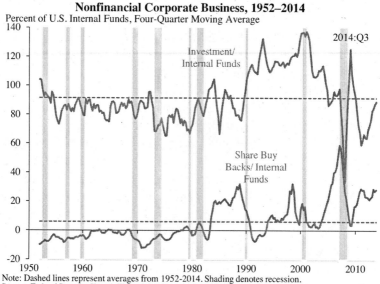

Note: Dashed lines represent averages from 1952-2014. Shading denotes recession.
Source: Federal Reserve Board, Financial Accounts of the United States.

manufacturing and trade businesses held sufficient inventories to supply 1.3 months of sales, roughly the same level as at year-end 2013.

State and Local Governments

When viewed over the current expansion, growth in State and local purchases has been the weakest of any business cycle recovery in the post-World War II period (Figure 2-26). The contribution of State and local purchases to real GDP growth was negative during the three years from 2010 to 2012 but finally turned positive in 2013 and 2014. Even during these past two years State and local governments contributed only 0.13 percentage point to the annual rate of real GDP growth. The recent weakly positive trend in this sector is also reflected in job gains as State and local governments have added 100,000 jobs since January 2013. Even so, employment in this sector remains 631,000 below its previous high. Almost 40 percent of this net job loss was in the educational services subsector.

Despite the positive signals during 2014, major obstacles to State and local expansion remain. State and local governments continue to spend more than they collect in revenues and their aggregate deficit during the first three quarters of 2014 amounted to 1.3 percent of nominal U.S. GDP ($233 billion), a deficit-to-GDP ratio that has been roughly stable for several

Figure 2-26
Real State and Local Government Purchases During Recoveries

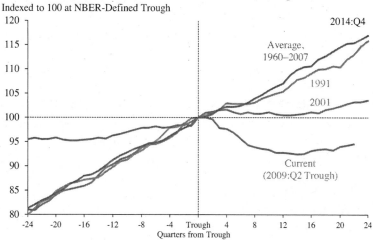

Note: The 1960–2007 average excludes the 1980 recession due to overlap with the 1981–1982 recession.
Source: Bureau of Economic Analysis, National Income and Product Accounts; National Bureau of Economic Research; CEA calculations.

years. In the first three quarters of 2014, expenditures remained roughly flat at about 14.0 percent of GDP, and revenues remained flat at about 12.7 percent of GDP. In addition, unfunded pension obligations place a heavy burden on State and local government finances. As can be seen in Figure 2-27, the size of these pension liabilities relative to State and local receipts ballooned immediately after the recession and remains elevated at a level that was about 57 percent of a year's revenue in 2014. Adding in State and local bond liabilities does not change the overall shape of the plot shown in Figure 2-27, though they elevate the liabilities-to-receipts ratio to about 200 percent of a year's revenue.

Labor Markets

Major labor market indicators showed a pronounced recovery in 2014. The unemployment rate dropped 1.2 percentage points in calendar year 2014, the fastest pace since 1984. Private employment increased by 3.0 million during the 12 months of 2014, substantially faster than the average pace of 2.4 million jobs during the three preceding years (Figure 2-28). The job gains were wide-spread across industries. Some notable growth included the construction industry, which continued to rebound, adding 338,000 jobs in 2014 (11 percent of the total increase in payroll employment), professional and business services (23 percent), and health care services (10 percent). The strengthening of the labor market is discussed in detail in Chapter 3, along with challenges that remain—including with respect to involuntary part-time work, long-term unemployment, labor force participation, the fluidity of labor markets, and job quality.

Long-term unemployment peaked in 2010 and has been falling steadily since then; declines in long-term unemployment accounted for 64 percent of the overall unemployment decline in 2014. While this progress is encouraging, long-term unemployment remains elevated above pre-recession levels (Figure 2-29). Data on job vacancies provided more encouraging news about the labor market in 2014. The number of job vacancies jumped 27 percent in the first 11 months of 2014. The number of job seekers per job vacancy stood at 1.8 in November, and is now below the 2.1 average during the previous expansion.

The labor force participation rate fell 3.2 percentage points between the fourth quarter of 2007 and the fourth quarter of 2014. CEA analysis finds that about one-half of this decline was due to the aging of the baby-boom generation into retirement, while the other half of this decline was due to a composition of cyclical factors, longer-standing secular trends, and factors specific to the recession. These demographic-related declines will become steeper in the near term, echoing the rise in the number of births from 1946

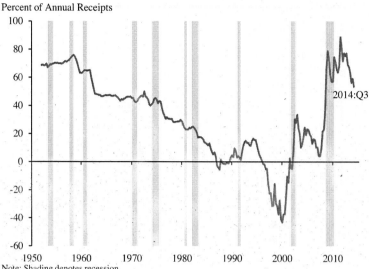

Figure 2-27
State and Local Pension Fund Liabilities, 1952–2014

Percent of Annual Receipts

2014:Q3

Note: Shading denotes recession.
Source: Federal Reserve Board, Financial Accounts of the United States.

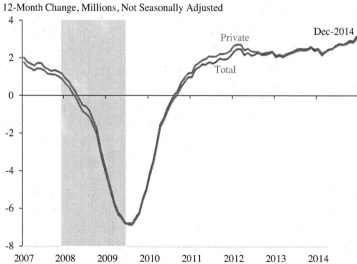

Figure 2-28
Nonfarm Payroll Employment, 2007–2014

12-Month Change, Millions, Not Seasonally Adjusted

Private   Dec-2014

Total

Note: Total excludes temporary decennial Census workers. Shading denotes recession.
Source: Bureau of Labor Statistics, Current Employment Statistics.

Figure 2-29
Unemployment Rate by Duration, 1990–2014
Percent of Civilian Labor Force

Unemployed for
26 Weeks or Less

Dec-2014

Unemployed for
27 Weeks and Over

Note: Shading denotes recession. Dashed lines represent averages from 2001-2007.
Source: Bureau of Labor Statistics, Current Population Survey.

through 1957. About a sixth of the participation-rate decline, however, was also due to the high unemployment rates from 2009 to 2014, which caused potential job-seekers to delay entry into the labor force or become discouraged. By the fourth quarter of 2014, the participation rate remained below what would occur if the labor market was fully recovered. Looking ahead, as the unemployment rate is projected to continue declining during 2015, the labor force participation rate is projected to be roughly flat, as the cyclical rebound roughly offsets the continued downward pull of the aging population. See Chapter 3 for further discussion.

The unemployment rate may not tell the whole story of the potential for increased employment. Measures of discouraged workers and those working part time for economic reasons indicate more slack than what is embodied in the official unemployment rate (see Chapter 3).

Labor Productivity in the Nonfarm Business Sector. Although employment growth is strong, the growth in output has not risen much; as such, the growth of labor productivity (that is, output per hour) has been below its long-term average pace. Because productivity moves with the business cycle, it should be measured over a long interval. When measured with product-side data from the national income and product accounts (the measure published by the Bureau of Labor Statistics), labor productivity—real nonfarm output per hour—rose at a 1.4-percent annual rate during the almost seven years since the business cycle peak in 2007. But when measured by the income-side measure, nonfarm productivity has risen at a 1.8-percent rate. The best measure of productivity growth is probably the average of these figures, similar to the average used for output in Figure 2-2, yielding an estimate of a 1.6-percent annual rate of growth in productivity thus far in this business cycle. This is a slower pace of growth than the 2.2 percent during the 54½-year period between the business-cycle peaks in 1953 and 2007, potentially at least in part due to the transitory after-effects of the severe recession, including reduced investment associated with the capital overhand discussed earlier.

How should recent productivity growth color forecasts of future productivity? In the absence of a structural change in the process generating productivity outcomes, the best way to forecast labor productivity is to draw on long-term data. Averaging productivity growth over the current business cycle with data from all the years since the business-cycle peak in 1953 yields an estimate of 2.1 percent a year, the figure that the Administration uses to project the long-term labor productivity growth rate, as discussed in the long-term outlook section below.

Price and wage inflation. Core consumer price inflation (that is, excluding food and energy prices) has been stable at around a 1.7-percent annual rate for the past two years. The overall (headline) consumer price index (CPI) was held down by declines in energy prices in 2013 and 2014, increasing just 1.5 percent and 0.8 percent during the 12 months of those two years (Figure 2-30). Food prices increased faster than overall inflation during 2014, partly reflecting the drought in California, with meat and milk prices up roughly 13 and 4 percent, respectively.

The price index for personal consumption expenditures in the national income accounts (the PCE price index) is largely a re-weighted version of the consumer price index. Because of a different method of aggregating the individual components, its annual increases have averaged about 0.3 percentage point a year less than the consumer price index (since 2002 when the Bureau of Labor Statistics started re-linking it with the pattern of expenditures every two years). During the 12 months of 2014, for example, the core PCE price index increased 1.3 percent, less than the 1.6 percent increase in the core CPI. As tabulated by the Survey of Professional Forecasters, measures of long-term expectations for CPI inflation have been well-anchored at around 2.3 percent (and 2.1 percent for the PCE price index), both during the last recession and more recently. This steadiness suggests market confidence in the Federal Reserve's ability to keep inflation under control.

Nominal hourly compensation increased 2.3 percent during 2014, as measured by the employment cost index (ECI) in the private sector (Figure 2-31). That pace was up slightly from the 1.8- and 2.0-percent rates observed

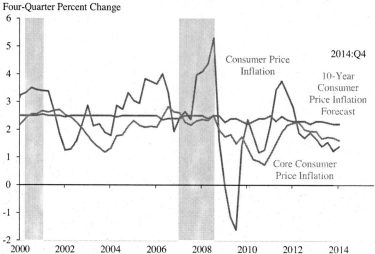

Figure 2-30
Inflation and Inflation Expectations Ten Years Forward, 2000–2014

Four-Quarter Percent Change

Note: Shading denotes recession. The 10-Year Consumer Price Inflation Forecast data come from the Survey of Professional Forecasters.
Source: Bureau of Labor Statistics; Federal Reserve Bank of Philadelphia, Survey of Professional Forecasters.

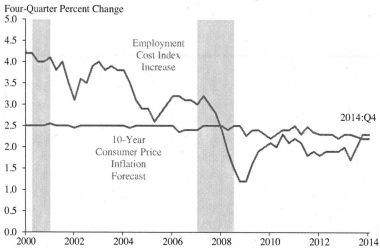

Figure 2-31
Hourly Compensation Increases vs. Inflation Expectations, 2000–2014

Four-Quarter Percent Change

Note: Shading denotes recession. The 10-Year Consumer Price Inflation Forecast data come from the Survey of Professional Forecasters.
Source: Bureau of Labor Statistics; Federal Reserve Bank of Philadelphia, Survey of Professional Forecasters.

during the preceding two years. The faster pace of growth in 2014 was accounted for by take-home wages and salaries as well as hourly benefits. It was not, however, in employer-paid health insurance, which slowed to a 2.4-percent increase during 2014, down from 3.0 percent during 2013. As can be seen from Figure 2-31, increases in nominal hourly compensation have been running lower than long-term price inflation expectations for the entire post-2008 period. The low increases in hourly compensation relative to prices are notable because—if the labor share of nonfarm business output were to be stable—hourly compensation growth would exceed output price inflation (in the nonfarm business sector) by the rate of productivity growth. That real hourly compensation growth has been below productivity growth suggests that the elevated unemployment rate and the overall slack in the labor market have suppressed hourly compensation growth since 2008.

THE LONG-TERM OUTLOOK

The 10-Year Forecast

Although real GDP growth averaged 2.2 percent during the four-year period, 2011 through 2014, major components of private domestic demand point to faster growth in 2015. Meanwhile, insofar as inflation remains low and stable, the supply side does not appear to impose near-term constraints. Although Federal fiscal policy has generally increased the level of output (as discussed in Chapter 3), the year-to-year decline in the deficit-to-GDP ratio implies that Federal fiscal policy subtracted from real GDP growth from FY 2010 through FY 2014. The Administration projects that the deficit-to-GDP ratio will edge up in FY 2015 under the terms of the bipartisan budget agreement for FY 2015 that Congress approved in mid-December 2014. With a strengthening State and local sector, fiscal actions will likely turn from being a drag to slightly expansionary in 2015. For consumers, faster job growth and a pickup in nominal and real wage gains in 2014 will probably boost spending in 2015. These income gains—following a multiyear period of successful deleveraging—leave consumers in an improved financial position. Beyond the income gains, the increases in housing and stock-market wealth during the past three years will probably also support strong growth in consumer spending in 2015. Business investment also shows brighter prospects for growth in 2015 than in earlier years. Businesses will need new facilities, equipment, and intellectual property to service growing demand. The decline in price of imported petroleum during the last quarter of 2014 will—if this lower price persists—save American businesses and consumers about $70 billion in 2015, or enough to boost real GDP by 0.4 percent.

Table 2-2
Administration Economic Forecast

	Nominal GDP	Real GDP (chain-type)	GDP price index (chain-type)	Con-sumer price index (CPI-U)	Unemp-loyment rate (percent)	Interest rate, 91-day Treasury bills (percent)	Interest rate, 10-year Treasury notes (percent)
	Percent change, Q4-to-Q4				Level, calendar year		
2013 (actual)	4.6	3.1	1.4	1.2	7.4	0.1	2.4
2014	3.5	2.1	1.4	1.5	6.2	0.0	2.6
2015	4.6	3.0	1.5	1.8	5.4	0.4	2.8
2016	4.8	3.0	1.7	2.0	5.1	1.5	3.3
2017	4.6	2.7	1.9	2.2	4.9	2.4	3.7
2018	4.5	2.5	2.0	2.3	4.9	2.9	4.0
2019	4.3	2.3	2.0	2.3	5.0	3.2	4.3
2020	4.3	2.3	2.0	2.3	5.1	3.3	4.5
2021	4.3	2.3	2.0	2.3	5.2	3.4	4.5
2022	4.3	2.3	2.0	2.3	5.2	3.4	4.5
2023	4.3	2.3	2.0	2.3	5.2	3.5	4.5
2024	4.3	2.3	2.0	2.3	5.2	3.5	4.5
2025	4.3	2.3	2.0	2.3	5.2	3.5	4.5

Note: These forecasts were based on data available as of November 20, 2014, and were used for the FY 2016 Budget. The interest rate on 91-day T-bills is measured on a secondary-market discount basis.
Source: The forecast was done jointly with the Council of Economic Advisers, the Department of the Treasury, and the Office of Management and Budget.

But not all signals are green, and the United States faces headwinds from abroad. The available 2014 indicators suggest that the economies of Japan and our euro area trading partners are sagging. A slowdown abroad not only reduces our exports, but also raises risks of financial and other spillovers to the U.S. economy.

With the unemployment rate in December 2014 at 5.6 percent, the labor force participation rate still below its expected level given demographic trends, the share of those working part-time for economic reasons still elevated, and the capacity utilization rate in manufacturing at about 78 percent, the economy still has room to utilize more of its potential.

The Administration's economic forecast, as finalized on November 20, 2014 and presented in Table 2-2, underpins the President's FY 2016 Budget. By long-standing convention, this forecast reflects the economic impact of the President's budgetary and other economic proposals which, in the FY 2016 Budget, primarily act to increase the growth rate of potential GDP as discussed in more detail in Box 2-5. The Administration expects real GDP growth to increase from a projected 2.1-percent annual rate during the four quarters of 2014 to 3.0 percent during 2015. (Data released after the final forecast show a faster-than-expected growth rate during 2014 of 2.5 percent rather than 2.1 percent.) The long-term projections for 2016 and beyond, as is standard for the Administration's Budget forecast, assume enactment of the President's policies, including substantial investments in infrastructure, reforms to the tax and immigration systems, liberalization of trade, and deficit reduction—all of which will work to support growth (Box 2-5).

Real GDP is projected to grow 3.0 percent at an annual rate during the eight quarters of 2015 and 2016 and then to grow 2.7 percent during 2017. All of these growth rates exceed the estimated rate of potential real GDP growth, which is 2.3 percent annually over the long run. As a consequence, the unemployment rate is likely to fall—eventually averaging 4.9 percent in 2016 and 2017. This level, below the Administration's estimate of 5.2 percent for the rate of unemployment consistent with stable inflation, can be expected to incrementally raise inflation. The core PCE price index increased by only 1.4 percent during the four quarters of 2014. By 2017, however, consumer price inflation is expected to stabilize at 2.0 percent for the PCE price index and 2.25 percent for the consumer price index.

Nominal interest rates are currently low because the economy has not fully healed from the last recession, while monetary policy has kept rates low across a wide range of debt securities with long maturities. Consistent with the Federal Reserve's forward policy guidance at the time of the forecast, interest rates are projected to rise as the expected period of very low short-term rates diminishes. Eventually, real interest rates (that is, nominal rates less the projected rate of inflation) are predicted to be near, but a bit below, their historical average. These interest-rate paths are close to those projected by professional economists. During the past several years, consensus forecasts for long-term interest rates and long-term economic growth have

Box 2-5: Policy Proposals to Raise Long-Run Potential Output

A key element of the Administration's economic forecast is the growth rate of real GDP in later years of the budget window once the economy's cyclical recovery is complete. Although there is considerable uncertainty around the longer-term outlook, this part of the forecast is critically important because it attempts to summarize the economy's long-run growth potential based solely on structural factors like the size of the labor force and worker productivity. The Administration projects that this long-run potential growth rate is 2.3 percent a year. For reference, the FOMC estimates a range of long-run output growth of 2.0 to 2.3 percent a year, the Congressional Budget Office (CBO 2015) puts this rate at 2.2 percent a year during 2018 to 2024, and the October 2014 Blue Chip consensus panel forecasts an average growth rate of 2.3 percent a year during the five years 2021 to 2025.

The Administration's forecast for long-run potential output growth is at the high end of this range because, consistent with long-standing Administration practice, it incorporates the economic impact of the assumed enactment of the President's policy proposals that would expand the labor force and increase productivity. These proposals include: the productivity increases associated with immigration reform; investments in surface transportation infrastructure and other areas; business tax reform; universal preschool and investments in child care that would boost female labor force participation; the Trans-Pacific Partnership and other policies to expand cross-border trade and investment; and approximately $1.6 trillion in primary (non-interest) deficit reduction.

The President's agenda is expected to deliver a substantial lift to the economy's future prospects and would raise the level of long-run potential output by several percentage points. The Organisation for Economic Co-operation and Development (OECD) and International Monetary Fund (IMF) estimated that the President's agenda would add 2.5 percent to GDP after five years, larger than their estimate for any other G-7 economy. CBO (2014b) also estimated positive effects from the President's proposals, although that assessment likely understates the benefits because it included neither trade agreements nor business tax reform.

Immigration reform. The policy proposal with the single largest effect on long-run potential output is immigration reform. The President continues to support comprehensive immigration reform along the lines of the bipartisan Border Security, Economic Opportunity, and Immigration Modernization Act that passed the U.S. Senate in June 2013. CBO (2013) has estimated that this legislation, if enacted, would raise the level of real GDP by 3.3 percent after 10 years. This effect is large because immigration reform would benefit the economy through a multitude of channels, including counteracting the effects of an aging native-born population, attracting highly skilled immigrants that engage in innovative or entrepreneurial activities, and enabling better job-matching for currently undocumented workers who are offered a path to earned citizenship. Much of the overall effect is due to an expanded workforce—a factor already reflected in the budget savings from immigration reform and thus not added to the forecast to avoid double counting. However, 0.7 percentage point of the total 10-year effect is due to increased total factor productivity, which may be included in the economic forecast without double counting. A portion of these benefits will be realized as a result of the administrative actions announced by President Obama in November 2014 (CEA 2014).

Investments in surface transportation infrastructure and other areas. The Administration's FY 2016 Budget includes $116 billion over 10 years in additional surface transportation infrastructure investment relative to a plausible baseline. The budget also provides for about $75 billion in additional funding in both the non-defense and defense discretionary categories over the next two years, with additional funding in future years. A substantial fraction of this spending will be devoted to investments in physical infrastructure, research and development, or education and training, all of which can help to boost productivity in the years ahead. Notably, the IMF (2014) recently found that given the current underutilization of resources in many advanced economies, a 1 percent of GDP permanent increase in public infrastructure investment could raise output by as much as 2.8 percent after 10 years.

Business tax reform. President Obama's framework for business tax reform, issued in 2012, sets out a series of changes that would strengthen the economy in three main ways. First, the President's plan would encourage investment in the United States. Second, by moving to a more neutral tax system, the proposal would result in a more efficient allocation of capital. And third, to the degree the new system better addresses externalities, for example with a more generous research and development credit, it would also increase total factor productivity and therefore growth. The precise effects of these changes are difficult to quantify but have the potential to be sizeable (See Chapter 5 of this *Report* for more discussion).

Policies to boost female labor force participation. President Obama has pursued policies that enable all workers to participate in the labor force to their fullest desire by making it easier for workers to balance career and family responsibilities. The Administration's FY 2016

Budget calls for tripling the maximum tax credit for child care to $3,000 for young children, while enabling more middle-class families to receive the maximum credit. In addition, the President has proposed, every year since 2013, a Federal-State partnership that would provide all four-year olds from low- and moderate-income families with access to high-quality preschool. Finally, the Budget calls for technical assistance to help States implement and develop paid parental leave programs. A growing empirical literature on the responsiveness of labor supply to family-friendly policies suggests that implementation of these measures could materially increase female labor force participation and GDP. (See Chapter 4 in this *Report* for more discussion.)

Policies to expand cross-border trade and investment. The Administration is pursuing a number of international agreements that would boost cross-border trade and investment, including the Trans-Pacific Partnership (TPP), the Transatlantic Trade and Investment Partnership (T-TIP), an expansion of the Information Technology Agreement, a Trade in Services Agreement, an Environmental Goods Agreement, and a Trade Facilitation Agreement. While the details of TPP are still evolving, one study supported by the Peterson Institute for International Economics (Petri and Plummer 2012) found that TPP could raise U.S. real income by 0.4 percent over approximately 12 years. The European Commission (2013) has estimated a roughly similar effect of T-TIP on the U.S. economy, amounting to an increase of 0.4 percent of GDP in 2027. (See Chapter 7 in this *Report* for more discussion.)

Deficit reduction. CBO's February 2013 analysis of the macroeconomic effects of alternative budgetary paths finds that a hypothetical $2 trillion in primary deficit reduction over 10 years raises the long-term level of real GDP by 0.5 percent. This effect arises because lower Federal deficits translate into higher national saving, lower interest rates, and in turn, greater private investment. The Administration's FY 2016 Budget proposal includes $1.6 trillion in primary deficit reduction relative to the Administration's plausible baseline, enough to stabilize and begin to reduce the National debt-to-GDP ratio.

fallen. The link between long-term growth prospects and long-term interest rates is examined in Box 2-6.

GDP Growth over the Long Term

As discussed earlier, the growth rate of the economy over the long run is determined by the growth of its supply-side components, including those governed by demographics and technological change. The growth rate that characterizes the long-run trend in real U.S. GDP—or potential GDP—plays an important role in guiding the Administration's long-run forecast. For the first three years of the forecast interval--2015, 2016, and 2017--real GDP growth is projected to average 2.9 percent at an annual rate as the economy moves back to its full potential, before shifting thereafter to an average of 2.3 percent, the Administration's estimate of the long-term rate of real GDP growth. These growth rates are slower than historical averages because of the aging of the baby-boom generation into the retirement years. The potential real GDP projections are based on the assumption that the President's full set of policy proposals, which would boost long-run output, are enacted (See Box 2-5)[11].

Table 2-3 shows the Administration's forecast for the contribution of each supply-side factor to the growth in potential real GDP: the working-age population, the rate of labor force participation, the employed share of the labor force, the ratio of nonfarm business employment to household employment, the length of the workweek, labor productivity, and the ratio of real GDP to nonfarm output. The two columns of Table 2-3 show the average annual growth rate for each factor during a long period of history and over the forecast horizon. The first column shows the long-run average growth rates between the business-cycle peak of 1953 and the latest quarter available when the forecast was finalized in mid-November 2014. Many of these variables show substantial fluctuations within business cycles, so that long-period growth rates must be examined to uncover underlying trends. The second column shows average projected growth rates between the third quarter of 2014 and the fourth quarter of 2025; that is, the entire 11¼-year interval covered by the Administration forecast.

The population is projected to grow 0.9 percent a year, on average, over the projection period (line 1, column 2), following the latest projection from the Social Security Administration. Over this same period, the labor force participation rate is projected to decline 0.4 percent a year (line 2, column 2). This projected decline in the labor force participation rate primarily reflects a negative demographic trend originating in the aging of the baby-boom generation into retirement. During the next couple of years, however, rising labor demand due to the continuing business-cycle

---

[11] The one exception is that the forecast does not reflect the increase in the size of labor force attributable to the President's immigration reform. The reason is that the budgetary impact of the added GDP associated with this change is already incorporated in the budget as a policy line, so including this effect in the economic forecast would, in effect, double count it. CBO estimates that the President's immigration reforms would also expand total factor productivity, but did not incorporate this effect into their budgetary estimates; as a result, the productivity effects are included in the Administration's forecast.

Box 2-6: Forecasting the Long-Run Interest Rate

A key input to the U.S. economic forecast is a projection for the long-run nominal interest rate. Recent patterns in bond markets raise a number of questions about the future path of interest rates. Nominal and real (inflation-adjusted) interest rates have been declining since the mid-1980s. In the aftermath of the financial crisis, the Federal Reserve conducted large-scale purchases of longer-term securities, pushing long-term real interest rates down, even below zero. Despite this low rate of return, there has been a strong global demand for U.S. government bonds as a safe haven for savings, including demand by foreign central banks for dollar reserves.

Figure 2-viii shows the nominal interest rate and the ex post real interest rate for 10-year Treasury securities. The *ex post* real interest rate is defined as the nominal rate less realized inflation (whereas the *ex ante* real interest rate is the nominal rate less expected inflation). The figure illustrates the 30-year decline in *ex post* real and nominal interest rates and the behavior of real and nominal rates across different monetary policy regimes.

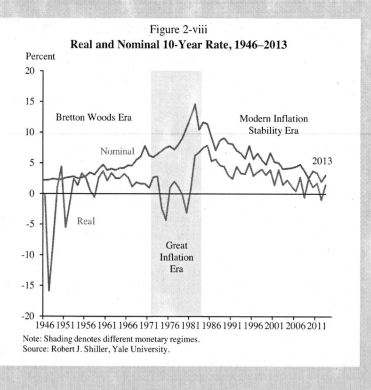

Figure 2-viii
Real and Nominal 10-Year Rate, 1946–2013

Note: Shading denotes different monetary regimes.
Source: Robert J. Shiller, Yale University.

Economic growth and the long-run real interest rate. The basic general equilibrium analysis of real and nominal interest rates originated with Irving Fisher (1930), who characterized the equilibrium relationship between the real return on investment and the compensation to savers for postponing consumption. The Ramsey optimal-growth model is a convenient framework for conveying these fundamental relationships. The model and its extensions characterize the behavior of the economy on its steady-state growth path (Ramsey 1928; Cass 1965; Koopmans 1965).

The Ramsey model is based on the dynamic saving and investment decisions of a representative household. In a balanced-growth equilibrium without uncertainty, optimal household decision-making implies a formula for the real interest rate:

$$r = MPK = \rho + \sigma g, \qquad (1)$$

Here, MPK denotes the marginal product of capital. When households have perfect foresight of the future, the marginal product of capital in steady state depends on the rate of discount on future income (ρ), the per capita growth rate of the economy (g), and the rate at which people are willing to substitute between current and future income ($1/\sigma$ is the intertemporal elasticity of substitution). If growth is expected to be high, people will wish to borrow against their future higher income to consume more now, and this will drive up the interest rate. At some point, the higher interest rate will discourage borrowing and restore equilibrium between the return on capital investment (which reflects the economy's ability to produce income in the future) and the household's willingness to postpone consumption.

In the balanced growth equilibrium (where all variables grow at the same rate), the marginal product of capital is constant. The rate of population growth does not affect the steady-state interest rate because, on the balanced growth path, the household saves enough for future generations to keep the ratio of capital per unit of effective labor constant. In a frictionless world where capital adjusts instantaneously to changes in the population or to productivity, (1) would hold at all times. More generally, capital adjusts with a lag and (1) is more appropriate as a characterization of the relationship between productivity and interest rates in the long run.

Under the illustrative assumptions that $\sigma = 1$ and $\rho = 0.4$, the most recent Administration forecast of labor productivity growth of 2.1 percent per year generates an approximation of the long-run real interest rate of 2.5 percent. (With these values for σ and ρ the Ramsey model's prediction is roughly consistent with actual real interest rates over the 1953-2007 period; however, the model's interest-rate implications are reasonably robust to a range of other σ, ρ combinations.) Note that this forecast abstracts from uncertainty so that there is no risk premium. This forecast also does not factor in inflation. Given the number of assumptions needed and the uncertainty about parameter values and future productivity growth, the forecast of the real rate of interest is approximate at best. What can be said with some confidence is that a reduction in future labor productivity growth should be reflected in a reduction in the long-run real interest rate.

Moving away from the strict assumptions of the model, other economic forces will potentially affect the interest rate. Such forces include declining rates of population growth, the aging of the population, and a decline in the government debt-to-GDP ratio. The magnitudes of these effects are hard to quantify but theory suggests that such shifts will exert downward pressure on interest rates.

Global factors are also likely to play a role. In a world with integrated markets, the global real interest rate is determined by the equality of the global supply of saving and world investment demand, as illustrated in Figure 2-ix. The gap between saving and investment in emerging markets was especially large in the mid-2000s, contributing to the "global saving glut" that helped to fuel asset bubbles in financial markets. The emerging market gap has declined and the IMF projects it will be near zero by the end of 2019. Figure 2-ix also shows that global saving and investment have trended up in the post-crisis period, and that trend is projected to continue for some years. If data measurement

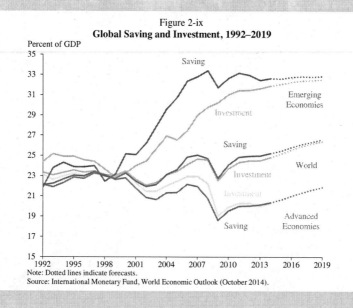

Figure 2-ix
Global Saving and Investment, 1992–2019

Note: Dotted lines indicate forecasts.
Source: International Monetary Fund, World Economic Outlook (October 2014).

were perfect, global saving would equal global investment exactly. Accordingly, it is not the gap but the *levels* of both series that are of interest. The large-scale deleveraging by households and by governments has resulted in an expansion of global saving that has exerted downward pressure on interest rates. Past experience with deleveraging suggests that this process could take a long while, indicating that low real interest rates may be part of the global landscape for some time to come.

Financial markets and the long-run nominal rate. An alternative forecast of the long-run rate is based on information from financial markets that incorporates real-world uncertainties into asset prices. The nominal interest rate on a long-term bond can be decomposed into three components: the real return on rolling over short-term assets during the holding period of the bond, the expected rate of inflation, and a term premium that compensates for the risk borne by the investor over the life of the bond. Precisely defined, the interest rate on long-term nominal bonds also includes a liquidity premium (because markets for some securities may be thin) and a credit risk premium reflecting the solvency of the lender. However, most financial economists assume these last two components are minuscule for the U.S. Treasury market. On those assumptions, forecasts of the short-term real interest rate, expected inflation, and the term premium suffice to forecast the long-run nominal interest rate.

Inflation expectations are a major determinant of the yield on Treasuries, which guarantee a nominal rate of return. The difference between nominal Treasury yields and the guaranteed real rate of return on Treasury Inflation-Protected Securities (TIPS) is usually referred to as the "breakeven" rate of inflation compensation. The current 10-year breakeven inflation compensation rate is 1.9 percent, and the 10-year breakeven inflation compensation rate starting in 2024 is 2.0 percent. Though often cited as a gauge of inflation expectations, the breakeven inflation compensation rate reflects more than market inflation expectations: also embedded in it are a risk premium that reflects the covariance of inflation with wealth, a liquidity premium that reflects the relative ease of converting the assets to cash, and other factors that reflect the relative demands for nominal and inflation-indexed securities. A point to note in interpreting the data is that TIPS are indexed to the CPI, whereas the Federal Reserve's inflation target of 2 percent a year applies to the PCE, which (as noted earlier in this chapter) tends to rise more slowly than the CPI. Inflation expectations can be inferred from surveys, however, and these indicate long-run rates of expected inflation close to the Federal Reserve's target.

The *expected short-term* rate is based on a forecast of monetary policy. The median projection released by the FOMC suggests a future Federal funds rate of 3.75 percent. Historically, the Federal funds rate is slightly higher than the rate on a three-month Treasury security, implying an expected three-month Treasury rate of roughly 3.5 percent. This rate would correspond to a projected short-term real interest rate of 1.5 percent a year with inflation expectations at 2 percent a year.

There is an extensive empirical literature that estimates the *term premium,* which reflects the extent to which the long-term nominal bond is a good hedge for other risks faced by the investor (for example, the covariance of the return on the bond with investor wealth and with inflation). Recent financial data indicate that the term premium has been falling and is in the neighborhood of 1 percent for a ten-year bond. It is possible that future changes in monetary policy or shifts in investor beliefs about the Federal Reserve's reaction function could reverse the downward trend in the term premium, but most forecasters predict that the term premium will remain low in the near future. Adding a term premium of 1.0 percent to the short-term nominal rate of 3.5 percent suggests a long-term (10-year) nominal rate of 4.5 percent.

Although reached through different reasoning, the rate on 10-year Treasury notes implied by financial markets is in the same neighborhood as that based on the steady-state prediction of a Ramsey model. This is not surprising – if the Ramsey model is a valid description of the economy, Federal Reserve policy and market expectations about the future will ultimately conform to the equilibrium conditions in the Ramsey model. There is a gap, however, between the rate implied by the Ramsey model presented here – which abstracts from inflation and uncertainty and therefore does not include a term premium – and the rate implied by financial markets, which in principle incorporate all risks but could be strongly affected by current economic conditions. Fully reconciling the two requires a lower expected productivity growth rate, a higher elasticity of intertemporal substitution, or a much smaller term premium than seems realistic to most economists.

recovery is expected to offset some of this downward trend. Young adults, in particular, have been preparing themselves for labor-force entry through additional education. The share of young adults aged 16 to 24 enrolled in school between January 2008 and December 2012 rose well above its trend, enough to account for the entire decline in the labor force participation rate for this age group over this period. As these young adults complete their education, most are expected to enter or reenter the labor force.

Table 2-3

**Supply-Side Components of Actual
and Potential Real GDP Growth, 1953–2024**

		Growth rate[a]	
		History	Forecast
	Component	1953:Q2 to 2014:Q3[b]	2014:Q3 to 2025:Q4
1	Civilian noninstitutional population aged 16+	1.4	0.9
2	Labor force participation rate	0.1	-0.4
3	Employed share of the labor force	-0.1	0.1
4	Ratio of nonfarm business employment to household employment	0.0	0.0
5	Average weekly hours (nonfarm business)	-0.2	0.0
6	Output per hour (productivity, nonfarm business)[c]	2.1	2.1
7	Ratio of real GDP to nonfarm business output[c]	-0.2	-0.3
8	Sum: Actual real GDP[c]	3.0	2.5
	Memo:		
9	Potential real GDP[d]	3.2	2.3
10	Output per worker differential: GDP vs nonfarm[e]	-0.3	-0.2

[a] All contributions are in percentage points at an annual rate, forecast finalized November 2014. Total may not add up due to rounding.

[b] 1953:Q2 was a business-cycle peak. 2014:Q3 is the latest quarter with available data.

[c] Real GDP and real nonfarm business output are measured as the average of income- and product-side measures.

[d] Computed as (real GDP, line 8) less 2*(the employed share of the labor force, line 3)

[e] Real GDP per household worker less nonfarm business output per nonfarm business worker. This can be shown to equal (line 7) - (line 4).

Note: Population, labor force, and household employment have been adjusted for discontinuities in the population series. Nonfarm business employment, and the workweek, come from the Labor Productivity and Costs database maintained by the Bureau of Labor Statistics.

Source: Bureau of Labor Statistics, Current Population Survey, Labor Productivity and Costs; Bureau of Economic Analysis, National Income and Product Accounts; Department of the Treasury; Office of Management and Budget; CEA calculations.

The employed share of the labor force—which is equal to one minus the unemployment rate—is expected to increase at an average 0.1 percent a year over the next 11 years. It is expected to be unchanged after 2018 when the unemployment rate converges to the rate consistent with stable inflation. The workweek is projected to be roughly flat during the forecast period, somewhat less of a decline than its long-term historical trend yearly growth of -0.2 percent. The workweek is expected to stabilize because some of the demographic forces pushing it down are largely exhausted, and because a longer workweek is projected to compensate for the anticipated decline in the labor force participation rate in what will eventually become an economy with a tight labor supply.

Labor productivity is projected to increase 2.1 percent a year over the entire forecast interval (line 6, column 2), the same as the average growth rate from 1953 to 2014 (line 6, column 1). Productivity tends to grow faster in the nonfarm business sector than for the economy as a whole, because productivity in the government and household sectors of the economy is presumed (by a national-income accounting convention) not to grow (that is, output in those two sectors grows only through the use of more production inputs). The difference in these growth rates is expected to subtract 0.2 percent a year during the 10-year projection period, similar to the 0.3 percent a year decline during the long-term historical interval (line 10, columns 1 and 2). This productivity differential can be shown to be equal to the sum of two other growth rates in the table: the ratio of nonfarm business employment to household employment (line 4) and the ratio of real GDP to nonfarm business output (line 7).

Summing the growth rates of all of its components, real GDP is projected to rise at an average 2.5 percent a year over the projection period (line 8, column 2), somewhat faster than the 2.3 percent annual growth rate for potential real GDP (line 9, column 2). Actual GDP is expected to grow faster than potential GDP primarily because of the projected rise in the employment rate (line 3, column 2) as millions of currently unemployed workers find jobs over the next two years.

Real potential GDP (line 9, column 2) is projected to grow more slowly than the long-term historical growth rate of 3.2 percent a year (line 9, column 1). As discussed earlier, the projected slowdown in real potential GDP growth primarily reflects the lower projected growth rate of the working-age population and the retirement of the baby-boom cohort. If the effects of immigration reform on labor-force size were incorporated into this forecast, however, then it would show a higher potential real GDP growth rate.

Upside and Downside of Forecast Risks. Like any forecast, the Administration's economic forecast comes with risk, but several are worth enumerating here. Among the upside risks is a sustained low price for imported petroleum. Much of the decline in petroleum prices occurred after the Administration forecast was finalized in mid-November 2014; at that time, oil-price futures markets anticipated general recovery in prices. Since then, the long-term futures prices have fallen. The housing sector also has some upside potential given the current low level of household formation and its potential for increase. On the downside, persistent European risks of deflation and slow growth continue to constrain the global economy. There are also concerns about a slowdown in China, and the speed with which Japan will rebound from the effects of the 2014 consumption tax hike. Over the longer-run, there are some downside risks to the estimate of potential growth insofar as more recent lower productivity growth rates continue.

CONCLUSION

The economy continued to strengthen during 2014, especially in the labor market with robust employment gains and deep declines in unemployment. The labor market saw the fastest pace of job gains since 1999, extending the longest streak of uninterrupted private-sector job growth on record and contributing to an American recovery that has outpaced most of its competitors and left a nation well-prepared for continued resilience. Conditions are ripe for another year of robust growth in 2015 as progress in consumer deleveraging and gains in household wealth have progressed in a way that should support further growth in consumer spending. Residential investment is also likely to expand as the financial constraints that have held back mortgage financing are gradually relaxed and demographic pressures for a larger housing stock become evident. Uncertainty over fiscal policy is lower than in earlier years because of Congress' December 2014 budget agreement. Recent declines in imported prices for petroleum will boost the real income of domestic consumers and reduce near-term inflation. Core inflation is low and below the Federal Reserve's target, and so some upward drift in inflation is projected.

The U.S. economy strengthened last year against a backdrop of relatively weak growth in the rest of the world. This differential is likely to persist into 2015 as growth projections for our major trading partners in Europe, Japan, and some emerging markets are currently less favorable than for the United States. This will dampen demand growth for U.S. exports. The last several years have seen an improvement in the U.S. current account balance (a falling deficit). Whether this trend continues will also depend, in part, on relative demand conditions at home and abroad.

Looking ahead, some of the most important decisions that we make as a Nation are the structural policies that influence long-term growth. The President's Budget sets forth a number of policies that can be expected to increase the long-term growth rate of potential GDP.

Such policies also aim to boost aggregate demand in the near term and to improve our long-term competitiveness, while promising fiscal restraint over the long run. They are an essential complement to policies that make sure this growth is shared by the middle class and those working to get into the middle class.

C H A P T E R   3

ACHIEVEMENTS AND CHALLENGES IN THE U.S. LABOR MARKET

A fundamental metric for judging an economy's performance is its success in providing abundant job opportunities that pay good wages
and provide an opportunity to get ahead. Five-and-one-half years ago—in
the wake of the worst financial crisis since the Great Depression—the
U.S. economy faced a massive challenge, as GDP shrank and the number
of jobless workers rose to more than 15 million. Since then, a successful
multifaceted policy response, including actions by the President, Congress,
and the Federal Reserve, combined with the determination of the American
people, has enabled the U.S. economy to dig out of that deep hole, putting
more people back to work, reducing the unemployment rate, and creating
a virtuous cycle in which higher consumer purchasing power supports
greater economic activity and job creation. After four years of recovery in
employment, in 2014, the unemployment rate declined at its most rapid rate
in nearly three decades. By the end of the year, it had fallen to 5.6 percent,
close to its pre-recession average of 5.3 percent.[1] But the United States labor
market still has more work to do to achieve the full health that comes with
not just low levels of unemployment, but also a labor market that encourages
labor force participation, supports quality jobs, and facilitates productive
matching of workers and positions—all of which are essential to creating
well-paying jobs and supporting robust family incomes.

This chapter begins by discussing the substantial progress that has
been made in healing the labor market since 2009, and the acceleration in
progress seen throughout 2014. By October 2014, the unemployment rate
had fallen more rapidly over the preceding 12 months than in any 12-month

---

[1] Bureau of Labor Statistics, Current Population Survey; CEA calculations. Throughout this
chapter, unless otherwise specified, data and statistics are from the Bureau of Labor Statistics
Current Population Survey or CEA calculations from these data.

period since 1984. The sharp drop in unemployment came amid a stabilization in the labor force participation rate and, for the year as a whole businesses added 3.0 million jobs—the most in any year since 1997. Moreover, nominal wage growth for production and nonsupervisory workers—a group that represents about 80 percent of workers who have lower earnings on average—continued to rise slightly faster than inflation, a reversal from what had been seen earlier in the recovery. Real wage growth was aided by low levels of inflation, including declining prices in the fourth quarter of 2014. Moreover, workers' take-home pay was helped by the fact that a typical worker's contribution to employer-sponsored family health insurance coverage rose at roughly one-half the rate seen on average prior to the recession, continuing a recent trend of subdued health cost growth. Finally, 2014 continued to see the economy shift away from part-time work toward full-time work, as all of the employment growth was in full-time jobs. Over the course of the recovery, the share of the labor market in full-time jobs has increased and by the end of 2014, the number of Americans holding full-time jobs had increased more from January 2010 than it had added total jobs over the same period.

Despite these positive developments, more work remains to both complete the cyclical recovery and address underlying structural issues that predate the recession, some of which have been present for decades. As described in Chapter 1, three key factors shape the economic situation of the middle class: productivity growth, the distribution of income, and labor force participation. As Chapter 1 also notes, due to a combination of long-term economic challenges and the Great Recession, the middle class has seen little improvement in real incomes since 1997 despite productivity growth, signaling at least one area where much work remains to be done in the labor market and overall economy.

After reviewing the notable progress in the labor market over 2014, this chapter steps back to consider a set of five long-run issues the labor market must address. These are: i) a long-standing decline in the participation rate that has been compounded by the recession and the retirement boom; ii) a rapidly recovering long-term unemployment rate that nonetheless remains elevated; iii) a similar pattern of rapid decline but continued elevation in the rate of people working part time but who are seeking full-time employment; iv) cyclical improvements in labor market fluidity that are set against a backdrop of a long-term decline in a variety of metrics of labor market fluidity, or labor market "churn"; and v) real wage growth that is beginning to pick up but is still insufficient. These phenomena have, to varying degrees, been building up in the years or decades before the Great Recession and, in many cases, are following patterns similar to those in other recent recessions, particularly those from 1980 on. This suggests that these issues are linked – for example, when a shock hits the economy, less labor market fluidity can result in more long-term unemployment and part-time employment and a lower participation rate than would occur if the labor market were more dynamic. In many cases, the increasingly rapid recovery in the labor market will help to address these challenges. In some cases, these trends may reflect a natural progression that would be undesirable to reverse, such as rising retirements among aging workers. However, additional policy steps are needed to counteract the continued effects of the Great Recession as well as longer-term trends that predated it. Consequently, this chapter concludes by laying out key elements of the President's middle-class economics agenda, which includes policies aimed at growing and supporting middle-class families, strengthening the labor market and expanding economic opportunity. As the past several years suggest, economic policies that focus on strengthening the middle class create a stronger foundation for shared and sustainable growth in the years to come.

THE STATE OF THE U.S. LABOR MARKET IN 2014

Since the end of the Great Recession in 2009, the economy has made enormous strides toward recovery, in terms of output, labor market indicators, consumer confidence, and numerous other measures. Perhaps no recent economic development has been more surprising than the rapid fall in the unemployment rate and commensurate pickup in the rate of job growth in 2014, which far outperformed forecast expectations. From its 2001-07 average of 5.3 percent, the unemployment rate hit 10.0 percent in October 2009; but as of December 2014, the rate stands at 5.6 percent, having recovered 93 percent of the way back to its pre-recession average.[2] Notably, 2014 marked the strongest year of job growth since 1999 and the strongest year of private-sector job growth since 1997. December's 5.6-percent unemployment rate was achieved roughly five years ahead of consensus forecasts made as recently as 2013, as shown in Figure 3-1.

In part due to a vigorous policy response to the economic crisis, the United States is in a sustained economic recovery. The Administration's early actions, including the American Recovery and Reinvestment Act of 2009 and middle-class tax cuts, helped catalyze this recovery: the Council of Economic Advisers (CEA) estimates that between early 2009 and the end of

---

[2] Throughout this chapter, the phrase "pre-recession average" refers to the average between December 2001 and December 2007, the most recent expansionary period before the Great Recession.

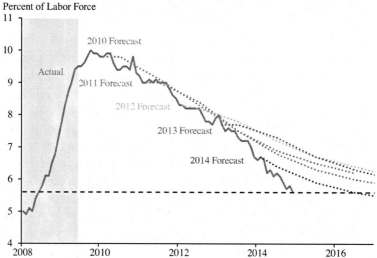

Figure 3-1
Actual and Consensus Forecast Unemployment Rate, 2008–2014

Percent of Labor Force

2010 Forecast

Actual

2011 Forecast

2012 Forecast

2013 Forecast

2014 Forecast

Note: Annual forecasts are current as of March of the stated year. Dashed line represents December 2014 value (5.6 percent). Shading denotes recession.
Source: Bureau of Labor Statistics, Current Population Survey; Blue Chip Economic Indicators.

2012, the Recovery Act added a total of more than 6.0 million job years to the economy (CEA 2014b).

In 2014, the rate of decline in the unemployment rate picked up to an average of 0.1 percentage point per month, higher than the rate of decline from 2010 to 2013, with much of the decline reflected in lower long-term unemployment. Although the long-term unemployed account for only about one-third of all unemployed, these reductions in long-term unemployment accounted for about two-thirds of the total unemployment decline in 2014. Falling long-term unemployment combined with a stable participation rate in 2014 suggests that the long-term unemployed are going back to work at higher rates (Cajner and Ratner 2014).

The improvement in the health of the labor market is also apparent in a range of labor market indicators, as shown in Figure 3-2. The headline unemployment rate accounts for jobless individuals who are actively seeking employment. Broader measures of labor market underutilization include individuals who are not looking for work because they believe no jobs are available (discouraged workers); others available for work but who have not looked for work in the past month (other marginally attached); and those who are working part-time but would like full-time work (part-time for economic reasons). All of these indicators tell a broadly consistent story: the U.S. economic recovery has made considerable progress, but it is not

Figure 3-2
Elevation and Recovery of Broader Measures of Unemployment

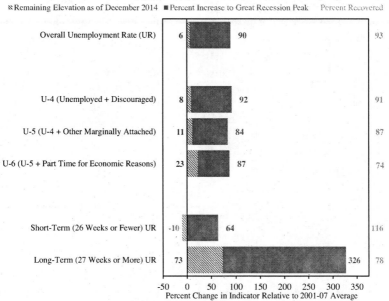

Note: All rates are expressed as a percent of the labor force and are seasonally adjusted.
Source: Bureau of Labor Statistics, Current Population Survey; CEA calculations.

yet complete. Important differences remain in the progress of the recovery across measures, however, including the continued elevation of long-term unemployment.

Relative to many other advanced economies, the United States experienced a large increase in unemployment during the crisis and yet has also had the strongest recovery since the peak of the crisis, as shown in Figure 3-3. Between the first quarter of 2008 and the final quarter of 2009, U.S. unemployment rose from 5.0 percent to 9.9 percent. Over the same period, unemployment in the Organisation for Economic Cooperation and Development (OECD) countries (excluding the United States) increased from an average of 5.1 percent to 7.8 percent.[3] Unemployment in the euro area over this period rose from 6.1 percent to 9.3 percent.

The most significant differences have emerged since early 2010. U.S. unemployment steadily declined and was down to 5.7 percent by the third quarter of 2014, over 40 percent below its recession maximum. In contrast, average unemployment in both the non-U.S. OECD and euro area has made

---

[3] CEA weighted OECD and euro area countries by GDP (in millions of USD), so that countries with larger economies received more weight than smaller countries. The United States is excluded from the OECD weighted average. Accordingly, these figures differ from OECD's published unweighted average unemployment rate across OECD countries.

Box 3-1: Unemployment Across Gender, Race, and Ethnicity Groups: The Situation for Men of Color

Men of color have much higher rates of unemployment than do White men. For example, in December 2014, adult African-American men had an unemployment rate of 11.0 percent—6.6 percentage points higher than that of adult White men. Among adult Hispanic men, the unemployment rate was 5.3 percent in December 2014, 0.9 percentage point higher than that of adult White men. Racial gaps in unemployment have narrowed over time, but less progress has been made among African-American men, for whom the gap in the unemployment rate relative to Whites has fallen the least.

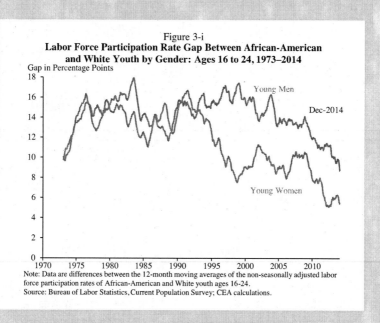

Figure 3-i
Labor Force Participation Rate Gap Between African-American and White Youth by Gender: Ages 16 to 24, 1973–2014

Note: Data are differences between the 12-month moving averages of the non-seasonally adjusted labor force participation rates of African-American and White youth ages 16-24.
Source: Bureau of Labor Statistics, Current Population Survey; CEA calculations.

In addition to higher unemployment rates, there are also differences in labor force participation, which mean that men of color often have even lower rates of employment than the unemployment rates alone would suggest. The gap in participation is especially problematic among young men, since early-life labor market experiences have significant impacts on later-life labor market success (Edelman, Holzer and Offner 2006; Raaum and Roed 2006).[1] The labor force participation rates of young White and African-American women have begun to converge since the 1990s, while convergence among young men largely

---

[1] The literature finds persistent and significant impacts of post-graduation labor market conditions and opportunities on later-in-life wages and employment.

stalled until the late 2000s. In December 2014, young African-American women's participation was 5 percentage points lower than young White women's, while young African-American men's participation was 9 percentage points lower than young White men's.

To speed U.S. progress in closing the racial disparities in labor market outcomes, the Administration has made tackling unemployment among minority men a priority under the My Brother's Keeper Initiative. The initiative supports the education and employment of African-American, Hispanic and Native American men, all of whom experience elevated unemployment and lower participation relative to men in other racial groups.

little progress. Unemployment across the OECD, excluding the United States, is, on average, roughly unchanged from its peak. As of the fourth quarter of 2013, the average unemployment rate across non-U.S. OECD countries was 7.6 percent. Unemployment across euro zone countries fared worse, with a decline in unemployment in 2010, followed by a sharp increase between 2011 and mid-2013. These international averages naturally abstract from varied experiences among OECD countries: Germany's unemployment rate fell between the first quarter of 2008 and the first quarter of 2010, while Spain's unemployment rate more than doubled. Nonetheless, the

Figure 3-3
**Unemployment in Non-U.S. OECD, Euro Area,
and United States, 2000–2013**

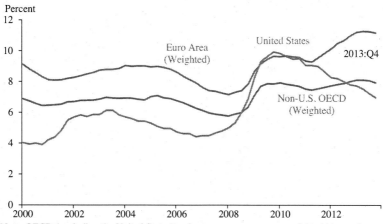

Note: OECD (excluding the United States) and euro area averages are weighted by member countries' GDP.
Source: Organisation for Economic Co-Operation and Development, Harmonized Unemployment Rate and GDP series; CEA calculations.

recovery in the U.S. unemployment rate compares favorably against the general experience of other advanced economies.

Behind the improvement in U.S. unemployment is a historic record of steady job growth, albeit one that follows historic job losses. As described in Chapter 2, total employment increased by 3.1 million jobs in 2014—the strongest year of the recovery—and average monthly job growth was 260,000, as shown in Figure 3-4. The private sector has added jobs for 58 consecutive months through December 2014, the longest period of continual job growth on record.

In 2014, private-sector employment growth was particularly strong in industries that traditionally provide good, middle-class jobs, such as construction and professional and business services. Since February 2010, more than 850,000 manufacturing jobs have been added, an increase of 7 percent. The average workweek for production and non-supervisory workers in manufacturing has also increased to near its highest level since World War II. Over the same period, 2.9 million jobs have been added in professional and business services, an 18 percent increase.

The labor market recovery has been generally shared across the full spectrum of American workers. Table 3-1 shows that looking across the

Figure 3-4
Average Monthly Job Growth by Year, 2007–2014

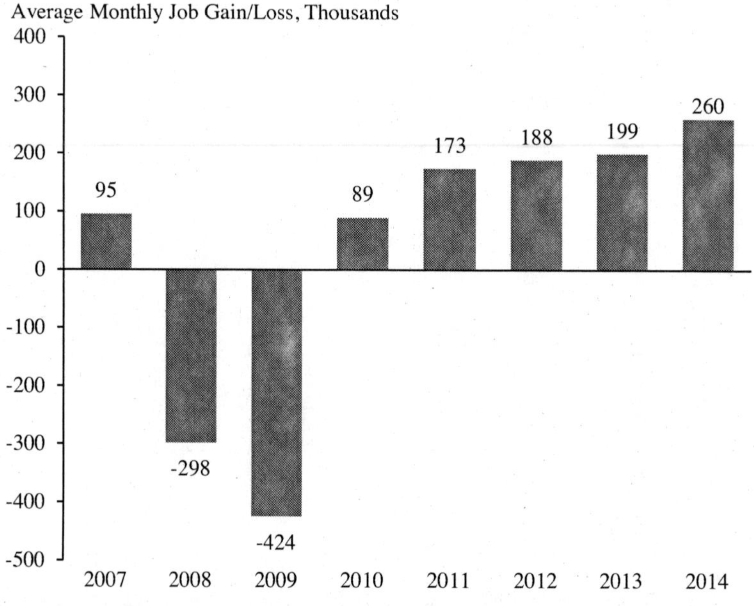

Source: Bureau of Labor Statistics, Current Employment Statistics.

Table 3-1
**Tracking the Recovery Across Race, Gender, Age, and
Level of Educational Attainment**

	Pre-Recession Average	Percent Increase to Great Recession Peak	Remaining Elevation as of December 2014 (Percent)	Percent Recovered
Overall Unemployment Rate (UR)	5.3	90	6	93
Male UR	5.4	106	8	93
Female UR	5.2	74	3	96
White UR	4.6	99	4	96
African-American UR	9.8	72	6	91
Hispanic UR	6.5	99	0	100
Asian UR	4.5	72	9	87
Less than High School UR	7.9	100	9	91
High School Graduates UR	4.8	127	9	93
Some College UR	4.1	117	20	83
College Graduates UR	2.5	99	15	85
Age 16-24 UR	11.4	71	8	88
Age 25-54 UR	4.3	108	8	92

Note: Asian unemployment rate is a 12-month moving average of not seasonally adjusted data.
Source: Bureau of Labor Statistics, Current Population Survey; CEA calculations.

population by racial, gender, and educational differences, most groups are at least 90 percent recovered, and those that have not reached that point are close to it.

The 1.2 percentage-point fall in the annual unemployment rate in 2014 was the largest such drop since 1984, and some groups experienced even larger declines in unemployment. Both the Hispanic and African-American annual unemployment rates fell by 1.7 percentage point in 2014, one of the largest declines in series history. As of December 2014, the African-American unemployment rate had recovered 91 percent of the way back to its pre-recession average, compared to 100 percent for Hispanics, 87 percent for Asians, and 96 percent for White workers.

The labor market gained strength in 2014, and numerous indicators illustrate that the recovery is robust. Now that much of the direct challenges of the recession are behind us, the United States must turn its attention to ensuring that the benefits of the recovery are widespread, benefiting more middle-class families. This requires addressing five longer-run challenges in the labor market. The following sections discuss each of these challenges in greater detail.

Labor Force Participation

The decline in the unemployment rate in the economic recovery has been driven by the increased pace of job creation. In addition to the decline in the traditional unemployment rate, a broader measure that also includes discouraged workers and people who would like to work if a job were available (U-5) has come down from a high of 11.4 percent in October 2009 to 6.9 percent in December 2014, or 87 percent of the way back to its pre-recession average.

At the same time, the economy has continued to go through a substantial change in labor force participation. Since peaking in the first quarter of 2000 at 67.3 percent, the labor force participation rate declined to 62.8 in the fourth quarter of 2014. A large portion of this decline is explained by the lower participation rates of an aging labor force and, in spite of continued demographic pressures in this direction, the participation rate has held steady since October 2013. This suggests that a stronger labor market is bringing people back into the labor force, partially off-setting the increasing size of the retirement-age population. Nevertheless, the participation rate is unlikely to return to its peak rate in the near future. This section examines the role of the aging baby boomers in driving declining participation, as well as the lesser but important roles of a decades-long downward trend in male labor force participation and a more recent slight trend decline in female labor force participation discussed in Chapter 1.

A Longer-Term Perspective on Labor Force Participation

The labor force participation rate, defined as the share of the population ages 16 and older who are working, or who are actively seeking employment, is an important measure of labor market potential and health. Labor force nonparticipation is not always a source of concern—many nonparticipators are seniors enjoying their retirements, young people investing in education, or parents caring for their children. However, low labor force participation—particularly among people of prime working age (ages 25 through 54) — is evidence that we can do more to create job prospects and support workers. Moreover, low labor force participation may mean that, even when good economic times return, mobilizing the pool of available workers will take more time.

Box 3-2: Changes in Labor Force Participation for Different Subpopulations

Overall, the most important factor affecting the aggregate participation rate in the recession and recovery has been the aging of the population. But there are a number of important trends and developments relevant for understanding the changes in participation of different subgroups of the population:

• Increased participation by older Americans, which may be attributable to an increase in skills among this population and also to changes in Social Security retirement benefits;

• Reduced participation by younger Americans as they stay in school longer;

• Continuation of an at least 65-year long trend of declining male labor force participation, which is especially stark for young minority men; and

• Tapering of the long-term trend of increasing female labor force participation, which dates back to before World War II.

All told, these different trends and factors roughly offset each other, but they are important for understanding these groups and for informing policy choices.

Table 3-i
Labor Force Participation Rate by Selected Groups

	2014:Q4	Average Change Per Year (Percentage Points)		
		1948*-1990	1990-2007	2007-2014
All	62.8	0.2	0.0	-0.5
Men	69.1	-0.2	-0.2	-0.6
Women	56.9	0.6	0.1	-0.3
Age 16-24	55.5	0.2	-0.5	-0.6
Age 25-54	80.8	0.4	0.0	-0.3
Age 55+	40.0	-0.3	0.5	0.2
White*	62.9	0.2	0.0	-0.5
Black*	61.4	0.2	0.0	-0.4
Hispanic*	66.2	0.4	0.1	-0.4

Source: Bureau of Labor Statistics, Current Population Survey; CEA calculations. Not all groups have information starting in 1948, for those groups (marked with a star), the 1948-1990 change is from the first year for which data is available.

Taking a longer view, as in Figure 3-5, the labor force participation rate increased from 60.8 percent to 66.6 percent between 1973 and 1995. As described in Chapter 1, this increase during the "Age of Participation" can be entirely accounted for by increased participation among women: over this

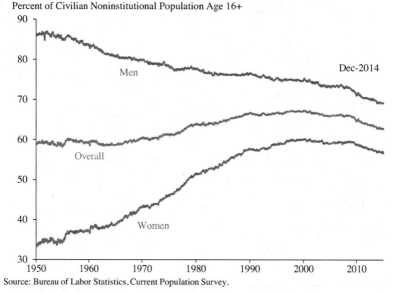

Figure 3-5
Labor Force Participation by Gender, 1950–2014
Percent of Civilian Noninstitutional Population Age 16+

Source: Bureau of Labor Statistics, Current Population Survey.

period, the female participation rate increased from 44.7 percent to 59.0 percent while the male participation rate fell from 78.8 percent to 75.0 percent.

Since 1995, however, the participation rate has fallen from 66.6 percent to 62.8 percent in the fourth quarter of 2014, with 3.2 percentage points of this decrease occurring since the fourth quarter of 2007. While some of this time period coincides with the Great Recession, it also coincides with the period when the eldest baby boomers entered their peak retirement years; the first baby boomers turned 62 in 2008, becoming eligible for Social Security. This demographic shift had been predicted to lower the participation rate well in advance of the Great Recession (Aaronson et al. 2006).

Although population aging explains much of the decline in labor force participation seen in recent years, longer-run trends, cyclical responses, and other factors also affect participation. CEA evaluated these various factors in its comprehensive report, *The Labor Force Participation Rate Since 2007: Causes and Policy Implications*, summarized in this chapter. This analysis finds that a combination of demographic changes and typical business-cycle effects can explain most, but not all, of the decrease since 2007.

Decomposing the Decline in Participation Since 2007

The decline in labor force participation between the fourth quarter of 2007 and the fourth quarter of 2014 can be decomposed into three parts: an

Figure 3-6
Labor Force Participation Decomposition, 2009–2014

Percent of Civilian Noninstitutional Population Age 16+

Note: Year axis denotes first quarter of year noted. See text for methodological details.
Source: Bureau of Labor Statistics, Current Population Survey; CEA calculations.

aging population, the economic downturn, and a residual that is attributable to other factors. Figure 3-6 shows the decomposition of this decline over time based on CEA modeling. By the close of 2014, the participation rate was down 3.2 percentage points since the end of 2007. Of this, CEA analysis attributes 1.7 points to long-run aging trends, and 0.5 point to poor business-cycle conditions. The remaining 0.9 point is not due to either standard business cycle or aging trends.[4] This residual component emerged in 2012 and grew over the subsequent few years.

CEA's finding that aging trends explain more than one-half of the decline in labor force participation over the course of the recession and recovery is consistent with a wide range of studies that have used a variety of methodological approaches to better understand the impact of various factors on the participation rate. These studies, summarized in Table 3-2, show that research finds that long-term trends such as aging account for between 25 and 82 percent of the participation decline over the recession. These findings are not directly comparable, as the time periods they study differ. Consequently, CEA's model is estimated over the same time period as each of these studies, with the results presented in the final two columns of Table 3-2. CEA's model finds an aging effect that is between 39 and 55 percent of the decline depending on the time period being analyzed. CEA's

---

[4] The three components do not sum to the whole due to rounding.

Table 3-2
Comparison of Participation Rate Estimates

	Time Period	Shares of the Total Decline		CEA Estimated Shares Over Same Time Period	
		Trend	Cycle	Trend	Cycle
CEA (2014c)	2007:Q4 – 2014:Q4	55%	17%		
Beginning in 2007					
CBO (2014)	2007:Q4 – 2013:Q4	50%	33%	48%	25%
S. Aaronson et al. (2014)	2007:Q4 – 2014:Q2	82%	11%	51%	21%
D. Aaronson et al. (2014)	2007: Q4 – 2014:Q3	74%	13%	54%	19%
Erceg and Levin (2013)	2007-2012	17%	55%	55%	42%
Fallick and Pingle (2013)	2007:Q4 – 2013:Q2	75%	16%	53%	35%
Kudlyak (2013)	2007-2012	80%	20%	55%	42%
Shierholz (2012)	2007-2011	31%	--	49%	59%
Van Zandweghe (2012)	2007-2011	42%	58%	49%	59%
Aaronson et al. (2006)	2007-2013	82%	--	48%	25%
Other time periods					
CEA (2014)	2011:Q1 – 2014:Q4	77%	-39%		
Fujita (2014)	2000:Q1 – 2013:Q4	65%	30%	39%	19%
Aaronson, Davis and Hu (2012)	2000-2011	40%	--	43%	43%

Source: Cited studies; CEA calculations.

estimate of the aging effects accounting for slightly more than one-half of the decline between 2007 and the end of 2014 is therefore roughly in the mid-range of the literature.

The variation across estimates of the cyclical component in the final column shows that different magnitudes of this component in the literature are largely driven by the time period of analysis, not variation in analytical methods. Comparing estimates from the literature to those from the CEA model in the same time period, the CEA estimate of the cyclical effect is roughly in the middle of the estimates. The roles of each factor in explaining the overall change in participation are addressed below.

Aging Population

Lower participation among baby boomers as they aged had been depressing the participation rate well before 2008, since participation begins to fall when workers reach their mid-50s. Both men and women decrease their participation by around 40 percentage points between ages 55 and 65 and participate at even lower rates thereafter. CEA concludes that the aging population is the single most important factor depressing the participation rate, accounting for 1.7 of the 3.2 percentage point decline, or more than

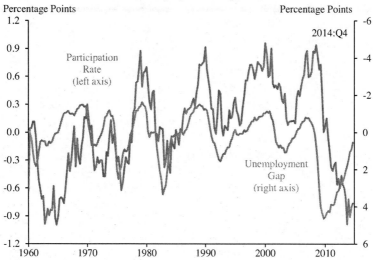

Figure 3-7
**Detrended Participation Rate and
(Inverted) Unemployment Gap, 1960–2014**

Source: Bureau of Labor Statistics, Current Population Survey; CEA calculations.

one-half of the decline, since the end of 2007. This finding is robust to different methods of modeling the effect of aging on participation, as described in more detail in *The Labor Force Participation Rate Since 2007: Causes and Policy Implications* (CEA 2014c). The effect of aging has also been growing in magnitude in recent years. The youngest baby boomers will not turn 65 until 2029, so aging will continue to depress labor force participation in coming years.

Business-Cycle Effects

Economic contractions historically result in both greater unemployment and lower labor force participation (Elsby, Hobijn, and Sahin 2010). Therefore, while movements in the participation rate over decades are driven largely by the long-term trends, in the short- and medium term, cyclical factors play a role.

Figure 3-7 shows the cyclicality of the participation rate by comparing the detrended participation rate and the (inverted) detrended unemployment gap, defined as the difference between the unemployment rate and CBO's estimate of the natural rate of unemployment.[5] For example, the detrended participation rate declined in the 1990s expansion and rose during the Great Recession. Visual inspection further suggests that move-

---

[5] Detrending was performed using the methods described in CEA (2014c). A trend component of each series was estimated using a semiparametric procedure. The trend components are then subtracted from the original data series to produce the series shown in Figure 3-7.

Box 3-3: Post-Recession Participation in the United States and United Kingdom

In late 2014, the U.S. and U.K. economies exhibited some striking similarities. The two countries' year-end unemployment rates were nearly identical, at 5.6 percent in the United States in December versus 5.8 percent in the United Kingdom as of the three months ending in November. Moreover, the International Monetary Fund predicted in October that the United Kingdom and the United States would see the fastest year-ahead GDP growth among G-7 economies, although output in the United States currently exceeds its pre-crisis peak by a substantially wider margin than in the United Kingdom.

However, some elements of the labor market have followed very different paths in the two economies. The United Kingdom has seen overall labor force participation hold roughly steady since 2007, despite the fact that the demographically adjusted participation series for the United Kingdom show a downtrend similar to that for the United States (Carney 2014). Yet more than a quarter of the increase in employment in the United Kingdom has been in part-time work, whereas all of the jobs added back in the United States have been full-time. And while average wages in the United States have been roughly keeping pace with inflation, U.K. workers have seen large declines in real earnings (Figure 3-iii). The average weekly inflation-adjusted paycheck for British private-sector workers is now more than 8 percent below its 2007 average. In short, the

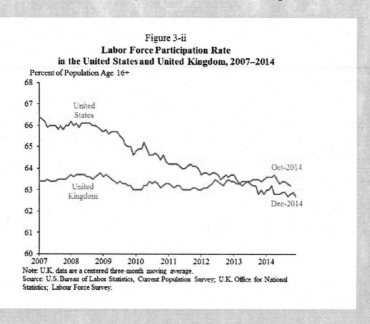

Figure 3-ii
**Labor Force Participation Rate
in the United States and United Kingdom, 2007–2014**

Note: U.K. data are a centered three-month moving average.
Source: U.S. Bureau of Labor Statistics, Current Population Survey; U.K. Office for National Statistics; Labour Force Survey.

United Kingdom experienced stable labor force participation at the same time that many jobs offered fewer work hours and lower pay.

To explain this set of circumstances, Bank of England Governor Mark Carney (2014) has argued that the United Kingdom experienced a labor supply surge in the wake of the crisis, with about 1.5 million people joining the U.K. labor force. Carney suggested this was likely fueled by a number of factors, including the need for households to rebuild savings or pay down debt in the wake of the financial crisis, as well as policy changes that have raised the retirement age for public-sector workers and introduced more stringent job-search requirements for some welfare recipients. The U.K. government has also undertaken efforts to improve job search assistance for unemployed workers, potentially facilitating faster matches of workers and positions.

Ultimately, the differences between the United States and United Kingdom on key labor market variables are a puzzle that is not yet fully understood. To an extent, some of the factors that have affected the United States and United Kingdom are similar—for instance a high number of indebted households. It is clear that both the United States and the United Kingdom face the challenge of facilitating transitions for workers currently employed in lower-wage and -hour jobs to jobs offering higher wages and more full-time work. Nevertheless, these different experiences are also a reminder of the many possible paths from recession to recovery.

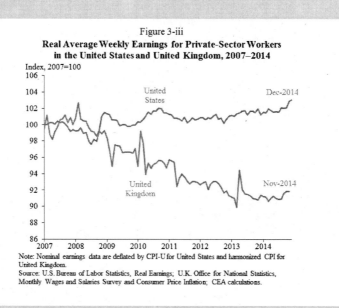

Figure 3-iii

Real Average Weekly Earnings for Private-Sector Workers in the United States and United Kingdom, 2007–2014

Index, 2007=100

Note: Nominal earnings data are deflated by CPI-U for United States and harmonized CPI for United Kingdom.
Source: U.S. Bureau of Labor Statistics, Real Earnings; U.K. Office for National Statistics, Monthly Wages and Salaries Survey and Consumer Price Inflation; CEA calculations.

ments in the participation rate lag movements in the unemployment rate by perhaps a year or so. CEA estimates that business-cycle effects explain 0.5 percentage point (about one-sixth) of the total decline in labor force participation between the end of 2007 and the end of 2014.[6]

As the labor market continues to recover, business cycle effects should wane. For example, cyclical factors depressed the participation rate by 1.1 percentage point in 2011 when the unemployment rate was about 9 percent, but by the fourth quarter of 2014, the unemployment rate had fallen to 5.7 percent and cyclical factors had shrunk to 0.5 percentage point.

Other Factors

While most of the decline in the participation rate since the end of 2007 is due to the combination of the aging population and standard cyclical effects, 0.9 percentage point, or a little over one-quarter, of the decline is not fully understood. CEA's analysis finds that this portion of the decline is not explained by either the aging of the population or the normal cyclical impact of the current recession. Between 2007 and 2012 the decline in participation is fully (and at some points more than fully) explained by the aging of the population and standard business-cycle effects. Beginning in 2012, however, the labor force participation rate decline began to exceed what was predicted from aging and cyclical factors. Since late 2013, the labor force participation rate has stabilized and the portion of the decline that was unexplained shrank, albeit slowly, between the second and fourth quarters of 2014 (Figure 3-6).

One driver of this unexplained component may be long-term trends within age groups. There was a general downward trend in participation rates prior to 2007, even after conditioning on age. In the case of prime-age men, the decline dates back to at least 1950; as noted in Chapter 1, prime-age male participation declined 0.1 percentage point a year between 1948 and 1973 and then 0.2 percentage point a year since 1973. More recently, prime-age female participation has declined at 0.1 percentage point a year on average since 1995. Because of these general trends toward lower participation, pre-recession models predicted a decline in participation over this period—greater than what would be predicted based on aging alone—even with the assumption of no major recession (Aaronson et al. 2006).

A second set of explanations is that the unexplained portion reflects the very severe nature of the Great Recession, which led to a greater-than-normal cyclical relationship between unemployment and participation.

---

[6] CEA uses the unemployment gap as a measure of the state of the business cycle. CEA regresses the quarter-on-quarter difference in the detrended labor force participation rate on the contemporaneous year-over-year difference in the detrended unemployment gap, along with a one-year lag and a two-year lag.

CEA's model assumes that the relationship between the unemployment rate and the labor force participation rate remained the same as in earlier, shallower recessions. However, the particularly long average duration of unemployment in the last recession might discourage participation even more. Adding unemployment duration to the model explains a part of the previously unexplained portion. Thus, the model suggests that a recession that leads to greater long-term unemployment leads to greater declines in labor force participation, conditional on the unemployment rate.

CEA's analysis finds no unusual rise in disability insurance in response to the recession—in fact, disability insurance rose less than would be predicted based on the severity of the recession—so this does not account for the unexplained decline in participation. The rise in schooling also does not account for the unexplained portion. Overall, it is likely that a combination of factors, including both non-aging trends and factors unique to the Great Recession, played a role in the participation-rate decline.

Outlook for the Participation Rate

While the evolution of the participation rate is subject to uncertainty, it is unlikely that the trend of decreasing labor force participation will reverse in the medium-term without policy changes. As of the fourth quarter of 2014, the cyclical effect depressed the labor force participation rate by 0.5 percentage point. In the short-run, as the economy fully recovers from the Great Recession, the cyclical component should dissipate, adding this 0.5 percentage point to the participation rate. At the same time, however, as more baby boomers retire, the aging population will depress the participation rate by roughly an additional 0.25 percentage point each year. The size of this aging effect is projected to grow gradually from 0.24 percentage point in 2015 to 0.27 percentage point in 2022, at which point the magnitude of the effect is expected to start receding. That older workers are able to retire is in many ways a positive development. But it also creates challenges, especially for overall fiscal policy and, in particular, for programs like Social Security and Medicare.

The unexplained component of the participation decline is subject to greater uncertainty. To the extent that the decline represents trends that pre-date the Great Recession, it could persist. However, if the unexplained portion primarily reflects temporary factors related to the Great Recession, as the economy recovers, the participation rate may increase more than what cyclical factors alone predict. However, under a range of feasible scenarios, it is likely the labor force participation rate will continue to decline in the medium-term.

Long-Term Unemployment

In 2014, not only did the annual unemployment rate fall by more than any year since 1984, but also most of the decline came from a decrease in long-term unemployment. The long-term unemployed, defined as those unemployed for 27 weeks or longer, accounted for 37 percent of the unemployed population as of December 2013. Nearly two-thirds of the 2014 decrease in unemployment resulted from a decrease in long-term unemployment, and by December 2014 they were 32 percent of the unemployed (Figure 3-8).

Broader measures of unemployment also fell slightly faster than the overall unemployment rate in 2014, while labor force participation was largely stable, suggesting that this reduction in long-term unemployment reflects workers finding employment rather than leaving the workforce or becoming discouraged. While this constitutes important progress, the long-term unemployment rate remains elevated relative to its pre-recession average.

Figure 3-8

Share of Recovery in Overall Unemployment Rate Due to Declines in Short- and Long-Term Unemployment

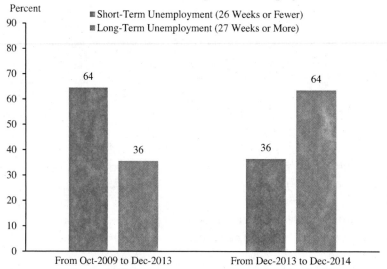

Source: Bureau of Labor Statistics, Current Population Survey; CEA calculations.

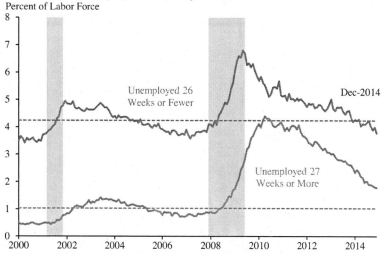

Figure 3-9
Unemployment Rate by Duration, 2000–2014

Percent of Labor Force

Note: Shading denotes recession. Dashed lines represent pre-Great Recession (December 2001-December 2007) averages.
Source: Bureau of Labor Statistics, Current Population Survey; CEA calculations.

Trends in Long-Term Unemployment

In the previous expansion, the short-term unemployment rate (workers unemployed for less than 27 weeks) averaged 4.2 percent of the labor force while the long-term unemployment rate averaged 1.0 percent. Both types of unemployment increased in the recession, with a markedly larger surge in long-term unemployment, as shown in Figure 3-9. Both have since substantially recovered, and Figure 3-9 shows that as of December 2014 the short-term unemployment rate was below its pre-recession average, although the long-term unemployment rate remained elevated. However, as discussed earlier, the long-term unemployment rate recovered more relative to the short-term unemployment rate in 2014.

The Great Recession saw a larger than typical increase in both the number and the share of the long-term unemployed. The number of long-term unemployed rose from 1.3 million at the end of 2007 to 6.8 million in April 2010, or 46 percent of all unemployed workers. By December 2014, however, this number had fallen to 2.8 million workers, or 32 percent of unemployed workers. By comparison, between 1948 and 2001, workers unemployed for at least 27 weeks accounted for about 12 percent of unemployed workers on average with a previous peak share of 26 percent in June 1983. The share of the unemployed who are long-term unemployed of longer durations also rose sharply in the recession, as shown in Figure 3-10.

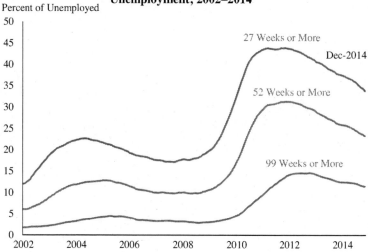

Figure 3-10
Share of Unemployed Workers by Duration of Unemployment, 2002–2014

Note: Calculations are a 12-month moving average of the share of unemployed by duration as a share of the overall unemployed population.
Source: Bureau of Labor Statistics, Current Population Survey; CEA calculations.

That figure also shows that even among the long-term unemployed, there have been greater improvements for those more recently unemployed.

This rise in the prevalence and severity of long-term unemployment in the Great Recession may in part be a continuation of longer-term trends in the cyclical pattern of long-term unemployment. Compared to recessions in earlier decades, the past several recessions have seen sharper increases in the share of the unemployed who are long-term unemployed as the unemployment rate climbs, as shown in Figure 3-11.

Moreover, aside from changes during business cycles, there appears to have been a secular increase in the long-term share of the unemployed for decades before the crisis occurred.[7] Figure 3-12 shows a gradual increase in the share long-term unemployed since 1948, when the data are first available.[8] The estimates suggest that, between 1948 and 2007, the share of the unemployed out of work for 27 weeks or more increased by about 0.2 percentage point a year on average.

If the share of unemployment that is long term returns to trend at the end of 2016, it would be about 20 percent, well above its October 2006 trough of 16 percent. However, recent cycles suggest that the long-term upward trend may be increasing even during expansionary periods.

---

[7] Also reported in Aaronson, Mazumder and Schechter (2010).
[8] The linear time trend is not adjusted for business cycles.

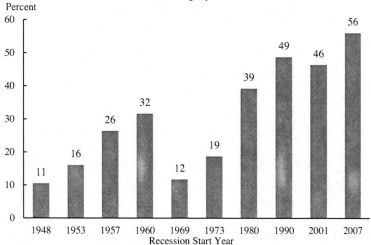

Figure 3-11
Increase in Long-Term Unemployment as a Percent of Increase in Overall Unemployment Rate

Note: Increases are measured from the first month of the recession to the peak in the overall unemployment rate. The 1980s recessions are consolidated into a single cycle.
Source: Bureau of Labor Statistics, Current Population Survey; CEA calculations.

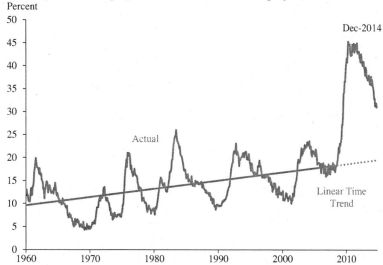

Figure 3-12
Long-term Unemployed as Share of Total Unemployed, 1960–2014

Note: Time trend projection is based on data from 1948 through 2007.
Source: Bureau of Labor Statistics, Current Population Survey; CEA calculations.

Moreover, during the Great Recession, long-term unemployment increased even more than would have been expected from the historical relationship (Aaronson, Mazumder, and Schechter 2010), suggesting that while long-run trends have contributed to higher rates of long-term unemployment, other factors may contribute to a more persistent increase.

Factors behind Elevated Rates of Long-Term Unemployment

The likelihood of finding new employment falls as an unemployment spell extends, as shown in Figure 3-13. During the Great Recession, the long-term unemployed were 20 to 40 percent less likely than the short-term unemployed to obtain employment within two years (Krueger, Cramer, and Cho 2014). In addition, audit studies show that callback rates from prospective employers decline with the length of unemployment (Kroft, Lange, and Notowidigdo 2013; Ghayad 2013).

The literature offers potential explanations for why the long-term unemployed are less likely to find employment than the short-term unemployed. One explanation, "worker heterogeneity," argues that the long-term unemployed are different from the short-term unemployed in ways that make them less attractive to employers, which extends how long they must search to land a new job (Pries 2008). However, this is less likely to be true following a deep recession. Moreover, research by Krueger, Cramer, and Cho (2014) and Mitchell (2013) find that the long-term unemployed resemble the short-term unemployed on many dimensions. Kroft et al. (2014) and Aaronson, Mazumder, and Schechter (2010) reach similar conclusions, and show that rates of long-term unemployment increased for nearly all demographic, occupation, industry, and regional groups during the Great Recession.

This research suggests that another explanation for why the long-term unemployed are less likely to be hired is more relevant to our recovery: that becoming long-term unemployed itself makes it harder to escape from unemployment. Employers may interpret a spell of long-term unemployment as a negative signal of a worker's ability because of stigma (Blanchard and Diamond 1994; Kroft, Lange, and Notowidigdo 2013). Additionally, employers' hiring processes may lead to discrimination against the long-term unemployed by, for example, screening out all workers with a long spell of unemployment regardless of their other qualifications (Ghayad 2013). Research has shown that the long-term unemployed conditional on all other characteristics remaining the same are less likely to get called for interviews (Kroft, Lange, and Notowidigdo 2013). Another explanation is that as people remain out of work for extended periods of time, their general and job-specific skills or connections to industry may deteriorate (Edin and

Figure 3-13
**Monthly Job Finding Rates by Duration of
Unemployment in Previous Month, December 2014**

Probability of Reemployment, Percent

Note: Seasonally-adjusted data as of December 2014. Data refer to the probability of reemployment in December 2014 based on duration of unemployment in November 2014.
Source: Bureau of Labor Statistics, Current Population Survey.

Gustavsson 2005; Autor et al. 2015). These explanations are not mutually exclusive, and both could affect the likelihood of transitioning from unemployment to employment (Jackman and Layard 1991).

Pre-recession patterns in the rate of transition from long-term unemployment to employment, controlling for duration of unemployment, do a good job predicting these transitions during this recovery (Kroft et al. 2014). This implies that, despite the much larger, more diverse pool of long-term unemployed as compared with past recessions or even non-recessionary periods, transitions from long-term unemployment back to employment are not any faster. Unemployment duration appears to be more important than worker characteristics in determining the transition back to employment. However, the long-term unemployed were more likely during the recession and recovery to stay in the labor market than past transition rates from long-term unemployed to out of the labor force would have predicted.[9] Some research suggests that the extensions of unemployment insurance encouraged the long-term unemployed to continue looking for work and reduced the likelihood that they exited the labor force (Krueger, Cramer,

---

[9] Specifically, Kroft et al. (2014) show that the transition probability from unemployment to non-employment fell markedly over the recession and began to recover around 2010. Their transition probabilities are constructed from a series in which monthly flows are harmonized to stocks for the employed, unemployed, and non-participants.

and Cho 2014; Aaronson, Mazumder, and Schechter 2010; Kroft et al. 2014; Rothstein 2011).

Why Long-term Unemployment Matters

Higher levels of long-term unemployment are concerning because they place greater strain on household resources and sometimes necessitate drastic changes in household behavior, such as selling a home or postponing medical care, which can have disruptive impacts on family members, the wider community, and the economy. Long-term earnings loss after resuming work also appears to increase with the duration of unemployment (Schmieder, von Wachter, and Bender 2013; Addison and Portugal 1989). Moreover, it does not appear that these earnings losses are unique to experiencing unemployment during an economic expansion or recovery, nor are they concentrated in the manufacturing or service sector (Couch and Placzek 2010). Former Federal Reserve Chairman Ben Bernanke has said that long-term unemployment "imposes economic costs on everyone, not just the unemployed themselves," as their loss of skills and lower rates of employment reduce the economy's overall productive capacity (Bernanke 2012).

PART-TIME WORK FOR ECONOMIC REASONS

Part-time employment tends to grow in recessions as some businesses hold on to workers by cutting their hours, and those businesses continuing to hire may need only part-time hours from new workers. Between December 2007 and December 2009, the share of the labor force usually working part-time rose from 16.1 percent to 17.9 percent. This increase was driven by a large rise in people working part-time for economic reasons, defined as employees who would prefer to have full-time work but either cannot find a full-time job or have a job that does not provide full-time hours (even if it once did). As the economy has recovered, the share of the labor force that is part-time has begun to recede as all the growth in employment has been driven by growth in full-time employment, as Figure 3-14 shows. Five years into the recovery, more than 9 million more people are working full-time, while the number of people employed in part-time jobs has been largely unchanged. Moreover, part-time jobs have been increasingly held by those who say they do not want to work full-time.

Rates of part-time employment for economic reasons doubled during the recession from 3 percent to 6 percent, exceeding the previous peak

Figure 3-14
**Net Change in Employment Since January 2010,
Household Survey Estimates**

Millions of Workers

Source: Bureau of Labor Statistics, Current Population Survey; CEA calculations.

reached in 1982, as shown in Figure 3-15.[10] The share of the labor force working part-time for economic reasons has since fallen, and the pace of the decline in this share picked up during 2014, declining 0.7 percentage point over the 12 months ending in December 2014. The rate is 4.3 percent as of December 2014, 54 percent of the way back to its pre-recession average, with over one-third of this overall progress occurring in 2014.

Patterns in Part-Time For Economic Reasons

As a general rule, the share of workers who are part-time but would prefer full-time work rises in a downturn and then trends slowly back down during the recovery and boom. As Figure 3-15 shows, in a typical business cycle rates of part-time employment rise and these jobs go disproportionately to those who would prefer full-time work, with rates of part-time work

---

[10] Care must be taken when comparing the share of workers who are part-time for economic reasons before and after the 1994 redesign of the Current Population Survey. CEA used the multiplicative adjustment factors reported by Polivka and Miller (1998) in order to place the pre-1994 estimates of the part-time for economic reasons rate on a comparable basis with post-redesign estimates. For the part-time series for which Polikva and Miller do not report suitable adjustment factors, the pre- and post-redesign series were spliced by multiplying the pre-1994 estimates by the ratio of the January 1994 rate to the December 1993 rate. This procedure generates similar results to the Polikva and Miller factors for series for which multiplicative factors are available.

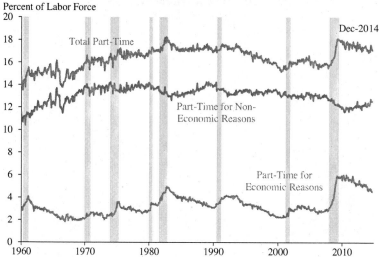

Figure 3-15
Rates of Part-Time Work, 1960–2014

Percent of Labor Force

Note: Shading denotes recession. See footnote 10 for details on comparability over time.
Source: Bureau of Labor Statistics, Current Population Survey; Polivka and Miller (1998); CEA calculations.

for other reasons declining. This shift likely reflects several factors: firms finding it easier to hire highly qualified workers for part-time jobs since fewer full-time jobs are available, and therefore hiring more people for part-time work who would prefer full-time work; firms cutting hours of full-time employees who are unable to find full-time work elsewhere; and workers in part-time jobs increasing their preferences for full-time work as household income falls (Bednarzik 1975; Bednarzik 1983; Maloney 1987).

Figure 3-15 also shows that, following some recessions, the rate did not fully recover to its prerecession low before rising again. This is partially a result of the fact that the relationship between unemployment and part-time for economic reasons has varied across recessions and may also be due partly due to differences in the length of the recovery period. Figure 3-16 reports the change in the share of the labor force working part-time for economic reasons relative to the change in the unemployment rate during contractions and expansions over the last five decades. Like the current cycle, both the 1980s recessions and the 2001 recession saw above-average increases in part-time employment for economic reasons for a given percentage point rise in the unemployment rate, but did not see commensurately rapid declines as the unemployment rate declined in the ensuing expansion.

Figure 3-17 uses the relationship between part-time employment for economic reasons and unemployment from prior recessions and the path of unemployment during the current business cycle to predict the path of

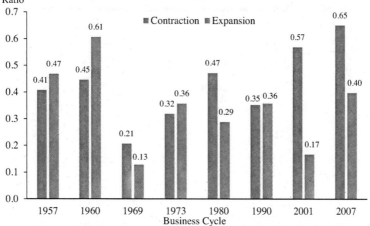

Figure 3-16
Change in Share Part-Time for Economic Reasons Per Percentage-Point Change in the Unemployment Rate, 1957–2014

Note: The 1980s recessions are consolidated into a single cycle. The expansion period runs through 22 quarters or until the next peak, whichever is earlier.
Source: Bureau of Labor Statistics, Current Population Survey; Polivka and Miller (1998); CEA calculations.

part-time employment for economic reasons. Consistent with the patterns described in the last paragraph, predictions based on the 1980s recessions and the 2001 recession generate a path similar to that observed during the current business cycle: a relatively sharp initial increase, followed by a recovery that, while steady, does not match the pace of the initial increase and, thus, leaves part-time employment for economic reasons elevated. Modeling the path in this recession using relationships from other post-1957 recessions generates a much smaller initial increase but a broadly similar pace of recovery.

Figures 3-16 and 3-17 imply that the mystery of part-time employment for economic reasons in the Great Recession (as well as of recessions in the 1980s and 2001) is the sharper increase of such work during the contraction, not a lack of full-time job creation during the recovery. Similarities across the 1980s and 2001 recessions suggest that the behavior of part-time employment for economic reasons in the 2007 recession may not be due to factors unique to the Great Recession, like its depth or duration. Instead, it may reflect longer-term changes in the cyclical sensitivity of this measure, suggesting that this challenge may return in future recessions.

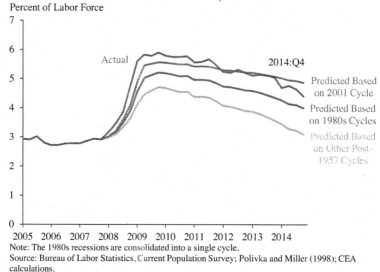

Figure 3-17
**Share Part-Time for Economic Reasons,
Actual and Predicted, 2005–2014**

Percent of Labor Force

Actual

2014:Q4

Predicted Based
on 2001 Cycle

Predicted Based
on 1980s Cycles

Predicted Based
on Other Post-
1957 Cycles

2005 2006 2007 2008 2009 2010 2011 2012 2013 2014

Note: The 1980s recessions are consolidated into a single cycle.
Source: Bureau of Labor Statistics, Current Population Survey; Polivka and Miller (1998); CEA
calculations.

The Outlook for the Rate of Part-Time for Economic Reasons

The question arises of whether the share of employees who work part-time for economic reasons will remain elevated over the long term. The answer depends in large part on the reasons behind this elevation.

One possibility is that this type of part-time employment remains elevated because it recovers later, even after the headline unemployment rate has fully recovered. The view suggests that part-time workers who prefer full-time work will accept more hours or a full-time job if it becomes available, and therefore they represent a pool of available workers to businesses wishing to expand employment. In this situation, a higher share of workers who are part-time for economic reasons indicates that there is more slack in the labor market than is suggested by a given unemployment rate. If this interpretation describes our current labor market, and the robust labor market momentum seen over 2014 continues, then the rate of part-time work for economic reasons should continue to decline in the years ahead, ultimately returning to pre-recession levels assuming the economy remains strong for long enough. Some evidence consistent with this scenario comes from the rapid decline in this rate in recent months, even measured relative to the increased pace of progress in reducing unemployment. Over 2014, the rate of part-time work for economic reasons has declined by 0.5 percentage point for each percentage-point reduction in the unemployment rate, whereas it declined, on average, by 0.3 percentage point for each percentage-point reduction in the unemployment rate since the start of 2010. Furthermore, experience from the late 1990s and mid-to-late 1960s provides historical precedent: part-time employment for economic reasons rapidly decreased relative to overall unemployment during these strong labor market periods.

On the other hand, another possibility is that recent recessions have accelerated ongoing structural changes that cause employers to demand more part-time workers relative to full-time workers. In this scenario, the part-time for economic reasons rate may remain elevated even once the unemployment rate has fully recovered, depending on the supply of part-time workers. The more rapid recovery in the goods sector relative to the service sector may provide some evidence that employer demand for part-time workers in the service sector has shifted. To the extent that the overall rate remains elevated mainly due to the incomplete recovery of the labor market, that incomplete recovery might be expected to affect both sectors similarly (Figure 3-18).

The timing of the shifts in part-time work also suggest that the Affordable Care Act's employer responsibility provision, which requires large employers to offer coverage to employees working 30 or more hours per week or pay a penalty, is not playing a meaningful role in recent trends in part-time work. First, both the share of the labor force working part-time and the share in part-time jobs who would prefer to be in full-time jobs declined more sharply in 2014 than in the earlier years of the recovery. In contrast, if the Affordable Care Act's employer responsibility provision was driving a substantial structural increase in the demand for part-time workers, one would, all else equal, have expected the opposite—that progress in reducing part-time employment would have slowed over the months leading up to the provision's implementation in 2015. Second, the most striking way in which the behavior of part-time employment, particularly among those who would prefer full-time, in the most recent recession and recovery differs from prior recessions is that it rose unusually sharply during the contraction, not that it has fallen unusually slowly during the recovery, as discussed above. This unusually sharp increase occurred essentially entirely before the Affordable Care Act became law in March 2010 and many years before employer responsibility took effect, so it cannot have been caused by the Affordable Care Act. Finally, as noted earlier, other recent recessions—most notably the 2001 recession and, to a lesser extent, the 1980s recession—also experienced sharp rises in the rate of involuntarily part-time workers that were not fully reversed by this point in the ensuing recovery, so the phenomenon may tell us more about a structural shift in the economy in the last several decades.

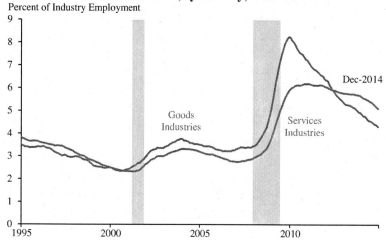

Figure 3-18
**Share of Employees Working Part-Time for
Economic Reasons, by Industry, 1995–2014**
Percent of Industry Employment

Note: Data are 12-month moving averages of non-seasonally adjusted data. Shading denotes recession.
Source: Bureau of Labor Statistics, Current Population Survey; CEA calculations.

LABOR MARKET FLUIDITY

Labor market fluidity (used interchangeably in this chapter with "dynamism" or "churn") refers broadly to the frequency of changes in who is working for whom in the labor market. From the worker's perspective, this is measured by hires and separations; from the firm's perspective, it is measured by new positions (job creation) and eliminated positions (job destruction). Although separations, hires, creation, destruction, and other measures capture different concepts of fluidity, increases in these measures generally indicate more fluidity.

A range of measures suggest that fluidity has risen in the labor market recovery, as shown in Figure 3-19.[11] The number of new workers hired has steadily increased: there were 5.0 million workers hired into new positions in November 2014, compared to 4.6 million in November of the previous year. The hires rate was 3.6 percent in November, a number that has nearly fully recovered to its rate of 3.7 percent in the month prior to the recession's start.

---

[11] The Longitudinal Employer-Household Dynamics (or LEHD) data are a restricted-access data source compiled and maintained by the Census Bureau. The LEHD data are the result of matching data across many sources—in particular, by matching household information from the Census and American Community Surveys to state administrative Unemployment Insurance system wage records and to employer data from economic censuses. For detail, see Abowd et al. (2005). The job-to-job (or J2J) data are newly available data constructed from the LEHD and published by Census. The J2J data provide information on the flows of workers joining, leaving or changing employers under various circumstances (Hyatt et al. 2014).

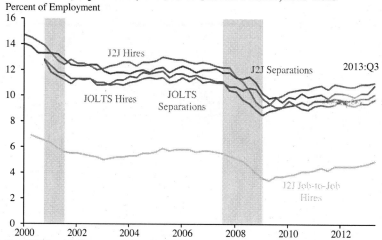

Figure 3-19
Hires, Separations, and Job-to-Job Flow Rates, 2000–2013

Note: J2J job-to-job hires are generally equal to J2J job-to-job separations (not shown). Shading denotes recession.
Source: Bureau of Labor Statistics, Job Openings and Labor Turnover Survey; Census Bureau, Job-to-Job Flows.

Direct transitions of workers from one job to another also show recovery. Worker flows out of jobs (separations), including voluntary quits, have also slowly risen during the recovery. Naturally, involuntary separations spiked during the recession, but recovery in voluntary separations indicates that workers are feeling comfortable in changing employers, which reflects the increasing strength of the labor market.

Consistent with the strong employment growth over the last 58 months, the rate of new job openings as a share of total positions is now above its pre-recession average after falling by more than 40 percent during the recession (Figure 3-20). This increase in job openings offers further opportunities for workers to change their employment status or situation if desired. Taken together, these data indicate that greater fluidity has accompanied the labor market strengthening.

While the short-term trend shows increased labor market dynamism, a growing body of evidence finds that there are long-run downward trends in fluidity that likely date back several decades. The recent gains in fluidity measures reflect the strength of the recovery and should therefore generally be viewed as positive. It is less clear, however, how the long-run decline should be viewed given that it has the potential for both positive aspects in terms of job stability and better matches, and negative aspects in terms of potentially less effective reallocation of labor to its highest productivity uses.

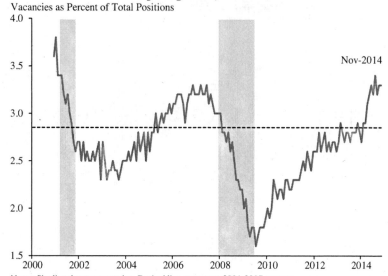

Figure 3-20
Job Opening Rates, 2000–2014

Vacancies as Percent of Total Positions

Nov-2014

Notes: Shading denotes recession. Dashed line represents 2001-2007 average.
Source: Bureau of Labor Statistics, Job Openings and Labor Turover Survey; CEA calculations.

This section examines these longer-run trends and their potential impact on the economy.

Trends in Labor Market Fluidity

Recent research has identified long-run declines in a variety of measures of worker mobility. Research has shown that workers are less likely to leave a job, are less likely to move to a new job, and are less likely to physically move for a job (Kaplan and Schulhofer-Wohl 2012; Molloy, Smith, and Wozniak 2014; Hyatt and Spletzer 2013). Research has also identified long-run declines in dynamism in firm-side measures, including job creation, job destruction, and the entry and exit of establishments from the marketplace (Decker et al. 2014; Davis and Haltiwanger 2014). Taken together, this body of work indicates a U.S. labor market characterized by considerably lower levels of fluidity of all kinds than was the case two to three decades ago.

Lower Hires and Separations Rates

Worker flows have declined since at least the late 1990s, including the entire period for which the best direct data on worker flows are available from the Job Openings and Labor Turnover Survey (JOLTS, available since 2001). Hyatt and Spletzer (2013) document declines of 10 percent (using Current Population Survey data) to 38 percent (using Longitudinal Employer-Household Dynamics data) in hires and separations since 2001, as shown in Figure 3-21.[12] Davis and Haltiwanger (2014) have a longer series on hires and separations that extends back to 1990, which shows a decline in worker flows over this longer period.

Other studies examine fluidity indirectly by looking at outcomes for which worker or job flows are likely important, such as flows between labor market statuses, long-distance migration, and transitions between industries and occupations. Some of these indirect measures can be calculated over longer historical periods and also point to long-term declines in fluidity. Hyatt and Spletzer (2013) find that job-to-job transitions declined by roughly 50 percent from 1998 to 2010. Davis et al. (2010) show that flows into and out of unemployment fell by nearly one-half over the two decades prior to the early 2000s. Long-distance migration in the United States, which typically involves a change of employer or labor force status, has been in a decades-long decline, falling by as much as 50 percent since the late 1970s (Molloy, Smith, and Wozniak 2014; Kaplan and Schulhofer-Wohl 2012). Industry, occupation, and employer transitions have also fallen markedly over a similar period, with declines in those measures accelerating since the 1990s, as shown in Figure 3-22.[13]

Lower Job Creation and Job Destruction Rates

More is known about job flows (job creation and destruction) than worker flows (hires and separations) since series data are available back to the 1980s. Literature based on these data concludes that job flows have markedly declined over the last 20 to 30 years. For example, Decker et al. (2014) and Davis and Haltiwanger (2014) document that job creation and job destruction fell from the late 1980s to just prior to the 2007 recession. Hyatt and Spletzer (2013) find larger declines, of roughly one-quarter to one-third, for both job creation and destruction between the late 1990s and 2010. To the degree that this reflects structural improvements in the economy that lead to more stable jobs, this would be an encouraging trend. But a potential concern is that it could reflect less reallocation of resources toward their most productive uses and thus fewer high-paying jobs.

Factors in Decreasing in Labor Market Fluidity

---

[12] Differences in the duration of jobs and types of establishments captured by the three series explain the level differences. The smaller decline in the Current Population Survey may be related to the fact that it misses more short-term jobs than does the Longitudinal Employer-Household Dynamics data (Abraham et al. 2013), and Hyatt and Speltzer (2013) show that the declining share of short-term jobs can explain some of the decline in hires and separations.

[13] A caveat is that some studies using CPS data find less clear trends in transitions for the 1980s to the 1990s, but again, for the late 1990s onward, the trend is clearly downward. Kambourov and Manovskii (2009) tabulate occupation mobility from the CPS and find an increasing trend. Moscarini and Thomsson (2007) characterize the trend in occupational mobility as weakly increasing in the 1980s. In addition, Stewart (2007) finds no trend in job-to-job flows from the 1980s to the 1990s using the annual retrospective question CPS question.

Figure 3-21
Trends in Hires and Separations, 1995–2012

Percent of Total Employment

Source: Hyatt and Spletzer (2013); Bureau of Labor Statistics, Current Population Survey; Bureau of Labor Statistics, Job Openings and Labor Turnover Survey; Census Bureau, Longitudinal Employer-Household Dynamics.

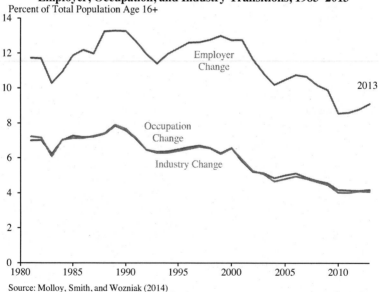

Figure 3-22
Employer, Occupation, and Industry Transitions, 1983–2013

Percent of Total Population Age 16+

Source: Molloy, Smith, and Wozniak (2014)

The empirical literature has only recently begun to examine why job and worker transitions have fallen. Two basic hypotheses have been explored: that firms or that workers have changed over time in ways that lower fluidity. Evidence shows that the first of these can explain a portion of declining fluidity. The average age and number of associated establishments per firm have both risen in recent decades (Davis and Haltiwanger 2014; CEA calculations). Older, larger firms are associated with lower job flows, as these firms are less likely to contract or expand rapidly. Consistent with this change in firm composition, rates of firm entry and exit have also declined over the last three decades (Figure 3-23). Because the change in the composition of firms has shifted in a way that, all else equal, would suggest fewer worker hires and separations, researchers have tested to see how much of the shift in worker flows can be explained by changes in firm composition. Hyatt and Spletzer (2013) and Davis and Haltiwanger (2014) decompose changes in worker flows into those due to job flows and those due to worker movements between existing jobs. They find that changes in job flows account for between one-third to one-half of the decline in worker flows. Because job flows are determined in part by firm size and age, changing firm characteristics contribute to the decline in worker flows (Hyatt and Spletzer 2013). In contrast, changes in characteristics of the average worker, like age and education, have been found to contribute little to declines in fluidity (Molloy, Smith, and Wozniak 2014; Davis and Haltiwanger 2014).

Potential Consequences of Reduced Fluidity

Some explanations for reduced fluidity may be benign. For example, employers may be increasing efforts to reduce turnover for a variety of reasons: increased cost of switching workers as job training requirements increase or better worker-firm matching at the point of hire, to name a few.[14] A reduced level of labor market transitions may also have benefits for workers, like more stable jobs with less disruption that allow them to invest more in skills that their employer values.

Reduced flows could be cause for concern, however, because they may undermine workers' abilities to improve their employment situations. In particular, reduced fluidity may preclude employees from realizing the wage gains of switching jobs or make it difficult for part-time workers to find full-time work or result in fewer high-paying jobs in productive industries.

---

[14] Cairo (2013) finds that job-training requirements have risen over time, which supports a theory that on-the-job experience has also become more important. Both would likely lead firms to want to lower turnover. No direct evidence exists on trends in the quality of worker-firm matches, but a substantial literature outlines the importance of this matching for wages (Nagypál 2007; Crane 2014; Jovanovic 1979).

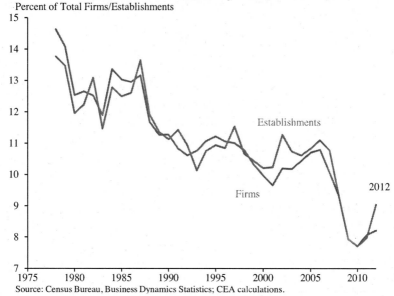

Figure 3-23
Firm and Establishment Entry Rates, 1978–2012
Percent of Total Firms/Establishments

Source: Census Bureau, Business Dynamics Statistics; CEA calculations.

A growing body of evidence finds that wages and earnings increase substantially when a worker changes jobs, as summarized in Table 3-3. In general, workers gain at rates considerably above inflation.

Even when workers ultimately stay with their employer, the potential for them to land better employment can generate wage growth as incumbent employers raise wages to retain these workers (Beaudry and DiNardo 1991). Lower fluidity may reduce workers' abilities to raise their wages by changing jobs, and consequently also their bargaining power with their incumbent employer. In this way, reduced fluidity may contribute to slower wage growth. Alternatively, lower fluidity may result from limited opportunities for wage growth through employer transitions. Regardless, Table 3-3 shows that the gains from switching jobs have varied over time. The largest wage gains from switching jobs were seen in the late 1990s, while wage gains from switching jobs in the 2000s were much lower.[15]

Other consequences of lower fluidity are perhaps more speculative but warrant careful observation nonetheless. Greater fluidity—or more precisely the conditions and institutions that enable greater fluidity—may prevent the share of long-term unemployed from rising, and may thereby reduce the negative consequences of long-term unemployment. More fluid labor

---

[15] Molloy, Smith, and Wozniak (2014) note that point estimates in both the PSID and NLSY are similar when the recession years are excluded.

Table 3-3
Wage and Earnings Gains Associated with Job Switching

	Data Source	Age Group	Time Period	Gain to Switching Jobs
Topel and Ward (1992)	LEED	18 to 34	1957:Q1 - 1972:Q4	9%
Molloy, Smith, and Wozniak (2014)	PSID	22 to 29	1983-1994	4%
			1995-2001	10%
			2003-2011	2%
	NLSY	22 to 29	1966-1981	7%
			1979-1994	3%
			2002-2011	4%
Fallick, Haltiwanger, and McEntarfer (2012)	LEHD	25 to 55	1995:Q2	8%
			1999:Q2	14%
			2001:Q2	6%

Note: Topel and Ward (1992) and Molloy, Smith, and Wozniak (2014) are wage regression models, while Fallick, Haltiwanger, and McEntarfer (2012) use sample earnings medians from job switchers. All regression estimates are statistically significant, except for the Molloy, Smith, and Wozniak (2014) estimates from the 2000s.

markets may also be more resistant to cyclical shocks, or, at minimum, may experience faster recoveries after a recession (Blanchard and Wolfers 2000). If this is the case, the slower recoveries in the shares of part-time for economic reasons and in long-term unemployment in recent recessions could in fact be related to the long-run decline in fluidity.

WAGE GROWTH AND JOB QUALITY

In 2014, average real wages for production and nonsupervisory workers increased 0.8 percent after increasing 0.7 percent in 2013. Although not sufficient, these increases are a marked improvement from the 2000s, including the pre-Great Recession years of 2001 to 2007, when real wage growth averaged 0.5 percent a year, as shown in Figure 1-4 of Chapter 1. While these recent wage gains are further evidence of a strengthening labor market, there is more work to be done to ensure that middle-class families fully share in the benefits of the recovery.

The evidence presented below shows that 2014 was a strong year for growth across almost all sectors, but it was particularly strong in several that have traditionally provided good, middle-class jobs. A longer-run perspective, however, shows that over the past several decades the composition of jobs has shifted toward both high- and low-skilled sectors while employment in the middle of the skill distribution has declined.

Job Growth in 2014

Not only was 2014 the strongest year for job growth since the 1990s, but the pickup in growth between 2013 and 2014 occurred more strongly in industries with higher average wages, as shown in Figure 3-24. For instance, average weekly earnings for manufacturing workers are about $170 higher than the average for all private-sector workers, and manufacturing job growth almost doubled from 10,000 a month in 2013 to 19,000 a month in 2014. Similarly, employment in the construction sector, which has average weekly earnings about $200 above the private-sector average, rose by an average of 28,000 a month in 2014, up from 18,000 a month in 2013.[16] It is important to note, however, that this—like any estimate of job growth by industry or occupation—does not necessarily tell the full story, which depends not just on job growth across sectors, but also on what is happening to job growth within sectors as well.

Patterns in Wage Growth since the 1980s

As discussed in Chapter 1 and shown in Table 3-4, for most workers, earnings gains have not kept pace with productivity gains over the last several decades.[17] The official estimate of labor productivity grew an average of 2.0 percent a year between 1980 and 2014. To make it comparable to the real wage and compensation data used below, CEA adjusted labor productivity using an index of consumer prices, the CPI-U-RS, yielding an estimate of 1.3 percent annual growth in productivity.[18] Over this period, hourly compensation for the average worker rose 0.9 percent annually, indicating that compensation did not keep up with productivity growth and that the share of gross domestic income going to capital was rising. Average hourly wages (calculated from wage and salary earnings in the CPS microdata) fell even

---

[16] Bureau of Labor Statistics, Current Employment Statistics; CEA calculations.

[17] All of the consumer price deflation in Table 3-4, and in this section, is done using the CPI-U-RS, as is common in the labor literature. The CPI-U-RS is the Consumer Price Index adjusted backwards to make a methodologically consistent historical series. Footnotes in this subsection indicate results using an alternative index, the price index for Personal Consumption Expenditure (PCE) from the National Income and Product Accounts. The PCE price index has the property relative to the CPI of not covering the same consumer basket as the one consumers purchase through their wages—for example, it includes Medicare costs for the government and the costs facing nonprofits. However, the PCE deflator also has the properties associated with using a chain-weighted index. As a result, PCE-adjustment implies real wage increases over time that are about 0.3 percentage point per year higher than CPI-based adjustment.

[18] The difference between the two estimates of productivity growth reflects slower growth in prices of investment goods and the terms of trade, relative to consumption good prices. As a result, the implicit price deflator used to deflate productivity rises more slowly than consumer prices over this period. If the labor share was constant, productivity adjusted for consumer prices should keep pace with wages adjusted for consumer prices.

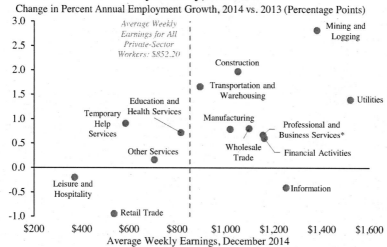

Figure 3-24
**Change in Job Growth vs. Average Earnings
by Industry, 2013–2014**

Change in Percent Annual Employment Growth, 2014 vs. 2013 (Percentage Points)

Average Weekly Earnings for All Private-Sector Workers: $852.20

Mining and Logging

Construction

Transportation and Warehousing

Utilities

Education and Health Services

Temporary Help Services

Manufacturing

Professional and Business Services*

Other Services

Wholesale Trade

Financial Activities

Leisure and Hospitality

Information

Retail Trade

Average Weekly Earnings, December 2014

Note: *Excludes Temporary Help Services (shown separately). Average earnings for Temporary Help Services are not seasonally adjusted.
Source: Bureau of Labor Statistics, Current Employment Statistics.

further short of productivity growth, rising only 0.6 percent a year, because they do not include the faster-growing components of compensation like employer-paid health insurance. Finally, median hourly wages grew only 0.3 percent per year—slower than average wages because the increase in wage inequality meant larger increases in wages for workers near the top, raising the average much more than the median. In total, the disconnect between the 2.0 percent annual productivity growth and the 0.3 percent annual growth in the median wage reflects the combination of these factors: a methodological issue involving different price indices, the rapid rise of benefit costs, and the increase in inequality.[19]

The slowdown in wage growth has been felt most in the middle and bottom of the wage distribution. Aside from the late 1990s—a period that saw rapid wage growth across the distribution—over most of the last three decades, wages have been stagnant or deteriorating for all except the highest earners. Figure 3-25 shows that these patterns have led to a widening in wage inequality since the late 1970s (Juhn, Murphy, and Pierce 1993; Lemieux 2006; Autor, Katz, and Kearney 2008). Between 1979 and 2014, real wages for the highest earners (the 90th percentile of the wage distribution) have grown by around 35 percent. At the same time, median wages rose by 8

---

[19] If Table 3-4 were produced using the PCE index, the average annual percent increase would be 1.6 for labor productivity; 1.2 for compensation; 0.9 for mean wages; and 0.6 for the median wage.

Table 3-4
Average Annual Percent Change in Real Productivity, Compensation, and Wages, 1980–2014

Real Labor Productivity	2.0
Labor Productivity*	1.3
Labor Compensation*	0.9
Mean Hourly Wage (CPS)*	0.6
Median Hourly Wage (CPS)*	0.3

Note: Series marked with (*) are adjusted for inflation using the CPI-U-RS. Wages are calculated using the same method as Figure 3-25.
Source: Bureau of Labor Statistics, Productivity and Costs; Bureau of Labor Statistics, Current Population Survey (Merged Outgoing Rotation Groups); Bureau of Labor Statistics, Consumer Price Index; CEA calculations.

percent while wages at the 10th percentile declined slightly.[20] As a result, the ratio between wages at the 90th and 10th percentiles widened by 37 percent since 1979. The 90th-to-50th percentile ratio grew by 26 percent, and the ratio between the 50th and 10th percentiles increased only slightly. As the figure shows, inequality at the bottom of the wage distribution—that is, between the 50th and 10th percentiles—grew rapidly during the 1980s and has been relatively constant since, whereas inequality between the highest earners and the rest of the distribution has grown since the late 1970s.

Figure 3-25 shows that the lack of wage growth in the lower half of the wage distribution has been a continuing challenge for more than three decades. Lee (1999) documents that an important factor explaining this decline is the erosion of the real value of the minimum wage. Increasing the value of the minimum wage in 2014 to its real average value in 1979 would have directly increased wages for the lowest 8 percent of wage earners.[21] Economists have found that the minimum wage can also "spill over" to increase wages for those with wages above the new minimum, since employers may adjust their compensation schedules to preserve relative pay among their workers (Autor, Manning, and Smith 2014). Autor, Manning, and Smith (2014) find that the effect of the minimum wage on inequality in the lower part of the wage distribution can be quite substantial: an approximately 10 percent increase in the minimum wage, relative to the median wage, reduces the 50-10 ratio by about 1.5 percent.

---

[20] Using the PCE deflator, 90th percentile wages would have grown by 50 percent, median wages by 20 percent, and 10th percentile wages by 10 percent. While the levels would be increased with this deflator, the evolution of inequality—the differences between the levels—is unaffected by the deflator.

[21] Bureau of Labor Statistics, Current Population Survey (Merged Outgoing Rotation Groups); CEA calculations. Inflation-adjusted using the CPI-U-RS. This is the percentage of workers making below the 1979 inflation-adjusted value of the minimum wage.

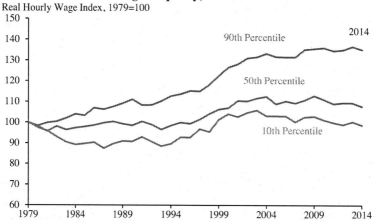

Figure 3-25
Wage Inequality, 1979–2014

Real Hourly Wage Index, 1979=100

Note: The figure depicts real hourly wage quantiles for workers age 18 to 64, excluding individuals who are self-employed, who have real wages below $0.50 or greater than $100 (in 1989 dollars), or whose wages are imputed. Top-coded earnings adjusted following Lemieux (2006). Inflation adjusted using the CPI-U-RS.
Source: Bureau of Labor Statistics, Current Population Survey (Merged Outgoing Rotation Groups); CEA calculations.

The Rise of the Skill Premium and Employment Growth in High- and Low-Skill Occupations

The rise in inequality shown in Figure 3-25 is also seen in earnings differentials for workers with different levels of education. Since the 1980s, the college income premium—the ratio of income among workers with at least a college education to workers with only a high school diploma—has increased. In 1963, men and women with college educations earned incomes 33 and 76 percent higher, respectively, than men and women with only high school diplomas. Since about 1980, however, these income gaps have widened so that by 2013, college-educated workers' incomes were more than twice the incomes of high school graduates.

Economists Claudia Goldin and Lawrence Katz (2010) explain this phenomenon as a "race" between technological advancements that increase the demand for highly-skilled workers and the supply of such workers. In particular, they document a slowdown in the growth of the college-educated workforce around 1980. This slowdown has meant that growth in the demand for skills (technology) outpaced growth in the supply of skills (educational attainment of workers), leading the college earnings premium to increase.

In spite of the long-term rise in demand for skill, employers appear to be offering less training than in the 1990s (Figure 3-27). To some extent,

Figure 3-26
College Income Premium by Gender, 1963–2013
Ratio of College Income to High School Income

Note: Income premia calculated using median annual income of persons 25 and older. Prior to 1991, "high school graduates" refers to respondents with 4 years of high school, and "college graduates" refers to respondents with at least 4 years of college.
Source: Bureau of Labor Statistics, Current Population Survey (Annual Social and Economic Supplement); CEA calculations.

these changes may reflect shifts in industry structure: historically, jobs with high vocational requirements are most likely to offer on-site training and financial assistance (Altonji and Spletzer 1991). Nevertheless, it appears that fewer workers are able to acquire new skills either on the job or with the support of their employer than in the past. Less access to training may contribute to inequality, since when employers invest in their workers' human capital by paying for training or offering training on the job site, workers also benefit in the form of future wage increases (Bartel 1992; Lynch 1991).

At the same time that wages and employment have been growing among high-skill workers, employment in middle-skill jobs has declined, especially relative to higher- and lower-skill jobs. Economists use the term polarization to describe this pattern: employment loss in the middle of the wage or job skill distribution combined with relative job growth at the bottom and at the top. The concept of polarization has its roots in the large literature on skill-biased technological change that developed to try to understand changes in wage inequality since the 1970s (Bound and Johnson 1995; Katz and Murphy 1992; Juhn, Murphy, and Pierce 1993). In the past decade, economists have refined the skill-biased technological change model, arguing that technology is a substitute for some, but not all, types of labor. For example, Autor, Levy, and Murnane (2003) and Acemoglu and Autor (2011) develop a model in which technology can replace labor in tasks that are easily automated, such as manual labor, and in which highly

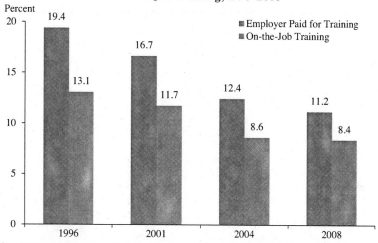

Figure 3-27
**Percent of Workers Receiving Employer-Sponsored
or On-the-Job Training, 1996–2008**

Note: Fraction of workers ages 18-65 receiving training of any duration in the last year.
Source: Census Bureau, Survey of Income and Program Participation (Employment and Training Topical Module); CEA calculations.

skilled managerial professions are complementary to labor. The tasks that are most easily automated tend to be in the middle of the skills distribution, so that over time employment moves to both the lower and higher ends of the occupational ranking, as shown in Figure 3-28, where occupations are ranked by average wage.

Figure 3-29 uses smoothed data from employment by occupations harmonized over a longer time period to show this pattern more clearly: since the late 1970s, employment growth has been greatest in the highest and lowest earning occupations. The middle of the distribution has actually experienced employment losses, with fewer workers employed in middle-wage occupations in 2012 than in 1979.

As demand falls for manual tasks, wages and employment in these positions also fall relative to highly-skilled workers, leading to greater inequality. The results from this research show that, in theory, automation can lead to both job and wage polarization (Acemoglu and Autor 2011; Goos, Manning, and Salomon 2007) and some have demonstrated a link between changing tasks and other forms of wage inequality (Black and Spitz-Oener 2010).

This stylized model, however, has not always matched the data. Some economists argue that the automation hypothesis cannot explain the timing of the trends in wage inequality and employment growth by real wage level (Card and DiNardo 2002; Mishel, Shierholz, and Schmitt 2013).

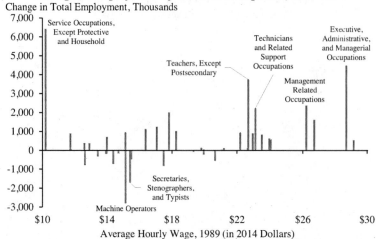

Figure 3-28
Change in Employment by Detailed Occupation, 1989–2014

Change in Total Employment, Thousands

Note: Excludes five occupational categories with outlying wages and relatively small changes in employment (Farm Occupations, Except Managerial; Private Household Occupations; Engineers, Architects, and Surveyors; Lawyers and Judges; and Health Diagnosing Occupations). Wages are calculated using the method of Figure 3-25 and are adjusted for inflation using the CPI-U-RS.
Source: Bureau of Labor Statistics, Current Population Survey; CEA calculations.

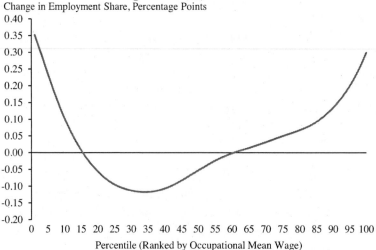

Figure 3-29
**Changes in Employment by Occupational
Wage Percentile, 1979–2012**

Change in Employment Share, Percentage Points

Source: Census Bureau, 1980 Census; Census Bureau, 2012 American Community Survey; calculations by David Autor and Brendan Price.

In particular, Mishel, Shierholz, and Schmitt (2013) find that changes in employment across occupations explains little of the rise in inequality in the overall wage distribution in contrast to what would be expected if occupations accurately reflect differences in tasks for which technology may have shifted demand.[22]

Broader Measures of Job Quality

Broader measures of compensation take into account the value of nonwage features of jobs. Sometimes these are benefits, like employer-provided retirement plans, paid vacation days, and employer-sponsored health insurance, but these can also be features like family-friendly scheduling practices and possibilities for advancement. Research has found that trends in the combination of employer-provided benefits plus wages and salary (called total compensation) broadly mirror those in wage compensation — both have become substantially more unequal since the early 1980s, though compensation inequality has generally grown more rapidly than wage inequality (Pierce 2001, 2010).

Coverage of major employer benefits—specifically health insurance and retirement plans—are tracked for long periods of time in surveys such as the National Health Interview Survey and the Current Population Survey. Changes in access to employer-sponsored health insurance and retirement plans are shown separately in Figures 3-30 and 3-31. Access to these benefits generally declined between 2000 and 2010, particularly for lower-skilled workers. Recently, these trends have stabilized or begun to reverse: in 2013, the share of employees with access to retirement plans increased, while access to employer-sponsored health insurance held relatively steady from 2012.

Other important aspects of job quality are the number of hours a worker is required to work, whether they are paid by salary, and whether they are eligible for overtime pay for hours they work over 40 hours a week. Figure 3-32 shows that since the mid-1990s, more full-time workers have been earning salaries. Prior to the recession, the share of full-time workers earning a salary was at or near its 1982 high. That share fell in the Great Recession, as it did in the 1991 and 2001 recessions, but has recently started to rise again. However, concern remains about the long hours of some salaried workers and whether they are properly compensated for those hours. The value of the threshold at which salaried workers qualify for overtime pay has eroded since it was last raised in 2004, and over this period the share of

---

[22] Mishel, Shierholz and Schmitt (2013) show that occupations explain a small and decreasing portion of the variance in wages.

Figure 3-30
**Share of Workers With an Offer of Employer-Sponsored
Insurance Coverage, by Education, 1997–2013**

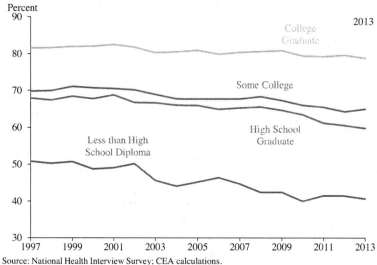

Source: National Health Interview Survey; CEA calculations.

Figure 3-31
**Share of Workers Included in Employer-Provided
Retirement Plan, by Education, 1997–2013**

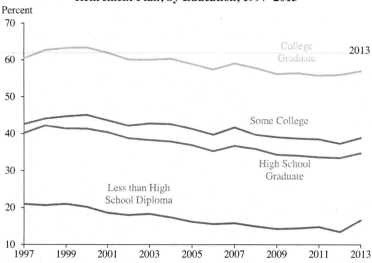

Source: Bureau of Labor Statistics, Current Population Survey (Annual Social and Economic
Supplement); CEA calculations.

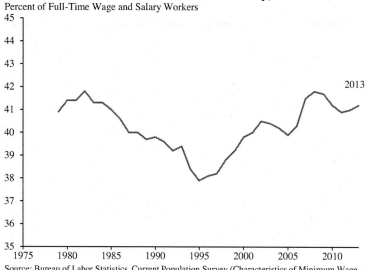

Figure 3-32
Share of Full-Time Workers Paid a Salary, 1979–2013
Percent of Full-Time Wage and Salary Workers

Source: Bureau of Labor Statistics, Current Population Survey (Characteristics of Minimum Wage
Workers, 2013).

salaried workers afforded overtime protection has fallen from 45 percent to
39 percent.

THE AGENDA FOR A STRONGER LABOR MARKET

This chapter has documented strong progress in the labor market over
the past year. The headline unemployment rate is now 93 percent returned
to its 2001-07 average, and broader measures of labor underutilization
show a similar pattern. Despite this progress, however, the labor market
continues to face five related challenges. These challenges pre-date the Great
Recession, although a recovery may lessen these challenges going forward.
Nevertheless, policy is also needed to overcome the many obstacles to a
better functioning labor market. The challenges described in this chapter—
decreased labor force participation; more long-term unemployed workers;
more part-time workers, particularly among those who would like full-
time hours; lower labor market fluidity; and insufficient real wage growth
amidst a more polarized job market—are potentially all inter-connected.
For example, decreased labor force participation; longer unemployment
durations; and more people working, at least temporarily, in part-time jobs
when they want full-time jobs might all be related to decreased labor market
fluidity. If transitions among jobs, employers, and firms are less common,
it can take longer for people to find work, leading to longer unemployment

durations. In addition, some of those workers may accept part-time work, at least temporarily, and some workers may stay out of the labor market because they are less likely to be aware of potential opportunities or find the longer searches needed too discouraging.

One key element of a successful strategy to address these challenges is providing workers with skills that help raise job security, earnings, and job quality—and a highly-trained workforce can also contribute to further long-term growth. The President's plans to improve access to education and training from birth through college are at the forefront of this strategy. The President's Fiscal Year 2016 Budget shows this commitment through a range of proposals, from funding for early learning initiatives, including ensuring that all 4-year-olds have access to pre-school, to proposing that two years of high-quality community college be free for hard-working students. In addition, he has proposed expanding apprenticeships and improving our workforce training systems by expanding career counseling and training in high-growth fields.

To further help workers access jobs that match their skills and qualifications, the President has also proposed working with states to spread best practices for occupational licensing systems and to reduce unnecessary training or high fees that keep people from doing jobs that best utilize their talents. This builds on the leadership that First Lady Michelle Obama and Dr. Jill Biden have undertaken to reduce licensing barriers for military spouses, through which 48 states have eased licensing requirements for current military spouses and veterans.

A second key aspect of the President's proposals to support and help build the middle class are policies that help working families stay in the labor force, by supporting flexible workplace practices, access to paid leave and paid sick days, and greater access to high quality child care. In addition to the work-family policies discussed in Chapter 4, the Administration's proposal for a new secondary earner credit recognizes the additional costs that families with two earners face and therefore would help dual-earning couples make ends meet.

Moreover, these policies are intricately linked to the President's early childhood education proposals since ensuring that children are well-cared for also supports their parents while they are at work. To this end, the Administration has proposed a continuum of early learning opportunities that could support working parents while benefiting children's cognitive and socio-emotional development. These initiatives include tripling the existing child care tax credit for families with very young children and expanding access to high-quality early education, including child care and preschool. These steps can help parents enter the labor market knowing that their children are cared for in a safe and nurturing environment, while also improving children's academic performance and future outcomes in adulthood.

Better skills and better employment supports are two key ingredients for higher wages and higher incomes, but they are not sufficient. That is why the President supports raising the minimum wage, a step that would help tens of millions of workers and help ensure that no full-time worker raises a family in poverty. Other institutional steps, like strengthening collective bargaining, would further help ensure that everyone shares in the benefits of growth.

Finally, the Administration continues to prioritize reducing long-term unemployment. The President's FY 2016 Budget proposes $16 billion for High-Growth Sector training grants, disbursed across states based on their unemployment rates, to double the number of dislocated workers who can receive the training necessary to transition to high-quality jobs. By making more funds available during economic downturns to provide training for those who face difficulties finding work in weak labor markets, this proposal could also reduce increases in long-term unemployment during future downturns. The President has also engaged businesses in hiring and recruiting the long-term unemployed.

The President's FY 2016 Budget also proposes a package of reforms to modernize the Unemployment Insurance (UI) program, which provides critical income support to those who are unemployed. These reforms will improve the solvency of state programs, strengthen the program's connection to work, and reach more workers who lose a job through no fault of their own. In addition, the proposal would make the UI program more targeted and responsive to economic downturns by implementing an Extended Benefits program that provides added benefits as soon as a state experiences a sharp rise in unemployment, even if a national increase in unemployment has not yet occurred.

Taking steps to foster more growth and high-quality jobs, better prepare workers for these jobs, and ensure that all workers share in the benefits of these jobs are the central tenets of the President's approach to middle class economics. All of these actions will help capitalize on the strengths of the U.S. economy while moving to address the long-standing challenges in the labor market.

Box 3-4: Immigration Reform and Labor Markets

A large body of academic research finds that, on balance, immigration has strong benefits for both the U.S. economy in general and U.S. labor markets in particular. Immigrants increase the productivity of the American workforce, both directly through increases in innovation and indirectly through spillovers to U.S. workers. For example, not only do high-skilled immigrants patent at a higher rate than their nonimmigrant peers, but their innovation also has spillover effects on patenting by native-born workers (Hunt and Gauthier-Loiselle 2010). At the same time, lower-skilled immigration can have positive effects on worker productivity by allowing for greater task specialization. While there is ongoing discussion in the academic literature about the direct wage and employment effects of immigration on native workers, it is important to note that researchers have found positive effects of immigration on these outcomes (for example, Peri, Shih, and Sparber 2014) as well as negative (for example, Borjas et al. 1997). Nevertheless, a number of recent studies suggest that complementarities between immigrant and nonimmigrant workers—interactions that indirectly raise the productivity, and thus wages, of both groups—may be substantial (e.g. Peri and Sparber 2009). In addition to these benefits, immigration has the potential to raise the overall labor force participation rate in the United States because immigrants participate in the workforce at higher rates than the native-born population (CBO 2015a). Researchers have shown that immigration is associated with a range of characteristics that may be related to greater labor force participation (Chiquiar and Hanson 2005; Butcher and Piehl 2007).

Despite these potential gains to the economy — and to American workers — from immigration, the U.S. immigration system remains badly broken. In November 2014, President Obama announced a series of executive actions to begin moving our immigration system into the 21st century. These provisions included actions designed to better attract high-skilled immigrants and foreign entrepreneurs and to allow advanced-degree holders in science, technology, engineering, and mathematics (STEM) fields to extend on-the-job training. The actions will also provide deferred action from removal to millions of undocumented workers who have substantial ties to the United States, pass a criminal background check, and pay payroll and income taxes. Drawing on a large body of research examining the economic effects of previous immigration reforms, the Council of Economic Advisers (2014a) estimated that the actions announced by the President would raise U.S. GDP by between 0.4 and 0.9 percent within ten years, equivalent to $90 to $210 billion in additional real GDP (in 2014 dollars) in 2024.

While these gains are substantial, they are small when compared with the potential economic effects of Congressional action on commonsense immigration reform. The Congressional Budget Office (2013) found that the Border Security, Economic Opportunity, and Immigration Modernization Act (S. 744) – the bipartisan immigration reform bill passed by the Senate in 2013 – would increase real GDP by 3.3 percent, or roughly $700 billion, over ten years and would raise average wages for all workers by 0.5 percent in twenty years. In addition, CEA estimates that the Senate's commonsense immigration reform bill would raise the overall labor force participation rate by approximately 0.3 percentage point in ten years.

CHAPTER 4

THE ECONOMICS OF FAMILY-FRIENDLY WORKPLACE POLICIES

W omen greatly increased their participation in the labor force beginning in the 20th century, marking the start of a fundamental change
in our workforce and families. In 1920, only 24 percent of women worked
outside the home, a share that rose to 43 percent by 1970. Today the majority
of women—57 percent—work outside the home.[1] A similar pattern is seen
in the participation rate of mothers with small children: 63 percent of whom
currently work outside the home, compared to only 31 percent in 1970.[2]

These gains in women's labor force participation, as well as their
increased educational attainment, have translated into large income gains
for American families and have benefited the U.S. economy overall.
Essentially all of the income gains that middle-class American families have
experienced since 1970 are due to the rise in women's earnings. By contrast,
wage growth for men over this same period has been flat. (For a broader
discussion of labor market trends, see Chapter 3.) For example, median family income in 2013 was nearly $11,000 higher than it was in 1970. If women
today still had the same labor force participation and working hours as they

---

[1] Women's labor force participation data for age 16 and over is calculated from the Decennial
Census in 1920 and taken from the published Bureau of Labor Statistics data series for 1970
and 2014.
[2] Data are from the 1970 and 2014 Current Population Survey's Annual Economic and Social
Supplement calculations that include women with their own children under age five living at
home in 1970 and 2014, using the share that are in the labor force during the survey reference
week.

did in 1970, median family income would be roughly $9,000 lower.[3] More generally, our economy is $2.0 trillion, or 13.5 percent, larger than it would be without women's increased participation in the labor force and hours worked since 1970.[4]

While mothers have become important contributors to family income, fathers have increasingly taken on caregiving responsibilities, shifting patterns in the organization of market work and non-market work within families. Today men are doing a larger share of household duties than in the past, though mothers still spend almost twice as much time on household work as fathers. Mothers in 2013 dedicated more than 12 hours a week to child care and related tasks, a slight increase from around 10 hours in 1965.[5] By comparison, fathers spent almost 7 hours a week on child care and related tasks in 2013, a nearly three-fold increase since 1965. Fathers are also becoming more likely to assume significant child-care roles, and today about 15 percent of all stay-at-home parents are men (Livingston 2014). More generally, caregiving responsibilities are shouldered by workers of both genders, all ages, and in a variety of family situations. More than one-half of workers provide care for others—including their children, elderly parents and relatives, spouses, adult children, and returning veterans with disabilities.[6]

Workplaces, however, have been slower to adapt to changing family dynamics. This has created greater conflicts between responsibilities at

---

[3] This is based on an accounting exercise that compares the median family income in 2013 to the (counterfactual) median that would have been obtained in 2013 had the distribution of women's work hours been the same as it was in 1970. The counterfactual is constructed by reweighting the 2013 family income distribution so that the reweighted distribution of family hours worked by women is identical to that observed in 1970, using the technique introduced by DiNardo, Fortin and Lemieux (1996; henceforth 'DFL'). The procedure effectively gives more weight to the family earnings of observations in 2013 that are more likely (based on the hours worked by women) to have been observed in 1970—that is, families with lower hours worked by women, and less weight to observations less likely to come from 1970. The calculation is based on data on primary families only (families within households containing the householder) from the 1971 and 2014 Current Population Survey ASEC. DFL weights are based on a logistic regression of an indicator variable for whether an observation is from 2013 (rather than 1970) on a set of indicator variables for categories of total hours (in 100-hour increments) worked by adult women in the family.

[4] CEA calculated this using a growth account formula that relates the level of output to the supply of labor. Using the Current Population Survey from 1970 to 2013, CEA calculated the increase in hours worked by women and assumed that the average product of labor was unchanged.

[5] Data are from the American Time Use Survey. Child care and related tasks are measured as any task identified under "caring for and helping household children." Data from 1965 are analyzed by Bianchi, Robinson, and Milkie (2006). CEA used a similar methodology to generate estimates for 2013.

[6] From the BLS release "Unpaid Eldercare in the United States 2011-2012" and BLS Current Population Survey, CEA calculated about 71 percent of workers have either elder care responsibilities or dependent children.

home and at work for men and women struggling to make ends meet and to help their children succeed. This interaction between family lives and work lives affects businesses and the economy. Many families deal with the challenges of work-family conflict as they attempt to balance breadwinning and caregiving responsibilities without the benefit of supportive family-friendly workplace policies. Too often, this forces workers to make trade-offs between the right job for their talents and the job that will allow them to best meet the needs of their families, including the choice of whether to work at all. Family-friendly workplace polices make it easier for people to make the choices that are right for them and their families.

Because workers often favor companies with family-friendly policies, the companies that adopt such policies are better able to attract and retain talent. For example, nearly 50 percent of working parents report that they have turned down a job offer because it would not have worked for their families (Nielsen 2014). As more companies adopt such policies and as public policies provide more of these benefits to all workers, people will have more freedom to choose their jobs according to where they will be most productive. Thus, family-friendly policies are a key component of the economic success of both families and businesses because they can help more workers succeed, regardless of caregiving responsibilities.

This chapter examines changes in American family life and the implications for work. The first section discusses how rising labor market participation among women and changing patterns of caregiving for fathers have helped grow household incomes and our economy, but has made the need for family-friendly workplace policies more acute. The next few sections examine access to important policies such as paid family leave, paid sick leave, and workplace flexibility, including outlining policies at the State and local level. The chapter then turns to analyzing the economics of family-friendly workplace policies, including addressing why some companies have implemented family-friendly workplace policies and others have not, and analyzing the evidence on how these policies can benefit both businesses and workers.

RECENT CHANGES IN AMERICAN FAMILY LIFE AND THEIR IMPLICATIONS FOR WORK

Recent changes in American family life have altered the composition of our workforce, daily routines, and how many of today's workers navigate dual roles as breadwinners and caregivers. These changes in the way that families organize their work and family lives have created a greater need for policies to help American workers better balance work and family needs.

Attachment to the Labor Force and Educational Attainment Have Increased Significantly Among American Women

One of the largest changes in work and family life occurred over the last century as women became more-equal participants in the labor force by increasing their participation in paid work, obtaining more education and training, and widening the scope of occupation types they entered. Since the beginning of the 1950s, women's labor force participation has increased by around 25 percentage points, while men's labor force participation has decreased by around 17 percentage points (Figure 4-1). While women on average still tend to work fewer hours each week than men, the gender gap in weekly hours worked has narrowed by around three hours since 1962.[7] As discussed in Chapter 1, prime-age women's labor force participation grew steadily between 1948 and 1973 at an average pace of 0.7 percentage point a year, and then accelerated to 1.1 percentage point a year between 1973 and 1995.

However, women's labor force participation and hours worked have declined in recent years. As described in Chapter 3, more than one-half of the decrease in labor force participation for both men and women since 2000 is due to the aging of the population, rather than changes in the choices people are making. Much of the rest of the decline reflects other trends, including a labor market still healing following the Great Recession.

In 2013, women accounted for 46.9 percent of all workers and 44.1 percent of all hours worked.[8] Because labor force participation is a key driver of economic growth, the greater attachment of women to the labor market has implications for both families and the economy. However, sheer volume is not the only, or even necessarily the most important, way that women's roles in the economy have changed. Women have also increased their labor market skills over this period by acquiring more education and training, receiving greater experience on the job, and moving into previously male-dominated professions.

Women's greater participation in the labor market has coincided with a record number of women earning higher education degrees (Figure 4-2). These are related trends: as more women have stayed in the labor force throughout their careers, chosen previously male-dominated occupations, and sought career advancement, they have invested in more education to

---

[7] CEA calculated this number using "hours worked last week" in the Current Population Survey ASEC in 1962 and 2014, since "usual hours worked" is not available in earlier years.
[8] Women's share of employment was calculated using the monthly Current Population Survey of workers ages 16 and older. Women's hours as a share of all hours were calculated using the Current Population Survey ASEC 2014. Aggregate hours were calculated by multiplying usual weekly hours last year by weeks worked last year.

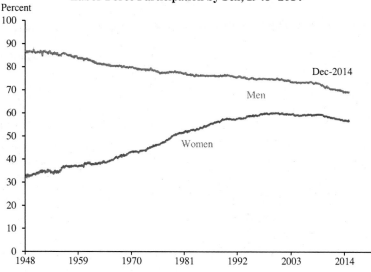

Figure 4-1
Labor Force Participation by Sex, 1948–2014

Percent

Dec-2014

Men

Women

Source: Bureau of Labor Statistics, Current Population Survey.

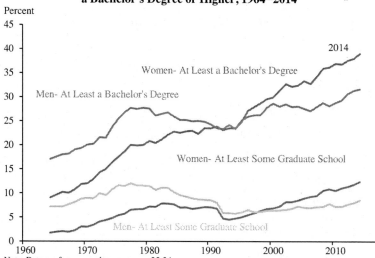

Figure 4-2
**Percent of Young Men and Women with
a Bachelor's Degree or Higher, 1964–2014**

Percent

2014

Women- At Least a Bachelor's Degree

Men- At Least a Bachelor's Degree

Women- At Least Some Graduate School

Men- At Least Some Graduate School

Note: Data are for men and women ages 25-34.
Source: Bureau of Labor Statistics, Current Population Survey; CEA calculations.

prepare themselves for these opportunities (Goldin and Katz 2002). As of academic year 2009-10, women received 57 percent of bachelor's degrees.[9] In addition, women have increasingly enrolled in formerly male-dominated professional and graduate degree programs. For example, today, women receive 52 percent of doctoral degrees (which includes PhDs, MDs, and law degrees), compared to 45 percent in academic year 1999-2000. If these patterns continue, women will soon represent a growing majority of highly educated workers.[10]

Rising educational attainment among women has opened up new career opportunities, which may have contributed to the decrease in occupational segregation. Today, women comprise much larger shares of many traditionally male occupations such as physicians, dentists, economists, and lawyers than they did fifty years ago (Goldin and Katz 2002). About two-thirds of occupations in 1970 were 80 percent or more male; today, about 40 percent of occupations fall into that category.[11]

Higher rates of labor force participation, combined with increased educational investments and broader career choice among women, have translated into earnings gains for women relative to men, and have markedly increased the importance of women's income in the household. More than 40 percent of mothers are now the sole or primary source of income for the household, reflecting both an increase in female-headed households and increased earnings among married women (Wang, Parker, and Taylor 2013). In 2013, employed married women's earnings comprised 44 percent of their family's earnings, up from 37 percent in 1970 (Figure 4-3).[12]

Families Are Adjusting to New Caregiving Needs

As mothers increasingly participate in the labor force and patterns of fathers' caregiving change, conflict between work and caregiving has grown. The result is ever more families trying to balance work and family

---

[9] Unless otherwise specified, data in this paragraph comes from U.S. Department of Education, National Center for Education Statistics (2012). "The Condition of Education 2012" (NCES 2012-045), Indicator 47.

[10] Restricting to those age 25 to 64, and assuming that as many female and male workers with college degrees enter the labor force at age 25 next year as entered this year, while those at age 64 leave, women would be 50.6 percent of workers with college degrees in 2015, while in 15 years women would be 53.9 percent of college-educated workers.

[11] CEA calculations using the Current Population Survey Annual Economic and Social Supplement in 1970 and 2014. Only those currently employed were included, and IPUMS 1950 occupational codes were used.

[12] CEA used the Current Population Survey Annual Economic and Social Supplement in 1971 and 2014 to calculate the portion of husband and wife wage and salary income from married women. Households where married women earned $0 or more than $2 million were omitted from analysis.

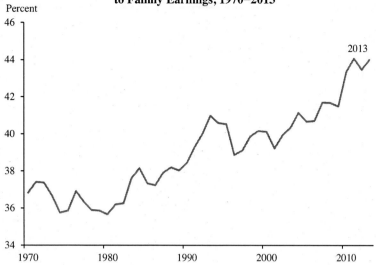

Figure 4-3
**Employed Married Women's Contribution
to Family Earnings, 1970–2013**

Source: Bureau of Labor Statistics, Current Population Survey; CEA calculations.

obligations, and an increasing proportion of households in which all parents work. Today, all parents are working in more than 6 out of every 10
households with children, up from 4 out of 10 in 1968 (Figure 4-4).[13] The
share of families with infants where all parents work has exhibited a similar
increase (Figure 4-4). These increases are due to two separate trends: the rise
in dual-earner families discussed previously and an increase in single-parent
families. As of 2013, 31.9 percent of families with children were headed by
a single parent, compared to 19.5 percent in 1980.[14] Over three-quarters
of the single-parent families in 2013 were headed by women. Partners in
two-parent families are increasingly sharing caregiving responsibilities more
equally, meaning that both parents have responsibility for both caregiving
and work. However, the rise in single-parent families means that a growing
number of households with children have only one adult and, as such, that
one adult has primary responsibility for both caregiving and work. For these
households, family-friendly workplace policies are especially important,
since it can be more difficult for single parents to make alternative arrangements when work-family conflicts arise.

As mothers have entered the labor force in greater numbers, fathers
are increasingly taking on child-care responsibilities. The share of fathers

---

[13] Including biological, step, and adoptive parents.
[14] Census Table FM-1

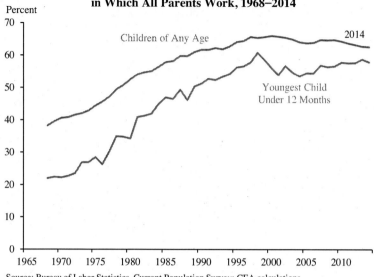

Figure 4-4
Percent of Households with Children in Which All Parents Work, 1968–2014

Percent

Source: Bureau of Labor Statistics, Current Population Survey; CEA calculations.

who stay at home while a spouse works has doubled in the last 25 years.[15] Today, around 15 percent of stay-at-home parents are fathers (Livingston 2014). The role of fathers is continuing to evolve and both employed and non-employed fathers are spending more time on child care than they did even a decade ago.[16] As shown in Figure 4-5, fathers are more likely now than a decade ago to help bathe and diaper, read to kids, and help with homework.[17]

On average, fathers spent 4.0 fewer hours a week on paid work in 2013 than in 1965, and 4.2 more hours a week on child care and 5.3 hours a week more on housework (Figure 4-6). So fathers are working more hours than in the past when the work of child care and household tasks is included, but a much larger share of their work is home production. Despite these shifts, social science surveys show that the majority of men and women believe that men should spend more time caring for children, possibly reflecting the fact that fathers, on average, still spend less time on child care than mothers.[18]

---

[15] Census Bureau Table MC-1
[16] CEA calculations using American Time Use Survey, based on Bianchi, Robinson, and Milkie (2006).
[17] Centers for Disease Control and Prevention, National Survey of Family Growth 2002-2010.
[18] In 2013, mothers spent 12.1 hours per week on child care according to the ATUS data used to calculate men's time spent on child care in Figure 4-6. Data from the 2002 wave of the General Social Survey show that 67 percent of men and 74 percent of women think that men should spend more time caring for children.

Figure 4-5
Fathers Reporting Role in Child Care Activities for Selected Years

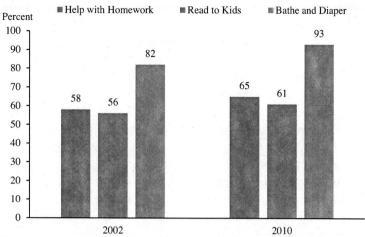

Note: Data show the percentage of resident fathers ages 15-44 who report they participate in the activity at least several times per week.
Source: Center for Disease Control and Prevention, National Survey of Family Growth, 2002-2010; CEA calculations.

Figure 4-6
Fathers' Average Weekly Time Use

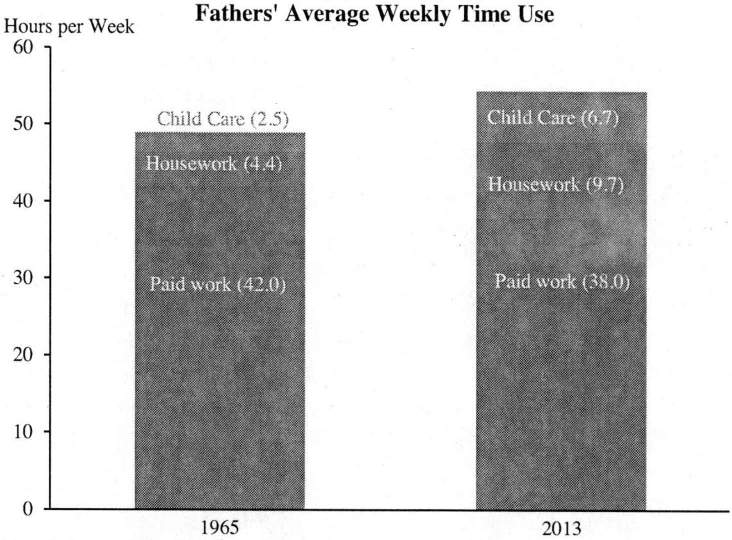

Hours per Week

Note: Fathers are defined as adult men ages 18-64 with children under 18.
Source: Bianchi et al. (2006); Bureau of Labor Statistics, American Time Use Survey, 2013; CEA calculations.

Greater longevity among older adults means that many workers also act as caregivers for other adults, such as the elderly or people with disabilities. Each year, approximately 40 million Americans (16 percent of the population aged 15 and older) provide unpaid care to an elderly relative or friend.[19] Most people providing eldercare are employed (63 percent), and about one-half work full-time.[20] Just as working parents must juggle caregiving and work responsibilities, many eldercare providers face similar—if not greater—competing demands.

While most eldercare providers are balancing work on top of their caregiving responsibilities (Figure 4-7), one-fifth of eldercare providers are also providing care for young children.[21] Despite the increased potential for work-family conflict, parents who provide eldercare have even higher rates of employment than eldercare providers without dependent children: 78 percent are employed and 62 percent work full-time. Now that baby boomers are entering retirement, it is likely that the "sandwich generation"—those caring for elderly relatives and young children—will continue to grow over the next 30 years (Figure 4-8).

The Effects of Work-Family Conflict

As both men and women increasingly perform multiple roles, many struggle to meet their work and family goals. Among dual-earning couples, the likelihood of reporting work-family conflict has become especially pronounced among fathers. In 2008, 60 percent of fathers in dual-earner couples reported work-family conflict, compared to 35 percent in 1977—a 25 percentage-point increase in just one generation (Figure 4-9; Galinsky, Aumann, and Bond 2011). Although in 1977 mothers in dual-earning couples were more likely to report work-family conflict than fathers, this pattern has since reversed; in 2008, fathers were more likely to report work-family conflict, consistent with the rise in time spent on child care among fathers.

Conflicts between work and family may arise because work obligations encroach on family responsibilities, but conflict can also arise when family encroaches on work. Both genders increasingly perceive that their work responsibilities interfere with their family obligations. In 2010, 46 percent of full-time working men and women reported that their job demands interfered with their family life sometimes or often, up from 41 percent in 2002 (Figure 4-10). In contrast, a smaller share of full-time workers report

---

[19] Bureau of Labor Statistics, American Time Use Survey 2011; CEA calculations.

[20] Bureau of Labor Statistics, American Time Use Survey 2011, 2012; CEA calculations; BLS release "Unpaid Eldercare in the United States 2011-2012."

[21] All data in this paragraph is from BLS release "Unpaid Eldercare in the United States 2011-2012."

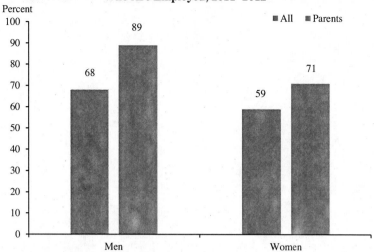

Figure 4-7
**Percent of All Unpaid Eldercare Providers
Who Are Employed, 2011–2012**

Source: Bureau of Labor Statistics, American Time Use Survey, 2011 and 2012; CEA calculations.

Figure 4-8
**Share of Households with Children Under 18
and Adults Over 65, 1968–2014**

Source: Bureau of Labor Statistics, Current Population Survey; CEA calculations.

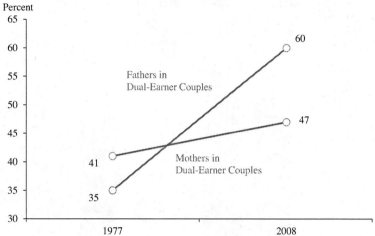

Figure 4-9
Percentage of Mothers and Fathers Reporting Work-Family Conflict for Selected Years

Source: Family and Work Institute, National Study of the Changing Workforce, 2008; Employment Standards Administration, Quality of Employment Survey, 1977, as analyzed in Galinsky, Aumann, and Bond (2011).

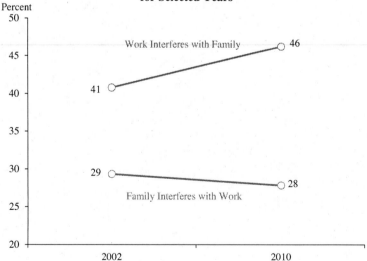

Figure 4-10
Percentage of Full-Time Workers Who Report Work-Family Conflict for Selected Years

Source: General Social Survey, 2002, 2010; CEA calculations.

that family responsibilities interfere with work, about 28 to 29 percent in both 2002 and 2010.[22]

Work and family conflict can also affect co-workers and employers as conflicts lead to greater absenteeism, lower productivity, and greater turnover.[23] Lessening the constraints families face as they seek to balance work and family can benefit more than just individual families, but also our overall economy. By expanding family-friendly workplace policies, caregivers have more options to make the right choice for them. For example, when workers must choose between spending the first few months at home with a new baby or keeping their job, families are put in a difficult position and the economy potentially loses a worker who would prefer to stay in the labor force if only they had time off. Similarly, policies that encourage workplace flexibility can help more families meet both their family and professional goals—something that is good for both them and our economy.

As discussed, the benefits of more flexible workplace policies will spill over to other workers, employers, and the overall economy. This chapter examines two major types of workplace policy, paid leave and the broader category of workplace flexibility policies. It also documents where these policies are found today, and what types of workers have access to them, including through State and local efforts to expand access. The chapter then turns to the economics of such policies, reviewing analysis that examines the benefits of these policies for business and the economy.

ACCESS TO FAMILY-FRIENDLY WORKPLACE POLICIES

Two of the most important policies that firms can offer to allow workers to better balance work and family are access to paid leave and workplace flexibility. Paid leave includes access to family leave, sick leave, and other leave that allow workers to take paid time off to care for themselves or a family member.

Workplace flexibility generally refers to arrangements that allow workers to shift the time or location of their work through flexible or alternative hours, telecommuting policies, or alternative work locations. It can also include partial employment options such as job sharing and phased retirement of older workers. Flexibility can include shifts in arrival and departure times, the schedule of breaks and overtime, and the number of days or hours worked per week, such as a compressed workweek or the ability to accrue and use comp time at the employee's discretion. Scheduling

---

[22] NORC at University of Chicago; General Social Survey 2002 and 2010; CEA calculations.
[23] See e.g. Dalton and Mesch (1990); NACEW (2013); Gov. UK (2014); Ton (2012); Baughman, DiNardi, and Holtz-Eakin (2003).

adjustments can be an important tool to address unexpected issues outside of work. For instance, if a family member is sick, allowing workers to work from home may be an alternative to the worker taking paid leave in some jobs. Workplace flexibility is not a substitute for leave policies, however. Instead, workplace flexibility can be a complement to leave policies, allowing workers to cope with emergencies with the least disruption to their work.

Access and Use of Leave in the United States

The 1993 Family Medical Leave Act (FMLA) significantly expanded access to leave by requiring employers to offer up to 12 weeks of unpaid leave for qualifying reasons, including the birth of a child. The FMLA increased unpaid leave use and coverage without reducing women's employment or wages (Waldfogel 1999). Many workers, however, are exempt from the FMLA, including employees who have been with the firm for less than 12 months and have worked fewer than 1,250 hours, those at private businesses with fewer than 50 employees, and those who work part-time.[24] A recent survey found that the FMLA covered only about 60 percent of workers (Klerman, Daley, and Pozniak 2014). As of 2011, almost one-third of workers reported no access to unpaid leave (Table 4-1). Further, the FMLA only guarantees access to unpaid leave for covered workers, not paid leave.

The distinction between paid and unpaid leave is important, especially for low-wage workers. Although unpaid leave may provide some flexibility, it is not a realistic option if workers cannot afford to take it. The implementation of paid family leave in California illustrates this point. The unpaid leave guaranteed by the FMLA enabled some mothers, mostly those with more education in higher-paying fields, to take maternity leave prior to California's paid family leave policy. However, it was not until California guaranteed access to paid family leave benefits through its State-based family leave plan that lower-income mothers began taking maternity leave in greater numbers (Rossin-Slater, Ruhm, and Waldfogel 2013). Although the expanded leave opportunities provided by FMLA made real progress for American workers two decades ago, the United States today significantly lags its international peers in leave provision, as discussed in Box 4-1. Approximately 4 percent of workers reported in 2011 that they wanted to take leave in a given week but could not do so, compared to 23 percent of

---

[24] The FMLA also excludes some employees of otherwise eligible employers (such as those with more than 50 employees in total); for example, those who work at a location where the employer has fewer than 50 employees within 75 miles.

Table 4-1
Access to Leave (ATUS), 2011

Reason	Percent Unpaid	Percent Paid
Vacation	60	56
Own Illness	73	53
Family	71	48

Source: Bureau of Labor Statistics, American Time Use Survey, 2011; CEA calculations.

workers who did take leave.[25] In addition, according to a recent FMLA survey, 6.1 percent of female employees had an unmet need for leave (compared to 3.2 percent of male employees), while 6.7 percent of workers of color had an unmet need for leave (compared to 3.8 percent of White workers) (Klerman, Daley, and Pozniak 2014).[26]

After vacation, sick leave is the most common type of paid leave employees have access to: approximately 53 percent of workers report having access to some form of paid leave they could take in the event of their own illness, but only 43 percent said they thought that they would be able to use paid leave to take care of ill family members. Overall, less than one-half of workers (48 percent) reported being able to take paid leave for any family-related reason. Even when workers have access to some forms of paid leave, it cannot always be used for all purposes. For instance, paid vacation days may be impractical to use for illness because an employer might require scheduling the time in advance.

Only a minority of workers–39 percent–report access to paid family leave for the birth of a child. Mothers are only slightly more likely than fathers to be able to access leave upon the birth of a child: 38 percent of working men say that they could take paid leave for the birth of a child, compared to 40 percent of working women. At the time of the American Time Use Survey, only residents of California and New Jersey, covering about 15 percent of the U.S. population, had State-run paid leave policies.[27] Since the

[25] Bureau of Labor Statistics, American Time Use Survey 2011; CEA calculations and published tables. The calculations in this paragraph and the ones following reflect responses to whether workers believe that they can take leave, assuming they receive their employer's approval, as asked in the American Time Use Survey (unless otherwise specified). To the extent that employers do not approve of leave, particularly unpaid leave, these statistics overstate the availability of leave.

[26] The study defined reasons for having an unmet need for leave as i) the individual is not eligible for FMLA, ii) the reason for leave is not covered by the FMLA, and iii) the individual has exhausted her available entitlement for the leave year. The study did not inquire about conditions that would necessitate leave (Klerman, Daley and Pozniak 2013).

[27] Since the American Time Use Survey paid leave module was conducted, Rhode Island has also implemented a paid family leave program.

**Box 4-1: International Comparisons: Access
to Paid Leave in Other Countries**

The United States is the only developed country in the world that does not ensure paid maternity leave (International Labour Organization 2014). Even in the developing world, only Papua New Guinea does not ensure paid maternity leave. In addition to guaranteeing paid maternity leave, other countries have acted to extend the amount and type of required parental leave. As of 2013, the majority of countries (53 percent of all countries and territories, and 95 percent of developed countries) surveyed by the International Labour Organization guaranteed paid maternity leave for a period of at least 14 weeks, the minimum duration recommended by the Maternity Protection Convention to ensure the health of mother and child (International Labour Organization 2014).

Other countries have also moved toward offering paternity leave in addition to maternity leave. As of 2013, 47 percent of countries and territories for which data are available provide both paternity and maternity leave, and paternity leave is paid in 90 percent of these countries. In contrast, just 28 percent of countries had statutory paternity leave provisions in 1994. Like maternity leave, the duration of paternity leave varies across countries, from one day in Tunisia to 90 days in Iceland, Slovenia, and Finland (International Labour Organization 2014).

Countries ensure paid maternity leave in different ways. The International Labour Organization contends that maternity leave should be provided through social insurance or public funds in order to provide broad coverage and mitigate discrimination against women in hiring that might arise if employers are fully responsible for financing maternity leave. In 2013, the majority of countries (58 percent) provided for maternity leave through social insurance programs, while a quarter relied solely on employer mandates. Sixteen percent of countries combine employer mandates and social insurance programs. In developed economies, 88 percent have programs financed exclusively through social contributions, while 10 percent have programs that involve an employer requirement. Since 1994, however, both developed and developing countries have shifted from employer mandates to more collective systems.

survey was conducted, Rhode Island has implemented a paid family leave program. The remainder of those reporting access to paid leave in the survey either had employers that voluntarily provided paid family leave, or could utilize other forms of paid leave, such as vacation time or compensation time, for the birth of a child. These responses also do not indicate the

Table 4-2

Access to Leave (NCS), 2014

Leave Type	Percent Paid Sick Leave	Percent Paid Vacation	Percent Paid Holidays
Civilian	65	74	75
Private Industry	61	77	76
State and Local Gov't	89	59	67

Source: Bureau of Labor Statistics, National Compensation Survey, Employee Benefits Survey, March 2014.

duration of leave; some of those who have access to paid family leave can take only a few paid days off work.

Access to paid leave varies by hours worked, firm size, and sector of employment. According to a nationally representative employer survey, 65 percent of employees have access to paid sick leave. Private employers, however, are much less likely to offer paid sick leave than public-sector employers (Table 4-2): 61 percent of private-sector employees have access to paid sick leave, compared to 89 percent among public-sector employees. In contrast, private employers were more likely than public-sector employers to offer either paid vacation or holiday time.[28]

However, employer surveys suggest that the availability of formal paid leave programs to workers is much lower than employee surveys indicate. According to an employer survey, only 11 percent of private-sector workers have access to a formal paid family leave policy, including only 4 percent of part-time workers (Van Giezen 2013). Workers at smaller firms also have less access to paid leave—only 8 percent of those at establishments with fewer than 100 workers (Van Giezen 2013). Although employer and employee surveys often give different impressions of benefits availability (Box 4-2), the discrepancy in this case may be due to workers reporting that they can use some paid time for caregiving—for example, paid sick days or accrued vacation time—but not necessarily that they have coverage by a formal paid leave program.

Even when workers have access to leave, they may not be able to use it. Some workers, especially lower-income workers and those who are their family's primary breadwinner, cannot forego wages by taking unpaid leave. Other workers may be pressured by their employer not to take leave. For these reasons, it is important to also examine the actual use of leave. As shown in Table 4-3, approximately 23 percent of workers took either paid or unpaid leave during a typical week.

---

[28] Bureau of Labor Statistics, National Compensation Survey 2014.

Box 4-2: Why is There Such a Large Difference in Reported Prevalence Between the American Time Use Survey, the National Compensation Survey, and the National Study of Employers?

One important reason for the difference between the three surveys is that employers report in the employer-based surveys that they provide flexibility for "some" or "most" workers, but do not otherwise indicate the prevalence. If many employers only provide a benefit to a minority of their workers, the percent of workers with a benefit will be smaller than the percent of firms offering the same benefit. In addition, there may be a difference between an organization's policies and their implementation. The National Study of Employers attempted to address this issue by asking if the organization "allows employees to…" or "provides the following benefits or programs…" rather than if it has "written policies." However, if workers are unaware that their managers would be willing to implement such practices, are unaware of such policies, or fear negative consequences from exercising such options, they will report less availability of such arrangements than will their employers.

Second, the National Study of Employers is a survey of employers in which the respondent is an organization rather than an individual. As a result, the data describe the formal benefits provided by a typical employer or how they are interpreted at the organizational level, rather than how they are experienced by a typical employee. Given that, by definition, larger employers represent more workers than do smaller firms, statistics about the average employer may not be representative of the experiences of the average worker.

The National Compensation Survey is also an employer survey, but unlike the National Study of Employers, it is weighted by the number of employees in a firm, so larger firms are given more weight. As such, the study reports statistics about the share of employees who are covered by a policy, not the share of employers who offer one. Also unlike the National Study of Employers, it only inquires about formal leave policies.

The American Time Use Survey (ATUS), in contrast, is based on employee responses to whether they are able to access leave and flexible work arrangements, and therefore captures informal policies and fungibility across different types of benefits. This survey also captures worker perceptions about having access to leave. But to the extent employers do not approve of leave, these statistics overstate the availability of leave. However, if workers are not informed of their company's policies, the ATUS may understate access to leave. Finally, the ATUS data on workers are from 2011 while those from the employers are from 2014. The prevalence of such practices may have grown in the interim.

Table 4-3
Leave Use and Hours, 2011

Utilization	Percent Who Used Leave in Last Week	Hours of Leave Taken Among Those Who Used Leave
Access to Paid or Unpaid Leave	23	15.1
Access to Paid Leave	25	15.8
Access to Unpaid Leave	23	15.3
Access to Schedule/Location Changes	21	–

Source: Bureau of Labor Statistics, American Time Use Survey, 2011; CEA calculations.

The most common reasons workers cited for not being able to take leave included "too much work" (26 percent) and "could not afford loss in income" (19 percent). An additional 12 percent reported not taking leave because they feared losing their job (Figure 4-11). Lower-wage workers were much more likely to cite "could not afford loss of income" as a reason they did not take desired leave while higher-wage workers were more likely to cite "too much work."[29] These responses demonstrate that there is unmet demand for leave policies, especially paid leave for low-income workers.

Workplace Flexibility Access in the United States

Workplace flexibility encompasses a range of policies that, broadly speaking, enable workers to adjust aspects of work as needed, including starting and ending time, days of work, and location. Many workplaces are able to accommodate some flexibility in scheduling, particularly when it concerns occasional changes in starting and quitting times. As shown below, 81 percent of employers report allowing at least some workers to periodically change their starting and quitting times, within some range of hours, in 2013. This is a slight increase from 2008 and a larger increase from 2005.[30] However, only 27 percent of employers allowed most or all employees to do so, indicating that this is often a benefit for only a few employees. Less than one-half of employers (41 percent) allowed at least some workers to change starting and quitting times on a daily basis and only 10 percent said that they allowed most or all of their workers to do so (Figure 4-12). Only 10 percent of firms report allowing workers to change their work times essentially at will or to alter the days on which they work (Figure 4-12).

As with paid leave, there are some differences across employer and worker responses on this issue. Around 53 percent of employees report that they have flexibility in when they work, but only 22 percent report flexibility

---

[29] Bureau of Labor Statistics, American Time Use Survey 2011; CEA calculations.
[30] Families and Work Institute, National Study of Employers 2005, 2008, and 2014.

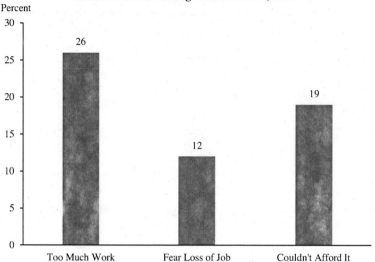

Figure 4-11
Reason for Not Taking Needed Leave, 2011

Percent

Note: Among workers who reported needing to take leave.
Source: Bureau of Labor Statistics, American Time Use Survey, 2011; CEA calculations.

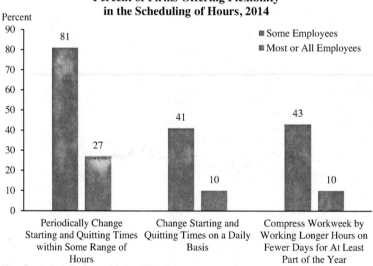

Figure 4-12
**Percent of Firms Offering Flexibility
in the Scheduling of Hours, 2014**

Percent

Note: Survey includes firms with over 50 employees.
Source: Families and Work Institute, National Study of Employers, 2014.

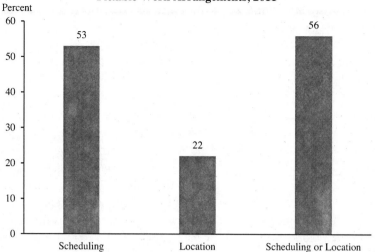

Figure 4-13
**Percent of Workers with Access to
Flexible Work Arrangements, 2011**

Source: Bureau of Labor Statistics, American Time Use Survey, 2011; CEA calculations.

in where they work (Figure 4-13). Flexibility in hours worked is more common for part-time workers at 56 percent (Bond, Galinsky, and Sakai 2008). In addition, though there is little data on the issue, there are anecdotal reports that low-wage workers face unpredictable schedules that they have little control over (Kantor 2014).

Flexibility in work location is less common than flexibility in either work days or hours, and there is substantial variation across industries and occupations. At least some of this difference is likely attributable to the fact that many jobs practically require an individual to be physically present at the worksite. For example, teachers, sales clerks, and assembly-line workers cannot fulfill many of their obligations from an off-site location. Managers and members of teams may need face-to-face contact. For other workers, however, a substantial fraction of their work could, in principle, be conducted from home or a satellite office. As a likely result of these factors, about 9 percent of workers in mining occupations report access to location flexibility, compared to over 40 percent of workers in information services.[31] One study estimated that, in 2000, more than one-half of all jobs were amenable to telecommuting, at least on a part-time basis (Potter 2003), and that fraction has likely increased since then as a result of the spread of high-speed Internet and mobile technology (Smith 2002).

---

[31] Statistics in this section are from Bureau of Labor Statistics, American Time Use Survey 2011; CEA calculations, unless otherwise specified.

While many employers allow some workers to telecommute, the vast majority of employers limit which employees have access to this option. As shown in Figure 4-14, 67 percent of employers reported allowing some workers to work at home occasionally, while only 8 percent of employers allowed most or all of their employees to do so (Figure 4-14). Similarly, 38 percent reported having some workers who worked from home on a regular basis, but only 3 percent had all or most of their employees based out of their home (Bond, Galinksy, and Sakai 2008).

In 2011, about 12 percent of workers who had access to flexible work arrangements changed either their schedule or location in the previous week. Of those who utilized workplace flexibility, about 22 percent changed their location. College-educated workers who used flexibility were more likely than less-educated workers to change their location (31 percent compared to 12 percent), and men were slightly more likely to change their location than were women. Men's greater access to flexibility in workplace location is partially due to differences in the industries and occupations in which men and women work.[32] About 6 percent of workers who used flexible arrangements combined location flexibility with scheduling flexibility.

Flexibility can also be used to help workers reduce the hours they need to work to stay in their jobs; for example, through job sharing. In 2014, 29 percent of employers reported allowing some workers to share jobs, and 36 percent reported allowing at least some individuals to move from full-time to part-time work, and back again, while remaining at the same position or level (Figure 4-15). Few firms allowed most or all employees to take advantage of these forms of flexibility (Matos and Galinsky 2014).

Disparities in Access to Paid Leave and Flexible Work Arrangements

Lack of access to paid leave or flexible work arrangements may, as has been suggested, relate to industry-specific practices or job requirements. However, this translates into uneven access across demographic and other worker characteristics, since those factors often correlate with job and sector choice. Family-friendly workplace policies are often a form of compensation, and groups that are more likely to be highly compensated are also more likely to have access to these policies. Evaluations have found that total compensation inequality (for example, access to health benefits and paid leave) was about 10 percent higher than wage inequality alone, and unequal leave access accounted for over one-third of this additional gap (Pierce 2010).

---

[32] In order to see if differences in industry and occupation explained men being more likely to change their location, CEA regressed likelihood to switch on gender, industry, and occupation.

Figure 4-14
Percent of Firms Offering Flexibility in the Location of Work, 2014

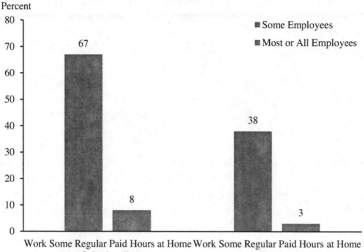

Note: Survey includes firms with over 50 employees.
Source: Families and Work Institute, National Study of Employers, 2014.

Figure 4-15
**Percent of Firms Offering Flexibility in the
Number of Hours of Work, 2014**

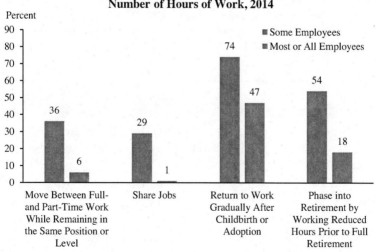

Note: Survey includes firms with over 50 employees.
Source: Families and Work Institute, National Study of Employers, 2014, as analyzed in Matos and Galinsky (2014).

> **Box 4-3: Small Business and Manufacturing**
>
> **Small Businesses.** Some argue that while flexible scheduling may work in large firms, each member of a small business team can be critical to business operations, making it too costly to implement such practices in small firms. However, flexibility can be a great advantage to small firms which may be better able to understand the flexibility needs of each of their employees and come up with a solution that benefits both the business and workers. Moreover, since flexibility can increase retention it may be particularly helpful for small businesses as losing members of a small business team can be particularly costly. In fact, data shows that small firms (50 to 99 employees) provide more flexibility to their employees than do large firms (1,000 and more employees) across five dimensions of flexibility: changing starting and quitting times, working some regular hours at home occasionally, having control over when to take breaks, returning to work gradually after childbirth or adoption, and taking time off during the workday to attend to important family or personal needs without loss of pay. (Matos and Galinsky 2014).
>
> **Manufacturing.** Manufacturing workers are less likely to have flexible work arrangements. This difference may be due to technological difficulties that limit the amount of flexibility manufacturing firms can give their workers. For firms that rely on formal shifts, employees may not be able to leave at non-standard times without disrupting their colleagues. In addition, the on-site physical nature of many manufacturing jobs may make telecommuting impossible. Despite these challenges, there are strategies that some manufacturing companies have used to increase workplace flexibility. Increasing the breadth of training can help ensure that workers can more effectively fill in or otherwise compensate for one another in case a worker cannot be present at a particular time.

Data do show substantial cross-industry differences in access to flexible scheduling. As shown in Figure 4-16, less than 40 percent of workers in construction and transportation and utilities have flexibility to change their hours or location, compared to about 70 percent in information and leisure and hospitality.

Paid leave access appears to be strongly related to the pay level of the industry, with high-wage industries offering more benefits. For example, in the leisure and hospitality sector where the average hourly wage is about $14, less than 25 percent of workers report having some form of paid leave, compared to almost 80 percent of workers in the financial-activities sector (Figure 4-17). In some industries, corporate culture may affect workers' willingness to take significant leave, suggesting that factors other than

Figure 4-16
Access to Scheduling and Location Flexibility by Industry, 2011

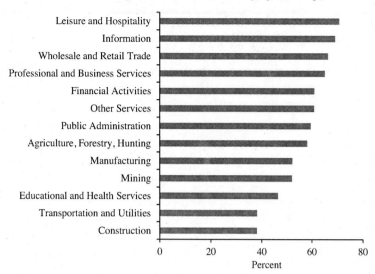

Source: Bureau of Labor Statistics, American Time Use Survey, 2011; CEA calculations.

Figure 4-17
Access to Paid and Unpaid Leave by Industry, 2011

Source: Bureau of Labor Statistics, American Time Use Survey, 2011; CEA calculations.

Table 4-4
Access to Leave and Workplace Flexibility by Demographic, Educational, and Worker Characteristics, 2011

Policy Type	Percent Access to Paid Leave	Percent Access to Unpaid Leave	Percent Flexibility in the Scheduling of Hours	Percent Flexibility in Days Worked	Percent Flexibility in the Location of Work	Percent Any Flexibility
Total	59	77	49	40	22	54
Demographic Characteristics						
Male	60	75	49	38	23	53
Female	57	78	48	42	21	55
White, Non-Hispanic	62	78	51	41	24	56
Black, Non-Hispanic	61	77	43	38	18	49
Asian, Non-Hispanic	62	72	54	44	31	60
Hispanic	43	71	39	34	15	45
Educational Attainment (Workers 25 and Older)						
Less than High School	35	70	27	28	12	32
High School	61	76	39	32	13	45
Some College	66	78	50	40	19	55
Bachelor's Degree or Higher	71	75	56	40	35	60
Weekly Earnings (Quartiles, 2011$)						
$0-$540	49	76	39	36	13	45
$541-$830	76	78	43	30	14	47
$831-$1,230	80	73	45	31	23	49
$1,230+	81	75	56	37	39	60
Hours Worked						
Full-Time	70	75	47	35	23	51
Part-Time	22	81	56	59	20	64

Note: Sample excludes self-employed workers. Weekly earnings are for full-time wage and salary workers with one job.
Source: Bureau of Labor Statistics, American Time Use Survey, 2011; CEA calculations.

compensation level alone are relevant for leave access and use (Bernard 2013).

Table 4-4 shows differences in reported workplace flexibility by worker characteristics and type of flexibility. The 2011 American Time Use Survey inquired about specific types of workplace flexibility workers can access. In general, workers who are likely to report flexibility in their schedule are also more likely to report having access to flexibility in where they do their work.

There are modest disparities in access to unpaid leave across demographic groups, likely because not all workers are covered under the Federal

Family and Medical Leave Act, which guarantees access to unpaid leave for workers that are covered by the law. Disparities in access to paid leave are typically more substantial. The largest differences in access to paid leave and workplace flexibility occur across Hispanics and non-Hispanics, with only 43 percent of Hispanics having access to paid leave compared to 62 percent among non-Hispanic Whites. This disparity is not fully explained by differences in the industries and occupations that Hispanics and non-Hispanics work in, nor is it fully explained by differences in wages and education. Accounting for differences in industry, occupation, wages, and education accounts for less than half of the difference in paid leave access between Hispanics and non-Hispanics.[33]

Higher-wage workers are significantly more likely to have access to paid leave compared to lower-wage workers, consistent with the finding above that higher-paying industries also offer more paid leave (Table 4-4). Employee surveys suggest that college-educated workers are twice as likely to have access to paid leave as workers without a high school degree (71 percent versus 35 percent). Comparing wage levels, full-time workers in the top income quartile are 1.7 times as likely to have access to paid leave as the workers in the bottom quartile (81 percent versus 49 percent). Therefore, the unequal availability of paid leave can exacerbate not only compensation inequality, but also inequality in well-being, since the highest-income workers are most likely to have access to policies that enable them to balance work and family.

STATE AND LOCAL INITIATIVES TO EXPAND ACCESS TO WORK-FAMILY FRIENDLY POLICIES

Beyond employers voluntarily providing access to paid leave for employees, some State and local governments have moved to expand access to family-friendly policies to all workers, spurred in part by worker demand for these policies, but also because some businesses recognize the value in a set of consistent policies for all workers. In fact, the vast majority of businesses see either positive or no effect from State paid leave policies (Appelbaum and Milkman 2011).

State Paid Family Leave

Currently three states have implemented paid family leave programs (Table 4-5). In addition, Washington State has passed paid leave legislation, but has not yet implemented the program. A number of states are also considering the feasibility of similar programs.[34] For example, in 2014 the U.S. Department of Labor awarded $500,000 in competitive Paid Leave Analysis Grants to the District of Columbia, Massachusetts, Montana, and Rhode Island to study the feasibility of state-wide paid leave programs. The grantees were selected from a larger pool of applicants. The Department of Labor announced in January 2015 that it will offer $1 million in new funding

---

[33] To conduct this analysis, CEA examined the relationship between access to leave and worker characteristics. After controlling for wages, education, industries, and occupations, 53 percent of the difference in access to leave between Hispanics and non-Hispanics remained unexplained.

[34] According to the National Partnership for Women and Families, around 20 states have pending legislation on some kind of paid leave program.

Table 4-5
State Leave Policies as of January 2015

State	Type	Year Effective	Duration	Implementation	Replacement Rate
California	Family Leave	2004	6 weeks	Temporary Disability Insurance	Approximately 55 percent, maximum of $1,104 per week
New Jersey	Family Leave	2009	6 weeks	Temporary Disability Insurance	66 percent, maximum of $604 per week
Rhode Island	Family Leave	2014	4 weeks	Temporary Disability Insurance	Around 60 percent, maximum of $770 per week
California	Sick Leave	2015	3 days	Paid by employers	100 percent
Connecticut	Sick Leave	2012	5 days	Paid by employers	100 percent
Massachusetts	Sick Leave	2015	40 hours	Paid by employers	100 percent
District of Columbia	Sick Leave	2008	3-7 days	Paid by employers	100 percent

Source: California Employment Department; New Jersey Department of Labor and Workforce Development; Rhode Island Department of Labor and Training; California Governor's Office of Business and Economic Development (2014); Connecticut Department of Labor (2014); Secretary of the Commonwealth of Massachusetts; District of Columbia (2008, 2013).

for the program, which could provide competitive grants to an additional 6 to 10 states or municipalities.

California implemented paid family leave in 2004. Under California law, paid family leave benefits are available to almost all workers. The program provides six weeks of paid family leave at approximately 55 percent of usual weekly earnings with a maximum weekly benefit of $1,104 as of 2015, which is indexed to the State's average weekly wage. The paid family leave program was developed as a component of the existing temporary disability insurance system. The system is funded through a payroll tax which is 0.9 percent of the first $104,378 of an employee's State Disability Insurance (SDI) taxable wages in 2015 (California Employment Development Department). This tax funds both the temporary disability insurance system and the paid leave system. By implementing paid leave through the existing disability insurance system, California was able to capitalize on their existing administrative and revenue collection institutions. Businesses may alternatively choose to cover employees through a voluntary plan that provides coverage, rights, and benefits that are at least as good as the state-mandated plan, with at least one greater right or benefit than provided by the State plan. Businesses choosing voluntary plans must also get the agreement of the majority of their employees.

Pew estimates that 1.5 million workers have used the California Paid Family Leave program since its inception (Pew Charitable Trusts 2014).

Because California enacted its policy a decade ago, some evidence on the policy's impacts in that state is available. Following implementation of the program, most businesses reported no negative effect on profitability. A survey of 253 employers affected by California's paid family leave initiative found that the vast majority—over 90 percent—reported no negative effect on profitability, turnover, or morale (Appelbaum and Milkman 2011). Empirical research also found that California's leave policy increased hours worked and earnings among mothers with one- to three-year-old children by up to 10 percent, particularly among lower-wage mothers who were unlikely to be able to afford to take unpaid leave (Rossin-Slater, Ruhm, and Waldfogel 2013).

New Jersey became the second state to provide its workers with access to paid family leave in 2009. The New Jersey program also piggybacks off of the state's Temporary Disability Insurance program to create Family Leave Insurance. All employees in New Jersey whose employers are subject to the New Jersey Unemployment Compensation law are covered regardless of the number of employees. Workers contribute 0.09 percent of their first $32,000 in earnings. Unlike California and Rhode Island, the revenue for the family leave insurance program is collected through a separate tax rate from the Temporary Disability Insurance program, although the wage base is the same as that that is used for both unemployment compensation and temporary disability insurance. Family Leave Insurance is available to workers with at least 20 calendar weeks of covered employment and at least $165 a week (or $8,300 annually) in earnings in the 52 weeks preceding leave. Covered workers are eligible for six weeks of partial wage replacement in the 12 months after becoming a parent or any time for the care of an ailing family member. The wage replacement is paid at two-thirds of the worker's average weekly wage, up to $604 a week. Employers can also choose to provide coverage through an approved Family Leave Insurance private plan and opt-out of the State plan. Private plans must, however, provide benefits that are at least as generous as the State plan and the cost to the worker cannot exceed the payroll tax they would face under the State plan (New Jersey Department of Labor and Workforce Development).

Rhode Island was the third State to enact paid family leave by extending its Temporary Disability Insurance program (which has been in place since 1942) to create a Temporary Caregiver Insurance program (TCI) and markedly expand access to paid leave among Rhode Island workers. TCI became effective at the start of 2014 and provides covered workers with income support when they take up to four weeks of paid time away from work to care for a new child or a seriously ill family member. Weekly Temporary Caregiver Insurance benefits total approximately 60 percent of an employee's weekly wage up to a maximum of $770.[35] Temporary Caregiver Insurance leverages the benefits of extending the Temporary Disability Insurance (TDI) program to incorporate new benefits for caregiving. Rhode Island covers the additional benefits under the previous payroll Temporary Disability Insurance Tax of 1.2 percent of a workers' first $64,200 in earnings. This employee paid tax covers both the TDI program and the TCI program. Additional benefits may be available to workers with children under the age of 18 and disabled children over 18. This weekly "dependency allowance" is paid as the greater of $10 or 7 percent of the standard benefit rate (Rhode Island Department of Labor and Training).

New York, Hawaii, and Puerto Rico also have temporary disability insurance systems and could easily implement programs similar to those in California, New Jersey, and Rhode Island. Washington was the first state to pass a paid leave law not administered through a disability insurance program, though it has not yet been implemented due to the lack of a financing mechanism.

State Paid Sick Leave

At the start of 2014, Connecticut was the only state, along with a few cities, that guaranteed workers the right to earn paid sick leave. But momentum was building at both the State and city level. By the end of the year, both California and Massachusetts had enacted paid sick leave policies, along with cities such as Eugene, Oregon, San Diego, and Oakland.

In 2008, the District of Columbia passed a paid sick leave law that provides paid sick leave to workers in most industries who have been with their employer for at least 90 days. Workers can use sick leave for illness, preventative care, or services related to domestic violence for themselves or a family member. The rate of sick leave accrual is based on employer size: employers with 100 or more employees are required to provide an hour of paid leave for every 37 hours worked, up to a maximum of 7 days, while employers with fewer than 25 employees must provide an hour of paid sick leave for every 87 hours worked, to a maximum of 3 days a year (District of Columbia 2008, 2013).

In 2012, Connecticut implemented legislation that required certain employers to offer paid sick leave to their workers. The law covers hourly (non-exempt) workers in the service sector employed by firms with at least 50 employees. Manufacturers and nationally chartered non-profits that provide recreation, child care, and education are not required to provide

---

[35] Benefits are 4.62 percent of the wages earned in the highest quarter of the base period. For workers who are earning a steady salary over the quarter this is approximately 60 percent of their weekly wages.

paid leave, and per diem and temporary workers are also not covered (Connecticut Department of Labor 2014). While only about 12 to 24 percent of Connecticut's workers are covered due to the many exceptions, most part-time workers were covered (Appelbaum et al. 2014). Covered workers in Connecticut earn an hour of paid leave for every 40 hours worked, up to a total of 40 hours of paid leave (5 days) in a calendar year. In addition to personal illness, workers are able to use this leave to care for a sick spouse, a sick child, or if they are a victim of family violence or sexual assault.

The California legislature passed paid sick leave legislation in September 2014. After July 1, 2015, all employers will be required to provide paid sick leave. Employees are eligible after working 30 days for an employer in California. Employees accrue at least an hour of sick leave for every 30 hours worked, which employers may limit to 3 days a year. In contrast to the laws in the District of Columbia and Connecticut, the California legislation extends to both small- and large-employers, but exempts some in-home service providers and some employees who are covered by collective bargaining arrangements. Like both the District of Columbia and Connecticut, California employees will be able to use paid sick leave to care for themselves or family members (California Governor's Office of Business and Economic Development 2014; Kalt 2014).

In November 2014, Massachusetts passed a ballot initiative requiring employers with at least 11 employees to offer paid sick leave (workers at smaller employers can take unpaid leave as provided for in the law). Workers earn at least an hour of sick leave for every 30 hours worked, up to a maximum of 40 hours a year. Workers can use this earned leave for illness or injury affecting the employee or his or her child, spouse, parent, or spouse's parent (or to attend routine medical appointments for the same group), or to address the effects of domestic violence on the employee or his or her dependent child. CEA estimates that, as of May 2015 when it becomes effective, approximately 90 percent of Massachusetts employees will have access to paid sick leave (Longitudinal Business Database 2012).[36]

Cities across the country have also enacted statutes providing covered employees with the opportunity to accrue paid sick leave. These include San Francisco; Oakland; Seattle; Portland, Oregon; New York City; Jersey City; and Newark. In addition, there are active campaigns in around 20 other States and cities to make paid sick leave mandatory. However, at least 10 States have legislation barring cities and counties from passing their own paid sick leave legislation.

---

[36] According to the Business Dynamics Survey, approximately 10.0 percent of employees in Massachusetts were employed at firms with 1-9 workers in 2012.

Right-to-Request Provisions

One way to help workers gain access to flexibility in the workplace is to make it easier for workers to simply ask for these benefits. This practice is spelled out in "right-to-request" policies, which lay out the circumstances and procedures by which workers can ask their supervisors to consider alternative work arrangements to meet their needs for flexibility. Workers may be hesitant to enquire about their employer's flexible scheduling policies because they fear this request will reflect poorly upon them or cause them to lose their job. One-fifth of American adults, and more than one-third of working parents and caregivers, report that they believe they have been denied a promotion, raise, or new job because they need a flexible work schedule (Nielsen 2014). In addition, anecdotal evidence—particularly from the service and retail sectors—suggest that even part-time employees can be penalized for requesting limits on their availability (Greenhouse 2014). Right-to-request laws attempt to reduce punitive behavior by employers when workers make a scheduling request. Under right-to-request laws, employers cannot retaliate against an employee who requests a flexible work arrangement. In addition, the laws create an incentive for employers to consider implementing flexible workplace policies.

Some local and State governments in the United States have already implemented right-to-request laws (Table 4-6). In 2013, San Francisco passed the Family Friendly Workplace Ordinance, which allows some workers to request flexible or predictable working arrangement to help meet their responsibilities in caring for children, elderly parents, or relatives with serious health conditions (City and County of San Francisco 2013). Vermont passed similar legislation that allows workers to request workplace flexibility for any reason (Vermont State Legislature 2013). These laws do not require the employer to accept the request; they only require employers to consider the requests, provide a written response, and not retaliate against workers for making such requests. Employers are able to deny requests that would negatively affect business performance or impose high business costs (City and County of San Francisco 2013; Vermont State Legislature 2013). As these policies were implemented recently, there is not yet empirical data on how businesses and employees have responded.

Other countries, including the United Kingdom, New Zealand, and Australia, have also adopted right-to-request laws.[37] Most requests are submitted by those with child care responsibilities and, in its early years of

---

[37] Under the "Act of Part-Time and Fixed-Term Contracts" (§ 8 TzBfG), employees in Germany who have been working for more than 6 months at a company with more than 15 employees can request to switch to part-time work. This request can only be declined for "business reasons." See Foster and Sule (2010).

**Box 4-5: Japan's Strategy to Grow the Economy
by Increasing Women's Involvement**

Japan has experienced decades of low growth. In response, Prime Minister Shinzō Abe has developed a strategy to put Japan back on a path to sustained growth. An important part of this strategy is creating a society in which women are supported in taking a more substantial role in work and decision making. Currently, many Japanese women must choose between career and family. As a result, the labor force participation rate among prime-age Japanese women has recently been well below that of other developed countries. It is currently around 74 percent, about 22 percentage points below that of Japanese men and about 2 percentage points above the Organisation for Economic Co-operation and Development (OECD) average. However, female labor force participation in Japan has risen about 7 percentage points since 2000. The focus on women's participation in Japan began in earnest in the last three years, and since 2011 there has been a notable uptick in female labor force participation.

The Abe policies are focused on creating a more broadly inclusive professional environment for women in Japan, with the goal of increasing economic growth by taking greater advantage of the talents of women in the labor market and government. The International Monetary Fund (IMF) estimates that increasing female labor force participation in Japan could add another 0.25 percent to growth each year and raise income per capita by 4 percent.

One avenue that the government is pursuing to raise female labor force participation is child care. Under Abe, the government is creating 400,000 new spaces in nursery schools to eliminate child care waiting lists and provide more high quality care and thereby enable women who want to continue to work after starting a family to do so. Currently, 60 percent of Japanese women leave work when they have their first child. Other policies include initiatives to increase the representation of women in leadership positions to 30 percent by 2020 and to encourage private businesses to add at least one woman to their boards. Japan provides 14 weeks of paid maternity leave at roughly two-thirds of pay and an additional 44 weeks of paid parental leave which makes it around average in the OECD for total leave available to mothers (OECD 2014). Japan also provides protections for pregnant workers: pregnant workers or workers who just had a baby cannot be assigned to work injurious to pregnancy, childbirth, nursing, and related matters (ILO 2014). These policies can provide important lessons for U.S. policy makers, in considering how to raise female labor force participation.

Table 4-6
Local Right to Request Laws

Locality	Date Effective	Covered Workers	Flexibility Uses	Employer Responsibilities
San Francisco (City and County)	January 1, 2014	Workers who have worked for their current employer for at least 6 months and who work at least 8 hours per week on a regular basis. Employers with fewer than 20 employees are exempt.	Caring for a child under the age of 18, a relative with a serious health condition, and/or a parent older than 65.	Employers must meet with the employee and respond to the request within 21 days of the meeting. Any denial must be in writing and describe the business reason for the denial.
Vermont	January 1, 2014	All public and private sector workers.	Workers can request flexible work arrangements or predictable schedules for any reason.	Employers must consider requests at least twice a year. Employers may deny if the request poses costs to the business.

Source: City and County of San Francisco (2013); Vermont State Legislature (2013).

implementation, employers fully or partially accepted more than 80 percent of these requests for flexibility (Georgetown University Federal Legislation Clinic 2006). Perhaps unsurprisingly, the percentage of employers offering workplace flexibility increased after the implementation of these laws. In the United Kingdom, for example, more than 90 percent of employers have flexible work arrangements in the workplace; only 50 percent of employers reported such arrangements in 1999 (NACEW 2013).

U.K. employers have realized business benefits from flexible work arrangements, including improved employee relations, better recruitment and retention, lower absenteeism, and increased productivity (NACEW 2013). The right-to-request law there was recently expanded to cover all workers, regardless of parent or caregiver status (Gov. UK 2014). The evidence suggests that right-to-request laws make it easier and more likely for employees to ask for and obtain flexible work arrangements. Flexible work arrangements can also lead to working environments better matched to employees' needs and a more productive workforce for employers.

The Administration recognizes that the benefits of workplace flexibility programs can only be realized if workers feel comfortable asking for them. With that understanding, the President signed a Presidential Memorandum in June 2014 encouraging every agency in the Federal Government to expand flexible workplace policies as much as possible. The memorandum also makes it clear that Federal workers have the right-to-request a flexible work arrangement without fear of retaliation. As a result, Federal agencies will periodically make their employees aware of the workplace flexibilities available to them and remind them that they may request any of those flexibilities without fear of retaliation. Supervisors must consider these requests carefully, confer with requesting employees, and render decisions in a timely fashion. Since workers may be unaware of their options with respect to workplace flexibility or the circumstances under which they are permitted to use them, this step will enable Federal employees to better balance their personal and professional obligations by providing clarity on those issues.

By instructing agencies to extend their flexibility policies and encouraging workers to request schedules that fit their needs, this memorandum builds on previous efforts to promote workplace flexibility in the Federal government. For example, increased telecommunication capacities developed in part under President Bill Clinton's direction have enabled Federal employees to work remotely through adverse weather situations. Workers' ability to change their work location has resulted in significant cost savings. For example, during the winter of 2009-10, telecommuting capabilities saved over $30 million for every day the Federal government was closed due to heavy snow, for a total savings of more than $150 million (CEA 2010).

The Economic Case for Family-Friendly Workplace Policies

Paid leave and workplace flexibility hold great potential to benefit businesses as well as our economy overall through improved economic productivity. A body of research finds that these practices can benefit employers by improving their ability to recruit and retain talent, lowering costly worker turnover, and minimizing loss of firm-specific skills and human capital, as well as by boosting morale and worker productivity. The following subsections present evidence on the impacts of paid leave and workplace flexibility on absenteeism and worker health, two dimensions of workforce quality performance about which there is a great deal of information, and then turn to the broader literature on other aspects of workforce performance, including turnover. Taken together, these two strands of research suggest that work-family friendly policies have significantly improved worker performance in firms and industries that have tried them.

While many companies do offer these benefits, many other companies do not: as previously shown, fewer than one-third of full-time workers have flexibility in their hours worked and less than one-half of workers have access to any kind of paid leave. The question of why these policies have not reached more workers is an important one, and the literature offers several explanations, reviewed in the sections below.

Impact of Leave and Flexibility on Worker Health and Absenteeism

Both paid leave and workplace flexibility policies can improve worker health, and workplace flexibility can reduce absenteeism. Improved worker health may indirectly improve productivity and morale, as healthy workers are able to work to their full potential.

Paid sick leave creates a healthier work environment by encouraging workers to stay home when they are sick, making them less likely to infect others and cause further productivity losses. For example, a study showed that employee absences fell more rapidly after the peak of the 2009 H1N1 pandemic among public sector workers (who had much higher access to paid sick leave) compared to private sector workers who were much less likely to have paid sick leave (Drago and Miller 2010).

Evidence suggests that, on net, paid sick days do not lower business profits. A survey of 253 employers affected by California's paid leave initiative found that around 90 percent reported no negative effect on profitability (Appelbaum and Milkman 2011). Another study examining the implementation of San Francisco's paid sick leave law in 2007 found no evidence of a negative economic effect. Relative to surrounding areas that did not have a paid sick leave law, total employment and the total number of businesses increased in San Francisco after the law's implementation (Petro 2010). In addition, a study of 251 employers in Connecticut after that State implemented a paid sick leave program found that employees did not abuse the policy by taking unnecessary sick days (Appelbaum 2014).

Research suggests that paid parental leave policies can provide health benefits that extend to children, such as higher birth weight and lower infant mortality. There are several channels through which improved health can occur. With paid leave, parents can better monitor their children's health (Ruhm 2000). In particular, Rossin-Slater (2011) found that, among college-educated mothers, an expansion of unpaid leave increased birth weight and decreased premature births and infant mortality. The existing evidence on child development emphasizes the importance of the early childhood and prenatal environment, so benefits of better health in infanthood are likely to persist as children age (Almond and Currie 2011). In support of this hypothesis, a study of Norway's maternity leave reform found children whose mothers were eligible for extended maternity leave had higher educational attainment, lower teen pregnancy rates, higher IQ scores, and higher adulthood earnings (Carneiro, Loken, and Salvanes 2011). In addition, more paternity leave taken at birth is associated with fathers being more involved in child care nine months later, which has benefits for both the child and the mother (Nepmonyaschy and Waldfogel 2007).

Flexible work arrangements can also improve worker health. A workplace intervention conducted at 12 Midwestern grocery stores found that workers supervised by family supportive managers reported improved physical and mental health (Work, Family, and Health Network 2008a). Another study found that a workplace intervention at a retail company to allow employees greater control over their work schedule resulted in employees being less likely to report feeling obligated to come to work, or not see a doctor, when they were sick. The intervention also improved sleep quality and energy and reduced psychological stress (Work, Family, and Health Network 2008b).

Workplace flexibility can also help reduce absenteeism, which can be costly to a firm by creating uncertainty over the workforce size and composition that a manager can expect on any given day. In companies where multiple workers perform similar tasks, workers can help compensate for missing colleagues. In smaller firms or firms where each worker's job is different and critical to a company's mission, however, unplanned absences may be especially costly. Studies that follow workers as they switch between firms that offer a flexible work schedule (such as work-at-home options) to those that did not found that workers tended to miss work more often in firms without flexible arrangements (Dionne and Dostie 2007; Yasbek 2004; Comfort, Johnson, and Wallace 2003; Akyeampong 2001). Perhaps the most compelling study of the impact of workplace flexibility on absenteeism comes from within a large public utility that temporarily allowed workers in one of its sub-units to choose their working hours without changing the total number of hours worked. The other sub-units retained the standard scheduling. The sub-unit with a flexible schedule reported a reduction in absences of more than 20 percent, while the absenteeism rate in other sub-units essentially remained unchanged (Figure 4-18; Dalton and Mesch 1990). When the company reverted back to standard scheduling for all of the sub-units after a one-year trial, the absenteeism rates of the two sub-unit groups became, once again, similar.

A recent Gallup Poll (2013) estimates that the annual cost of workforce absences due to poor health was $84 billion. If the findings in Dalton and Mesch (1990) generalize across industries, and if all of this reduction

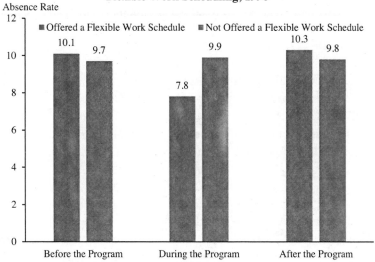

Figure 4-18
**Average Absence Rates With and Without
Flexible Work Scheduling, 1990**

Absence Rate

Source: Dalton and Mesch (1990).

translates into lower costs for employers, then the implied savings due to offering flexibility could be around $17 billion a year.[38]

The Role of Family-Friendly Policies in Worker Recruitment, Retention, and Productivity

Paid leave and flexible work arrangements are forms of compensation, similar to wages or health and retirement benefits. Employers have discretion over which benefits to provide to their employees, resulting in differing compensation "packages." Economists have long considered the total wage and benefits "bundle" to be important to workers in selecting jobs (Bauman 1970; Woodbury 1983; Eberts and Stone 1985; Summers 1989; Gruber and Krueger 1991; Sheiner 1999; Olson 2002). There is evidence that workers take into account the entire compensation package—not only wages—when considering job offers. For example, workers must be paid higher wages to accept jobs without health insurance, partly to help pay for their health expenses (CEA 2010). Similarly, analysis of data on 120 employers found that, when offered little workplace flexibility, workers require higher wages to help pay for services such as emergency child care and

---

[38] As discussed earlier, Dalton and Mesch (1990) find that a flexible schedule reduced absences by more than 20 percent. Applying that percentage to $84 billion translates to savings of about $17 billion a year.

eldercare (Baughman, DiNardi, and Holtz-Eakin 2003). These studies show clearly that workers value family-friendly benefits and that offering these benefits is a form of compensation. Research shows that higher compensation improves business' ability to attract and retain talent as well as generally improving worker performance (Dal Bo, Finan, and Rossi 2013; Cappelli and Chauvin 1991; Akerlof and Yellen 1986; Bewley 1999). Therefore it is not surprising that firms that offer these benefits have been shown to be more productive (Bloom, Krestchmer, and Van Reenen 2006; Bloom et al. 2013; A Better Balance 2008; Corporate Voices for Working Families 2005; NACEW 2013).

In addition to the academic analyses cited above, survey evidence also indicates that employees highly value access to leave and flexibility. Nearly one-half of working parents say they have chosen to pass up a job they felt would conflict with family obligations (Nielsen 2014). As shown in Figure 4-19, a very high share of Americans support such policies, and more than one-half of workers feel they could do their job better if allowed a more flexible schedule (Nielsen 2014). In another survey of 200 human resource managers, two-thirds cited family-supportive policies such as flexible hours as the single most important factor in attracting and retaining employees (Williams 2001). Employers that have adopted these practices cite many economic benefits, such as reduced worker absenteeism and turnover, improvements in their ability to attract and retain workers, and other positive changes that translate into increased worker productivity (A Better Balance 2008; Corporate Voices for Working Families 2005).

Research by Claudia Goldin has focused on a new reason for gender segregation, particularly in high-skill occupations: highly educated women are more often choosing career paths in which the wage penalties for flexibility are smaller—such as dentistry, veterinary medicine, optometry, and pharmacy—and where the slowdown in wage growth for small periods of time out of the labor force is less (Goldin 2014). However, survey evidence suggests that both men and women value family-friendly workplace policies and men are increasingly also prioritizing jobs that allow more flexibility or include paid parental leave. For example, a 2014 survey of high-skilled working fathers conducted by researchers at Boston College found that 89 percent said that the availability of paid paternity leave was an important consideration in seeking a new job if they planned to have another child. Likewise, 95 percent reported that workplace flexibility policies allowing them to actively engage with their children were an important job characteristic (Harrington et al. 2014).

Recruitment and retention are particularly important channels through which work-family friendly policies can improve productivity and

Figure 4-19
The Need for Workplace Flexibility, 2014

Nine in ten Americans believe employers should offer workers flexibility to meet their families' needs, so long as their work gets done.

Over half of workers feel they could do their job better if they were allowed a more flexible schedule.

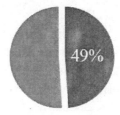

More than a third of working parents believe they've been "passed over" for a promotion, a raise, or a new job due to a need for a flexible work schedule.

Nearly half of working parents say they have have chosen to pass up a job they felt would conflict with family obligations.

Source: Nielsen (2014) Harris Poll of 4,096 U.S. adults (aged 18+), conducted online May-27-30, 2014.

the bottom line for businesses. More successful recruiting means firms can get the employees they want faster, and improved retention saves the direct and indirect costs of turnover. These costs can be considerable: for example, one study found that hiring costs account for more than $2,500 per hire in large firms, or approximately 3 percent of total annual labor costs for a full-time equivalent worker.[39] Low retention is particularly costly for firms that extensively train their workers with skills specific to their workplace (Becker 1964; Mincer 1974; Lazear 2003). One study notes that "visible" costs such as advertising and orientation costs account for only 10 to 15 percent of total turnover costs (Baughman, DiNardi, and Holtz-Eakin 2003). But after including costs such as productivity losses related to training new employees, another study estimates that the median cost of turnover was 21 percent of an employee's annual salary (Boushey and Glynn 2012). It is not surprising, therefore, that firms have strong incentives to reduce voluntary turnovers (Pencavel 1972). Research has shown that firms that invest in

---

[39] The study included more than 300 large organizations. Data referred to the 2007 calendar year. The average size of the company in the report has annual revenue of $5.7 billion and roughly 17,000 employees. See PriceWaterhouseCoopers LLP (2009).

their workforce with higher pay, fuller training, better benefits, and more convenient schedules outperform their competitors (Ton 2012).

There are several ways that paid leave and flexible work arrangements can help reduce turnover. A 2011 Gallup Poll found that access to flexible work arrangements was highly correlated with greater worker engagement and higher well-being (Harter and Agrawal 2012). In a survey of 120 randomly selected employers in New York, employers that offered sick leave and child care assistance had significantly lower rates of turnover (Baughman, DiNardi and Holtz-Eakin 2003). Other studies report that firms with more flexible telecommuting practices had lower turnover (Yasbek 2004; Computer Economics 2008). Case studies of firms, highlighted in Box 4-6, also provide qualitative insights into perceived benefits.

Paid parental leave in particular can help businesses retain talented workers after childbirth. Studies show that paid maternity leave increases the likelihood that mothers return to their employer following the birth of a child, and particularly when combined with statutory job protection, paid maternity leave can increase mothers' wages and employment in the long run (Rossin-Slater, Ruhm, and Waldfogel 2013; Waldfogel, Higuchi, and Abe 1999). At a macroeconomic level, paid leave could contribute to higher labor force participation and a stronger economy, and can also raise business profits if the costs of providing paid leave are lower than the costs of turnover costs.

In addition to the evidence on recruitment and retention, several studies document a positive relationship between workplace flexibility and worker productivity. For example, a study of over 700 firms in the United States, United Kingdom, France, and Germany found a significant positive relationship between work-life balance practices and total factor productivity (Bloom, Krestchmer, and Van Reenen 2006). The authors argue that this correlation could be driven by a third factor—good management. Well-managed firms both have higher productivity and often embrace flexible workplace practices. But importantly, the study finds no evidence that workplace flexibility harms productivity. In a randomized evaluation designed to eliminate a role for management in affecting worker productivity, call center employees at a travel agency in China found productivity increased when workers chose where they worked. When workers were allowed to choose the optimal place to work based on their preferences and circumstances—whether from home or the office—productivity increased 22 percent (Bloom et al. 2013).

The Business Case for Wider Adoption of Flexible Workplace Practices and Policies

The evidence cited above suggests that paid leave and flexible work arrangements benefit workers and employers. Workers are happier, healthier, and more likely to remain with the more flexible firm; for firms, this means lower turnover, less absenteeism, easier recruiting of talent, and more productive workers. Yet despite these benefits, many firms have still not adopted such practices. If these practices generate such large economic benefits for both workers and firms, why do more workers not already have access to them?

Researchers have put forth two explanations for this puzzle. One broad explanation is that managers either are unaware that these policies can benefit them, or they simply do not have the capacity to implement these policies. A second explanation posits that firms differ in the benefits that family-friendly policies can provide, with some firms benefiting greatly and others much less so. Under this explanation, managers are aware of the benefits of such practices to their firms, and implementation rates reflect the fact that only some managers will find it worthwhile to enact these policies.

Research has found considerable evidence for the first of these explanations. Economists find that lack of information is one factor that may contribute to the incomplete adoption of the best management practices (Bloom and Van Reenen 2010). For example, even in manufacturing where productivity is relatively easily quantified, managers sometimes appear to fail to make profit-maximizing choices (Romer 2006; Bloom and Van Reenen 2010; Levitt 2006; Cho and Rust 2010; Bloom, Kretschmer, and Van Reenen 2006; Yasbek 2004). This may be because it takes time for managers to learn and incorporate new techniques and policies, or because firms can be persuaded to adopt such policies under only intense outside pressure. In addition, as the labor force changes, the best practices from previous years may not be best-suited to today's workforce (Griliches 1957; Cohen and Levinthal 1990; Levitt and March 1988; Nelson and Winter 1985). If implementing new work-family policies is costly for firms, adoption may lag, leaving firms with outdated human resources practices until either labor-market competition forces a change or until new management arrives.

The second possible explanation holds that costs and benefits of family-friendly practices may differ across firms. For example, it might be possible for financial services employees to occasionally work from home, while it is often infeasible for food service employees. Theory then predicts that firms and industries with the greatest potential net gains from adopting flexible practices should be among the first to embrace them. Since existing studies of the effect of flexible arrangements come from firms that have already adopted these practices, the evidence presented above may overstate the economic benefits that some firms without flexible arrangements would enjoy if such flexibility were widely adopted. On the other hand, if flexible arrangements were coordinated across firms or part of a Federal program, costs would be spread out among employers, making such offerings more beneficial for them. In addition, it would prevent employers who refuse to provide flexibility to their workers from pricing their goods and services lower than competitors who do provide flexibility.

However, there is still an economic rationale for why employers and the U.S. economy could benefit from wider adoption of flexible workplace practices. Promoting work-life balance may help society in ways that are not taken into account by either employers or employees (what economists call social benefits or positive externalities). For example, some economic models have emphasized that firms may be reluctant to offer benefits packages that are particularly attractive to workers for whom the benefits are most costly to provide. The classic example is health insurance, which may attract the sickest workers. If a similar dynamic operates with flexible workplace arrangements, then too few employers may offer such arrangements and those that do will pay a higher cost. Summers (1989) explains this as an example of asymmetric information. Suppose that providing the benefit is costly and that a firm does not have accurate information about an individual's probability of using the benefit. A firm-offered benefit attracts the workers who value it most. If the benefit is most costly to provide to these workers, the firm's cost of offering the benefit will increase. The cost would be lower if all firms offered the same benefit, allowing more workers to benefit from the increased flexibility (Levine 1991 provides a related argument). In addition, on average, adopting flexible practices likely encourages labor force participation among those workers that would otherwise find it too "costly" to work or invest in workplace skills. For example, Goldin (2006) documents that as women perceived more options for long-term future careers, their educational attainment increased. In this way, when potential workers are better able to envision a long-term attachment to the labor force, their skill development may increase.

Family-friendly practices can also help encourage better bonding between parents and children, which has been shown to lead to better outcomes for children in adulthood. For instance, researchers have shown that children of women who receive paid maternity leave earn 5 percent higher wages at age 30 (Carneiro, Loken, and Salvanes 2011). Enabling workers who are sick, or who have sick children, to stay home can also benefit others as illness is more quickly curtailed in schools and the workplace.

In decision making, firms may be best persuaded by evidence of impacts on other firms' bottom lines. An innovative paper studying the impact on firm profits tracked the announcements of new work-life balance policies (such as dependent care or flexible work arrangements) by Fortune 500 companies in *The Wall Street Journal*. The paper found that, on average, firms' stock prices rose in the days following announcements of work-life balance initiatives (Arthur 2003). Such evidence indicates that flexible practices boost investors' perceptions of the value of a firm, which may derive from their beliefs about the impact of the policies on worker productivity. It may also be due to a perception about the value of working parents and caregivers in the company and the effect of work-life balance initiatives on these employees. Greater representation of women in top management positions is associated with better firm performance on several dimensions (Catalyst 2004), and research also finds that women can help drive innovation and better target female customers and employees (Hewlett, Marshall, and Sherbin 2013).

CONCLUSION

With women and men increasingly sharing breadwinning and caregiving responsibilities, today's working families need a modern workplace—one with workplace flexibility, paid family and sick leave, access to family-supporting and work-supporting policies like quality child care and eldercare to allow them to make the choices that best fit their needs. Such policies lead to higher labor force participation, greater labor productivity and work engagement, and better allocation of talent across the economy. The International Monetary Fund and the Organisation for Economic Cooperation and Development have both identified child care policies and paid leave as important drivers of female labor force participation (Elborgh-Woytek et al. 2013). Caregivers will continue to face complex decisions about whether to combine their caregiving duties with participation in the labor force, and many will choose to stay out of the labor force or reduce their work hours in order to best meet the needs of their families. However, policies should make it easier for those who, by choice or necessity, are combining caregiving with paid work. Not only are such policies helpful to parents, but access to policies like paid leave better facilitate children's development and therefore their long-run outcomes including higher wages as adults.

While many employers have already adapted to the changing realities of the American workforce, there is still a long way to go. More than one-half of workers believe they could do their jobs better with more flexibility, and almost one-half of parents say they have passed up a job because of its conflict with family obligations. An increasing share of parents in dual-earner families report that work interferes with their home life. More than one-quarter of workers report that they have no access to any form of leave, even unpaid; less than one-half of workers have access to paid leave for the birth or adoption of a child. These numbers also contain important disparities by ethnicity, income, education, and sector of employment.

As in all business decisions, the critical factors that determine adoption of a new management strategy are the costs and benefits of a program. Almost one-third of firms cite costs or limited funds as obstacles to implementing workplace flexibility arrangements. Yet there is evidence that adopting workplace flexibility arrangements leads to significant benefits for employers, in the form of reduced turnover, improved recruitment, and increased productivity. Implementing these practices may also reduce costs for employers by improving employee health and decreasing absenteeism.

The wider adoption of such practices would result in benefits to society (in the form of improved employment outcomes and more efficient allocation of workers to employers) that may be even greater than the gains to individual firms and workers. The best available evidence suggests that encouraging more firms to consider adopting flexible practices can potentially boost productivity, improve morale, and benefit the U.S. economy as a whole. To put a number on it, if women's employment increased enough to close the male-female employment gap, that would raise GDP by 9 percent.[40]

---

[40] CEA calculated this number by raising the employment-to-population ratio and work week for women to the average level for men and applying this to a growth-accounting model that holds the average product of labor constant. For a similar calculation, see Goldman Sachs (2007), which estimates an increase of up to 9 percent.

CHAPTER 5

BUSINESS TAX REFORM AND ECONOMIC GROWTH

The U.S. tax system, for both individuals and businesses, is overdue for reform. On the individual side, the system should do more to encourage and reward work, increase the accumulation of human capital, and ensure that economic gains are widely shared. The necessary reforms should also make the system simpler and more efficient and should reduce the deficit. Business tax reform should increase productivity, output, and living standards—complementing other efforts to improve the productivity of the U.S. economy, like additional investments in infrastructure. The focus of this chapter is business tax reform; individual reforms are discussed in Box 5-3.

The U.S. corporate income tax combines the highest statutory rate among advanced economies with a base narrowed by loopholes, tax expenditures, and tax planning strategies. In addition to the corporate income tax, the United States operates a second, parallel system of business taxation for pass-through entities—businesses whose earnings are taxed on the owners' income tax returns rather than a separate entity-level return. The U.S. system of business taxation allows some companies to avoid significant tax liability, while others pay tax at a high rate. It distorts important economic decisions about where to produce, how to finance investments, and what industries and assets to invest in. The system is also too complicated, and that complexity hurts America's small businesses and allows large corporations to reduce their tax liability by shifting profits around the globe.

The current system of business taxation reduces productivity, output, and wages through its impact on the quantity of investment, the location of production and profits, the means of financing new investments, and the allocation of investment across assets and industries. The high statutory rate and complicated rules for taxing income in different countries discourage locating highly profitable investments in the United States. Reduced investment in turn reduces U.S. productivity and output. Loopholes that allow multinational firms to shift profits to low-tax jurisdictions abroad require higher taxes on domestic businesses and families. The significant tax preference for debt encourages excessive borrowing, which in turn increases bankruptcy costs and financial fragility, and thus reduces macroeconomic stability. Tax expenditures that privilege certain industries and assets encourage investment in low-return, lightly taxed projects while high-return, heavily taxed projects are ignored.

Business tax reform can increase the quantity and quality of investment in the United States by reducing the economic distortions caused by disparities in tax rates across jurisdictions, across industries, across assets, across means of financing, and across different forms of business. The quality of investment refers, not to the dollar value of investment expenditure, but to the kinds of investments American firms make. The quality of investment increases when high-return projects are prioritized over low-return projects. Quality increases when businesses choose to finance their investments using the financial products that best share risk, and not those that generate the largest tax savings. And the quality of investment increases when firms make decisions to invest in one country instead of another based on considerations such as the quality of the workforce, the strength of economic institutions, and the location of customers, rather than where the tax rates are lowest.

Tax reform is not just about removing policy-induced distortions that lead to inefficient decisions by businesses. In some carefully delineated cases, tax policy can play a role in remedying distortions fundamental to private markets that lead firms to, for example, underinvest in research or clean energy because the firm does not capture the full economy-wide benefits of their expenditures. The quality of investment also increases when businesses recognize the benefits and costs their investments create for others, such as the spillovers associated with new research insights or the harm associated with polluting activities.

Improvements in both the quantity and quality of investment increase productivity and, in doing so, increase American living standards. Since 1948, increases in productivity have more than quadrupled the amount of output each American worker generates per hour worked. If a worker has access to the most useful equipment, not the equipment that receives the best tax treatment, she or he will be able to produce more per hour worked. If firms pursue all research for which the benefits exceed the costs, workers will then be able to leverage those new innovations to increase output.

The President's approach to business tax reform reduces disparities in tax rates across jurisdictions, across industries, across assets, across means of financing, and across different forms of business. In doing so, it encourages domestic investment and increases the quality of investment and productivity. Specifically, the approach broadens the tax base, lowers the top corporate rate, and reforms the taxation of income earned abroad. It moderates the incentives to shift profits to tax havens and encourages high-return domestic investment. This approach significantly simplifies the tax system for small businesses and corrects for externalities—benefits and costs that firms' actions have on unrelated individuals. In addition, the one-time revenue that is generated by reform is used to fund a substantial, six-year increase in public infrastructure investment.

This chapter reviews the role of productivity in long-run growth and summarizes the international context for business tax reform. It then describes the President's approach to business tax reform and examines how that approach can increase productivity and output. The chapter concludes with a consideration of alternative approaches to reform.

THE SOURCES OF PRODUCTIVITY GROWTH

Long-term growth in output comes from two sources: increases in the number of hours worked and increases in the output per hour worked, otherwise known as labor productivity. Large changes in the quantity of labor are typically driven by demographic forces such as births, deaths, and immigration. For example, the movement of the baby boom generation into retirement will be a major driver of changes in the quantity of labor in the next decade (Council of Economic Advisers 2014). However, the longer-term trend in participation will also be affected by Americans' personal choices about family, work, and retirement. Chapter 3 analyzes trend changes in participation as well as other labor market challenges that may affect participation decisions. Chapter 4 examines policies affecting participation among working families in particular, including paid leave and access to more flexible work environments.

Labor productivity depends on three factors: labor quality, the amount of capital workers have at their disposal, and total factor productivity (TFP). Labor quality reflects worker characteristics such as education and experience, which generally allow workers to produce more output per hour worked. The capital stock is the land, buildings, machinery, and equipment workers have at their disposal. Increases in the quantity of capital each worker has at his or her disposal, referred to as capital deepening, also boost output per hour worked. Lastly, TFP determines the amount of output that can be produced from a given amount of capital and labor. TFP includes things like the quality of technology, which allows workers to produce more with less, as well as other difficult to measure aspects of productivity such as the quality of the match between a worker and his or her job and workers' ability to focus on their work. Put differently, growth in TFP is any increase in output not accounted for by an increase in inputs. TFP increases with scientific breakthroughs, organizational innovations, the development of new applications for existing technologies, and any efficiency improvements not uniquely associated with a single input. Figure 5-1 shows how each of these three factors has contributed to productivity growth over the last 60 years, splitting that growth into the three broad periods discussed in Chapter 1.[1]

Figure 5-1 contains three important lessons:

Productivity has increased tremendously. On average, workers in 2013 could produce more than four times as much as their counterparts more than 60 years ago. This four-fold improvement reflects the cumulative effect of annual productivity growth averaging 2.3 percent each year since 1948. Roughly one-half of the increase in productivity is due to higher TFP, about 40 percent to workers today having more capital at their disposal, and about 10 percent to increased education and training.

Annual productivity growth varied substantially over the last 60 years. Productivity growth was especially rapid in the post-war decades, slowed in the 1970s, and sped up again in the 1990s. As noted in Chapter 1, slower productivity growth since 1973 has had a very large impact on household incomes—in fact, if the 1948 to 1973 productivity growth rate had continued, incomes would have been 58 percent higher in 2013.

Variation in the growth rate of productivity is almost entirely due to variation in the growth rate of TFP. The increase in productivity due to capital deepening and improvements in labor quality varied only modestly across the three periods shown in Figure 5-1. However, variations in the growth rate of TFP were large and economically meaningful. The growth rate of TFP between 1948 and 1973, at its highest, was more than four times the growth rate of TFP between 1973 and 1995, at its lowest.

THE HISTORICAL AND INTERNATIONAL CONTEXT FOR BUSINESS TAX REFORM

Since the last major reform of the U.S. system of business taxation in 1986, the international environment has changed significantly. In the early 1980s, the top U.S. statutory corporate income tax rate was close to the average for the Organisation for Economic Cooperation and Development (OECD), an association of developed, market economies (Figure 5-2). The United States cut the corporate tax rate well below the OECD average in

---

[1] The estimates presented in Figure 5-1 differ slightly from those presented in Chapter 1 as they rely on a different data series produced by the Bureau of Labor Statistics (BLS).

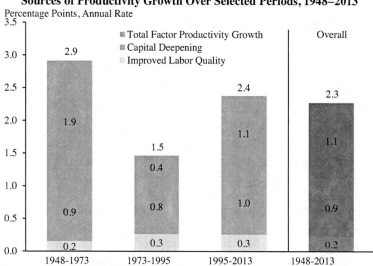

Figure 5-1
Sources of Productivity Growth Over Selected Periods, 1948–2013

Percentage Points, Annual Rate

Source: Bureau of Labor Statistics, Multifactor Productivity; CEA Calculations.

Figure 5-2
Statutory Corporate Tax Rates in the U.S. and OECD, 1981–2013

Percent

Source: OECD StatExtracts and World Tax Database; CEA Calculations.

1986, but other countries soon followed suit and, by 2014, the U.S. rate was roughly 10 percentage points above the OECD average (Figure 5-3).

This section focuses on international comparisons of corporate income taxes, as the share of large businesses accounted for by pass-through entities in the United States is unusually high relative to the share in other countries; also, the U.S. pass-through regime itself is somewhat atypical (Treasury 2007). The rates presented reflect corporate income taxes imposed by both the central government and sub-central government. In the United States, the Federal statutory corporate tax rate is 35 percent and, after accounting for their deductibility from Federal taxes, State corporate taxes increase the rate by 4 percent.

While the top U.S. statutory corporate income tax rate is the highest among OECD economies, other measures of corporate tax rates show a different picture. The effective tax rate, which accounts for differences in the definition of the taxable income across countries, is slightly below the average for the other large, advanced economies of the G-7 (Figure 5-4). The effective tax rate is the ratio of corporate taxes paid to pre-tax income. On average, for the years 2006 to 2009, corporations headquartered in the United States paid an effective tax rate, aggregated across all countries, of 27.7 percent. The average rate for the G-7 over this period was 29.2 percent.

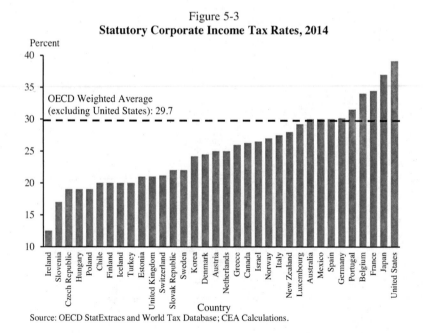

Figure 5-3
Statutory Corporate Income Tax Rates, 2014

Source: OECD StatExtracs and World Tax Database; CEA Calculations.

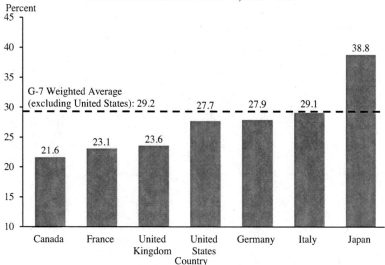

Figure 5-4
Effective Tax Rates in the G-7, 2006–2009

Percent

G-7 Weighted Average
(excluding United States): 29.2

Canada: 21.6
France: 23.1
United Kingdom: 23.6
United States: 27.7
Germany: 27.9
Italy: 29.1
Japan: 38.8

Country

Source: PwC and Business Roundtable (2011); OECD StatExtracts; CEA Calculations.

As with the statutory corporate rate, effective tax rates varied substantially across countries from a low of 21.6 percent for Canada to a high of 38.8 percent for Japan. Note, however, that several countries have enacted significant corporate tax legislation since 2006, including Canada, Germany, Japan, and the United Kingdom.

Similarly, the U.S. effective marginal tax rate is only modestly above the average for the other countries of the G-7 (Figure 5-5). The effective marginal tax rate is the tax rate that would apply to a hypothetical project earning the minimum required return sufficient to obtain financing. The U.S. effective marginal tax rate on a domestic investment in 2014 was 23.9 percent, while the average for the other G-7 countries was 20.6 percent. Importantly, the rates presented in Figure 5-5 exclude the effects of temporary policies. For example, the United States has offered a temporary bonus depreciation provision that allows firms to deduct their investment expenses more rapidly in every year since 2008, which is excluded from these estimates. Incorporating bonus depreciation into the analysis would reduce the estimated effective marginal tax rate on new investment.

Each of these tax rates—the statutory rate, the effective rate, and the effective marginal rate—are relevant for different economic decisions:

The *statutory rate* is the amount of additional tax paid on an additional dollar of profit without any accompanying changes in deductions for business expenses. It thus captures the relevant financial incentive for

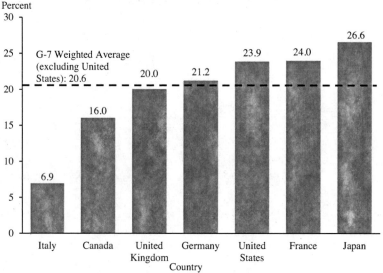

Figure 5-5
Effective Marginal Tax Rates in the G-7, 2014

Percent

G-7 Weighted Average (excluding United States): 20.6

Italy 6.9
Canada 16.0
United Kingdom 20.0
Germany 21.2
United States 23.9
France 24.0
Japan 26.6

Country

Source: U.S. Department of the Treasury; OECD StatExtracts; CEA Calculations.

decisions about tax planning strategies that shift profits between countries without changes in the underlying economic activity. Every dollar of profit moved from the United States, where it is subject to a 39-percent statutory rate, to a country with, for example, a 20-percent statutory rate would reduce corporate taxes by 19 cents.

The *effective rate* is the total amount of tax paid as a share of pre-tax income. If a company could relocate the entirety of its operations and income from one country to another, the effective tax rate would be the relevant one for making such a decision. However, because firms operate and pay corporate taxes in multiple countries, effective tax rates would generally be computed for, and apply to, decisions about locating particular projects or investments in different countries. The effective tax rate for these discrete decisions is known as the *effective average tax rate* and differs for each project depending on its precise characteristics.

The *effective marginal rate* is the effective rate for a project that generates the minimum return sufficient to obtain financing under prevailing market conditions. It is the relevant tax rate for firms deciding precisely when to stop scaling up their investment spending under the assumption that each increase in spending generates a slightly smaller return. Facing such a decision, firms will stop increasing spending when the last dollar spent generates a return just large enough to first pay tax at the effective marginal rate and then to pay investors the required return. This last dollar of investment is known as the marginal dollar of investment, leading to the label effective marginal rate.

The corporate income tax affects all of these decisions simultaneously, and the analysis of any potential approach to tax reform must consider its impact on each of them. Tax reform that seeks lower rates without reducing revenue—reform financed by closing loopholes and broadening the tax base—must prioritize between lowering the statutory rate, the effective average rate, and the effective marginal rate, as lowering any one rate reduces revenue.

The U.S. corporate income tax is often described as a tax on worldwide income and therefore out of step with the territorial systems used elsewhere. A pure worldwide system would tax all income earned anywhere in the world; in contrast, a pure territorial system would exempt all foreign income from taxation. In practice, all systems—including the U.S. corporate income tax—reflect some combination of worldwide and territorial concepts. While U.S. corporations owe tax on income earned anywhere in the world, this tax is only due if, and when, foreign earnings are paid to a U.S. parent company by its foreign subsidiaries. Taxation of foreign earnings can be deferred indefinitely by keeping the earnings in foreign subsidiaries. This aspect of the U.S. system is known as deferral and means that, in practice, the U.S. approach to corporate taxation is far from that of a pure worldwide system. (For the role of deferral in encouraging the recent wave of corporate inversions, see Box 5-1.)

Incorporating deferral and other complex rules for the taxation of U.S. multinationals into the analysis, simulations by Rosanne Altshuler and Harry Grubert (2013) illustrate how far from a worldwide system the U.S. corporate income tax is. Their analysis assumes a statutory corporate rate of 30 percent, but otherwise matches the features of current U.S. law.[2] The simulations show that the effective marginal tax rate on investments by a hypothetical U.S. multinational in a low-tax country is -24 percent after accounting for shifting of intangibles, and the effective marginal tax rate on investments in a high-tax country is 13 percent after accounting for earnings stripping (Figure 5-6). For these computations, the low-tax country is assumed to have a statutory rate of 5 percent and the high-tax country a rate of 25 percent. The activities in each country and the associated tax planning strategies correspond to typical behavior of U.S. companies in such countries. These simulations suggest that, though the United States

---

[2] The authors use a 30-percent statutory rate because "[t]here seems to be a growing consensus that the United States should reduce its corporate statutory rate in response to the dramatic and continuing decline in corporate statutory rates abroad." Thus, even though their analysis does not use the current rate, it is particularly relevant to discussions of the U.S. approach to taxing multinational corporations in the context of reform.

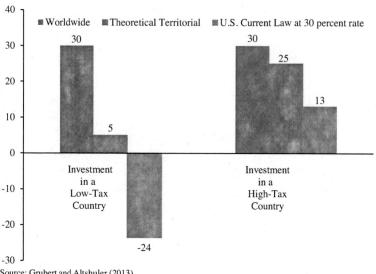

Figure 5-6
Effective Marginal Tax Rates in Several Tax Systems

Source: Grubert and Altshuler (2013).

ostensibly imposes a worldwide tax, the difference in effective marginal tax rates between high- and low-tax jurisdictions abroad can look more like a territorial system. Moreover, the tax rates in both high- and low-tax countries can be well below the rates that would apply under either a true worldwide system or even a theoretically ideal territorial system unaffected by base erosion or profit shifting.

Over the last 30 years, the dual challenges of base erosion and profit shifting have increased significantly (Clausing 2009). Base erosion refers to the disappearance of corporate income (the tax base) as a result of tax planning strategies (see Box 5-2). Profit shifting is a particular form of base erosion in which firms report profits in low-tax jurisdictions rather than in high-tax jurisdictions, reducing their global tax liability. The revenue loss attributable to earnings missing from the U.S. corporate tax base as a result of base erosion may amount to 30 percent of corporate tax receipts (Clausing 2011).

Table 5-1 updates the estimates of Gravelle (2013) that show U.S. controlled foreign corporation profits in a particular country as a share of GDP for each country. In 2010, U.S. controlled foreign corporation profits reported in Bermuda were more than 15 times the size of Bermuda's economy. Even in the Netherlands, which has a much larger economy than Bermuda, U.S. controlled foreign corporation profits amounted to 15 percent of GDP. It is unlikely that the high concentration of U.S. profits for

Box 5-1: Corporate Inversions

Under the U.S. corporate income tax system, American firms pay tax on profits earned anywhere in the world. However, these taxes are due only if, and when, the money is paid as a dividend to the U.S parent by its foreign subsidiaries. As a result, American firms have accumulated as much as $2 trillion of overseas profits. The significant and growing value of these profits has spurred interest among U.S. firms in finding ways to use or distribute them without paying tax. One strategy for avoiding tax is an inversion—a maneuver whereby a U.S. parent firm merges with a foreign parent, such that the shareholders of the foreign company own at least 20 percent of the equity in the combined entity, and then declares that the foreign company is the parent company for tax purposes. Because the original foreign subsidiaries of the U.S. firm continue to be subsidiaries of a U.S. firm, such a maneuver does not exempt their future earnings from tax. However, the new foreign parent can facilitate financial transactions that provide low-tax access to the earnings of those subsidiaries. For example, once inverted, the foreign subsidiaries can lend money directly to the new parent company without going through the U.S. parent. These transactions are known as hopscotch loans and, until recently, such loans did not trigger any tax liability since the funds never pass through the U.S. company.

The benefits of an inversion extend beyond low-tax access to the earnings of foreign subsidiaries. For example, inversions can also facilitate earnings stripping, a strategy in which firms shift profits that would be taxed in the United States into other lower-tax countries. One easy way of accomplishing earnings stripping is for an inverted U.S. corporation to borrow from its new foreign parent. The interest payments of the U.S. corporation are deductible at the high statutory rate that applies under the U.S. corporate tax, and the interest income is taxed to the foreign parent at its lower rate. Rules that restrict the ability of U.S. corporations to avoid taxation on passive income abroad limit non-inverted entities' ability to use this strategy. However, the interest income of the foreign parent is not subject to these rules; an inverted firm's ability to use this strategy is limited only by weaker rules restricting interest deductions.

In September 2014, the U.S. Department of the Treasury released a notice announcing forthcoming regulations that would limit some of the benefits of inverting. These rules restricted firms' ability to structure the hopscotch loan transactions described above, as well as making several other changes. While these actions make inversions less attractive, legislation is needed to fully address the incentives to invert—both through broader reforms that reduce the value of post-inversion tax planning strategies and specific measures that limit a company's ability to invert.

> The Administration has proposed increasing the ownership threshold that must be met for a foreign affiliate to become the parent of a U.S. company through an inversion from the current 20-percent threshold to a 50-percent threshold. The higher threshold would eliminate inversions—in which a small foreign company becomes the parent of a large U.S. company—that are not justified by business considerations other than the tax benefits.

the countries shown in Table 5-1 reflects the actual business activity of these firms rather than tax planning.

An important limitation of the international comparisons presented in this section is that they focus only on taxes imposed on corporate profits. Other taxes paid by corporations can also significantly affect the profitability of business investments. In particular, real estate taxes on land and buildings, property taxes on equipment and inventories, and sales taxes on purchases of business inputs increase both effective tax rates and effective marginal tax rates. Incorporating these factors into the analysis tends to increase tax rates in the United States relative to other countries.

Table 5-1

U.S. Controlled Foreign Corporation Profits Relative to GDP, 2010

Country	Foreign Corporation Profits Relative to GDP (%)
Bahamas	104
Bermuda	1,578
British Virgin Islands	1,009
Cayman Islands	1,430
Cyprus	13
Ireland	38
Luxembourg	103
Netherlands	15
Netherlands Antilles	25

Source: IRS Statistics of Income; United Nations; CEA calculations.

Box 5-2: Base Erosion and Profit Shifting

The related challenges of base erosion and profit shifting hurt the global economy, weaken government budgets, and heighten public concern about the equitable distribution of tax burdens. Base erosion refers to the disappearance of business income (the tax base) as a result of tax planning strategies. Examples of corporate tax planning strategies include: exploiting differences in how income or residency is defined by different countries; choosing low-tax jurisdictions to hold intellectual property and other assets; and manipulating the terms of intra-firm transactions to control where earnings are taxed. Profit shifting is one form of base erosion in which firms shift profits from one, typically high-tax country to another, typically low-tax country to reduce their overall, worldwide tax liability.

Tax planning strategies hurt the global economy because they lead to socially wasteful expenditures on the accounting, legal, and other advisory services required to structure the financial transactions and legal arrangements that minimize tax payments. Reforms that harmonize the treatment of income and deduction items across countries, as well as address other harmful tax practices, improve productivity and well-being by allowing firms to compete on the merits of their services and not the quality of their tax advisors. Historically, a primary objective for international tax negotiations was to prevent double taxation. Today, countries must solve the problem of double non-taxation, the creation of stateless income that slips through the gaps between tax systems and is not taxed in any country.

In recognition of the challenges posed by base erosion and profit shifting, the G-20 and OECD have led a coordinated international response that seeks to improve tax policy and tax administration. The OECD developed an action plan, released in July 2013 and endorsed by G-20 leaders in September 2013 (OECD 2013). The action plan articulates 15 actions and a series of deliverables—reports, recommendations, and model tax rules—to be completed by December 2015. In September 2014, the OECD released a set of recommendations to address 7 of the 15 actions (OECD 2014). Discussion drafts for the remaining eight items are scheduled to be released over the course of 2015.

Recent announcements show that the OECD Base Erosion and Profit Shifting Project, in combination with other legal and economic developments, is having an impact on international tax policy. In October 2014, Ireland announced policy changes that would effectively shut down a widely used tax avoidance strategy, the Double Irish, which allows some multinational firms to legally pay extremely low effective tax rates (Noonan 2014). The Double Irish and its variants let firms funnel profits through Ireland into low- or zero-tax jurisdictions and dramatically reduce the tax paid on the associated sales. The strategy relies on a provision of Irish law that allows firms to incorporate in Ireland while being resident for tax purposes in other countries. Like other mismatches between the tax systems that operate in different countries, this mismatch in residence and tax treatment facilitates base erosion and profit shifting.

Subsequently, in November 2014, the United Kingdom and Germany reached agreement on a joint proposal for dealing with preferential intellectual property (IP) regimes. The proposal would require the United Kingdom to close its current preferential IP regime to new entrants in June 2016 and to abolish it entirely by June 2021. Preferential IP regimes can fall under the heading of harmful tax practices: policies that seek to attract highly mobile income with no economic relationship to the taxing country by offering very low rates on that income. Such policies are harmful because they encourage firms to aggressively shift profits between countries solely to reduce tax liability. The agreement between the United Kingdom and Germany endorsed an approach that allows countries to offer reduced rates for IP provided that the property derives from significant economic activity in the country. This approach ensures that countries can implement their preferred policies to promote innovation and economic development, but discourages policies designed primarily to siphon off tax revenue from other countries.

The action plan also includes efforts to neutralize hybrid mismatches, limit treaty shopping, reduce earnings stripping through intra-firm financial transactions, stop the creation of stateless income, and improve dispute resolution, among others. As one example of these efforts, consider the action item on hybrid mismatches. A hybrid mismatch occurs when a particular financial instrument or business entity is treated differently by two different countries. For example, a financial security may be treated as a debt security in one country and an equity security in another. In certain cases, companies can obtain two deductions for one act of borrowing or generate a deduction without a corresponding income inclusion. The Base Erosion and Profit Shifting Project proposes to combat such mismatches by increasing the coherence of international tax laws. Concretely, this action item encourages steps such as drafting model treaties, encouraging member countries to adopt laws that deny domestic deductions for payments also deductible in another jurisdiction, and issuing guidance for tie-breaker rules if multiple countries apply incompatible rules to a single transaction.

The Administration firmly supports the G-20/OECD Base Erosion and Profit Shifting Project and continues to actively engage with the international community to develop new and effective solutions to the tax compliance challenges raised by our modern economy. The President's Budget for Fiscal Year 2016 also proposes specific changes to U.S. tax law that will make it harder to create stateless income or achieve double non-taxation. These proposals will benefit the American public because, when gaps between tax systems allow firms to shift profits out of the United States and reduce their tax liability, the burden of financing our public programs shifts to other businesses and individuals. Moreover, as home to some of the world's most recognizable and innovative companies, we benefit when companies are able to play by clear, well-defined rules.

THE PRESIDENT'S APPROACH TO BUSINESS TAX REFORM

The President's approach to business tax reform seeks to improve the quantity and quality of U.S. investment and thus productivity and output. The reserve for revenue-neutral business tax reform in the President's Fiscal Year 2016 Budget details numerous specific reform proposals, including a comprehensive discussion of the President's international reform proposals. The Administration's overall approach to reform has been described previously in *The President's Framework for Business Tax Reform*, released in 2012. The President's approach would:

Cut the corporate rate to 28 percent, paid for by closing loopholes and structural reforms. At 28 percent, down from 35 percent, the U.S. corporate rate would be generally in line with other large OECD economies. The rate cut would be paid for in part by closing loopholes—provisions that benefit a specific industry without a sound justification in broader spillovers. The special provisions for oil and gas that President Ronald Reagan unsuccessfully targeted for elimination in his tax reform plan are one clear example. Closing loopholes alone, however, would not raise sufficient funds to pay for the rate reduction nor would it sufficiently address the disparities in tax rates across means of financing and different business activities that reduce the quality of investment. As a result, this approach would also require additional structural reforms: addressing accelerated depreciation—deductions for the depreciation of tangible capital at a more rapid pace than the assets lose value—and reducing the tax preference for debt-financed investment. Sound combinations of these measures would result in more similar taxation of different types of investment and forms of financing.

Make permanent, expand, and reform key incentives. The test for any incentive is whether it is motivated by a positive externality, which, as discussed below, leads to inefficiently low levels of the corresponding business activity in the private economy. The *Framework* identified three categories of incentives as passing this test: incentives for research, for clean energy, and for manufacturing. The reserve for revenue-neutral tax reform in the FY 2016 Budget includes proposals that would make permanent and improve the Research and Experimentation Tax Credit and the Renewable Electricity Production Tax Credit, make permanent the Investment Tax Credit for clean energy projects, and provide a new investment tax credit for projects that provide for carbon capture and sequestration. The Budget also includes a fee on large, highly leveraged financial institutions, to reflect the negative externalities that financial firm size and leverage can impose on the broader economy.

Simplify and reduce taxes for small businesses. Small businesses are disproportionately organized as pass-through entities, and, while many base-broadening reforms apply to both corporate and pass-through businesses, rate reductions only benefit corporations. The reserve for revenue-neutral reform in the FY 2016 Budget includes proposals that would simplify complex accounting rules for small businesses and allow more generous depreciation deductions for tangible investment for small businesses, both simplifying and reducing their taxes. With appropriate reforms for small businesses like these, business tax reform can be implemented on a stand-alone basis without broader individual reform.

Establish a hybrid international system with a minimum tax on the earnings of foreign subsidiaries. The current U.S. system applies the full statutory rate to foreign earnings, but only if, and when, those earnings are repatriated. The President's approach would replace the current system of indefinite deferral with a new hybrid system based on a minimum tax. The minimum tax would apply a 19-percent rate to the active foreign earnings of U.S. companies at the time the income is earned. Once the minimum tax has been paid, earnings could be repatriated without incurring any further tax liability. Foreign tax credits would be allowed only against the minimum tax liability for the country in which the foreign tax is paid and for only 85 percent of the amount of foreign taxes paid. Firms would also receive an allowance for corporate equity. This allowance, a deduction from the minimum tax base, would provide businesses with a modest return on equity invested in active business assets. This system would be more effective at preventing base erosion than the current system and would reduce the importance of tax considerations for some location decisions, while also having the potential to improve the global competitiveness of U.S. corporations. A smarter hybrid reflects a balance of competing neutrality concepts in rejecting both a pure territorial system—one that exempts all foreign income from taxation—and a pure worldwide system. It would also eliminate the inefficiencies associated with the ability to choose the timing of repatriations under the current system. This comprehensive reform proposal stands in contrast to proposals for a repatriation holiday, which would exacerbate the inefficiencies of the current international system while also losing revenue.

Impose a toll charge on the existing stock of accumulated foreign profits as part of the transition to the new international system and use the revenue to finance infrastructure investment. Under current law, the existing stock of accumulated profits is subject to tax if repatriated but need not be repatriated. Under the new system, repatriation would incur no tax liability. To avoid a windfall from the transition, the President's Budget proposes a one-time toll charge of 14 percent on accumulated foreign profits. The revenue raised by this toll would be used to pay for infrastructure investment.

Add nothing to the deficit in either the short or long run. Most plans consistent with the President's approach generate one-time revenue during the transition to the new system. This transition revenue can obscure significant future revenue loses if reform is viewed from a short-run perspective. It is essential to measure the revenue impact of business tax reform when fully in effect so that reform does not add to the deficit in the longer term. A long-term view is particularly important when reform includes measures like moving to economic depreciation, which shifts the timing of revenue collected but not the total amount of revenue. Since that shift pulls revenue forward into the traditional 10-year budget window, it results in inflated savings. The President's approach to business tax reform would not add to the deficit in either the short or long run.

THE POTENTIAL FOR BUSINESS TAX REFORM TO BOOST PRODUCTIVITY

Productivity is a primary long-run determinant of living standards, together with factors like how growth is shared and who is able to participate in the economy that are discussed in Chapter 1 and throughout this Report. The President's approach to business tax reform boosts productivity and living standards through four channels: encouraging domestic investment, improving the quality of investment, reducing the inefficiencies of the international tax system, and investing in infrastructure. This section reviews each of these channels in turn.

Encouraging Domestic Investment

Business tax reform can increase domestic investment in two ways. First, reform can reduce effective marginal tax rates for businesses, which

Box 5-3: Improving the Tax Code for Families

The President's approach to business tax reform complements his plan to improve the tax code for individuals and families, making it fairer by eliminating some of the biggest loopholes and using the savings to pay for investments that help middle-class families get ahead—part of an overall approach the President has termed "middle-class economics."

As in previous years, the Budget baseline assumes the continuation of the expansions of the Earned Income Tax Credit (EITC) and the Child Tax Credit enacted in the American Recovery and Reinvestment Act of 2009, benefitting 16 million families with 29 million children. Studies have shown that previous EITC expansions have significantly increased employment among eligible individuals, and the Recovery Act expansions implement the same pro-work model (Executive Office of the President and U.S. Treasury Department 2014). In addition, recent research suggests that the EITC and Child Tax Credit can improve health and educational outcomes for the children whose parents receive the credits (Chetty, Friedman, and Rockoff 2011; Hoynes, Miller, and Simon 2013; Manoli and Turner 2014).

Simplify and expand child care tax benefits. The Budget proposes to make the Child and Dependent Care Tax Credit available in full for families with incomes up to $120,000 and expands the credit for families with children under age five to pay for one-half the cost of care up to $6,000 (a $3,000 maximum credit). This proposal is designed to make it easier for families to afford high-quality child care because that both helps working families manage what is often their largest expense and invests more in the next generation by supporting child development. Under current law, there are two types of tax benefits for families: a tax credit for child and dependent care expenses and employer-provided tax-preferred flexible spending accounts to pay for child care expenses. For some families, obtaining the maximum benefit from current policies requires using both the credit and a flexible spending account. The Budget repeals dependent care flexible spending accounts so that families need not perform calculations to compare tax benefits under multiple competing tax benefits and invests the savings in a single, improved child care tax credit.

Support employment. Building on the EITC and Child Tax Credit expansions enacted in the Recovery Act, the Budget proposes an expansion of the EITC for workers without children and for noncustodial parents. The EITC is a highly effective antipoverty policy, but the maximum credit for workers without children is only about $500. Expanding the credit for this population would benefit 13 million low-income workers and extend the pro-work impacts of the policy to a broader population

(Executive Office of the President and U.S. Department of the Treasury 2014).

The Budget also proposes a tax benefit based on the earnings of the lower-earning spouse in two-earner families. When both spouses work, families incur additional expenses for commuting, professional obligations, child care, and elder care. When layered on top of other costs, including Federal and State taxes, these work-related costs can lead to a high implicit tax rate on work, especially for parents of young children and couples caring for aging parents (Kearney and Turner 2013). This proposal for a new second-earner credit helps ensure that the tax code supports work by offsetting a portion of the additional costs that a family incurs when both spouses are working, such as commuting and child-care expenses. The new $500 second-earner tax benefit would benefit 24 million American families.

Consolidate and improve tax benefits for education. Building on bipartisan Congressional proposals, the Budget proposes a significant simplification of the tax benefits for education combined with an expansion targeted to those individuals least likely to attend college without financial aid. In most cases, students and their families can claim one of three tax benefits based on current educational expenses: the American Opportunity Tax Credit, the Lifetime Learning Credit, and the tuition and fees deduction. Choosing and claiming education tax benefits can require complex calculations and, under current law, the benefits often flow to those families in which children are most likely to attend college even without any additional assistance. One analysis found that 27 percent of individuals claiming the tuition and fees deduction would have received a larger benefit if they claimed a tax credit instead (GAO 2012). The Budget proposes that the three tax benefits based on current educational expenses be combined into a single, improved American Opportunity Tax Credit.

Expand access to workplace retirement savings. The Budget also calls for the creation of a new automatic Individual Retirement Account (IRA) for workers whose employers do not offer another retirement plan. The automatic IRA would guarantee every American working at a firm with more than 10 employees access to easy, payroll-based retirement savings. Americans face a daunting array of choices when it comes to their retirement savings, and, while some workers are automatically enrolled in a retirement savings plan by their employer with an option to opt out, others have to open an account, manage contributions, and research and select investments on their own. However, the evidence is clear: individuals with access to an easy way to save at work will save, and those who lack such access rarely receive any tax benefits for retirement at all (Choi et al. 2004). The automatic IRA would allow individuals to begin saving for retirement without needing to confront complicated choices about which tax-preferred vehicle to use and what portfolio to select.

Reform the taxation of capital income. The Budget proposes to close the single largest loophole allowing capital income to go untaxed: the step up in basis at death. Families that spend down their wealth during their lifetimes must pay tax on their capital gains as they sell their assets, but the tiny fraction of families wealthy enough that they never need to sell their assets can pass those assets to their heirs without ever paying the tax on the capital gain. Moreover, if the heirs ever sell the assets, the cost at which they are considered to have acquired the assets is the value at the time the assets are inherited. This treatment creates an inefficiency known as the lock-in effect in which older individuals for whom the best course of action would be to sell their assets and invest in a new enterprise, instead hold on to the assets to avoid paying any capital gains tax. In addition, the President's Budget would increase the top tax rate on capital gains and dividends from 23.8 percent under current law to 28 percent.

Close loopholes and limit tax expenditures. Consistent with previous Budgets, the FY 2016 Budget proposes a limit on tax expenditures for high-income families. Deductions and exclusions from income generate a tax benefit for each dollar of the tax-advantaged activity equal to the individual's marginal rate. Because marginal rates typically rise with income, these tax benefits, such as the mortgage interest deduction, charitable deduction, and deduction for State and local taxes, provide more value to high-income families than for middle-income families and can lead to inefficiencies by excessively subsidizing certain taxpayer behavior. The FY 2016 Budget proposes to limit the value of these tax benefits to 28 percent. If a taxpayer's marginal rate is 35 percent—such that under current law a dollar of tax-preferred activity generates 35 cents of tax savings—under the proposal it would generate only 28 cents. By reducing the tax savings associated with these deductions, the proposal reduces the corresponding inefficiencies. In addition, the Budget includes additional proposals that would implement the Buffett Rule, the principle that no household making over $1 million each year should pay a smaller share of their income in taxes than middle-class families pay.

will increase investment, the size of the capital stock, and output. Second, reform can reduce the effective average tax rate on highly profitable business investments, which will encourage firms to locate mobile, high-return investments in the United States.

As discussed above, the effective marginal tax rate is the ratio of tax paid to pre-tax income for a project yielding the minimum required return to obtain financing under prevailing market conditions. When effective marginal rates are higher, potential projects need to generate more income if the business is to pay the tax and still provide investors with the required return. Businesses will therefore limit their activities to higher-return projects. Thus, all else equal, a higher effective marginal rate for businesses will tend to reduce the level of investment, and a lower effective marginal rate will tend to encourage additional projects and a larger capital stock.[3] Increases in the capital available for each worker's use, also referred to as capital deepening, boost productivity, wages, and output.

One approach to business tax reform would prioritize changes that reduce effective marginal tax rates for businesses. The core of such a reform is allowing firms to immediately deduct the full cost of their investments, known as expensing. Expensing reduces the effective tax rate on equity-financed investments that generate the minimum required return to zero. That is, it reduces the effective marginal tax rate on equity-financed investments to zero. However, a corporate tax system with expensing would continue to impose a positive tax on investments that generate a higher return.[4] In contrast, a reform that reduces the effective marginal tax rate to zero by lowering the statutory rate to zero would eliminate taxation on high-return investments as well and thus come at a much greater revenue loss. An additional benefit of an approach oriented around expensing is that it cuts taxes only on new investments. Investments made in the past would be unaffected. Because tax cuts today do not spur additional investment in the past, the revenue loss associated with tax cuts on past investment spurs no additional investment and generates no increase in productivity. (See Box 5-4 for a discussion of the use of expensing as a temporary policy during economic downturns.)

However, while expensing has a number of attractive features, the exclusive focus on the marginal investment misses several critical points that are increasingly important in the modern, global economy. Firms face other important decisions that are also affected by the business tax system. To take one example, consider a firm deciding where to locate a plant. When a project's return substantially exceeds investors' required return, there is no

---

[3] See, for example, Cummins et al. (1994), Chirinko et al. (1999), Hassett and Hubbard (2002), Hassett and Newmark (2008).

[4] The discussion in this section focuses on business income taxes in isolation. Even with expensing, the effective marginal tax rate could remain positive as a result of other taxes, such as sales and property taxes. While incorporating other taxes into the analysis would affect the level of tax, they would not affect any of the conclusions about the changes in tax rates resulting from the policy changes discussed in this section.

question a firm will pursue the project. But the firm has flexibility over the choice of country. For this decision, the value of accelerated depreciation deductions is small relative to the profit the plan generates. The tax on these higher returns, sometimes referred to as excess returns, will depend largely on the statutory rate. As the excess returns grow in size, the relevant tax rate converges to the statutory rate. These types of investment location decisions are increasingly important in an interconnected global economy, and may be particularly important for the type of investment we most want to attract and retain (Devereux and Griffith 1998, 2003).

An alternative approach to reform therefore focuses on reducing the statutory rate to reduce the effective average tax rate on highly profitable investments. The effective average tax rate is the ratio of taxes paid to pre-tax profits for a particular investment. If an investment yields only enough to pay the required return after taxes, the effective average tax rate on that investment is equal to the effective marginal tax rate. However, if the investment return exceeds that minimum amount, the effective average tax rate on the investment exceeds the effective marginal tax rate. Therefore, reductions in the statutory rate are essential to encourage additional internationally mobile, high-return investments in the United States.

Moreover, many of the disparities in tax rates across industries and assets, across means of financing, and across organizational forms that damage the quality of investment (discussed next) are reduced at lower statutory rates. Lower statutory rates can also relieve some of the otherwise irreducible tension between capital export neutrality and capital ownership neutrality in international taxation (discussed below). Finally, it is worth considering the nearly universal view among business people and tax practitioners that the statutory rate is particularly salient in business decisionmaking.

In total, given the tension between reform that exclusively targets the effective marginal tax rate by accelerating depreciation and reform that lowers the statutory tax rate with an eye toward attracting mobile, high-return investment and reducing other distortions, the President's approach to business tax reform targets the statutory rate. Such an approach encourages additional domestic investment by reducing the disparity in tax rates across jurisdictions and also reduces disparities in tax rates across industry, asset, means of financing, and organizational form.

Improving the Quality of Investment

It is not just the quantity of investment that matters for the economy, but also the quality. Quality does not mean more expensive, higher-tech machinery, but instead means that each dollar is invested in the area where it generates the highest return and in the form that most efficiently allocates risks and managerial talents.[5] The quality of investment depends, not on the level of taxation, but on its form. In particular, maximizing the quality of investment requires a tax system that does not distort business decisions except in the cases where markets, by themselves, would not result in optimal outcomes.

Reducing Distortions in the Allocation of Investment by Industry and Asset. Targeted tax preferences lead to dispersion in tax rates across industries and assets. According to the Congressional Budget Office (CBO), effective marginal tax rates for businesses subject to the corporate income range from 12 percent for the broadcasting and telecommunications industry to 25 percent for certain manufacturing sectors, motion picture and sound recording, and some financial sectors (CBO 2014). As a result of these disparities, for any given level of the capital stock, firms will pursue lower-return projects in tax-preferred sectors rather than higher-return projects in tax-disadvantaged sectors. These disparities in tax rates also exist across asset types, and the cross-asset disparities can be much larger. CBO estimates that the effective marginal tax rate on mining structures is only 1 percent while the effective marginal tax rate on prepackaged software is 30 percent.

By reducing these distortions, the economy can become more productive even with no change in the level of investment and savings. One recent study concluded that 4 percent of the aggregate capital stock appears to be misallocated as a result of corporate tax distortions (Fatica 2013). Inefficient capital allocation lowers productivity and living standards (Auerbach and Hassett 1992). The President's approach to reform would take significant steps to reduce the disparities in tax rates across industry and asset. For example, the FY 2016 Budget calls for the elimination of numerous fossil fuel preferences that not only advantage fossil fuel production in general, but also pick winners and losers among fossil fuel technologies. The Budget also proposes repeal of an excise tax credit for certain distilled spirits that can lead to distortions even within a relatively small class of production activities.

Reducing Distortions in the Financing of Investment. The current U.S. system of business taxation imposes a substantially higher tax burden on equity-financed investment than debt-financed investment. Tax reform that reduces this disparity can reduce overleveraging, which increases financial fragility since firms have less of a cushion in downturns, and prevent fire

---

[5] In Chapter 4 and throughout this *Report*, policies are discussed that can help ensure that workers are better allocated to the activities in which they will be most productive. For example, implementing policies that reduce unnecessary distortions in workers' choices, such as improving work-family balance, result in more workers choosing jobs based on where they will be most productive.

Box 5-4: Temporary Countercyclical Policies to Promote Investment

Policies that temporarily reduce effective marginal tax rates can play an important role in increasing the quantity of investment and output in the short run, when the economy is operating below its potential. One example of such a policy is the bonus depreciation provision that was enacted on an emergency basis to help combat the Great Recession. Bonus depreciation accelerates the timing of the depreciation deductions firms take for their tangible investment; it operates as a de facto interest-free loan—firms get larger deductions today, reducing current tax payments, and smaller deductions in the future, increasing future tax payments.

When credit markets seized up during the financial crisis, some businesses had difficulty borrowing at any interest rate. As a result, if they did not have sufficient cash on hand to finance all of their ongoing projects, they had to reduce investment below their desired level. Bonus depreciation moderated the economic damage of dysfunctional credit markets by providing firms making at least some new investment with a substantial infusion of cash that they could use to increase investment further. Research by Eric Zwick and James Mahon (2014) finds that bonus depreciation increased investment by 30 percent between 2008 and 2010, with the largest effects among financially constrained firms. These temporary business tax cuts contributed to the fact that business investment has increased at a 5.3-percent annual rate over the course of this economic recovery, which is notably faster than the pace seen in the 2000s recovery.

Moreover, while firms limited by borrowing constraints could direct every dollar of this cash infusion into new investment, the cost to the Federal Government was only the interest charge incurred by deferring a tax payment that would have been due today into the future. Because interest rates on Federal debt fell at the outset of the crisis and rates have remained low since that time, the cost of financing the implicit loan has been modest. As a result, the impact on output per dollar cost to the government of stimulus policies like this one can be quite high.

This same logic applies to targeted policies that expand expensing for small businesses. Bonus depreciation allows firms to deduct a portion of their investment expenses immediately; expensing allows them to deduct the entire cost. Small businesses are more likely to be credit constrained than large businesses. This logic also helps explain why policies such as extending net operating loss carrybacks, which allows firms to take deductions for operating losses immediately that they would otherwise not be able to claim until future years, may be effective in spurring investment in the midst of a financial crisis even though such policies do not affect the effective marginal tax rate in standard economic models.

Permanent business tax reform, however, focuses on long-run growth, not short-term challenges. The overall strengthening of the economy, combined with the fact that more credit is flowing to businesses, means both the effectiveness and desirability of bonus depreciation are considerably less today than they were in the recent past. Moreover, making bonus depreciation permanent—or indefinitely extending it—would cost more than $200 billion over the next 10 years. As a result, the President's Budget would allow bonus depreciation to lapse at the end of 2014.

sales, contagion, and larger and less efficient macroeconomic fluctuations (de Mooij 2011, Slemrod 2009). Firms' decisions with regard to financing their investments also affect bankruptcy risk, the extent to which investment risk is distributed in the population, and potentially also the management quality of the firm itself (Weichenrieder and Klautke 2008). The tax advantage for interest arises because firms can deduct interest payments, but not dividend payments, from taxable income, while individuals must pay tax on both interest and dividend income, though they pay tax on dividends at a reduced rate.

The Treasury Department estimates that the effective marginal tax rate on equity-financed investment is 27.3 percent, while the effective marginal tax rate on debt-financed investment is -38.9 percent (Figure 5-7). (Tax rates can be negative if the tax benefits of the activity, such as additional credits or deductions, exceed the additional tax paid on the associated income. In the case of debt-financed investment, the combination of interest deductions and accelerated depreciation more than offset the tax paid at the corporate level.) The Treasury Department estimates that, as of 2014, the United States had the second-lowest tax rate on debt-financed investment in machinery in the OECD and the largest debt-equity disparity for such investments. Even taking into account individual-level taxes, which tax equity returns more lightly than interest payments, the disparity is still large, with a 35.5 percent tax rate for equity investment and a -0.2 percent rate for debt. By reducing the statutory rate, the President's approach to business tax reform would moderate the debt-equity disparity. Since the statutory rate determines the value of an additional deduction, a reduction in the statutory rate reduces the value of the deduction for interest payments. Additional reforms to the treatment of interest expense could further moderate the disparity.

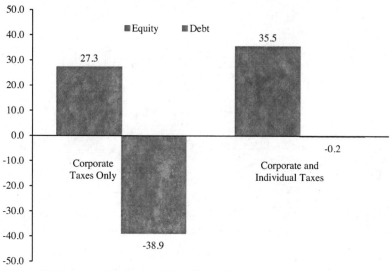

Figure 5-7
Effective Marginal Tax Rates by Source of Financing, 2014

Source: U.S. Department of the Treasury, Office of Tax Analysis.

Addressing Positive and Negative Externalities of Business Behavior.
Business activity often generates spillovers that impact other firms and
the general public, even when they are not involved in the activity. These
spillover effects are known as externalities, and can be either positive or
negative. For example, future generations of Americans benefit from the
research and development activity we undertake today in the form of new
products and services, which they will be able to enjoy, and the higher wages
resulting from increased productivity. Research and development generates
positive externalities. Polluting activities, such as burning fossil fuels, generate negative externalities through increases in carbon dioxide emissions and
particulate matter.

The quality of American investment is maximized when firms'
financial incentives to make particular investments reflect the externalities
those investments impose on others. Business tax reform can play a role in
aligning the social and private incentives for different activities by appropri-
ately subsidizing or penalizing activities where research conclusively estab-
lishes positive or negative spillovers. *The President's Framework for Business
Tax Reform* identified three areas where targeted incentives are appropriate:
research and development, clean energy, and manufacturing. The FY 2016
Budget identifies one further area where a tax is appropriate: highly leveraged financial firms.

Numerous studies find that the total returns to research and development are significantly larger than the private returns earned by the investors who fund it (Hall, Mairesse, and Mohnen 2010; Tyson and Linden 2012). This evidence suggests that the social returns range from one to two times the private returns, a disparity which leads to private-sector underinvestment in the absence of policies such as the Research and Experimentation Tax Credit. Studies that directly evaluate the Research and Experimentation Tax Credit find that each dollar of foregone tax revenue through the credit generally causes firms to invest at least one dollar in research and development (Hall 1995; Hall and Van Reenen 2000; Executive Office of the President and U.S. Department of the Treasury 2012).

While energy production is essential for the modern economy, polluting activities also pose significant harm. Greenhouse gas emissions will lead to significant environmental costs for future generations and other pollutants, such as particulate matter and ozone, lead to immediate health consequences. Appropriate subsidies for clean energy can help address these challenges and ensure that Americans benefit from high-quality investment in the energy sector. (See Chapter 6 for additional discussion of the Administration's energy strategy.)

Spillovers also provide the argument for policies that focus specifically on the manufacturing sector. Encouraging manufacturing investment and production may support higher-wage jobs. Investment in new production capacity and proximity to the manufacturing process create spillovers across firms and industries, leading to the ideas, capabilities, and technologies that enable innovation (Greenstone, Hornbeck, and Moretti 2010). To the degree these effects are operating in the economy, targeted incentives for manufacturing investment would be justified.

The FY 2016 Budget includes a fee on large, highly leveraged financial institutions. This fee would apply to banks and other financial institutions with assets of at least $50 billion, affecting approximately 100 firms. Excessive leverage entails potentially serious costs to American families and other businesses in cases of default, and the problem is most acute in the financial sector, where balance sheets may be particularly fragile. Excessive borrowing may arise because these costs are not entirely borne by the firms deciding how much to borrow. By increasing the cost to firms and therefore discouraging excessively risky financing decisions for large financial institutions, the financial fee will reduce the resources devoted to addressing the corresponding damages of default and increase American families' wellbeing.

Reducing Distortions in the Choice of Business Form. Business owners can choose between several different legal structures for their operations.

For tax purposes, the primary distinction is between the C corporation, a corporation subject to the corporate income tax, and alternative structures treated as pass-through entities. Many rules, such as those for determining depreciation deductions, are similar for C corporations and pass-through entities. However, there are important differences, the most notable of which are the rate structure and the treatment of distributions. The top Federal corporate tax rate is 35 percent while the top individual tax rate is 39.6 percent. Thus, corporations pay at a maximum rate of 35 percent while owners of pass-through entities pay a maximum rate of 39.6 percent on their business earnings. However, distributions to business owners are tax-free for the owners of pass-through businesses and taxable for the owners of C corporations.

Overall, the tax system currently advantages large pass-through entities over large C corporations. This advantage arises because the combination of corporate income taxes and individual income taxes faced by owners of a C corporation exceeds the single layer of taxation faced by owners of a pass-through entity. As a result, according to the Treasury Department's analysis shown in Figure 5-8, C corporations face a 30.3 percent effective marginal tax rate while pass-through entities face a 25.2 percent rate. Similar estimates by the Congressional Budget Office put the effective tax rate for C corporations at 31 percentage points and the rate for pass-through entities at 27 percentage points (CBO 2014).

As the tax treatment of corporate and pass-through businesses is not identical, the tax system encourages firms to change their corporate structure in order to reduce their tax liability. Empirical research confirms that these differences induce changes in the ownership structure of firms.[6] By changing the legal structures under which businesses operate relative to what they would be in the absence of these taxes, the distortion in business form reduces productivity and output. For example, in most cases, publicly traded businesses are taxed as C corporations. However, the tax bias against C corporations may discourage some businesses from accessing public capital markets and therefore lead to inefficient ownership structures.

The difference between the top corporate tax rate and the top individual tax rate has changed over time, and the increase in this disparity in the late 1980s—when the top corporate rate went from 4 percentage points above the individual rate to 6 percentage points below—led to a large shift in the distribution of revenue across business forms (CBO 2012). The share of business receipts accounted for by C corporations has continued to fall since that time as a result of other tax and non-tax changes in the economy.

---

[6] See, for example, Goolsbee (1998, 2004), Gordon and MacKie-Mason (1994), and MacKie-Mason and Gordon (1997).

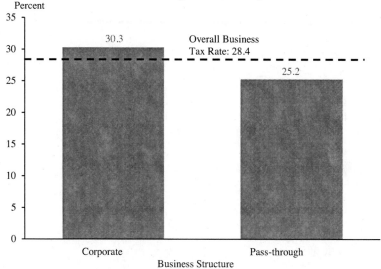

Figure 5-8
Effective Marginal Tax Rates, 2014

Source: U.S. Department of the Treasury, Office of Tax Analysis.

Overall, since 1980, the C corporation share of business receipts has fallen from nearly 90 percent to just above 60 percent (Figure 5-9). To the degree this trend has been driven by tax considerations, it represents an inefficient way for businesses to choose to organize themselves and a bias against the C corporate form. By reducing the statutory rate on C corporations, the President's approach to business tax reform would reduce the current bias against investment in the corporate form.

Reducing the Inefficiencies of the International Tax System

Business tax reform can also increase productivity and output by reducing disparities in tax rates across countries and across activities. The structure of production processes, corporate ownership relations, and intra-firm financing are all influenced by tax considerations. Higher tax rates on corporate earnings in a particular country reduce investment in that country.[7] Because corporate income tax liability can depend on the country of residence of a business's corporate parent, corporate taxes can also affect the ownership structure of firms. One example of this effect is the series of high-profile corporate inversions—rearrangements of the ownership structure of U.S. corporations so as to obtain a foreign parent for tax purposes—that

---

[7] See, for example, Cummins and Hubbard (1995), Devereux and Griffith (1998, 2003), Desai et al. (2004), Grubert and Mutti (1991, 2000), Hines (1996, 1999).

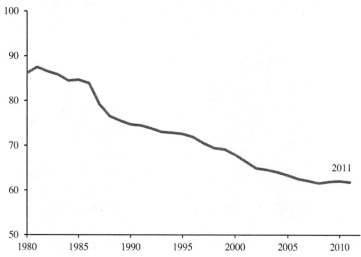

Figure 5-9
C Corporation Share of Total Business Receipts, 1980–2011

Note: RICs and REITs excluded from both C corporation share and total.
Source: IRS Statistics of Income; CEA calculations.

has received significant press attention over the last year (see Box 5-1). In addition, differences in tax rates across countries can lead firms to engage in complicated financial transactions to shift profits from high-tax countries to low-tax countries (Bartelsman and Beetsma 2003, Huizinga and Laeven 2008, Dharmapala 2014).

Unfortunately, achieving neutrality with respect to all of these business decisions simultaneously is difficult because, for any country acting alone, reforms that move toward neutrality on one dimension often move away from neutrality on another. For example, a firm will structure its production processes in an efficient manner across countries if it pays the same tax rate in every country. This neutrality concept is known as capital export neutrality. On the other hand, a local firm will be owned by the parent that generates the most economic value if all parent companies face the same tax rate on local production regardless of which country the parent firm is based in. This concept is referred to as capital ownership neutrality. Under the first objective, features of the current U.S. tax system such as indefinite deferral—which allows firms to defer paying tax on foreign income until it is repatriated—are a problem and should be eliminated. Under the second objective, foreign income should be exempt from taxation entirely, not just deferred. Moving in either direction makes the other problem worse. Moreover, these two notions of neutrality are only two of many widely discussed notions of neutrality when it comes to the taxation of multinational firms.

The President's hybrid approach to international taxation reflects a sensible compromise between competing neutrality concepts, moderates the challenges of base erosion and profit shifting, and reduces inefficiencies generated by the current system of indefinite deferral. By imposing a minimum level of tax, the value of setting up shell corporations in tax havens with tax rates near zero is dramatically reduced. Under current law, a firm might establish a subsidiary in a low- or zero-tax jurisdiction and then arrange its affairs so that as much income is reported by that subsidiary as possible. However, the President's approach would impose a minimum tax of 19 percent on earnings in every country, paid when the income is earned. Thus, while a firm would see a modest benefit if it shifts profits from a country with a tax rate above 19 percent to a country with a tax rate below that level, the incentive to find tax havens that offer a zero tax rate is substantially reduced.

In isolation, a minimum tax might encourage other countries to target subsidiaries of U.S. multinationals for specific taxes intended to soak up the revenue of the minimum tax. While treaty provisions limit the ability of foreign governments to target American firms by virtue of their being American firms, a modest reduction in the value of foreign tax credits for purposes of the minimum tax computation further protects against efforts by other countries to soak up the minimum tax revenue. This reduction ensures that U.S. corporations are not completely indifferent to the level of tax, while achieving the objective of dramatically reducing the impact of rate differentials across countries.

An allowance for corporate equity for purposes of computing the minimum tax ensures that American firms can compete on an even footing anywhere in the world when it comes to productive investment. Thus, the minimum tax would include a deduction for firms based on their equity investments abroad. This allowance would serve to reduce effective marginal tax rates on American firms when it comes to buying foreign businesses or performing productive activity abroad.

Finally, tax-free repatriation means that firms will no longer have an incentive to stockpile profits in their foreign affiliates. Instead, once they have paid the minimum tax, they could repatriate their earnings at any time without any additional tax liability. Critically, the President's approach to business tax reform would allow tax-free repatriation under a fully reformed system. Allowing a repatriation holiday under the current system would both lose revenue and exacerbate its inefficiencies, compounding our existing challenges.

While the harms of so-called trapped cash can be over-stated, under the President's minimum tax proposal there would no longer be any reason for it to exist, provided the existing stock of accumulated profits is effectively taxed at the outset. However, allowing tax-free repatriation of existing profits—which would incur tax if repatriated today—would provide an unmerited windfall. To avoid this outcome, implementation of the minimum tax and tax-free repatriation would be accompanied by a toll charge on accumulated profits. These profits could then be repatriated with no additional tax under the new system.

Investing in Infrastructure

Business tax reform is part of the President's broader approach to improving the economy and raising productivity. The transition to a new international system would raise substantial one-time revenue. The President's Budget proposes to use these funds for a six-year investment in infrastructure—ensuring that temporary revenues are matched to temporary costs so that the business tax reform as a whole does not raise the long-run deficit.

A quality transportation network is essential to a vibrant economy. Investments by previous generations of Americans—from the Erie Canal, to the Transcontinental Railroad, to the Interstate Highway System—were instrumental in increasing productivity and generating economic growth. A high-performing transportation network keeps jobs in America, allows businesses to expand, and lowers prices on household goods for American families. Better infrastructure allows businesses to manage their inventories and transport goods more cheaply and efficiently, as well as access a variety of suppliers and markets for their products, making it more cost-effective for manufacturers to keep production in, or move production to, the United States.

The economic benefits of smart infrastructure investment are long-term competitiveness, productivity, innovation, lower prices, and higher incomes (Gramlich 1994, Munnell 1992). The costs of inadequate infrastructure investment are exhibited all around us. Americans spend 5.5 billion hours in traffic each year, costing families more than $120 billion in extra fuel and lost time (Schrank, Eisele, and Lomax 2012). American businesses pay $7.8 billion a year in direct freight transportation costs due to bottlenecks (White and Grenzeback 2007).

Infrastructure investment is a natural partner for business tax reform, as both are motivated by the goal of increasing investment, productivity, and ultimately the well-being of American families. Devoting transition revenue raised by business tax reform to infrastructure investment boosts the overall productivity impact of tax reform.

Four Alternative Approaches
to Business Tax Reform

Analysts have offered four primary alternative approaches to reform. This section considers the merits of each approach.

Eliminate the Corporate Income Tax

Numerous commentators have called for complete repeal of the corporate income tax. However, the details of what repeal could plausibly mean vary widely. One version would repeal the corporate income tax and make no other changes to the tax system. Such an approach suffers from insurmountable compliance problems and would lead to revenue losses far in excess of current corporate tax receipts. Income would rapidly shift into the now-untaxed corporate form, allowing individuals to indefinitely defer taxes, and evasion strategies that disguise more heavily taxed wage income as lightly taxed dividend income would become widespread. Moreover, repealing the corporate income tax without increasing the deficit would require massive, deeply damaging cuts to important programs like Medicare, Medicaid, and Social Security, as well as federal investments in areas such as national security, research, and education.

A somewhat more nuanced approach to corporate income tax repeal would combine repeal with an increase in the tax rate on capital gains and dividends to match tax rates on earned income. However, taxing capital gains and dividends at the rate on earned income would be unlikely to raise enough money to cut the corporate rate by even 3 percentage points, let alone 35. Increasing rates on capital gains and dividends can finance only a small reduction in the corporate rate for three primary reasons. First, these forms of income are already subject to partial taxation. Second, individuals can use a variety of strategies, such as timing shifts in financial transactions, to avoid realization-based capital income taxes. And third, substantial capital income avoids individual-level taxation because it is held by tax-exempt entities such as pension funds and foundations. In the presence of a corporate tax, the corporations in which these tax-exempt entities have invested, of course, are subject to tax.

Absent a much larger overhaul of capital taxation—which would need to include accrual accounting for capital gains, retaining the corporate income tax as a withholding tax to address tax-exempt entities and tax evasion, and providing credits or deductions when corporate earnings are distributed to owners who are not tax-exempt—purely individual-level capital taxation is not a viable policy. Eric Toder and Alan Viard (2014) have recently advanced a more fleshed-out proposal that would repeal the corporate income tax, tax capital gains on accrual for publicly traded companies, and tax companies that are not publicly traded under a pass-through regime. Instead of paying tax on the proceeds of asset sales, shareholders of publicly traded corporations would pay tax on the change in market value of their shares each year and no additional tax when the assets are ultimately sold. However, even if the substantive and political challenges in transitioning to a new system could be overcome, their framework replaces only one-half of the revenue from the corporate tax.

Cut the Top Individual Rate in Parallel with the Corporate Rate

The desire for neutrality with respect to organizational form and the desire to cut taxes on pass-through businesses have been used to justify arguments that individual and corporate tax reform need to be done together and, in particular, that there should be parity between the top individual rate and the top corporate rate. This argument is motivated by valid concerns. Different rates on activities with different labels create opportunities for gamesmanship; for example, building up income inside a corporation rather than paying annual tax on it at the individual level. But overall, this argument suffers from serious economic and practical objections. On the economic merits, it is important to remember that C-corporation income is partially taxed at two levels while pass-through income is only taxed at one level. As a result, C corporations face an effective marginal rate that is 5 percentage points higher than that on pass-through businesses, as discussed above. Although the President's approach would cut and simplify taxes for small business, including small pass-through entities, for larger businesses reform should move in the direction of greater parity—with the goal of equal effective rates for C corporations and pass-through entities when individual and corporate taxes are combined—a goal that would not be served by parallel reductions in individual and corporate tax rates. Meanwhile, lowering the top individual rate across-the-board is both expensive and regressive, while significantly lowering the individual rate only for pass-through businesses—but not for individual taxpayers—would greatly exacerbate the existing compliance problems associated with relabeling wages and salaries as business income by high-income individuals.

Finally, while reducing the top individual rate is often motivated by reference to small business, reducing it is an inefficient way to target small businesses. Already, 96 percent of small businesses pay tax at rates of 28 percent or below (Knittel et al. 2011). Most of the revenue loss from a top rate cut reflects the expense of a tax cut for high-income individuals. Tools like expanding expensing for small businesses and reforming accounting requirements can be used to ensure that reform, taken as a whole, both simplifies and cuts taxes for small businesses—without cutting the tax rate on high-income professionals and large firms.

Adopt a Territorial Tax System

It is sometimes argued that all other major economies use a territorial tax system, though in practice many of them deviate significantly from a pure territorial system. A country that operates a pure territorial system would tax firms only on the income earned in that country, and exclude from taxation all income earned elsewhere in the world. Territorial taxation ensures that local firms are owned by the parent company that generates the largest economic benefits from ownership. However, this result comes at the expense of an inefficient global allocation of capital and production. Firms operating in a low-tax country pay less tax, and firms will respond by attempting to shift as much production as possible to low-tax countries.

A territorial approach exacerbates the problems of inefficient allocation of capital around the world, with excess capital in countries with low tax rates. Low-return investments are pursued in low-tax countries; however, high-return investments in higher-tax countries are not. In addition, a territorial system exacerbates the challenges of base erosion and profit shifting as it increases the financial rewards of shifting income abroad. Countries around the world are facing difficult questions about how to address base erosion (see Box 5-2). While explicit anti-erosion provisions can moderate these effects, they will not eliminate them. Offsetting the revenue loss arising from base erosion by multinationals will require higher tax rates on domestic U.S. companies, further discouraging investment in the United States, or higher tax rates on individuals. And, while it is often asserted that moving to a territorial system eliminates the incentive for corporations to invert, this is an overstatement. The incentive to relocate abroad is eliminated if the tax system is residence-neutral. Relocating can still be desirable if it facilitates tax-avoidance strategies such as earnings stripping, which can be more effective with a foreign parent even under a territorial system.

Substituting a fully territorial tax system privileges a single neutrality concept above—and at the expense of—all other neutrality concepts and exacerbates several challenges associated with tax avoidance. The hybrid international system in the President's approach reflects a sensible compromise between competing neutrality concepts, moderates the challenges of base erosion and profit shifting, and reduces the economic waste associated with the current system of indefinite deferral.

Allow Expensing for New Investment

Another alternative paradigm for business tax reform would focus on reducing the effective marginal tax rate for businesses with the objective of spurring additional investment and ultimately a larger capital stock. This alternative approach would feature two major components: full expensing and full repeal of interest deductibility. Rather than eliminating accelerated depreciation, this approach would go in the opposite direction by allowing immediate deductions for new investment. Since the combination of expensing and interest deductibility results in negative effective tax rates, this approach would also repeal the tax deduction for net interest.

The primary advantage of this alternative approach is potentially larger impacts on productivity and output, compared to an approach that focuses on reducing the statutory rate. By reducing the effective marginal tax rate on new business investment, it would boost investment, the capital stock, and productivity. In addition, a well-designed tax system based around expensing may be better suited to achieving neutrality between debt and equity financing than reforms within the current corporate tax paradigm. Expensing would also avoid the need to determine depreciation schedules for tax purposes (though not for accounting purposes) and therefore reduce the bookkeeping required to track assets' tax basis.

The primary disadvantage of the proposal is the additional revenue cost associated with more generous depreciation schedules, which would require either a smaller rate reduction or other offsetting tax increases. If the cost of expensing is offset with a smaller rate reduction, the impact of the plan on average tax rates and the ability to attract mobile, high-return investment under the proposal is reduced. This could lead to smaller effects of reform on productivity and a smaller reduction in costly tax avoidance behavior. Moreover, if, as some argue, depreciation provisions have only a modest impact on investment decisions, this alternative paradigm would be bad for investment and growth. It would provide businesses with a large tax benefit that has little impact on their investment decisions (expensing), while taking away a benefit that has a larger impact on their investment decisions (interest deductibility) and providing a smaller rate cut.

In addition, an expensing approach that does not repeal interest deductibility would exacerbate the non-neutralities of the current system by reducing the effective marginal tax rate on debt-financed projects even further below zero—effectively subsidizing them—and thus encouraging investments that are socially wasteful. Finally, shifting to such a system would face significant technical challenges both with structuring the transition and with handling the taxation of financial institutions, and would require corresponding reforms to taxation of capital income at the individual level.

Conclusion

Longer-term economic growth relies on continued increases in productivity that enable each American worker to produce more for every hour on the job. Business tax reform offers the potential to boost productivity by improving the quantity and quality of investment in the United States. However, it can only do this if it is done carefully and does not exacerbate other challenges; for example, by adding to the medium- or long-term deficit or crowding out other public investments. Rather, business tax reform can and should complement the rest of the growth agenda—including by funding investments in infrastructure—as well as a broader agenda involving individual tax reform and a set of other policies that guarantees all Americans can share in this growth.

CHAPTER 6

THE ENERGY REVOLUTION: ECONOMIC BENEFITS AND THE FOUNDATION FOR A LOW-CARBON ENERGY FUTURE

O ver the past ten years, the U.S. economy has undergone a revolution in the production and consumption of energy. Increasing production of oil, natural gas, and renewable energy has contributed broadly to employment and gross domestic product (GDP) growth during the recovery from the Great Recession. Energy efficiency has increased, with gasoline consumption falling 2 percent over the last decade despite a 17 percent increase in real GDP. Declining net oil imports have helped reduce the U.S. trade deficit and improve energy security. On balance, the energy revolution lays the foundation for U.S. leadership in global efforts to address climate change and paves the way toward a low-carbon energy future.

Recent changes in the energy sector, and their consequences for economic growth and combating climate change, have been remarkable. Breakthroughs in unconventional oil and natural gas extraction technology have reversed the decades-long decline in their production. Continued technological progress in wind, solar, and biofuels, as well as innovation and deployment policies at the local, State, and Federal levels, has caused an equally dramatic boom in the use of renewables. The composition of the Nation's energy sources has begun to shift: petroleum and coal are now being replaced by the growing use of natural gas and renewables, which are cleaner sources with lower, or even zero, carbon emissions. In 2014, renewable energy sources accounted for one-half of new installed capacity, and natural gas units comprised most of the remainder. These developments have contributed to a dramatic drop in the price of oil amidst geopolitical tension that might otherwise have caused oil prices to increase. Although oil prices will continue to fluctuate, the energy-sector developments will have a durable impact on our economy and our climate over the longer run regardless of future fluctuations in the price of oil.

To further build on this progress, foster continuing economic growth, and ensure that growth is sustainable for future generations, the President will continue his aggressive All-of-the-Above strategy for a cleaner energy future. The strategy has three elements, the first of which is to support economic growth and job creation. Expanded production of oil, natural gas, and renewables has raised employment in these industries during a period of labor market slack. Technological innovation and greater production help reduce energy prices, to the benefit of energy-consuming businesses and households. These developments have contributed broadly to employment and GDP growth, and will continue to do so.

The second element of the President's energy strategy is improving energy security. Lower net oil imports reduce the macroeconomic vulnerability of the United States to foreign oil supply disruptions. In today's domestic liquid fuels markets and globally integrated oil markets, a sudden international supply disruption means a sharp jump in prices. The combination of declining gasoline demand, increasing domestic crude oil production, and increasing use of biofuels, however, enhances the resilience of the U.S. economy to these oil price shocks. Although international oil supply shocks and oil price volatility will always present risks, reductions in net petroleum imports and the lower domestic oil consumption will reduce those risks. To further reduce net oil imports in the long run, the Administration has taken steps to curb petroleum demand by aggressively raising standards for vehicle fuel economy. Efforts are also being made to boost the use of biofuels, electric vehicles, natural gas, and other petroleum substitutes.

The third element of the All-of-the-Above Energy Strategy addresses the challenges of global climate change. The need to act now to stem climate change is clear; delaying would only lead to larger costs for future generations. Delaying action is costly because it means less incentive for research and development of effective carbon-reducing technologies, while at the same time encouraging investments in older and carbon-intensive technologies. After having delayed, making up for lost time requires more stringent and costly policies in the future. In practice, delay also may render unrealistic the climate targets that are within reach today. Delaying action imposes greater mitigation costs and economic damages than would have otherwise occurred. Higher temperatures, more acidic oceans, and increasingly severe storms, droughts, and wildfires could all result from avoidable higher greenhouse gas emissions.

The energy revolution lays the groundwork for reducing domestic greenhouse gas emissions. From 2005 through 2012, the United States cut its total carbon dioxide (CO2) pollution by 12 percent, partly reflecting a domestic shift toward cleaner natural gas, increased use of renewables, and improved energy efficiency. Although the reductions in CO2 emissions represent an historic shift from past trends, much more work remains.

The Climate Action Plan is the centerpiece of the President's efforts to confront climate change. With this plan, the President has put in motion steps that will immediately and substantially reduce greenhouse gas emissions. These steps include direct regulation of emissions, such as the Clean Power Plan, which will further the shift toward cleaner sources of electricity and complement carbon regulations already in place for other sectors, such as fuel economy and greenhouse gas standards for light, medium, and heavy-duty vehicles.

The President's Climate Action steps also include a strategy to reduce methane emissions (a potent greenhouse gas). Through a recent announcement, the Administration identified opportunities to further reduce methane emissions from the oil and gas sector; this topic is also a focus of the Quadrennial Energy Review. Additionally, the Administration supports research, development, and commercialization of technologies that help to bring down the costs of renewables; for example, through solar programs such as the U.S. Department of Energy's SunShot initiative, which seeks to make solar energy cost-competitive with other forms of electricity by 2020. These efforts support continuing U.S. leadership in global efforts to address climate change, as evidenced by the November 2014 joint announcement of climate targets with China.

This chapter discusses the three elements of the All-of-the-Above Energy Strategy, and takes stock of both the progress that has been made to date and the work that remains to be done to transition to a low-carbon energy system. The third element, laying the foundation for a clean energy future, dovetails with the President's Climate Action Plan, which is the focus of the final section in this chapter. The chapter builds on two previous Council of Economic Advisers (CEA) reports: The All-of-the-Above Energy Strategy as a Path to Sustainable Economic Growth (CEA 2014a), and The Cost of Delaying Action to Stem Climate Change (CEA 2014b).

THE ENERGY REVOLUTION: HISTORICAL PERSPECTIVE AND ECONOMIC BENEFITS

The Energy Revolution in Historical Perspective

Over the past two centuries, the amount of energy consumed in the United States has increased dramatically and our energy sources have become more convenient. As Figure 6-1 shows, wood was the main U.S. energy source through the middle of the 19th century. The use of coal rose sharply through the early 20th century, plateaued, and then increased in the 1970s for the generation of electricity. For most of the 20th century, petroleum consumption grew sharply, dropping off temporarily after the oil crises of the 1970s but then resuming its growth, albeit at a slower pace than previously. Natural gas consumption spread during the second half of the 20th century, with greater use of this fuel in homes and industry and to meet peak electricity demand. During the last quarter of the 20th century, nuclear electricity generation burgeoned to the point that it now supplies 19 percent of electricity, and wood—the original biofuel—saw a small regional resurgence (primarily for home heating) because of the increases in home heating oil prices in the 1970s. Meanwhile, production of renewables—which includes biomass and biofuels, hydroelectric, wind, solar, and geothermal energy—has approached nuclear energy production levels.

Energy consumption trends have already shifted dramatically in the 21st century (Figure 6-1b): coal consumption dropped by 21 percent between its 2005 peak and 2013; and total petroleum consumption declined by 13 percent between its 2005 peak and 2013. Natural gas consumption has risen sharply, with much of this increase displacing coal for electricity generation. In addition, total energy obtained from renewables rose 77 percent between 2005 and 2013.

The decline in petroleum consumption, starting in 2006, was unexpected. In the case of energy, industry-standard benchmark projections are produced annually by the Energy Information Administration (EIA) in its Annual Energy Outlook. Revisions to those projections include the effects of unforeseen developments in the energy sector. Figure 6-2a shows U.S. petroleum consumption since 1950 and projected consumption from the 2006, 2010, and 2014 editions of the Annual Energy Outlook. Only nine years ago, EIA projected an increase in petroleum consumption during the subsequent 25 years. But events dramatically affected subsequent projections: by 2010, EIA had reduced both the level and rate of growth of its projection; its 2014 outlook now projects petroleum consumption to decline through 2030 after a slight increase over the next five years. The reversal in projected petroleum consumption is led by the reversal in actual and projected gasoline consumption (Figure 6-2b): the 2014 EIA projection of consumption in 2030 is 44 percent below the projection made in 2006. Actual gasoline consumption declined between 2006 and 2010 mainly due to the recession and rising fuel prices, but much of the revision to the 2030 levels reflects the largely unexpected fuel economy improvements stemming from the Energy Independence and Security Act of 2007 and the Administration's subsequent

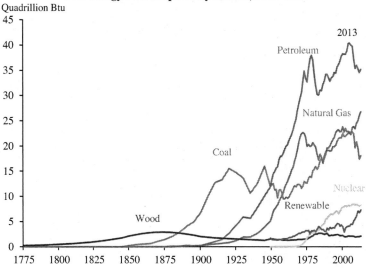

Figure 6-1a
U.S. Energy Consumption by Source, 1775–2013

Source: Energy Information Administration, Energy Perspectives (1949-2011) and Monthly Energy Review (Dec 2014).

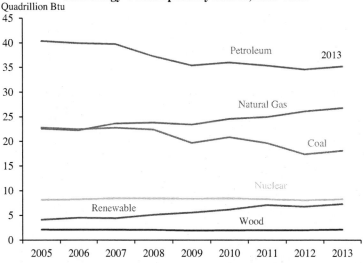

Figure 6-1b
U.S. Energy Consumption by Source, 2005–2013

Source: Energy Information Administration, Monthly Energy Review (Dec 2014).

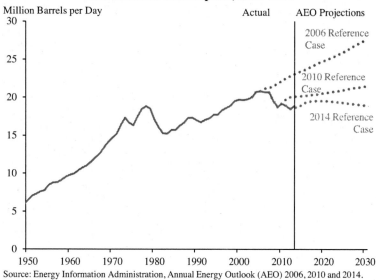

Figure 6-2a
U.S.Petroleum Consumption, 1950–2030

Million Barrels per Day

Actual   AEO Projections

2006 Reference Case

2010 Reference Case

2014 Reference Case

Source: Energy Information Administration, Annual Energy Outlook (AEO) 2006, 2010 and 2014.

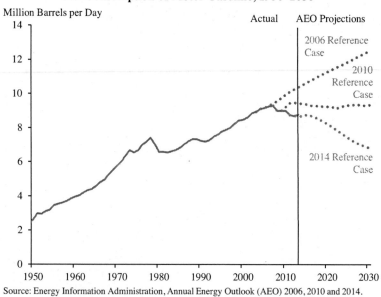

Figure 6-2b
U.S. Consumption of Motor Gasoline, 1950–2030

Million Barrels per Day

Actual   AEO Projections

2006 Reference Case

2010 Reference Case

2014 Reference Case

Source: Energy Information Administration, Annual Energy Outlook (AEO) 2006, 2010 and 2014.

tightening of those standards. The 2014 projections further reflect the 2012 light-duty vehicle fuel economy and greenhouse gas emissions rate standards, which apply to model years 2017 through 2025. The Administration's fuel economy and greenhouse gas standards for medium and heavy-duty trucks also contribute to the reduction in projected petroleum consumption between the 2010 and 2014 Outlooks.

The recent increase in U.S. petroleum production was equally unforeseen. As Figure 6-3 shows, domestic petroleum production peaked in 1970 at 11 million barrels per day (bpd). Production plateaued through the mid-1980s and then declined steadily through the late 2000s as producers depleted conventional domestic deposits. Since then, however, entrepreneurs adapted horizontal drilling and hydraulic fracturing technology that had previously been more widely used for natural gas. The newer technology enables the extraction of oil from within rocky formations once considered uneconomic, like the Eagle Ford in Texas, and development of new regions such as the Bakken in North Dakota. This chapter uses the term "unconventional oil" to describe oil produced from shale and other relatively impermeable formations, and produced using new drilling methods. These unforeseen technological developments are recent: most of the revision to EIA's earlier projections has occurred since 2010, and now EIA projects

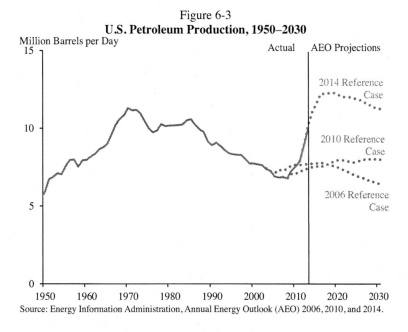

Figure 6-3
U.S. Petroleum Production, 1950–2030

Source: Energy Information Administration, Annual Energy Outlook (AEO) 2006, 2010, and 2014.

production to surpass its earlier 1970 peak this year. The EIA Reference case, which includes the baseline assumptions, projects production to decline slowly after 2019. But because extraction technology is still advancing, there is considerable uncertainty about the United States' economically recoverable resource potential.

The decline in demand for petroleum and increase in production have triggered a sharp turnaround in net petroleum imports (Figure 6-4). U.S. net petroleum imports fell from a peak of 12 million bpd in 2005 to 6 million bpd in 2013, representing a decrease of 6 million bpd compared to EIA's 2006 projection of 2013 imports. Comparing actual 2013 imports and the 2006 projection of 2013 imports, roughly 4 million bpd, or 65 percent, of the reduction stem from the fall in consumption; and 2 million bpd, or 35 percent, are due to the unforeseen increase in production.

The Administration has supported oil production on Federal and Indian lands. In fiscal year 2013, onshore oil production on Federal and Indian lands increased 58 percent compared with 2008. In 2014, the U.S. Interior Department held 25 onshore lease sales, generating about $200 million in revenue for States, Tribes, and the American taxpayer. The Administration has also promoted the environmentally responsible development of offshore resources through the Interior Department's Five-Year Outer Continental Shelf Oil and Gas Leasing Program. In early 2015 the

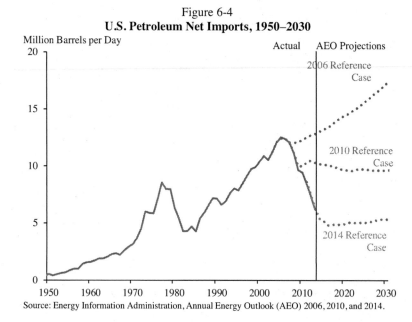

Figure 6-4
U.S. Petroleum Net Imports, 1950–2030

Source: Energy Information Administration, Annual Energy Outlook (AEO) 2006, 2010, and 2014.

Interior Department announced a Draft Proposed Program for 2017 to 2022 that includes potential lease sales in the Gulf of Mexico, off the Alaska coast, and in the Atlantic. Following the Deepwater Horizon incident in 2010, the Interior Department has implemented new safety standards for new wells. In 2014, the Interior Department issued 68 new deep water well permits.

The rise in unconventional natural gas production preceded the rise in unconventional oil production (unconventional gas is defined similarly to unconventional oil, as gas produced from impermeable formations using new drilling methods). Figure 6-5, which presents domestic natural gas production and historical EIA projections, shows that the EIA's 2014 projections indicate an upswing in natural gas production through 2030. Already, well over one-half of natural gas production is from unconventional formations (tight gas and shale gas), a fraction that is projected to increase as the conventional resource base becomes less productive and competitive. The resulting benefits of these innovations to natural gas producers and consumers are discussed in a subsequent subsection.

Domestic use of renewable energy sources has also increased substantially since 2000. Figure 6-6 shows that the use of liquid biofuels—primarily ethanol from corn and biodiesel from various sources including waste oil and soy oil—grew sharply in the mid-2000s. Several factors contributed to this growth, including the Renewable Fuel Standard, which mandates

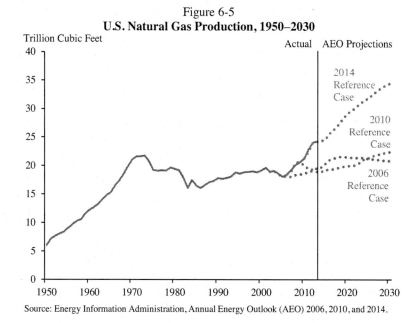

Figure 6-5
U.S. Natural Gas Production, 1950–2030

Source: Energy Information Administration, Annual Energy Outlook (AEO) 2006, 2010, and 2014.

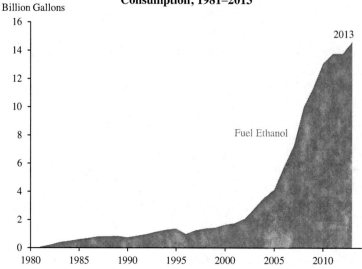

Figure 6-6
U.S. Fuel Ethanol and Biodiesel Consumption, 1981–2013

Source: Energy Information Administration, Monthly Energy Review (Dec 2014).

ethanol volumes under the 2005 Energy Policy Act and was modified by the 2007 Energy Independence and Security Act. The combined effect of increased production of natural gas, oil, and liquid biofuels has positioned the United States as the leading petroleum, natural gas, and biofuels producer in the world (Figure 6-7).

The U.S. energy revolution also encompasses a dramatic rise in the use of renewables for electricity generation. At the end of 2013, wind generation capacity totaled 61 gigawatts, which was more than double its 2008 level.[1] Wind generator construction has occurred throughout the Midwest, Southwest, West Coast, and New England (Figure 6-8) and a record 13 gigawatts of new wind power capacity was installed in 2012 alone, roughly double the amount of newly installed capacity in 2011. This new wind capacity represented the largest share of addition by a single fuel source to total U.S. electric generation capacity in 2012. As a result, wind-powered electricity generation nearly tripled from a monthly rate of 17 thousand gigawatt hours at the beginning of 2009 to 50 thousand gigawatt hours at the beginning of 2014 (Figure 6-9). Similarly, solar-powered electricity generation nearly quadrupled from a monthly rate of just above two thousand gigawatt hours to more than eight thousand gigawatt hours over the same period.

---

[1] One gigawatt is equal to 1 billion watts, and is a common unit of generation capacity; the entire U.S. power system contains roughly 1,100 gigawatts of installed capacity.

Figure 6-7
Petroleum, Biofuels, and Natural Gas Production, 2008–2013

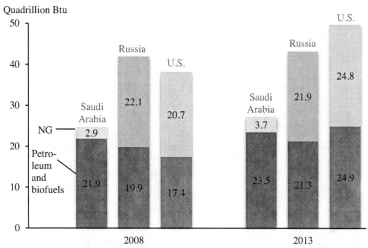

Note: Petroleum production includes crude oil, natural gas liquids, condensates, refinery processing gains and other liquids including biofuels.
Source: Energy Information Administration, International Energy Statistics.

Figure 6-8
Change in Wind Power Generation Capacity, 2010–2013

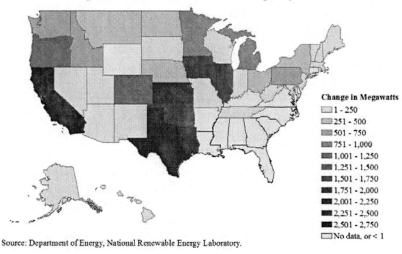

Source: Department of Energy, National Renewable Energy Laboratory.

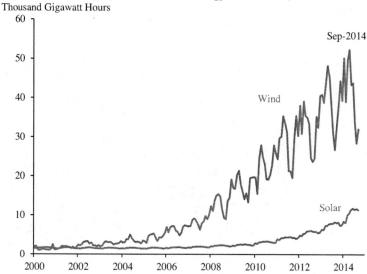

Figure 6-9
Total Monthly Wind and Solar Energy Production, 2000–2014

Thousand Gigawatt Hours

Source: Energy Information Administration, Monthly Energy Review (Dec 2014).

In 2013, wind accounted for 66 percent of non-hydro renewable electricity generation, biomass for 24 percent, solar for 4 percent, and geothermal for 6 percent; between 2009 and 2013, wind and solar had the fastest growth rates among non-hydro renewables.

The American Recovery and Reinvestment Act of 2009 played a significant role in the rising use of renewables for electricity generation. Since the early 1990s, the Federal Government has helped spur most wind and solar investments by offering tax credits. Investors in wind projects that began construction before the end of 2013 received a tax credit of $23 for each megawatt-hour of electricity generation; solar projects are currently eligible for a tax credit of 30 percent of the up-front investment cost. The Recovery Act provided eligible wind, solar, and other low-carbon projects the option of a grant from the U.S. Treasury equal to 30 percent of the project's cost, rather than a tax credit. Since 2009, the program has provided almost $22 billion in grants for 22 gigawatts of wind capacity and 5 gigawatts of solar capacity. The President's approach to business tax reform includes proposals to make permanent and more effective tax incentives for renewable energy (see further discussion in Chapter 5).

GDP, Jobs, and the Trade Deficit

The U.S. energy revolution has contributed to economic growth, both in terms of net economic output as measured by GDP and overall employment. It has also contributed to a declining trade deficit as the Nation has recovered from the Great Recession. CEA estimates that the oil and natural gas sectors alone contributed more than 0.2 percentage point to real GDP growth between 2012 and 2014, in contrast to a slight negative contribution on average from 1995 to 2005 (Figure 6-10). The contribution between 2012 and 2014, which does not count all economic spillovers, added substantially to the 2.4 percent average annualized rate of U.S. economic growth over these three years.

Growth in oil and gas production has directly and indirectly created jobs over the past several years. As Figure 6-11 shows, total employment in the oil and natural gas industries, which includes extraction and support activities, increased by 133,000 jobs between 2010 and 2013, and continued to grow through 2014 (not shown); coal employment has also edged up only slightly over this period. Much oil and gas job growth has been concentrated in a handful of states like Texas, Pennsylvania, and North Dakota that are at the forefront of developing new energy resources (Cruz, Smith and Stanley 2014). The oil and gas employment increase in Figure 6-11 understates the

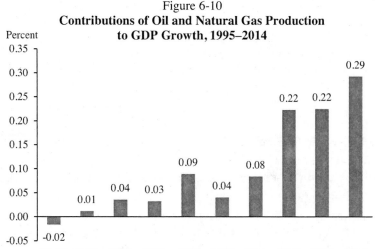

Figure 6-10
Contributions of Oil and Natural Gas Production to GDP Growth, 1995–2014

Note: CEA calculations use physical quantity data for oil and natural gas production and implicitly include contributions from the sectors that service and sell equipment to the oil and gas drilling industry. 2014 contribution is estimated based on partial data for the year as a whole.
Source: Energy Information Administration, Spot Prices for Crude Oil and Petroleum Products and Short-Term Energy Outlook (Jan 2015); CEA calculations.

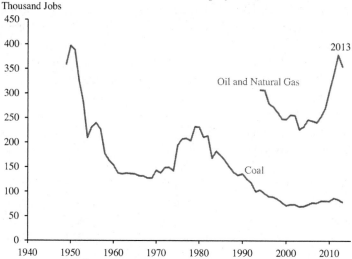

Figure 6-11
Coal, Oil and Natural Gas Employment, 1949–2013

Note: Both series include extraction/mining as well as support activities for the industry.
Source: Bureau of Labor Statistics, Current Employment Statistics and National Industry Specific Occupational Employment and Wage Estimates.

full short-run effect of oil and gas development on U.S. employment for two reasons. First, jobs have also been created in companies that provide goods and services to the oil and gas industries, including manufacturing, transportation, and leisure and hospitality. Second, workers in all of these industries create additional jobs when they spend their incomes, as do State and local governments that spend additional tax revenue. As a result, new oil and gas regions have seen employment growth in schools, retail, health care, and other sectors. Because of labor market slack reflected in elevated unemployment rates during the recovery, the number of additional jobs created by spending tax revenue and income could be quite large—perhaps equal to one-half the increase in the oil and gas industries, or about 65,000 additional jobs in 2013 compared to 2010 (CEA 2014c).[2]

Expansion of renewable energy capacity has similarly contributed to economic growth. Employment in the renewable sector spans several categories in Federal data collection systems, which complicates direct estimation of job growth and output in the sector. However, trade association data suggest that, in addition to rapid expansion in wind and solar electricity generation, there has also been a sharp rise in employment. As Figure 6-12 shows, from 2010 to 2014, employment in the solar energy industry grew by more than 85 percent. Moreover, employment in the solar industry is

---

[2] CEA (2014c) provides estimates of the fiscal multiplier for the Recovery Act.

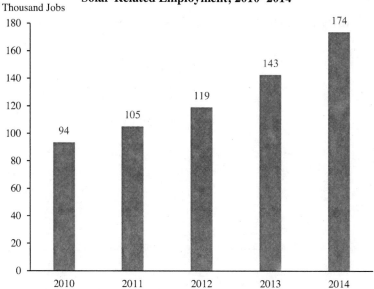

Figure 6-12
Solar-Related Employment, 2010–2014

Source: The Solar Foundation, National Solar Jobs Census 2014.

projected to increase by another 21 percent in 2015.[3] Wind industry employ-ment totaled roughly 50,000 workers in 2013.[4] The solar and wind employ-ment levels are not directly comparable to the oil, gas, and coal employment levels shown in Figure 6-11; the solar and wind employment figures include a broader range of related activities.

The increase in domestic oil production, combined with reduced demand for oil, has also led to a sharp drop in net petroleum imports and, as a result, a decline in the Nation's trade deficit. In 2006, the total trade deficit was 5.4 percent of GDP, the highest ever recorded for the United States. By the end of 2013, the trade deficit had fallen to 2.8 percent of GDP, which, excluding the crisis-affected year of 2009, was the lowest since 1999 (Figure 6-13). While the U.S. trade balance is subject to a number of influences and depends in large part on domestic and global macroeconomic conditions, the rise in domestic energy production has been a substantial factor in the recent improvement. Of the 2.7 percentage-point decline in the trade deficit

---

[3] Estimates of employment related to the solar energy industry are from the Solar Foundation's 2014 National Solar Jobs Census. The National Solar Jobs Census uses a statistical survey methodology broadly comparable to the Bureau of Labor Statistics' Quarterly Census of Employment and Wages and Current Employment Statistics surveys.
[4] Estimates of national employment related to the wind power sector come from the 2013 American Wind Energy Association's U.S. Wind Industry Annual Market Report.

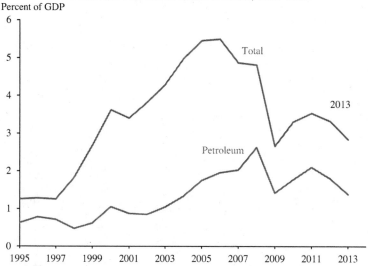

Figure 6-13
Total and Petroleum Trade Deficits, 1995–2013

Percent of GDP

Source: Census Bureau, U.S. International Trade in Goods and Services; Bureau of Economic Analysis,
National Income and Product Accounts.

since 2006, about 0.6 percentage point (or just over one-fifth) is accounted
for by a shrinking trade deficit in petroleum products.

Energy Prices, Households, and Businesses

Since 2006, natural gas prices have fallen well below crude oil prices
on an energy-equivalent basis, providing a cheaper source of energy to consumers and businesses in the United States (Figure 6-14). This price decrease
has created widespread benefits and opportunities for the U.S. economy.

The decrease in U.S. natural gas prices has opened a gap between U.S.
and international prices, presenting an export opportunity for domestic natural gas producers (see Box 6-1). The gap reflects the undeveloped nature of
international gas markets combined with the expense of international trade.
Liquefaction, transportation from the United States to Europe, and regasification have been estimated to add $6 to $9 per million British Thermal
Unit (Btu), which would roughly double the price of U.S. gas entering the
pipeline in Europe relative to the Henry Hub price.[5] Under the Natural Gas
Act of 1938, as amended, the Department of Energy (DOE) must authorize
any natural gas exports. As of November 2014, the DOE has conditionally
approved approximately 12 billion cubic feet per day of liquefied natural gas

[5] The Henry Hub price is a benchmark price for natural gas, and it measures the price at a
pipeline distribution point in Louisiana.

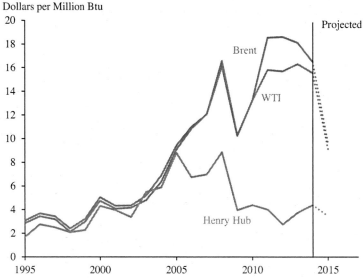

Figure 6-14
Annual Crude Oil and Natural Gas Spot Prices, 1995–2015

Dollars per Million Btu

Source: Energy Information Administration, Short-Term Energy Outlook (Jan 2015).

(LNG) export capacity, though the enormous capital expenditure required for LNG facilities raises the possibility that some of this capacity might not actually be built. Because of high transport costs, even if a global market for LNG were to develop, domestic natural gas prices are likely to remain well below prices in the rest of the world for an extended period of time.

Low wholesale natural gas prices broadly benefit the U.S. economy in several direct and indirect ways. Residential natural gas prices have followed the decline in wholesale natural gas prices, and the 12-month average price has declined by 18 percent from its 2009 high (Figure 6-15a). Households, which accounted for about one-fifth of U.S. natural gas consumption in 2014, pay lower gas bills and can either spend or save the difference. Commercial and industrial businesses, which accounted for about 40 percent of domestic consumption in 2014, also benefit from lower gas prices, which raise business profits. Lower gas prices benefit consumers indirectly to the extent that businesses pass on lower energy prices to consumers in the form of lower product prices. Finally, low wholesale natural gas prices have supported a switch in fuels in the electric power sector from coal to natural gas. With natural gas prices falling from 2007 to 2012, retail electricity prices have increased at a slower rate than they had during the previous 15 years (Figure 6-15b). In other words, electricity consumers—businesses and

Figure 6-15a
Wholesale and Residential Natural Gas Prices, 1995–2014

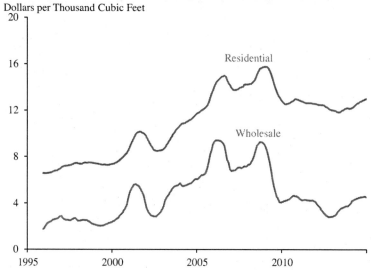

Note: Prices illustrated are twelve-month moving averages.
Source: Energy Information Administration, Short-Term Energy Outlook (Jan 2015).

Figure 6-15b
Retail Electricity Prices and Fuel Costs, 1995–2014

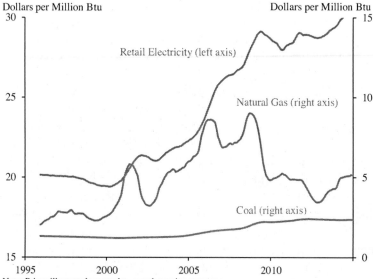

Note: Prices illustrated are twelve-month moving averages.
Source: Energy Information Administration, Short-Term Energy Outlook (Jan 2015).

Box 6-1: Natural Gas Exports

Over the last decade, U.S. natural gas production increased by roughly 40 percent. This sharp increase in domestic production has widened the gap between domestic natural gas prices and natural gas prices in other countries (Figure 6-i), creating potential profitable export opportunities for domestic natural gas producers. In 2014, the United States surpassed Qatar to become the world's largest exporter of Liquefied Petroleum Gas (LPG),[1] for which there is already export capacity in the Gulf region for 400 thousand barrels per day (bpd), with another 700 thousand bpd expected by 2016. The Energy Information Administration (EIA) projects that the United States will become a net exporter of liquefied natural gas (LNG) by 2016 (Figure 6-ii). However, expansion of U.S. natural gas exports requires both governmental action and the construction of additional exporting infrastructure.

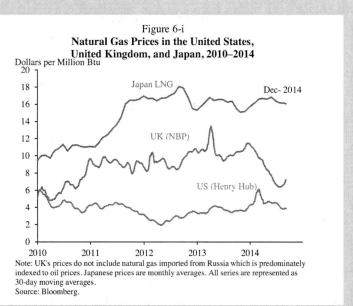

Figure 6-i
**Natural Gas Prices in the United States,
United Kingdom, and Japan, 2010–2014**

Note: UK's prices do not include natural gas imported from Russia which is predominately indexed to oil prices. Japanese prices are monthly averages. All series are represented as 30-day moving averages.
Source: Bloomberg.

Both transportation costs and government-imposed barriers to trade have caused prices among countries to differ. The gap between U.S. natural gas prices and prices in other countries reflects two main trade impediments. First, transportation costs—liquefaction, transportation abroad, and regasification—roughly double the price of gas entering Europe relative to the price at its origin in the United States. Transport charges must cover substantial infrastructure investments and capital

_____

[1] A group of hydrocarbon gases derived from crude oil refining or natural gas processing.

expenditure—for example, the cost of building a liquefaction terminal that can export up to 2.76 billion cubic feet (bcf) per day for 20 years can be around $12 billion.[2] The second impediment is the Natural Gas Act of 1938 (NGA) and subsequent amendments, which restrict natural gas exports. Under the NGA, natural gas exports require approval from the U.S. Department of Energy (DOE).[3] As of November 2014, DOE has approved applications for the export of about 12 bcf per day of LNG, although some of the approvals are contingent on approval by the Federal Energy Regulatory Commission. Because the recent technological developments have given the United States a natural comparative advantage in gas production over importing regions, both trade impediments – natural and government mandated – depress U.S. gas prices relative to those paid abroad.

What will happen as more export infrastructure comes on line and DOE approves higher volumes of gas exports? When barriers to trade are reduced between a low-cost country (the United States) and

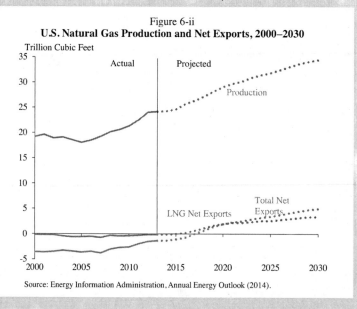

Figure 6-ii
U.S. Natural Gas Production and Net Exports, 2000–2030

Source: Energy Information Administration, Annual Energy Outlook (2014).

---

[2] Over 15 bcf per day of export capacity is under construction or has been proposed, though cost considerations make it unlikely that all proposed projects will be completed. By comparison, the United States produces almost 70 bcf per day.

[3] Approval is even required for exports to countries with which the U.S. has a free trade agreement, though an amendment to the NGA in 1992 required that applications to authorize exports to free trade partners be granted without modification or delay. As a result, conclusion of the Trans-Pacific Partnership and the Transatlantic Trade and Investment Partnership would vastly increase the range of countries to which U.S. producers could export without administrative barriers (see Chapter 7).

high-cost countries (importers in the rest of the world), basic economic theory predicts a convergence of prices. As U.S. natural gas enters the global market, it will increase global supply and push global prices down. Meanwhile, domestic prices will rise as natural gas leaves the domestic market, reducing supply in the United States. A recent study by EIA estimates that an increase in exports of 12 bcf per day by 2020 would raise U.S. residential retail prices by 2 percent between 2015 and 2040, although the EIA considers such a large exports increase by 2020 to be almost impossible. An increase in U.S. exports of natural gas, and the resulting price changes, would have a number of mostly beneficial effects on natural gas producers, employment, U.S. geopolitical security, and the environment.

- **Higher prices for domestic producers increase domestic production.** Increased production, in turn, spurs investment, increasing U.S. GDP. EIA (2014) estimates that the increase in GDP could range from 0.05 percent to 0.17 percent in different export scenarios ranging from 12 to 20 bcf per year, phased in at different rates beginning in 2015.

- **An increase in exports can create jobs in the short run.** Estimates suggest that natural gas exports of six bcf per year could support as many as 65,000 jobs (Levi 2012). These jobs would arise both in gas production and along the supply chain (for example, in manufacturing machines and parts used as downstream inputs).

- **Lower natural gas prices around the world have a positive geopolitical impact for the United States.** Increased U.S. supply builds liquidity in the global natural gas market, and reduces European dependence on the current primary suppliers, Russia and Iran.

- **More U.S. exports could help promote the use of cleaner energy abroad, including in developing countries that now rely heavily on coal.** Lower foreign emissions would help to counteract global warming and therefore are a direct benefit for the United States. As natural gas becomes cheaper for the rest of the world, countries overseas will replace dirtier, coal-fired power with natural gas. Cheaper natural gas could also replace low-carbon sources and increase electricity consumption abroad; the net global impact is ambiguous. The effects of the natural gas price increase in the United States are also complex. Higher gas prices tend to curb overall emissions by reducing total energy consumption and inducing substitution toward renewable sources of power. However, higher prices might also cause some U.S. substitution toward coal, raising our emissions.

- **U.S. manufacturers would still have a competitive cost advantage in natural gas, albeit smaller than what they would otherwise have.** Because of transportation costs, in equilibrium, U.S. natural gas prices would still be expected to be persistently lower than prices overseas. The cost advantage, however, would be smaller than it would otherwise be—but any potential impact on manufacturing is likely to be small because in 2010, on average, the cost of natural gas represented less than 2 percent of the value of manufacturing shipments. This suggests that a 2 percent increase in the price of natural gas would raise average production costs by only about 0.04 percent. For the most intensive users—such as producers of flat glass or nitrogen fertilizers—the increase in costs will be higher. But these gas-intensive industries represent only a small share of total manufacturing employment and output. In particular, the top 15 gas-intensive industries account for only 2 percent of total manufacturing employment and 3 percent of manufacturing value added. Businesses with very thin profit margins may also be adversely affected. In contrast, expanded natural gas exports will create new jobs in a range of sectors including natural gas extraction, infrastructure investment, and transportation.

households—have also benefited from the slower growth of electricity prices caused by lower wholesale natural gas prices.

Oil prices decreased dramatically in the second half of 2014. Box 6-2 shows the drop in crude prices, and notes the range of global factors behind the drop, including the boom in U.S. oil production. Retail gasoline prices are closely linked to global crude oil prices, so households now pay less for gasoline. Seasonally adjusted gasoline prices decreased by roughly $0.80 per gallon between June and December 2014. EIA estimates that lower gasoline prices in 2015, compared to 2014, will save the average household about $750. Oil-consuming businesses would also enjoy huge gains—in the tens of billions of dollars. In addition, the fact that lower oil prices are expected to boost the global economy will create additional spillovers for U.S. economic activity by creating higher demand for the products and services we export. On the other hand, these gains are partially offset by the fact that lower crude oil prices reduce the profits and investments of oil producers. On net, however, the recent oil price decrease benefits the U.S. economy (see Chapter 2 for further discussion of the macroeconomic effects of oil prices).

Infrastructure Implications of the Energy Revolution

Expanding domestic energy supply has challenged the U.S. energy infrastructure in different ways. Since some of the best wind and solar resources are located far from population and economic hubs, adding substantially more wind and central-station solar generation usually requires

Box 6-2: U.S. Oil Production in a Global Perspective, and Implications for U.S. GDP

U.S. crude oil production has expanded dramatically since 2008. Technological innovations in horizontal drilling, hydraulic fracturing, and seismic imaging have led to a surge in domestic production from an average of about 5 million barrels per day in 2008 to more than 7 million barrels per day in 2013. Figure 6-iii shows that this growth is largely a U.S. phenomenon. Excluding the United States, the top 15 oil-producing countries experienced an average increase of 0.2 million barrels per day between 2008 and 2013, compared to the 2.4 million barrel per day increase experienced in the United States.

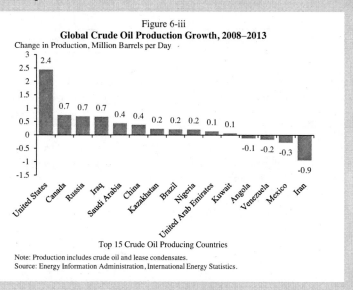

Figure 6-iii
Global Crude Oil Production Growth, 2008–2013

Note: Production includes crude oil and lease condensates.
Source: Energy Information Administration, International Energy Statistics.

Crude oil prices decreased dramatically in the second half of 2014. Between 2011 and the third quarter of 2014, prices were typically between $100 and $120 per barrel (see Figure 6-iv). Crude prices—as measured by the Brent price index, which is a standard global price index—dropped 40 percent between August and the end of December, to about $60 per barrel. Explanations for this price decline include: the major gains in U.S. oil production over the last several years; recent decreases in forecasted global oil demand; and sustained, high levels of production from the Organization of the Petroleum Exporting Countries (OPEC) that has, in fact, produced above its official target in each month from April to October and decided in November not to reduce this target.

Lower crude oil prices have translated into lower prices for petroleum products like gasoline, diesel, heating oil, propane, and jet fuel

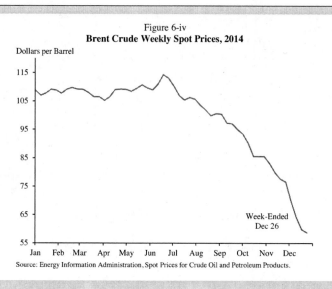

Figure 6-iv
Brent Crude Weekly Spot Prices, 2014

Dollars per Barrel

Source: Energy Information Administration, Spot Prices for Crude Oil and Petroleum Products.

(Figure 6-v). In the United States, gasoline accounts for about one-half of crude oil consumption, distillates (diesel and heating oil) for about 20 percent, and propane and jet fuel for about 6 and 7 percent. Lower petroleum product prices increase households' real income and boost businesses' profits, which translate into higher GDP. Prices fell roughly $40 per barrel between August and the end of 2014. Chapter 2 provides an estimate that, if this price decrease is sustained for the next year, GDP will be 0.4 percentage point higher in 2015 that it would be if oil prices were to remain at their mid-2014 levels.

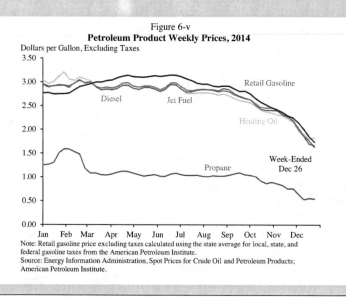

Figure 6-v
Petroleum Product Weekly Prices, 2014

Dollars per Gallon, Excluding Taxes

Note: Retail gasoline price excluding taxes calculated using the state average for local, state, and federal gasoline taxes from the American Petroleum Institute.
Source: Energy Information Administration, Spot Prices for Crude Oil and Petroleum Products; American Petroleum Institute.

new construction or upgrades of existing transmission lines. For example, installed wind generator capacity in Texas grew between 2000 and 2008 from 0.17 gigawatts to 10 gigawatts, but most of the new generators were installed in West Texas. Little existing transmission capacity connected the wind generators to electricity demand centers in East Texas. During certain times, such as at night or during the spring, available wind generation in the West exceeded local electricity demand. If there had been sufficient transmission capacity, the excess wind generation could have been transported to East Texas, relieving fossil fuel-fired generators there. But because transmission capacity did not keep pace with wind generation, electricity costs and emissions were higher than they needed to be. Texas recently completed a major transmission project that alleviates these problems, providing an important example of infrastructure investments that can support the energy revolution.

Another reason for insufficient infrastructure is that much of the recent growth in natural gas and oil production has occurred in regions with little recent history of energy production. Oil production in North Dakota increased from 0.1 million bpd in January 2008 to 1.2 million bpd in October 2014. However, transportation bottlenecks have contributed to crude oil prices, particularly in the U.S. interior, falling below international benchmarks. Responding to these bottlenecks, according to EIA estimates, shipments of crude oil by rail increased from nearly zero to about 750 thousand bpd during roughly the same time period. Recent high-profile rail accidents involving crude oil shipments have raised concerns about the safety and environmental consequences of increasing reliance on rail for shipping crude. Recognizing these concerns, the Department of Transportation recently proposed strengthened safety regulations for rail cars transporting crude oil and other flammable materials.

The Administration launched the first Quadrennial Energy Review in January 2014, in part to support long-term planning of energy infrastructure. The first phase of the Review, to be completed by early 2015, focuses on infrastructure for energy transport, storage, and distribution. Subsequent phases will address other dimensions of U.S. energy security and sustainability, thereby providing a multiyear roadmap for Federal energy policy.

THE ENERGY REVOLUTION AND ENERGY SECURITY: A MACROECONOMIC PERSPECTIVE

The term energy security is used to mean different things in different contexts, and broadly covers energy supply availability, reliability, affordability, and geopolitical considerations.[6] This section focuses on macroeconomic energy security, which means the extent to which a country's economy is exposed to energy supply risks—specifically, international energy supply disruptions that lead to product unavailability, price shocks, or both. The concept of macroeconomic energy security encompasses domestic risks as well as international supply risks such as disruptions to foreign oil production. In the United States, domestic energy security considerations are important and domestic supply breakdowns can have large costs. For example, CEA and DOE, and other Federal agencies, have estimated substantial costs of electricity-grid outages associated with storms (CEA/DOE 2013). Historically, however, energy supply disruptions of foreign origin have had the greatest overall macroeconomic impact. Foreign oil supply disruptions played a role in the recessions of the 1970s as well as the 1990-91 recession, though disagreement remains about the magnitude of that role. For this reason, this section focuses on the vulnerability of the U.S. economy to international energy supply disruptions rather than to domestic ones.

Because most U.S. energy import dollars are spent on petroleum, the main threats to U.S. macroeconomic energy security come from international oil supply disruptions. During the 1973-74 OPEC oil embargo, price controls and lack of product led to gasoline rationing and long lines at service stations. But in today's global oil market with many producers and domestically deregulated petroleum prices, petroleum products will still be available in the event of a foreign supply disruption, just at a higher price. Today, macroeconomic energy security concerns the resilience of the U.S. economy to temporary unexpected price hikes—price shocks—of foreign origin.

Historically, temporary oil price shocks arising from foreign supply disruptions have cut GDP growth and reduced employment. These events have been studied and debated in depth in the economics literature (see Hamilton 2009 and Kilian 2008b, 2014 for surveys). Table 6-1 presents a list of the major oil supply disruptions from 1973 to 2005 identified in Kilian

---

[6] In a joint statement released May 6, 2014, the G-7 energy ministers stated: "We believe that the path to energy security is built on a number of core principles: Development of flexible, transparent and competitive energy markets, including gas markets; Diversification of energy fuels, sources and routes, and encouragement of indigenous sources of energy supply; Reducing our greenhouse gas emissions, and accelerating the transition to a low carbon economy, as a key contribution to enduring energy security; Enhancing energy efficiency in demand and supply, and demand response management; Promoting deployment of clean and sustainable energy technologies and continued investment in research and innovation; Improving energy systems resilience by promoting infrastructure modernization and supply and demand policies that help withstand systemic shocks; [and] Putting in place emergency response systems, including reserves and fuel substitution for importing countries, in case of major energy disruptions."

Table 6-1
Major Oil Disruptions, 1973–2005

Event Name	Date	Duration (months)	Gross Peak Global Supply Loss (millions of barrels per day)	Percent Change in Oil Prices
Arab Oil Embargo & Arab-Israeli War	Oct-73 to Mar-74	6	4.3	45%
Iranian Revolution	Nov-78 to Apr-79	6	5.6	53%
Iran-Iraq War	Oct-80 to Jan-81	3	4.1	40%
Persian Gulf War	Aug-90 to Jan-91	6	4.3	32%
Civil Unrest in Venezuela	Dec-02 to Mar-03	4	2.6	28%
Iraq War	Mar-03 to Dec-03	10	2.3	28%

Source: Events as identified in Kilian (2008a) and Hamilton (2009). Dates and gross peak supply loss figures as identified in IEA(2012). Price changes for events over select windows as specified in Hamilton (2009) and price changes before 1982 measured using crude petroleum PPI as in Hamilton (2009).

(2008a) and Hamilton (2009), the estimated gross peak global supply loss, and the percentage change in oil prices in the aftermath of the disruption. For example, in the months following the Iranian Revolution in November 1978, oil prices increased by 53 percent. This link is not perfect, and not every oil price shock has led to an economic slowdown, but as is discussed below in more detail, the empirical evidence points to a negative link between oil price spikes and economic activity.

Trends in Oil Import Prices and Shares

The price of oil plays a central role in macroeconomic energy security. Figure 6-16 shows the price of oil in nominal (current) dollars and in 2013 dollars (deflated by the price index for consumer spending). Jumps in the price of oil are visible around the disruptions described in Table 6-1, as well as during more gradual increases such as in 2007 to 2008. Oil prices in November 2014, of roughly $75 per barrel, are comparable, in real terms,

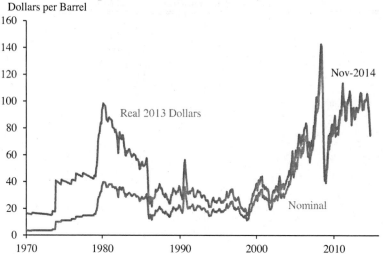

Figure 6-16
WTI Spot Price: Nominal and Real, 1970–2014

Dollars per Barrel

Note: Nominal prices deflated using overall PCE price index.
Source: Energy Information Administration, Spot Prices for Crude Oil and Petroleum
Products; Bureau of Economic Analysis, Personal Consumption Expenditures.

with those in the early 1980s, but are roughly twice the real prices of the 1990s.

The expenditure share of net petroleum imports measures the fraction of GDP that is spent on net imports of petroleum. Ignoring compositional differences, this share is the product of net barrels of petroleum imports times the price per barrel, divided by GDP. Figure 6-17 presents two measures of the expenditure share of GDP that is net imports. The first uses a narrow definition of net imports of crude, gasoline, distillates, and fuel oil. The second, which is only available starting in 1973, uses a broader definition that includes other refined products, such as jet fuel. The alternative definition slightly increases the share relative to the narrow measure but does not materially change the overall time series pattern. In order to observe longer-term movements, the Figure also presents smoothed trends of the two measures, which reduce the influence of high frequency fluctuations in these series due to short-term price volatility. During the 1990s, the price of oil was low even though physical imports were higher than in previous years, which kept the expenditure share relatively low. In contrast, between early 2011 and mid-2014, high oil prices have produced a relatively high expenditure share, though this share has declined noticeably over the past few years as domestic demand has declined and domestic oil production has increased. The high correlation of the net import share with

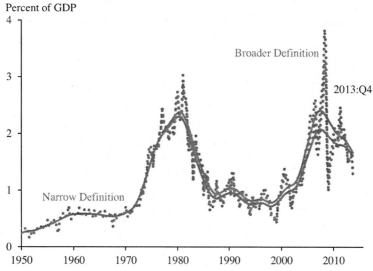

Figure 6-17
Net Import Shares of Petroleum Products, 1950–2013

Percent of GDP

Source: Energy Information Administration, Monthly Energy Review (Apr 2014); CEA calculations.

price indicates that the short-term price elasticity of demand for petroleum products is quite low, meaning that consumers do not reduce their demand very much when the price rises.

Macroeconomic Channels of Oil Price Shocks

Oil price shocks can affect GDP through several channels, including demand for goods and services, supply (production), and physical product rationing. As Kilian (2009) and Blinder (2009) point out, these channels are conceptually distinct and can have different macroeconomic effects.

Via the demand channel, an increase in the price of oil reduces spending on other goods and services, reducing GDP. Because, as noted above, the short-run demand for petroleum products is quite price-inelastic, the share of expenditures by consumers and firms on petroleum rises when the oil price increases.[7] Because the United States is a net importer of oil, expenditures on net imports also rise when the oil price increases. If the oil shock is known to be temporary, the life-cycle theory of consumption sug-

---

[7] For example, Kilian and Murphy (2014) estimate the short-run price elasticity of demand for oil to be approximately -0.3, meaning that a one percent oil price increase reduces consumption by 0.3 percent. Earlier estimates show short-run elasticities of even smaller magnitudes. If demand for energy-intensive imported products is similarly insensitive to price changes, an oil price increase would strongly raise U.S. spending on those imported products and therefore strongly diminish the income available to spend on other goods.

gests that consumers would make minimal adjustments to the rest of their consumption and would temporarily finance the additional oil expenditure by drawing down savings. However, in practice consumers do not know the duration of a price hike and many, or most, would instead reduce their consumption of other goods and services to pay for the more expensive fuel needed for daily life. Because expenditures on oil imports go abroad and not to the domestic economy, the additional spending on fuel does not count toward GDP. As a result, the immediate effect of a price increase on an imported good like oil, which has price-inelastic demand, is to decrease consumption of domestic goods and services and, as a result, to decrease GDP. This demand-reducing effect works just as if consumers' wealth had been reduced, so this channel is sometimes referred to as the wealth channel. The wealth channel can be large; for instance, if net oil imports are 2 percent of GDP, as they were in the late 1970s and late 2000s, a 10-percent jump in the price of oil causes a corresponding reduction in spending on everything else and reduces GDP by about 0.2 percent. The wealth channel can be offset by other factors, however, depending on the source of the oil price increase. For example, an increase in overall world economic activity that drives up the demand for, and the price of, oil would also expand U.S. exports, at least partially offsetting the macroeconomic effects of the increased price of oil imports.

There are two other ways, besides the wealth effect, by which an oil price increase can affect demand. First, an oil price increase, like a change in the relative price of any other good, also changes the composition of demand as consumers shift spending from items that are indirectly affected by the price increase (like air travel and cars with low fuel economy) to goods and services that are less energy-intensive. Thus, products of energy-intensive sectors become relatively more expensive and those sectors will see a reduction in demand. Even within sectors, demand can shift across products, such as to cars with greater fuel economy. Moreover, to the extent that shifting from energy-intensive goods reduces purchases of durables such as automobiles or refrigerators, spending today is shifted into the future, depressing aggregate demand. Although this temporal shift increases demand in less energy-intensive sectors, it takes time for displaced workers to find alternative employment in those sectors, so incomes decline and unemployment rises (see for example Hamilton 1988).

Second, an oil price increase can depress domestic demand if it raises uncertainty. Concerns about the economic future can lead consumers to postpone major purchases and convince firms to postpone investment and hiring, which slows the economy (for example, Bernanke 1983, Dixit and Pindyck 1994, Bloom 2009; and for oil investment specifically, Kellogg

2010). Oil price volatility can be causal (the volatility creates uncertainty that postpones investment, hiring, or durables consumption), or the volatility can simply reflect broader market uncertainty about future economic or geopolitical events. Another potential demand-side channel is a fall in aggregate consumption because an oil price rise is regressive and transfers income from individuals with a high marginal propensity to consume to individuals with a lower marginal propensity to consume (for example, Nordhaus 2007).

Oil price increases can also reduce economic activity through the supply side of the economy. To the extent that energy prices more broadly move with oil prices, an increase in oil prices makes energy a more expensive factor of production and increases costs to businesses and households, who will strive to reduce energy consumption and expenditures. Although high energy prices could cause firms and households to shift toward less energy-intensive technology in the long run; in the short run, with fixed technology, higher energy costs can result in layoffs in energy-intensive firms and industries (Linn 2008 and 2009). Because it takes time for displaced workers to find jobs, incomes decline and unemployment rises. This supply-side channel matters most if price increases are long lasting. Because capital and labor are being used less efficiently, this channel also could harm productivity growth. However, because of economy-wide improvements in energy efficiency over the last several decades, as shown in Figure 6-19 below, this supply-side channel is less important today than it has been in the past.

The channels discussed above concern changes in the relative price of oil and assume that oil is available. If, however, prices are not flexible and instead oil or petroleum products are rationed, the effect on GDP can be severe. On the production side, because technology is fixed in the short run, many workers cannot do their jobs without oil. Time spent waiting in line for gasoline is time not spent productively. In such cases, output falls, and even relatively small dollar volumes of unavailable supply can have an outsized influence on the economy. Fortunately, the development of global crude oil markets and deregulated domestic retail markets have made widespread petroleum product rationing a thing of the past, outside of occasional temporary regional events stemming from weather-related supply chain disruptions. Such events can have significant, even life-threatening impacts on the individuals involved, and minimizing those impacts through improving supply chain resilience is an important goal (and indeed is a central topic of the Quadrennial Energy Review). But the temporary nature of these events and regional scope means that the macroeconomic impact of the resulting petroleum product unavailability is limited.

CEA (2014a) presents reduced-form empirical evidence on the relative importance of the different effects of energy supply shocks on the

U.S. economy and on the changing correlations among energy prices. The results of this analysis suggest that a lower share of net oil imports in GDP enhances the resilience of the economy to oil price shocks. Specifically, the same oil-price increase reduces GDP much less in 2015 than it did in 2006, and will reduce GDP even less at the lower import level that EIA projects for 2017. This analysis suggests that the unconventional oil boom and lower oil demand have significantly improved U.S. energy security.

A Path to a Low-Carbon Future

Most anthropogenic emissions of greenhouse gases are energy-related, particularly from the combustion of fossil fuels (EPA 2010). A central challenge of energy and environmental policy is to find a responsible path that balances the economic benefits of low-cost energy with the social and environmental costs to future generations associated with conventional energy production. Addressing these challenges is a central part of the President's All-of-the-Above Energy Strategy, which several recent policy achievements demonstrate. As part of the 2009 Conference of the Parties to the United Nations Framework Convention on Climate Change in Copenhagen, the United States pledged to cut its CO_2 and other greenhouse gas emissions in the range of 17 percent below 2005 levels by 2020. Under the President's Climate Action Plan, the United States is expected to meet this target. Moreover, in November 2014 President Obama and President Xi Jinping of China jointly announced historic post-2020 climate targets. Specifically, China committed to peak its emissions by around 2030 and to double the share of non-fossil (nuclear and renewable) energy in its overall economy from about 10 percent today to around 20 percent by 2030. At the same time, the United States announced a new goal to reduce emissions 26 to 28 percent below 2005 levels by 2025. The United States and China also agreed to work together on energy innovation and toward a successful global agreement as part of the continuing United Nations climate negotiations.

A Case for Climate Action

From an economist's perspective, greenhouse gas emissions generate a negative externality. A negative externality occurs when the production or consumption of a good imposes harm on individuals not involved in the production or consumption of that good. For example, a business burning oil to run a generator or a person driving a gasoline-powered car emits greenhouse gasses, which negatively affect other people—including future generations. Economically efficient policies to address this negative externality would require those responsible—the business burning the oil or the person driving the car—to pay the true cost of their additional—or marginal—emissions, which takes into account the harm they caused to third parties. Compelling businesses and individuals to pay the true incremental costs encourages them to produce and consume less of the fuels, and also encourages technological solutions that reduce the externality, such as cars with higher fuel economy. On a larger scale, greenhouse gas emissions from the United States affect residents in other countries and vice versa. In fact, U.S. emissions have the same effect on the global climate as emissions from any other country. Putting a price on emissions that is equal to the global cost of an additional ton of emissions would cause those responsible for the emissions to pay the incremental costs of their actions.

A recent CEA report (2014b) examines the economic consequences of delaying implementing such policies and reaches two main conclusions, both of which point to the benefits of swiftly implementing mitigation policies and to the high costs of delaying such actions. First, although delaying action can reduce costs in the short run, on net, delaying action to limit the effects of climate change is costly. Because CO_2 accumulates in the atmosphere, delay allows CO_2 concentrations to increase more quickly. Thus, if a policy delay ultimately leads to higher future CO_2 concentrations, that delay produces persistent economic damages due to the higher temperatures and CO_2 concentrations that result. Alternatively, if a delayed policy still aims to achieve a given climate target, such as limiting CO_2 concentration to a given level, then a delay means that when implemented, the policy must be more stringent and thus more costly in subsequent years. In either case, delay is costly.

Costs of delay will take the form of either greater damages from climate change or higher costs associated with implementing more rapid reductions in greenhouse gas emissions. In practice, both forms are possible and potentially large. Based on a leading aggregate damage estimate in the climate economics literature, a delay that results in warming of 3° Celsius above preindustrial levels, instead of 2°, could increase economic damages by approximately 0.9 percent of global output (CEA 2014b, based on Nordhaus 2013). To put this percentage in perspective, 0.9 percent of estimated 2014 U.S. GDP is approximately $150 billion. The incremental cost of an additional degree of warming beyond 3° Celsius would be even greater. Moreover, these costs are not one-time, but instead are incurred year after year because of the recurring damage caused by permanently increased climate warning resulting from the delay.

An analysis of research on the effect of delay on the cost of achieving a specified climate target (typically, a given concentration of greenhouse gases) suggests that net mitigation costs increase, on average, by approximately 40 percent for each decade of delay (CEA 2014b). These costs are higher for more aggressive climate goals: since each year of delay means more CO2 emissions, it becomes increasingly difficult, or even infeasible, to hit a climate target that would result in only moderate temperature increases.

The second conclusion explained in the CEA report (2014b) is that climate policy can be thought of as "climate insurance" taken out against the most severe and irreversible potential consequences of climate change. Events such as the rapid melting of ice sheets and the consequent swell in global sea levels, or temperature rises on the higher end of the range of scientific uncertainty, could pose such severe economic consequences that they could reasonably be thought of as climate catastrophes. Reducing the possibility of such climate catastrophes will require taking prudent steps now to reduce the future chances of the most severe consequences of climate change. The longer that action is postponed, the greater the concentration of CO2 in the atmosphere will be and the greater the risk of severe climate events. Just as businesses and individuals guard against severe financial risks by purchasing various forms of insurance, policymakers can take actions now that reduce expected climate damages. And, unlike conventional insurance policies, climate policy that serves as climate insurance is an investment that also leads to cleaner air (Parry et al. 2014), energy security, and benefits that are difficult to monetize, such as biological diversity.

Two other recent reports underscore these conclusions about the cost of delaying climate action. As part of the Fifth Assessment Report, the Intergovernmental Panel on Climate Change (IPCC) recently released its Synthesis Report, which integrates the Fifth Assessment's separate reports on physical science, impacts, and mitigation (released over the past two years). The Synthesis Report summarizes the literature quantifying the impacts of projected climate change by sector. Impacts include: decreased agricultural production; coastal flooding, erosion, and submergence; increases in heat-related illness and other stresses due to extreme weather events; reduction in water availability and quality; displacement of people and increased risk of violent conflict; and species extinction and biodiversity loss. Although effects vary by region, and some are not well-understood, evidence of these impacts has grown in recent years. The IPCC also cites simulation studies showing that delay is costly, both when all countries delay action and when there is partial delay, with some countries delaying action while awaiting a more coordinated international effort; CEA (2014b) expands on that analysis by including additional studies.

Combining climate projections with empirically based estimates of the links between climate and the U.S. economy, the Risky Business report (Risky Business Project 2014) echoes many of the IPCC's conclusions. The

Risky Business report predicts that, in the coming decades, climate change will likely impose significant costs on many regions and facets of the U.S. economy. The report describes the effects of rising sea levels, storms and flooding, and droughts and extreme heat waves. The report's authors estimate that $66 billion to $106 billion of existing coastal property will likely be below sea level by 2050. Within just the next 15 years, the average costs of coastal storms on the East Coast and Gulf of Mexico will likely increase by $2 billion to $3.5 billion a year. By 2050, the average American likely will annually experience two to three times more days that reach 95°F, to the detriment of human health and labor productivity. Higher temperatures and different weather patterns likely will affect agricultural productivity—with gains for Northern farmers and losses for Midwestern and Southern farmers. Overall, the report emphasizes the considerable risk that climate change is imposing on the U.S. economy.

The Climate Action Plan

Recognizing the case for immediate and strong climate action, the President called on Congress in his 2013 State of the Union address to pass legislation that would provide a market-based mechanism for reducing emissions. Thus far, Congress has failed to act but the President has taken other actions, including direct regulation of greenhouse gas emissions under the Clean Air Act.[8]

To address the broad challenges associated with climate change, the President's Climate Action Plan has three central goals: a) reduce domestic emissions, b) prepare for the impacts of climate change, and c) provide international leadership to address climate change. The remainder of this

---

[8] Regulations have costs and benefits, and computing the monetary benefits of reducing CO_2 emissions requires an estimate of the net present value of the economic cost of an additional, or marginal, ton of CO_2 emissions. This cost—which covers health, property damage, agricultural impacts, the value of ecosystem services, and other costs of climate change—is often referred to as the "social cost of carbon" (SCC). In 2010, a Federal interagency working group, led by the CEA and the Office of Management and Budget, produced a Technical Support Document that outlined a methodology for estimating the SCC and provided numeric estimates (White House 2010). Since then, the SCC has been used at various stages of rulemaking by the Department of Transportation, the Environmental Protection Agency, and the Department of Energy. The SCC estimate is updated as the science and models underlying the SCC progress, and in November 2013 public comments were invited on the most recent update of the SCC, which produced an estimate of $39 per metric ton CO_2 in 2015 (2011 dollars). The SCC increases over time as the economy grows and emissions cause greater damage, and reaches $76 per metric ton CO_2 in 2050.

Reducing greenhouse gas emissions is likely to yield additional benefits, besides the climate benefits, which are often referred to as co-benefits (Parry et al. 2014). For example, policies that reduce fuel consumption at coal-fired electricity generators cause lower emissions of particulates and other pollutants that harm human health.

section describes the initiatives under the first goal, reducing domestic emissions. As explained below, the first part of the Climate Action Plan includes a broad range of actions, from providing research, demonstration, and deployment funding for new energy technologies to the direct regulation of carbon emissions under the Clean Air Act. For example, in the Clean Power Plan, the Environmental Protection Agency has proposed regulations to reduce electricity-sector CO_2 emissions. The proposal is projected to reduce CO_2 emissions by about 30 percent from 2005 levels, and the total benefits of emissions reductions are expected easily to outweigh the costs. Box 6-3 provides a list of selected initiatives under the Climate Action Plan.

To date, the United States has made important progress in reducing greenhouse gas emissions, but more work remains. As Figure 6-18 shows, U.S. energy-related CO_2 emissions have fallen 10 percent from their peak in 2007. Given a counterfactual, or baseline, path for CO_2 emissions, one can attribute the reduction in CO_2 emissions to changes in the carbon content of energy, energy efficiency, and in the level of GDP, relative to the baseline path.[9]

The baseline path is computed using a combination of historical trends and published forecasts as of 2005. Relative to this baseline, the decline in post-2013 projected emissions is due to policy-driven improvements, market-driven shifts to cleaner energy, and slower growth than was initially projected in 2005; that is, because of the decline in economic activity as a result of the Great Recession. Importantly, the post-2013 projected emissions exclude the portions of the Climate Action Plan yet to be finalized—notably, the Clean Power Plan and new actions to address methane pollution. Policy and market-driven shifts to cleaner energy make a large contribution to the decline in post-2013 projected emissions. These shifts include the reduction in electricity generated by coal and the increase in cleaner natural gas and zero-emissions wind and solar generation. Improvements in energy efficiency, partly due to vehicle, equipment, and appliance standards, also made a contribution. The recent reduction in emissions shows that while progress has been made, given the magnitude of the climate challenges, policies currently in progress and under development will be important to reaching our 2020 and post-2020 climate targets, but more remains to be done.

---

[9] Specifically, CO_2 emissions are the product of $(CO_2/Btu) \times (Btu/GDP) \times GDP$, where CO_2 represents U.S. CO_2 emissions in a given year, Btu represents energy consumption in that year, and GDP is that year's GDP. Taking logarithms of this expression, and then subtracting the actual values from the baseline, gives a decomposition of the CO_2 reduction into contributions from clean energy, energy efficiency, and the recent recession.

Box 6-3: Selected Administration Initiatives under the Climate Action Plan

A broad range of Administration initiatives promote the development and adoption of technologies that reduce greenhouse gas emissions. The Administration has:

Electricity

• Proposed the Clean Power Plan, which will help cut CO_2 pollution from the electricity sector by 30 percent from 2005 levels. The proposal sets rates of CO_2 emissions for each State, and provides States flexibility to meet those standards by 2030.

• Issued about $30 billion in loan guarantees to kick-start utility-scale solar; supported "first mover" advanced nuclear reactors with enhanced safety features in Georgia; and enabled the auto industry to retool for very efficient and electric vehicles.

• In partnership with industry, invested in 4 commercial-scale and 24 industrial-scale coal projects that will store more than 15 million metric tons of CO_2 per year.

• Under the Recovery Act, supported more than 90,000 projects by leveraging nearly $50 billion in private, regional, and state dollars to deploy enough renewable electricity to power 6.5 million homes annually.

• As part of a commitment to improvements in permitting and transmission for renewables, approved 50 utility-scale renewable energy proposals and associated transmission, including 27 solar, 11 wind, and 12 geothermal projects since 2009, enough to power 4.8 million homes. Thirteen of the projects are already in operation.

Transportation

• In 2012, finalized national standards to double the fuel economy of light-duty cars and trucks by 2025 and slash greenhouse gas emissions by 6 billion metric tons over the lifetime of the vehicles sold during this period.

• Building on the first-ever medium- and heavy-duty truck fuel economy and greenhouse gas standards released in 2011, began collaborating with industry to develop standards for trucks beyond model year 2018, which will yield large savings in fuel, lower CO_2 emissions, and health benefits from reduced particulate matter and ozone.

Energy Efficiency

• In the second term alone, finalized energy conservation standards for 13 products. These standards—when taken together with the final rules already issued under this Administration—mean that more than 70 percent of the President's goal of reducing cumulative carbon pollution by 3 billion metric tons by 2030 through appliance efficiency standards will be achieved, over which time Americans will save hundreds of billions of dollars in energy costs.

• Launched the Better Buildings Challenge in 2011 to help American buildings become at least 20 percent more energy efficient by 2020. More than 190 diverse organizations, representing over 3 billion square feet, 600 manufacturing plants, and close to $2 billion in energy efficiency financing stepped up to the President's Challenge. Participation has grown rapidly and participating organizations include states, cities, school districts, multifamily housing organizations, retailers, food and hospitality service providers, and manufacturing organizations.

• Beginning in 2009, created weatherization programs that helped low-income households save $250 to $500 per year on their energy bills, and provided energy efficiency improvements to nearly 2 million homes.

The President, as part of his FY 2016 Budget, is also proposing new initiatives to:

• Invest $5 billion in funding for clean energy technology activities at the Department of Energy, including $900 million for programs and infrastructure that support nuclear energy technologies, $900 million to increase affordability and convenience of advanced vehicles and renewable fuels, and $5 million in cleaner energy from fossil fuels.

• Put $1 billion toward advancing the goals of the Global Climate Change Initiative (GCCI) and the President's Climate Action Plan by supporting bilateral and multilateral engagement with major and emerging economies.

Reducing Emissions through Improved Efficiency

The amount of energy used to produce a dollar of real GDP has declined steadily over the past four decades, and today stands at less than one-half of what it was in 1970 (Figure 6-19). This improvement in overall energy efficiency, which has averaged 1.6 percent a year since 1960, is due both to more efficient use of energy resources to complete the same or similar tasks and to shifts in the types of tasks undertaken. The first contribution is reflected in the Economy-Wide Energy Intensity Index (also shown in Figure 6-19) developed by DOE, which estimates the amount of energy needed to produce a given basket of goods in one year compared to the amount required the year before. Between 1985 and 2011, the Energy Intensity Index fell by 14 percent. The second contribution to the decrease in the energy-to-GDP ratio arises from such factors as shifts in production from more to less energy-intensive sectors of the economy, as well as shifts to imports rather than production of energy-intensive goods. These latter

Figure 6-18
Energy Related Carbon Dioxide Emissions, 1980–2030

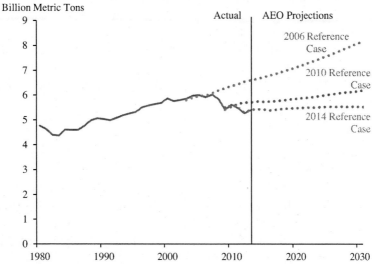

Source: Energy Information Administration, Annual Energy Outlook (AEO) 2006, 2010, and 2014.

Figure 6-19
U.S. Energy Intensity, 1950–2011

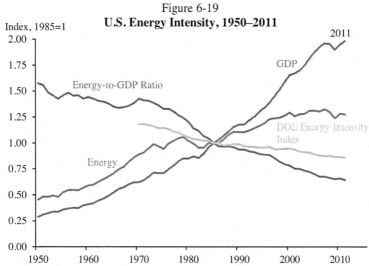

Note: The DOE Energy Intensity Index illustrates the amount of energy needed to produce a set basket of goods over time. The Energy-to-GDP ratio shows energy use per dollar of overall output.
Source: Department of Energy, Energy Information Administration and Office of Energy Efficiency and Renewable Energy.

factors and the efficiency increases together produced a drop of 36 percent in the ratio of energy to GDP between 1985 and 2011.

Both market forces and government programs spur energy efficiency improvements. For example, as Figure 6-20a shows, gasoline consumption per capita rose through the early 2000s and plateaued in the mid-2000s before dropping substantially during the Great Recession. As the economy recovered, however, gasoline consumption per capita continued to fall. Some of this continued decline stems from the relatively high real gasoline prices shown in Figure 6-20a, but only in part. Increasing fuel economy brought about by Federal fuel economy standards also played a role. In 2012, the Administration finalized fuel economy standards that, together with the Administration's first round of standards, will roughly double the fuel economy of light-duty vehicles from 2010 levels to the equivalent of 54.5 miles per gallon by the 2025 model year (Figure 6-20b). Further, beginning in model year 2014, medium- and heavy-duty trucks have had to meet their own fuel economy and greenhouse gas standards, which are projected to increase their fuel economy by 10 to 20 percent by 2018. Finally, the Accelerate Energy Productivity 2030 initiative (being undertaken by the Department of Energy with two private-sector partners: the Council on Competitiveness and the Alliance to Save Energy) is supporting the President's goal of doubling energy productivity (GDP per unit of energy use) from its 2010 level by 2030.

The Role of Natural Gas in Lowering CO_2 Emissions

Natural gas is already playing a central role in the transition to a clean energy future. According to the decomposition mentioned in Footnote 12, nearly one-half of the CO2 emissions reductions from 2005 through 2013 stem from fuel switching, primarily switching from the use of coal to natural gas, wind, and solar for the purpose of generating electricity. Unconventional natural gas development has opened a vast resource and, as shown in Figure 6-21, the EIA Reference case (which includes the base-line assumptions for economic growth, oil prices, and technology) projects increasing quantities of natural gas production and steady price growth over the coming two decades.

Price is the leading reason for the increased use of natural gas in elec-tricity generation. As Figure 6-22 shows, steep declines in natural gas prices in 2008 through 2009 and in 2012 induced substitution of natural gas for coal in electricity generation. Confirming the link between natural gas prices and fuel substitution is the fact that rising natural gas prices have the oppo-site effect. In 2013, the benchmark natural gas price increased from $3.33 per million Btu in January 2013 to $4.24 per million Btu in December 2013;

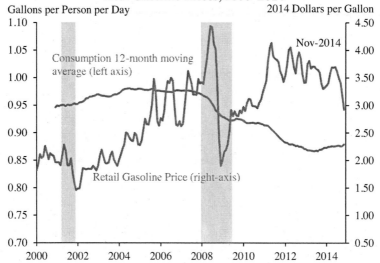

Figure 6-20a
**U.S. Per Capita Consumption of Gasoline and
Real Gasoline Prices, 2000–2014**

Gallons per Person per Day   2014 Dollars per Gallon

Note: Retail gasoline prices deflated using consumer price index (1982-84=100).
Source: Energy Information Administration; Department of Commerce, Census Bureau; CEA
calculations.

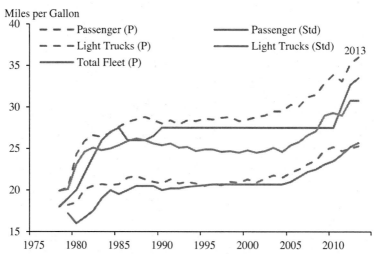

Figure 6-20b
Corporate Average Fuel Economy Standard

Miles per Gallon

Note: Dotted lines represent actual performance (P) and solid lines represent the relevant fuel
economy standard (Std).
Source: Energy Information Administration, Annual Energy Outlook.

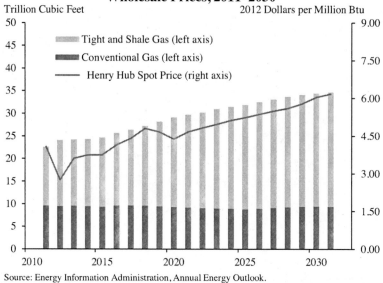

Figure 6-21
**U.S. Natural Gas Production and
Wholesale Prices, 2011–2030**

Trillion Cubic Feet

2012 Dollars per Million Btu

Tight and Shale Gas (left axis)

Conventional Gas (left axis)

Henry Hub Spot Price (right axis)

Source: Energy Information Administration, Annual Energy Outlook.

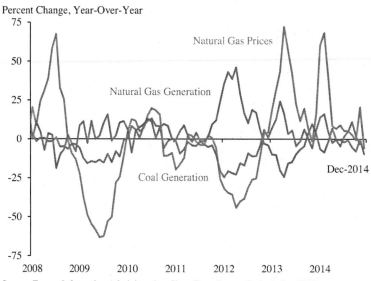

Figure 6-22
Change in Monthly Electricity Generation and Prices, 2008–2014

Percent Change, Year-Over-Year

Natural Gas Prices

Natural Gas Generation

Coal Generation

Dec-2014

Source: Energy Information Administration, Short-Term Energy Outlook (Jan 2015).

and as natural gas prices rose relative to coal, the use of coal for electricity generation increased while the use of natural gas decreased. Looking ahead, the price of natural gas will make it an economically attractive alternative fuel as market forces as well as state and federal policies further reduce coal-fired electricity generation.

The Administration is taking steps to ensure that the expansion of natural gas and oil production be done responsibly and with environmental safeguards. Environmental concerns include both climate impacts of fugitive methane emissions and flaring, as well as local environmental issues associated with water and land use for hydraulic fracturing operations.[10] The Climate Action Plan includes a strategy both to reduce methane emissions and to address gaps in current methane emissions data. The regulatory structure for addressing local environmental concerns, especially around land and water use, exists primarily at the State and local level. Research that is actively under way will inform prudent local environmental regulation of hydraulic fracturing.

Looking further ahead, the current development of natural gas generation infrastructure prepares the Nation for future widespread deployment of wind and solar generation. Wind and solar are non-dispatchable, meaning that electricity generation depends on how strongly the wind is blowing or the sun is shining, in contrast to fossil fuel-fired generators, whose power output can be largely adjusted as needed. Consequently, high market penetration of both wind and solar would benefit from either storage or backup generation capacity. Developing natural gas infrastructure today facilitates its use tomorrow for peak demand and renewable backup generation.

Supporting Renewables, Nuclear, Cleaner Coal, and Cleaner Transportation

Low- and zero-carbon renewable and nuclear technologies, as well as cleaner coal and transportation technologies, have a central role to play in a clean energy future. Consequently, the President's All-of-the-Above Energy Strategy makes a strong commitment to supporting these low-carbon technologies.

---

[10] Natural gas is composed primarily of methane, which is a potent greenhouse gas. Fugitive methane refers to methane that leaks from wells, pipelines, or other parts of the natural gas delivery system. Flaring refers to burning excess gas. Because flared gas emits CO_2 rather than methane, the greenhouse gas footprint is smaller when the gas is flared rather than emitted directly to the atmosphere. However, both fugitive emissions and flaring increase the total greenhouse gas footprint of natural gas. Fugitive methane emissions and flaring are relevant to both natural gas and oil production, because many oil wells contain significant amounts of natural gas.

Electricity from Wind and Solar Energy. Historically, tax incentives for wind and solar energy have been based on the avoided-pollution-emissions and infant-industry arguments. Wind and solar generation are zero-emission sources of energy and thus do not create a negative climate externality.

The market demand for these alternative sources is sub-optimally low from society's point of view since emitters do not bear the incremental cost of their emissions-related damages and therefore have little incentive to switch away from more carbon-intensive energy sources. The potential market profits of wind and solar projects, therefore, do not reflect the broad benefits to society of their zero emissions, so policies such as tax incentives are justified. Moreover, offering tax incentives to immature technologies could spur innovation that reduces the costs of renewables in the long run. In a wide range of contexts, both inside and outside of the energy sector, new technologies experience periods of rapid learning. If firms can profit from their own learning—say by improving their products or reducing manufacturing costs—then firms have every incentive to spend resources on learning and improving technology. But with new technologies—so-called infant industries—a market failure could cause too little investment in their research, development, and demonstration. Specifically, a business that learns and improves its technology may see its competitors take those improvements and reduce their own costs or improve their own products (for example, without violating any patents). If the first business anticipates that its competitors will benefit from its own learning, then that business is less likely to spend the resources needed to learn and potential improvements in technology will suffer. In such cases, where learning spills over across firms, private markets create less innovation than is socially optimal. Accordingly, the Administration supports research and early deployment projects aimed at bringing down the ultimate market price of immature renewable energy technologies.

Increasing competitiveness of wind and photovoltaic electricity production, renewable portfolio standards that many states have adopted, and other government policies have together increased the share of electricity generated by non-hydro renewables from roughly 2 percent in 2005 to 7 percent in 2014 (Figure 6-23). The total installed costs of new photovoltaic systems have dropped sharply since around 2008, with the total installed cost of a new system falling by almost 50 percent for residential and commercial-scale systems and by 40 percent for utility-scale systems (Barbose et al. 2014).

The Administration has also supported solar deployment. Five years ago, no significant wind or solar energy projects existed on public lands. Today, the Interior Department is on track to permit enough solar and wind

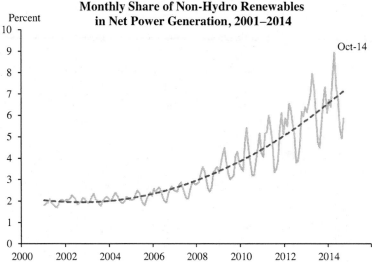

Figure 6-23
Monthly Share of Non-Hydro Renewables in Net Power Generation, 2001–2014

Percent

Oct-14

Note: Solid line shows actual data and dotted line is a smoothed trend, shown to dampen the strong seasonal patterns (the share of non-hydro renewables drops during the winter and summer--both seasons of high power generation demand).
Source: Energy Information Administration, Net Generation for All Sectors.

projects on public lands by 2020 to power more than 6 million homes; the Defense Department has set a goal to deploy three gigawatts of renewable energy—including solar, wind, biomass, and geothermal—on Army, Navy, and Air Force installations by 2025; and, as part of the Climate Action Plan, the Federal Government has committed to sourcing 20 percent of the energy consumed in Federal buildings from renewable sources by 2020.

Nuclear and Cleaner Coal. Nuclear energy provides zero-carbon base load electricity and, through DOE, the Administration is supporting nuclear research and deployment. A high priority of DOE has been to help accelerate the timelines for the commercialization and deployment of small modular reactor (SMR) technologies through the SMR Licensing Technical Support program. Small modular reactors offer the advantage of lower initial capital investment, scalability, and siting flexibility at locations unable to accommodate more traditional larger reactors. They also have the potential for enhanced safety and security; for example, through built-in passive safety systems. DOE is committing $452 million to support first-of-a-kind SMR activities through cost-sharing arrangements with industry partners.

DOE is also supporting deployment of advanced large-scale reactors. In February 2014, the Department issued $6.5 billion in loan guarantees to support the construction of the nation's next generation of advanced nuclear reactors. The two new 1100 megawatt reactors, which will be located in

Georgia, feature advanced safety components and could provide a standard-ized design for the U.S. utilities market.

The Administration is also advancing lower GHG emission coal technology. DOE's R&D program is focused on improving advanced power generation and carbon capture, utilization, and storage technologies by increasing overall system efficiencies and reducing capital costs. In the near-term, advanced technologies are being developed that both increase the power generation efficiency for new plants, and incorporate new technologies to capture CO_2. The longer-term goals are to increase coal plant efficiencies and reduce both the energy and capital costs of CO_2 capture and storage from coal plants. As part of its $6 billion commitment to coal technology, the Administration, partnered with industry, is investing in commercial-scale carbon capture and storage projects at power plants and industrial sites, and in research and development on new technologies. In addition, the Department of Energy has made available $8 billion in loan guarantees for advanced fossil energy products that avoid, reduce, or sequester greenhouse gas emissions.

Meeting the Challenge of the Transportation Sector. Low-carbon vehicle technologies and fuels must play an important role in the transportation sector. Promising low-emission alternatives include hybrids, electric vehicles, hydrogen, natural gas, and biofuels. The effective emissions from an electric vehicle depend on the source of electricity, and they will fall as the electric power sector reduces its CO_2 emissions. Different fuels are likely to be relatively better suited for different needs; for example, natural gas for busses and heavy-duty fleet vehicles and electricity for private vehicles in urban settings. But the transformation of the transportation sector is in its infancy, and the Administration is supporting research and development of a wide range of advanced transportation fuel options.

The convenience of high-energy content liquid fuels means that their role in the transportation sector could persist for decades. If so, renewable liquid fuels with a low greenhouse gas footprint would prove important for reducing the climate impact of the transportation sector. Already, the U.S. transportation sector uses ethanol, biodiesel, renewable diesel, and lesser quantities of other renewable fuels. Ethanol boosts octane and is blended into nearly all of the U.S. gasoline supply to produce E10, which is 10 percent ethanol by volume. Demand for renewable transportation fuels is further supported by the Renewable Fuel Standard (RFS). To qualify under the RFS as conventional renewable fuel, the fuel must achieve a 20 percent life-cycle greenhouse gas emissions reduction, relative to petroleum gasoline. The legislation authorizing the RFS, which was expanded under the Energy Independence and Security Act of 2007, mandated increasing amounts of renewable fuels over time. As Figure 6-24 shows, blending of ethanol into E10 has already reduced the amount of petroleum in gasoline substantially. The 2007 legislation envisioned conventional renewable fuels such as corn ethanol to be transitional and that their market share would decrease as the market share of advanced renewable fuels would increase. The long-term environmental goal of the RFS is to support the development of advanced biofuels, which have life cycle greenhouse gas emissions reductions of at least 50 percent, and especially to support cellulosic biofuels, which have life cycle greenhouse gas emissions reductions of at least 60 percent (cellulosic biofuels use feedstocks such as corn stover, which includes parts of the corn plant besides the kernels; conventional ethanol production does not use stover).

International Leadership

Actions taken to reduce domestic emissions, the first goal of the Climate Action Plan, provide the foundation for meeting the Plan's third objective: providing international leadership to address climate change. From 2005 to 2012 (the last year of data available from the EIA), the United States reduced its total carbon pollution (measured in tons of CO_2-equivalent) more than any other nation on Earth. And, as noted above, the

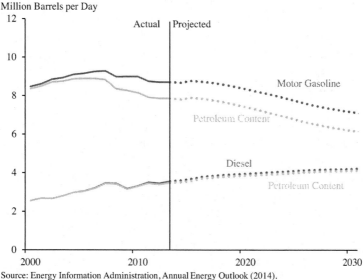

Figure 6-24
U.S. Motor Gasoline and Diesel Fuel Consumption, 2000–2030

Source: Energy Information Administration, Annual Energy Outlook (2014).

United States is further reducing its greenhouse gas emissions by: improving energy efficiency; taking advantage of unconventional natural gas as a transitional fuel; supporting renewable, nuclear, and clean coal energy sources; and regulating emissions under the Clean Air Act. But curbing greenhouse gas emissions is ultimately an international challenge, as is climate change. The United States produces approximately 16 percent of global energy-related CO_2 emissions, second only to China (Figure 6-25). As the economies in the developing world expand, however, their energy needs will increase. Business-as-usual projections indicate that an increasing share of greenhouse gas emissions will come from outside the United States and from the developing world in particular. Fully solving the problem of excessive emissions will therefore require a broad global response.

U.S. leadership is vital to the success of international negotiations to set meaningful reduction goals. This leadership is multifaceted. Through low-carbon technologies developed and demonstrated in the United States (including unconventional natural gas production technology), this Nation can help the rest of the world reduce its dependence on high-carbon fuels. The President's initiative under the Climate Action Plan to lead efforts to eliminate international public financing for new conventional coal plants, except in the poorest countries without economically feasible alternatives, will further help the world move toward cleaner fuels for electric power. Investing in research in new technologies such as carbon capture and storage for cleaner coal and natural gas, as well as biomass co-firing, and advanced renewable liquid fuels, pushes forward these frontiers, and supports U.S. technology leadership in clean energy. More broadly, clean energy technologies developed here, as well as domestically manufactured clean energy products, provide global benefits when they are used abroad to reduce greenhouse gas emissions. And by taking strong steps to reduce emissions at home, the Administration is in a strong position to secure similar commitments from other nations—both in discussions with individual countries and at the United Nations climate negotiations to be held in Paris in 2015. The domestic steps include new initiatives such as the second round of medium and heavy-duty truck greenhouse gas standards, programs to reduce methane emissions and other non-CO_2 gases outside the energy sector, and regulation of CO_2 emissions from the electric power sector, combined with the large and growing effects of enacted policies such as fuel economy standards for passenger vehicles. This strength is demonstrated by the recent historic joint announcement of post-2020 climate targets with China. In combination, the Administration's efforts lay the foundation for a cleaner energy future that is economically efficient, upholds our

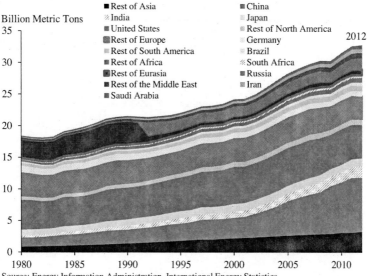

Figure 6-25
World Carbon Dioxide Emissions, 1980–2012

Billion Metric Tons

Source: Energy Information Administration, International Energy Statistics.

responsibility to future generations, and provides positive net economic benefits, both directly and through the example we set for other countries.

CONCLUSION

The U.S. energy sector has changed profoundly over the past decade. Technological innovations and government policies have reversed the decline in oil and gas production and have caused an explosion in renewable energy production. Building on these developments, the Administration's All-of-the-Above Energy Strategy supports job creation and economic growth, while improving the Nation's energy security. The energy revolution has benefited not only domestic energy sectors, but also the energy-consuming businesses and households that enjoy lower energy prices.

Recognizing the need to address climate change domestically and to provide international climate leadership, the President's Climate Action Plan includes a broad range of initiatives to reduce domestic emissions aggressively. These efforts lay the foundation for leadership in securing international agreements to reduce emissions and prepare for climate change. The Administration's energy strategy has built the framework for a sustainable energy future.

CHAPTER 7

THE UNITED STATES IN
A GLOBAL ECONOMY

The world's economies are more intertwined than ever before. Since the middle of the last century, declining policy barriers, transportation costs, and communication costs have driven a swift rise in world exports and foreign investment, far outpacing the growth in world output. Even so, the potential economic gains from trade for the United States are far from exhausted, as U.S. businesses must overcome an average tariff hurdle of 6.8 percent and countless non-tariff measures to serve the roughly three-quarters of world purchasing power and almost 95 percent of world consumers that are outside America's borders.

Expanding trade allows production inputs such as labor and capital to be used more efficiently, which raises overall productivity. U.S. businesses that grow in response to increased market access abroad create new jobs. These firms are more productive and rely more on capital and skilled workers, on average, than similar non-exporting firms. Partly because of this, the wages paid by exporting firms tend to be higher than wages paid by non-exporters in the same industry. In particular, evidence for the United States suggests that, in manufacturing, average wages in exporting firms and industries are up to 18 percent higher than average wages in non-exporting firms and industries.

In addition, international trade helps U.S. households' budgets go further. Because our trading partners also specialize in the goods and services for which they are relatively more productive, the prices for those goods and services in the United States are lower than if we could only consume what we produce. Trade also offers a much greater diversity of consumption opportunities, from year-round fresh fruit to affordable clothing.

By increasing global production and consumption opportunities, international trade can promote world economic growth and development. Trade among nations offers a mechanism potentially to reduce global poverty, which may decrease child labor and pull developing country workers into jobs with improved working conditions. Trade can be a force toward the empowerment of traditionally marginalized groups; for example, some empirical evidence suggests that decreased discrimination against women is related to the effects of global competition brought about by trade. Research also shows that bilateral trade agreements can reduce the likelihood of bilateral conflict, as economic cooperation promotes political cooperation, though the relationship is less clear in a multilateral setting, perhaps because multilateral trade reduces the dependence of any one country on another. Trade can also facilitate the spread of new green technologies throughout the world, which decreases emissions, potentially outweighing any additional emissions associated with an increased scale of production, consumption, and transportation.

However, because the process of globalization spurs the shifting of resources within national economies, it can also create challenges in areas like income inequality. For this reason, it is critical that globalization is managed—in terms of both the types of trade agreements the United States enters into and the domestic policies that are in place—in a way that ensures that more Americans can take advantage of the opportunities afforded by trade, while being better insulated from any challenges trade creates. Therefore, President Obama's "values-driven" trade policy seeks to do what's best for U.S. businesses and workers by enforcing international agreements that improve labor and environmental standards around the world, combat corruption, and strengthen the rule of law abroad. Encouraging such trade agreements maximizes globalization's benefits while minimizing globalization's unwanted side effects. For example, new U.S. trade agreements promote and enforce the rights of workers abroad, "leveling up" rather than "leveling down" and risking workers' rights in the United States. The Administration's domestic policies, such as skills training, infrastructure investment, and business tax reform, allow workers and firms to take better advantage of the opportunities trade offers. At the same time, policies like Trade Adjustment Assistance and the Affordable Care Act help protect workers from some of the challenges associated with broader, less-mindful globalization.

An additional aspect of the global economy, beyond trade in goods and services, is international financial markets, which also offer mutual benefits to trading economies. International financial transactions, through which countries diversify risks globally and undertake international borrowing and lending, can promote higher and more stable consumption levels throughout the world economy. But, they can also pose major risks to national and global stability, as was starkly manifested in a series of global financial crises in recent decades. To maximize benefits, increased financial integration must be accompanied by sustained and coordinated monitoring and regulation of financial institutions and markets.

This chapter starts by reviewing data on the growth in world exports and the role of trade agreements in facilitating this growth. In particular, the chapter reviews the proposed Trans-Pacific Partnership (TPP) and the Transatlantic Trade and Investment Partnership (T-TIP), which embody the President's "values-driven" approach to trade policy, by seeking to level the playing field for American workers and businesses, including by promoting enforceable standards for workers and strengthening environmental protections. The chapter next looks at the considerable benefits of trade, especially for workers in export-intensive industries, and the challenges faced by workers displaced as a result of trade. The chapter concludes by surveying the rapid growth of international financial markets. This last section of the chapter outlines the benefits and risks from international financial integration and the steps global policymakers have taken to contain those risks, while preserving the benefits.

Multilateral Trade

Multilateral efforts to promote trade liberalization for goods and services date back to the General Agreement on Tariffs and Trade (GATT), signed by the United States and 22 other countries in October 1947. As a complement to the Bretton Woods financial system established in 1944, GATT was inspired by the belief that trade liberalization would promote international prosperity, peace, and security, and thus contribute to the U.S.-led effort to rebuild after World War II and avert another sequel. Average tariffs in advanced economies have fallen dramatically from about 40 percent when GATT began in 1947 to about 3 percent in 2012. Including developing countries, the decline is even more substantial. Non-tariff barriers (NTBs), for instance, on items related to government procurement, arbitrary product standards, local content requirements, and other regulatory barriers have also been eased.

As of the end of 2014, the World Trade Organization (WTO), established in 1995, has 160 members. Currently, the United States is engaged in discussions at the WTO on a wide range of topics. Among them are formalizing the Trade Facilitation Agreement, which seeks to reduce costs associated with customs-related and other cross-border procedures and provide support to developing countries in this capacity. In addition, the United States is negotiating to expand the Information Technology Agreement, which will eliminate tariffs on a wider range of information and communications technology (ICT) products, as well as the Environmental

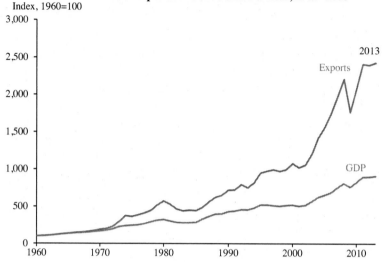

Figure 7-1
Global GDP and Exports of Goods and Services, 1960–2013
Index, 1960=100

Note: All values in real 2009 dollars, deflated using the U.S. GDP deflator.
Source: World Bank, World Development Indicators.

Goods Agreement and the Trade in Services Agreement to reduce barriers to trade in, respectively, green technologies and services such as telecommunications, insurance, and distribution systems. The United States is also participating in efforts to evaluate prospects for a conclusion of the Doha Development Agenda round of multilateral trade negotiations.

The Growth of U.S. and World Trade

Worldwide flows of goods and services as a share of the global economy are at an all-time high, thanks in no small part to the solid foundations put in place by the WTO to govern countries' policies toward trade flows. Figure 7-1 illustrates the progress of worldwide goods and services trade integration since 1960. Over this period, real global exports of goods and services have increased by a factor of 24, almost triple the pace of real world output growth.[1]

The increase in trade volumes is partly a function of broader trends in globalization, including reductions in transportation costs, improved inventory management, the entry of major new economies into the global trading system, and increased dispersion of production. Declining trade policy barriers around the world have also played an important role in increasing

---

[1] A large contraction in world trade followed the Great Recession, but it has since rebounded, albeit at a slower pace of growth in the last few years than prior to the recession.

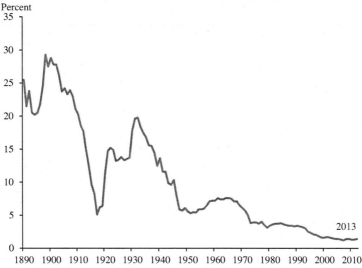

Figure 7-2
Ratio of U.S. Duties Collected to Total Imports, 1891–2013

Note: Total imports measured as the customs value of imports for consumption.
Source: U.S. International Trade Commission, Office of Analysis and Research Services.

the global volume of trade. The U.S. International Trade Commission has recorded U.S. duties collected as a share of total imports since 1891 (see Figure 7-2).[2] The U.S. average ad valorem equivalent tariff has been below 5 percent since the mid-1970s, below 2 percent since 1999, and currently stands at 1.4 percent.

As advanced nations generally have low tariff barriers, the most recent global tariff reductions have come as historically protectionist emerging and developing economies entered the global trading system, recognizing the benefits of open markets. Figure 7-3 shows the relative pace of tariff declines across three broad world income groups, as defined by the World Bank, since the early 1990s. High-income countries, with already low tariff levels, decreased tariffs from 3.6 percent on average in 1988 to 2.6 percent on average in 2012. By contrast, middle-income economies decreased tariff levels by a sharp 7.2 percentage points (from 14.8 percent on average in 1996 to 7.6 percent on average in 2012), and low-income countries decreased tariffs by an even greater 21.3 percentage points over the same time (from 33 percent

---

[2] Tariff rates were high prior to World War I, in part, because they were a primary revenue source for the Federal government. The Revenue Act of 1913, which passed following ratification of the Sixteenth Amendment, lowered tariffs sharply while replacing the lost revenue with a Federal income tax. Tariff rates in the 1920s and 1930s were relatively high as a result of the Fordney-McCumber Tariff Act of 1922 and the Smoot-Hawley Act of 1930. U.S. unilateral tariff reductions began even before GATT, once the Reciprocal Trade Act of 1934 authorized President Franklin Roosevelt to negotiate tariff reductions with trade partners.

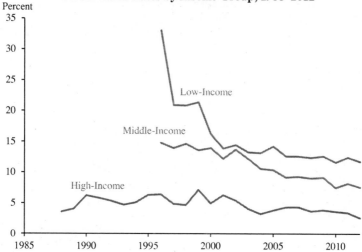

Figure 7-3
Global Tariff Rates by Income Group, 1988–2012

Percent

Low-Income

Middle-Income

High-Income

Note: Tariffs are calculated as the simple average of the applied tariff rate across all products within country groups.
Source: World Bank, World Development Indicators.

on average in 1996 to 16.2 percent on average in 2000, then to 11.7 percent on average in 2012).

The Rise of Services Trade. Services industries comprise 62 percent of the U.S. economy, and employ 86 percent of American workers. Despite the prevalence of services in the economy, there is a dearth of research investigating the impact of international trade in services. The cross-border flow of physical goods is easy to measure as goods pass through customs authorities. Services trade, on the other hand, is less straightforward to document, as many services are delivered digitally and thus have no single point of crossing.[3]

Apart from limited data, the lack of research on services trade also reflects that services, which require interaction between producers and customers, were long thought to be non-tradable—the classic example of the

---

[3] The General Agreement on Trade in Services, a WTO agreement that came into force in 1995, defines four modes of services trade. First, services trade occurs when a service produced in one country is consumed in another country; for instance, when Hollywood movies show in theaters abroad. Second, services trade occurs when consumers from abroad purchase local services, such as when foreigners travel to the United States for vacation, for an education, or for health care services. The third mode of services trade occurs through foreign direct investment; for instance, when a U.S. bank opens a branch abroad to offer financial services in other countries. Finally, the fourth mode of services trade occurs when individual service providers from one country travel to supply services in another country. An example would be an American academic giving an educational seminar abroad for an honorarium.

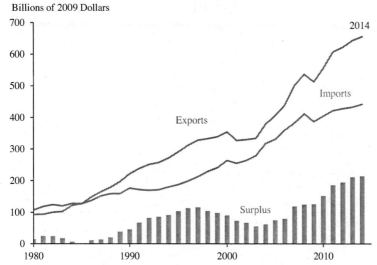

Figure 7-4
U.S. Trade in Services, 1980–2014

Billions of 2009 Dollars

Note: All values in real 2009 dollars, deflated using the U.S. GDP deflator. Data post-1998 are based on BEA's restructured U.S. Trade in Services series.
Source: Bureau of Economic Analysis, International Economic Accounts; Haver Analytics.

non-tradable service being the haircut. While haircuts are still unlikely to be traded, the growth in information technology and declining transportation costs have facilitated a strong rise in trade in services like education, health care, tourism, as well as the many business and professional services associated with trade in goods (telecommunications, finance, distribution, insurance, and more). The spread of multinational firms and the worldwide subdivision of production processes have also contributed to this rise.

In 2014, U.S. services exports measured approximately $710 billion, or 30 percent of total U.S. exports, while imports of services were about $479 billion, or 17 percent of total U.S. imports. Together, services trade accounted for almost 6.9 percent of U.S. gross domestic product (GDP) in 2014. As depicted in Figure 7-4, these levels reflect rapid growth since 1980; real U.S. services exports grew by 613 percent over the 34-year period to 2014, or at a 5.6-percent average annual rate. Despite an overall trade deficit, the United States maintains a strong and growing surplus in services.

FREE TRADE AGREEMENTS

U.S. free trade agreements (FTAs) play a central role in continuing progress toward more open markets. Table 7-1 lists the current U.S. bilateral and regional FTAs, beginning with the first FTA to enter into force with Israel in 1985. Canada signed an FTA with the United States

Box 7-1: Trade in Ideas

In 2013, U.S. companies paid $39 billion in royalties and licensing fees to foreign companies, and were paid $129 billion by foreign companies seeking access to intellectual property held in the United States. While this "trade in ideas" represents just 14.6 percent of all U.S. trade in services, it generates 40 percent of our $225 billion services trade surplus. Figure 7-i shows the level of imports and exports in 2013 for each of the four major categories of trade in intellectual property. Roughly two-thirds of this trade is intra-firm, with a greater share of this intra-company trade occurring in the trademark and franchise fees category (76 percent) than for industrial processes (69 percent), software (58 percent), or audio-visual materials (42 percent).

Trade in ideas is partly influenced by differences in countries' intellectual property laws; as such, harmonizing the international treatment of intellectual property rights has become an important, and sometimes controversial, aspect of international trade negotiations. For example, the WTO Agreement on Trade Related Aspects of Intellectual Property Rights established minimum standards for various forms of intellectual property protection. Several economic studies, such as papers by Branstetter, Fisman, and Foley (2006) and Cockburn, Lanjouw, and Schankerman (2014), suggest that stronger patent protection in destina-

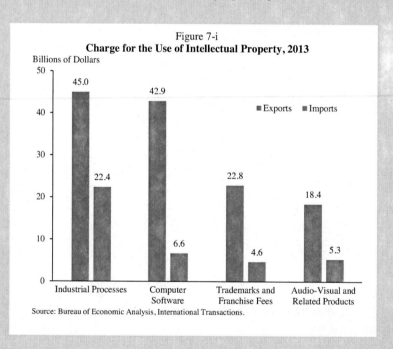

Figure 7-i
Charge for the Use of Intellectual Property, 2013

Source: Bureau of Economic Analysis, International Transactions.

tion countries does promote outbound technology transfer, both within and between firms.

One reason that trade in intellectual property can be controversial is that ideas are non-rival goods that can be used by many parties at the same time, with little or no incremental cost per user. This feature of intellectual property also creates challenges for measuring international technology transfer because it implies that the location of an idea, which determines the direction of trade flows, is somewhat arbitrary. To compound that problem, there is no obvious market price for many intra-company transactions, so both the magnitude and direction of intra-company trade in ideas may reflect corporate tax and legal strategies, as much as they do business or economic realities.

All of these complications can produce some unusual outcomes in the trade statistics. For example, U.S. intellectual property exports to Bermuda were $3 billion in 2013, with 98 percent of that trade occurring between affiliated companies, a trade that largely occurs for tax reasons rather than economic reasons, as discussed in Chapter 5 of this *Report*. These intellectual property exports are about two-thirds the size of Bermuda's $4.5 billion GDP. In the same year, U.S. intellectual property exports to France, whose GDP is 600 times larger than Bermuda's, totaled $3.4 billion, with only 42 percent transpiring between related companies. Lipsey (2010) shows that foreign affiliates of U.S. multinationals located in a variety of low-tax countries report unusually high levels of intangible assets relative to both employees and physical capital.

While it is difficult to estimate the size of any measurement bias created by geographic reallocation of intellectual property within multinational firms, it is possible to say something about the likely impact on trade statistics. In particular, transfers of intellectual capital abroad at below-market rates and intra-company pricing that shifts income outside the United States will lead the official statistics to underestimate the true size of the U.S. services trade surplus—that is, what would be observed under competitive market prices or in a tax neutral environment. For example, the true value of intellectual property exports in Figure 7-i may be higher, and the value of imports lower, particularly for trade in ideas related to trademark and franchise fees, where the share of intra-company transactions is highest. This type of bias would also make U.S. companies that trade in intellectual property appear less productive, by artificially lowering their revenues and inflating their costs. The continued growth of intra-company cross-border trade within large multinationals suggests that these measurement challenges will only grow in importance for both tax authorities and government statisticians.

Table 7-1
U.S. Free Trade Agreements

Agreement	Date of Entry Into Force	Bilateral Goods Trade (in Billions, 2014)	As Percent of Total U.S. Goods Trade (2014)
Israel	Aug-85	38	1
Canada	Jan-89	658	16.6
NAFTA	Jan-94	1,193	30
Jordan	Dec-01	3	0.1
Chile	Jan-04	26	0.7
Singapore	Jan-04	47	1.2
Australia	Jan-05	37	0.9
Bahrain	Jan-06	2	0.1
Morocco	Jan-06	3	0.1
CAFTA-DR	Mar-06	60	1.5
Oman	Jan-09	3	0.1
Peru	Feb-09	16	0.4
Korea	Mar-12	114	2.9
Colombia	May-12	39	1
Panama	Oct-12	11	0.3
Total in Force		**1,592**	**40.1**
TPP	TBD	1,609	40.5
T-TIP	TBD	695	18
Total		**2,623**	**66.1**

Note: Individual rows do not sum to the total, since individual countries may be represented in multiple agreements (e.g., Canada in NAFTA).
Source: U.S. Census Bureau, Foreign Trade Statistics; World Trade Organization, Regional Trade Agreements Information System.

in 1989, and together, these parties joined with Mexico in 1994 to form the North American Free Trade Agreement (NAFTA). Since then, the United States has also signed agreements with countries in the Middle East (Jordan, Morocco, Bahrain, and Oman), in Asia (Singapore and Korea), in Oceania (Australia), in South America (Chile, Peru, and Colombia), and in Central America (the Dominican Republic-Central American Free Trade Agreement—or CAFTA-DR[4]—and Panama). In total, current U.S. FTAs cover 40 percent of total U.S. goods trade.

With a few minor exceptions, all of this trade is duty-free. Therefore, it is little surprise that the United States has experienced a large increase in trade activity with these partners in the years following entry into force of the agreements. Notably, however, higher trade with FTA partners is not

---

[4] CAFTA-DR includes five Central American countries (Costa Rica, El Salvador, Guatemala, Honduras, and Nicaragua) and the Dominican Republic.

accompanied by reduced trade with non-FTA countries. Figure 7-5 summarizes the growth in U.S. goods trade with our free trade partners before and after the enactment of all 14 FTAs. For comparison, the analysis also presents the growth in U.S. trade with non-FTA partners before and after the FTAs entered into force. By construction, time zero is the date of entry into force. Looking at GDP-weighted averages of trade across all FTA partners and non-partners suggests that, on average, trade with both country groups was growing around 3 percent a year before the enactment of the agreements. After entry into force of the agreements, trade grew at about 10 percent a year with FTA partners, and also grew at about 6 percent a year with non-partners. Research by Baier and Bergstrand (2007) on free trade agreements for 96 different countries supports these findings. The authors report that, on average, an FTA approximately doubles two members' bilateral trade flows after 10 years. Our estimates based on the GDP-weighted average of trade with FTA partners suggests a 95 percent increase in trade flows after 10 years (see Figure 7-5).[5]

Current Trade Negotiations

In recent years, the United States has been focusing on negotiations toward two major multi-continental FTAs: TPP would encompass 12 Pacific nations across the Asia-Pacific, and T-TIP is a proposed free trade agreement between the United States and the 28 member states of the European Union. A key goal of U.S. free trade agreements is to secure tariff reductions abroad. As discussed earlier, the average tariff in the United States is a low 1.4 percent, while many of our trading partners maintain relatively high tariffs. At the same time, tariffs are just one of many policy instruments available to governments. Trade agreements bring about reductions in non-tariff measures, while also liberalizing investment regimes and services trade (where NTBs are especially severe). Bringing down our trading partners' tariff and non-tariff barriers is essential for American firms to be able to compete on a level playing field in the global economy.

The Administration's policy is to encourage trade agreements to promote a "values-driven" trade regime that maximizes globalization's benefits while addressing globalization's problematic side-effects. Environmental and labor commitments, included as a core part of our agreements, can help to level the playing field for U.S. businesses and workers, while also contributing to safer and greener policies worldwide. In addition, our trade agreements ensure that American businesses remain competitive in a global market in which our trading partners are also gaining preferential access

---

[5] The estimates rely on incomplete data, as a full 10 years has not yet passed for some U.S. FTAs.

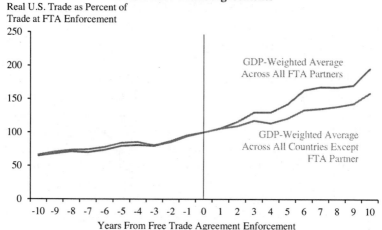

Figure 7-5

Growth in Real U.S. Goods Trade
Around Free Trade Agreements

Real U.S. Trade as Percent of
Trade at FTA Enforcement

GDP-Weighted Average
Across All FTA Partners

GDP-Weighted Average
Across All Countries Except
FTA Partner

Years From Free Trade Agreement Enforcement

Note: Trade is defined as the sum of goods imports and exports. All values in real 2009 dollars, deflated using the U.S. GDP deflator.
Source: U.S. Census Bureau, Foreign Trade Statistics; Bureau of Economic Analysis; International Monetary Fund, World Economic Outlook; CEA calculations.

to foreign markets through negotiations of their own bilateral and regional agreements. The Administration's efforts will also pave the way for future high-standard agreements around the world, and trade pacts with TPP and T-TIP countries will help advance U.S. strategic and geopolitical interests. Finally, it is important to understand that these agreements are not meant to represent the end of the process. TPP is designed to allow others to join in the future, and both TPP and T-TIP are intended to spur further multilateral trade liberalization.

Trans-Pacific Partnership. The TPP is a proposed regional FTA that the United States is negotiating with 11 other countries: Australia, Brunei Darussalam, Canada, Chile, Japan, Malaysia, Mexico, New Zealand, Peru, Singapore, and Vietnam. Based on the most recent data, TPP partners account for 37 percent of world GDP, 11 percent of the world's population, and 23 percent of world exports of goods and services. In 2013, TPP countries received $699 billion in U.S. merchandise exports and $199 billion in U.S. services exports, making the region as a whole the top export destination for the United States. In addition, included among the partners are some of the fastest-growing economies in the world; according to some measures, the number of middle-class consumers in Asia is expected to grow to 2.7 billion by 2030—an enormous increase in the potential export market for U.S. goods and services. The region is already an important location for

U.S. investment; in 2013, U.S. companies invested $695 billion in the Asia-Pacific area.

TPP Leaders have expressed their intent to achieve a "comprehensive and high-standard" FTA that will broadly liberalize regional trade and investment, strengthening economic ties between the parties. In addition to addressing tariff barriers, the TPP countries are seeking to address a range of outstanding non-tariff barriers, such as import licensing restrictions, as well as to open services and government procurement markets in the region. The United States and its partners are seeking to negotiate rules that will provide transparent protections for investors and citizens, support the digital economy, promote innovation through strong supervision of intellectual property rights, and offer guidance on competitive practices associated with state-owned enterprises.

In addition, when concluded, TPP will place strong labor commitments at the core of the agreement, making them enforceable and subject to dispute settlement, as with other commercial provisions. TPP will constitute the largest expansion of enforceable labor rights in history, more than quadrupling the number of people around the world covered by enforceable labor standards. TPP will also contain strong commitments on the environment, including commitments to protect our oceans, combat wildlife trafficking, and eliminate illegal logging. As with the labor provisions of TPP, these commitments will be enforceable through dispute settlement, allowing for trade sanctions against countries that fail to abide by the commitments.

Failing to secure a TPP agreement would place U.S. workers and businesses at a distinct disadvantage, by allowing other countries to set the rules of the global trading system—rules that would likely be adverse to U.S. interests. Comprehensive trade agreements like TPP offer the United States a way to shape globalization's rules in the best interest of American workers and firms and to ensure that global standards include important issues like worker and environmental protections.

Transatlantic Trade and Investment Partnership. The United States and the European Union already maintain the world's largest bilateral trade relationship. In 2013, together both regions account for nearly one-half of world GDP and about 42 percent of global exports of goods and services. Based on the most recent data, U.S. companies have approximately $2.4 trillion invested in the European Union, while European companies have $1.7 trillion invested in the United States. These already strong economic relationships would be strengthened through the formalization of T-TIP.

Despite their large size and close ties, the European Union and the United States have not achieved the full potential of their economic relationship. Negotiations toward the ambitious T-TIP began in earnest in June

2013. Since tariff barriers between the two partners are already very low, the agreement strives to increase market access by also addressing NTBs. Importantly, both sides seek agreement on cross-cutting disciplines on regulatory coherence and transparency—including early consultation on major regulations and use of regulatory impact assessment—for the development and implementation of efficient, cost-effective, and more-compatible regulations for goods and services. Adoption and use of good regulatory practices will ultimately raise the standards and promote trade beyond just the United States and the European Union. In addition, the governments intend to commit to liberalize services trade, promote foreign direct investment, and cooperate on the development of rules and policies on global issues of common concern.

THE IMPLICATIONS OF TRADE

The process of globalization offers many new economic opportunities, but it also has created challenges. Globalization is a result of both worldwide economic developments and specific policy changes. Analyzing globalization's general impact is different from analyzing any particular trade agreement. Understanding the impact of any particular agreement requires both historical research, as well as an analysis of the relative tariffs of trading partners, NTBs, and the relevant standards (for instance, labor, environment, and intellectual property).

Nevertheless, historical experience does underscore the potentially large gains from trade. In the past half-century, as trade barriers around the world have diminished, these gains have multiplied and are increasingly shared across different countries and different industries. Among these classic gains from trade are lower prices for consumers and producers, greater variety of goods and services available for purchase, enhanced productivity, and increased innovative activity.

Classic Gains from Trade

Enhanced Productivity. Long-established theories of international trade suggest that trade liberalization will improve a nation's economic productivity through several different channels.[6] First, trade can improve economy-wide productivity by allowing each country to focus on its comparative advantage. This follows from the classic trade theory expounded by economist David Ricardo in the early 1800s. Productivity gains can also

---

[6] Productivity is defined as the amount of output that can be generated with a given level of inputs, so a more productive firm can produce more than a less productive firm with the same resources.

occur within an industry if there is some heterogeneity between firms in that industry (Melitz 2003), as labor and resources shift, in response to lower trade costs, to the most efficient firms—those best able to take advantage of the opportunity to export—thereby improving productivity in that sector. Several studies find evidence of this phenomenon in U.S. manufacturing. One study, which compares high- and low-productivity plants during a time of falling tariffs and transportation costs finds that industry productivity rises when trade costs fall (Bernard et al. 2006). Ebenstein et al. (2011) find that industries where employment growth is highest in China tend to be the industries in the United States that have declining unit labor costs and increased productivity growth in the United States. This suggests that Chinese import competition in the United States could be driving improvements in productivity.

A separate line of research considers that increases in export activity offer firms opportunities to learn about foreign markets—perhaps even gaining technical expertise from foreign buyers—leading to increased productivity. Productivity gains through exporting may also occur through increased competition from foreign producers. This "learning-by-exporting" theory has support in a literature spanning many countries and time periods. By contrast, Clerides, Lach, and Tybout (1998) argue that the well-established relationship between exporting and productivity is explained by the selection of more productive firms into global markets.

Lower Prices. Perhaps the most broadly shared benefit of increased trade is lower prices for consumers and producers in the domestic market. By allowing our trading partners to produce the goods in which they are relatively more efficient, the United States can import at lower prices than would prevail if we were to produce the goods ourselves. This "specialize in what you do best, trade for the rest" philosophy makes everyday goods and services more affordable and enhances the real earning power of American workers. In addition, recent estimates suggest that over one-half of all U.S. imports are intermediate inputs into the production process; that international trade lowers prices on such inputs allows U.S. businesses to expand by reducing input costs.

Greater Variety. Another underappreciated benefit of trade liberalization is increased variety for domestic consumers and producers. With new importers come new products. This expanded selection increases the welfare of consumers who appreciate having more choice. Broda and Weinstein (2006) examine historical trade statistics and determine that the variety of imported goods increased approximately three-fold between 1972 and 2001. Conventional import price indices have trouble incorporating the value of increased choice, so this finding suggests that import prices have effectively fallen even further than the conventional import price index would suggest. The researchers estimate that this increased variety has provided U.S. consumers with value equivalent to 2.6 percent of GDP, or approximately $450 billion in 2014. Mostashari (2010) updates the calculations in Broda and Weinstein (2006) and reports that the number of varieties of goods imported into the United States increased 33 percent between 1989 and 2007.

More Innovation. A related strand of literature shows that when trade barriers fall, domestic industries often respond through innovation and self-improvement. Blundell et al. (1999) find that British firms in industries with higher import penetration spent more on innovation. Bloom et al. (2011) study how industries in 12 European countries fared after the elimination of import quotas as part of the WTO Agreement on Textiles and Clothing. They find that the increased trade catalyzed growth for high-tech, high-innovation firms. For these firms, spending on research and development increased, use of ICT intensified, and total factor productivity improved.

The Labor Market Implications of Trade

Trade also has notable impacts on labor markets, many of them a direct result of the classic gains from trade in terms of increased productivity and innovation. U.S. businesses that expand in response to the increased foreign market access due to U.S. trade agreements support—and may even create—new jobs. The importance of such export-led job growth for the Nation's income is reinforced by the fact that wages in export-intensive manufacturing industries tend to be higher than wages in non-export-intensive industries. Of course, while the aggregate benefits of trade may be large, trade can also have adverse effects for some workers. Domestic policies the Administration supports, such as investment in infrastructure, worker training, and education, can help our labor force take advantage of the considerable opportunities that trade opens up. For displaced workers and their families, effective policies can help smooth the adjustment into new, potentially higher-paying jobs.

Wages. Expanding U.S. market access abroad has important implications for the workforce at home. A very long literature spanning decades and many different countries highlights that exporting firms are systematically different from non-exporting firms even within the same industrial category. Bernard and Jensen (1995) were the first to document this fact for the United States. They note that exporting plants are larger in terms of employment, more productive in terms of value added per worker, more capital-intensive, and pay higher wages. These differences persist even within detailed industrial categories, and controlling for firms' regional locations.

Figure 7-6
Characteristics of Export-Intensive and
Non-Export-Intensive Industries, 1989–2009

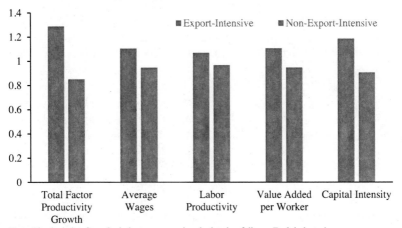

Note: The deviation from the industry average is calculated as follows. Each industry's characteristic is measured relative to the industry average within the year and then averaged over the 1989-2009 period and across export-intensive and non-export-intensive industry groups.
Source: National Bureau of Economic Research-Center for Economic Studies, Manufacturing Industry Database; U.S. Cenusu Bureau, Foreign Trade Statistics.

Figure 7-6 offers descriptive evidence relying on data from the U.S. Census Bureau's Foreign Trade Statistics matched to the National Bureau of Economic Research's (NBER) Manufacturing Industry Database (Becker, Gray, and Marvakov 2013). Export-intensive industries are defined as those industries with above-average values of exports as a fraction of total shipments (the export share) in 1989, and non-export-intensive industries are those industries with below-average values of the export share in 1989.[7] For ease of illustration, in order to report the various characteristics in comparable units, the Figure shows deviations from the industry average, calculated as described in the Figure note. On average over the 1989 to 2009 period of data availability, relative to non-export-intensive industries, export-intensive industries report 51 percent higher total factor productivity growth, 17 percent higher average wages (total wage bill per worker), 10 percent higher levels of labor productivity (total shipments per worker), 17 percent higher value added per worker, and 31 percent higher capital intensity (total real capital stock per worker), consistent with the findings in the academic research.

---

[7] The average export share across the 377 6-digit NAICS (North American Industrial Classification System) industries was 12.7 percent in 1989.

Box 7-2: Employment Impacts of Trade with China

The seismic event of the last three decades in the global economy has been the emergence of China. Until 1979, the People's Republic of China was, as a matter of policy, essentially closed off from the global economy. Over the subsequent two decades, over 730 million Chinese workers integrated into the global labor force. Estimates of the direct impact of these dynamics vary widely. Using variation in regional exposure to Chinese imports across U.S. labor markets to control for broad, economy-wide changes in employment, Autor, Dorn, and Hanson (2013) estimate that Chinese import competition can explain 44 percent of the aggregate decline in U.S. domestic manufacturing employment over this period. In a more recent expansion of this work, Acemoglu et al. (forthcoming) find that increased Chinese exports to the United States were directly responsible for roughly 10 percent of the manufacturing jobs lost between 1999 and 2011.

These studies, however, do not capture the full story because they do not incorporate how expanded U.S. exports boost employment and the economy. To provide a rough sense of the relative magnitudes of these effects, but without the same degree of causal certainty, CEA performed an analysis of 377 six-digit NAICS manufacturing industries from 1989 to 2009, using a specification similar to that of Autor, Dorn, and Hanson (2013). The analysis confirms the view that increased import penetration over the 1990s and 2000s is associated with decreasing U.S. manufacturing employment. The analysis also finds, however, that a 10 percentage-point rise in an industry's export share is associated with about a 1.8 percent increase in industry employment. As the average industry experienced about a 30 percentage-point increase in the export share over this time period, exports are associated with more than a 5 percent increase in manufacturing employment for the average industry.

Taken together, the results suggest that, though increases in import penetration were related to declines in manufacturing employment in recent decades, increases in exports can, in many cases, offer some offsetting effects. Future research into the relationship between exports and employment can help to refine the estimates.

That exporters pay higher wages than similar non-exporters is a well-established feature of the data across many countries and over decades. For the United States, estimates for the exporter wage premium (the amount by which exporting industries and firms pay higher wages than non-exporting industries and firms) range between 6 percent and 18 percent. Riker (2010) estimates that workers employed in exporting manufacturing industries earned approximately 18 percent more than similar workers employed in domestically-oriented manufacturing industries between 2006 and 2008.[8] Controlling for industry differences, Bernard, Jensen, Redding, and Schott (2007) document a 6-percent exporter wage premium in 2002: the average annual wage at exporting manufacturing firms is 6 percent higher than the average annual wage at domestically-oriented manufacturing firms. In a simple analysis using data on individual-level annual earnings from the Current Population Survey for the years 1989 to 2009, the Council of Economic Advisers (CEA) confirms an exporter wage premium. Controlling for time-invariant industry, state, and year factors, CEA's analysis suggests that the strong increase in exports over the 1990s and 2000s translates into an additional $1,300 in annual earnings for workers in today's dollars.

Inequality. Inequality has increased substantially since the 1970s. Many countries, including China, began integrating into the global economy beginning in the 1980s. The resulting increase of about 3.5 billion in the globally integrated population led many to question the relationship between increased globalization and inequality. Classic economic theory—specifically, the Stolper-Samuelson effect (Stolper and Samuelson 1941)—predicts that globalization will lead to an increase in wages for low-skilled labor relative to high-skilled labor in countries where low-skilled labor is abundant. The reverse is predicted to occur in high-skilled labor abundant countries. Driving this effect, according to the theory, is that changes in production patterns across countries change the relative demand for workers of different skill levels. But this effect was not seen in the data over the 1980s and 1990s. Instead, the education skill premium increased in a wide range of countries during this time, including many relatively poor countries (Goldberg and Pavcnik 2007).

Researchers, therefore, began to explore alternative explanations. If classic trade theory is correct, the data should show reallocations of workers toward skill-intensive industries in the United States. Instead, Berman, Bound, and Griliches (1994) documented that between-industry shifts in employment were smaller than within-industry shifts in employment in the United States and the United Kingdom over this time period. Based on this evidence, they hypothesized that technological change played a more important role than other factors in rising wage inequality in both the developed and developing world, as those workers trained to use more advanced information technology were increasingly in demand.

Alternative explanations subsequently surfaced, including differences in factor intensity across firms, even within narrowly defined industrial categories. As described earlier, exporting firms tend to be larger, more

---

[8] In follow-up work, Riker and Thurner (2011) demonstrate that the relationship holds in services industries as well.

productive, more capital intensive, and they generally pay higher wages than domestically oriented firms in the same industry. Bernard and Jensen (1995, 1997) document shifts of employment and wages within an industry, suggesting gains in the more productive, higher-wage exporting firms. There may also be factor intensity differences across different stages of the production process. As illustrated in Feenstra and Hanson (1997, 1999), cross-border movements of capital can increase the skill intensity of production, increasing the demand for skilled labor in both rich and poor countries—a Stolper-Samuelson effect for trade in intermediate inputs. Finally, the nature of international trade has changed dramatically in recent decades, including reductions in ICT costs and the increased importance of emerging economies in the global market.

Another question relates to the impact of trade agreements. In making an assessment of any particular trade agreement, it is important to differentiate between the overall effects of globalization and the specific effects of that agreement. A review of the evidence suggests that the largest factors behind the rise in inequality are likely technological change, the slowing trend in educational attainment, and changes in labor market institutions (such as the erosion of the real minimum wage and reduced unionization). For most of our work force, the dominant influences on wages originate in the domestic labor market (for example, see Blinder and Krueger 2013). But the process of globalization, while creating generally higher-paying jobs, can also be a contributor to wage inequality. This globalization, which has been driven by massive demographic and technological changes that brought billions more people into an increasingly connected global economy, would occur regardless of whether any particular trade agreement enters into force or not. Any particular agreement must be assessed based on an analysis of its tariff provisions, its reduction of NTBs to exports, and its provisions that promote higher standards. This can lead to a quite different outcome than globalization more broadly. Labor and environmental protections in trade agreements, in particular, would likely push in the opposite direction of globalization-driven increases in inequality.

Development Benefits of Trade

The United States engages in international trade and free trade agreements to increase market-access opportunities for U.S. businesses and workers and to lower prices and increase options for U.S. consumers. In addition to these benefits, it is important to recognize the impact trade has on global growth and security. U.S. trade policy also has implications for labor rights in our trading partners, gender equality, and environmental sustainability.

Global Growth

When countries specialize in the goods and services for which they are relatively efficient and trade for the rest, world production and consumption increase as existing resources are more efficiently utilized. Simple international trade theory, therefore, suggests that increased international trade can boost incomes. However straightforward this may seem, it is actually quite difficult to discern empirically a causal relationship between trade and income.[9] Frankel and Romer (1999) were among the first to report a positive causal effect of trade on income. More recently, Feyrer (2009) relies on a unique event in world history to identify changes in distance between country-pairs—the closure and re-opening of the Suez Canal between 1967 and 1975. The closure of the canal increased the effective distance between several country-pairs, and in some cases trade between affected country-pairs decreased substantially. Since some country-pairs were not affected by the closing, this event offers a unique experiment to test how trade impacts income. The author concludes that every dollar of increased trade raises income by about 25 cents.

Poverty. As developing countries entered the world trading system, concerns mounted about the impacts of trade on the well-being of the poor. The literature on the impact of trade on GDP suggests a potential for poverty to fall with increased international commerce. Unfortunately, if most of the benefits accrue to the wealthy when a country's income rises, the least well-off citizens may not benefit enough to escape poverty. A large amount of evidence suggests otherwise, however. Though within-country inequality generally increased in the aftermath of globalization (see the earlier discussion), across-country global income inequality witnessed the first decline since the Industrial Revolution, according to Milanovic (2013).

Hanson (2007) investigates the case of Mexico in the decade surrounding the implementation of NAFTA. Using state-level variation, the author documents that individuals born in states with high-exposure to globalization have relatively higher wages than individuals born in states with low-exposure to globalization. McCaig (2011) uses the 2001 U.S.-Vietnam Bilateral Trade Agreement (BTA) to study the effects of increased market access to rich countries on poverty in developing countries and finds that a one standard deviation decrease in provincial tariffs is associated with a two-year rate of poverty reduction of between 33 and 40 percent. By contrast, work by Topalova (2007, 2010) on India's 1991 trade liberalization provides

---

[9] For instance, perhaps countries trade more because they are richer. Richer countries have better trading infrastructure, such as ports, and better access to information about opportunities abroad. The fundamental challenge for statistical inference, then, is that trade may affect income, but income also affects trade.

a different view. Although the incidence of poverty in rural India fell 13 percentage points around the liberalization—from 37 percent in 1987 to 24 percent in 1999—areas of that country more exposed to trade experienced progress toward poverty reduction that was not as rapid as other areas.

Working Conditions. A common argument against trade integration with countries in the developing world is the poor labor standards of those countries. However, research finds that expanding access to U.S. markets promotes higher-quality employment in less-developed countries as workers shift from informal to formal employment, with little empirical evidence that local tariff reductions have an offsetting effect—meaning that the forces unleashed by trade itself complement the effort to include enforceable labor standards in free trade agreements.[10] A recent paper by McCaig and Pavcnik (2014) finds that employment shifts from the household business (informal) sector to the formal enterprise sector in Vietnam in the aftermath of large U.S. tariff reductions as part of the U.S.-Vietnam BTA. Similarly, Paz (2014) reports that decreases in foreign market tariffs decrease domestic informal employment in Brazil, while early work by Goldberg and Pavcnik (2003), supported in Menezes-Filho and Muendler (2011), finds no evidence of a link between declining import tariffs in Brazil and informal employment. More importantly, work by Edmonds and Pavcnik (2005) documents a decrease in child labor associated with increased international trade in Vietnam.

Therefore, trade agreements that expand U.S. market access for countries at a lower level of development can provide a market-based approach to improving labor conditions in the developing world. High standard U.S. trade agreements also contain commitments to promote and enforce workers' rights. A recent study by the U.S. Department of Labor (DOL) documents the improvement in labor conditions in countries engaged in trade agreements with the United States (DOL 2014).[11]

Gender Equality

Promoting gender equality is a key development goal in both the developing world and in the United States. Importantly, since trade promotes international competition, it may also reduce firms' leeway to discriminate against women. The classic Becker (1957) model of discrimination predicts that costly discrimination cannot persist with increased market

---

[10] Jobs in the informal sector are associated with lower wages, lower employee benefits, worse working conditions, and lower job "quality" (Chapter 3 of this *Report* considers measures of job quality in the United States).

[11] For example, seven Latin American countries "significantly advanced" in terms of DOL's assessment of labor policies and practice related to child labor in 2013 from 2012. Five of the seven countries have free trade agreements with the United States.

competition. Therefore, as trade liberalization results in increased competition in the domestic market, the gender wage gap should narrow. In line with the theory, by investigating trade-affected manufacturing industries in the United States between 1976 and 1993, Black and Brainerd (2004) find that the residual gender wage gap narrowed more rapidly in initially more concentrated industries that experienced larger increases in competition with trade reform than in initially more competitive industries.

Political Cooperation

Strong economic ties between countries tend to coincide with strong political cooperation. This notion was one of the foundational beliefs behind the GATT texts in the aftermath of World War II, as well as a motivation for the European Coal and Steel Community (known today as the European Union) and the Southern Cone Common Market (Mercosur) between Argentina, Brazil, Paraguay, and Uruguay. Basic intuition about the benefits of trade match these assertions; that is, two countries with a robust trading partnership would be loath to make war on one another and would be eager to cooperate on a variety of fronts, lest the substantial benefits of trade are in any way adversely affected. In addition, international trade in goods and services brings countries into contact with one another, reducing initial prejudices.

Relying on data across 177 countries and 30 years, Blomberg and Hess (2006) estimate that the presence of conflict acts as a tariff barrier—as much as a 30-percent tariff on trade—larger than traditional policy barriers. Martin, Mayer, and Thoenig (2008) find that countries with high barriers to trade are more likely to make war because the opportunity cost of the forgone trading relationship is low, but only for pairs of countries. The relationship disappears in the multilateral setting, perhaps reflecting how multilateral trade reduces the dependence of any one country on another, thus lessening the trade-based costs of war for any given pair. Martin, Mayer, and Thoenig (2012), therefore, suggest that international trade has changed the nature of conflict. However, as with trade and income, identifying a causal relationship between trade and conflict is complex, and as such, remains one of the important open questions in international economics.

Environmental Protection

Trade agreements can raise environmental standards in countries that otherwise would not be motivated to raise standards on their own. In fact, the United States has a long history of pursuing mutually supportive trade and environmental policies, and has found that strong, enforceable environmental provisions pursued as part of our bilateral and regional trade agreements can help raise environmental standards in our trading partners, leveling the playing field for workers and businesses in America.

In addition to this values-driven approach to trade policy, there are two broad channels through which trade can impact the environment: by changing the level of economic activity within trading countries, and by changing the composition of economic activity among trading countries. In each channel, there are ways in which trade can help encourage sustainable development and promote environmental protection.

It is well-established that increases in trade activity among countries go hand in hand with increases in their overall economic activity. Environmentalists often point to this increase, known as the "scale effect," as a cause for worry. A greater scale of economic activity likely means increases in transportation, shipping, production, and consumption—all pollution-emitting activities. Note, however, that much of this concern would apply to any policy that increases productivity growth, including expanded research and education.

Higher productivity is associated with higher real incomes. Greater prosperity, in turn, can benefit the environment in multiple ways. Higher real incomes create opportunities for investment in research and development in clean technology, allowing countries to "clean-up" production techniques. Higher real incomes can also generate greater ability and willingness to adopt, enforce, and pay for higher standards of environmental quality. For example, with more disposable income, families might be willing to pay a little extra to buy a hybrid car, or install solar panels for home-electricity generation.

Ultimately, increased economic activity both generates and curbs pollution; the overall effect on the environment depends on the relative magnitudes of each change. Empirical studies have produced relatively consistent results showing that trade does increase pollution, but also that accompanying emissions reductions from cleaner technology are enough to offset that increase. For instance, Antweiler, Copeland, and Taylor (2001) remark that if trade liberalization raises GDP per capita by 1 percent, then pollution concentrations fall by about 1 percent. The authors decompose this effect as follows: a 1 percent increase in the scale of economic activity raises pollution by around 0.5 percent, but the increase in income associated with international trade drives down pollution by around 1.5 percent. Similarly, Copeland and Taylor (2003) estimate the technique elasticity of pollution reduction with respect to income to be negative and greater than -1; that is, a given increase in real income is associated with an even greater reduction in pollution in percentage terms. Grether, Mathys, and de Melo (2010) analyze data on 62 countries and 7 manufacturing sectors and show that increases in worldwide trade flows between 1990 and 2000 are associated with a 2 to 3 percent decrease in global sulfur dioxide emissions. Further, they show that manufacturing industries have become much cleaner over time—while, globally, industry's employment and output levels rose 10 to 20 percent between 1990 and 2000, manufacturing emissions decreased by 10 percent. In other words, the evidence suggests that, likely due to a global shift toward cleaner technology, the net effect of increased trade on pollution is less than or equal to zero.

Compositional changes that occur in the economies of trading partners as trade promotes production specialization are a second mechanism behind trade's environmental impacts. A popular assumption is that specialization will send the most heavily polluting industries from rich countries with stricter environmental regulation to poor countries, which have relatively lax regulation. Theoretically, this migration would lead to an increase in world pollution levels and the creation of "pollution havens" in developing countries that, as exporters of the "dirtiest" goods, would bear a disproportionate amount of global pollution burdens. In a worst-case scenario, environmentalists say, a "race to the bottom" in environmental regulation could ensue if developed countries saw an incentive to slow down efforts to raise environmental protection in an effort to forestall the "dirty" industries' emigration. True, not all parties in a trade relationship can specialize in the cleanest industries, but concerns about "pollution havens" and "races to the bottom" are belied by the empirical evidence. In fact, there is reason to believe that compositional changes could actually yield net environmental benefits.

Developed countries tend to be the best equipped for production of high-polluting goods since the most-polluting industries, which include manufacture of chemicals, metals, and paper, and oil refining, are capital intensive. The basic economic theory of comparative advantage suggests that those industries belong in countries with abundant capital—the richer, developed countries. Poorer countries with less capital on hand are more likely to specialize in industries that are more service-oriented and labor-intensive, and less polluting. If this is true, the compositional effects of trade could actually lead to reductions in global emissions, as pollution-intensive production would occur in countries with stricter standards.

Of course, the issue is slightly more complicated, as environmental regulation can increase the marginal cost of production in polluting industries, driving them to less regulated countries. According to a 1999 WTO report, however, the increased marginal cost of pollution abatement in developed countries is no more than 1 percent of production costs for the average polluter (a maximum of 5 percent for the worst polluters). Such small costs are likely not powerful enough to deter production and send it elsewhere and, according to the WTO, the developed-country share of global production in polluting industries has remained relatively constant at around 75 to 80 percent over the past few decades (Nordstrom and Vaughan 1999). Regardless of environmental regulation, standard non-environmental comparative advantage considerations seem to dominate location decisions.

FINANCIAL FLOWS

Financial flows are motivated by opportunities for mutual gain analogous to those driving trade in goods and services. In a world with uncertainty, cross-border flows of financial assets broaden the scope for diversifying risk. The gains from international risk sharing are largest when the sources of risk are country-specific; in that case, for example, a fall in the returns to investment in one country can be offset by increases in returns in other countries. Global financial markets also facilitate international borrowing and lending. If such activity across borders were prohibited, domestic investment would be limited by the supply of national saving. With integrated capital markets, however, the global supply of saving can be invested in the locations where it is most productive and therefore yields the highest returns. When markets function without distortions, the ability to diversify across countries and to allocate investment to its most productive use results in a globally efficient allocation of capital, higher returns to investment, and reduced wealth volatility—all shared by people around the world. In particular, net export deficits, which require foreign financing, do not necessarily imply lower economic growth, and may well be associated with higher growth (see Box 7-3).

Along with the benefits of financial market integration come substantial risks, as was amply demonstrated by the waves of crises that have swept through global financial markets since the 1980s. The increasingly tight interconnections among financial systems mean that disturbances in one market have the potential to reverberate around the globe. As discussed in this chapter, given the interdependence among national financial systems, it is not enough for national regulators to "keep one's own house in order," but governments must work together to develop and implement policies to safeguard global stability.

Figure 7-7 illustrates the expansion of global financial flows relative to the growth in world trade in goods and services and world GDP since 1985. In this Figure, trade is measured as the average of global exports and imports and gross global asset flows are the average of inflows and outflows. Both global trade and GDP have grown since the 1980s, trade faster than GDP.

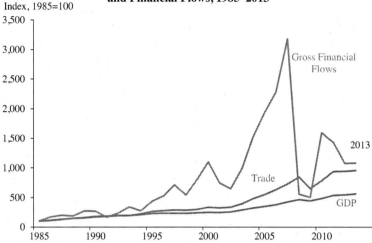

Figure 7-7
**Growth of Global GDP, Trade in Goods and Services,
and Financial Flows, 1985–2013**

Index, 1985=100

Note: All data are in nominal U.S. dollars. Global trade is defined as the average of global exports and imports of goods and services. Gross global financial flows are defined as the sum of direct investment, portfolio investment, and foreign exchange reserves. Values are obtained by averaging inflows and outflows to account for measurement error.
Source: UNCTAD; IMF, International Financial Statistics.

But even the pace of trade growth pales in comparison with that of international financial flows in the early to mid-2000s. Some of the increased asset trade can be attributed to the removal of capital controls and other barriers to cross-border investment. The advanced economies were the first to lower barriers to capital flow as countries moved from fixed to flexible exchange rates in the early 1970s. Emerging markets followed suit in the 1990s as they became more integrated into global markets. But the pace of globalization in financial markets exploded in the 2000s, reaching its zenith on the eve of the global financial crisis in 2007, driven primarily by cross-border bank loans. A notable retrenchment of cross-border asset trade occurred in 2008; and in 2012 and 2013 the volume of global financial flows has hovered around $4 trillion, or roughly 5.5 percent of world GDP.

The expansion of financial flows coincided with increased financialization within countries and the expansion of banking services across countries. Between 1980 and 2000, the share of the financial sector in the United States doubled from 4 to 8 percent of GDP (Philippon and Reshef, 2013). Up until the 1990s, international banking expanded in line with the growth in international trade and foreign direct investment as banks provided services supporting the international operations of business firms. There was a sharp liftoff in global banking activity in the 2000s as both the volume of cross-border banking and the number of international subsidiaries and branches expanded. At its peak in 2007, international claims of banks (cross-border claims and local claims in foreign currency) accounted for over 60 percent of global GDP (Goldberg 2013).

Composition of International Capital Flows

International financial markets offer genuine opportunities for investment and risk sharing, but they also serve as conduits for the cross-border transmission of economic shocks, as well as for arbitrage between national regulatory and tax systems. From a stability perspective, the composition of international financial flows matters, as does the economic motivation underlying these transactions. Table 7-2 shows the breakdown of total global financial flows into foreign direct investment, equity transactions, and debt and loans. Each of these flows is discussed in turn.

Foreign direct investment involves the acquisition of an ownership stake of 10 percent or more in a foreign firm. Economic studies suggest that FDI is associated with the transfer of technology and that foreign-owned firms tend to be more productive than domestic firms.[12] Alquist, Mukherjee, and Tesar (2014) find that FDI also serves as a source of liquidity in emerging markets where borrowing conditions are tight. This is especially beneficial during periods of financial stress in the local market, when the firm might otherwise be forced to liquidate assets, but instead can borrow from its parent. FDI has become an increasingly important form of cross-border capital investment. Its share of total financial inflows has increased in both advanced countries and emerging markets. In 2013, FDI accounted for almost one-half of international financial flows though the increase in the share is in part driven by the fall off in portfolio debt and loans. One reason for the growth of FDI is the desire of multinational firms to establish more finely articulated global supply chains that better exploit the scope for international specialization of production tasks.

Not all capital flows through multinationals are benign, however. International differences in tax rates can provide incentives for firms to engage in transactions that shift income from high-tax to low-tax jurisdictions in order to minimize their global tax liability. In one example of "earnings stripping," a U.S. firm with a parent in a low-tax jurisdiction outside the United States simply borrows from its foreign parent. The interest payments on that loan are deductible in the United States and are taxed abroad, reducing the firm's overall global tax liability. While this shifting of profits

---

[12] For evidence on technology transfer and productivity gains from FDI in the U.S., see Keller and Yeaple (2009) and Haskel, Perreira, and Slaughter (2007) for evidence from the UK. See Poole (2013) on wage and productivity spillovers from FDI in Brazil and Kee (2014) on evidence from Bangladesh.

Table 7-2
Gross Global Financial Flows, 1985-2013

Gross Global Financial Flows	1985	1990	1995	2000	2005	2010	2013
Levels (Billions of U.S. Dollars)							
Total	385	1031	1688	4244	7429	6150	4170
Direct Investment	59	250	365	1503	1392	1740	1944
Portfolio Equity	19	16	130	756	929	719	803
Portfolio Debt and Loans	307	765	1192	1985	5109	3691	1423
Of which: FX Reserves	*14*	*90*	*190*	*178*	*632*	*1181*	*723*
Shares	100%	100%	100%	100%	100%	100%	100%
Direct Investment	15%	24%	22%	35%	19%	28%	47%
Portfolio Equity	5%	2%	8%	18%	13%	12%	19%
Portfolio Debt and Loans	80%	74%	71%	47%	69%	60%	34%

Note: Levels represented in nominal dollars. FX reserves are foreign exchange reserves.
Source: International Monetary Fund, Balance of Payments Statistics.

is achieved without changing the consolidated balance sheet of the firm, the transaction does artificially inflate global gross financial flows by generating two offsetting international debt transactions, the only purpose of which is tax avoidance.[13] Transactions can be much more complicated than this simple example and can be very difficult to track. And to be sure, not all such transactions are for tax avoidance purposes. The full amount of revenue lost to the U.S. Treasury through tax avoidance is difficult to estimate but the Treasury Department estimates that a single proposal to limit interest deductions for U.S. firms with much more debt than their foreign parent and its affiliates abroad would raise $64 billion over the period 2016 to 2025. See Chapter 5 for a detailed discussion of the international ramifications of the President's approach to business tax reform.

Portfolio equity investment involves the purchase of shares in foreign companies. Share prices tend to be volatile and when markets in different countries fall together, as happened in the 2007-08 crisis, even a globally diversified portfolio of equity does not provide much insurance. An advantage of equities, however, is that the international distribution of payoffs happens automatically through changing share values and dividend payments without the risk of default, which can adversely affect financial market stability when debtors' problems impair the perceived creditworthiness of their creditors.

---

[13] Suppose the foreign parent lends a $1 bank deposit in London to its U.S. affiliate, which moves the $1 to its own London account. Then there is a financial inflow to the United States (the foreign borrowing by the U.S. affiliate) and an offsetting financial outflow from the U.S. (the U.S. affiliate acquires a $1 deposit in London). Corporate debt interest rates generally exceed bank deposit rates, however, so profits are indeed shifted out of the U.S. In the process, the global level of gross international financial flows rises by $2.

Box 7-3: Have U.S. Trade Deficits Reduced Output and Employment?

Countries that engage in free international trade rarely have balanced trade—the state in which exports and imports are equal in value. Instead, they may lend to other countries when exports exceed imports, or borrow from them in the opposite case. The U.S. economy has run trade deficits in every year since 1976, borrowing from abroad in international financial markets to make up the difference between spending and income.

Economic commentators sometimes argue that these trade deficits have been a drag on the Nation's economic growth and employment, and that reducing trade deficits (perhaps by restricting international trade) would have resulted in more U.S. output and jobs. On the surface, their argument seems straightforward: demand for imports, if somehow re-directed to U.S. goods, would raise domestic demand, presumably generating more production by U.S. businesses and more employment to support that production. The truth, however, is substantially more complicated.

The factors that give rise to higher imports often raise demand for domestic goods at the same time. Eliminating those sources of higher import demand would therefore reduce, not raise, output and jobs. Moreover, measures a government might take to reduce imports can have effects elsewhere in the economy that counteract any anticipated improvement in the trade deficit. For example, a protective tariff may, in the first instance, make imports more expensive, but, by moving the balance of payments toward a surplus, the tariff will also lead the home currency to appreciate against foreign currencies, making imports cheaper again and exports less competitive. That change is likely to neutralize most or all of the trade-balance effect of the tariff, but at the cost of a more distorted allocation of resources (which lowers output below potential).

Another way to see the fallacy is to realize that a trade deficit, which requires funding from foreign lenders, also means that our own saving is insufficient to finance domestic investment; whereas a trade surplus means that our saving is more than sufficient, with the excess of saving over domestic investment being lent to foreigners (who themselves must be running a trade deficit in this case). Trade balance improvement therefore requires some combination of a rise in saving or a fall in investment, neither of which generally causes higher output or job growth.

Because of this relationship, the U.S. trade balance is highly countercyclical, tending to register bigger deficits when the economy is stronger, not weaker (as Figure 7-ii shows). Not surprisingly, this same pattern holds across most industrial economies. For advanced economies in general, bigger trade deficits are associated with stronger, not weaker, growth because they tend to reflect higher overall demand that raises imports at the same time as it raises output. True, if imports were lower and nothing else in the economy changed, output would have to be higher to balance domestic supply with demand. In reality, however, it is impossible for policies to change imports without affecting a range of other macroeconomic variables in ways that will not necessarily help economic growth, and may well hurt it.

The preceding discussion of the short-term relation between trade deficits and economic performance is only part of the story, of course. On the one hand, countries that have trade deficits because their higher investment levels are financing productive ventures will also see faster growth over the medium to long terms. But countries with poor investment allocation will eventually see their national income reduced, meaning that the short-run demand boost from higher investment will result in a long-run cost for the economy. In addition, large current account deficits can lead to financial instability—especially for emerging economies.

The bottom line is that the relationship between the trade balance and growth depends on circumstances and can vary according to the factors that cause the trade balance to change. Understanding those factors is essential, however, before we can decide if policies to alter the trade balance are desirable, and if so, what the proper policy choice would be.

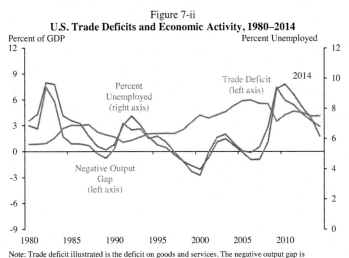

Figure 7-ii
U.S. Trade Deficits and Economic Activity, 1980–2014

Note: Trade deficit illustrated is the deficit on goods and services. The negative output gap is calculated by subtracting potential GDP from actual GDP.
Source: Bureau of Economic Analysis; Bureau of Labor Statistics; International Monetary Fund.

Viewed through the lens of optimal portfolio diversification, holdings of cross-border equity are still low, even in advanced economies. Figure 7-8 shows the degree of "home equity bias" in the U.S. equity portfolio. Home equity bias measures the percent of their shares that U.S. stock owners invest in the U.S. market, adjusted for the size of the U.S. stock market in the world market. If U.S. investors maximized their diversification by investing in home equities exactly in proportion to the size of the U.S. stock market in the world stock market, the degree of their home bias would be zero.[14] But if they invested nothing abroad, their home bias would be 100 percent. As shown in Figure 7-8, home bias has been declining since 2000 but still remains above 60 percent. Of course, setting portfolio weights equal to market shares is just one benchmark from which to judge the extent of home bias. Other benchmarks would emerge from a portfolio allocation strategy based on an assumption about how investors trade off risk and return. The advantage of the market-share benchmark is that it is simple to interpret and the implied shares are stable over time.

Far from being just a U.S. phenomenon, home bias is a fairly universal description of national portfolio choice. Using data from other countries, Coeurdacier and Rey (2013) report home bias ratios in 2008 ranging from 50 percent for individual euro area countries to 99 percent in Brazil and China. In emerging markets, extensive home bias is still likely to reflect barriers to international capital flows. In advanced economies, however, other factors such as limited information about foreign markets, institutional frictions, and perceptions about the riskiness of foreign markets continue to affect portfolio decisions. The chief takeaway here is that, as globalized as financial markets seem to be, there remains scope for further diversification gains through trade in equity shares. It is remarkable that home equity bias persists despite the high volumes of activity in international financial markets and the very large gross external asset and liability positions—sometimes multiples of GDP—that many (especially industrial) countries have developed.

A major weakness in the current financial system is the strong bias toward debt finance and flows of debt finance through banks. Though debt flows have declined as a share of total flows and home bias in debt portfolios has declined, debt transactions remain central to international finance. And, as was learned in the recent financial crisis, debt contracts have features that can be extremely damaging in some (and not altogether rare) circumstances.

Unlike equities, payoffs on debt contracts are fixed and do not take account of unexpected economic shocks that may make full repayment

---

[14] If s is the share of their stocks that U.S. residents invest in the U.S. stock market and s^* is the share of the U.S. stock market in the global stock market, then the degree of U.S. investors' home bias is defined as $100 \times \dfrac{s - s^*}{1 - s^*}$.

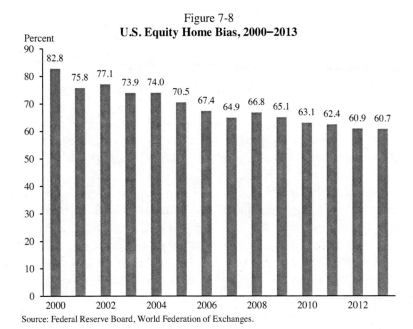

Figure 7-8
U.S. Equity Home Bias, 2000–2013

Percent

Source: Federal Reserve Board, World Federation of Exchanges.

difficult or impossible. If the borrower hits hard times, the options are to renegotiate with the lender or default. The advantage of debt contracts is that they are structurally and informationally quite simple—payoffs on debt are not contingent on the performance of either party (provided there is no default), avoiding some types of moral hazard. Given this simple structure, debt contracts can easily be priced, securitized, and re-sold to third parties under tranquil financial market conditions. The disadvantage, as repeated debt crises have demonstrated, is that in the event the borrower is unwilling or unable to pay, the amount of the payoff is unknown and depends on the enforceability of the original contract. Further, widespread borrower stress can lead to lender runs—refusals to roll over maturing debts—along with evaporation of market liquidity and a breakdown in the market's ability to fairly price some debt securities. The institutions supporting debt contracts vary from place to place, and may change over time. International lenders learned the hard way that, for example, mortgages in the United States are non-recourse loans, meaning that the loan is secured by a pledge of collateral (the house itself) but the borrower is not personally liable for the loan. In many other countries, the lender can place a lien against the borrower's income or seize other assets in the event of default.

The international financial system is strongly biased toward debt for several reasons. One is deposit insurance and implicit bailout guarantees, which effectively subsidize bank intermediation and, in some countries, result in globally active banks that are too big to fail. Second, tax laws tend to favor debt over equity, tilting investment portfolios toward debt and away from equity, as discussed in Chapter 5. Third, equity markets remain under-developed in some poorer developing countries, where the returns to investment are arguably still high. Fourth, national policies to promote home ownership effectively subsidize mortgage lending and the resulting securitized instruments.

An important caveat to the data in Table 7-2 is that they may under-state the degree of debt bias in international financial flows. Official statistics classify cross-border lending between affiliated nonfinancial companies as FDI, even though these transactions take the form of debt. Thus, some FDI actually has no equity component, and instead is associated with some of the same risks as conventional lending flows (see Avdjiev, Chui, and Shin 2014). And as described above, some of these debt flows are motivated by tax avoidance. On the other hand, the amount of debt in the system could be overstated if it is measured both when debt is issued by the foreign affiliate and when it flows back to the headquarter firm.

The widespread global bias toward debt was a key contributor to the severity of the recent financial crisis and its global transmission. As is now well understood, the seeds of the crisis were sown in the U.S. mortgage mar-ket. Securitization of subprime loans meant that exposure to delinquent U.S. mortgages was spread throughout the financial system, in the United States and abroad. The troubled mortgage problem was not confined to the United States, however, as real estate values and credit volumes rose rapidly in many countries during the 2000s. Lax regulation and asset booms occurred simul-taneously, and, for somewhat different reasons, in Iceland, Ireland, Spain, the United Kingdom and many other countries. At the same time, high lev-els of global saving kept world interest rates low, making debt cheap relative to other forms of finance. At a national level, low borrowing costs allowed some governments to finance macro imbalances through easy foreign bor-rowing and to postpone tough policy choices. Optimism about the euro project resulted in low sovereign debt spreads in the euro area's peripheral economies that did not reflect the actual risk of their national balance sheets, especially given the sizes and vulnerabilities of their banks. Ultimately, as housing prices started to fall and as different parts of the financial system suffered lender runs, the close interconnections among highly levered finan-cial institutions threatened to destabilize the entire system.

Challenges in Regulating Global Financial Markets

The global crisis exposed regulatory gaps and inconsistencies across countries, exacerbated by the free flow of capital across borders. With hindsight, the problems are easy to list: excessive leverage of banks and other financial institutions; lack of transparency and regulation in derivatives markets; increased importance of financial activity outside of the regulated banking sector (the "shadow banks"); and failure on the part of regulators to recognize the way in which risks were transferred across borders, between different types of financial institutions, and between the financial system and governments. The risks of new financial instruments were not well understood and few connected the dots between global imbalances, globally rapid credit expansion, and asset price bubbles, especially in housing markets.

In the United States, the passage of the Dodd-Frank Wall Street Reform and Consumer Protection Act in 2010 was an important step toward addressing problems at the core of the financial crisis. Wall Street Reform addressed difficult systemic problems by: appointing a new Financial Stability Oversight Council to monitor the stability of the U.S. financial system as a whole, not just the safety and soundness of individual institutions; creating a process to resolve "too big to fail" firms without government bailouts; increasing transparency into previously unreported and unregulated financial products and services, to allow trading partners and investors to more accurately assess the risks associated with a contract or investment; centralizing previously scattered consumer financial protection authority under a single, new regulator; and better aligning the incentives for financial firms and their executives with the long-term health of both the firm and the broader economy. Several of these measures are still being enacted, but Wall Street Reform has already reined in many practices that led to the financial crisis. It is essential for domestic and global stability that Wall Street Reform be fully implemented.

However, the tight interconnections between domestic and international financial institutions mean that individual nations' efforts to "keep one's own house in order" are insufficient fully to attain global financial stability. Particularly challenging in the international context is the presence of currency risk—since internationally active banks do business in several major currencies—and regulatory arbitrage that exploits gaps and inconsistencies among national regulatory frameworks. The Basel process of international regulatory coordination emerged as a response to these challenges. The United States has provided strong leadership in developing and implementing the resulting international guidelines for monitoring and regulating international banking.

The Basel process has developed under the auspices of the Bank for International Settlements (BIS) and has its roots in the financial market turmoil that followed the collapse of the Bretton Woods system of managed exchange rates in the 1970s (BIS 2014). In 1974, central bank governors of the G-10 countries established the Committee on Banking and Regulation and Supervisory Practices and agreed to a set of principles regarding minimal capital standards and rules for regulating and sharing information among national regulators (the "Concordat"). At the outset, the concern was that international supervisory coverage be expanded so that no foreign banking establishment would be outside of the scope of supervision and that such supervision be consistent across member jurisdictions.

The outbreak of the debt crisis in Latin America in the early 1980s threatened the solvency of a number of large international banks and prompted revision of the Basel rulebook. The committee's attention shifted toward capital adequacy standards, now referred to as Basel I. The 1988 Accord called for a minimum capital ratio of capital to risk-weighted assets and the need to include off-balance sheet transactions. Ultimately, these capital provisions were adopted by all countries with active international banks. The Basel agreements were amended over time as banking activity expanded and broadened in scope. Basel II, finalized in June 2004, included three "pillars": minimal capital requirements; supervisory review of a bank's capital adequacy and its internal assessment process; and effective use of disclosure to strengthen market discipline.

The recent financial crisis has resulted in a third round of major revisions, which now involve the full G-20 membership, with a target date of 2019 for full implementation. The Basel III package strengthens the Basel II standards and contains the additional components enumerated in Table 7-3.

Other international institutions play a supporting role in global financial regulation. The BIS is also known as the "central bankers' bank": it supports central banks in implementing the Basel III measures, and also houses the global Financial Stability Board established in its present form by the G-20 in 2009. The International Monetary Fund is a central institution for policy analysis, data reporting, and the provision of a global safety net through its lending operation and conditionality. The World Bank provides policy advice and financial assistance, particularly to low- to middle-income countries.

While the Basel process is a critical step forward in the global regulation of the financial sector, some important challenges remain. First, the Basel rules formally apply only to internationally active banks and the measures are focused almost exclusively on building ex ante capital and liquidity buffers at banks to prevent a crisis and less on tools that governments might use in the event of a crisis. There is broad consensus that there is a need for more capital and less liquidity risk in the banking system, especially for large systemically important institutions. There is less agreement that augmented bank capital and liquidity standards alone will be sufficient for preventing a

Table 7-3
Additional Basel III Components

Component	Description
Capital Protection	A supplemental layer of common equity that, when infringed upon, prohibits the distribution of earnings to assist in protecting the minimum common equity requirement.
Countercyclical Capital Preservation	A constraint placed on banks during credit booms with the intention of reducing their losses in the event of a credit bust.
Leverage Percentage	A minimum amount of loss-absorbing capital relative to the bank's assets and off-balance sheet liabilities irrespective of risk-weighting.
Liquidity Reserves	A minimum liquidity ratio to distribute enough cash to cover funding necessities over a month-long period of stress.
Additional Measures to Govern Vital Banks	Such as requirements for additional capital, fortified arrangements for cross-border management, and resolution for banks that are large enough to destabilize the financial system.

Source: Bank for International Settlements.

future crisis, particularly in light of the wide-ranging activities undertaken by non-bank financial institutions. The Federal Reserve has imposed stricter capital standards than Basel for U.S. banks, is proposing an even larger capital requirement for systemically important U.S. banks, and has required foreign banking organizations with U.S. non-branch assets over $50 billion to set up holding companies subject to Federal Reserve regulation (Tarullo 2014).

A second challenge is the implementation of the Basel policies. Not all G-20 members have fully implemented the recommended policies, and there remains the general problem that financial regulation and supervision remain largely at the national level but the externalities of weak financial institutions are potentially global. As Mervyn King, former Governor of the Bank of England, observed: "Financial institutions are global in life, but national in death." That is, liquid financial institutions are everyone's bank in the good times, but become the government's bank in the event of a liquidity shortage or insolvency. For many countries, particularly in Europe, the size of the banking sector (indeed in some cases, the size of individual banks), remains larger than national GDP. Yet mechanisms are not in place to mobilize massive liquidity in multiple currencies in the event of a creditor run. And if a bank is not just illiquid but also insolvent and needs to be resolved, its size could overwhelm the resources of its home government. Moreover, processes for unwinding large globally active systemic institutions, especially when several governments are involved, remain imperfect.

Another challenge that is particular to global regulation is that countries are inherently different, with different sizes and business models of financial institutions and differing degrees of dependence on those institutions. This creates a trade-off between rules that apply equally to all countries, and the need for regulation that is sensitive to macroeconomic and financial conditions at different times and in different places. In other words, there may be a tradeoff between the rules that create a level playing field, where all financial actors are treated equally, and the rules that create a safe playing field that recognizes asymmetries across players.

Deeper coordination does eventually seem to happen when minds become concentrated on the brink of disaster. But that is not enough and it has been harder to sustain cooperative momentum in periods of calm. Yet it is precisely in periods of calm when the investments and preparation for the next crisis need to occur. It is critical to maintain the pressure for financial reform while the memory of the last financial crisis is still fresh. Ultimately, international financial markets are necessary for risk mitigation, growth, and innovation, not just in the United States but in the global economy. For these markets to provide maximum benefits, however, governments must recognize potential risks and continue to collaborate in containing and managing them, just as they have collaborated in creating institutions and rules for the international trading system.

Conclusion

Through trade and financial linkages, the world's economies are more interdependent than at any time in history. This interdependence has been supported not only by steep declines in the costs of international communication and shipping, but also by a reduction in governmental barriers to the cross-border movement of goods, services, investment, and portfolio assets. Increasingly, economies are linked by production processes that cross international borders so as to minimize costs by better exploiting local comparative advantages.

The post-World War II process of globalization has delivered important benefits for U.S. consumers, workers, and businesses by increasing economies' productivity, opening new markets for exports, and expanding the range of products available for purchase. Expanded trade has also improved peoples' lives in other, indirect ways, for example, raising living and working standards in other countries, and locking in meaningful environmental protections.

Since the benefits of trade are often unevenly distributed, it is important that globalization be accompanied by domestic and international safeguards that prevent unfair trade practices. Such safeguards include policies that limit damage to the environment, protect displaced workers, and regulate risky financial practices that could cause financial instability.

Domestic U.S. policies are essential to help our economy take advantage of the opportunities afforded by trade along with measures to counteract the potentially negative side effects of trade. But beyond these purely domestic safeguards, an evolving structure of multilateral and regional agreements has worked to lower international trade barriers while reining in predatory trade practices and negative side effects. The World Trade Organization is central to that effort. In addition, the Administration is pursing comprehensive, high-quality free trade agreements that provide U.S. exporters with enhanced market access while insisting that our trading partners do not compete on the basis of low worker- or environmental-protection standards. In the financial sphere, international governmental collaboration and a set of central organizations including the Basel Committee, the Financial Stability Board, and the International Monetary Fund are key components in constructing a global safety net for crisis prevention and management.

REFERENCES

CHAPTER 1

Blau, Francine D., and Lawrence M. Kahn. 2013. "Female Labor Supply: Why is the US Falling Behind?" *American Economic Review* 103(3): 251-256.

Mishkin, F. S. 1978. "The Household Balance Sheet and the Great Depression." *Journal of Economic History* 38: 918-937.

Saez, Emmanuel. 2015. United States Income Inequality Data, http://eml.berkeley.edu/~saez/TabFig2013prel.xls. Updating: Piketty, Thomas, and Emmanuel Saez. 2003. "Income Inequality in the United States, 1913-1998." *Quarterly Journal of Economics* 118(1): 1-39.

CHAPTER 2

Abe, Prime Minister Shinzo. 2014. "Press Conference by Prime Minister Abe." Tokyo, Japan, November 18 (http://japan.kantei.go.jp/96_abe/statement/201411/1118kaiken.html).

Arezki, Rabah and Olivier Blanchard. 2014. "Seven Questions About the Recent Oil Price Slump" (blog). iMFdirect. International Monetary Fund. December 22. http://blog-imfdirect.imf.org/2014/12/22/seven-questions-about-the-recent-oil-price-slump.

Bank of Japan (BOJ). 2014a. "Statement on Monetary Policy: March 11, 2014." https://www.boj.or.jp/en/announcements/release_2014/k141031a.pdf.

____. 2014b. "Expansion of the Quantitative and Qualitative Monetary Easing: October 31, 2014."

https://www.boj.or.jp/en/announcements/release_2014/k141031a.pdf.

___. 2015. "Monthly Report of Recent Economic and Financial Developments: January 2015." http://www.boj.or.jp/en/mopo/gp_2015/gp1501b.pdf.

Bloomberg News. 2014. "Xi says China Must Adapt to 'New Normal' of Slower Growth." May. http://www.bloomberg.com/news/2014-05-11/xi-says-china-must-adapt-to-new-normal-of-slower-growth.html.

Blue Chip Economic Indicators. 2014. "Top Analysts' Forecasts of the U.S. Economic Outlook for the Year Ahead." *Blue Chip Economic Indicators* 39, no. 10 (October): 1-21.

Board of Governors of the Federal Reserve System. 2013. "Press release: June 19, 2013." http://www.federalreserve.gov/mediacenter/files/FOMCpresconf20130619.pdf.

Board of Governors of the Federal Reserve System. 2014. "In the shadow of the Great Recession: Experiences and perspectives of young workers." http://www.federalreserve.gov/econresdata/2014-survey-young-workers-young-workers-outlook.htm.

Board of Governors of the Federal Reserve System. 2015a. "Press release: January 28, 2015." http://www.federalreserve.gov/newsevents/press/monetary/20150128a.htm.

Board of Governors of the Federal Reserve System. 2015b. "The January 2015 Senior Loan Officer Opinion Survey on Bank Lending Practices." http://www.federalreserve.gov/boarddocs/snloansurvey/201502/fullreport.pdf.

Cass, David. 1965. "Optimum Growth in an Aggregative Model of Capital Accumulation." *The Review of Economic Studies* 32, no. 3 (July): 233-240.

Congressional Budget Office (CBO). 2013a. "Macroeconomic Effects of Alternative Budgetary Paths." February. http://www.cbo.gov/sites/default/files/43769_AlternativePaths_2012-2-5_0.pdf.

Congressional Budget Office (CBO). 2013b. "The Economic Impact of S. 744, the Border Security, Economic Opportunity and Immigration Modernization Act." June. https://www.cbo.gov/sites/default/files/44346-Immigration.pdf.

Congressional Budget Office (CBO). 2014. "The Economic Effects of the President's 2015 Budget." July. https://www.cbo.gov/sites/default/files/45540-Economic_APB.pdf.

Congressional Budget Office (CBO). 2015. "The Budget and Economic Outlook: 2015 to 2025." January. http://www.cbo.gov/sites/default/files/cbofiles/attachments/49892-Outlook2015.pdf.

Council of Economic Advisers (CEA). 2009. *The Economic Impact of the American Recovery and Reinvestment Act of 2009: First Quarterly Report.* September.

http://www.whitehouse.gov/assets/documents/CEA_ARRA_Report_Final.pdf.

Council of Economic Advisers (CEA). 2014a. The Economic Report of the President. March.

http://www.whitehouse.gov/sites/default/files/docs/full_2014_economic_report_of_the_president.pdf

Council of Economic Advisers (CEA). 2014b. "15 Economic Facts about Millennials." October. http://www.whitehouse.gov/sites/default/files/docs/millennials_report.pdf.

Council of Economic Advisers (CEA). 2014c. "The Economic Effects of Administrative Action on Immigration." November. http://www.whitehouse.gov/sites/default/files/docs/cea_2014_economic_effects_of_immigration_executive_action.pdf.

European Central Bank (ECB). 2012a. "Press release: July 26, 2012." http://www.ecb.europa.eu/press/key/date/2012/html/sp120726.en.html.

European Central Bank (ECB). 2012b. "Press release: August 2, 2012." http://www.ecb.europa.eu/press/pressconf/2012/html/is120802.en.html.

European Central Bank (ECB). 2012c. "Press release: September 6, 2012." http://www.ecb.europa.eu/press/pr/date/2012/html/pr120906_1.en.html.

European Central Bank (ECB). 2014. "Press release: November 21, 2014." http://www.ecb.europa.eu/press/key/date/2014/html/sp141121.en.html.

European Central Bank (ECB). 2015. "Press release: January 22, 2015." http://www.ecb.europa.eu/press/pressconf/2015/html/is150122.en.html.

European Commission. 2013. "Transatlantic Trade and Investment Partnership: The Economic Analysis Explained." September. http://trade.ec.europa.eu/doclib/docs/2013/september/tradoc_151787.pdf.

Fannie Mae. 2014. News Release. "Americans' Personal Finance Sentiment Strengthens, Housing Optimism Follows Suit." http://www.

fanniemae.com/portal/about-us/media/corporate-news/2014/6192. html.

Federal Reserve Bank of Philadelphia. 2014. "Survey of Professional Forecasters, Fourth Quarter 2014." http://www.philadelphiafed.org/research-and-data/real-time-center/survey-of-professional-forecasters/2014/spfq414.pdf.

Fisher, Irving. 1930. The Theory of Interest. New York: The McMillan Company.

Gallup. 2014. "Americans' Views of Job Market Hold Steady." http://www.gallup.com/poll/179483/americans-perceptions-job-market-hold-steady.aspx.

International Monetary Fund (IMF). 2010. "World Economic Outlook, April 2010: Rebalancing Growth." https://www.imf.org/external/pubs/ft/weo/2010/01/pdf/text.pdf.

International Monetary Fund (IMF). 2013. "World Economic Outlook, April 2013: Hopes, Realities, Risks." http://www.imf.org/external/pubs/ft/weo/2013/01/pdf/text.pdf.

International Monetary Fund (IMF). 2014. "World Economic Outlook, October 2014: Legacies, Clouds, Uncertainties." http://www.imf.org/external/pubs/ft/weo/2014/02/pdf/text.pdf.

International Monetary Fund (IMF). 2015. "World Economic Outlook Update, January 2015: Cross Currents." http://www.imf.org/external/pubs/ft/weo/2015/update/01/pdf/0115.pdf.

Koopmans, Tjalling C. 1965. "On the Concept of Optimal Economic Growth." The Economic Approach to Development Planning. Amsterdam: North-Holland Press.

Office of Management and Budget (OMB). 2014. "OMB Director Shaun Donovan on the Passage of H.R. 83, Consolidated and Further Continuing Appropriations Act, 2015." December. https://www.whitehouse.gov/blog/2014/12/17/omb-director-shaun-donovan-passage-hr-83-consolidated-and-further-continuing-appropr.

Office of Management and Budget (OMB). 2015. "The President's Budget for Fiscal Year 2016." February. http://www.whitehouse.gov/omb/budget/.

Petri, Peter A. and Michael G. Plummer. 2012. "The Trans-Pacific Partnership and Asia-Pacific Integration: Policy Implications." Peterson

Institute for International Economics Policy Brief. Number PB12-16. http://www.iie.com/publications/pb/pb12-16.pdf.

Ramsey. F. P. 1928. "A Mathematical Theory of Saving." The Economic Journal 38, no. 152 (December): 543-559.

Saez, Emmanuel and Gabriel Zucman. 2014. "Wealth inequality in the United States since 2013: Evidence from capitalized income tax data." Working Paper 20625. Cambridge, Mass.: National Bureau of Economic Research (October).

Shiller, Robert. 2014. "Online Data." http://www.econ.yale.edu/~shiller/data.htm.

The World Bank Group. 2015. "Global Economic Prospects, January 2015: Having Fiscal Space and Using It." http://www.worldbank.org/content/dam/Worldbank/GEP/GEP2015a/pdfs/GEP15a_web_full.pdf.

The Urban Institute. 2015. "Housing Finance at a Glance, January 2015: A Monthly Chartbook." http://www.urban.org/UploadedPDF/2000075-Housing-Finance-At-A-Glance.pdf.

The White House, Office of the Press Secretary. 2015. "FACT SHEET: Making Homeownership More Accessible and Sustainable." January. http://www.whitehouse.gov/the-press-office/2015/01/07/fact-sheet-making-homeownership-more-accessible-and-sustainable.

Chapter 3

Aldy, Joseph E. 2013. "A Preliminary Assessment of the American Recovery and Reinvestment Act's Clean Energy Package." *Review of Environmental Economics and Policy* 7(1): 136-155.

Alesina, Alberto,and Silvia Ardagna. 2010. "Large Changes in Fiscal Policy: Taxes versus Spending." *Tax Policy and the Economy* 24: 35-68.

Angrist, Joshua D., and Jörn-Steffen Pischke. 2010. "The Credibility Revolution in Empirical Economics: How Better Research Design Is Taking the Con out of Econometrics." *Journal of Economic Perspectives* 24, no. 2: 3-30.

Auerbach, Alan J., and Daniel Feenberg. 2000. "The Significance of Federal Taxes as Automatic Stabilizers." *Journal of Economic Perspectives* 14(3): 37-56.

Auerbach, Alan, and Yuriy Gorodnichenko. 2012. "Measuring the Output Responses to Fiscal Policy." *American Economic Journal: Economic Policy* 4(2): 1-27.

Barro, Robert J. 1974. "Are Government Bonds Net Wealth?" *Journal of Political Economy* 82(6): 1095-1117.

Ball, Laurence M. 2009. "Hysteresis in Unemployment: Old and New Evidence." Working Paper 14818. Cambridge, MA: National Bureau of Economic Research.

Bastiat, Frédéric. 1848. "Selected Essays on Political Economy." Seymour Cain, trans. 1995. *Library of Economics and Liberty.* 3 February 2014.

Blanchard, Olivier, Giovanni Dell'Ariccia, and Paolo Mauro. 2010. "Rethinking Macroeconomic Policy." IMF Staff Position Note. Washington: International Monetary Fund.

Blanchard, Olivier, and Daniel Leigh. 2013. "Growth Forecast Errors and Fiscal Multipliers." IMF Working Paper.

Blanchard, Olivier, and Roberto, Perotti. 2002. "An Empirical Characterization of the Dynamic Effects of Changes in Government Spending and Taxes on Output." *Quarterly Journal of Economics.*

Blanchard, Olivier, and Lawrence H. Summers. 1986. "Hysteresis and the European Unemployment Problem." NBER Macroeconomics Annual, 1, 15-90. Cambridge, MA: National Bureau of Economic Research.

Blinder, Alan S., and Mark Zandi. 2010. "How the Great Recession was Brought to an End." Princeton University and Moody's Analytics.

Card, David and Phillip Levine. 2000. "Extended Benefits and the Duration of UI Spells: Evidence from the New Jersey Extended Benefit Program." *Journal of Public Economics* 78: 107-38.

Chetty, Raj. 2008. "Moral Hazard vs Liquidity and Optimal Unemployment Insurance." Working Paper 13967. Cambridge, MA: National Bureau of Economic Research.

Chodorow-Reich, Gabriel, Laura Feiveson, Zachary Liscow, and William Gui Woolston. 2012. "Does State Fiscal Relief During Recessions Increase Employment? Evidence from the American Recovery and Reinvestment Act." *American Economic Journal: Economic Policy* 4, no. 3: 118-145.

Christiano, Lawrence, Martin Eichenbaum, and Sergio Rebelo. 2011. "When Is the Government Spending Multiplier Too Large?" *Journal of Political Economy* 119(1): 78-121.

Coenen, Gunter, et al. 2012. "Effects of Fiscal Stimulus in Structural Models." *American Economic Journal: Macroeconomics* 4(1): 22-68.

Cogan, John F., et al. 2010 "New Keynesian versus old Keynesian government spending multipliers." *Journal of Economic Dynamics and Control* 34(3): 281-295.

Congressional Budget Office (CBO). 2009a. "Health Information Technology for Economic and Clinical Health Act."

___. 2009b. "Cost Estimate: H.R. 1, American Recovery and Reinvestment Act of 2009."

___. 2009c. "Cost Estimate: H.R. 3548, Worker, Homeownership, and Business Assistance Act of 2009."

___. 2010a. "The Budget and Economic Outlook: Fiscal Years 2010 to 2020."

___. 2010b. "The Budget and Economic Outlook: An Update."

___. 2010c. "Cost Estimate: H.R. 4691, the Temporary Extension Act of 2010, As Introduced on February 25, 2010."

___. 2010d. "Cost Estimate: Budgetary Effects of Hiring Incentives to Restore Employment Act, as Introduced by Senator Reid on February 11, 2010."

___. 2010e. "Cost Estimate: Amendment No. 3721 to H.R. 4851, the Continuing Extension Act, 2010, as Proposed by Senator Baucus."

___. 2010f. "Cost Estimate: Budgetary Effects of Senate Amendment 4425, the Unemployment Compensation Extension Act of 2010."

___. 2010g. "Cost Estimate: CBO Estimate of Changes in Revenues and Direct Spending for Senate Amendment 4594 in the Nature of a Substitute to H.R. 5297, the Small Business Jobs and Credit Act of 2010."

___. 2010h. "Cost Estimate: CBO Estimate of Changes in Revenues and Direct Spending for S.A. 4753, an amendment to H.R. 4852, the Tax Relief, Unemployment Insurance Reauthorization, and Job Creation Act of 2010."

___. 2010i. "Cost Estimate: Budgetary Effects of Senate Amendment 4575, containing proposals related to education, state fiscal relief, the Supplemental Nutrition Assistance Program, rescissions, and revenue offsets."

___. 2011a. "The Budget and Economic Outlook: Fiscal Years 2011 to 2021."

___. 2011b. "Cost Estimate: Budgetary Effects of Senate Amendment 927 to H.R. 674, as proposed by Senator Reid for Senator Tester."

___. 2011c. "Cost Estimate: H.R. 5297, the Small Business Jobs Act of 2010."

___. 2011d. "Cost Estimate: Budgetary Effects of the Temporary Payroll Tax Cut Continuation Act of 2011, as Posted on the Website of the House Committee on Rules on December 22, 2011."

___. 2012a. "The Budget and Economic Outlook: Fiscal Years 2012 to 2022."

___. 2012b. "Cost Estimate: Budgetary effects of the Conference Agreement for H.R. 3630, the Middle Class Tax Relief and Job Creation Act of 2012, as Posted on the Web Site of the House Committee on Rules on February 16, 2012."

___. 2012c. "Cost Estimate: Budgetary effects of the Conference Agreement for H.R. 3630, the Middle Class Tax Relief and Job Creation Act of 2012, as Posted on the Web Site of the House Committee on Rules on February 16, 2012."

___. 2013a. "Estimated Impact of the American Recovery and Reinvestment Act on Employment and Economic Output from October 2012 Through December 2012."

___. 2013b. "Cost Estimate: Estimate of Budgetary Effects of H.R. 8, the American Taxpayer Relief Act of 2012, as passed by the Senate on January 1, 2013."

___. 2014. "The budget and Economic Outlook: 2014 to 2024."

Conley, Timothy, and Bill Dupor. 2013. "The American Recovery and Reinvestment Act: Public Sector Jobs Saved, Private Sector Jobs Forestalled." Journal of Monetary Economics.

Council of Economic Advisers (CEA). 2009a. "Estimates of Job Creation from the American Recovery and Reinvestment Act of 2009."

___. 2009b. "The Economic Impact of the American Recovery and Reinvestment Act of 2009." First Quarterly Report. September.

___. 2010a. "The Economic Impact of the American Recovery and Reinvestment Act of 2009." Second Quarterly Report. January.

___. 2010b. "The Economic Impact of the American Recovery and Reinvestment Act of 2009." Third Quarterly Report. April.

___. 2010c. "The Economic Impact of the American Recovery and Reinvestment Act of 2009." Fourth Quarterly Report. July.

___. 2011. "The Economic Impact of the American Recovery and Reinvestment Act of 2009." Sixth Quarterly Report. March.

___. 2013a. "The Economic Impact of the American Recovery and Reinvestment Act of 2009." Ninth Quarterly Report. February.

___. 2013b. "Economic Report of the President." March.

Council of Economic Advisers and the Department of Labor. 2014. "The Economic Benefits of Extending Unemployment Insurance." January.

Delong, J. Bradford, and Lawrence H. Summers. 2012. "Fiscal Policy in a Depressed Economy." *Brookings Papers on Economic Activity.* Spring.

Department of Education. 2011. "FY 2012 Department of Education Justifications of Appropriation Estimates to the Congress: Student Financial Assistance" in President's FY 2012 Budget Request for the U.S. Department of Education.

Department of the Treasury. 2010a. "The Case for Temporary 100 Percent Expensing: Encouraging Business to Expand now by Lowering the Cost of Investment."

___. 2010b. "The American Opportunity Tax Credit."

___. 2011. "Treasury Analysis of Build America Bonds Issuance and Savings."

Department of the Treasury and Council of Economic Advisers. 2012. "A New Economic Analysis of Infrastructure Investment." March.

Eggertson, Gauti B. 2001. "Real Government Spending in a Liquidity Trap." New York Federal Reserve.

Elmendorf, Douglas W., and Jason Furman. 2008. "If, When, How: A Primer on Fiscal Stimulus." Washington: Brookings Institution.

(EPA) Environmental Protection Agency. 2013. "American Recovery and Reinvestment Act Quarterly Performance Report – FY2013 Quarter 4 Cumulative Results as of September 30, 2013."

Executive Office of the President and Office of the Vice President. 2010. "The Recovery Act: Transforming the American Economy through Innovation". The White House.

Farhi, Emmanuel, and Ivan Werning. 2012. "Fiscal Multipliers: Liquidity Traps and Currency Unions." Working Paper 18321. Cambridge, MA: National Bureau of Economic Research.

Favero, Carlo, and Francesco Giavazzi. 2012. "Measuring Tax Multipliers: The Narrative Method in Fiscal VARs." *American Economic Journal: Economic Policy* 4(2): 69–94.

Fernald, John G. 1999. "Roads to Prosperity? Assessing the Link between Public Capital and Productivity," *The American Economic Review*, Vol. 89, No. 3:619-638.

Feyrer, James, and Bruce Sacerdote. 2011. "Did the Stimulus Stimulate? Real Time Estimates of the Effects of the American Recovery and Reinvestment Act." Working Paper 16759. National Bureau of Economic Research.

Financial Crisis Inquiry Commission. 2011. *The Financial Crisis Inquiry Report*. New York: PublicAffairs.

Follette, Glenn, and Byron Lutz. 2010. "Fiscal Policy in the United States: Automatic Stabilizers, Discretionary Fiscal Policy Actions, and the Economy." Finance and Economics Discussion Series. Washington: Federal Reserve Board.

Guajardo, Jaime, Daniel Leigh, and Andrea Pescatori. Forthcoming. "Expansionary Austerity? New International Evidence." *Journal of the European Economic Association*.

Hall, Bronwyn H., Jacques Mairesse, Pierre Mohnen. 2009. "Measuring the Returns to R&D." Working Paper 15622. Cambridge, MA: National Bureau of Economic Research.

House, Christopher L., and Matthew D. Shapiro. 2008. "Temporary Investment Tax Incentives: Theory with Evidence from Bonus Depreciation." *American Economic Review* 98(3): 737-768.

Ilzetski, Ethan, Enrique G. Mendoza, and Carlos A. Vegh. 2011. "How Big (Small?) are Fiscal Multipliers?" IMF Working Paper.

(IMF) International Monetary Fund. 2009 "What's the Damage? Medium Term Dynamics after Financial Crises." *World Economic Outlook* October 2009: Sustaining the Recovery Chapter 4, p. 121-151.

___. 2012. World Economic Outlook April 2012: Growth Resuming, Dangers Remain."

Johnson, David S., Jonathan A. Parker, and Nicholas S. Souleles. 2006. "Household Expenditure and the Income Tax Rebates of 2001." *American Economic Review* 96(5): 1589-1610.

Joint Committee on Taxation. 2009. "Estimated Budget Effects of the Revenue Provisions Contained in the Conference Agreement for

H.R.1, The 'American Recovery and Reinvestment Tax Act of 2009.'"

____. 2010a. "Estimated Budget Effects of the Revenue Provisions Contained in Senate Amendment #4594 to H.R. 5297, The 'Small Business Jobs Act of 2010,' Scheduled for Consideration by the United States Senate on September 16, 2010."

____. 2010b. "Estimated Revenue Effects of the House Amendment to the Senate Amendment to H.R. 4853, The 'Middle Class Tax Relief Act of 2010,' Scheduled for Consideration by the House of Representatives on December 2, 2010."

____. 2012. "Estimated Revenue Effects of H.R. 8, The 'Job Protection and Recession Prevention Act of 2012.'"

Katz, Lawrence F. and Bruce D. Meyer. 1990. "Unemployment Insurance, Recall Expectations, and Unemployment Outcomes." *Quarterly Journal of Economics* 105, no. 4: 973-1002.

Kroft, Kory and Matthew Notowidigdo. 2011. "Should Unemployment Insurance Vary with the Local Unemployment Rate? Theory and Evidence." Working Paper.

Laeven, Luc, and Fabian Valencia. 2012. "Systemic Banking Crises Database: An Update."Working Paper WP/12/163. Washington: International Monetary Fund.

Ljungqvist, Lars, and Thomas J. Sargent. 1998. "The European Unemployment Dilemma." Journal of Political Economy 106(3): 514-550.

Mertens, Karel, and Morten O. Ravn. 2012. "Empirical Evidence on the Aggregate Effects of Anticipated and Unanticipated US Tax Policy Shocks." *American Economic Journal*: Economic Policy 4(2): 145–181.

Mertens, Karel, and Morten Ravn. 2013. "The Dynamic Effects of Personal and Corporate Income Tax Changes in the United States." *American Economic Review*. June.

Meyer, Bruce D. 1990. "Unemployment Insurance and Unemployment Spells." Econometrica 58, no.4: 757–782.

Munnell, Alicia H, 1992. "Infrastructure Investment and Economic Growth," *Journal of Economic Perspectives*, vol. 6(4), pages 189-98, Fall. Pittsburg, PA: American Economic Association.

Nakamura, Emi, and Jón Steinsson. 2011. "Fiscal Stimulus in a Monetary Union: Evidence from U.S. Regions." Unpublished paper, New York: Columbia University.

Office of Science and Technology Policy, and The National Economic Council. 2013. "Four Years of Broadband Growth." The White House.

Parker, Jonathan A. 2011. "On Measuring the Effects of Fiscal Policy in Recessions." Working Paper 17240. Cambridge, MA: National Bureau of Economic Research.

Parker, Jonathan A., Nicholas S. Souleles, David S. Johnson, and Robert McClelland. 2011. "Consumer Spending and the Economic Stimulus Payments of 2008." Working Paper 16684. Cambridge, MA: National Bureau of Economic Research.

Perotti, Roberto. 2011. "The Austerity Myth: Gain Without Pain?" Working Paper 17571. Cambridge, MA: National Bureau of Economic Research.

Phelps, Edmund. 1972. "Inflation policy and unemployment theory." New York: WW Norton and Company.

Poterba, James M. 1994. "State Responses to Fiscal Crises: The Effects of Budgetary Institutions and Politics." *Journal of Political Economy* 102(4): 799-821.

Ramey, Valerie A. 2011a. "Identifying Government Spending Shocks: It's All in the Timing" *Quarterly Journal of Economics* 126, no. 1: 1-50.

___. 2011b. "Can Government Purchases Stimulate the Economy?" *Journal of Economic Literature* 49, no. 3: 673-85.

Ramey, Valerie A, and Matthew Shapiro. 1998. "Costly Capital Reallocation and the Effects of Government Spending." Carnegie-Rochester Conference on Public Policy 48: 145-94.

Reichling, Felix, and Charles Whalen. 2012. "Assessing the Short-Term Effects on Output Changes in Federal Fiscal Policies." Working Paper 2012-08. Congressional Budget Office.

Reinhart, Carmen M., and Kenneth S. Rogoff. 2009. *This time is different: Eight Centuries of Financial Folly.* Princeton, NJ: Princeton University Press.

___. Forthcoming. "Recovery from Financial Crises: Evidence from 100 Episodes." *American Economic Review.*

Reifschneider, Dave, William L. Wascher, and David Wilcox. 2013. "Aggregate Supply in the United States: Recent Developments and Implications for the Conduct of Monetary Policy." 14th Jacques Polak Annual Research Conference. Washington: International Monetary Fund.

Romer, Christina D. 2011. "Back from the Brink." In The International Financial Crisis: Have the Rules of Finance Changed? Edited by Asli Demirgüç-Kunt, Douglas D. Evanoff, George G. Kaufman, pp. 15-31. World Scientific Publishing Company.

___. 2012. "Fiscal Policy in the Crisis: Lessons and Policy Implications." University of California-Berkeley, Department of Economics.

Romer, Christina D., and David H. Romer. 2010. "The Macroeconomic Effects of Tax Changes: Estimates Based on a New Measure of Fiscal Shocks." *American Economic Review* 100(3): 763-801.

Rothstein, Jesse. 2011. "Unemployment Insurance and Job Search in the Great Recession." *Brookings Papers on Economic Activity*, Fall.

Schmieder, Johannes F., Till Von Wachter, and Stefan Bender. 2012. "The Long-term Effects of UI Extensions on Employment." *American Economic Review*, Papers and Proceedings.

Shoag, Daniel. 2013. "Using state pension shocks to estimate fiscal multipliers since the Great Recession." *American Economic Review* 103(3): 121-124.

Sims, Christopher A. 2010. "But Economics Is Not an Experimental Science." *Journal of Economic Perspectives* 24, no. 2: 59-68.

Smets, Frank, and Rafael Wouters. 2007. "Shocks and Frictions in US Business Cycles: a Bayesian DSGE Approach." *American Economic Review* 97(3): 586-606.

Sperling, Gene. 2007. "Ways to Get Economic Stimulus Right This Time." Bloomberg.com. December 17.

Stock, James H. 2010. "The Other Transformation in Econometric Practice: Robust Tools for Inference." *Journal of Economic Perspectives* 24, no. 2: 83-94.

Stock, James H. and Mark W. Watson. 2012. "Disentangling the Channels of the 2007–09 Recession," *Brookings Papers on Economic Activity*. Spring.

Stock, James H., and Mark W. Watson. 2010. *Introduction to Econometrics*. 3rd ed. Boston, MA: Addison-Wesley.

Suarez Serrato, Juan Carlos, and Philippe Wingender. 2011. "Estimating the Incidence of Government Spending."

Summers, Lawrence H. 2007. "The State of the US Economy." Presentation at Brookings Institution Forum on December 19th, 2007.

____. 2008. Speech at the Wall Street Journal-CEO Council Conference. Washington, D.C., November 19.

Taylor, John B. 2011. "An Empirical analysis of the Revival of Fiscal Activism in the 2000s." *Journal of Economic Literature* 49(3): 686:702.

____. Forthcoming. "The Role of Policy in the Great Recession and the Weak Recovery." *American Economic Review*, Papers and Proceedings.

Transportation Research Board of the National Academies. 2013. "Transportation Investments in Response to Economic Downturns, Special Report 312."

Wilson, Daniel J. 2012. "Fiscal Spending Jobs Multipliers: Evidence from the 2009 American Recovery and Reinvestment Act." *American Economic Journal: Economic Policy.*

Wimer, Christopher, Liana Fox, Irwin Garfinkel, Neeraj Kaushal, and Jane Waldfogel. 2013. "Trends in Poverty with an Anchored Supplemental Poverty Measure." Working Paper 1- 25. New York: Columbia Population Research Center.

Woodford, Michael. 2011. "Simple Analytics of the Government Expenditure Multiplier." *American Economic Journal: Macroeconomics* (3), p. 1-35.

CHAPTER 4

A Better Balance. 2008. "The Business Case for Workplace Flexibility." March. New York, NY.

Akyeampong, E. 2001. "Fact Sheet on Work Absences – Perspectives on Labour and Income." Ottawa, ON: Statistics Canada.

Almond, Douglas, and Janet Currie. 2011. "Killing Me Softly: The Fetal Origins Hypothesis." *Journal of Economic Perspectives* 25(3): 153-172.

Appelbaum, Eileen and Ruth Milkman. 2011. "Paid Family Leave Pays Off in California." Harvard Business Review Blog Network.

Appelbaum, Eileen. 2014. "Paid Sick Days in Connecticut Not a Burden for Employers." Center for Economic and Policy Research.

Appelbaum, Eileen, Ruth Milkman, Luke Elliott, and Teresa Kroeger. 2014. "Good for Business? Connecticut's Paid Sick Leave Law." Center for Economic and Policy Research.

Akerlof, George, and Janet Yellen. 1986. *Efficiency Wage Models of the Labor Market.*

Cambridge: Cambridge University Press.

Arthur, Michelle. 2003. "Share Price Reactions to Work-Family Initiatives: An Institutional Perspective." *Academy of Management Journal* 46(4): 497-505.

Baughman, Reagan, Daniela DiNardi, and Douglas Holtz-Eakin. 2003. "Productivity and Wage Effects of 'Family-friendly' Fringe Benefits." *International Journal of Manpower* 24(3): 247-259.

Bauman, Alvin. 1970. "Measuring employee compensation in U.S. industry." *Monthly Labor Review*: 17-24.

Becker, Gary S. 1964. *Human Capital.* Chicago, IL: University of Chicago Press.

Bernard, Tara Siegel. "The Unspoken Stigma of Workplace Flexibility." New York Times. 14 June 2013.

Bewley, Truman. 1999. *Why Wages Don't Fall During a Recession.* Cambridge, MA: Harvard   University Press.

Bianchi, S. M., J.P. Robinson and M. Milkie. 2006. "Changing Rhythms of American Family Life." New York: Russell Sage Foundation.

Bloom, Nick, and John Van Reenen. 2010. "Why Do Management Practices Differ across Firms and Countries?" *Journal of Economic Perspectives* 24(1): 203–24.

Bloom, Nicholas, James Liang, John Roberts, and Zhichun Jenny Ying. 2013. "Does Working from Home Work? Evidence from a Chinese Experiment." NBER Working Paper 18871.

Bloom, Nick, Tobias Krestchmer, and John Van Reenen. 2006. "Work-Life Balance, Management Practices and Productivity." Centre for Economic Performance, London School of Economics.

Bureau of Labor Statistics (BLS). 2011. "Access to and Use of Leave 2011: Data from the American Time Use Survey." U.S. Department of Labor.

_____. 2013. "Unpaid Eldercare in the United States 2011-2012: Data from the American Time Use Survey." U.S. Department of Labor.

Bond, James, Ellen Galinsky, and Kelly Sakai. 2008. "2008 National Study of Employers." New

York, NY: Families and Work Institute.

Boushey, Heather and Sarah Glynn. 2012. "There are Significant Business Costs to Replacing Employees." Center for American Progress.

California Governor's Office of Business and Economic Development. 2014. "Employee Benefits." Accessed December 16, 2014. https://www. business.ca.gov/StartaBusiness/AdministeringEmployees/Employ-eeBenefits.aspx.

California Employment Development Department. 2014. "Paid Family Leave Benefits." Accessed December 14, 2014. http://www.edd. ca.gov/disability/PFL_Benefit_Amounts.htm.

California Employment Development Department 2014. "State Disability Insurance (SDI) Tax" Accessed December 16, 2014. http://www. edd.ca.gov/payroll_taxes/State_Disability_Insurance_Tax.htm.

Cappelli, Peter and Keith Chauvin. 1991. "An Interplant Test of the Efficiency Wage Hypothesis." *Quarterly Journal of Economics* 106(3): 769-787.

Catalyst. 2004. "The Bottom Line: Connecting Corporate Performance and Gender Diversity." http://www.catalyst.org/knowledge/bottom-line-connecting-corporate-performance-and-gender-diversity.

Carneiro, Pedro, Katrine V. Loken and Kjell G. Salvanes. 2011. "A Flying Start? Maternity Leave Benefits and Long Run Outcomes of Children." Institute for the Study of Labor (IZA) Discussion Paper 5793.

Cho, Sungjin, and John Rust. 2010. "The Flat Rental Puzzle." *The Review of Economic Studies* 77: 560-594.

City and County of San Francisco. 2013. "Family Friendly Workplace Ordinance (FFWO)". San Francisco Administrative Code Chapter 12 Z.

Cohen, Wesley, and Daniel Levinthal. 1990. "Absorptive Capacity: A New Perspective on Learning and Innovation." *Administrative Science Quarterly* 35: 128–152.

Comfort, Derrick, Karen Johnson, and David Wallace. 2003. "Part-time work and Family-Friendly Practices in Canadian Workplaces." The Evolving Workplace Series. Ottawa, Canada: Statistics Canada and Human Resources Development Canada (June).

Computer Economics. 2008. "Telecommuting Policies Can Lower IT Employee Turnover." Irvine, CA.

Connecticut Department of Labor 2014. "An Overview of the Paid Sick Leave Law." Accessed December 16, 2014. http://www.ctdol.state.ct.us/wgwkstnd/sickleave.htm.

Corporate Voices for Working Families. 2005. "Business Impacts of Flexibility: An Imperative for Expansion." July. Washington, D.C.

Council of Economic Advisers. 2010. "Work-Life Balance and the Economics of Workplace Flexibility."

Dal Bo, Ernesto; Frederico Finan; and Martin A. Rossi. 2013. "Strengthening State Capabilities:

The Role of Financial Incentives in the Call to Public Service." Quarterly Journal of Economics 128(3): 1169-1218.

Dalton, Dan R., and Debra J. Mesch. 1990. "The Impact of Flexible Scheduling on Employee Attendance and Turnover." *Administrative Science Quarterly* 35(2): 370–387.

DiNardo, John, Nicole M. Fortin, and Thomas Lemieux. 1996. "Labor Market Institutions and the Distribution of Wages, 1973-1992: A Semiparametric Approach." Econometrica 64(5): 1001-1044.

Dionne, Georges, and Benoit Dostie. 2007. "New Evidence on the Determinants of Absenteeism Using Linked Employer-Employee Data." *Industrial and Labor Relations Review*: 108-120.

District of Columbia, Department of Employment Services. 2008. "Accrued Sick and Safe Leave Act of 2008."

District of Columbia, Department of Employment Services. 2013. "Earned Sick and Safe Leave Amendment Act of 2013."

Drago, Robert, and Kevin Miller. 2010. "Sick at Work: Infected Employees in the Workplace during the H1N1 Pandemic." Institute for Women's Policy Research.

Eberts, Randall W., and Joe A. Stone. 1985. "Wages, Fringe Benefits, and Working Conditions: An Analysis of Compensating Differentials." *Southern Economic Journal*: 274-280.

Elborgh-Woytek, Katrin, Monique Newiak, Kalpana Kochhar, Stefania Fabrizio, Kangni Kpodar, Philippe Wingender, Benedict Clements and Gerd Schwartz. 2013. "Women, Work and the Economy: Macroeconomic Gains from Gender Equity." International Monetary Fund (IMF) Staff Discussion Note.

Foster, Nigel and Satish Sule. 2010. "German Legal System and Laws," New York: Oxford University Press: 586.

Galinsky, Ellen, Kerstin Aumann, and James T. Bond. 2011. "Times are Changing: Gender and Generation at Work and at Home." Families and Work Institute: 2008 National Study of the Changing Workforce.

Gallup. 2013. "In U.S., Poor Health Tied to Big Losses for All Job Types."

Georgetown University Federal Legislation Clinic. 2006. "The United Kingdom Flexible Working Act."

Goldin, Claudia. 2006. "The Quiet Revolution That Transformed Women's Employment, Education, and Family." *American Economic Review*, Papers and Proceedings 96: 1–26.

Goldin, Claudia. 2014. "A grand gender convergence: Its last chapter." *American Economic Review* 104(4): 1091-1119.

Goldin, Claudia and Lawrence F. Katz. 2002. "The Power of the Pill: Oral Contraceptives and Women's Career and Marriage Decisions." *Journal of Political Economy* 110(4): 730-770.

Goldman Sachs. 2007. "Gender Inequality, Growth and Global Ageing." Goldman Sachs Economic Research Global Economics Paper.

Gov.UK, 2014. "Flexible Working."

Greenhouse, Steven. "Part-Time Schedules, Full-Time Headaches." *New York Times*. 18 July 2014.

Griliches, Zvi. 1957. "Hybrid corn: An Exploration in the Economics of Technological Change." *Econometrica* 25(4): 501–522.

Gruber, Jonathan and Alan B. Krueger. 1991. "The Incidence of Mandated Employer-Provided Insurance: Lessons From Workers' Compensation Insurance." In *Tax Policy and the Economy* 5, ed. David Bradford. Cambridge, MA: MIT Press: 111-144.

Harrington, Brad, Fred Van Deusen, Jennifer Sabatini Fraone and Samantha Eddy. 2014. "The New Dad: Take Your Leave." Center for Work & Family, Carroll School of Management. Boston.

Harter, James K and Sangeeta Agrawal. 2012. "Engagement at Work: Working Hours, Flextime, Vacation Time, and Wellbeing." Gallup Inc.

Hewlett, Sylvia Ann, Melinda Marshall, and Laura Sherbin. 2013. "Innovation, Diversity, and Market Growth." Center for Talent Innovation.

International Labour Organization (ILO). 2014. "Maternity and Paternity at Work: Law and Practice Across the World."

Kalt, Michael S. 2014. "California Enacts Law Requiring Employers to Provide Paid Sick Leave." Society for Human Resource Management. http://www.shrm.org/legalissues/stateandlocalresources/pages/calif.-enacts-paid-sick-leave.aspx.

Kantor, Jodi. "Working Anything but 9 to 5." New York Times. 13 August 2014.

Klerman, Jacob Alex, Kelly Daley, and Alyssa Pozniak. 2014. "Family and Medical Leave in 2012: Technical Report." Cambridge, MA: Abt Associates Inc. http://www.dol.gov/asp/evaluation/fmla/FMLA-2012-Technical-Report.pdf.

Lazear, Edward P. 2003. "Firm-Specific Human Capital: A Skill-Weights Approach." NBER Working Paper 9679.

Levine, David I. 1991. "Just-Cause Employment Policies in the Presence of Worker Adverse Selection." *Journal of Labor Economics* 9(3): 294–305.

Levitt, Barbara, and James G. March. 1988. "Organizational Learning." *Annual Review of Sociology* 14: 319–40.

Levitt, Steven. 2006. "An Economist Sells Bagels: A Case Study in Profit Maximization." NBER Working Paper 12152.

Livingston, Gretchen. 2014. "Chapter 1: The Likelihood of Being a Stay-at-Home Father." In Growing Number of Dads Home with the Kids. Pew Research Center.

Matos, Kenneth and Ellen Galinsky. 2014. "2014 National Study of Employers." Families and Work Institute: National Study of Employers.

Mincer, Jacob. 1974. *Schooling, Experience, and Earnings*. New York: Columbia University Press.

National Advisory Council on the Employment of Women (NACEW). 2013. "Flexible Work Arrangements: Literature Review." http://womenatwork.org.nz/assets/Uploads/Files-PDFs-Docs/flexible-working-literature-review.pdf.

National Center for Education Statistics. 2012. "The Condition of Education 2012." U.S. Department of Education. http://nces.ed.gov/pubs2012/2012045.pdf.

National Partnership for Women and Families. "Advancing a Family Friendly America: How Family Friendly Is Your State?" Accessed

January 27, 2015. http://www.nationalpartnership.org/issues/work-family/family-friendly-america/family-friendly-america-map.html.

Nelson, Richard R., and Sidney G. Winter. 1985. *An Evolutionary Theory of Economic Change*. Harvard University Press.

Nepomnyaschy, Lenna, and Jane Waldfogel. 2007. "Paternity Leave and Fathers' Involvement With Their Young Children: Evidence from the American Ecls–B." Community, Work and Family 10(4): 427-453.

New Jersey Department of Labor and Workforce Development. 2014. "Family Leave Insurance: Cost to the Worker." Accessed December 16, 2014. http://lwd.state.nj.us/labor/fli/content/cost.html.

New Jersey Division of Temporary Disability Insurance. 2013. "Your Guide to Family Leave Insurance in New Jersey." http://lwd.state.nj.us/labor/forms_pdfs/tdi/WPR-119.pdf.

Nielsen Holdings. 2014. "Harris Poll: Vast Majority of Americans Favor Flexible Workplace Policies."

Olson, Craig. 2002. "Do Workers Accept Lower Wages in Exchange for Health Benefits?" *Journal of Labor Economics* 20(S2): S91-S114.

Organisation for Economic Co-operation and Development (OECD). 2014. "PF2.1: Key Characteristics of parental leave systems." http://www.oecd.org/els/soc/PF2_1_Parental_leave_systems_1May2014.pdf.

Pencavel, John H. 1972. "Wages, Specific Training, and Labor Turnover in U.S. Manufacturing Industries." *International Economic Review* 13(1): 53–64.

Petro, John. 2010. "Paid Sick Leave Does Not Harm Business Growth or Job Growth." Drum Major Institution for Public Policy.

Pew Charitable Trusts. 2014. "Paid Family Leave Hits a Snag in States." Stateline.

Pierce, Brooks. 2010. "Recent Trends in Compensation Inequality." In *Labor in the New Economy*: 63-98. University of Chicago Press.

Potter, Edward E. 2003. "Telecommuting: The Future of Work, Corporate Culture, and American Society." *Journal of Labor Research* 24(1): 73–84.

PricewaterhouseCoopers LLP. 2009. "US Human Capital Effectiveness Report." New York, NY.

Rhode Island Department of Labor and Training. 2014. "Temporary Disability Insurance/ Temporary Caregiver Insurance." Accessed December 14, 2014, http://www.dlt.ri.gov/tdi/.

Romer, David. 2006. "Do Firms Maximize? Evidence from Professional Football." *Journal of Political Economy* 114(2): 340–65.

Rossin-Slater, Maya. 2011."The Effects of Maternity Leave on Children's Birth and Infant Health Outcomes in the United States." *Journal of Health Economics* 30(2): 221-239.

Rossin-Slater, Maya, Christopher J. Ruhm, and Jane Waldfogel. 2013. "The Effects of California's Paid Family Leave Program on Mothers' Leave-Taking and Subsequent Labor Market Outcomes." *Journal of Policy Analysis and Management* 32(2): 224-245.

Ruhm, Christopher J. 2000. "Parental Leave and Child Health." *Journal of Health Economics* 19(6): 931-960.

Secretary of the Commonwealth of Massachusetts. "Question 4: Law Proposed by Initiative Petition." Accessed February 10, 2015. http://www.sec.state.ma.us/ele/ele14/pip144.htm.

Sheiner, Louise. 1999. "Health Care Costs, Wages, and Aging." Federal Reserve Board of Governors.

Smith, Mark. 2002. "5 Ways to Equip Telecommuters." Connected Home Media (May 6).

Summers, Lawrence H. 1989. "Some Simple Economics of Mandated Benefits." *American Economic Review* 79(2): 177-183.

Ton, Zeynep. 2012. "Why" good jobs" are good for retailers." *Harvard Business Review* 90(1-2): 124-31.

Van Giezen, Robert. 2013. "Paid Leave in Private Industry Over the Past 20 Years." Beyond the Numbers: Pay & Benefits 2(18).

Vermont State Legislature. 2013. "No. 31. An Act Relating to Equal Pay."

Waldfogel, Jane. 1999. "The impact of the family and medical leave act." *Journal of Policy Analysis and Management* 18(2): 281-302.

Waldfogel, Jane, Yoshio Higuchi, and Masahiro Abe. 1999. "Family Leave Policies and Women's Retention After Childbirth: Evidence from the United States, Britain, and Japan." *Journal of Population Economics* 12(4): 523-545.

Wang, Wendy, Kim Parker, and Paul Taylor. 2013. "Breadwinner Moms." Pew Research Center. http://www.pewsocialtrends.org/2013/05/29/breadwinner-moms/.

Williams, Joan. 2001. *Unbending Gender: Why Work and Family Conflict and What to Do About It.* Oxford University Press.

Woodbury, Stephen A. 1983. "Substitution Between Wage and Nonwage Benefits." *American Economic Review* 73(1): 166-182.

Work, Family, & Health Network. 2008a. "A Behavioral Measure of Supervisory Support." Portland, OR.

––––––. 2008b. "Flexible Work and Well-Being Center." Portland, OR.

Yasbek, Philippa. 2004. "The Business Case for Firm-Level Work-Life Balance Policies: A Review of the Literature." Wellington, UK: Department of Labour (January).

Chapter 5

Auerbach, Alan J., and Kevin Hassett. "Tax policy and business fixed investment in the United States." *Journal of Public Economics* 47, no. 2 (1992): 141-170.

Bartelsman, Eric J., and Roel MWJ Beetsma. 2003. "Why pay more? Corporate tax avoidance through transfer pricing in OECD countries." *Journal of Public Economics* 87, no. 9: 2225-2252.

Chetty, Raj, John N. Friedman, and Jonah Rockoff. 2011. "New Evidence on the Long-Term Impacts of Tax Credits," IRS Statistics of Income Working Paper Series. http://www.irs.gov/pub/irs-soi/11rpchettyfriedmanrockoff.pdf.

Chirinko, Robert S., Steven M. Fazzari, and Andrew P. Meyer. 1999. "How responsive is business capital formation to its user cost?: An exploration with micro data." *Journal of Public Economics* 74, no. 1: 53-80.

Choi, James J., David Laibson, Brigitte C. Madrian, and Andrew Metrick. 2004. "For Better or For Worse: Default Effects and 401(k) Savings Behavior." In *Perspectives in the Economics of Aging*, edited by David A. Wise pp. 81–121. Chicago: University of Chicago Press.

Clausing, Kimberly A. 2009. "Multinational Firm Tax Avoidance and Tax Policy." *National Tax Journal* 62, no. 4: 703-725.

Clausing, Kimberly A. 2011. "The revenue effects of multinational firm income shifting." Tax Notes, March 28.

Congressional Budget Office. 2012. "Taxing Businesses Through the Individual Income Tax."

Congressional Budget Office. 2014. "Taxing Capital Income: Effective Marginal Tax Rates Under 2014 Law and Selected Policy Options."

Council of Economic Advisers. 2014. "The Labor Force Participation Rate Since 2007: Causes and Policy Implications."

Cummins, Jason G., et al. 1994. "A reconsideration of investment behavior using tax reforms as natural experiments." Brookings Papers on Economic Activity: 1-74.

Cummins, Jason, and R. Glenn Hubbard. 1995. "The tax sensitivity of foreign direct investment: evidence from firm-level panel data." In *The Effects of Taxation on Multinational Corporations*, pp. 123-152. University of Chicago Press.

de Mooij, Ruud A. 2011. "The tax elasticity of corporate debt: A synthesis of size and variations." IMF Working Papers: 1-27.

Desai, Mihir A., C. Fritz Foley, and James R. Hines Jr. 2004. "A multinational perspective on capital structure choice and internal capital markets." *The Journal of Finance* 59, no. 6: 2451-2487.

Devereux, Michael P., and Rachel Griffith. 1998. "Taxes and the Location of Production: Evidence from a Panel of US Multinationals." *Journal of Public Economics* 68, no. 3: 335-367.

Devereux, Michael P., and Rachel Griffith. 2003. "Evaluating tax policy for location decisions." *International Tax and Public Finance* 10, no. 2: 107-126.

Dharmapala, Dhammika. 2014. What Do We Know About Base Erosion and Profit Shifting? A Review of the Empirical Literature. CESifo Working Paper No. 4612.

Executive Office of the President and U.S. Department of the Treasury. 2012. "The President's Framework for Business Tax Reform." Washington. http://www.treasury.gov/resource-center/tax-policy/Documents/The-Presidents-Framework-for-Business-Tax-Reform-02-22-2012.pdf.

Executive Office of the President and U.S. Department of the Treasury. 2014. "The President's Proposal to Expand the Earned Income Tax Credit." Washington. http://www.whitehouse.gov/sites/default/files/docs/eitc_report_0.pdf.

Fatica, Serena. 2013. Do corporate taxes distort capital allocation? Cross-country evidence from industry-level data. No. 503. Directorate General Economic and Monetary Affairs (DG ECFIN), European Commission.

Goolsbee, Austan. 1998. "Taxes, Organizational Form, and the Deadweight Loss of the Corporate Income Tax." *Journal of Public Economics* 69, no. 1: 143-152.

Goolsbee, Austan. 2004. "The impact of the corporate income tax: evidence from state organizational form data." *Journal of Public Economics* 88, no. 11: 2283-2299.

Gordon, Roger H., and Jeffrey K. MacKie-Mason. 1994. "Tax distortions to the choice of organizational form." *Journal of Public Economics* 55, no. 2: 279-306.

Gramlich, Edward M. 1994. "Infrastructure Investment: A Review Essay." Journal of Economic Literature 32, (September): 1177-1196.

Gravelle, Jane G. 2013. "Tax Havens: International Tax Avoidance and Evasion." Congressional Research Service. Report for Congress R40623.

Greenstone, Michael, Richard Hornbeck, and Enrico Moretti. 2010. "Identifying Agglomeration Spillovers: Evidence from Winners and Losers of Large Plant Openings." *Journal of Political Economy* 118, no. 3: 536-598.

Grubert, Harry, and Rosanne Altshuler. 2013. "Fixing the system: an analysis of alternative proposals for the reform of international tax." *National Tax Journal* 66, (September): 671–712.

Grubert, Harry, and John Mutti. 1991. "Taxes, tariffs and transfer pricing in multinational corporate decision making." *The Review of Economics and Statistics*: 285-293.

Grubert, Harry, and John Mutti. 2000. "Do taxes influence where US corporations invest?" *National Tax Journal*: 825-839.

Hall, Bronwyn H. 1995. "Effectiveness of Research and Experimentation Tax Credits: Critical Literature Review and Research Design." Report for the Office of Technology Assessment, Congress of the United States.

Hall, Bronwyn H., Jacques Mairesse, and Pierre Mohnen. 2010. "Measuring the Returns to R&D." In *Handbook of the Economics of Innovation 2*, edited by Bronwyn H. Hall and Nathan Rosenberg. Elsevier.

Hall, Bronwyn H., and John Van Reenen. 2000. "How effective are fiscal incentives for R&D? A review of the evidence." *Research Policy* 29 (May): 449-469.

Hassett, Kevin A., and R. Glenn Hubbard. 2002. "Tax policy and business investment." *Handbook of Public Economics* 3: 1293-1343.

Hassett, Kevin A., and Kathryn Newmark. 2008. "Taxation and business behavior: A review of the recent literature." In *Fundamental Tax Reform: Issues, Choices and Implications*. MIT Press: 191-214.

Hines, Jr., James R. 1996. "Tax policy and the activities of multinational corporations." National Bureau of Economic Research Working Paper No. w5589.

Hines, Jr., James R. 1999. "Lessons from behavioral responses to international taxation." *National Tax Journal*: 305-322.

Hoynes, Hilary W., Douglas L. Miller, and David Simon. 2013. "Income, The Earned Income Tax Credit, and Infant Health." https://gspp.berkeley.edu/assets/uploads/research/pdf/Hoynes-Miller-Simon-10-3-13.pdf.

Huizinga, Harry, and Luc Laeven. 2008. "International profit shifting within multinationals: A multi-country perspective." *Journal of Public Economics* 92, no. 5: 1164-1182.

Kearney, Melissa S., and Lesley Turner. 2013. "Giving Secondary Earners a Tax Break: A Proposal to Help Low-and Middle-Income Families." The Hamilton Project Discussion Paper 2013-07, Washington: Brookings Institution.

Knittel, Matthew, et al. 2011. "Methodology to Identify Small Businesses and Their Owners." Department of the Treasury, Office of Tax Analysis Technical Paper 4.

Mackie-Mason, Jeffrey K., and Roger H. Gordon. 1997. "How much do taxes discourage incorporation?" *The Journal of Finance* 52, no. 2: 477-506.

Manoli, Dayanand S. and Nicholas Turner, 2014. "Cash-on-Hand and College Enrollment: Evidence from Population Tax Data and Policy Nonlinearities," National Bureau of Economic Research Working Paper No. 19836. http://www.nber.org/papers/w19836.

Munnell, Alicia H. 1992. "Policy watch: infrastructure investment and economic growth." *The Journal of Economic Perspectives* 6, no. 4: 189-198.

Noonan, T.D. Minister Michael D. 2014. "Financial Statement of the Minister for Finance." Dublin. http://www.budget.gov.ie/Budgets/2015/FinancialStatement.aspx.

Organization for Economic Cooperation and Development. 2013. Action Plan on Base Erosion and Profit Shifting. Paris: OECD Publishing.

Organization for Economic Cooperation and Development. 2014. "Explanatory Statement: 2014 Deliverables." OECD/G20 Base Erosion and Profit Shifting Project, OECD. www.oecd.org/tax/beps-2014-deliverables-explanatory-statement.pdf.

PwC and Business Roundtable. 2011. "Global Effective Tax Rates." http://businessroundtable.org/sites/default/files/Effective_Tax_Rate_Study.pdf.

Schrank, David, Bill Eisele, and Tim Lomax. 2012. "TTI's 2012 Urban Mobility Report," Texas Transportation Institute.

Slemrod, Joel. 2009. "Lessons for tax policy in the Great Recession." *National Tax Journal*: 387-397.

Toder, Eric J., and Alan D. Viard. 2014. "Major Surgery Needed: A Call for Structural Reform of the US Corporate Income Tax." Washington: Urban Institute and American Enterprise Institute.

Tyson, Laura and Greg Linden. 2012. "The Corporate R&D Tax Credit and U.S. Innovation and Competitiveness: Gauging the Economic and Fiscal Effectiveness of the Credit." Washington: Center for American Progress.

U.S. Department of the Treasury. 2007. Treasury Conference on Business Taxation and Global Competitiveness, Background Paper. Washington.

U.S. Government Accountability Office. 2012. "Improved Tax Information Could Help Families Pay for College." GAO-12-560.

Weichenrieder, Alfons J., and Tina Klautke. 2008. "Taxes and the efficiency costs of capital distortions." CESifo working paper No. 2431.

White, Karen, and Lance R. Grenzeback. 2007. "Understanding freight bottlenecks." *Public Roads* 70, no. 5.

Zwick, Eric, and James Mahon. 2014. "Do Financial Frictions Amplify Fiscal Policy? Evidence from Business Investment Stimulus." Harvard University.

CHAPTER 6

Barbose, Galen, Samantha Weaver, and Naim Darghouth. 2014. Tracking the Sun VII: An Historical Summary of the Installed Price of Photovoltaics in the United States from 1998-2013. Lawrence Berkeley National Laboratory Report LBNL-6808E.

Bernanke, Ben S. 1983. "Irreversibility, Uncertainty, and Cyclical Investment." *Quarterly Journal of Economics*, vol. 98, pp. 85–106.

Blinder, Alan. 2009. "Comment on Hamilton, Causes and Consequences of the Oil Shock of 2007-08." *Brookings Papers on Economic Activity*, no. 1: 262–267.

Bloom, Nicholas. 2009. "The Impact of Uncertainty Shocks." *Econometrica* 77:623–85.

Cruz, Jennifer, Peter W. Smith, and Sara Stanley. 2014. "The Marcellus Shale Gas Boom in Pennsylvania: Employment and Wage Trends." *Bureau of Labor Statistics Monthly Labor Review*, February, at http://www.bls.gov/opub/mlr/2014/article/the-marcellus-shale-gas-boom-in-pennsylvania.htm

Council of Economic Advisers and Department of Energy. 2013. "Economic Benefits of Increasing Grid Resilience to Weather Outages."

Council of Economic Advisers. 2014a. "The All-of-the-Above Energy Strategy as a Path to Sustainable Economic Growth."

Council of Economic Advisers. 2014b. "The Cost of Delaying Action to Stem Climate Change."

Council of Economic Advisers. 2014c. "The Economic Impact of the American Recovery and Reinvestment Act Five Years Later."

Dixit, Avinash K. and Robert S. Pindyck. *Investment under Uncertainty*. Princeton, NJ: Princeton University Press, 1994.

Edelstein, Paul and Lutz Kilian. 2009. "How Sensitive are Consumer Expenditures to Retail Energy?" *Journal of Monetary Economics* 56, 766–779.

Energy Information Administration. 2014. "Effect of Increased Levels of Liquefied Natural Gas Exports on U.S. Energy Markets."

Environmental Protection Agency. 2010. "Inventory of U.S. Greenhouse Gas Emissions and Sinks: 1990-2010." http://www.epa.gov/climatechange/ghgemissions/usinventoryreport.html.

Hamilton, James D. 1988. "A Neoclassical Model of Unemployment and the Business Cycle." *Journal of Political Economy* 96, no. 3: 593–617.

Hamilton, James D. 2009. "Causes and Consequences of the Oil Shock of 2007–08." *Brookings Papers on Economic Activity*, no. 1: 215–83.

Intergovernmental Panel on Climate Change. 2014.

Interagency Working Group on Social Cost of Carbon, United States Government. 2010. "Technical Support Document: - Social Cost of Carbon for Regulatory Impact Analysis Under Executive Order 12866".

Kellogg, Ryan. 2010. "The Effect of Uncertainty on Investment: Evidence from Texas Oil Drilling." NBER Working Paper 16541.

Kilian, Lutz. 2008a. "Exogenous Oil Supply Shocks: How Big Are They and How Much Do They Matter for the U.S. Economy?" *Review of Economics and Statistics* 90, no. 2: 216–40.

Kilian, Lutz. 2008b. "The Economic Effect of Energy Price Shocks." *Journal of Economic Literature* 46, no. 4: 871–909.

Kilian, Lutz. 2009. "Not All Oil Price Shocks Are Alike: Disentangling Demand and Supply Shocks in the Crude Oil Market." *American Economic Review* 99, no. 3: 1053–69.

Kilian, Lutz and Daniel P. Murphy. 2014. "The Role of Inventories and Speculative Trading in the Global Market for Crude Oil." *Journal of Applied Economics*, vol. 29, pp. 454–478.

Levi, Michael. 2012. "A Strategy for U.S. Natural Gas Exports." The Hamilton Project, Discussion Paper 2012-04. Washington: Brookings Institution (June).

Linn, Joshua. 2008. Energy Prices and the Adoption of Energy-Saving Technology. *The Economic Journal*, vol. 118, pp. 1986–2012.

Linn, Joshua. 2009. Why Do Oil Shocks Matter? The Role of Inter-Industry Linkages. *Economic Inquiry*, vol. 47, pp. 153–176.

Nordhaus, William D. 2007. "Who's Afraid of a Big Bad Oil Shock?" *Brookings Papers on Economic Activity*, no. 2:219–238.

Parry, Ian, Chandara Veung, and Dirk Heine. 2014. How Much Carbon Pricing is in Countries' Own Interests? The Critical Role of Co-Benefits. IMF Working Paper 14/174.

The Risky Business Project. 2014. Risky Business: The Economic Risks of Climate Change in the United States.

CHAPTER 7

Acemoglu, et al. Forthcoming. "Import Competition and the Great U.S. Employment Sag of the 2000s." *Journal of Labor Economics.*

Alquist, Ron, Rahul Mukherjee, and Linda Tesar. 2014. "Liquidity-Driven FDI." Economics Section, no. 17. The Graduate Institute of International Studies.

Antweiler, Werner, Brian R. Copeland, and M. Scott Taylor. 2001. "Is Free Trade Good for the Environment?" *American Economic Review* 91, no. 4: 877-908.

Autor, David H., David Dorn, and Gordon H. Hanson. 2013. "The China Syndrome: Local Labor Market Effects of Import Competition in the United States." *American Economic Review* 103, no. 6: 2121-68.

Avdjiev, Stefan, Michael Chui, and Hyun Song Shin. 2014. "Non-Financial Corporations from Emerging Market Economies and Capital Flows." *BIS Quarterly Review*, December: 67-77.

Baier, Scott L., and Jeffrey H. Bergstrand. 2007. "Do Free Trade Agreements Actually Increase Members' International Trade?" *Journal of International Economics* 71, no. 1: 72-95.

Becker, Gary S. 1957. "The Economics of Discrimination." The University of Chicago Press, 2nd edition.

Becker, Randy, Wayne Gray, and Jordan Marvakov. 2013. "NBER-CES Manufacturing Industry Database." Cambridge, Mass.: National Bureau of Economic Research.

Berman, Eli, John Bound, and Zvi Griliches. 1994. "Changes in Demand for Skilled Labor within U.S. Manufacturing Industries: Evidence from the Annual Survey of Manufacturing." The *Quarterly Journal of Economics* 109, no. 2: 367-97.

Bernard, Andrew B., and J. Bradford Jensen. 1995. "Exporters, Jobs, and Wages in U.S. Manufacturing: 1976-1987." *Brookings Papers on Activity: Microeconomics* 1995: 67-112.

_____. 1997. "Exceptional Exporter Performance: Cause, Effect, or Both?" *Journal of International Economics* 47, no. 1: 1-25.

Bernard, Andrew B., J. Bradford Jensen, Stephen J. Redding, and Peter K. Schott. 2007. "Firms in International Trade." *Journal of Economic Perspectives* 21, no. 3: 105-130.

Bernard, Andrew B., J. Bradford Jensen, and Peter K. Schott. 2006. "Trade Costs, Firms and Productivity." *Journal of Monetary Economics* 53, no. 5: 917-37.

Black, Sandra E., and Elizabeth Brainerd. 2004. "Importing Equality? The Impact of Globalization on Gender Discrimination." *Industrial and Labor Review* 57, no. 4: 540-59.

Blinder, Alan S., and Alan B. Krueger. 2013. "Alternative Measures of Offshorability: A Survey Approach." *Journal of Labor Economics* 31, no. 2, pt. 2: S97-S128.

Blomberg, S. Brock, and Gregory D. Hess. 2006. "How Much Does Violence Tax Trade?" *Review of Economics and Statistics* 88, no. 4: 599-612.

Bloom, Nicholas, Mirko Draca, and John Van Reenen. 2011. "Trade Induced Technical Change? The Impact of Chinese Imports on Innovation, IT and Productivity." Centre for Economic Performance Discussion Paper no. 1000.

Blundell, Richard, Rachel Griffith, and John Van Reenen. 1999. "Market Share, Market Value and Innovation in a Panel of British Manufacturing Firms." *Review of Economic Studies* 66, no. 3: 529-54.

Branstetter, Lee G., Raymond Fisman, and C. Fritz Foley. 2006. "Do Stronger Intellectual Property Rights Increase International Technology Transfer? Empirical Evidence from U.S. Firm-Level Panel Data." *Quarterly Journal of Economics* 121, no. 1: 321-49.

Broda, Christian, and David E. Weinstein. 2006. "Globalization and the Gains from Variety." *Quarterly Journal of Economics* 121, no. 2: 541-85.

Clerides, Sofronis K., Saul Lach, and James R. Tybout. 1998. "Is Learning by Exporting Important? Micro-dynamic Evidence from Colombia, Mexico, and Morocco." *Quarterly Journal of Economics* 113, no. 3: 903-07.

Cockburn, Iain M., Jean O. Lanjouw, and Mark Schankerman. 2014. "Patents and the Global Diffusion of New Drugs." Working Paper 20492. Cambridge, Mass.: National Bureau of Economic Research.

Coeurdacier, Nicolas, and Hélene Rey. 2013. "Home Bias in Open Economy Financial Macroeconomics." *Journal of Economic Literature* 51, no. 1: 63-115.

Copeland, Brian R., and M. Scott Taylor. 2003. "Trade and the Environment." Princeton University Press.

Ebenstein, et al. 2011. "Understanding the Role of China in the "Decline" of U.S. Manufacturing." Hebrew University of Jerusalem.

Edmonds, Eric V., and Nina Pavcnik. 2005. "The Effect of Trade Liberalization on Child Labor." *Journal of International Economics* 65, no. 2: 401-19.

Feenstra, Robert C., and Gordon H. Hanson. 1997. "Productivity Measurement and the Impact of Trade and Technology on Wages: Estimates for the U.S. 1972-1990." Working Paper 6052. Cambridge, Mass.: National Bureau of Economic Research.

_____. 1999. "The Impact of Outsourcing and High-Technology Capital on Wages: Estimates for the United States, 1979-1990." *Quarterly Journal of Economics* 114, no. 3: 907-40.

Feyrer, James. 2009. "Distance, Trade, and Income—The 1967 to 1975 Closing of the Suez Canal as a Natural Experiment." Working Paper 15557. Cambridge, Mass.: National Bureau of Economic Research.

Frankel, Jeffrey A., and David Romer. 1999. "Does Trade Cause Growth?" *American Economic Review* 90, no. 3: 379-99.

Goldberg, Linda S. 2013. "Banking Globalization, Transmission, and Monetary Policy Autonomy." *Sveriges Riksbank Economic Review* 3: 161-93.

Goldberg, Pinelopi K., and Nina Pavcnik. 2003. "The Response of the Informal Sector to Trade Liberalization." *Journal of Development Economics* 72, no. 2: 463-96.

_____. 2007. "Distributional Effects of Globalization in Developing Countries." *Journal of Economic Literature*, 45, no. 1: 39-82.

Grether, Jean-Marie, Nicole A. Mathys, and Jaime De Melo. 2010. "Global Manufacturing SO2 Emissions: Does Trade Matter?" *Review of World Economics* 145, no. 4: 713-29.

Hanson, Gordon H. 2007. "Globalization, Labor Income, and Poverty in Mexico." *Globalization and Poverty*, pp. 417-56. University of Chicago Press.

Haskel, Jonathan E., Sonia C. Pereira, and Matthew J. Slaughter. 2007. "Does Inward Foreign Direct Investment Boost the Productivity of Domestic Firms?" *Review of Economics and Statistics* 89, no. 3: 482-96.

Kee, Hiau Looi. 2014. "Local Intermediate Inputs and the Shared Supplier Spillovers of Foreign Direct Investment." World Bank Policy Research Working Paper 7050.

Keller, Wolfgang, and Stephen R. Yeaple. 2009. "Multinational Enterprises, International Trade, and Productivity Growth: Firm-Level Evidence from the United States." *Review of Economics and Statistics* 91, no. 4: 821-31.

Lipsey, Robert E. 2010. "Measuring the Location of Production in a World of Intangible Productive Assets, FDI, and Intrafirm Trade." *Review of Income and Wealth* 56, no. S1:S99-S110.

Martin, Philippe, Thierry Mayer, and Mathias Thoenig. 2008. "Make Trade not War?" *Review of Economic Studies* 75, no. 3: 865-900.

_____. 2012. "The Geography of Conflicts and Regional Trade Agreements." *American Economic Journal: Macroeconomics* 4, no. 4: 1-35.

McCaig, Brian. 2011. "Exporting out of Poverty: Provincial Poverty in Vietnam and U.S. Market Access." *Journal of International Economics* 85, no. 1: 102-13.

McCaig, Brian, and Nina Pavcnik. 2014. "Export Markets and Labor Allocation in a Low-Income Country." Working Paper 20455. Cambridge, Mass.: National Bureau of Economic Research.

Melitz, Marc J. 2003. "The Impact of Trade on Intra-Industry Reallocations and Aggregate Industry Productivity." *Econometrica* 71, no. 6: 1695-1725.

Menezes-Filho, Naércio Aquino, and Marc-Andreas Muendler. 2011. "Labor Reallocation Response to Trade Reform." Working Paper 17372. Cambridge, Mass.: National Bureau of Economic Research.

Milanovic, Branko. 2013. "Global Income Inequality in Numbers: In History and Now." *Global Policy* 4, no. 2. Washington, D.C.: World Bank (May).

Mostashari, Shalah M. 2010. "Expanding Variety of Goods Underscores Battle for Comparative Advantage." Economic Letter 5, no. 15. Federal Reserve Bank of Dallas.

Nordström, Håkan, and Scott Vaughan. 1999. "Trade and Environment." *Special Studies* 4. The World Trade Organization.

Paz, Lourenço S. 2014. "The Impacts of Trade Liberalization on Informal Labor Markets: A Theoretical and Empirical Evaluation of the Brazilian Case." *Journal of International Economics* 92, no. 2: 330-48.

Philippon, Thomas, and Ariell Reshef. 2013. "An International Look at the Growth of Modern Finance." *Journal of Economic Perspectives* 27, no. 2: 73-96.

Poole, Jennifer. 2013. "Knowledge Transfers from Multinational to Domestic Firms: Evidence from Worker Mobility." *Review of Economics and Statistics* 95, no. 2: 393-406.

Riker, David. 2010. "Do Jobs in Export Industries Still Pay More? And Why?" Manufacturing and Services Economics Brief no. 2, International Trade Administration, U.S. Department of Commerce.

Riker, David, and Brandon Thurner. 2011. "Weekly Earnings in Export-Intensive U.S. Services Industries." Manufacturing and Services Economics Brief no. 4, International Trade Administration, U.S. Department of Commerce.

Stolper, Wolfgang F., and Paul A. Samuelson. 1941. "Protection and Real Wages." *Review of Economic Studies* 9, no. 1: 58-73.

Tarullo, Daniel K. 2014. "Regulating Large Foreign Banking Organizations." Speech at the Harvard Law School Symposium on Building the Financial System of the Twenty-first Century: An Agenda for Europe and the United States. Armonk, NY, March 27.

Topalova, Petia. 2007. "Trade Liberalization, Poverty, and Inequality: Evidence from Indian Districts." *Globalization and Poverty*, pp. 291-336. University of Chicago Press.

_____. 2010. "Factor Immobility and the Regional Impacts of Trade Liberalization: Evidence on Poverty from India." *American Economic Journal: Applied Economics* 2, no. 4: 1-41.

U.S. Department of Labor. 2014. 2013 Findings on the Worst Forms of Child Labor.

REPORT TO THE PRESIDENT ON THE ACTIVITIES OF THE COUNCIL OF ECONOMIC ADVISERS DURING 2014

LETTER OF TRANSMITTAL

COUNCIL OF ECONOMIC ADVISERS
Washington, D.C., December 31, 2014

MR. PRESIDENT:

The Council of Economic Advisers submits this report on its activities during calendar year 2014 in accordance with the requirements of the Congress, as set forth in section 10(d) of the Employment Act of 1946 as amended by the Full Employment and Balanced Growth Act of 1978.

Sincerely yours,

Jason Furman, *Chairman*
Betsey Stevenson, *Member*
Maurice Obstfeld, *Member*

Council Members and Their Dates of Service

Name	Position	Oath of office date	Separation date
Edwin G. Nourse	Chairman	August 9, 1946	November 1, 1949
Leon H. Keyserling	Vice Chairman	August 9, 1946	
	Acting Chairman	November 2, 1949	
	Chairman	May 10, 1950	January 20, 1953
John D. Clark	Member	August 9, 1946	
	Vice Chairman	May 10, 1950	February 11, 1953
Roy Blough	Member	June 29, 1950	August 20, 1952
Robert C. Turner	Member	September 8, 1952	January 20, 1953
Arthur F. Burns	Chairman	March 19, 1953	December 1, 1956
Neil H. Jacoby	Member	September 15, 1953	February 9, 1955
Walter W. Stewart	Member	December 2, 1953	April 29, 1955
Raymond J. Saulnier	Member	April 4, 1955	
	Chairman	December 3, 1956	January 20, 1961
Joseph S. Davis	Member	May 2, 1955	October 31, 1958
Paul W. McCracken	Member	December 3, 1956	January 31, 1959
Karl Brandt	Member	November 1, 1958	January 20, 1961
Henry C. Wallich	Member	May 7, 1959	January 20, 1961
Walter W. Heller	Chairman	January 29, 1961	November 15, 1964
James Tobin	Member	January 29, 1961	July 31, 1962
Kermit Gordon	Member	January 29, 1961	December 27, 1962
Gardner Ackley	Member	August 3, 1962	
	Chairman	November 16, 1964	February 15, 1968
John P. Lewis	Member	May 17, 1963	August 31, 1964
Otto Eckstein	Member	September 2, 1964	February 1, 1966
Arthur M. Okun	Member	November 16, 1964	
	Chairman	February 15, 1968	January 20, 1969
James S. Duesenberry	Member	February 2, 1966	June 30, 1968
Merton J. Peck	Member	February 15, 1968	January 20, 1969
Warren L. Smith	Member	July 1, 1968	January 20, 1969
Paul W. McCracken	Chairman	February 4, 1969	December 31, 1971
Hendrik S. Houthakker	Member	February 4, 1969	July 15, 1971
Herbert Stein	Member	February 4, 1969	
	Chairman	January 1, 1972	August 31, 1974
Ezra Solomon	Member	September 9, 1971	March 26, 1973
Marina v.N. Whitman	Member	March 13, 1972	August 15, 1973
Gary L. Seevers	Member	July 23, 1973	April 15, 1975
William J. Fellner	Member	October 31, 1973	February 25, 1975
Alan Greenspan	Chairman	September 4, 1974	January 20, 1977
Paul W. MacAvoy	Member	June 13, 1975	November 15, 1976
Burton G. Malkiel	Member	July 22, 1975	January 20, 1977
Charles L. Schultze	Chairman	January 22, 1977	January 20, 1981
William D. Nordhaus	Member	March 18, 1977	February 4, 1979
Lyle E. Gramley	Member	March 18, 1977	May 27, 1980
George C. Eads	Member	June 6, 1979	January 20, 1981
Stephen M. Goldfeld	Member	August 20, 1980	January 20, 1981
Murray L. Weidenbaum	Chairman	February 27, 1981	August 25, 1982
William A. Niskanen	Member	June 12, 1981	March 30, 1985

Council Members and Their Dates of Service

Name	Position	Oath of office date	Separation date
Jerry L. Jordan	Member	July 14, 1981	July 31, 1982
Martin Feldstein	Chairman	October 14, 1982	July 10, 1984
William Poole	Member	December 10, 1982	January 20, 1985
Beryl W. Sprinkel	Chairman	April 18, 1985	January 20, 1989
Thomas Gale Moore	Member	July 1, 1985	May 1, 1989
Michael L. Mussa	Member	August 18, 1986	September 19, 1988
Michael J. Boskin	Chairman	February 2, 1989	January 12, 1993
John B. Taylor	Member	June 9, 1989	August 2, 1991
Richard L. Schmalensee	Member	October 3, 1989	June 21, 1991
David F. Bradford	Member	November 13, 1991	January 20, 1993
Paul Wonnacott	Member	November 13, 1991	January 20, 1993
Laura D'Andrea Tyson	Chair	February 5, 1993	April 22, 1995
Alan S. Blinder	Member	July 27, 1993	June 26, 1994
Joseph E. Stiglitz	Member	July 27, 1993	
	Chairman	June 28, 1995	February 10, 1997
Martin N. Baily	Member	June 30, 1995	August 30, 1996
Alicia H. Munnell	Member	January 29, 1996	August 1, 1997
Janet L. Yellen	Chair	February 18, 1997	August 3, 1999
Jeffrey A. Frankel	Member	April 23, 1997	March 2, 1999
Rebecca M. Blank	Member	October 22, 1998	July 9, 1999
Martin N. Baily	Chairman	August 12, 1999	January 19, 2001
Robert Z. Lawrence	Member	August 12, 1999	January 12, 2001
Kathryn L. Shaw	Member	May 31, 2000	January 19, 2001
R. Glenn Hubbard	Chairman	May 11, 2001	February 28, 2003
Mark B. McClellan	Member	July 25, 2001	November 13, 2002
Randall S. Kroszner	Member	November 30, 2001	July 1, 2003
N. Gregory Mankiw	Chairman	May 29, 2003	February 18, 2005
Kristin J. Forbes	Member	November 21, 2003	June 3, 2005
Harvey S. Rosen	Member	November 21, 2003	
	Chairman	February 23, 2005	June 10, 2005
Ben S. Bernanke	Chairman	June 21, 2005	January 31, 2006
Katherine Baicker	Member	November 18, 2005	July 11, 2007
Matthew J. Slaughter	Member	November 18, 2005	March 1, 2007
Edward P. Lazear	Chairman	February 27, 2006	January 20, 2009
Donald B. Marron	Member	July 17, 2008	January 20, 2009
Christina D. Romer	Chair	January 29, 2009	September 3, 2010
Austan D. Goolsbee	Member	March 11, 2009	
	Chairman	September 10, 2010	August 5, 2011
Cecilia Elena Rouse	Member	March 11, 2009	February 28, 2011
Katharine G. Abraham	Member	April 19, 2011	April 19, 2013
Carl Shapiro	Member	April 19, 2011	May 4, 2012
Alan B. Krueger	Chairman	November 7, 2011	August 2, 2013
James H. Stock	Member	February 7, 2013	May 19, 2014
Jason Furman	Chairman	August 4, 2013	
Betsey Stevenson	Member	August 6, 2013	
Maurice Obstfeld	Member	July 21, 2014	

REPORT TO THE PRESIDENT ON THE ACTIVITIES OF THE COUNCIL OF ECONOMIC ADVISERS DURING 2014

The Council of Economic Advisers was established by the Employment Act of 1946 to provide the President with objective economic analysis and advice on the development and implementation of a wide range of domestic and international economic policy issues. The Council is governed by a Chairman and two Members. The Chairman is appointed by the President and confirmed by the United States Senate. The Members are appointed by the President.

THE CHAIRMAN OF THE COUNCIL

Jason Furman was confirmed by the U.S. Senate on August 1, 2013. Prior to this role, Furman served as Assistant to the President for Economic Policy and the Principal Deputy Director of the National Economic Council.

From 2007 to 2008 Furman was a Senior Fellow in Economic Studies and Director of the Hamilton Project at the Brookings Institute. Previously, he served as a Staff Economist at the Council of Economic Advisers, a Special Assistant to the President for Economic Policy at the National Economic Council under President Clinton and Senior Adviser to the Chief Economist and Senior Vice President of the World Bank. Furman was the Economic Policy Director for Obama for America. Furman has also served as Visiting Scholar at NYU's Wagner Graduate School of Public Service, a visiting lecturer at Yale and Columbia Universities, and a Senior Fellow at the Center on Budget and Policy Priorities.

THE MEMBERS OF THE COUNCIL

Betsey Stevenson was appointed by the President on August 6, 2013. She is on leave from the University of Michigan's Gerald R. Ford School of Public Policy and the Economics Department where she is an Associate

Professor of Public Policy and Economics. She served as the Chief Economist of the US Department of Labor from 2010 to 2011.

Maurice Obstfeld was appointed by the President on July 21, 2014. He is on leave from the University of California, Berkeley, where he is the Class of 1958 Professor of Economics. He joined Berkeley In 1989 as a professor, following appointments at Columbia (1979-1986) and the University of Pennsylvania (1986-1989).

James H. Stock resigned as Member of the Council of May 19, 2014 to return to Harvard University, where he is the Harold Hitchings Burbank Professor of Political Economy and a member of the faculty at Harvard Kennedy School of Government.

AREAS OF ACTIVITIES

A central function of the Council is to advise the President on all economic issues and developments. In the past year, as in the four previous years, advising the President on policies to spur economic growth and job creation, and evaluating the effects of the policies on the economy, have been a priority.

The Council works closely with various government agencies, including the National Economic Council, the Office of Management and Budget, White House senior staff, and other officials and engages in discussions on numerous policy matters. In the area of international economic policy, the Council coordinates with other units of the White House, the Treasury Department, the State Department, the Commerce Department, and the Federal Reserve on matters related to the global financial system.

Among the specific economic policy areas that received attention in 2014 were: college affordability and ratings; health care cost growth and the Affordable Care Act; infrastructure investment; regulatory measures; trade policies; poverty and income inequality; unemployment insurance and the minimum wage; labor force participation; job training; corporate taxation; regional development; the economic cost of carbon pollution; renewable fuel standards; energy policy; intellectual property and innovation; and foreign direct investment. The Council also worked on several issues related to the quality of the data available for assessing economic conditions.

The Council prepares for the President, the Vice President, and the White House senior staff a daily economic briefing memo analyzing current economic developments and almost-daily memos on key economic data releases. Chairman Furman also presents a monthly briefing on the state of the economy and the Council's energy analysis to senior White House officials.

The Council, the Department of Treasury, and the Office of Management and Budget—the Administration's economic "troika"— are responsible for producing the economic forecasts that underlie the Administration's budget proposals. The Council initiates the forecasting process twice each year, consulting with a wide variety of outside sources, including leading private sector forecasters and other government agencies.

The Council was an active participant in the trade policy process, participating in the Trade Policy Staff Committee and the Trade Policy Review Group. The Council provided analysis and opinions on a range of trade-related issues involving the enforcement of existing trade agreements, reviews of current U.S. trade policies, and consideration of future policies. The Council also participated on the Trade Promotion Coordinating Committee, helping to examine the ways in which exports may support economic growth in the years to come. In the area of investment and security, the Council participated on the Committee on Foreign Investment in the United States (CFIUS), reviewing individual cases before the committee.

The Council is a leading participant in the Organisation for Economic Co-operation and Development (OECD), an important forum for economic cooperation among high-income industrial economies. The Council coordinated and oversaw the OECD's review of the U.S. economy. Chairman Furman is chairman of the OECD's Economic Policy Committee, and Council Members and staff participate actively in working-party meetings on macroeconomic policy and coordination and contribute to the OECD's research agenda.

The Council issued a wide range of reports in 2014 and early 2015. In March, the Council released a report analyzing the effect of a minimum wage increase on the gender wage gap. In May, the Council released a report examining the economic benefits of an "all-of-the-above" energy strategy. In June, the Council worked with the Domestic Policy Council to study the impact of student loan debt and highlighted the benefits of the Administration's actions to make college more affordable. Also in June, the Council released a report examining data on access to paid and unpaid leave in the workplace and emphasizing the importance of paid and unpaid leave options. In July, the Council released a report quantifying several consequences of States' decisions not to expand Medicaid. Also In July, the Council released a report examining the economic consequences of delaying implementation of policies to stem climate change. The same month, the Council released a report analyzing labor force participation rates since 2007, with a focus on the effects that the Great Recession and the retirement of the baby boomers had on labor force participation. The Council also worked with NEC on a report to highlight the economic benefits of infrastructure investment, including long-term competitiveness, productivity, lower prices, and higher Incomes. In October, the Council released a report describing the economic returns to investments in childhood development and early education. All of the afore-mentioned reports can be found on the Council's website and some of them are incorporated into this annual report as well. (http://www.whitehouse.gov/administration/eop/cea/factsheets-reports.)

The Council continued its efforts to improve the public's under-standing of economic developments and of the Administration's economic policies through briefings with the economic and financial press, speeches, discussions with outside economists, and regular updates on major data releases and postings of CEA's Reports on the White House and CEA blogs. The Chairman and Members also regularly met to exchange views on the economy with the Chairman and Members of the Board of Governors of the Federal Reserve System.

PUBLIC INFORMATION

The Council's annual Economic Report of the President is an impor-tant vehicle for presenting the Administration's domestic and international economic policies. It is available for purchase through the Government Printing Office, and is viewable on the Internet at www.gpo.gov/erp.

The Council frequently prepared reports and blog posts in 2014, and the Chairman and Members gave numerous public speeches. The reports, posts and texts of speeches are available at the Council's website, www.whitehouse.gov/cea. Finally, the Council published the monthly Economic Indicators, which is available online at www.gpo.gov/economicindicators.

THE STAFF OF THE COUNCIL OF ECONOMIC ADVISERS

The staff of the Council consists of the senior staff, senior economists, economists, staff economists, research economists, a research assistant, and the administrative and support staff. The staff at the end of 2014 was:

Senior Staff

Jessica Schumer	Chief of Staff & General Counsel
Steven N. Braun	Director of Macroeconomic Forecasting
Anna Y. Lee	Director of Finance and Administration
Jordan D. Matsudaira	Chief Economist
Adrienne Pilot	Director of Statistical Office

Senior Economists

Jane K. Dokko	Housing
Matthew Fiedler	Health
Gregory Leiserson	Tax, Retirement
Joshua Linn	Energy, Environment
Cynthia J. Nickerson	Agriculture, Environment, Evaluation
Jennifer P. Poole	International Trade
Timothy Simcoe	Innovation, Technology, Industrial Organization
Linda L. Tesar	Macroeconomics
Abigail Wozniak	Labor, Education

Staff Economists and Policy Analysts

Martha Gimbel	Labor
Timothy Hyde	Macro, Labor, Energy, Environment
Noah Mann	Education
Gabriel Scheffler	Health, Labor
Eric Van Nostrand	Macroeconomics

Research Economists

Krista Ruffini	Labor

Research Assistants

Lydia Cox	Energy, Trade, Agriculture
Harris R. Eppsteiner	Labor, Immigration
Samuel F. Himel	Housing, Infrastructure, Industrial Organization
Brian David Moore	Tax, Retirement
Emma Rackstraw	Labor, Education
Susannah Scanlan	Macroeconomics, International

Statistical Office

The Statistical Office gathers, administers, and produces statistical information for the Council. Duties include preparing the statistical appendix to the Economic Report of the President and the monthly publication Economic Indicators. The staff also creates background materials for economic analysis and verifies statistical content in Presidential memoranda. The Office serves as the Council's liaison to the statistical community.

Brian A. Amorosi .... Statistical Analyst
Wenfan Chen .... Economic Statistician

Office of the Chairman and Members

Andrea Taverna .... Deputy Staff Director and Special Assistant to the Chairman
Matthew Aks* .... Special Assistant to the Chairman and Research Economist
Jeff Goldstein .... Special Assistant to the Members
Katie Rodihan.................. Special Assistant

Administrative Office

The Administrative Office provides general support for the Council's activities. This includes financial management, human resource management, travel, operations of facilities, security, information technology, and telecommunications management support.

Doris T. Searles................. Administrative and Information Management Specialist

* Matthew Aks received the Robert M. Solow Award for Distinguished Service in 2014, after serving CEA for more than two years.

Interns

Student interns provide invaluable help with research projects, day-to-day operations, and fact-checking. Interns during the year were: Alexander Abramowitz, Brian Bernard, Emma Brody, Carter Casady, Maddy Dunn, Laura Elmendorf, Joshua Feinzig, Lauren Iannolo, Amelia Keyes, Jin Han Kim, Paige Kirby, Audrey Lee, James Lim, Charles Matula, David Mkrtchian, Gabrielle Orfield, Stephen Orians, Nirav Patel, Curtis Powell, Austin Rochon, Rahul Singh, Hershil Shah, Sara Sperling, Kyle Sullivan, Benjamin Summers, Lacoya Theus, Meiyao Tysinger, Jayson Wang, Veronica Weis, Leigh West, and Felix Zhang.

Departures in 2014

The senior economists who resigned in 2014 (with the institutions to which they returned after leaving the Council in parentheses) were: David J. Balan (Federal Trade Commission), Marco Cagetti (Federal Reserve), Tracy M. Gordon (Urban-Brookings Tax Policy Center), Douglas Kruse (Rutgers University), Ronald J. Shadbegian (Environmental Protection Agency), and Kenneth A. Swinnerton (U.S. Department of Labor).

The staff economists who departed in 2014 were Zachary Y. Brown, John Coglianese, and Kevin Rinz.

The research economists who departed in 2014 were Philip K. Lambrakos, Cordaye T. Ogletree, and Rudy Telles Jr, and Katie Wright.

The Research Assistants who departed in 2014 were Brendan Mochoruk, Jenny Shen, and David Wasser.

Alexander G. Krulic resigned from his position as General Counsel. Natasha Lawrence resigned from her position as Special Assistant to the Members.

STATISTICAL TABLES RELATING TO INCOME, EMPLOYMENT, AND PRODUCTION

C O N T E N T S

INTEREST RATES, MONEY STOCK, AND GOVERNMENT FINANCE
—Continued

GENERAL NOTES

Detail in these tables may not add to totals due to rounding.

Because of the formula used for calculating real gross domestic product (GDP), the chained (2009) dollar estimates for the detailed components do not add to the chained-dollar value of GDP or to any intermediate aggregate. The Department of Commerce (Bureau of Economic Analysis) no longer publishes chained-dollar estimates prior to 1999, except for selected series.

Because of the method used for seasonal adjustment, the sum or average of seasonally adjusted monthly values generally will not equal annual totals based on unadjusted values.

Unless otherwise noted, all dollar figures are in current dollars.

Symbols used:
    p Preliminary.
    ... Not available (also, not applicable).

Data in these tables reflect revisions made by source agencies through February 6, 2015, unless otherwise noted.

Excel versions of these tables are available at *www.gpo.gov/erp.*

Table B–1. Percent changes in real gross domestic product, 1965–2014

[Percent change from preceding period; quarterly data at seasonally adjusted annual rates]

Year or quarter	Gross domestic product	Personal consumption expenditures			Gross private domestic investment							
		Total	Goods	Services	Total	Fixed investment						Change in private inventories
						Total	Nonresidential				Residential	
							Total	Structures	Equipment	Intellectual Property Products		
1965	6.5	6.3	7.1	5.5	13.8	10.4	16.7	15.9	18.2	12.7	-2.6	
1966	6.6	5.7	6.3	4.9	9.0	6.2	12.3	6.8	15.5	13.2	-8.4	
1967	2.7	3.0	2.0	4.1	-3.5	-.9	-.3	-2.5	-1.0	7.8	-2.6	
1968	4.9	5.7	6.2	5.3	6.0	7.0	4.8	1.4	6.1	7.5	13.5	
1969	3.1	3.7	3.1	4.4	5.6	5.9	7.0	5.4	8.3	5.4	3.1	
1970	.2	2.4	.8	3.9	-6.1	-2.1	-.9	.3	-1.8	-.1	-5.2	
1971	3.3	3.8	4.2	3.5	10.3	6.9	.0	-1.6	.8	.4	26.6	
1972	5.2	6.1	6.5	5.8	11.3	11.4	8.7	3.1	12.7	7.0	17.4	
1973	5.6	5.0	5.2	4.7	10.9	8.6	13.2	8.2	18.5	5.0	-.6	
1974	-.5	-.8	-3.6	1.9	-6.6	-5.6	.8	-2.2	2.1	2.9	-19.6	
1975	-.2	2.3	.7	3.8	-16.2	-9.8	-9.0	-10.5	-10.5	.9	-12.1	
1976	5.4	5.6	7.0	4.3	19.1	9.8	5.7	2.4	6.1	10.9	22.1	
1977	4.6	4.2	4.3	4.1	14.3	13.6	10.8	4.1	15.5	6.6	20.5	
1978	5.6	4.4	4.1	4.6	11.6	11.6	13.8	14.4	15.1	7.1	6.7	
1979	3.2	2.4	1.6	3.1	3.5	5.8	10.0	12.7	8.2	11.7	-3.7	
1980	-.2	-.3	-2.5	1.6	-10.1	-5.9	.0	5.9	-4.4	5.0	-20.9	
1981	2.6	1.5	1.2	1.7	8.8	2.7	6.1	8.0	3.7	10.9	-8.2	
1982	-1.9	1.4	.7	2.0	-13.0	-6.7	-3.6	-1.6	-7.6	6.2	-18.1	
1983	4.6	5.7	6.4	5.2	9.3	7.5	-.4	-10.8	4.6	7.9	42.0	
1984	7.3	5.3	7.2	3.9	27.3	16.2	16.7	13.9	19.4	13.7	14.8	
1985	4.2	5.3	5.3	5.3	-.1	5.5	6.6	7.1	5.5	9.0	2.3	
1986	3.5	4.2	5.6	3.2	.2	1.8	-1.7	-11.0	1.1	7.0	12.4	
1987	3.5	3.4	1.8	4.5	2.8	.6	.1	-2.9	.4	3.9	2.0	
1988	4.2	4.2	3.7	4.5	2.5	3.3	5.0	.7	6.6	7.1	-.9	
1989	3.7	2.9	2.5	3.2	4.0	3.2	5.7	2.0	5.3	11.7	-3.2	
1990	1.9	2.1	.6	3.0	-2.6	-1.4	1.1	1.5	-2.1	8.4	-8.5	
1991	-.1	.2	-2.0	1.6	-6.6	-5.1	-3.9	-11.1	-4.6	6.4	-8.9	
1992	3.6	3.7	3.2	4.0	7.3	5.5	2.9	-6.0	5.9	6.0	13.8	
1993	2.7	3.5	4.2	3.1	8.0	7.7	7.5	-.3	12.7	4.2	8.2	
1994	4.0	3.9	5.3	3.1	11.9	8.2	7.9	1.8	12.3	4.0	9.0	
1995	2.7	3.0	3.0	3.0	3.2	6.1	9.7	6.4	12.1	7.3	-3.4	
1996	3.8	3.5	4.5	2.9	8.8	8.9	9.1	5.7	9.5	11.3	8.2	
1997	4.5	3.8	4.8	3.2	11.4	8.6	10.8	7.3	11.1	13.0	2.4	
1998	4.5	5.3	6.7	4.6	9.5	10.2	10.8	5.1	13.1	10.8	8.6	
1999	4.7	5.3	7.9	3.9	8.4	8.8	9.7	.1	12.5	12.4	6.3	
2000	4.1	5.1	5.2	5.0	6.5	6.9	9.1	7.8	9.7	8.9	.7	
2001	1.0	2.6	3.0	2.4	-6.1	-1.6	-2.4	-1.5	-4.3	.5	.9	
2002	1.8	2.6	3.9	1.9	-.6	-3.5	-6.9	-17.7	-5.4	-.5	6.1	
2003	2.8	3.1	4.8	2.2	4.1	4.0	1.9	-3.9	3.2	3.8	9.1	
2004	3.8	3.8	5.1	3.2	8.8	6.7	5.2	-.4	7.7	5.1	10.0	
2005	3.3	3.5	4.1	3.2	6.4	6.8	7.0	1.7	9.6	6.5	6.6	
2006	2.7	3.0	3.6	2.7	2.1	2.0	7.1	7.2	8.6	4.5	-7.6	
2007	1.8	2.2	2.7	2.0	-3.1	-2.0	5.9	12.7	3.2	4.8	-18.8	
2008	-.3	-.3	-2.5	.8	-9.4	-6.8	-.7	6.1	-6.9	3.0	-24.0	
2009	-2.8	-1.6	-3.0	-.9	-21.6	-16.7	-15.6	-18.9	-22.9	-1.4	-21.2	
2010	2.5	1.9	3.4	1.2	12.9	1.5	2.5	-16.4	15.9	1.9	-2.5	
2011	1.6	2.3	3.1	1.8	5.2	6.3	7.7	2.3	13.6	3.6	.5	
2012	2.3	1.8	2.8	1.3	9.2	8.3	7.2	13.1	6.8	3.9	13.5	
2013	2.2	2.4	3.4	1.9	4.9	4.7	3.0	-.5	4.6	3.4	11.9	
2014 ᵖ	2.4	2.5	3.5	2.0	6.0	5.2	6.1	8.0	6.3	4.6	1.6	
2011: I	-1.5	2.0	2.9	1.6	-7.2	-.9	-.9	-27.1	12.1	1.4	-.8	
II	2.9	.8	-.8	1.6	16.4	8.2	8.8	30.6	4.4	3.2	5.4	
III	.8	1.8	.9	2.2	1.1	17.3	19.4	25.6	27.7	5.1	8.1	
IV	4.6	1.4	3.9	.1	32.1	9.9	9.5	13.8	9.4	6.8	11.7	
2012: I	2.3	2.8	4.7	1.8	6.9	9.1	5.8	18.7	3.6	.7	25.5	
II	1.6	1.3	1.3	1.3	5.8	4.4	4.4	10.5	1.0	5.1	4.3	
III	2.5	1.9	3.2	1.3	1.6	3.1	.8	-1.4	.7	2.6	14.1	
IV	.1	1.9	2.9	1.4	-5.3	6.6	3.6	-6.7	8.1	5.1	20.4	
2013: I	2.7	3.6	5.9	2.4	7.6	2.7	1.5	-11.5	4.8	6.5	7.8	
II	1.8	1.8	1.3	2.0	6.9	4.9	1.6	7.3	1.5	-2.0	19.0	
III	4.5	2.0	3.5	1.3	16.8	6.6	5.5	11.2	4.7	2.8	11.2	
IV	3.5	3.7	3.7	3.7	3.8	6.3	10.4	12.8	14.1	3.6	-8.5	
2014: I	-2.1	1.2	1.0	1.3	-6.9	.2	1.6	2.9	-1.0	4.6	-5.3	
II	4.6	2.5	5.9	.9	19.1	9.5	9.7	12.6	11.2	5.5	8.8	
III	5.0	3.2	4.7	2.5	7.2	7.7	8.9	4.8	11.0	8.8	3.2	
IV ᵖ	2.6	4.3	5.4	3.7	7.4	2.3	1.9	2.6	-1.9	7.1	4.1	

See next page for continuation of table.

TABLE B–1. Percent changes in real gross domestic product, 1965–2014—*Continued*

[Percent change from preceding period; quarterly data at seasonally adjusted annual rates]

Year or quarter	Net exports of goods and services			Government consumption expenditures and gross investment					Final sales of domestic product	Gross domestic purchases [1]	Gross domestic income [2]	Gross national product [3]
	Net exports	Exports	Imports	Total	Federal			State and local				
					Total	National defense	Non-defense					
1965		2.8	10.6	3.2	0.8	-1.3	7.9	6.6	5.9	6.9	6.4	6.5
1966		6.9	14.9	8.7	10.7	12.9	3.6	6.2	6.1	6.9	6.0	6.5
1967		2.3	7.3	7.9	10.1	12.5	1.9	5.0	3.3	3.0	3.0	2.7
1968		7.9	14.9	3.4	1.5	1.6	1.3	6.0	5.1	5.2	5.0	4.9
1969		4.9	5.7	.2	-2.4	-4.1	3.9	3.5	3.2	3.2	3.3	3.1
1970		10.7	4.3	-2.0	-6.1	-8.2	1.0	2.9	.9	-.1	-.1	.2
1971		1.7	5.3	-1.8	-6.4	-10.2	5.6	3.1	2.7	3.5	3.0	3.3
1972		7.8	11.3	-.5	-3.1	-6.9	7.2	2.2	5.2	5.4	5.5	5.3
1973		18.8	4.6	-.3	-3.6	-5.1	.2	2.8	5.2	4.8	5.8	5.9
1974		7.9	-2.3	2.3	.7	-1.0	4.6	3.7	-.3	-1.2	-.6	-.4
1975		-.6	-11.1	2.2	.5	-1.0	3.9	3.6	1.0	-1.1	-.5	-.4
1976		4.4	19.5	.5	.2	-.5	1.6	.8	4.0	6.5	5.1	5.5
1977		2.4	10.9	1.2	2.2	1.0	4.7	.4	4.4	5.3	4.8	4.7
1978		10.5	8.7	2.9	2.5	.8	6.0	3.3	5.5	5.5	5.5	5.5
1979		9.9	1.7	1.9	2.3	2.7	1.7	1.5	3.6	2.5	2.4	3.5
1980		10.8	-6.6	1.9	4.4	3.9	5.4	-.2	.6	-1.9	-.1	-.3
1981		1.2	2.6	1.0	4.5	6.2	1.0	-2.0	1.5	2.7	3.0	2.4
1982		-7.6	-1.3	1.8	3.7	7.2	-3.6	.1	-.6	-1.3	-1.0	-1.8
1983		-2.6	12.6	3.8	6.5	7.3	4.7	1.3	4.3	5.9	3.3	4.5
1984		8.2	24.3	3.6	3.3	5.2	-1.4	3.8	5.4	8.7	7.8	7.1
1985		3.3	6.5	6.8	7.9	8.8	5.7	5.7	5.4	4.5	4.0	3.9
1986		7.7	8.5	5.4	5.9	6.9	3.1	5.0	3.8	3.7	3.0	3.3
1987		10.9	5.9	3.0	3.8	5.1	.2	2.2	3.1	3.2	4.3	3.4
1988		16.2	3.9	1.3	-1.3	-.2	-4.3	3.9	4.4	3.3	5.1	4.3
1989		11.6	4.4	2.9	1.7	-.2	7.2	4.0	3.5	3.1	2.5	3.7
1990		8.8	3.6	3.2	2.1	.3	7.3	4.1	2.1	1.5	1.5	2.0
1991		6.6	-.1	1.2	.0	-1.0	2.4	2.2	.2	-.7	.0	-.2
1992		6.9	7.0	.5	-1.5	-4.5	5.9	2.1	3.3	3.6	3.3	3.5
1993		3.3	8.6	-.8	-3.5	-5.1	.0	1.2	2.7	3.3	2.2	2.7
1994		8.8	11.9	.1	-3.5	-4.9	-.8	2.8	3.4	4.4	4.4	3.9
1995		10.3	8.0	.5	-2.6	-4.0	.0	2.7	3.2	2.6	3.4	2.8
1996		8.2	8.7	1.0	-1.2	-1.6	-.5	2.4	3.8	3.9	4.3	3.8
1997		11.9	13.5	1.9	-.8	-2.7	2.8	3.6	4.0	4.7	5.1	4.4
1998		2.3	11.7	2.1	-.9	-2.1	1.3	3.8	4.5	5.5	5.3	4.4
1999		2.6	10.1	3.4	2.0	1.5	2.7	4.2	4.7	5.5	4.4	4.8
2000		8.6	13.0	1.9	.3	-.9	2.3	2.8	4.2	4.8	4.7	4.2
2001		-5.8	-2.8	3.8	3.9	3.5	4.7	3.7	1.9	1.2	1.1	1.1
2002		-1.7	3.7	4.4	7.2	7.0	7.4	2.9	1.3	2.3	1.4	1.7
2003		1.8	4.5	2.2	6.8	8.5	4.1	-.4	2.8	3.1	2.3	2.9
2004		9.8	11.4	1.6	4.5	6.0	2.0	-.1	3.4	4.3	3.7	3.9
2005		6.3	6.3	.6	1.7	2.0	1.3	.0	3.4	3.5	3.6	3.3
2006		9.0	6.3	1.5	2.5	2.0	3.5	.9	2.6	2.6	4.0	2.4
2007		9.3	2.5	1.6	1.7	2.5	.3	1.5	2.0	1.1	.1	2.2
2008		5.7	-2.6	2.8	6.8	7.5	5.5	.3	.2	-1.3	-.8	.0
2009		-8.8	-13.7	3.2	5.7	5.4	6.2	1.6	-2.0	-3.8	-2.6	-2.9
2010		11.9	12.7	.1	4.4	3.2	6.4	-2.7	1.1	2.9	2.7	2.8
2011		6.9	5.5	-3.0	-2.7	-2.3	-3.4	-3.3	1.7	1.6	2.2	1.8
2012		3.3	2.3	-1.4	-1.8	-3.3	1.0	-1.2	2.2	2.2	3.4	2.1
2013		3.0	1.1	-2.0	-5.7	-6.6	-4.1	.5	2.2	1.9	2.2	2.2
2014 P		3.1	3.9	-.2	-1.9	-2.2	-1.5	.9	2.3	2.6		
2011: I		2.1	3.1	-7.5	-10.6	-14.0	-4.3	-5.3	-.6	-1.2	.5	-1.2
II		6.2	3.0	-.4	1.6	6.7	-6.9	-1.8	1.9	2.5	1.9	2.9
III		4.3	3.3	-2.5	-4.0	1.9	-14.0	-1.4	3.0	.8	2.6	1.4
IV		4.1	4.5	-1.6	-2.6	-9.5	11.4	-.8	1.8	4.6	3.3	4.9
2012: I		1.3	1.7	-2.7	-3.0	-7.4	5.3	-2.6	2.5	2.3	7.2	1.3
II		4.8	4.0	-.4	-.9	-1.3	-.4	.0	1.4	1.6	.6	1.4
III		2.1	-.6	2.7	7.5	11.9	.4	-.6	2.7	2.0	1.3	2.1
IV		1.5	-3.5	-6.0	-13.0	-20.1	.6	-.8	1.9	-.7	4.2	.3
2013: I		-.8	-.3	-3.9	-9.9	-10.9	-8.2	.3	2.0	2.7	1.4	2.3
II		6.3	8.5	.2	-3.5	-2.1	-5.8	2.7	1.5	2.2	2.7	1.9
III		5.1	.6	.2	-1.2	.4	-3.9	1.1	3.0	3.8	1.9	4.8
IV		10.0	1.3	-3.8	-10.4	-11.4	-8.6	.6	3.9	2.3	1.8	3.7
2014: I		-9.2	2.2	-.8	-.1	-4.0	6.6	-1.3	-1.0	-.4	-.8	-2.8
II		11.1	11.3	1.7	-.9	.9	-3.8	3.4	3.2	4.8	4.0	4.6
III		4.5	-.9	4.4	9.9	16.0	.4	1.1	5.0	4.1	4.7	5.3
IV P		2.8	8.9	-2.2	-7.5	-12.5	1.7	1.3	1.8	3.6		

[1] Gross domestic product (GDP) less exports of goods and services plus imports of goods and services.
[2] Gross domestic income is deflated by the implicit price deflator for GDP.
[3] GDP plus net income receipts from rest of the world.

Note: Percent changes based on unrounded GDP quantity indexes.

Source: Department of Commerce (Bureau of Economic Analysis).

Table B–2. Gross domestic product, 2000–2014

[Quarterly data at seasonally adjusted annual rates]

Year or quarter	Gross domestic product	Personal consumption expenditures			Gross private domestic investment							
		Total	Goods	Services	Total	Fixed investment						Change in private inventories
						Total	Nonresidential				Residential	
							Total	Structures	Equipment	Intellectual Property Products		
Billions of dollars												
2000	10,284.8	6,792.4	2,452.9	4,339.5	2,033.8	1,979.2	1,493.8	318.1	766.1	409.5	485.4	54.5
2001	10,621.8	7,103.1	2,525.2	4,577.9	1,928.6	1,966.9	1,453.9	329.7	711.5	412.6	513.0	−38.3
2002	10,977.5	7,384.1	2,598.6	4,785.5	1,925.0	1,906.5	1,348.9	282.9	659.6	406.4	557.6	18.5
2003	11,510.7	7,765.5	2,721.6	5,044.0	2,027.9	2,008.7	1,371.7	281.8	669.0	420.9	636.9	19.3
2004	12,274.9	8,260.0	2,900.3	5,359.8	2,276.7	2,212.8	1,463.1	301.8	719.2	442.1	749.7	63.9
2005	13,093.7	8,794.1	3,080.3	5,713.8	2,527.1	2,467.5	1,611.5	345.6	790.7	475.1	856.1	59.6
2006	13,855.9	9,304.0	3,235.8	6,068.2	2,680.6	2,613.7	1,776.3	415.6	856.1	504.6	837.4	67.0
2007	14,477.6	9,750.5	3,361.6	6,388.9	2,643.7	2,609.3	1,920.6	496.9	885.8	537.9	688.7	34.5
2008	14,718.6	10,013.6	3,375.7	6,637.9	2,424.8	2,456.8	1,941.0	552.4	825.1	563.4	515.9	−32.0
2009	14,418.7	9,847.0	3,198.4	6,648.5	1,878.1	2,025.7	1,633.4	438.2	644.3	550.9	392.2	−147.6
2010	14,964.4	10,202.2	3,362.8	6,839.4	2,100.8	2,039.3	1,658.2	362.0	731.8	564.3	381.1	61.5
2011	15,517.9	10,689.3	3,596.5	7,092.8	2,239.9	2,198.1	1,812.1	381.6	838.2	592.2	386.0	41.8
2012	16,163.2	11,083.1	3,741.9	7,341.3	2,479.2	2,414.3	1,972.0	446.9	904.1	621.0	442.3	64.9
2013	16,768.1	11,484.3	3,851.2	7,633.2	2,648.0	2,573.9	2,054.0	457.2	949.7	647.1	519.9	74.1
2014 ᵖ	17,420.7	11,928.4	3,969.0	7,959.3	2,855.8	2,765.4	2,206.4	506.1	1,015.6	684.7	559.0	90.4
2011: I	15,238.4	10,523.5	3,534.0	6,989.6	2,123.5	2,097.2	1,722.4	343.2	798.3	580.9	374.8	26.3
II	15,460.9	10,651.4	3,588.0	7,063.4	2,212.7	2,149.6	1,768.5	371.3	809.7	587.5	381.1	63.0
III	15,587.1	10,754.5	3,613.0	7,141.4	2,228.2	2,243.1	1,854.5	397.1	861.7	595.7	388.6	−14.9
IV	15,785.3	10,827.9	3,650.9	7,177.0	2,395.2	2,302.5	1,902.9	415.0	883.3	604.6	399.6	92.6
2012: I	15,956.5	10,959.7	3,709.6	7,250.1	2,445.4	2,364.3	1,942.0	437.0	894.9	610.1	422.3	81.1
II	16,094.7	11,030.6	3,717.2	7,313.3	2,489.3	2,397.1	1,968.8	452.5	897.1	619.2	428.3	92.2
III	16,268.9	11,119.8	3,751.9	7,367.9	2,500.4	2,424.7	1,978.3	452.2	901.4	624.7	446.4	75.7
IV	16,332.5	11,222.6	3,788.8	7,433.8	2,481.5	2,471.0	1,998.7	445.9	922.8	630.0	472.3	10.4
2013: I	16,502.4	11,351.1	3,832.2	7,518.9	2,543.3	2,499.1	2,010.3	435.4	933.1	641.8	488.9	44.2
II	16,619.2	11,414.3	3,821.0	7,593.2	2,594.6	2,543.8	2,026.9	448.5	937.0	641.4	516.9	50.8
III	16,872.3	11,518.7	3,865.3	7,653.4	2,708.9	2,598.1	2,060.2	463.0	948.8	648.4	538.0	110.7
IV	17,078.3	11,653.3	3,886.1	7,767.2	2,745.2	2,654.6	2,118.7	481.7	980.0	657.0	535.9	90.5
2014: I	17,044.0	11,728.5	3,890.6	7,837.8	2,714.4	2,674.3	2,134.6	487.9	979.5	667.2	539.7	40.1
II	17,328.2	11,870.7	3,964.5	7,906.2	2,843.6	2,743.4	2,191.2	504.4	1,008.6	678.2	552.2	100.3
III	17,599.8	12,002.0	4,011.5	7,990.4	2,905.1	2,810.6	2,244.3	513.3	1,038.2	692.7	566.4	94.5
IV ᵖ	17,710.7	12,112.3	4,009.4	8,102.9	2,960.2	2,833.3	2,255.7	518.8	1,036.1	700.8	577.6	126.9
Billions of chained (2009) dollars												
2000	12,559.7	8,170.7	2,588.3	5,599.3	2,375.5	2,316.2	1,647.7	533.5	726.9	426.1	637.9	66.2
2001	12,682.2	8,382.6	2,666.6	5,731.0	2,231.4	2,280.0	1,608.4	525.4	695.7	428.0	643.7	−46.2
2002	12,908.8	8,598.8	2,770.2	5,838.2	2,218.2	2,201.1	1,498.0	432.5	658.0	425.9	682.7	22.5
2003	13,271.1	8,867.6	2,904.5	5,966.9	2,308.7	2,289.5	1,526.1	415.8	679.0	442.2	744.5	22.6
2004	13,773.5	9,208.2	3,051.9	6,156.6	2,511.3	2,443.9	1,605.4	414.1	731.2	464.9	818.9	71.4
2005	14,234.2	9,531.8	3,177.2	6,353.4	2,672.6	2,611.0	1,717.4	421.2	801.6	495.0	872.6	64.3
2006	14,613.8	9,821.7	3,292.5	6,526.6	2,730.0	2,662.5	1,839.6	451.5	870.8	517.5	806.6	71.6
2007	14,873.7	10,041.6	3,381.8	6,656.4	2,644.1	2,609.6	1,948.4	509.0	898.3	542.4	654.8	35.5
2008	14,830.4	10,007.2	3,297.8	6,708.6	2,396.0	2,432.6	1,934.4	540.2	836.1	558.8	497.7	−33.7
2009	14,418.7	9,847.0	3,198.4	6,648.5	1,878.1	2,025.7	1,633.4	438.2	644.3	550.9	392.2	−147.6
2010	14,783.8	10,036.3	3,308.7	6,727.6	2,120.4	2,056.2	1,673.8	366.3	746.7	561.3	382.4	58.2
2011	15,020.6	10,263.5	3,411.8	6,851.4	2,230.4	2,186.7	1,802.3	374.7	847.9	583.1	384.5	37.6
2012	15,369.2	10,449.7	3,506.5	6,942.4	2,435.9	2,368.0	1,931.8	423.8	905.6	603.7	436.5	57.0
2013	15,710.3	10,699.7	3,626.0	7,073.1	2,556.2	2,479.2	1,990.6	421.7	947.2	624.1	488.4	63.5
2014 ᵖ	16,089.8	10,967.8	3,752.2	7,216.1	2,710.7	2,608.1	2,112.7	455.3	1,006.6	653.0	496.3	78.8
2011: I	14,881.3	10,217.1	3,404.9	6,812.0	2,125.9	2,098.4	1,724.1	343.0	810.6	571.9	374.4	25.1
II	14,989.6	10,237.7	3,398.2	6,839.2	2,208.0	2,140.2	1,761.0	366.7	819.3	576.3	379.3	57.5
III	15,021.1	10,282.2	3,405.5	6,876.6	2,214.0	2,227.5	1,840.8	388.2	871.0	583.5	386.8	−13.0
IV	15,190.3	10,316.8	3,438.5	6,877.7	2,373.7	2,280.6	1,883.1	400.9	890.8	593.3	397.6	80.8
2012: I	15,275.0	10,387.6	3,478.0	6,908.8	2,413.7	2,330.7	1,910.1	418.5	898.7	594.4	420.8	70.9
II	15,336.7	10,420.2	3,489.0	6,930.5	2,448.0	2,355.6	1,930.6	429.0	900.9	601.8	425.3	78.9
III	15,431.3	10,470.4	3,516.9	6,952.8	2,457.7	2,373.7	1,934.5	427.5	902.5	605.6	439.5	71.2
IV	15,433.7	10,520.6	3,542.3	6,977.5	2,424.3	2,412.0	1,951.9	420.1	920.4	613.2	460.3	7.2
2013: I	15,538.4	10,613.7	3,593.7	7,019.3	2,469.0	2,428.0	1,959.0	407.5	931.3	622.8	469.0	33.4
II	15,606.6	10,660.4	3,605.2	7,054.5	2,510.7	2,457.0	1,966.8	414.7	934.8	619.8	489.8	43.4
III	15,779.9	10,713.3	3,636.1	7,076.6	2,610.3	2,496.8	1,993.3	425.8	945.6	624.1	503.0	95.6
IV	15,916.2	10,811.4	3,669.0	7,141.9	2,634.7	2,535.0	2,043.3	438.8	977.2	629.6	491.9	81.8
2014: I	15,831.7	10,844.3	3,678.3	7,165.4	2,588.2	2,536.1	2,051.5	441.9	974.8	636.8	483.5	35.2
II	16,010.4	10,912.6	3,731.6	7,181.4	2,703.7	2,594.5	2,099.6	455.2	1,001.1	645.4	495.6	84.8
III	16,205.6	10,999.5	3,774.5	7,225.9	2,750.8	2,643.3	2,144.8	460.6	1,027.6	659.2	499.6	82.2
IV ᵖ	16,311.6	11,114.9	3,824.3	7,292.0	2,800.2	2,658.5	2,154.8	463.6	1,022.8	670.7	504.6	113.1

See next page for continuation of table.

TABLE B–2. Gross domestic product, 2000–2014—*Continued*

[Quarterly data at seasonally adjusted annual rates]

Year or quarter	Net exports of goods and services			Government consumption expenditures and gross investment					Final sales of domestic product	Gross domestic purchases [1]	Gross domestic income [2]	Gross national product [3]
	Net exports	Exports	Imports	Total	Federal			State and local				
					Total	National defense	Non-defense					
Billions of dollars												
2000	−375.8	1,096.8	1,472.6	1,834.4	632.4	391.7	240.7	1,202.0	10,230.2	10,660.6	10,384.3	10,321.8
2001	−368.7	1,026.7	1,395.4	1,958.8	669.2	412.7	256.5	1,289.5	10,660.1	10,990.5	10,736.8	10,673.6
2002	−426.5	1,002.5	1,429.0	2,094.9	740.6	456.8	283.8	1,354.3	10,959.0	11,404.0	11,050.3	11,026.1
2003	−503.7	1,040.3	1,543.9	2,220.8	824.8	519.9	304.9	1,396.0	11,491.4	12,014.3	11,524.3	11,577.8
2004	−619.2	1,181.5	1,800.7	2,357.4	892.4	570.2	322.1	1,465.0	12,211.1	12,894.1	12,283.5	12,364.1
2005	−721.2	1,308.9	2,030.1	2,493.7	946.3	608.3	338.1	1,547.4	13,034.1	13,814.9	13,129.2	13,186.3
2006	−770.9	1,476.3	2,247.3	2,642.2	1,002.0	642.4	359.6	1,640.2	13,788.9	14,626.8	14,073.2	13,923.5
2007	−718.5	1,664.6	2,383.2	2,801.9	1,049.8	678.7	371.0	1,752.2	14,443.2	15,196.2	14,460.1	14,603.2
2008	−723.1	1,841.9	2,565.0	3,003.2	1,155.6	754.1	401.5	1,847.6	14,750.6	15,441.6	14,619.2	14,890.6
2009	−395.4	1,587.7	1,983.2	3,089.1	1,217.7	788.3	429.4	1,871.4	14,566.3	14,814.2	14,343.4	14,569.8
2010	−512.7	1,852.3	2,365.0	3,174.0	1,303.9	832.8	471.1	1,870.2	14,902.8	15,477.0	14,915.2	15,170.3
2011	−580.0	2,106.4	2,686.4	3,168.7	1,303.5	836.9	466.5	1,865.3	15,476.2	16,097.9	15,556.3	15,764.6
2012	−568.3	2,194.2	2,762.5	3,169.2	1,291.4	818.0	473.4	1,877.8	16,098.3	16,731.5	16,372.3	16,390.5
2013	−508.2	2,262.2	2,770.4	3,143.9	1,231.5	769.9	461.6	1,912.4	16,694.0	17,276.2	16,980.0	16,992.4
2014 p	−538.0	2,334.2	2,872.3	3,174.5	1,219.0	761.4	457.6	1,955.5	17,330.3	17,958.7	....	....
2011: I	−562.5	2,033.3	2,595.8	3,153.8	1,298.1	823.4	474.7	1,855.8	15,212.1	15,800.8	15,282.5	15,466.5
II	−586.9	2,108.3	2,695.3	3,183.8	1,314.9	844.9	470.0	1,869.0	15,397.9	16,047.9	15,467.7	15,692.0
III	−572.4	2,142.9	2,715.3	3,170.8	1,305.9	851.5	454.5	1,870.9	15,602.0	16,159.5	15,661.8	15,842.6
IV	−598.1	2,141.0	2,739.1	3,160.4	1,294.9	828.0	466.9	1,865.5	15,692.7	16,383.5	15,813.1	16,057.1
2012: I	−614.8	2,162.4	2,777.1	3,166.2	1,291.4	818.6	472.8	1,874.8	15,875.4	16,571.3	16,175.6	16,195.0
II	−588.5	2,192.5	2,781.1	3,163.3	1,290.0	817.1	472.9	1,873.3	16,002.5	16,683.2	16,276.3	16,325.0
III	−541.7	2,203.2	2,745.0	3,190.5	1,314.3	840.9	473.4	1,876.2	16,193.2	16,810.7	16,403.5	16,484.0
IV	−528.2	2,218.5	2,746.7	3,156.6	1,269.9	795.4	474.4	1,886.8	16,322.1	16,860.7	16,633.8	16,558.0
2013: I	−528.0	2,219.4	2,747.4	3,135.9	1,241.9	775.1	466.8	1,894.0	16,458.2	17,030.4	16,752.7	16,711.2
II	−532.0	2,236.4	2,768.4	3,142.4	1,234.1	772.2	461.9	1,908.3	16,568.4	17,151.2	16,909.3	16,834.0
III	−509.9	2,268.4	2,778.3	3,154.7	1,233.9	774.9	459.0	1,920.7	16,761.6	17,382.2	17,060.0	17,103.1
IV	−462.9	2,324.6	2,787.5	3,142.7	1,216.2	757.5	458.7	1,926.5	16,987.8	17,541.2	17,197.8	17,321.2
2014: I	−538.0	2,284.7	2,822.7	3,139.1	1,208.1	749.9	458.2	1,931.0	17,003.9	17,582.0	17,221.5	17,255.0
II	−549.2	2,344.3	2,893.5	3,163.1	1,210.5	754.6	455.9	1,952.6	17,228.0	17,877.5	17,481.7	17,541.7
III	−516.5	2,366.5	2,883.0	3,209.3	1,241.3	784.0	457.3	1,968.0	17,505.3	18,116.3	17,743.5	17,829.6
IV p	−548.5	2,341.3	2,889.8	3,186.7	1,216.2	757.0	459.2	1,970.5	17,583.8	18,259.2	....	....
Billions of chained (2009) dollars												
2000	−477.8	1,258.4	1,736.2	2,498.2	817.7	512.3	305.4	1,689.1	12,494.9	13,057.9	12,681.2	12,608.8
2001	−502.1	1,184.9	1,687.0	2,592.4	849.8	530.0	319.7	1,751.5	12,729.6	13,208.5	12,819.5	12,747.9
2002	−584.3	1,164.5	1,748.8	2,705.8	910.8	567.3	343.3	1,802.4	12,888.9	13,518.4	12,994.4	12,969.8
2003	−641.9	1,185.0	1,826.9	2,764.3	973.0	615.4	357.5	1,795.3	13,249.0	13,938.5	13,286.8	13,352.1
2004	−734.8	1,300.6	2,035.3	2,808.2	1,017.1	652.7	364.5	1,792.8	13,702.2	14,531.7	13,783.1	13,877.3
2005	−782.3	1,381.9	2,164.2	2,826.2	1,034.8	665.5	369.4	1,792.3	14,168.8	15,040.3	14,272.7	14,338.4
2006	−794.3	1,506.8	2,301.0	2,869.3	1,060.9	678.8	382.1	1,808.8	14,542.3	15,431.6	14,842.9	14,688.6
2007	−712.6	1,646.4	2,359.0	2,914.4	1,078.7	695.6	383.1	1,836.1	14,836.2	15,606.8	14,855.8	15,005.7
2008	−557.8	1,740.8	2,298.6	2,994.8	1,152.3	748.1	404.2	1,842.4	14,865.7	15,399.4	14,730.2	15,004.8
2009	−395.4	1,587.7	1,983.2	3,089.1	1,217.7	788.3	429.4	1,871.4	14,566.3	14,814.2	14,343.4	14,569.8
2010	−458.8	1,776.6	2,235.4	3,091.4	1,270.7	813.5	457.1	1,820.8	14,722.2	15,244.9	14,735.2	14,970.8
2011	−459.4	1,898.3	2,357.7	2,997.4	1,236.4	795.0	441.4	1,761.0	14,979.0	15,483.9	15,057.1	15,241.0
2012	−452.5	1,960.1	2,412.6	2,953.9	1,214.4	768.7	445.7	1,739.5	15,304.3	15,824.6	15,568.1	15,567.3
2013	−420.4	2,019.8	2,440.3	2,894.5	1,145.3	717.7	427.5	1,748.4	15,636.7	16,131.0	15,908.8	15,902.4
2014 p	−452.6	2,082.5	2,535.1	2,889.3	1,123.4	702.2	421.0	1,764.9	15,991.7	16,544.1	....	....
2011: I	−466.2	1,862.3	2,328.5	3,012.2	1,241.2	788.4	452.7	1,771.1	14,855.3	15,351.6	14,924.4	15,086.5
II	−455.2	1,890.7	2,345.9	3,009.0	1,246.0	801.3	444.7	1,763.0	14,924.5	15,448.3	14,996.1	15,195.1
III	−454.3	1,910.6	2,364.9	2,990.0	1,233.3	805.1	428.2	1,756.8	15,035.1	15,479.5	15,093.1	15,249.1
IV	−461.7	1,929.7	2,391.3	2,978.3	1,225.2	785.3	439.9	1,753.1	15,101.0	15,656.1	15,217.0	15,433.2
2012: I	−465.7	1,936.0	2,401.7	2,957.8	1,216.0	770.4	445.6	1,741.7	15,195.6	15,744.7	15,484.9	15,484.6
II	−466.7	1,958.9	2,425.5	2,954.9	1,213.1	767.9	445.2	1,741.7	15,248.2	15,807.6	15,509.8	15,538.1
III	−453.0	1,969.1	2,422.1	2,974.4	1,235.4	789.8	445.6	1,739.2	15,350.9	15,887.2	15,559.0	15,617.5
IV	−424.5	1,976.5	2,401.0	2,928.7	1,193.0	746.7	446.3	1,735.5	15,422.6	15,859.0	15,718.4	15,629.1
2013: I	−427.2	1,972.3	2,399.5	2,899.8	1,162.5	725.5	436.9	1,736.8	15,499.6	15,966.0	15,774.1	15,717.2
II	−446.0	2,002.8	2,448.8	2,901.2	1,152.2	721.8	430.4	1,748.3	15,555.5	16,054.5	15,879.1	15,790.6
III	−424.6	2,027.7	2,452.3	2,902.4	1,148.7	722.6	426.1	1,753.0	15,671.0	16,205.0	15,955.4	15,977.6
IV	−384.0	2,076.5	2,460.5	2,874.5	1,117.8	701.0	416.7	1,755.7	15,820.7	16,298.6	16,027.6	16,124.3
2014: I	−447.2	2,026.9	2,474.1	2,868.5	1,117.4	693.9	423.4	1,750.2	15,782.6	16,280.4	15,996.4	16,009.8
II	−460.4	2,080.7	2,541.1	2,880.6	1,114.9	695.4	419.4	1,764.7	15,905.9	16,473.2	16,152.2	16,189.8
III	−431.4	2,104.0	2,535.3	2,911.9	1,141.6	721.7	419.8	1,769.5	16,102.8	16,637.7	16,337.9	16,399.3
IV p	−471.5	2,118.4	2,589.9	2,896.0	1,119.7	697.9	421.6	1,775.2	16,175.6	16,785.1	....	....

[1] Gross domestic product (GDP) less exports of goods and services plus imports of goods and services.
[2] For chained dollar measures, gross domestic income is deflated by the implicit price deflator for GDP.
[3] GDP plus net income receipts from rest of the world.

Source: Department of Commerce (Bureau of Economic Analysis).

TABLE B–3. Quantity and price indexes for gross domestic product, and percent changes, 1965–2014

[Quarterly data are seasonally adjusted]

Year or quarter	Index numbers, 2009=100						Percent change from preceding period [1]					
	Gross domestic product (GDP)			Personal consumption expenditures (PCE)		Gross domestic purchases price index	Gross domestic product (GDP)			Personal consumption expenditures (PCE)		Gross domestic purchases price index
	Real GDP (chain-type quantity index)	GDP chain-type price index	GDP implicit price deflator	PCE chain-type price index	PCE less food and energy price index		Real GDP (chain-type quantity index)	GDP chain-type price index	GDP implicit price deflator	PCE chain-type price index	PCE less food and energy price index	
1965	27.580	18.744	18.702	18.681	19.325	18.321	6.5	1.8	1.8	1.4	1.3	1.7
1966	29.399	19.271	19.227	19.155	19.762	18.830	6.6	2.8	2.8	2.5	2.3	2.8
1967	30.205	19.831	19.786	19.637	20.367	19.346	2.7	2.9	2.9	2.5	3.1	2.7
1968	31.688	20.674	20.627	20.402	21.240	20.164	4.9	4.3	4.3	3.9	4.3	4.2
1969	32.683	21.691	21.642	21.326	22.238	21.149	3.1	4.9	4.9	4.5	4.7	4.9
1970	32.749	22.836	22.784	22.325	23.281	22.287	.2	5.3	5.3	4.7	4.7	5.4
1971	33.833	23.996	23.941	23.274	24.377	23.450	3.3	5.1	5.1	4.3	4.7	5.2
1972	35.609	25.035	24.978	24.070	25.165	24.498	5.2	4.3	4.3	3.4	3.2	4.5
1973	37.618	26.396	26.337	25.368	26.126	25.888	5.6	5.4	5.4	5.4	3.8	5.7
1974	37.424	28.760	28.703	28.009	28.196	28.511	–.5	9.0	9.0	10.4	7.9	10.1
1975	37.350	31.431	31.361	30.348	30.558	31.116	–.2	9.3	9.3	8.4	8.4	9.1
1976	39.361	33.157	33.083	32.013	32.415	32.821	5.4	5.5	5.5	5.5	6.1	5.5
1977	41.175	35.209	35.135	34.091	34.495	34.977	4.6	6.2	6.2	6.5	6.4	6.6
1978	43.466	37.680	37.602	36.479	36.802	37.459	5.6	7.0	7.0	7.0	6.7	7.1
1979	44.846	40.790	40.706	39.714	39.479	40.730	3.2	8.3	8.3	8.9	7.3	8.7
1980	44.736	44.480	44.377	43.978	43.093	44.963	–.2	9.0	9.0	10.7	9.2	10.4
1981	45.897	48.658	48.520	47.908	46.857	49.088	2.6	9.4	9.3	8.9	8.7	9.2
1982	45.020	51.624	51.530	50.553	49.881	51.876	–1.9	6.1	6.2	5.5	6.5	5.7
1983	47.105	53.658	53.565	52.729	52.466	53.697	4.6	3.9	3.9	4.3	5.2	3.5
1984	50.525	55.564	55.466	54.724	54.645	55.483	7.3	3.6	3.5	3.8	4.2	3.3
1985	52.666	57.341	57.240	56.661	56.898	57.151	4.2	3.2	3.2	3.5	4.1	3.0
1986	54.516	58.504	58.395	57.887	58.850	58.345	3.5	2.0	2.0	2.2	3.4	2.1
1987	56.403	59.935	59.885	59.650	60.719	59.689	3.5	2.4	2.6	3.0	3.2	2.8
1988	58.774	62.036	61.982	61.974	63.290	62.092	4.2	3.5	3.5	3.9	4.2	3.5
1989	60.937	64.448	64.392	64.641	65.869	64.516	3.7	3.9	3.9	4.3	4.1	3.9
1990	62.107	66.841	66.773	67.440	68.492	67.040	1.9	3.7	3.7	4.3	4.0	3.9
1991	62.061	69.057	68.996	69.652	70.886	69.112	–.1	3.3	3.3	3.3	3.5	3.1
1992	64.267	70.632	70.569	71.494	73.021	70.720	3.6	2.3	2.3	2.6	3.0	2.3
1993	66.032	72.315	72.248	73.279	75.008	72.324	2.7	2.4	2.4	2.5	2.7	2.3
1994	68.698	73.851	73.785	74.803	76.680	73.835	4.0	2.1	2.1	2.1	2.2	2.1
1995	70.566	75.393	75.324	76.356	78.324	75.421	2.7	2.1	2.1	2.1	2.1	2.1
1996	73.245	76.767	76.699	77.981	79.801	76.729	3.8	1.8	1.8	2.1	1.9	1.7
1997	76.531	78.088	78.012	79.327	81.196	77.852	4.5	1.7	1.7	1.7	1.7	1.5
1998	79.937	78.935	78.859	79.936	82.200	78.359	4.5	1.1	1.1	.8	1.2	.7
1999	83.682	80.065	80.065	81.110	83.291	79.579	4.7	1.4	1.5	1.5	1.3	1.6
2000	87.107	81.890	81.887	83.131	84.747	81.644	4.1	2.3	2.3	2.5	1.7	2.6
2001	87.957	83.755	83.754	84.736	86.281	83.209	1.0	2.3	2.3	1.9	1.8	1.9
2002	89.528	85.040	85.039	85.873	87.750	84.360	1.8	1.5	1.5	1.3	1.7	1.4
2003	92.041	86.735	86.735	87.572	89.047	86.196	2.8	2.0	2.0	2.0	1.5	2.2
2004	95.525	89.118	89.120	89.703	90.751	88.729	3.8	2.7	2.7	2.4	1.9	2.9
2005	98.720	91.985	91.988	92.261	92.711	91.851	3.3	3.2	3.2	2.9	2.2	3.5
2006	101.353	94.812	94.814	94.729	94.786	94.783	2.7	3.1	3.1	2.7	2.2	3.2
2007	103.156	97.340	97.337	97.102	96.832	97.372	1.8	2.7	2.7	2.5	2.2	2.7
2008	102.855	99.218	99.246	100.065	98.827	100.244	–.3	1.9	2.0	3.1	2.1	2.9
2009	100.000	100.000	100.000	100.000	100.000	100.000	–2.8	.8	.8	–.1	1.2	–.2
2010	102.532	101.226	101.221	101.653	101.286	101.527	2.5	1.2	1.2	1.7	1.3	1.5
2011	104.174	103.315	103.311	104.149	102.800	103.970	1.6	2.1	2.1	2.5	1.5	2.4
2012	106.592	105.174	105.166	106.062	104.678	105.738	2.3	1.8	1.8	1.8	1.8	1.7
2013	108.957	106.739	106.733	107.333	106.084	107.105	2.2	1.5	1.5	1.2	1.3	1.3
2014 ᵖ	111.590	108.309	108.272	108.757	107.575	108.587	2.4	1.5	1.4	1.3	1.4	1.4
2011: I	103.208	102.409	102.399	103.002	101.974	102.936	–1.5	1.8	1.8	3.0	1.4	3.0
II	103.959	103.170	103.145	104.043	102.593	103.906	2.9	3.0	2.9	4.1	2.5	3.8
III	104.178	103.770	103.768	104.595	103.110	104.395	.8	2.3	2.4	2.1	2.0	1.9
IV	105.351	103.913	103.917	104.956	103.522	104.641	4.6	.6	.6	1.4	1.6	.9
2012: I	105.939	104.461	104.461	105.510	104.063	105.249	2.3	2.1	2.1	2.1	2.1	2.3
II	106.367	104.937	104.942	105.860	104.546	105.533	1.6	1.8	1.9	1.3	1.9	1.1
III	107.023	105.475	105.428	106.204	104.871	105.858	2.5	2.1	1.9	1.3	1.2	1.2
IV	107.039	105.821	105.824	106.675	105.230	106.313	.1	1.3	1.5	1.8	1.4	1.7
2013: I	107.766	106.172	106.204	106.951	105.606	106.634	2.7	1.3	1.4	1.0	1.4	1.2
II	108.238	106.495	106.488	107.074	105.875	106.837	1.8	1.2	1.1	.5	1.0	.8
III	109.440	106.943	106.923	107.520	106.252	107.284	4.5	1.7	1.6	1.7	1.4	1.7
IV	110.386	107.347	107.301	107.789	106.603	107.667	3.5	1.5	1.4	1.0	1.3	1.4
2014: I	109.799	107.694	107.658	108.156	106.922	108.030	–2.1	1.3	1.3	1.4	1.2	1.4
II	111.039	108.261	108.231	108.782	107.447	108.553	4.6	2.1	2.1	2.3	2.0	2.0
III	112.393	108.643	108.603	109.116	107.821	108.925	5.0	1.4	1.4	1.2	1.4	1.4
IV ᵖ	113.128	108.638	108.578	108.975	108.111	108.840	2.6	.0	–.1	–.5	1.1	–.3

[1] Quarterly percent changes are at annual rates.

Source: Department of Commerce (Bureau of Economic Analysis).

TABLE B-4. Growth rates in real gross domestic product by area and country, 1996–2015

[Percent change]

Area and country	1996–2005 annual average	2006	2007	2008	2009	2010	2011	2012	2013	2014[1]	2015[1]
World	3.9	5.6	5.7	3.0	0.0	5.4	4.1	3.4	3.3	3.3	3.5
Advanced economies	2.8	3.1	2.8	.1	-3.4	3.1	1.7	1.2	1.3	1.8	2.4
Of which:											
United States	3.4	2.7	1.8	-.3	-2.8	2.5	1.6	2.3	2.2	2.4	3.6
Euro area[2]	2.1	3.3	3.0	.4	-4.5	1.9	1.6	-.7	-.5	.8	1.2
Germany	1.2	3.9	3.4	.8	-5.1	3.9	3.4	.9	.2	1.5	1.3
France	2.3	2.4	2.4	.2	-2.9	2.0	2.1	.3	.3	.4	.9
Italy	1.4	2.2	1.7	-1.2	-5.5	1.7	.4	-2.4	-1.9	-.4	.4
Spain	3.7	4.1	3.5	.9	-3.8	-.2	.1	-1.6	-1.2	1.4	2.0
Japan	1.0	1.7	2.2	-1.0	-5.5	4.7	-.5	1.5	1.6	.1	.6
United Kingdom	3.4	2.8	3.4	-.8	-5.2	1.7	1.1	.3	1.7	2.6	2.7
Canada	3.3	2.6	2.0	1.2	-2.7	3.4	2.5	1.7	2.0	2.4	2.3
Other advanced economies	3.8	4.8	5.1	1.8	-1.0	5.9	3.3	2.0	2.2	2.8	3.0
Emerging market and developing economies	5.2	8.2	8.6	5.8	3.1	7.5	6.2	5.1	4.7	4.4	4.3
Regional groups:											
Commonwealth of Independent States[3]	4.2	8.9	9.0	5.4	-6.2	5.0	4.8	3.4	2.2	.9	-1.4
Russia	3.8	8.2	8.5	5.2	-7.8	4.5	4.3	3.4	1.3	.6	-3.0
Excluding Russia	5.1	11.0	10.3	5.6	-2.3	6.1	6.1	3.6	4.3	1.5	2.4
Emerging and Developing Asia	6.9	10.1	11.2	7.1	7.5	9.5	7.7	6.7	6.6	6.5	6.4
China	9.2	12.7	14.2	9.6	9.2	10.4	9.3	7.7	7.8	7.4	6.8
India[4]	6.4	9.3	9.8	3.9	8.5	10.3	6.6	4.7	5.0	5.8	6.3
ASEAN-5[5]	3.6	5.5	6.2	4.9	2.1	6.9	4.7	6.2	5.2	4.5	5.2
Emerging and Developing Europe	4.0	6.4	5.3	3.2	-3.6	4.7	5.5	1.4	2.8	2.7	2.9
Latin America and the Caribbean	2.9	5.7	5.8	3.9	-1.3	6.0	4.5	2.9	2.8	1.2	1.3
Brazil	2.4	4.0	6.1	5.2	-.3	7.5	2.7	1.0	2.5	.1	.3
Mexico	3.4	5.0	3.1	1.4	-4.7	5.1	4.0	4.0	1.4	2.1	3.2
Middle East, North Africa, Afghanistan, and Pakistan	4.9	6.7	5.8	5.2	2.3	5.3	4.4	4.8	2.2	2.8	3.3
Saudi Arabia	3.3	5.6	6.0	8.4	1.8	7.4	8.6	5.8	2.7	3.6	2.8
Sub-Saharan Africa	5.4	7.0	7.9	6.3	4.1	6.9	5.1	4.4	5.2	4.8	4.9
Nigeria	9.6	8.8	9.6	8.6	9.6	10.6	4.9	4.3	5.4	6.1	4.8
South Africa	3.3	5.6	5.5	3.6	-1.5	3.1	3.6	2.5	2.2	1.4	2.1

[1] All figures are forecasts as published by the International Monetary Fund. For the United States, advance estimates by the Department of Commerce show that real GDP rose 2.4 percent in 2014.

[2] For 2015, includes data for: Austria, Belgium, Cyprus, Estonia, Finland, France, Germany, Greece, Ireland, Italy, Latvia, Luxembourg, Malta, Netherlands, Portugal, Slovak Republic, Slovenia, and Spain.

[3] Includes Georgia and Turkmenistan, which are not members of the Commonwealth of Independent States but are included for reasons of geography and similarity in economic structure.

[4] Data and forecasts are presented on a fiscal year basis and output growth is based on GDP at market prices.

[5] Consists of Indonesia, Malaysia, Philippines, Thailand, and Vietnam.

Note: For details on data shown in this table, see *World Economic Outlook*, October 2014, and *World Economic Outlook Update*, January 2015, published by the International Monetary Fund.

Sources: International Monetary Fund and Department of Commerce (Bureau of Economic Analysis).

TABLE B–5. Real exports and imports of goods and services, 1999–2014

[Billions of chained (2009) dollars; quarterly data at seasonally adjusted annual rates]

Year or quarter	Exports of goods and services					Imports of goods and services				
	Total	Goods [1]			Services [1]	Total	Goods [1]			Services [1]
		Total	Durable goods	Nondurable goods			Total	Durable goods	Nondurable goods	
1999	1,159.1	819.4	533.8	288.0	338.6	1,536.2	1,286.9	724.4	572.8	245.4
2000	1,258.4	902.2	599.3	301.9	354.3	1,736.2	1,455.4	834.4	624.4	276.4
2001	1,184.9	846.7	549.5	300.1	336.6	1,687.0	1,408.4	782.2	641.1	274.6
2002	1,164.5	817.8	518.7	305.7	345.7	1,748.8	1,461.1	815.3	659.3	283.6
2003	1,185.0	833.1	528.0	312.0	350.8	1,826.9	1,533.0	850.4	698.9	289.6
2004	1,300.6	904.5	586.0	323.4	395.4	2,035.3	1,704.1	969.3	745.7	326.4
2005	1,381.9	970.6	641.0	333.2	410.3	2,164.2	1,817.9	1,051.6	774.8	341.1
2006	1,506.8	1,062.0	710.1	355.2	443.5	2,301.0	1,925.4	1,145.2	787.7	370.5
2007	1,646.4	1,141.5	770.8	373.9	504.1	2,359.0	1,960.9	1,174.5	794.2	393.5
2008	1,740.8	1,211.5	810.2	404.2	528.3	2,298.6	1,887.9	1,129.0	766.1	408.2
2009	1,587.7	1,065.1	671.6	393.5	522.6	1,983.2	1,590.3	893.8	696.5	392.9
2010	1,776.6	1,218.3	784.8	434.0	558.0	2,235.4	1,826.7	1,095.2	735.8	407.8
2011	1,898.3	1,297.6	852.0	448.2	600.6	2,357.7	1,932.1	1,197.9	745.9	424.2
2012	1,960.1	1,344.9	891.3	457.9	614.7	2,412.6	1,973.1	1,283.0	716.2	438.7
2013	2,019.8	1,382.9	908.4	477.4	636.6	2,440.3	1,991.5	1,326.8	698.7	448.4
2014 ᵖ	2,082.5	1,438.4	940.5	500.3	643.5	2,535.1	2,071.6	1,418.7	697.8	462.9
2011: I	1,862.3	1,274.0	828.7	446.6	588.0	2,328.5	1,917.7	1,177.7	748.6	408.7
II	1,890.7	1,289.5	849.5	443.1	601.2	2,345.9	1,921.3	1,175.5	753.7	423.5
III	1,910.6	1,300.5	859.2	444.8	610.3	2,364.9	1,931.8	1,206.6	739.2	432.4
IV	1,929.7	1,326.2	870.7	458.1	603.0	2,391.3	1,957.8	1,231.7	742.2	432.4
2012: I	1,936.0	1,331.2	893.6	443.7	604.2	2,401.7	1,967.2	1,274.2	718.1	433.2
II	1,958.9	1,348.5	890.7	461.5	609.7	2,425.5	1,986.8	1,288.3	723.9	437.5
III	1,969.1	1,355.3	892.6	466.0	613.2	2,422.1	1,981.2	1,284.8	721.7	440.1
IV	1,976.5	1,344.7	888.1	460.3	631.8	2,401.0	1,957.2	1,284.6	701.1	443.8
2013: I	1,972.3	1,341.8	887.5	458.2	630.4	2,399.5	1,959.8	1,288.3	700.7	439.2
II	2,002.8	1,368.9	913.3	460.8	633.6	2,448.8	2,000.1	1,324.1	708.1	448.2
III	2,027.7	1,388.0	910.5	480.2	639.3	2,452.3	2,000.8	1,339.8	696.7	451.2
IV	2,076.5	1,433.0	922.3	510.5	642.9	2,460.5	2,005.3	1,354.9	689.2	455.1
2014: I	2,026.9	1,388.1	913.1	478.2	638.4	2,474.1	2,017.7	1,352.2	701.8	456.3
II	2,080.7	1,435.4	939.5	498.3	644.7	2,541.1	2,077.8	1,423.9	699.2	462.5
III	2,104.0	1,461.6	959.7	504.9	641.6	2,535.3	2,071.0	1,428.8	689.7	463.7
IV ᵖ	2,118.4	1,468.6	949.8	519.9	649.1	2,589.9	2,119.9	1,469.8	700.4	469.1

[1] Certain goods, primarily military equipment purchased and sold by the Federal Government, are included in services. Repairs and alterations of equipment are also included in services.

Source: Department of Commerce (Bureau of Economic Analysis).

TABLE B–6. Corporate profits by industry, 1965–2014

[Billions of dollars; quarterly data at seasonally adjusted annual rates]

Year or quarter	Total	Corporate profits with inventory valuation adjustment and without capital consumption adjustment												Rest of the world
		Domestic industries												
		Total	Financial			Nonfinancial								
			Total	Federal Reserve banks	Other	Total	Manu-factur-ing	Trans-porta-tion[1]	Utilities	Whole-sale trade	Retail trade	Infor-mation	Other	
SIC:[2]														
1965	81.9	77.2	9.3	1.3	8.0	67.9	42.1	11.4		3.8	4.9		5.7	4.7
1966	88.3	83.7	10.7	1.7	9.1	73.0	45.3	12.6		4.0	4.9		6.3	4.5
1967	86.1	81.3	11.2	2.0	9.2	70.1	42.4	11.4		4.1	5.7		6.6	4.8
1968	94.3	88.6	12.9	2.5	10.4	75.7	45.8	11.4		4.7	6.4		7.4	5.6
1969	90.8	84.2	13.6	3.1	10.6	70.6	41.6	11.1		4.9	6.4		6.5	6.6
1970	79.7	72.6	15.5	3.5	12.0	57.1	32.0	8.8		4.6	6.1		5.8	7.1
1971	94.7	86.8	17.9	3.3	14.6	69.0	40.0	9.6		5.4	7.3		6.7	7.9
1972	109.3	99.7	19.5	3.3	16.1	80.3	47.6	10.4		7.2	7.5		7.6	9.5
1973	126.6	111.7	21.1	4.5	16.6	90.6	55.0	10.2		8.8	7.0		9.6	14.9
1974	123.3	105.8	20.8	5.7	15.1	85.1	51.0	9.1		12.2	2.8		10.0	17.5
1975	144.2	129.6	20.4	5.6	14.8	109.2	63.0	11.7		14.3	8.4		11.8	14.6
1976	182.1	165.6	25.6	5.9	19.7	140.0	82.5	17.5		13.7	10.9		15.3	16.5
1977	212.8	193.7	32.6	6.1	26.5	161.1	91.5	21.2		16.4	12.8		19.2	19.1
1978	246.7	223.8	40.8	7.6	33.1	183.1	105.8	25.5		16.7	13.1		22.0	22.9
1979	261.0	226.4	41.8	9.4	32.3	184.6	107.1	21.6		20.0	10.7		25.2	34.6
1980	240.6	205.2	35.2	11.8	23.5	169.9	97.6	22.2		18.5	7.0		24.6	35.5
1981	252.0	222.3	30.3	14.4	15.9	192.0	112.5	25.1		23.7	10.7		20.1	29.7
1982	224.8	192.2	27.2	15.2	12.0	165.0	89.6	28.1		20.7	14.3		12.3	32.6
1983	256.4	221.4	36.2	14.6	21.6	185.2	97.3	34.3		21.9	19.3		12.3	35.1
1984	294.3	257.7	34.7	16.4	18.3	223.0	114.2	44.7		30.4	21.5		12.1	36.6
1985	289.7	251.6	46.5	16.3	30.2	205.1	107.1	39.1		24.6	22.8		11.4	38.1
1986	273.3	233.8	56.4	15.5	40.8	177.4	75.6	39.3		24.4	23.4		14.7	39.5
1987	314.6	266.5	60.3	16.2	44.1	206.2	101.8	42.0		18.9	23.3		20.3	48.0
1988	366.2	309.2	66.9	18.1	48.8	242.3	132.8	46.8		20.4	19.8		22.5	57.0
1989	373.1	305.9	78.3	20.6	57.6	227.6	122.3	41.9		22.0	20.9		20.5	67.1
1990	391.2	315.1	89.6	21.8	67.8	225.5	120.9	43.5		19.4	20.3		21.3	76.1
1991	434.2	357.8	120.4	20.7	99.7	237.3	109.3	54.5		22.3	26.9		24.3	76.5
1992	459.7	386.6	132.4	18.3	114.1	254.2	109.8	57.7		25.3	28.1		33.4	73.1
1993	501.9	425.0	119.9	16.7	103.2	305.1	122.9	70.1		26.5	39.7		45.8	76.9
1994	589.3	511.3	125.9	18.5	107.4	385.4	162.6	83.9		31.4	46.3		61.2	78.0
1995	667.0	574.0	140.3	22.9	117.3	433.7	199.8	89.0		28.0	43.9		73.1	92.9
1996	741.8	639.8	147.9	22.5	125.3	492.0	220.4	91.2		39.9	52.0		88.5	102.0
1997	811.0	703.4	162.2	24.3	137.9	541.2	248.5	81.0		48.1	63.4		100.3	107.6
1998	743.8	641.1	138.9	25.6	113.3	502.1	220.4	72.6		50.6	72.3		86.3	102.8
1999	762.2	640.2	154.6	26.7	127.9	485.6	219.4	49.3		46.8	72.5		97.6	122.0
2000	730.3	584.1	149.7	31.2	118.5	434.4	205.9	33.8		50.4	68.9		75.4	146.2
NAICS:[2]														
1998	743.8	641.1	138.9	25.6	113.3	502.1	193.5	12.8	33.3	57.3	62.5	33.1	109.7	102.8
1999	762.2	640.2	154.6	26.7	127.9	485.6	184.5	7.2	34.4	55.6	59.5	20.8	123.5	122.0
2000	730.3	584.1	149.7	31.2	118.5	434.4	175.6	9.5	24.3	59.5	51.3	−11.9	126.1	146.2
2001	698.7	528.3	195.0	28.9	166.1	333.3	75.1	−7	22.5	51.1	71.3	−26.4	140.2	170.4
2002	795.1	636.3	270.7	23.5	247.2	365.6	75.1	−6.0	11.1	55.8	83.7	−3.1	149.0	158.8
2003	959.9	793.3	306.5	20.1	286.5	486.7	125.3	4.8	13.5	59.3	90.5	16.3	177.1	166.6
2004	1,215.2	1,010.1	349.4	20.0	329.4	660.7	182.7	12.0	20.5	74.7	93.2	52.7	224.9	205.0
2005	1,621.2	1,382.1	409.7	26.6	383.1	972.4	277.7	27.7	30.8	96.2	121.7	91.3	327.2	239.1
2006	1,815.7	1,559.6	415.1	33.8	381.3	1,144.4	349.7	41.2	55.1	105.9	132.5	107.0	353.1	256.2
2007	1,708.9	1,355.5	301.5	36.0	265.5	1,054.0	321.9	23.9	49.5	103.2	119.0	108.4	328.2	353.4
2008	1,345.5	938.8	95.4	35.1	60.4	843.4	240.6	28.8	30.1	90.6	80.3	92.2	280.8	406.7
2009	1,479.2	1,122.0	362.9	47.3	315.5	759.2	171.4	22.4	23.8	89.3	108.7	81.2	262.3	357.2
2010	1,799.7	1,404.5	406.3	71.6	334.8	998.2	287.6	44.7	30.3	102.4	118.6	95.1	319.5	395.2
2011	1,738.5	1,316.6	375.9	75.9	300.0	940.7	298.1	30.4	9.8	94.4	114.3	83.8	309.9	421.9
2012	2,126.6	1,724.8	488.9	71.7	417.2	1,235.9	404.2	51.9	12.9	136.6	157.2	101.1	372.0	401.8
2013	2,238.7	1,835.6	533.5	79.6	453.9	1,302.1	402.4	62.6	20.9	154.5	171.2	108.3	382.2	403.1
2012: I	2,088.6	1,680.1	468.8	73.4	395.4	1,211.3	402.7	51.8	21.0	123.6	153.2	100.7	358.3	408.6
II	2,130.7	1,725.8	470.7	72.6	398.1	1,255.1	419.8	53.9	11.6	142.1	155.8	111.6	360.4	405.0
III	2,141.8	1,750.4	524.4	67.5	456.9	1,226.0	392.6	53.3	12.1	134.4	149.2	102.5	381.9	391.4
IV	2,145.3	1,742.9	491.6	73.3	418.3	1,251.2	401.5	48.5	6.9	146.4	170.8	89.6	387.6	402.4
2013: I	2,167.3	1,781.2	504.9	71.2	433.7	1,276.3	388.4	60.3	6.8	158.1	166.2	109.7	386.8	386.1
II	2,235.0	1,841.9	525.5	75.2	450.2	1,316.4	383.7	61.5	31.1	157.1	179.1	114.6	389.3	393.1
III	2,273.7	1,864.2	554.1	82.3	471.8	1,310.1	392.3	62.8	30.0	154.8	175.4	103.2	391.7	409.6
IV	2,278.6	1,855.1	549.4	89.6	459.8	1,305.7	445.4	65.7	15.8	147.9	164.2	105.6	361.1	423.5
2014: I	2,272.6	1,875.1	480.8	88.7	392.2	1,394.2	432.5	73.6	42.3	152.0	168.1	123.0	402.6	397.5
II	2,437.4	2,043.5	514.5	93.1	421.4	1,528.9	504.4	83.5	50.4	157.6	176.7	142.9	413.4	393.9
III	2,501.1	2,090.7	530.7	94.2	436.5	1,560.0	523.7	82.1	54.5	174.4	175.8	129.1	420.5	410.4

[1] Data on Standard Industrial Classification (SIC) basis include transportation and public utilities. Those on North American Industry Classification System (NAICS) basis include transporation and warehousing. Utilities classified separately in NAICS (as shown beginning 1998).
[2] SIC-based industry data use the 1987 SIC for data beginning in 1987 and the 1972 SIC for prior data. NAICS-based data use 2002 NAICS.

Note: Industry data on SIC basis and NAICS basis are not necessarily the same and are not strictly comparable.

Source: Department of Commerce (Bureau of Economic Analysis).

TABLE B–7. Real farm income, 1950–2014

[Billions of chained (2009) dollars]

Year	Income of farm operators from farming [1]						Production expenses	Net farm income
	Gross farm income							
	Total [2]	Value of farm sector production				Direct Government payments		
		Total	Crops [3, 4]	Livestock [4]	Forestry and services			
1950	240.8	238.8	96.0	132.0	10.8	2.1	141.5	99.3
1951	260.9	258.9	95.6	152.1	11.2	1.9	152.3	108.6
1952	251.7	249.9	102.2	135.7	12.0	1.8	152.0	99.8
1953	226.8	225.4	93.1	120.1	12.2	1.4	141.3	85.4
1954	222.7	221.1	94.0	115.3	11.8	1.7	142.1	80.6
1955	215.1	213.6	91.6	110.0	12.0	1.5	142.4	72.6
1956	210.9	207.5	89.7	106.2	11.6	3.4	141.0	69.9
1957	208.8	202.7	81.9	109.0	11.7	6.1	142.2	66.5
1958	228.5	222.1	88.0	121.9	12.2	6.4	151.3	77.2
1959	219.3	215.4	85.5	116.8	13.1	3.9	157.3	62.0
1960	220.3	216.3	89.5	113.5	13.4	4.0	156.3	64.0
1961	229.0	220.5	89.3	117.4	13.8	8.4	161.4	67.5
1962	236.2	226.5	92.9	119.5	14.0	9.7	168.9	67.3
1963	239.2	229.9	98.9	116.4	14.6	9.4	174.3	64.9
1964	229.8	218.0	91.7	111.2	15.1	11.8	172.8	57.0
1965	248.3	235.2	101.5	118.4	15.3	13.1	179.5	68.8
1966	261.9	244.9	95.0	134.2	15.6	17.0	189.4	72.4
1967	254.8	239.2	96.9	126.0	16.3	15.5	192.5	62.2
1968	250.8	234.0	91.5	126.3	16.2	16.7	191.2	59.6
1969	260.1	242.6	90.7	135.2	16.6	17.5	194.2	65.9
1970	257.6	241.3	89.9	134.7	16.7	16.3	194.7	62.9
1971	258.9	245.8	97.6	131.1	17.0	13.1	196.3	62.6
1972	284.2	268.4	103.7	147.4	17.3	15.8	206.5	77.7
1973	374.7	364.8	163.1	183.2	18.5	9.9	244.6	130.2
1974	341.6	339.8	170.9	148.9	20.0	1.8	246.8	94.8
1975	319.9	317.4	160.4	136.8	20.2	2.6	238.8	81.2
1976	310.4	308.2	145.9	140.6	21.7	2.2	249.5	60.8
1977	308.9	303.7	145.3	134.4	24.1	5.2	252.4	56.5
1978	340.9	332.8	150.2	156.2	26.4	8.0	274.0	66.9
1979	369.5	366.1	163.4	174.5	28.2	3.4	302.3	67.2
1980	335.6	332.7	144.7	158.1	29.9	2.9	299.3	36.3
1981	341.8	337.8	162.2	144.7	31.0	4.0	286.6	55.2
1982	318.0	311.2	139.1	136.6	35.5	6.8	271.8	46.2
1983	286.7	269.4	106.0	130.5	32.9	17.3	260.2	26.6
1984	302.3	287.1	139.9	129.6	17.6	15.2	255.6	46.7
1985	280.9	267.5	128.5	120.3	18.7	13.4	231.2	49.7
1986	266.9	246.7	108.2	120.9	17.5	20.2	213.7	53.2
1987	281.0	253.0	107.6	126.4	19.1	27.9	217.6	63.4
1988	286.8	263.5	111.7	126.8	25.0	23.3	222.9	63.9
1989	297.3	280.4	126.4	129.5	24.5	16.9	225.2	72.1
1990	295.9	282.0	124.5	134.7	22.8	13.9	226.7	69.2
1991	278.1	266.2	117.6	126.3	22.3	11.9	219.8	58.3
1992	283.9	271.0	126.1	123.4	21.5	13.0	212.9	71.0
1993	283.5	265.0	114.3	127.2	23.5	18.5	218.9	64.6
1994	292.6	282.0	136.1	121.5	24.4	10.7	221.4	71.2
1995	279.6	270.0	127.2	116.4	26.4	9.7	226.9	52.8
1996	307.2	297.6	150.7	119.9	27.0	9.6	230.4	76.8
1997	304.8	295.2	144.1	123.3	27.8	9.6	239.1	65.7
1998	294.7	279.0	129.4	119.3	30.3	15.7	235.0	59.7
1999	293.4	266.6	115.9	118.9	31.8	26.9	233.9	59.6
2000	295.1	266.8	116.0	121.0	29.8	28.4	233.2	61.9
2001	298.4	271.6	113.5	127.0	31.1	26.8	232.8	65.5
2002	271.1	256.5	115.1	109.9	31.5	14.6	225.1	46.0
2003	298.3	279.2	125.2	121.1	33.0	19.1	228.0	70.3
2004	330.9	316.3	140.4	139.4	36.5	14.6	232.8	98.1
2005	324.5	298.0	124.3	137.5	36.1	26.5	238.9	85.6
2006	306.0	289.4	125.2	125.9	38.3	16.7	245.5	60.6
2007	348.8	336.6	155.2	142.2	39.2	12.2	276.9	71.9
2008	376.3	363.9	180.8	140.9	42.3	12.3	296.3	80.0
2009	339.5	327.4	166.9	117.8	42.7	12.2	283.0	56.6
2010	358.3	346.1	168.9	138.2	39.0	12.2	284.0	74.3
2011	412.6	402.5	197.4	158.2	47.0	10.1	302.5	110.1
2012	423.1	413.0	207.9	159.2	45.9	10.1	325.6	97.5
2013	450.6	440.3	218.9	170.6	50.8	10.3	329.8	120.8
2014 p	428.7	419.0	184.0	189.5	45.5	9.7	339.4	89.3

[1] The GDP chain-type price index is used to convert the current-dollar statistics to 2009=100 equivalents.
[2] Value of production, Government payments, other farm-related cash income, and nonmoney income produced by farms including imputed rent of farm dwellings.
[3] Crop receipts include proceeds received from commodities placed under Commodity Credit Corporation loans.
[4] The value of production equates to the sum of cash receipts, home consumption, and the value of the change in inventories.

Note: Data for 2014 are forecasts.

Source: Department of Agriculture (Economic Research Service).

[Thousands; monthly data at seasonally adjusted annual rates]

Year or month	New housing units started — Total	1 unit	2 to 4 units [2]	5 units or more	New housing units authorized [1] — Total	1 unit	2 to 4 units	5 units or more	New housing units completed	New houses sold
1970	1,433.6	812.9	84.9	535.9	1,351.5	646.8	88.1	616.7	1,418.4	485
1971	2,052.2	1,151.0	120.5	780.9	1,924.6	906.1	132.9	885.7	1,706.1	656
1972	2,356.6	1,309.2	141.2	906.2	2,218.9	1,033.1	148.6	1,037.2	2,003.9	718
1973	2,045.3	1,132.0	118.2	795.0	1,819.5	882.1	117.0	820.5	2,100.5	634
1974	1,337.7	888.1	68.0	381.6	1,074.4	643.8	64.4	366.2	1,728.5	519
1975	1,160.4	892.2	64.0	204.3	939.2	675.5	63.8	199.8	1,317.2	549
1976	1,537.5	1,162.4	85.8	289.2	1,296.2	893.6	93.1	309.5	1,377.2	646
1977	1,987.1	1,450.9	121.7	414.4	1,690.0	1,126.1	121.3	442.7	1,657.1	819
1978	2,020.3	1,433.3	125.1	462.0	1,800.5	1,182.6	130.6	487.3	1,867.5	817
1979	1,745.1	1,194.1	122.0	429.0	1,551.8	981.5	125.4	444.8	1,870.8	709
1980	1,292.2	852.2	109.5	330.5	1,190.6	710.4	114.5	365.7	1,501.6	545
1981	1,084.2	705.4	91.2	287.7	985.5	564.3	101.8	319.4	1,265.7	436
1982	1,062.2	662.6	80.1	319.6	1,000.5	546.4	88.3	365.8	1,005.5	412
1983	1,703.0	1,067.6	113.5	522.0	1,605.2	901.5	133.7	570.1	1,390.3	623
1984	1,749.5	1,084.2	121.4	543.9	1,681.8	922.4	142.6	616.8	1,652.2	639
1985	1,741.8	1,072.4	93.5	576.0	1,733.3	956.6	120.1	656.6	1,703.3	688
1986	1,805.4	1,179.4	84.0	542.0	1,769.4	1,077.6	108.4	583.5	1,756.4	750
1987	1,620.5	1,146.4	65.1	408.7	1,534.8	1,024.4	89.3	421.1	1,668.8	671
1988	1,488.1	1,081.3	58.7	348.0	1,455.6	993.8	75.7	386.1	1,529.8	676
1989	1,376.1	1,003.3	55.3	317.6	1,338.4	931.7	66.9	339.8	1,422.8	650
1990	1,192.7	894.8	37.6	260.4	1,110.8	793.9	54.3	262.6	1,308.0	534
1991	1,013.9	840.4	35.6	137.9	948.8	753.5	43.1	152.1	1,090.8	509
1992	1,199.7	1,029.9	30.9	139.0	1,094.9	910.7	45.8	138.4	1,157.5	610
1993	1,287.6	1,125.7	29.4	132.6	1,199.1	986.5	52.4	160.2	1,192.7	666
1994	1,457.0	1,198.4	35.2	223.5	1,371.6	1,068.5	62.2	241.0	1,346.9	670
1995	1,354.1	1,076.2	33.8	244.1	1,332.5	997.3	63.8	271.5	1,312.6	667
1996	1,476.8	1,160.9	45.3	270.8	1,425.6	1,069.5	65.8	290.3	1,412.9	757
1997	1,474.0	1,133.7	44.5	295.8	1,441.1	1,062.4	68.4	310.3	1,400.5	804
1998	1,616.9	1,271.4	42.6	302.9	1,612.3	1,187.6	69.2	355.5	1,474.2	886
1999	1,640.9	1,302.4	31.9	306.6	1,663.5	1,246.7	65.8	351.1	1,604.9	880
2000	1,568.7	1,230.9	38.7	299.1	1,592.3	1,198.1	64.9	329.3	1,573.7	877
2001	1,602.7	1,273.3	36.6	292.8	1,636.7	1,235.6	66.0	335.2	1,570.8	908
2002	1,704.9	1,358.6	38.5	307.9	1,747.7	1,332.6	73.7	341.4	1,648.4	973
2003	1,847.7	1,499.0	33.5	315.2	1,889.2	1,460.9	82.5	345.8	1,678.7	1,086
2004	1,955.8	1,610.5	42.3	303.0	2,070.1	1,613.4	90.4	366.2	1,841.9	1,203
2005	2,068.3	1,715.8	41.1	311.4	2,155.3	1,682.0	84.0	389.3	1,931.4	1,283
2006	1,800.9	1,465.4	42.7	292.8	1,838.9	1,378.2	76.6	384.1	1,979.4	1,051
2007	1,355.0	1,046.0	31.7	277.3	1,398.4	979.9	59.6	359.0	1,502.8	776
2008	905.5	622.0	17.5	266.0	905.4	575.6	34.4	295.4	1,119.7	485
2009	554.0	445.1	11.6	97.3	583.0	441.1	20.7	121.1	794.4	375
2010	586.9	471.2	11.4	104.3	604.6	447.3	22.0	135.3	651.7	323
2011	608.8	430.6	10.9	167.3	624.1	418.5	21.6	184.0	584.9	306
2012	780.6	535.3	11.4	233.9	829.7	518.7	25.9	285.1	649.2	368
2013	924.9	617.6	13.6	293.7	990.8	620.8	29.0	341.1	764.4	429
2014 p	1,005.8	648.0	13.9	343.9	1,038.5	630.3	27.5	380.7	883.0	435
2013: Jan	896	618		267	947	597	29	321	726	453
Feb	951	650		291	976	611	36	329	723	448
Mar	994	613		356	926	605	26	295	805	440
Apr	848	591		243	1,040	622	28	390	699	452
May	915	597		307	1,010	624	29	357	719	431
June	831	601		219	938	627	29	282	763	459
July	898	596		283	977	616	30	331	779	367
Aug	885	617		255	948	631	25	292	763	379
Sept	863	582		271	993	617	29	347	761	399
Oct	936	603		322	1,067	625	30	412	815	450
Nov	1,105	710		386	1,037	645	27	365	826	445
Dec	1,034	675		338	1,022	617	30	375	775	442
2014: Jan	897	583		306	939	598	26	315	850	457
Feb	928	589		328	1,011	593	23	395	866	432
Mar	950	635		301	1,000	600	28	372	874	403
Apr	1,063	649		405	1,059	597	26	436	832	413
May	984	634		341	1,005	615	27	363	898	458
June	909	593		294	973	634	30	309	809	409
July	1,098	652		430	1,057	631	30	396	860	399
Aug	963	641		305	1,003	627	31	345	908	448
Sept	1,028	663		353	1,031	631	24	376	950	456
Oct	1,092	716		359	1,092	647	32	413	915	462
Nov p	1,043	679		354	1,052	638	28	386	872	431
Dec p	1,089	728		339	1,058	668	27	363	927	481

[1] Authorized by issuance of local building permits in permit-issuing places: 20,000 places beginning with 2004; 19,000 for 1994–2003; 17,000 for 1984–93; 16,000 for 1978–83; 14,000 for 1972–77; and 13,000 for 1970–71.

[2] Monthly data do not meet publication standards because tests for identifiable and stable seasonality do not meet reliability standards.

Note: One-unit estimates prior to 1999, for new housing units started and completed and for new houses sold, include an upward adjustment of 3.3 percent to account for structures in permit-issuing areas that did not have permit authorization.

Source: Department of Commerce (Bureau of the Census).

TABLE B–9. Median money income (in 2013 dollars) and poverty status of families and people, by race, 2004-2013

Race, Hispanic origin, and year	Families [1]						People below poverty level		Median money income (in 2013 dollars) of people 15 years old and over with income [2]			
			Below poverty level						Males		Females	
	Number (mil-lions)	Median money income (in 2013 dol-lars) [2]	Total		Female householder, no husband present		Number (mil-lions)	Percent	All people	Year-round full-time workers	All people	Year-round full-time workers
			Number (mil-lions)	Percent	Number (mil-lions)	Percent						
TOTAL (all races) [3]												
2004 [4]	76.9	$66,670	7.8	10.2	4.0	28.3	37.0	12.7	$37,633	$51,385	$21,788	$39,607
2005	77.4	67,053	7.7	9.9	4.0	28.7	37.0	12.6	37,318	50,340	22,166	39,682
2006	78.5	67,481	7.7	9.8	4.1	28.3	36.5	12.3	37,277	51,942	23,123	40,425
2007	77.9	68,931	7.6	9.8	4.1	28.3	37.3	12.5	37,295	51,932	23,505	40,633
2008	78.9	66,560	8.1	10.3	4.2	28.7	39.8	13.2	35,877	51,693	22,576	39,693
2009 [5]	78.9	65,257	8.8	11.1	4.4	29.9	43.6	14.3	34,953	53,394	22,760	40,437
2010 [6]	79.6	64,356	9.4	11.8	4.8	31.7	46.3	15.1	34,408	53,581	22,196	41,068
2011	80.5	63,152	9.5	11.8	4.9	31.2	46.2	15.0	34,164	52,114	21,856	40,067
2012	80.9	63,145	9.5	11.8	4.8	30.9	46.5	15.0	34,397	51,419	21,833	40,601
2013 [7]	81.2	63,815	9.1	11.2	4.6	30.6	45.3	14.5	35,228	50,943	22,063	40,597
WHITE, non-Hispanic [8]												
2004 [4]	54.3	75,220	3.5	6.5	1.5	20.8	16.9	8.7	41,533	57,940	22,735	43,068
2005	54.3	75,360	3.3	6.1	1.5	21.5	16.2	8.3	42,175	57,417	23,210	42,714
2006	54.7	76,098	3.4	6.2	1.6	22.0	16.0	8.2	42,244	58,281	23,947	42,616
2007	53.9	78,573	3.2	5.9	1.5	20.7	16.0	8.2	41,988	57,820	24,365	43,454
2008	54.5	75,809	3.4	6.2	1.5	20.7	17.0	8.6	40,473	56,634	23,530	42,703
2009 [5]	54.5	73,134	3.8	7.0	1.7	23.3	18.5	9.4	39,950	56,983	23,826	43,729
2010 [6]	53.8	73,616	3.9	7.2	1.7	24.1	19.3	9.9	39,695	58,391	23,200	44,159
2011	54.2	72,324	4.0	7.3	1.8	23.4	19.2	9.8	39,511	57,755	23,020	42,851
2012	54.0	72,517	3.8	7.1	1.7	23.4	18.9	9.7	39,314	57,064	23,235	42,784
2013 [7]	53.8	72,624	3.7	6.9	1.6	22.6	18.8	9.6	40,122	56,456	23,780	42,784
BLACK [8]												
2004 [4]	8.9	43,346	2.0	22.8	1.5	37.6	9.0	24.7	27,982	39,118	21,408	35,943
2005	9.1	42,317	2.0	22.1	1.5	36.1	9.2	24.9	27,030	40,848	21,038	36,230
2006	9.3	44,214	2.0	21.6	1.5	36.6	9.0	24.3	28,958	40,988	22,071	35,742
2007	9.3	45,100	2.0	22.1	1.5	37.3	9.2	24.5	29,011	41,272	22,191	35,492
2008	9.4	43,145	2.1	22.0	1.5	37.2	9.4	24.7	27,323	41,775	21,851	34,822
2009 [5]	9.4	41,713	2.1	22.7	1.5	36.7	9.9	25.8	25,780	42,748	21,145	35,263
2010 [6]	9.6	41,234	2.3	24.1	1.7	38.7	10.7	27.4	24,889	40,304	20,990	36,371
2011	9.7	41,942	2.3	24.2	1.7	39.0	10.9	27.6	24,314	41,712	20,461	36,402
2012	9.8	41,106	2.3	23.7	1.6	37.8	10.9	27.2	25,285	40,395	20,312	35,600
2013 [7]	9.9	41,588	2.3	22.8	1.6	38.5	11.0	27.2	24,855	41,630	20,044	35,381
ASIAN [8]												
2004 [4]	3.1	80,678	.2	7.4	.0	13.6	1.2	9.8	40,720	57,733	25,308	45,155
2005	3.2	82,282	.3	9.0	.1	19.7	1.4	11.1	40,826	59,337	25,823	43,926
2006	3.3	86,203	.3	7.8	.1	15.4	1.4	10.3	43,230	60,195	25,650	46,501
2007	3.3	86,657	.3	7.9	.1	16.1	1.3	10.2	41,786	57,537	27,362	46,417
2008	3.5	79,605	.3	9.8	.1	16.7	1.6	11.8	39,605	56,027	25,002	47,829
2009 [5]	3.6	81,482	.3	9.4	.1	16.9	1.7	12.5	40,542	58,025	26,437	48,466
2010 [6]	3.9	80,361	.4	9.3	.1	21.1	1.9	12.2	38,273	56,096	25,175	44,787
2011	4.2	75,604	.4	9.7	.1	19.1	2.0	12.3	37,632	58,294	22,826	42,890
2012	4.1	78,995	.4	9.4	.1	19.2	1.9	11.7	40,812	61,129	23,674	47,045
2013 [7]	4.4	76,402	.4	8.7	.1	14.9	1.8	10.5	40,153	60,154	24,840	45,076
HISPANIC (any race) [8]												
2004 [4]	9.5	43,706	2.0	20.5	.9	38.9	9.1	21.9	26,584	33,172	17,823	29,961
2005	9.9	45,184	1.9	19.7	.9	38.9	9.4	21.8	26,357	32,177	17,941	29,857
2006	10.2	46,214	1.9	18.9	.9	36.0	9.2	20.6	27,095	34,165	18,206	29,686
2007	10.4	45,575	2.0	19.7	1.0	38.4	9.9	21.5	27,470	34,214	18,816	30,507
2008	10.5	43,781	2.2	21.3	1.0	39.2	11.0	23.2	25,969	33,776	17,762	29,689
2009 [5]	10.4	43,148	2.4	22.7	1.1	38.8	12.4	25.3	24,171	34,360	17,605	30,282
2010 [6]	11.3	41,988	2.7	24.3	1.3	42.6	13.5	26.5	23,953	34,021	17,406	31,086
2011	11.6	41,492	2.7	22.9	1.3	41.2	13.2	25.3	24,579	33,234	17,430	31,177
2012	12.0	41,356	2.8	23.5	1.3	40.7	13.6	25.6	24,949	32,989	16,968	29,937
2013 [7]	12.1	42,269	2.6	21.6	1.3	40.4	12.7	23.5	25,411	32,949	17,762	30,799

[1] The term "family" refers to a group of two or more persons related by birth, marriage, or adoption and residing together. Every family must include a reference person.
[2] Adjusted by consumer price index research series (CPI-U-RS).
[3] Data for American Indians and Alaska natives, native Hawaiians and other Pacific Islanders, and those reporting two or more races are included in the total but not shown separately.
[4] For 2004, figures are revised to reflect a correction to the weights in the 2005 Annual Social and Economic Supplement (ASEC).
[5] Beginning with data for 2009, the upper income interval used to calculate median incomes was expanded to $250,000 or more.
[6] Reflects implementation of Census 2010-based population controls comparable to succeeding years.
[7] For 2013, data are based on the 2014 ASEC sample of 68,000 addresses that received income questions similar to those used in the 2013 ASEC. The 2014 ASEC also included redesigned income questions that were provided to a separate 30,000 addresses.
[8] The Current Population Survey allows respondents to choose more than one race. Data shown are for "white alone, non-Hispanic," "black alone," and "Asian alone" race categories. ("Black" is also "black or African American.") Family race and Hispanic origin are based on the reference person.

Note: Poverty thresholds are updated each year to reflect changes in the consumer price index (CPI-U).
For details see publication Series P–60 on the Current Population Survey and Annual Social and Economic Supplements.

Source: Department of Commerce (Bureau of the Census).

[For all urban consumers; percent change]

December to December	All items	All items less food and energy					Food			Energy[4]		C-CPI-U[5]
		Total[1]	Shelter[2]	Medical care[3]	Apparel	New vehicles	Total[1]	At home	Away from home	Total[1]	Gasoline	
1946	18.1			8.3	18.1		31.3				7.8	
1947	8.8			6.9	8.2		11.3				16.4	
1948	3.0			5.8	5.1	11.5	-.8	-1.1			6.2	
1949	-2.1			1.4	-7.4	4.0	-3.9	-3.7			1.6	
1950	5.9			3.4	5.3	.2	9.8	9.5			1.6	
1951	6.0			5.8	5.7	9.7	7.1	7.6			2.1	
1952	.8			4.3	-2.9	4.4	-1.0	-1.3			.5	
1953	.7		3.2	3.5	.7	-1.7	-1.1	-1.6			10.1	
1954	-.7		1.8	2.3	-.7	1.3	-1.8	-2.3	0.9		-1.4	
1955	.4		.9	3.3	.5	-2.3	-.7	-1.0	1.4		4.2	
1956	3.0		2.6	3.2	2.5	7.8	2.9	2.7	2.7		3.1	
1957	2.9		3.4	4.7	.9	2.0	2.8	3.0	3.9		2.2	
1958	1.8	1.7	.8	4.5	.2	6.1	2.4	1.9	2.1	-.9	-3.8	
1959	1.7	2.0	2.0	3.8	1.3	-.2	-1.0	-1.3	3.3	4.7	7.0	
1960	1.4	1.0	1.6	3.2	1.5	-3.0	3.1	3.2	2.4	1.3	1.2	
1961	.7	1.3	.8	3.1	.4	.2	-.7	-1.6	2.3	-1.3	-3.2	
1962	1.3	1.3	.8	2.2	.6	-1.0	1.3	1.3	3.0	2.2	3.8	
1963	1.6	1.6	1.9	2.5	1.7	-.4	2.0	1.6	1.8	-.9	-2.4	
1964	1.0	1.2	1.5	2.1	.4	-.6	1.3	1.5	1.4	.0	.0	
1965	1.9	1.5	2.2	2.8	1.3	-2.9	3.5	3.6	3.2	1.8	4.1	
1966	3.5	3.3	4.0	6.7	3.9	.0	4.0	3.2	5.5	1.7	3.2	
1967	3.0	3.8	2.8	6.3	4.2	2.8	1.2	.3	4.6	1.7	1.5	
1968	4.7	5.1	6.5	6.2	6.3	1.4	4.4	4.0	5.6	1.7	1.5	
1969	6.2	6.2	8.7	6.2	5.2	2.1	7.0	7.1	7.4	2.9	3.4	
1970	5.6	6.6	8.9	7.4	3.9	6.6	2.3	1.3	6.1	4.8	2.5	
1971	3.3	3.1	2.7	4.6	2.1	-3.2	4.3	4.3	4.4	3.1	-.4	
1972	3.4	3.0	4.0	3.3	2.6	.2	4.6	5.1	4.2	2.6	2.8	
1973	8.7	4.7	7.1	5.3	4.4	1.3	20.3	22.0	12.7	17.0	19.6	
1974	12.3	11.1	11.4	12.6	8.7	11.4	12.0	12.4	11.3	21.6	20.7	
1975	6.9	6.7	7.2	9.8	2.4	7.3	6.6	6.2	7.4	11.4	11.0	
1976	4.9	6.1	4.2	10.0	4.6	4.8	.5	-.8	6.0	7.1	2.8	
1977	6.7	6.5	8.8	8.9	4.3	7.2	8.1	7.9	7.9	7.2	4.8	
1978	9.0	8.5	11.4	8.8	3.1	6.2	11.8	12.5	10.4	7.9	8.6	
1979	13.3	11.3	17.5	10.1	5.5	7.4	10.2	9.7	11.4	37.5	52.1	
1980	12.5	12.2	15.0	9.9	6.8	7.4	10.2	10.5	9.6	18.0	18.9	
1981	8.9	9.5	9.9	12.5	3.5	6.8	4.3	2.9	7.1	11.9	9.4	
1982	3.8	4.5	2.4	11.0	1.6	1.4	3.1	2.3	5.1	1.3	-6.7	
1983	3.8	4.8	4.7	6.4	2.9	3.3	2.7	1.8	4.1	-.5	-1.6	
1984	3.9	4.7	5.2	6.1	2.0	2.5	3.8	3.6	4.2	.2	-2.5	
1985	3.8	4.3	6.0	6.8	2.8	3.6	2.6	2.0	3.8	1.8	3.0	
1986	1.1	3.8	4.6	7.7	.9	5.6	3.8	3.7	4.3	-19.7	-30.7	
1987	4.4	4.2	4.8	5.8	4.8	1.8	3.5	3.5	3.7	8.2	18.6	
1988	4.4	4.7	4.5	6.9	4.7	2.2	5.2	5.6	4.4	.5	-1.8	
1989	4.6	4.4	4.9	8.5	1.0	2.4	5.6	6.2	4.6	5.1	6.5	
1990	6.1	5.2	5.2	9.6	5.1	2.0	5.3	5.8	4.5	18.1	36.8	
1991	3.1	4.4	3.9	7.9	3.4	3.2	1.9	1.3	2.9	-7.4	-16.2	
1992	2.9	3.3	2.9	6.6	1.4	2.3	1.5	1.5	1.4	2.0	2.0	
1993	2.7	3.2	3.0	5.4	.9	3.3	2.9	3.5	1.9	-1.4	-5.9	
1994	2.7	2.6	3.0	4.9	-1.6	3.3	2.9	3.5	1.9	2.2	6.4	
1995	2.5	3.0	3.5	3.9	.1	1.9	2.1	2.0	2.2	-1.3	-4.2	
1996	3.3	2.6	2.9	3.0	-.2	1.8	4.3	4.9	3.1	8.6	12.4	
1997	1.7	2.2	3.4	2.8	1.0	-.9	1.5	1.0	2.6	-3.4	-6.1	
1998	1.6	2.4	3.3	3.4	-.7	.0	2.3	2.1	2.5	-8.8	-15.4	
1999	2.7	1.9	2.5	3.7	-.5	-.3	1.9	1.7	2.3	13.4	30.1	
2000	3.4	2.6	3.4	4.2	-1.8	.0	2.8	2.9	2.4	14.2	13.9	2.6
2001	1.6	2.7	4.2	4.7	-3.2	-.1	2.8	2.6	3.0	-13.0	-24.9	1.3
2002	2.4	1.9	3.1	5.0	-1.8	-2.0	1.5	.8	2.3	10.7	24.8	2.0
2003	1.9	1.1	2.2	3.7	-2.1	-1.8	3.6	4.5	2.3	6.9	6.8	1.7
2004	3.3	2.2	2.7	4.2	-.2	.6	2.7	2.4	3.0	16.6	26.1	3.2
2005	3.4	2.2	2.6	4.3	-1.1	-.4	2.3	1.7	3.2	17.1	16.1	2.9
2006	2.5	2.6	4.2	3.6	.9	-.9	2.1	1.4	3.2	2.9	6.4	2.3
2007	4.1	2.4	3.1	5.2	-.3	-.3	4.9	5.6	4.0	17.4	29.6	3.7
2008	.1	1.8	1.9	2.6	-1.0	-3.2	5.9	6.6	5.0	-21.3	-43.1	.2
2009	2.7	1.8	.3	3.4	1.9	4.9	-.5	-2.4	1.9	18.2	53.5	2.5
2010	1.5	.8	.4	3.3	-1.1	-.2	1.5	1.7	1.3	7.7	13.8	1.3
2011	3.0	2.2	1.9	3.5	4.6	3.2	4.7	6.0	2.9	6.6	9.9	2.9
2012	1.7	1.9	2.2	3.2	1.8	1.6	1.8	1.3	2.5	.5	1.7	1.5
2013	1.5	1.7	2.5	2.0	.6	.4	1.1	.4	2.1	.5	-1.0	1.3
2014	.8	1.6	2.9	3.0	-2.0	.5	3.4	3.7	3.0	-10.6	-21.0	.3

[1] Includes other items not shown separately.
[2] Data beginning with 1983 incorporate a rental equivalence measure for homeowners' costs.
[3] Commodities and services.
[4] Household energy—electricity, utility (piped) gas service, fuel oil, etc.–and motor fuel.
[5] Chained consumer price index (C-CPI-U) introduced in 2002. Reflects the effect of substitution that consumers make across item categories in response to changes in relative prices. Data for 2014 are subject to revision.

Note: Changes from December to December are based on unadjusted indexes.
Series reflect changes in composition and renaming beginning in 1998, and formula and methodology changes in 1999.

Source: Department of Labor (Bureau of Labor Statistics).

TABLE B–11. Civilian population and labor force, 1929–2014

[Monthly data seasonally adjusted, except as noted]

Year or month	Civilian noninstitutional population [1]	Civilian labor force					Not in labor force	Civilian labor force participation rate [2]	Civilian employment/population ratio [3]	Unemployment rate, civilian workers [4]
		Total	Employment			Unemployment				
			Total	Agricultural	Nonagricultural					
	Thousands of persons 14 years of age and over							Percent		
1929	....	49,180	47,630	10,450	37,180	1,550	....	....	....	3.2
1930	....	49,820	45,480	10,340	35,140	4,340	....	....	....	8.7
1931	....	50,420	42,400	10,290	32,110	8,020	....	....	....	15.9
1932	....	51,000	38,940	10,170	28,770	12,060	....	....	....	23.6
1933	....	51,590	38,760	10,090	28,670	12,830	....	....	....	24.9
1934	....	52,230	40,890	9,900	30,990	11,340	....	....	....	21.7
1935	....	52,870	42,260	10,110	32,150	10,610	....	....	....	20.1
1936	....	53,440	44,410	10,000	34,410	9,030	....	....	....	16.9
1937	....	54,000	46,300	9,820	36,480	7,700	....	....	....	14.3
1938	....	54,610	44,220	9,690	34,530	10,390	....	....	....	19.0
1939	....	55,230	45,750	9,610	36,140	9,480	....	....	....	17.2
1940	99,840	55,640	47,520	9,540	37,980	8,120	44,200	55.7	47.6	14.6
1941	99,900	55,910	50,350	9,100	41,250	5,560	43,990	56.0	50.4	9.9
1942	98,640	56,410	53,750	9,250	44,500	2,660	42,230	57.2	54.5	4.7
1943	94,640	55,540	54,470	9,080	45,390	1,070	39,100	58.7	57.6	1.9
1944	93,220	54,630	53,960	8,950	45,010	670	38,590	58.6	57.9	1.2
1945	94,090	53,860	52,820	8,580	44,240	1,040	40,230	57.2	56.1	1.9
1946	103,070	57,520	55,250	8,320	46,930	2,270	45,550	55.8	53.6	3.9
1947	106,018	60,168	57,812	8,256	49,557	2,356	45,850	56.8	54.5	3.9
	Thousands of persons 16 years of age and over									
1947	101,827	59,350	57,038	7,890	49,148	2,311	42,477	58.3	56.0	3.9
1948	103,068	60,621	58,343	7,629	50,714	2,276	42,447	58.8	56.6	3.8
1949	103,994	61,286	57,651	7,658	49,993	3,637	42,708	58.9	55.4	5.9
1950	104,995	62,208	58,918	7,160	51,758	3,288	42,787	59.2	56.1	5.3
1951	104,621	62,017	59,961	6,726	53,235	2,055	42,604	59.2	57.3	3.3
1952	105,231	62,138	60,250	6,500	53,749	1,883	43,093	59.0	57.3	3.0
1953	107,056	63,015	61,179	6,260	54,919	1,834	44,041	58.9	57.1	2.9
1954	108,321	63,643	60,109	6,205	53,904	3,532	44,678	58.8	55.5	5.5
1955	109,683	65,023	62,170	6,450	55,722	2,852	44,660	59.3	56.7	4.4
1956	110,954	66,552	63,799	6,283	57,514	2,750	44,402	60.0	57.5	4.1
1957	112,265	66,929	64,071	5,947	58,123	2,859	45,336	59.6	57.1	4.3
1958	113,727	67,639	63,036	5,586	57,450	4,602	46,088	59.5	55.4	6.8
1959	115,329	68,369	64,630	5,565	59,065	3,740	46,960	59.3	56.0	5.5
1960	117,245	69,628	65,778	5,458	60,318	3,852	47,617	59.4	56.1	5.5
1961	118,771	70,459	65,746	5,200	60,546	4,714	48,312	59.3	55.4	6.7
1962	120,153	70,614	66,702	4,944	61,759	3,911	49,539	58.8	55.5	5.5
1963	122,416	71,833	67,762	4,687	63,076	4,070	50,583	58.7	55.4	5.7
1964	124,485	73,091	69,305	4,523	64,782	3,786	51,394	58.7	55.7	5.2
1965	126,513	74,455	71,088	4,361	66,726	3,366	52,058	58.9	56.2	4.5
1966	128,058	75,770	72,895	3,979	68,915	2,875	52,288	59.2	56.9	3.8
1967	129,874	77,347	74,372	3,844	70,527	2,975	52,527	59.6	57.3	3.8
1968	132,028	78,737	75,920	3,817	72,103	2,817	53,291	59.6	57.5	3.6
1969	134,335	80,734	77,902	3,606	74,296	2,832	53,602	60.1	58.0	3.5
1970	137,085	82,771	78,678	3,463	75,215	4,093	54,315	60.4	57.4	4.9
1971	140,216	84,382	79,367	3,394	75,972	5,016	55,834	60.2	56.6	5.9
1972	144,126	87,034	82,153	3,484	78,669	4,882	57,091	60.4	57.0	5.6
1973	147,096	89,429	85,064	3,470	81,594	4,365	57,667	60.8	57.8	4.9
1974	150,120	91,949	86,794	3,515	83,279	5,156	58,171	61.3	57.8	5.6
1975	153,153	93,775	85,846	3,408	82,438	7,929	59,377	61.2	56.1	8.5
1976	156,150	96,158	88,752	3,331	85,421	7,406	59,991	61.6	56.8	7.7
1977	159,033	99,009	92,017	3,283	88,734	6,991	60,025	62.3	57.9	7.1
1978	161,910	102,251	96,048	3,387	92,661	6,202	59,659	63.2	59.3	6.1
1979	164,863	104,962	98,824	3,347	95,477	6,137	59,900	63.7	59.9	5.8
1980	167,745	106,940	99,303	3,364	95,938	7,637	60,806	63.8	59.2	7.1
1981	170,130	108,670	100,397	3,368	97,030	8,273	61,460	63.9	59.0	7.6
1982	172,271	110,204	99,526	3,401	96,125	10,678	62,067	64.0	57.8	9.7
1983	174,215	111,550	100,834	3,383	97,450	10,717	62,665	64.0	57.9	9.6
1984	176,383	113,544	105,005	3,321	101,685	8,539	62,839	64.4	59.5	7.5
1985	178,206	115,461	107,150	3,179	103,971	8,312	62,744	64.8	60.1	7.2
1986	180,587	117,834	109,597	3,163	106,434	8,237	62,752	65.3	60.7	7.0
1987	182,753	119,865	112,440	3,208	109,232	7,425	62,888	65.6	61.5	6.2
1988	184,613	121,669	114,968	3,169	111,800	6,701	62,944	65.9	62.3	5.5
1989	186,393	123,869	117,342	3,199	114,142	6,528	62,523	66.5	63.0	5.3

[1] Not seasonally adjusted.
[2] Civilian labor force as percent of civilian noninstitutional population.
[3] Civilian employment as percent of civilian noninstitutional population.
[4] Unemployed as percent of civilian labor force.

See next page for continuation of table.

TABLE B-11. Civilian population and labor force, 1929-2014—*Continued*

[Monthly data seasonally adjusted, except as noted]

Year or month	Civilian noninstitu- tional population [1]	Civilian labor force					Not in labor force	Civilian labor force participa- tion rate [2]	Civilian employ- ment/ population ratio [3]	Unemploy- ment rate, civilian workers [4]
		Total	Employment			Unemploy- ment				
			Total	Agricultural	Non- agricultural					
	Thousands of persons 16 years of age and over							Percent		
1990	189,164	125,840	118,793	3,223	115,570	7,047	63,324	66.5	62.8	5.6
1991	190,925	126,346	117,718	3,269	114,449	8,628	64,578	66.2	61.7	6.8
1992	192,805	128,105	118,492	3,247	115,245	9,613	64,700	66.4	61.5	7.5
1993	194,838	129,200	120,259	3,115	117,144	8,940	65,638	66.3	61.7	6.9
1994	196,814	131,056	123,060	3,409	119,651	7,996	65,758	66.6	62.5	6.1
1995	198,584	132,304	124,900	3,440	121,460	7,404	66,280	66.6	62.9	5.6
1996	200,591	133,943	126,708	3,443	123,264	7,236	66,647	66.8	63.2	5.4
1997	203,133	136,297	129,558	3,399	126,159	6,739	66,837	67.1	63.8	4.9
1998	205,220	137,673	131,463	3,378	128,085	6,210	67,547	67.1	64.1	4.5
1999	207,753	139,368	133,488	3,281	130,207	5,880	68,385	67.1	64.3	4.2
2000 [5]	212,577	142,583	136,891	2,464	134,427	5,692	69,994	67.1	64.4	4.0
2001	215,092	143,734	136,933	2,299	134,635	6,801	71,359	66.8	63.7	4.7
2002	217,570	144,863	136,485	2,311	134,174	8,378	72,707	66.6	62.7	5.8
2003	221,168	146,510	137,736	2,275	135,461	8,774	74,658	66.2	62.3	6.0
2004	223,357	147,401	139,252	2,232	137,020	8,149	75,956	66.0	62.3	5.5
2005	226,082	149,320	141,730	2,197	139,532	7,591	76,762	66.0	62.7	5.1
2006	228,815	151,428	144,427	2,206	142,221	7,001	77,387	66.2	63.1	4.6
2007	231,867	153,124	146,047	2,095	143,952	7,078	78,743	66.0	63.0	4.6
2008	233,788	154,287	145,362	2,168	143,194	8,924	79,501	66.0	62.2	5.8
2009	235,801	154,142	139,877	2,103	137,775	14,265	81,659	65.4	59.3	9.3
2010	237,830	153,889	139,064	2,206	136,858	14,825	83,941	64.7	58.5	9.6
2011	239,618	153,617	139,869	2,254	137,615	13,747	86,001	64.1	58.4	8.9
2012	243,284	154,975	142,469	2,186	140,283	12,506	88,310	63.7	58.6	8.1
2013	245,679	155,389	143,929	2,130	141,799	11,460	90,290	63.2	58.6	7.4
2014	247,947	155,922	146,305	2,237	144,068	9,617	92,025	62.9	59.0	6.2
2012: Jan	242,269	154,445	141,633	2,206	139,423	12,812	87,824	63.7	58.5	8.3
Feb	242,435	154,739	141,911	2,196	139,771	12,828	87,696	63.8	58.5	8.3
Mar	242,604	154,765	142,069	2,251	139,847	12,696	87,839	63.8	58.6	8.2
Apr	242,784	154,589	141,953	2,215	139,716	12,636	88,195	63.7	58.5	8.2
May	242,966	154,899	142,231	2,297	139,945	12,668	88,066	63.8	58.5	8.2
June	243,155	155,088	142,400	2,236	140,156	12,688	88,068	63.8	58.6	8.2
July	243,354	154,927	142,270	2,223	139,994	12,657	88,427	63.7	58.5	8.2
Aug	243,566	154,726	142,277	2,108	140,066	12,449	88,840	63.5	58.4	8.0
Sept	243,772	155,060	142,953	2,165	140,819	12,106	88,713	63.6	58.6	7.8
Oct	243,983	155,491	143,350	2,152	141,379	12,141	88,491	63.7	58.8	7.8
Nov	244,174	155,305	143,279	2,101	141,154	12,026	88,870	63.6	58.7	7.7
Dec	244,350	155,553	143,280	2,053	141,229	12,272	88,797	63.7	58.6	7.9
2013: Jan	244,663	155,825	143,328	2,053	141,208	12,497	88,838	63.7	58.6	8.0
Feb	244,828	155,396	143,429	2,077	141,379	11,967	89,432	63.5	58.6	7.7
Mar	244,995	155,026	143,374	2,030	141,291	11,653	89,969	63.3	58.5	7.5
Apr	245,175	155,401	143,665	2,059	141,616	11,735	89,774	63.4	58.6	7.6
May	245,363	155,562	143,868	2,109	141,819	11,671	89,801	63.4	58.6	7.5
June	245,552	155,761	144,025	2,111	141,900	11,736	89,791	63.4	58.7	7.5
July	245,756	155,632	144,275	2,188	142,036	11,357	90,124	63.3	58.7	7.3
Aug	245,959	155,529	144,288	2,204	141,994	11,241	90,430	63.2	58.7	7.2
Sept	246,168	155,548	144,297	2,186	142,134	11,251	90,620	63.2	58.6	7.2
Oct	246,381	154,615	143,453	2,171	141,450	11,161	91,766	62.8	58.2	7.2
Nov	246,567	155,304	144,490	2,104	142,358	10,814	91,263	63.0	58.6	7.0
Dec	246,745	155,047	144,671	2,211	142,460	10,376	91,698	62.8	58.6	6.7
2014: Jan	246,915	155,486	145,206	2,171	143,010	10,280	91,429	63.0	58.8	6.6
Feb	247,085	155,688	145,301	2,148	143,196	10,387	91,398	63.0	58.8	6.7
Mar	247,258	156,180	145,796	2,155	143,560	10,384	91,077	63.2	59.0	6.6
Apr	247,439	155,420	145,724	2,167	143,566	9,696	92,019	62.8	58.9	6.2
May	247,622	155,629	145,868	2,054	143,843	9,761	91,993	62.8	58.9	6.3
June	247,814	155,700	146,247	2,165	144,078	9,453	92,114	62.8	59.0	6.1
July	248,023	156,048	146,401	2,161	144,192	9,648	91,975	62.9	59.0	6.2
Aug	248,229	156,018	146,451	2,265	144,111	9,568	92,210	62.9	59.0	6.1
Sept	248,446	155,845	146,607	2,377	144,254	9,237	92,601	62.7	59.0	5.9
Oct	248,657	156,243	147,260	2,402	144,982	8,983	92,414	62.8	59.2	5.7
Nov	248,844	156,402	147,331	2,392	144,939	9,071	92,442	62.9	59.2	5.8
Dec	249,027	156,129	147,442	2,358	145,101	8,688	92,898	62.7	59.2	5.6

[5] Beginning in 2000, data for agricultural employment are for agricultural and related industries; data for this series and for nonagricultural employment are not strictly comparable with data for earlier years. Because of independent seasonal adjustment for these two series, monthly data will not add to total civilian employment.

Note: Labor force data in Tables B–11 through B–13 are based on household interviews and usually relate to the calendar week that includes the 12th of the month. Historical comparability is affected by revisions to population controls, changes in occupational and industry classification, and other changes to the survey. In recent years, updated population controls have been introduced annually with the release of January data, so data are not strictly comparable with earlier periods. Particularly notable changes were introduced for data in the years 1953, 1960, 1962, 1972, 1973, 1978, 1980, 1990, 1994, 1997, 1998, 2000, 2003, 2008 and 2012. For definitions of terms, area samples used, historical comparability of the data, comparability with other series, etc., see *Employment and Earnings* or concepts and methodology of the CPS at http://www.bls.gov/cps/documentation.htm#concepts.

Source: Department of Labor (Bureau of Labor Statistics).

TABLE B-12. Civilian unemployment rate, 1970–2014

[Percent [1]; monthly data seasonally adjusted, except as noted]

Year or month	All civilian workers	Males			Females			Both sexes 16–19 years	By race				Hispanic or Latino ethnicity [3]	Married men, spouse present	Women who maintain families [4]
		Total	16–19 years	20 years and over	Total	16–19 years	20 years and over		White [2]	Black and other [2]	Black or African American [2]	Asian [2]			
1970	4.9	4.4	15.0	3.5	5.9	15.6	4.8	15.3	4.5	8.2				2.6	5.4
1971	5.9	5.3	16.6	4.4	6.9	17.2	5.7	16.9	5.4	9.9				3.2	7.3
1972	5.6	5.0	15.9	4.0	6.6	16.7	5.4	16.2	5.1	10.0	10.4			2.8	7.2
1973	4.9	4.2	13.9	3.3	6.0	15.3	4.9	14.5	4.3	9.0	9.4		7.5	2.3	7.1
1974	5.6	4.9	15.6	3.8	6.7	16.6	5.5	16.0	5.0	9.9	10.5		8.1	2.7	7.0
1975	8.5	7.9	20.1	6.8	9.3	19.7	8.0	19.9	7.8	13.8	14.8		12.2	5.1	10.0
1976	7.7	7.1	19.2	5.9	8.6	18.7	7.4	19.0	7.0	13.1	14.0		11.5	4.2	10.1
1977	7.1	6.3	17.3	5.2	8.2	18.3	7.0	17.8	6.2	13.1	14.0		10.1	3.6	9.4
1978	6.1	5.3	15.8	4.3	7.2	17.1	6.0	16.4	5.2	11.9	12.8		9.1	2.8	8.5
1979	5.8	5.1	15.9	4.2	6.8	16.4	5.7	16.1	5.1	11.3	12.3		8.3	2.8	8.3
1980	7.1	6.9	18.3	5.9	7.4	17.2	6.4	17.8	6.3	13.1	14.3		10.1	4.2	9.2
1981	7.6	7.4	20.1	6.3	7.9	19.0	6.8	19.6	6.7	14.2	15.6		10.4	4.3	10.4
1982	9.7	9.9	24.4	8.8	9.4	21.9	8.3	23.2	8.6	17.3	18.9		13.8	6.5	11.7
1983	9.6	9.9	23.3	8.9	9.2	21.3	8.1	22.4	8.4	17.8	19.5		13.7	6.5	12.2
1984	7.5	7.4	19.6	6.6	7.6	18.0	6.8	18.9	6.5	14.4	15.9		10.7	4.6	10.3
1985	7.2	7.0	19.5	6.2	7.4	17.6	6.6	18.6	6.2	13.7	15.1		10.5	4.3	10.4
1986	7.0	6.9	19.0	6.1	7.1	17.6	6.2	18.3	6.0	13.1	14.5		10.6	4.4	9.8
1987	6.2	6.2	17.8	5.4	6.2	15.9	5.4	16.9	5.3	11.6	13.0		8.8	3.9	9.2
1988	5.5	5.5	16.0	4.8	5.6	14.4	4.9	15.3	4.7	10.4	11.7		8.2	3.3	8.1
1989	5.3	5.2	15.9	4.5	5.4	14.0	4.7	15.0	4.5	10.0	11.4		8.0	3.0	8.1
1990	5.6	5.7	16.3	5.0	5.5	14.7	4.9	15.5	4.8	10.1	11.4		8.2	3.4	8.3
1991	6.8	7.2	19.8	6.4	6.4	17.5	5.7	18.7	6.1	11.1	12.5		10.0	4.4	9.3
1992	7.5	7.9	21.5	7.1	7.0	18.6	6.3	20.1	6.6	12.7	14.2		11.6	5.1	10.0
1993	6.9	7.2	20.4	6.4	6.6	17.5	5.9	19.0	6.1	11.7	13.0		10.8	4.4	9.7
1994	6.1	6.2	19.0	5.4	6.0	16.2	5.4	17.6	5.3	10.5	11.5		9.9	3.7	8.9
1995	5.6	5.6	18.4	4.8	5.6	16.1	4.9	17.3	4.9	9.6	10.4		9.3	3.3	8.0
1996	5.4	5.4	18.1	4.6	5.4	15.2	4.8	16.7	4.7	9.3	10.5		8.9	3.0	8.2
1997	4.9	4.9	16.9	4.2	5.0	15.0	4.4	16.0	4.2	8.8	10.0		7.7	2.7	8.1
1998	4.5	4.4	16.2	3.7	4.6	12.9	4.1	14.6	3.9	7.8	8.9		7.2	2.4	7.2
1999	4.2	4.1	14.7	3.5	4.3	13.2	3.8	13.9	3.7	7.0	8.0		6.4	2.2	6.4
2000	4.0	3.9	14.0	3.3	4.1	12.1	3.6	13.1	3.5		7.6	3.6	5.7	2.0	5.9
2001	4.7	4.8	16.0	4.2	4.7	13.4	4.1	14.7	4.2		8.6	4.5	6.6	2.7	6.6
2002	5.8	5.9	18.1	5.3	5.6	14.9	5.1	16.5	5.1		10.2	5.9	7.5	3.6	8.0
2003	6.0	6.3	19.3	5.6	5.7	15.6	5.1	17.5	5.2		10.8	6.0	7.7	3.8	8.5
2004	5.5	5.6	18.4	5.0	5.4	15.5	4.9	17.0	4.8		10.4	4.4	7.0	3.1	8.0
2005	5.1	5.1	18.6	4.4	5.1	14.5	4.6	16.6	4.4		10.0	4.0	6.0	2.8	7.8
2006	4.6	4.6	16.9	4.0	4.6	13.8	4.1	15.4	4.0		8.9	3.0	5.2	2.4	7.1
2007	4.6	4.7	17.6	4.1	4.5	13.8	4.0	15.7	4.1		8.3	3.2	5.6	2.5	6.5
2008	5.8	6.1	21.2	5.4	5.4	16.2	4.9	18.7	5.2		10.1	4.0	7.6	3.4	8.0
2009	9.3	10.3	27.8	9.6	8.1	20.7	7.5	24.3	8.5		14.8	7.3	12.1	6.6	11.5
2010	9.6	10.5	28.8	9.8	8.6	22.8	8.0	25.9	8.7		16.0	7.5	12.5	6.8	12.3
2011	8.9	9.4	27.2	8.7	8.5	21.7	7.9	24.4	7.9		15.8	7.0	11.5	5.8	12.4
2012	8.1	8.2	26.8	7.5	7.9	21.1	7.3	24.0	7.2		13.8	5.9	10.3	4.9	11.4
2013	7.4	7.6	25.5	7.0	7.1	20.3	6.5	22.9	6.5		13.1	5.2	9.1	4.3	10.2
2014	6.2	6.3	21.4	5.7	6.1	17.7	5.6	19.6	5.3		11.3	5.0	7.4	3.4	8.6
2013: Jan	8.0	8.2	27.0	7.5	7.8	20.8	7.3	23.9	7.1		13.7	6.4	9.7	4.6	11.3
Feb	7.7	7.8	27.1	7.0	7.6	23.2	7.0	25.2	6.8		13.9	6.0	9.6	4.5	11.0
Mar	7.5	7.5	25.8	6.9	7.5	22.5	6.9	24.1	6.7		13.1	5.0	9.3	4.2	10.7
Apr	7.6	7.8	26.2	7.1	7.3	22.0	6.7	24.1	6.7		13.1	5.3	9.2	4.4	10.3
May	7.5	7.8	26.8	7.1	7.1	21.5	6.5	24.2	6.7		13.4	4.5	9.0	4.4	9.9
June	7.5	7.7	26.9	7.0	7.3	19.5	6.8	23.3	6.6		13.8	4.7	9.0	4.3	10.7
July	7.3	7.7	26.7	7.0	6.9	19.6	6.4	23.2	6.5		12.4	5.4	9.3	4.3	10.5
Aug	7.2	7.7	24.9	7.0	6.7	20.1	6.2	22.5	6.4		13.0	5.2	9.2	4.3	11.0
Sept	7.2	7.7	24.0	7.1	6.7	18.0	6.2	21.1	6.3		13.1	5.4	9.0	4.4	8.8
Oct	7.2	7.6	24.8	6.9	6.8	19.4	6.3	22.2	6.3		13.0	5.3	9.0	4.5	9.5
Nov	7.0	7.2	23.8	6.7	6.6	18.2	6.2	20.9	6.1		12.4	5.2	8.7	4.2	9.7
Dec	6.7	6.8	21.3	6.3	6.5	19.5	6.0	20.4	6.0		11.8	4.1	8.4	3.9	8.7
2014: Jan	6.6	6.8	22.9	6.3	6.4	18.8	5.9	20.8	5.7		12.1	4.8	8.3	3.8	9.1
Feb	6.7	6.9	24.2	6.3	6.4	18.5	5.9	21.3	5.8		12.0	5.9	8.1	3.8	9.1
Mar	6.6	6.7	24.0	6.0	6.6	17.7	6.2	20.9	5.7		12.2	5.4	7.9	3.7	9.0
Apr	6.2	6.4	21.0	5.9	6.1	17.2	5.7	19.1	5.3		11.4	5.9	7.5	3.5	8.5
May	6.3	6.4	20.7	5.9	6.2	17.7	5.7	19.2	5.4		11.4	5.6	7.7	3.3	8.4
June	6.1	6.3	22.7	5.7	5.9	18.7	5.3	20.7	5.3		10.7	4.8	7.6	3.4	8.1
July	6.2	6.2	21.8	5.7	6.1	18.2	5.7	20.0	5.3		11.4	4.2	7.6	3.3	9.1
Aug	6.1	6.2	21.2	5.7	6.1	17.6	5.6	19.4	5.3		11.6	4.6	7.4	3.2	9.3
Sept	5.9	5.9	21.8	5.3	6.0	17.8	5.5	19.8	5.1		11.0	4.5	7.0	2.9	8.3
Oct	5.7	5.6	19.5	5.1	5.9	17.8	5.4	18.7	4.9		10.9	5.0	6.8	3.0	8.7
Nov	5.8	5.9	17.8	5.4	5.7	17.2	5.2	17.5	4.9		11.0	4.7	6.6	3.2	8.2
Dec	5.6	5.8	19.2	5.3	5.3	14.2	5.0	16.8	4.8		10.4	4.2	6.5	3.0	7.8

[1] Unemployed as percent of civilian labor force in group specified.
[2] Beginning in 2003, persons who selected this race group only. Prior to 2003, persons who selected more than one race were included in the group they identified as the main race. Data for "black or African American" were for "black" prior to 2003. Data discontinued for "black and other" series. See *Employment and Earnings* or concepts and methodology of the CPS at http://www.bls.gov/cps/documentation.htm#concepts for details.
[3] Persons whose ethnicity is identified as Hispanic or Latino may be of any race.
[4] Not seasonally adjusted.

Note: Data relate to persons 16 years of age and over.
See Note, Table B–11.

Source: Department of Labor (Bureau of Labor Statistics).

TABLE B-13. Unemployment by duration and reason, 1970–2014

[Thousands of persons, except as noted; monthly data seasonally adjusted [1]]

Year or month	Un-employ-ment	Duration of unemployment						Reason for unemployment					
		Less than 5 weeks	5–14 weeks	15–26 weeks	27 weeks and over	Average (mean) duration (weeks) [2]	Median duration (weeks)	Job losers [3]			Job leavers	Re-entrants	New entrants
								Total	On layoff	Other			
1970	4,093	2,139	1,290	428	235	8.6	4.9	1,811	675	1,137	550	1,228	504
1971	5,016	2,245	1,585	668	519	11.3	6.3	2,323	735	1,588	590	1,472	630
1972	4,882	2,242	1,472	601	566	12.0	6.2	2,108	582	1,526	641	1,456	677
1973	4,365	2,224	1,314	483	343	10.0	5.2	1,694	472	1,221	683	1,340	649
1974	5,156	2,604	1,597	574	381	9.8	5.2	2,242	746	1,495	768	1,463	681
1975	7,929	2,940	2,484	1,303	1,203	14.2	8.4	4,386	1,671	2,714	827	1,892	823
1976	7,406	2,844	2,196	1,018	1,348	15.8	8.2	3,679	1,050	2,628	903	1,928	895
1977	6,991	2,919	2,132	913	1,028	14.3	7.0	3,166	865	2,300	909	1,963	953
1978	6,202	2,865	1,923	766	648	11.9	5.9	2,585	712	1,873	874	1,857	885
1979	6,137	2,950	1,946	706	535	10.8	5.4	2,635	851	1,784	880	1,806	817
1980	7,637	3,295	2,470	1,052	820	11.9	6.5	3,947	1,488	2,459	891	1,927	872
1981	8,273	3,449	2,539	1,122	1,162	13.7	6.9	4,267	1,430	2,837	923	2,102	981
1982	10,678	3,883	3,311	1,708	1,776	15.6	8.7	6,268	2,127	4,141	840	2,384	1,185
1983	10,717	3,570	2,937	1,652	2,559	20.0	10.1	6,258	1,780	4,478	830	2,412	1,216
1984	8,539	3,350	2,451	1,104	1,634	18.2	7.9	4,421	1,171	3,250	823	2,184	1,110
1985	8,312	3,498	2,509	1,025	1,280	15.6	6.8	4,139	1,157	2,982	877	2,256	1,039
1986	8,237	3,448	2,557	1,045	1,187	15.0	6.9	4,033	1,090	2,943	1,015	2,160	1,029
1987	7,425	3,246	2,196	943	1,040	14.5	6.5	3,566	943	2,623	965	1,974	920
1988	6,701	3,084	2,007	801	809	13.5	5.9	3,092	851	2,241	983	1,809	816
1989	6,528	3,174	1,978	730	646	11.9	4.8	2,983	850	2,133	1,024	1,843	677
1990	7,047	3,265	2,257	822	703	12.0	5.3	3,387	1,028	2,359	1,041	1,930	688
1991	8,628	3,480	2,791	1,246	1,111	13.7	6.8	4,694	1,292	3,402	1,004	2,139	792
1992	9,613	3,376	2,830	1,453	1,954	17.7	8.7	5,389	1,260	4,129	1,002	2,285	937
1993	8,940	3,262	2,584	1,297	1,798	18.0	8.3	4,848	1,115	3,733	976	2,198	919
1994	7,996	2,728	2,408	1,237	1,623	18.8	9.2	3,815	977	2,838	791	2,786	604
1995	7,404	2,700	2,342	1,085	1,278	16.6	8.3	3,476	1,030	2,446	824	2,525	579
1996	7,236	2,633	2,287	1,053	1,262	16.7	8.3	3,370	1,021	2,349	774	2,512	580
1997	6,739	2,538	2,138	995	1,067	15.8	8.0	3,037	931	2,106	795	2,338	569
1998	6,210	2,622	1,950	763	875	14.5	6.7	2,822	866	1,957	734	2,132	520
1999	5,880	2,568	1,832	755	725	13.4	6.4	2,622	848	1,774	783	2,005	469
2000	5,692	2,558	1,815	669	649	12.6	5.9	2,517	852	1,664	780	1,961	434
2001	6,801	2,853	2,196	951	801	13.1	6.8	3,476	1,067	2,409	835	2,031	459
2002	8,378	2,893	2,580	1,369	1,535	16.6	9.1	4,607	1,124	3,483	866	2,368	536
2003	8,774	2,785	2,612	1,442	1,936	19.2	10.1	4,838	1,121	3,717	818	2,477	641
2004	8,149	2,696	2,382	1,293	1,779	19.6	9.8	4,197	998	3,199	858	2,408	686
2005	7,591	2,667	2,304	1,130	1,490	18.4	8.9	3,667	933	2,734	872	2,386	666
2006	7,001	2,614	2,121	1,031	1,235	16.8	8.3	3,321	921	2,400	827	2,237	616
2007	7,078	2,542	2,232	1,061	1,243	16.8	8.5	3,515	976	2,539	793	2,142	627
2008	8,924	2,932	2,804	1,427	1,761	17.9	9.4	4,789	1,176	3,614	896	2,472	766
2009	14,265	3,165	3,828	2,775	4,496	24.4	15.1	9,160	1,630	7,530	882	3,187	1,035
2010	14,825	2,771	3,267	2,371	6,415	33.0	21.4	9,250	1,431	7,819	889	3,466	1,220
2011	13,747	2,677	2,993	2,061	6,016	39.3	21.4	8,106	1,230	6,876	956	3,401	1,284
2012	12,506	2,644	2,866	1,859	5,136	39.4	19.3	6,877	1,183	5,694	967	3,345	1,316
2013	11,460	2,584	2,759	1,807	4,310	36.5	17.0	6,073	1,136	4,937	932	3,207	1,247
2014	9,617	2,471	2,432	1,497	3,218	33.7	14.0	4,878	1,007	3,871	824	2,829	1,086
2013: Jan	12,497	2,757	3,107	1,862	4,683	35.5	16.2	6,627	1,183	5,444	1,000	3,550	1,283
Feb	11,967	2,712	2,769	1,723	4,695	36.7	17.5	6,443	1,095	5,348	957	3,309	1,271
Mar	11,653	2,478	2,840	1,773	4,531	36.9	17.7	6,260	1,114	5,147	983	3,163	1,296
Apr	11,735	2,502	2,870	1,934	4,381	36.5	17.1	6,329	1,183	5,145	873	3,194	1,276
May	11,671	2,664	2,666	1,962	4,349	36.9	17.0	6,111	989	5,122	933	3,317	1,270
June	11,736	2,679	2,852	1,917	4,352	35.9	16.6	6,087	1,180	4,906	1,024	3,300	1,259
July	11,357	2,507	2,790	1,791	4,269	37.1	16.3	5,897	1,182	4,715	961	3,218	1,244
Aug	11,241	2,477	2,725	1,712	4,297	37.4	16.8	5,909	1,019	4,890	877	3,105	1,302
Sept	11,251	2,609	2,657	1,817	4,138	37.2	16.5	5,857	1,106	4,750	978	3,157	1,199
Oct	11,161	2,798	2,659	1,772	4,046	35.5	16.1	6,214	1,524	4,690	859	3,064	1,212
Nov	10,814	2,420	2,581	1,719	4,059	36.8	17.0	5,762	1,118	4,643	880	3,047	1,154
Dec	10,376	2,323	2,525	1,680	3,877	36.8	17.0	5,421	1,014	4,408	860	3,027	1,198
2014: Jan	10,280	2,449	2,428	1,699	3,628	35.3	15.9	5,354	996	4,359	815	2,911	1,181
Feb	10,387	2,388	2,558	1,597	3,804	36.9	16.2	5,403	1,037	4,366	816	2,972	1,232
Mar	10,384	2,477	2,584	1,669	3,682	35.2	15.9	5,416	1,046	4,370	807	3,027	1,157
Apr	9,696	2,451	2,346	1,509	3,413	34.8	15.6	5,153	1,014	4,139	786	2,631	1,052
May	9,761	2,553	2,401	1,451	3,351	34.3	14.5	4,959	1,002	3,958	872	2,869	1,063
June	9,453	2,423	2,418	1,516	3,076	33.3	13.2	4,791	1,031	3,760	848	2,701	1,059
July	9,648	2,583	2,435	1,423	3,166	32.5	13.5	4,830	992	3,838	857	2,860	1,080
Aug	9,568	2,609	2,444	1,500	2,966	31.9	13.3	4,813	1,106	3,708	851	2,845	1,064
Sept	9,237	2,372	2,495	1,423	2,951	31.8	13.3	4,521	924	3,597	816	2,805	1,094
Oct	8,983	2,455	2,322	1,416	2,904	32.9	13.5	4,349	847	3,501	782	2,856	1,058
Nov	9,071	2,505	2,378	1,403	2,822	33.0	12.8	4,480	1,070	3,410	835	2,761	1,045
Dec	8,688	2,375	2,293	1,274	2,785	32.8	12.6	4,325	959	3,366	798	2,701	971

[1] Because of independent seasonal adjustment of the various series, detail will not sum to totals.
[2] Beginning with January 2011, includes unemployment durations of up to 5 years; prior data are for up to 2 years.
[3] Beginning with January 1994, job losers and persons who completed temporary jobs.

Note: Data relate to persons 16 years of age and over.
See Note, Table B–11.

Source: Department of Labor (Bureau of Labor Statistics).

TABLE B–14. Employees on nonagricultural payrolls, by major industry, 1970–2014

[Thousands of jobs; monthly data seasonally adjusted]

Year or month	Total non-agricultural employment	Private industries									
		Total private	Goods-producing industries						Private service-providing industries		
			Total	Mining and logging	Construction	Manufacturing			Total	Trade, transportation, and utilities [1]	
						Total	Durable goods	Non-durable goods		Total	Retail trade
1970	71,006	58,318	22,179	677	3,654	17,848	10,762	7,086	36,139	14,144	7,463
1971	71,335	58,323	21,602	658	3,770	17,174	10,229	6,944	36,721	14,318	7,657
1972	73,798	60,333	22,299	672	3,957	17,669	10,630	7,039	38,034	14,788	8,038
1973	76,912	63,050	23,450	693	4,167	18,589	11,414	7,176	39,600	15,349	8,371
1974	78,389	64,086	23,364	755	4,095	18,514	11,432	7,082	40,721	15,693	8,536
1975	77,069	62,250	21,318	802	3,608	16,909	10,266	6,643	40,932	15,606	8,600
1976	79,502	64,501	22,025	832	3,662	17,531	10,640	6,891	42,476	16,128	8,966
1977	82,593	67,334	22,972	865	3,940	18,167	11,132	7,035	44,362	16,765	9,359
1978	86,826	71,014	24,156	902	4,322	18,932	11,770	7,162	46,858	17,658	9,879
1979	89,933	73,865	24,997	1,008	4,562	19,426	12,220	7,206	48,869	18,303	10,180
1980	90,533	74,158	24,263	1,077	4,454	18,733	11,679	7,054	49,895	18,413	10,244
1981	91,297	75,117	24,118	1,180	4,304	18,634	11,611	7,023	50,999	18,604	10,364
1982	89,689	73,706	22,550	1,163	4,024	17,363	10,610	6,753	51,156	18,457	10,372
1983	90,295	74,284	22,110	997	4,065	17,048	10,326	6,722	52,174	18,668	10,635
1984	94,548	78,389	23,435	1,014	4,501	17,920	11,050	6,870	54,954	19,653	11,223
1985	97,532	81,000	23,585	974	4,793	17,819	11,034	6,784	57,415	20,379	11,733
1986	99,500	82,661	23,318	829	4,937	17,552	10,795	6,757	59,343	20,795	12,078
1987	102,116	84,960	23,470	771	5,090	17,609	10,767	6,842	61,490	21,302	12,419
1988	105,378	87,838	23,909	770	5,233	17,906	10,969	6,938	63,929	21,974	12,808
1989	108,051	90,124	24,045	750	5,309	17,985	11,004	6,981	66,079	22,510	13,108
1990	109,527	91,112	23,723	765	5,263	17,695	10,737	6,958	67,389	22,666	13,182
1991	108,427	89,981	22,588	739	4,780	17,068	10,220	6,848	67,293	22,281	12,896
1992	108,802	90,015	22,095	689	4,608	16,799	9,946	6,853	67,921	22,125	12,828
1993	110,935	91,946	22,219	666	4,779	16,774	9,901	6,872	69,727	22,378	13,021
1994	114,398	95,124	22,774	659	5,095	17,020	10,132	6,889	72,350	23,128	13,491
1995	117,407	97,975	23,156	641	5,274	17,241	10,373	6,868	74,819	23,834	13,897
1996	119,836	100,297	23,409	637	5,536	17,237	10,486	6,751	76,888	24,239	14,143
1997	122,951	103,287	23,886	654	5,813	17,419	10,705	6,714	79,401	24,700	14,389
1998	126,157	106,248	24,354	645	6,149	17,560	10,911	6,649	81,894	25,186	14,609
1999	129,240	108,933	24,465	598	6,545	17,322	10,831	6,491	84,468	25,771	14,970
2000	132,019	111,230	24,649	599	6,787	17,263	10,877	6,386	86,581	26,225	15,280
2001	132,074	110,956	23,873	606	6,826	16,441	10,336	6,105	87,083	25,983	15,239
2002	130,628	109,115	22,557	583	6,716	15,259	9,485	5,774	86,558	25,497	15,025
2003	130,318	108,735	21,816	572	6,735	14,509	8,964	5,546	86,918	25,287	14,917
2004	131,749	110,128	21,882	591	6,976	14,315	8,925	5,390	88,246	25,533	15,058
2005	134,005	112,201	22,190	628	7,336	14,227	8,956	5,271	90,010	25,959	15,280
2006	136,398	114,424	22,530	684	7,691	14,155	8,981	5,174	91,894	26,276	15,353
2007	137,936	115,718	22,233	724	7,630	13,879	8,808	5,071	93,485	26,630	15,520
2008	137,170	114,661	21,335	767	7,162	13,406	8,463	4,943	93,326	26,293	15,283
2009	131,233	108,678	18,558	694	6,016	11,847	7,284	4,564	90,121	24,906	14,522
2010	130,275	107,785	17,751	705	5,518	11,528	7,064	4,464	90,034	24,636	14,440
2011	131,842	109,756	18,047	788	5,533	11,726	7,273	4,453	91,708	25,065	14,668
2012	134,104	112,184	18,420	848	5,646	11,927	7,470	4,457	93,763	25,476	14,841
2013	136,393	114,541	18,738	863	5,856	12,020	7,548	4,472	95,803	25,862	15,079
2014 P	139,042	117,179	19,223	896	6,138	12,188	7,685	4,503	97,956	26,383	15,364
2013: Jan	135,293	113,416	18,581	855	5,746	11,980	7,516	4,464	94,835	25,683	14,939
Feb	135,607	113,713	18,660	860	5,798	12,002	7,527	4,475	95,053	25,699	14,956
Mar	135,722	113,852	18,681	860	5,815	12,006	7,535	4,471	95,171	25,690	14,951
Apr	135,909	114,046	18,676	857	5,813	12,006	7,537	4,469	95,370	25,723	14,973
May	136,128	114,271	18,700	860	5,833	12,007	7,537	4,470	95,571	25,756	15,004
June	136,255	114,443	18,722	861	5,856	12,005	7,538	4,467	95,721	25,800	15,043
July	136,419	114,605	18,698	861	5,854	11,983	7,513	4,470	95,907	25,836	15,084
Aug	136,675	114,818	18,741	864	5,866	12,011	7,545	4,466	96,077	25,899	15,120
Sept	136,825	114,986	18,781	866	5,893	12,022	7,559	4,463	96,205	25,966	15,150
Oct	137,050	115,221	18,827	869	5,918	12,040	7,570	4,470	96,394	26,001	15,185
Nov	137,367	115,524	18,896	871	5,953	12,072	7,587	4,485	96,628	26,065	15,217
Dec	137,476	115,648	18,894	871	5,937	12,086	7,593	4,493	96,754	26,159	15,274
2014: Jan	137,642	115,831	18,984	876	6,006	12,102	7,597	4,505	96,847	26,155	15,257
Feb	137,830	116,006	19,031	877	6,032	12,122	7,614	4,508	96,975	26,141	15,238
Mar	138,055	116,229	19,073	880	6,062	12,131	7,628	4,503	97,156	26,190	15,265
Apr	138,385	116,542	19,131	886	6,103	12,142	7,640	4,502	97,411	26,260	15,308
May	138,621	116,780	19,156	888	6,114	12,154	7,659	4,495	97,624	26,297	15,318
June	138,907	117,052	19,190	892	6,121	12,177	7,678	4,499	97,862	26,362	15,357
July	139,156	117,295	19,243	900	6,152	12,191	7,693	4,498	98,052	26,413	15,382
Aug	139,369	117,504	19,277	903	6,169	12,205	7,709	4,496	98,227	26,427	15,379
Sept	139,619	117,739	19,315	910	6,191	12,214	7,719	4,495	98,424	26,467	15,410
Oct	139,840	117,957	19,349	911	6,201	12,237	7,740	4,497	98,608	26,517	15,436
Nov	140,263	118,371	19,425	912	6,231	12,282	7,768	4,514	98,946	26,615	15,498
Dec P	140,592	118,691	19,498	915	6,275	12,308	7,789	4,519	99,193	26,669	15,505

[1] Includes wholesale trade, transportation and warehousing, and utilities, not shown separately.

Note: Data in Tables B–14 and B–15 are based on reports from employing establishments and relate to full- and part-time wage and salary workers in nonagricultural establishments who received pay for any part of the pay period that includes the 12th of the month. Not comparable with labor force data (Tables B–11 through B–13), which include proprietors, self-employed persons, unpaid family workers, and private household workers; which count persons as

See next page for continuation of table.

TABLE B–14. Employees on nonagricultural payrolls, by major industry, 1970–2014—*Continued*

[Thousands of jobs; monthly data seasonally adjusted]

Year or month	Private industries—Continued						Government			
	Private service-providing industries—Continued									
	Information	Financial activities	Professional and business services	Education and health services	Leisure and hospitality	Other services	Total	Federal	State	Local
1970	2,041	3,532	5,267	4,577	4,789	1,789	12,687	2,865	2,664	7,158
1971	2,009	3,651	5,328	4,675	4,914	1,827	13,012	2,828	2,747	7,437
1972	2,056	3,784	5,523	4,863	5,121	1,900	13,465	2,815	2,859	7,790
1973	2,135	3,920	5,774	5,092	5,341	1,990	13,862	2,794	2,923	8,146
1974	2,160	4,023	5,974	5,322	5,471	2,078	14,303	2,858	3,039	8,407
1975	2,061	4,047	6,034	5,497	5,544	2,144	14,820	2,882	3,179	8,758
1976	2,111	4,155	6,287	5,756	5,794	2,244	15,001	2,863	3,273	8,865
1977	2,185	4,348	6,587	6,052	6,065	2,359	15,258	2,859	3,377	9,023
1978	2,287	4,599	6,972	6,427	6,411	2,505	15,812	2,893	3,474	9,446
1979	2,375	4,843	7,312	6,768	6,631	2,637	16,068	2,894	3,541	9,633
1980	2,361	5,025	7,544	7,077	6,721	2,755	16,375	3,000	3,610	9,765
1981	2,382	5,163	7,782	7,364	6,840	2,865	16,180	2,922	3,640	9,619
1982	2,317	5,209	7,848	7,526	6,874	2,924	15,982	2,884	3,640	9,458
1983	2,253	5,334	8,039	7,781	7,078	3,021	16,011	2,915	3,662	9,434
1984	2,398	5,553	8,464	8,211	7,489	3,186	16,159	2,943	3,734	9,482
1985	2,437	5,815	8,871	8,679	7,869	3,366	16,533	3,014	3,832	9,687
1986	2,445	6,128	9,211	9,086	8,156	3,523	16,838	3,044	3,893	9,901
1987	2,507	6,385	9,608	9,543	8,446	3,699	17,156	3,089	3,967	10,100
1988	2,585	6,500	10,090	10,096	8,778	3,907	17,540	3,124	4,076	10,339
1989	2,622	6,562	10,555	10,652	9,062	4,116	17,927	3,136	4,182	10,609
1990	2,688	6,614	10,848	11,024	9,288	4,261	18,415	3,196	4,305	10,914
1991	2,677	6,561	10,714	11,556	9,256	4,249	18,545	3,110	4,355	11,081
1992	2,641	6,559	10,970	11,948	9,437	4,240	18,787	3,111	4,408	11,267
1993	2,668	6,742	11,495	12,362	9,732	4,350	18,989	3,063	4,488	11,438
1994	2,738	6,910	12,174	12,872	10,100	4,428	19,275	3,018	4,576	11,682
1995	2,843	6,866	12,844	13,360	10,501	4,572	19,432	2,949	4,635	11,849
1996	2,940	7,018	13,462	13,761	10,777	4,690	19,539	2,877	4,606	12,056
1997	3,084	7,255	14,335	14,185	11,018	4,825	19,664	2,806	4,582	12,276
1998	3,218	7,565	15,147	14,570	11,232	4,976	19,909	2,772	4,612	12,525
1999	3,419	7,753	15,957	14,939	11,543	5,087	20,307	2,769	4,709	12,829
2000	3,630	7,783	16,666	15,247	11,862	5,168	20,790	2,865	4,786	13,139
2001	3,629	7,900	16,476	15,801	12,036	5,258	21,118	2,764	4,905	13,449
2002	3,395	7,956	15,976	16,377	11,986	5,372	21,513	2,766	5,029	13,718
2003	3,188	8,078	15,987	16,805	12,173	5,401	21,583	2,761	5,002	13,820
2004	3,118	8,105	16,394	17,192	12,493	5,409	21,621	2,730	4,982	13,909
2005	3,061	8,197	16,954	17,630	12,816	5,395	21,804	2,732	5,032	14,041
2006	3,038	8,367	17,566	18,099	13,110	5,438	21,974	2,732	5,075	14,167
2007	3,032	8,348	17,942	18,613	13,427	5,494	22,218	2,734	5,122	14,362
2008	2,984	8,206	17,735	19,156	13,436	5,515	22,509	2,762	5,177	14,571
2009	2,804	7,838	16,579	19,550	13,077	5,367	22,555	2,832	5,169	14,554
2010	2,707	7,695	16,728	19,889	13,049	5,331	22,490	2,977	5,137	14,376
2011	2,674	7,697	17,332	20,228	13,353	5,360	22,086	2,859	5,078	14,150
2012	2,676	7,784	17,932	20,698	13,768	5,430	21,920	2,820	5,055	14,045
2013	2,706	7,886	18,515	21,097	14,254	5,483	21,853	2,769	5,046	14,037
2014 ᵖ	2,740	7,980	19,096	21,474	14,710	5,573	21,863	2,728	5,061	14,074
2013: Jan	2,668	7,838	18,217	20,937	14,035	5,457	21,877	2,807	5,033	14,037
Feb	2,700	7,851	18,306	20,954	14,085	5,458	21,894	2,811	5,046	14,037
Mar	2,699	7,857	18,361	20,999	14,115	5,450	21,870	2,792	5,054	14,024
Apr	2,698	7,869	18,422	21,049	14,153	5,456	21,863	2,794	5,049	14,020
May	2,710	7,882	18,490	21,066	14,196	5,471	21,857	2,776	5,049	14,032
June	2,707	7,888	18,526	21,067	14,253	5,480	21,812	2,769	5,034	14,009
July	2,718	7,905	18,569	21,102	14,293	5,484	21,814	2,760	5,027	14,027
Aug	2,691	7,901	18,600	21,162	14,332	5,492	21,857	2,752	5,044	14,061
Sept	2,709	7,900	18,625	21,162	14,342	5,501	21,839	2,750	5,049	14,040
Oct	2,721	7,909	18,671	21,188	14,395	5,509	21,829	2,741	5,052	14,036
Nov	2,728	7,912	18,737	21,231	14,442	5,513	21,843	2,744	5,058	14,041
Dec	2,724	7,914	18,735	21,230	14,466	5,526	21,828	2,743	5,056	14,029
2014: Jan	2,724	7,918	18,771	21,249	14,494	5,536	21,811	2,731	5,053	14,027
Feb	2,720	7,931	18,840	21,279	14,526	5,538	21,824	2,730	5,061	14,033
Mar	2,723	7,933	18,879	21,314	14,565	5,552	21,826	2,727	5,057	14,042
Apr	2,728	7,942	18,951	21,353	14,610	5,567	21,843	2,726	5,060	14,057
May	2,723	7,951	19,005	21,409	14,667	5,572	21,841	2,726	5,054	14,061
June	2,735	7,968	19,079	21,452	14,698	5,568	21,855	2,726	5,057	14,072
July	2,740	7,984	19,124	21,497	14,721	5,573	21,861	2,724	5,051	14,086
Aug	2,753	7,997	19,180	21,539	14,746	5,585	21,865	2,727	5,042	14,096
Sept	2,757	8,007	19,231	21,585	14,795	5,582	21,880	2,725	5,062	14,093
Oct	2,754	8,014	19,271	21,613	14,850	5,589	21,883	2,720	5,067	14,096
Nov	2,761	8,042	19,367	21,664	14,892	5,605	21,892	2,729	5,072	14,091
Dec ᵖ	2,765	8,051	19,447	21,712	14,939	5,610	21,901	2,731	5,080	14,090

Note (cont'd): employed when they are not at work because of industrial disputes, bad weather, etc., even if they are not paid for the time off; which are based on a sample of the working-age population; and which count persons only once—as employed, unemployed, or not in the labor force. In the data shown here, persons who work at more than one job are counted each time they appear on a payroll.

Establishment data for employment, hours, and earnings are classified based on the 2012 North American Industry Classification System (NAICS). For further description and details see *Employment and Earnings*.

Source: Department of Labor (Bureau of Labor Statistics).

TABLE B–15. Hours and earnings in private nonagricultural industries, 1970–2014 [1]

[Monthly data seasonally adjusted]

Year or month	Average weekly hours			Average hourly earnings			Average weekly earnings, total private			
	Total private	Manufacturing		Total private		Manu-facturing (current dollars)	Level		Percent change from year earlier	
		Total	Overtime	Current dollars	1982–84 dollars [2]		Current dollars	1982–84 dollars [2]	Current dollars	1982–84 dollars [2]
1970	37.0	39.8	2.9	$3.40	$8.72	$3.24	$125.79	$322.54	4.2	−1.4
1971	36.7	39.9	2.9	3.63	8.92	3.45	133.22	327.32	5.9	1.5
1972	36.9	40.6	3.4	3.90	9.26	3.70	143.87	341.73	8.0	4.4
1973	36.9	40.7	3.8	4.14	9.26	3.97	152.59	341.36	6.1	−.1
1974	36.4	40.0	3.2	4.43	8.93	4.31	161.61	325.83	5.9	−4.5
1975	36.0	39.5	2.6	4.73	8.74	4.71	170.29	314.77	5.4	−3.4
1976	36.1	40.1	3.1	5.06	8.85	5.10	182.65	319.32	7.3	1.4
1977	35.9	40.3	3.4	5.44	8.93	5.55	195.58	321.15	7.1	.6
1978	35.8	40.4	3.6	5.88	8.96	6.05	210.29	320.56	7.5	−.2
1979	35.6	40.2	3.3	6.34	8.67	6.57	225.69	308.74	7.3	−3.7
1980	35.2	39.6	2.8	6.85	8.26	7.15	241.07	290.80	6.8	−5.8
1981	35.2	39.8	2.8	7.44	8.14	7.87	261.53	286.14	8.5	−1.6
1982	34.7	38.9	2.3	7.87	8.12	8.36	273.10	281.84	4.4	−1.5
1983	34.9	40.1	2.9	8.20	8.22	8.70	286.43	287.00	4.9	1.8
1984	35.1	40.6	3.4	8.49	8.22	9.05	298.26	288.73	4.1	.6
1985	34.9	40.5	3.3	8.74	8.18	9.40	304.62	284.96	2.1	−1.3
1986	34.7	40.7	3.4	8.93	8.22	9.60	309.78	285.25	1.7	.1
1987	34.7	40.9	3.7	9.14	8.12	9.77	317.39	282.12	2.5	−1.1
1988	34.6	41.0	3.8	9.44	8.07	10.05	326.48	279.04	2.9	−1.1
1989	34.5	40.9	3.8	9.80	7.99	10.35	338.34	275.97	3.6	−1.1
1990	34.3	40.5	3.9	10.20	7.91	10.78	349.63	271.03	3.3	−1.8
1991	34.1	40.4	3.8	10.51	7.83	11.13	358.46	266.91	2.5	−1.5
1992	34.2	40.7	4.0	10.77	7.79	11.40	368.20	266.43	2.7	−.2
1993	34.3	41.1	4.4	11.05	7.78	11.70	378.89	266.64	2.9	.1
1994	34.5	41.7	5.0	11.34	7.79	12.04	391.17	268.66	3.2	.8
1995	34.3	41.3	4.7	11.65	7.78	12.34	400.04	267.05	2.3	−.6
1996	34.3	41.3	4.8	12.04	7.81	12.75	413.25	268.17	3.3	.4
1997	34.5	41.7	5.1	12.51	7.94	13.14	431.86	274.02	4.5	2.2
1998	34.5	41.4	4.8	13.01	8.15	13.45	448.59	280.90	3.9	2.5
1999	34.3	41.4	4.9	13.49	8.27	13.85	463.15	283.79	3.2	1.0
2000	34.3	41.3	4.7	14.02	8.30	14.32	480.99	284.78	3.9	.3
2001	34.0	40.3	4.0	14.54	8.38	14.76	493.74	284.58	2.7	−.1
2002	33.9	40.5	4.2	14.97	8.51	15.29	506.60	288.00	2.6	1.2
2003	33.7	40.4	4.2	15.37	8.55	15.74	517.82	288.00	2.2	.0
2004	33.7	40.8	4.6	15.69	8.50	16.14	528.89	286.66	2.1	−.5
2005	33.8	40.7	4.6	16.12	8.44	16.56	544.05	284.84	2.9	−.6
2006	33.9	41.1	4.4	16.75	8.50	16.81	567.39	287.97	4.3	1.1
2007	33.8	41.2	4.2	17.42	8.59	17.26	589.27	290.61	3.9	1.0
2008	33.6	40.8	3.7	18.07	8.56	17.75	607.53	287.86	3.1	−.9
2009	33.1	39.8	2.9	18.61	8.88	18.24	616.01	293.86	1.4	2.1
2010	33.4	41.1	3.8	19.05	8.90	18.61	636.25	297.36	3.3	1.2
2011	33.6	41.4	4.1	19.44	8.77	18.93	653.19	294.79	2.7	−.9
2012	33.7	41.7	4.2	19.74	8.73	19.08	665.82	294.31	1.9	−.2
2013	33.7	41.8	4.3	20.13	8.78	19.30	677.67	295.51	1.8	.4
2014 [p]	33.7	42.0	4.5	20.61	8.85	19.56	694.89	298.53	2.5	1.0
2013: Jan	33.6	41.7	4.3	19.94	8.76	19.15	669.98	294.23	1.3	−.2
Feb	33.8	41.9	4.4	19.99	8.72	19.22	675.66	294.82	2.3	.4
Mar	33.8	41.9	4.4	20.02	8.76	19.21	676.68	296.16	2.2	.9
Apr	33.7	41.8	4.3	20.04	8.79	19.22	675.35	296.26	1.7	.8
May	33.7	41.7	4.3	20.06	8.78	19.24	676.02	295.94	2.2	.9
June	33.7	41.8	4.3	20.12	8.78	19.28	678.04	295.75	2.0	.3
July	33.5	41.7	4.3	20.14	8.77	19.26	674.69	293.74	1.6	−.4
Aug	33.6	41.9	4.4	20.18	8.78	19.33	678.05	295.01	2.2	.7
Sept	33.7	41.8	4.3	20.22	8.79	19.35	681.41	296.12	2.5	1.5
Oct	33.6	41.9	4.4	20.26	8.81	19.37	680.74	295.86	2.3	1.5
Nov	33.7	42.0	4.5	20.31	8.82	19.42	684.45	297.24	2.3	1.2
Dec	33.6	41.9	4.5	20.34	8.81	19.44	683.42	295.96	1.9	.4
2014: Jan	33.5	41.6	4.4	20.40	8.82	19.44	683.40	295.55	2.0	.4
Feb	33.5	41.6	4.3	20.48	8.85	19.48	686.08	296.56	1.5	.6
Mar	33.7	42.0	4.5	20.50	8.84	19.52	690.85	298.06	2.1	.6
Apr	33.7	41.9	4.4	20.52	8.83	19.49	691.52	297.50	2.4	.4
May	33.7	42.2	4.6	20.55	8.81	19.53	692.54	296.93	2.4	.3
June	33.7	42.1	4.5	20.59	8.80	19.55	693.88	296.60	2.3	.3
July	33.7	42.0	4.4	20.63	8.81	19.59	695.23	296.96	3.0	1.1
Aug	33.7	42.0	4.4	20.68	8.86	19.63	696.92	298.45	2.8	1.2
Sept	33.7	42.1	4.5	20.68	8.85	19.62	696.92	298.16	2.3	.7
Oct	33.7	42.1	4.4	20.72	8.87	19.65	698.26	298.98	2.6	1.1
Nov	33.8	42.2	4.6	20.77	8.93	19.64	702.03	301.83	2.6	1.5
Dec [p]	33.9	42.1	4.6	20.73	8.96	19.61	702.75	303.68	2.8	2.6

[1] For production employees in goods-producing industries and for nonsupervisory employees in private, service-providing industries; total includes private industry groups shown in Table B–14.
[2] Current dollars divided by the consumer price index for urban wage earners and clerical workers on a 1982–84=100 base.

Note: See Note, Table B–14.

Source: Department of Labor (Bureau of Labor Statistics).

TABLE B-16. Productivity and related data, business and nonfarm business sectors, 1965-2014

[Index numbers, 2009=100; quarterly data seasonally adjusted]

Year or quarter	Output per hour of all persons — Business sector	Output per hour of all persons — Nonfarm business sector	Output[1] — Business sector	Output[1] — Nonfarm business sector	Hours of all persons[2] — Business sector	Hours of all persons[2] — Nonfarm business sector	Compensation per hour[3] — Business sector	Compensation per hour[3] — Nonfarm business sector	Real compensation per hour[4] — Business sector	Real compensation per hour[4] — Nonfarm business sector	Unit labor costs — Business sector	Unit labor costs — Nonfarm business sector	Implicit price deflator[5] — Business sector	Implicit price deflator[5] — Nonfarm business sector
1965	39.5	41.5	25.0	25.0	63.5	60.3	9.2	9.5	57.2	58.7	23.3	22.8	21.9	21.4
1966	41.1	43.0	26.7	26.8	65.1	62.4	9.8	10.0	59.4	60.5	23.9	23.3	22.4	21.8
1967	42.0	43.8	27.3	27.3	64.9	62.4	10.4	10.6	60.9	62.1	24.7	24.2	23.0	22.5
1968	43.5	45.3	28.7	28.8	65.9	63.5	11.2	11.4	63.0	64.1	25.7	25.1	23.9	23.4
1969	43.7	45.4	29.6	29.7	67.6	65.3	12.0	12.2	63.9	64.9	27.4	26.8	25.0	24.4
1970	44.6	46.1	29.5	29.6	66.3	64.3	12.9	13.0	65.0	65.7	28.9	28.3	26.1	25.5
1971	46.4	47.9	30.7	30.7	66.1	64.1	13.7	13.8	66.0	66.8	29.4	28.9	27.2	26.6
1972	47.9	49.5	32.7	32.8	68.1	66.2	14.5	14.7	67.9	68.9	30.3	29.7	28.1	27.4
1973	49.3	51.0	34.9	35.2	70.7	68.9	15.7	15.8	69.0	69.8	31.7	31.0	29.6	28.4
1974	48.5	50.2	34.4	34.6	70.9	69.0	17.1	17.3	68.0	68.8	35.3	34.5	32.5	31.4
1975	50.2	51.6	34.0	34.1	67.8	66.0	19.0	19.2	68.9	69.7	37.8	37.2	35.6	34.7
1976	51.9	53.3	36.3	36.5	70.1	68.4	20.5	20.6	70.4	71.0	39.5	38.7	37.5	36.6
1977	52.8	54.2	38.4	38.6	72.7	71.1	22.1	22.3	71.4	72.1	41.9	41.2	39.7	38.9
1978	53.4	55.0	40.8	41.1	76.5	74.8	24.0	24.2	72.3	73.2	44.9	44.1	42.5	41.5
1979	53.4	54.8	42.3	42.5	79.1	77.5	26.3	26.6	72.4	73.1	49.2	48.5	46.1	45.0
1980	53.4	54.8	41.9	42.1	78.4	76.8	29.1	29.4	72.2	72.9	54.5	53.7	50.2	49.3
1981	54.6	55.7	43.1	43.1	78.9	77.4	31.9	32.3	72.1	73.0	58.4	58.0	54.8	54.0
1982	54.2	55.1	41.8	41.7	77.1	75.7	34.2	34.6	73.0	73.8	63.1	62.8	58.0	57.4
1983	56.2	57.5	44.1	44.4	78.5	77.2	35.8	36.2	73.2	74.0	63.6	62.9	60.0	59.2
1984	57.7	58.8	48.0	48.1	83.1	81.9	37.3	37.7	73.4	74.2	64.7	64.2	61.7	60.9
1985	59.0	59.7	50.2	50.2	85.0	84.0	39.2	39.6	74.6	75.2	66.5	66.3	63.5	62.9
1986	60.7	61.5	52.0	52.1	85.7	84.7	41.4	41.8	77.4	78.1	68.3	68.0	64.3	63.8
1987	61.0	61.8	53.9	54.0	88.2	87.2	43.0	43.4	77.7	78.5	70.5	70.2	65.6	65.1
1988	62.0	62.8	56.2	56.4	90.7	89.8	45.3	45.7	78.9	79.5	73.1	72.6	67.7	67.1
1989	62.7	63.4	58.3	58.5	93.1	92.2	46.7	47.0	77.9	78.5	74.5	74.1	70.2	69.5
1990	64.1	64.7	59.3	59.4	92.5	91.8	49.7	49.9	79.1	79.4	77.6	77.2	72.5	71.8
1991	65.2	65.9	58.9	59.0	90.3	89.6	52.1	52.4	80.0	80.5	79.9	79.6	74.5	74.1
1992	68.1	68.7	61.4	61.4	90.1	89.4	55.2	55.6	82.7	83.2	81.0	80.9	75.7	75.3
1993	68.2	68.8	63.2	63.3	92.6	92.1	56.0	56.2	81.9	82.2	82.1	81.8	77.5	77.0
1994	68.8	69.4	66.2	66.3	96.3	95.4	56.6	56.9	80.9	81.5	82.2	82.0	78.9	78.5
1995	69.0	69.9	68.3	68.6	99.0	98.1	57.7	58.1	80.6	81.1	83.5	83.0	80.2	79.8
1996	71.1	71.8	71.5	71.7	100.6	99.8	60.1	60.4	81.8	82.3	84.5	84.2	81.5	80.9
1997	72.4	73.0	75.3	75.4	103.9	103.3	62.3	62.5	82.9	83.3	85.9	85.7	82.7	82.3
1998	74.7	75.2	79.2	79.4	106.0	105.6	65.9	66.2	86.6	87.0	88.3	88.0	83.1	82.8
1999	77.3	77.7	83.6	83.8	108.1	107.9	68.8	68.9	88.6	88.7	89.1	88.8	83.7	83.6
2000	79.9	80.2	87.3	87.5	109.3	109.0	73.9	74.0	92.0	92.2	92.4	92.3	85.3	85.2
2001	82.1	82.4	87.9	88.1	107.0	106.9	77.3	77.3	93.6	93.6	94.1	93.8	86.8	86.6
2002	85.6	86.0	89.5	89.7	104.5	104.3	79.0	79.0	94.1	94.2	92.2	91.9	87.4	87.3
2003	88.9	89.1	92.3	92.5	103.8	103.7	82.0	82.0	95.6	95.6	92.1	92.0	88.6	88.5
2004	91.8	91.9	96.5	96.6	105.1	105.1	85.8	85.7	97.4	97.3	93.4	93.3	90.7	90.3
2005	93.7	93.8	100.1	100.2	106.8	106.9	88.8	88.8	97.6	97.6	94.8	94.7	93.5	93.4
2006	94.6	94.7	103.3	103.4	109.1	109.3	92.3	92.3	98.2	98.2	97.6	97.5	96.0	96.0
2007	96.0	96.2	105.5	105.8	109.8	110.0	96.4	96.3	99.8	99.6	100.4	100.1	98.2	97.9
2008	96.8	96.9	104.2	104.4	107.7	107.8	99.0	98.9	98.6	98.6	102.2	102.1	99.8	99.4
2009	100.0	100.0	100.0	100.0	100.0	100.0	100.0	100.0	100.0	100.0	100.0	100.0	100.0	100.0
2010	103.3	103.3	103.2	103.2	99.9	99.9	101.9	102.0	100.2	100.3	98.6	98.7	101.1	101.0
2011	103.3	103.5	105.3	105.5	101.9	101.9	104.0	104.2	99.2	99.4	100.7	100.7	103.3	102.8
2012	104.3	104.5	108.6	108.9	104.2	104.2	107.0	107.1	99.9	100.0	102.6	102.4	105.2	104.7
2013	105.5	105.4	111.6	111.7	105.7	105.9	108.5	108.3	99.9	99.7	102.8	102.7	106.7	106.1
2014 p	106.1	106.3	114.8	115.1	108.2	108.3	110.8	110.8	100.4	100.4	104.4	104.2	108.1	107.5
2011: I	103.1	103.1	104.1	104.1	101.0	100.9	104.5	104.7	101.0	101.2	101.4	101.5	102.3	101.9
II	103.3	103.5	105.1	105.2	101.7	101.7	104.0	104.1	99.3	99.4	100.6	100.6	103.1	102.6
III	103.1	103.2	105.3	105.5	102.2	102.2	104.5	104.7	99.1	99.3	101.4	101.4	103.8	103.2
IV	103.9	104.0	106.9	107.0	102.9	102.9	103.3	103.4	97.6	97.7	99.4	99.4	104.0	103.5
2012: I	103.9	104.1	107.7	107.9	103.7	103.7	106.1	106.3	99.8	99.9	102.2	102.1	104.5	103.9
II	104.3	104.5	108.3	108.5	103.8	103.8	106.3	106.5	99.6	99.7	101.9	101.8	105.0	104.5
III	104.7	105.0	109.2	109.5	104.3	104.3	106.4	106.4	99.2	99.3	101.6	101.4	105.6	105.0
IV	104.2	104.4	109.1	109.5	104.8	104.9	109.1	109.1	101.2	101.1	104.7	104.4	105.9	105.2
2013: I	104.7	104.7	110.0	110.2	105.1	105.3	107.5	107.3	99.4	99.2	102.7	102.5	106.3	105.5
II	104.9	104.8	110.6	110.7	105.4	105.7	108.6	108.3	100.3	100.0	103.5	103.4	106.5	105.9
III	105.8	105.7	112.2	112.2	106.0	106.2	108.6	108.5	99.8	99.7	102.7	102.6	106.9	106.4
IV	106.6	106.6	113.5	113.5	106.4	106.5	109.1	109.0	99.9	99.9	102.3	102.3	107.2	106.7
2014: I	105.3	105.4	112.5	112.9	106.9	107.1	110.9	110.7	101.1	101.0	105.4	105.1	107.5	106.9
II	106.0	106.1	114.1	114.4	107.6	107.8	110.6	110.5	100.1	100.0	104.3	104.1	108.2	107.5
III	106.9	107.1	115.9	116.1	108.4	108.5	110.8	110.8	100.0	100.1	103.7	103.5	108.5	107.9
IV p	106.3	106.6	116.8	117.0	109.9	109.8	111.0	111.1	100.5	100.6	104.3	104.2	108.3	107.8

[1] Output refers to real gross domestic product in the sector.
[2] Hours at work of all persons engaged in sector, including hours of employees, proprietors, and unpaid family workers. Estimates based primarily on establishment data.
[3] Wages and salaries of employees plus employers' contributions for social insurance and private benefit plans. Also includes an estimate of wages, salaries, and supplemental payments for the self-employed.
[4] Hourly compensation divided by consumer price series. The consumer price series for 1978-2013 is based on the consumer price index research series (CPI-U-RS), and for recent quarters is based on the consumer price index for all urban consumers (CPI-U).
[5] Current dollar output divided by the output index.

Source: Department of Labor (Bureau of Labor Statistics).

Table B–17. Bond yields and interest rates, 1945–2014

[Percent per annum]

| Year and month | U.S. Treasury securities | | | | | Corporate bonds (Moody's) | | High-grade municipal bonds (Standard & Poor's) | New-home mort-gage yields [4] | Prime rate charged by banks [5] | Discount window (Federal Reserve Bank of New York) [5, 6] | | Federal funds rate [7] |
| | Bills (at auction) [1] | | Constant maturities [2] | | | | | | | | | | |
	3-month	6-month	3-year	10-year	30-year	Aaa [3]	Baa				Primary credit	Adjustment credit	
1945	0.375	....	....	....		2.62	3.29	1.67	....	1.50	....	[8]1.00	....
1946	.375	....	....	....		2.53	3.05	1.64	....	1.50	....	[8]1.00	....
1947	.594	....	....	....		2.61	3.24	2.01	....	1.50–1.75	....	1.00	....
1948	1.040	....	....	....		2.82	3.47	2.40	....	1.75–2.00	....	1.34	....
1949	1.102	....	....	....		2.66	3.42	2.21	....	2.00	....	1.50	....
1950	1.218	....	....	....		2.62	3.24	1.98	....	2.07	....	1.59	....
1951	1.552	....	....	....		2.86	3.41	2.00	....	2.56	....	1.75	....
1952	1.766	....	....	....		2.96	3.52	2.19	....	3.00	....	1.75	....
1953	1.931	....	2.47	2.85		3.20	3.74	2.72	....	3.17	....	1.99	....
1954	.953	....	1.63	2.40		2.90	3.51	2.37	....	3.05	....	1.60	....
1955	1.753	....	2.47	2.82		3.06	3.53	2.53	....	3.16	....	1.89	1.79
1956	2.658	....	3.19	3.18		3.36	3.88	2.93	....	3.77	....	2.77	2.73
1957	3.267	....	3.98	3.65		3.89	4.71	3.60	....	4.20	....	3.12	3.11
1958	1.839	....	2.84	3.32		3.79	4.73	3.56	....	3.83	....	2.15	1.57
1959	3.405	3.832	4.46	4.33		4.38	5.05	3.95	....	4.48	....	3.36	3.31
1960	2.93	3.25	3.98	4.12		4.41	5.19	3.73	....	4.82	....	3.53	3.21
1961	2.38	2.61	3.54	3.88		4.35	5.08	3.46	....	4.50	....	3.00	1.95
1962	2.78	2.91	3.47	3.95		4.33	5.02	3.18	....	4.50	....	3.00	2.71
1963	3.16	3.25	3.67	4.00		4.26	4.86	3.23	5.89	4.50	....	3.23	3.18
1964	3.56	3.69	4.03	4.19		4.40	4.83	3.22	5.83	4.50	....	3.55	3.50
1965	3.95	4.05	4.22	4.28		4.49	4.87	3.27	5.81	4.54	....	4.04	4.07
1966	4.88	5.08	5.23	4.93		5.13	5.67	3.82	6.25	5.63	....	4.50	5.11
1967	4.32	4.63	5.03	5.07		5.51	6.23	3.98	6.46	5.63	....	4.19	4.22
1968	5.34	5.47	5.68	5.64		6.18	6.94	4.51	6.97	6.31	....	5.17	5.66
1969	6.68	6.85	7.02	6.67		7.03	7.81	5.81	7.81	7.96	....	5.87	8.21
1970	6.43	6.53	7.29	7.35		8.04	9.11	6.51	8.45	7.91	....	5.95	7.17
1971	4.35	4.51	5.66	6.16		7.39	8.56	5.70	7.74	5.73	....	4.88	4.67
1972	4.07	4.47	5.72	6.21		7.21	8.16	5.27	7.60	5.25	....	4.50	4.44
1973	7.04	7.18	6.96	6.85		7.44	8.24	5.18	7.96	8.03	....	6.45	8.74
1974	7.89	7.93	7.84	7.56		8.57	9.50	6.09	8.92	10.81	....	7.83	10.51
1975	5.84	6.12	7.50	7.99		8.83	10.61	6.89	9.00	7.86	....	6.25	5.82
1976	4.99	5.27	6.77	7.61		8.43	9.75	6.49	9.00	6.84	....	5.50	5.05
1977	5.27	5.52	6.68	7.42	7.75	8.02	8.97	5.56	9.02	6.83	....	5.46	5.54
1978	7.22	7.58	8.29	8.41	8.49	8.73	9.49	5.90	9.56	9.06	....	7.46	7.94
1979	10.05	10.02	9.70	9.43	9.28	9.63	10.69	6.39	10.78	12.67	....	10.29	11.20
1980	11.51	11.37	11.51	11.43	11.27	11.94	13.67	8.51	12.66	15.26	....	11.77	13.35
1981	14.03	13.78	14.46	13.92	13.45	14.17	16.04	11.23	14.70	18.87	....	13.42	16.39
1982	10.69	11.08	12.93	13.01	12.76	13.79	16.11	11.57	15.14	14.85	....	11.01	12.24
1983	8.63	8.75	10.45	11.10	11.18	12.04	13.55	9.47	12.57	10.79	....	8.50	9.09
1984	9.53	9.77	11.92	12.46	12.41	12.71	14.19	10.15	12.38	12.04	....	8.80	10.23
1985	7.47	7.64	9.64	10.62	10.79	11.37	12.72	9.18	11.55	9.93	....	7.69	8.10
1986	5.98	6.03	7.06	7.67	7.78	9.02	10.39	7.38	10.17	8.33	....	6.32	6.80
1987	5.82	6.05	7.68	8.39	8.59	9.38	10.58	7.73	9.31	8.21	....	5.66	6.66
1988	6.69	6.92	8.26	8.85	8.96	9.71	10.83	7.76	9.19	9.32	....	6.20	7.57
1989	8.12	8.04	8.55	8.49	8.45	9.26	10.18	7.24	10.13	10.87	....	6.93	9.21
1990	7.51	7.47	8.26	8.55	8.61	9.32	10.36	7.25	10.05	10.01	....	6.98	8.10
1991	5.42	5.49	6.82	7.86	8.14	8.77	9.80	6.89	9.32	8.46	....	5.45	5.69
1992	3.45	3.57	5.30	7.01	7.67	8.14	8.98	6.41	8.24	6.25	....	3.25	3.52
1993	3.02	3.14	4.44	5.87	6.59	7.22	7.93	5.63	7.20	6.00	....	3.00	3.02
1994	4.29	4.66	6.27	7.09	7.37	7.96	8.62	6.19	7.49	7.15	....	3.60	4.21
1995	5.51	5.59	6.25	6.57	6.88	7.59	8.20	5.95	7.87	8.83	....	5.21	5.83
1996	5.02	5.09	5.99	6.44	6.71	7.37	8.05	5.75	7.80	8.27	....	5.02	5.30
1997	5.07	5.18	6.10	6.35	6.61	7.26	7.86	5.55	7.71	8.44	....	5.00	5.46
1998	4.81	4.85	5.14	5.26	5.58	6.53	7.22	5.12	7.07	8.35	....	4.92	5.35
1999	4.66	4.76	5.49	5.65	5.87	7.04	7.87	5.43	7.04	8.00	....	4.62	4.97
2000	5.85	5.92	6.22	6.03	5.94	7.62	8.36	5.77	7.52	9.23	....	5.73	6.24
2001	3.44	3.39	4.09	5.02	5.49	7.08	7.95	5.19	7.00	6.91	....	3.40	3.88
2002	1.62	1.69	3.10	4.61	5.43	6.49	7.80	5.05	6.43	4.67	....	1.17	1.67
2003	1.01	1.06	2.10	4.01	....	5.67	6.77	4.73	5.80	4.12	2.12	....	1.13
2004	1.38	1.57	2.78	4.27	....	5.63	6.39	4.63	5.77	4.34	2.34	....	1.35
2005	3.16	3.40	3.93	4.29	....	5.24	6.06	4.29	5.94	6.19	4.19	....	3.22
2006	4.73	4.80	4.77	4.80	4.91	5.59	6.48	4.42	6.63	7.96	5.96	....	4.97
2007	4.41	4.48	4.35	4.63	4.84	5.56	6.48	4.42	6.41	8.05	5.86	....	5.02
2008	1.48	1.71	2.24	3.66	4.28	5.63	7.45	4.80	6.05	5.09	2.39	....	1.92
2009	.16	.29	1.43	3.26	4.08	5.31	7.30	4.64	5.14	3.25	.50	....	.16
2010	.14	.20	1.11	3.22	4.25	4.94	6.04	4.16	4.80	3.25	.72	....	.18
2011	.06	.10	.75	2.78	3.91	4.64	5.66	4.29	4.56	3.25	.75	....	.10
2012	.09	.13	.38	1.80	2.92	3.67	4.94	3.14	3.69	3.25	.75	....	.14
2013	.06	.09	.54	2.35	3.45	4.24	5.10	3.96	4.00	3.25	.75	....	.11
2014	.03	.06	.90	2.54	3.34	4.16	4.85	3.78	4.22	3.25	.75	....	.09

[1] High bill rate at auction, issue date within period, bank-discount basis. On or after October 28, 1998, data are stop yields from uniform-price auctions. Before that date, they are weighted average yields from multiple-price auctions.

See next page for continuation of table.

[Percent per annum]

Year and month	U.S. Treasury securities					Corporate bonds (Moody's)		High-grade municipal bonds (Standard & Poor's) [1]	New-home mortgage yields [4]	Prime rate charged by banks [5]	Discount window (Federal Reserve Bank of New York) [5,6]		Federal funds rate [7]
	Bills (at auction) [1]		Constant maturities [2]										
	3-month	6-month	3-year	10-year	30-year	Aaa [3]	Baa				Primary credit	Adjustment credit	
										High-low	High-low	High-low	
2010: Jan	0.06	0.15	1.49	3.73	4.60	5.26	6.25	4.22	5.04	3.25–3.25	0.50–0.50	....	0.11
Feb	.10	.18	1.40	3.69	4.62	5.35	6.34	4.23	5.08	3.25–3.25	0.75–0.50	....	.13
Mar	.15	.22	1.51	3.73	4.64	5.27	6.27	4.22	5.09	3.25–3.25	0.75–0.75	....	.16
Apr	.15	.24	1.64	3.85	4.69	5.29	6.25	4.24	5.21	3.25–3.25	0.75–0.75	....	.20
May	.16	.23	1.32	3.42	4.29	4.96	6.05	4.15	5.12	3.25–3.25	0.75–0.75	....	.20
June	.12	.19	1.17	3.20	4.13	4.88	6.23	4.18	5.00	3.25–3.25	0.75–0.75	....	.18
July	.16	.20	.98	3.01	3.99	4.72	6.01	4.11	4.87	3.25–3.25	0.75–0.75	....	.18
Aug	.15	.19	.78	2.70	3.80	4.49	5.66	3.91	4.67	3.25–3.25	0.75–0.75	....	.19
Sept	.15	.19	.74	2.65	3.77	4.53	5.66	3.76	4.52	3.25–3.25	0.75–0.75	....	.19
Oct	.13	.17	.57	2.54	3.87	4.68	5.72	3.83	4.40	3.25–3.25	0.75–0.75	....	.19
Nov	.13	.17	.67	2.76	4.19	4.87	5.92	4.30	4.26	3.25–3.25	0.75–0.75	....	.19
Dec	.15	.20	.99	3.29	4.42	5.02	6.10	4.72	4.44	3.25–3.25	0.75–0.75	....	.18
2011: Jan	.15	.18	1.03	3.39	4.52	5.04	6.09	5.02	4.75	3.25–3.25	0.75–0.75	....	.17
Feb	.14	.17	1.28	3.58	4.65	5.22	6.15	4.92	4.94	3.25–3.25	0.75–0.75	....	.16
Mar	.11	.16	1.17	3.41	4.51	5.13	6.03	4.70	4.98	3.25–3.25	0.75–0.75	....	.14
Apr	.06	.12	1.21	3.46	4.50	5.16	6.02	4.71	4.91	3.25–3.25	0.75–0.75	....	.10
May	.04	.08	.94	3.17	4.29	4.96	5.78	4.34	4.86	3.25–3.25	0.75–0.75	....	.09
June	.04	.10	.71	3.00	4.23	4.99	5.75	4.22	4.61	3.25–3.25	0.75–0.75	....	.09
July	.03	.08	.68	3.00	4.27	4.93	5.76	4.24	4.55	3.25–3.25	0.75–0.75	....	.07
Aug	.05	.09	.38	2.30	3.65	4.37	5.36	3.92	4.29	3.25–3.25	0.75–0.75	....	.10
Sept	.02	.05	.35	1.98	3.18	4.09	5.27	3.79	4.36	3.25–3.25	0.75–0.75	....	.08
Oct	.02	.06	.47	2.15	3.13	3.98	5.37	3.94	4.19	3.25–3.25	0.75–0.75	....	.07
Nov	.01	.05	.39	2.01	3.02	3.87	5.14	3.95	4.26	3.25–3.25	0.75–0.75	....	.08
Dec	.02	.05	.39	1.98	2.98	3.93	5.25	3.76	4.18	3.25–3.25	0.75–0.75	....	.07
2012: Jan	.02	.06	.36	1.97	3.03	3.85	5.23	3.43	4.09	3.25–3.25	0.75–0.75	....	.08
Feb	.08	.11	.38	1.97	3.11	3.85	5.14	3.25	4.01	3.25–3.25	0.75–0.75	....	.10
Mar	.09	.14	.51	2.17	3.28	3.99	5.23	3.51	3.72	3.25–3.25	0.75–0.75	....	.13
Apr	.08	.14	.43	2.05	3.18	3.96	5.19	3.47	3.93	3.25–3.25	0.75–0.75	....	.14
May	.09	.14	.39	1.80	2.93	3.80	5.07	3.21	3.88	3.25–3.25	0.75–0.75	....	.16
June	.09	.14	.39	1.62	2.70	3.64	5.02	3.30	3.80	3.25–3.25	0.75–0.75	....	.16
July	.10	.14	.33	1.53	2.59	3.40	4.87	3.14	3.76	3.25–3.25	0.75–0.75	....	.16
Aug	.11	.14	.37	1.68	2.77	3.48	4.91	3.07	3.67	3.25–3.25	0.75–0.75	....	.13
Sept	.10	.13	.34	1.72	2.88	3.49	4.84	3.02	3.62	3.25–3.25	0.75–0.75	....	.14
Oct	.10	.15	.37	1.75	2.90	3.47	4.58	2.89	3.58	3.25–3.25	0.75–0.75	....	.16
Nov	.11	.15	.36	1.65	2.80	3.50	4.51	2.68	3.46	3.25–3.25	0.75–0.75	....	.16
Dec	.08	.12	.35	1.72	2.88	3.65	4.63	2.73	3.40	3.25–3.25	0.75–0.75	....	.16
2013: Jan	.07	.11	.39	1.91	3.08	3.80	4.73	2.93	3.41	3.25–3.25	0.75–0.75	....	.14
Feb	.10	.12	.40	1.98	3.17	3.90	4.85	3.09	3.49	3.25–3.25	0.75–0.75	....	.15
Mar	.09	.11	.39	1.96	3.16	3.93	4.85	3.27	3.61	3.25–3.25	0.75–0.75	....	.14
Apr	.06	.09	.34	1.76	2.93	3.73	4.59	3.22	3.66	3.25–3.25	0.75–0.75	....	.15
May	.05	.08	.40	1.93	3.11	3.89	4.73	3.39	3.55	3.25–3.25	0.75–0.75	....	.11
June	.05	.09	.58	2.30	3.40	4.27	5.19	4.02	3.64	3.25–3.25	0.75–0.75	....	.09
July	.04	.08	.64	2.58	3.61	4.34	5.32	4.51	4.07	3.25–3.25	0.75–0.75	....	.09
Aug	.04	.07	.70	2.74	3.76	4.54	5.42	4.77	4.33	3.25–3.25	0.75–0.75	....	.08
Sept	.02	.04	.78	2.81	3.79	4.64	5.47	4.74	4.44	3.25–3.25	0.75–0.75	....	.08
Oct	.05	.08	.63	2.62	3.68	4.53	5.31	4.50	4.47	3.25–3.25	0.75–0.75	....	.09
Nov	.07	.10	.58	2.72	3.80	4.63	5.38	4.51	4.39	3.25–3.25	0.75–0.75	....	.08
Dec	.07	.09	.69	2.90	3.89	4.62	5.38	4.55	4.37	3.25–3.25	0.75–0.75	....	.09
2014: Jan	.05	.07	.78	2.86	3.77	4.49	5.19	4.38	4.45	3.25–3.25	0.75–0.75	....	.07
Feb	.06	.08	.69	2.71	3.66	4.45	5.10	4.25	4.04	3.25–3.25	0.75–0.75	....	.07
Mar	.05	.08	.82	2.72	3.62	4.38	5.06	4.16	4.35	3.25–3.25	0.75–0.75	....	.08
Apr	.04	.05	.88	2.71	3.52	4.24	4.90	4.02	4.33	3.25–3.25	0.75–0.75	....	.09
May	.03	.06	.83	2.56	3.39	4.16	4.76	3.80	4.01	3.25–3.25	0.75–0.75	....	.09
June	.03	.06	.90	2.60	3.42	4.25	4.80	3.72	4.27	3.25–3.25	0.75–0.75	....	.10
July	.03	.06	.97	2.54	3.33	4.16	4.73	3.75	4.25	3.25–3.25	0.75–0.75	....	.09
Aug	.03	.05	.93	2.42	3.20	4.08	4.69	3.53	4.25	3.25–3.25	0.75–0.75	....	.09
Sept	.02	.05	1.05	2.53	3.26	4.11	4.80	3.55	4.23	3.25–3.25	0.75–0.75	....	.09
Oct	.02	.05	.88	2.30	3.04	3.92	4.69	3.35	4.23	3.25–3.25	0.75–0.75	....	.09
Nov	.02	.07	.96	2.33	3.04	3.92	4.79	3.49	4.16	3.25–3.25	0.75–0.75	....	.09
Dec	.04	.11	1.06	2.21	2.83	3.92	4.74	3.39	4.14	3.25–3.25	0.75–0.75	....	.12

[2] Yields on the more actively traded issues adjusted to constant maturities by the Department of the Treasury. The 30-year Treasury constant maturity series was discontinued on February 18, 2002, and reintroduced on February 9, 2006.

[3] Beginning with December 7, 2001, data for corporate Aaa series are industrial bonds only.

[4] Effective rate (in the primary market) on conventional mortgages, reflecting fees and charges as well as contract rate and assuming, on the average, repayment at end of 10 years. Rates beginning with January 1973 not strictly comparable with prior years.

[5] For monthly data, high and low for the period. Prime rate for 1947–1948 are ranges of the rate in effect during the period.

[6] Primary credit replaced adjustment credit as the Federal Reserve's principal discount window lending program effective January 9, 2003.

[7] Since July 19, 1975, the daily effective rate is an average of the rates on a given day weighted by the volume of transactions at these rates. Prior to that date, the daily effective rate was the rate considered most representative of the day's transactions, usually the one at which most transactions occurred.

[8] Through April 24, 1946, a preferential rate of 0.50 percent was in effect for advances secured by Government securities maturing in one year or less.

Sources: Department of the Treasury, Board of Governors of the Federal Reserve System, Federal Housing Finance Agency, Moody's Investors Service, and Standard & Poor's.

TABLE B–18. Money stock and debt measures, 1974–2014

[Averages of daily figures, except debt end-of-period basis; billions of dollars, seasonally adjusted]

Year and month	M1 Sum of currency, demand deposits, travelers checks, and other checkable deposits	M2 M1 plus savings deposits, retail MMMF balances, and small time deposits [2]	Debt [1] Debt of domestic nonfinancial sectors	Percent change		
				From year or 6 months earlier [3]		From previous period [4]
				M1	M2	Debt
December:						
1974	274.2	902.1	2,069.8	4.3	5.4	9.2
1975	287.1	1,016.2	2,260.4	4.7	12.6	9.3
1976	306.2	1,152.0	2,503.7	6.7	13.4	10.9
1977	330.9	1,270.3	2,825.1	8.1	10.3	12.8
1978	357.3	1,366.0	3,209.3	8.0	7.5	13.8
1979	381.8	1,473.7	3,596.5	6.9	7.9	12.0
1980	408.5	1,599.8	3,943.2	7.0	8.6	9.4
1981	436.7	1,755.5	4,349.2	6.9	9.7	10.3
1982	474.8	1,906.4	4,770.6	8.7	8.6	10.4
1983	521.4	2,123.8	5,344.2	9.8	11.4	12.0
1984	551.6	2,306.8	6,138.2	5.8	8.6	14.9
1985	619.8	2,492.6	7,111.8	12.4	8.1	15.6
1986	724.7	2,729.2	7,953.5	16.9	9.5	11.9
1987	750.2	2,828.8	8,656.8	3.5	3.6	9.1
1988	786.7	2,990.6	9,439.6	4.9	5.7	9.1
1989	792.9	3,154.4	10,141.0	.8	5.5	7.2
1990	824.7	3,272.7	10,827.2	4.0	3.8	6.5
1991	897.0	3,371.6	11,296.4	8.8	3.0	4.4
1992	1,024.9	3,423.1	11,813.9	14.3	1.5	4.6
1993	1,129.6	3,472.4	12,496.1	10.2	1.4	5.6
1994	1,150.7	3,485.0	13,141.4	1.9	.4	5.1
1995	1,127.5	3,626.7	13,797.9	−2.0	4.1	4.9
1996	1,081.3	3,804.9	14,479.4	−4.1	4.9	4.9
1997	1,072.3	4,017.4	15,239.2	−.8	5.6	5.3
1998	1,095.0	4,356.6	16,223.8	2.1	8.4	6.5
1999	1,122.2	4,617.0	17,265.4	2.5	6.0	6.2
2000	1,087.8	4,903.7	18,121.5	−3.1	6.2	4.9
2001	1,182.3	5,405.7	19,211.1	8.7	10.2	6.1
2002	1,219.2	5,740.4	20,580.1	3.1	6.2	7.1
2003	1,305.2	6,035.2	22,222.9	7.1	5.1	7.8
2004	1,375.5	6,388.4	24,945.4	5.4	5.9	9.0
2005	1,374.8	6,654.1	27,179.7	−.1	4.2	9.0
2006	1,368.3	7,046.0	29,513.7	−.5	5.9	8.4
2007	1,376.6	7,452.4	31,903.3	.6	5.8	8.2
2008	1,607.1	8,177.0	33,756.0	16.7	9.7	6.2
2009	1,698.4	8,482.4	34,470.1	5.7	3.7	3.3
2010	1,841.8	8,782.9	35,617.9	8.4	3.5	4.1
2011	2,168.2	9,635.8	36,759.6	17.7	9.7	3.6
2012	2,457.7	10,423.6	38,427.6	13.4	8.2	5.0
2013	2,654.0	10,984.9	39,771.9	8.0	5.4	3.8
2014	2,906.6	11,625.6		9.5	5.8	
2013: Jan	2,467.6	10,451.9		13.2	8.4	
Feb	2,470.4	10,448.6		10.6	6.9	
Mar	2,474.8	10,518.9	38,797.7	7.7	6.6	4.1
Apr	2,511.0	10,552.5		7.9	6.1	
May	2,522.0	10,586.4		8.2	5.6	
June	2,518.0	10,639.1	39,059.2	4.9	4.1	3.0
July	2,545.7	10,700.7		6.3	4.8	
Aug	2,557.4	10,754.6		7.0	5.9	
Sept	2,579.0	10,809.5	39,369.1	8.4	5.5	3.5
Oct	2,620.3	10,920.5		8.7	7.0	
Nov	2,622.0	10,929.8		7.9	6.5	
Dec	2,654.0	10,984.9	39,771.9	10.8	6.5	4.4
2014: Jan	2,682.7	11,037.5		10.8	6.3	
Feb	2,718.5	11,118.9		12.6	6.8	
Mar	2,745.9	11,162.6	40,178.9	12.9	6.5	4.2
Apr	2,772.4	11,218.8		11.6	5.5	
May	2,785.3	11,283.8		12.5	6.5	
June	2,814.3	11,331.8	40,508.8	12.1	6.3	3.4
July	2,840.7	11,404.9		11.8	6.7	
Aug	2,814.4	11,440.4		7.1	5.8	
Sept	2,857.5	11,480.9	40,946.9	8.1	5.7	4.4
Oct	2,861.3	11,520.6		6.4	5.4	
Nov	2,874.9	11,562.2		6.4	4.9	
Dec	2,906.6	11,625.6		6.6	5.2	

[1] Consists of outstanding credit market debt of the U.S. Government, State and local governments, and private nonfinancial sectors.
[2] Money market mutual fund (MMMF). Savings deposits include money market deposit accounts.
[3] Annual changes are from December to December; monthly changes are from six months earlier at a simple annual rate.
[4] Annual changes are from fourth quarter to fourth quarter. Quarterly changes are from previous quarter at annual rate.

Note: For further information on the composition of M1 and M2, see the H.6 release of the Federal Reserve Board. The Federal Reserve no longer publishes the M3 monetary aggregate and most of its components. Institutional money market mutual fund balances are published as a memorandum item in the H.6 release, and measures of large-denomination time deposits are published in the H.8 and Z.1 releases. For details, see H.6 release of March 23, 2006.

Source: Board of Governors of the Federal Reserve System.

TABLE B–19. Federal receipts, outlays, surplus or deficit, and debt, fiscal years, 1948–2016

[Billions of dollars; fiscal years]

Fiscal year or period	Total Receipts	Total Outlays	Total Surplus or deficit (–)	On-budget Receipts	On-budget Outlays	On-budget Surplus or deficit (–)	Off-budget Receipts	Off-budget Outlays	Off-budget Surplus or deficit (–)	Federal debt (end of period) Gross Federal	Federal debt (end of period) Held by the public	Addendum: Gross domestic product
1948	41.6	29.8	11.8	39.9	29.4	10.5	1.6	0.4	1.2	252.0	216.3	262.4
1949	39.4	38.8	.6	37.7	38.4	–.7	1.7	.4	1.3	252.6	214.3	276.8
1950	39.4	42.6	–3.1	37.3	42.0	–4.7	2.1	.5	1.6	256.9	219.0	279.0
1951	51.6	45.5	6.1	48.5	44.2	4.3	3.1	1.3	1.8	255.3	214.3	327.4
1952	66.2	67.7	–1.5	62.6	66.0	–3.4	3.6	1.7	1.9	259.1	214.8	357.5
1953	69.6	76.1	–6.5	65.5	73.8	–8.3	4.1	2.3	1.8	266.0	218.4	382.5
1954	69.7	70.9	–1.2	65.1	67.9	–2.8	4.6	2.9	1.7	270.8	224.5	387.7
1955	65.5	68.4	–3.0	60.4	64.5	–4.1	5.1	4.0	1.1	274.4	226.6	407.0
1956	74.6	70.6	3.9	68.2	65.7	2.5	6.4	5.0	1.5	272.7	222.2	439.0
1957	80.0	76.6	3.4	73.2	70.6	2.6	6.8	6.0	.8	272.3	219.3	464.2
1958	79.6	82.4	–2.8	71.6	74.9	–3.3	8.0	7.5	.5	279.7	226.3	474.3
1959	79.2	92.1	–12.8	71.0	83.1	–12.1	8.3	9.0	–.7	287.5	234.7	505.6
1960	92.5	92.2	.3	81.9	81.3	.5	10.6	10.9	–.2	290.5	236.8	535.1
1961	94.4	97.7	–3.3	82.3	86.0	–3.8	12.1	11.7	.4	292.6	238.4	547.6
1962	99.7	106.8	–7.1	87.4	93.3	–5.9	12.3	13.5	–1.3	302.9	248.0	586.9
1963	106.6	111.3	–4.8	92.4	96.4	–4.0	14.2	15.0	–.8	310.3	254.0	619.3
1964	112.6	118.5	–5.9	96.2	102.8	–6.5	16.4	15.7	.6	316.1	256.8	662.9
1965	116.8	118.2	–1.4	100.1	101.7	–1.6	16.7	16.5	.2	322.3	260.8	710.7
1966	130.8	134.5	–3.7	111.7	114.8	–3.1	19.1	19.7	–.6	328.5	263.7	781.9
1967	148.8	157.5	–8.6	124.4	137.0	–12.6	24.4	20.4	4.0	340.4	266.6	838.2
1968	153.0	178.1	–25.2	128.1	155.8	–27.7	24.9	22.3	2.6	368.7	289.5	899.3
1969	186.9	183.6	3.2	157.9	158.4	–.5	29.0	25.2	3.7	365.8	278.1	982.3
1970	192.8	195.6	–2.8	159.3	168.0	–8.7	33.5	27.6	5.9	380.9	283.2	1,049.1
1971	187.1	210.2	–23.0	151.3	177.3	–26.1	35.8	32.8	3.0	408.2	303.0	1,119.3
1972	207.3	230.7	–23.4	167.4	193.5	–26.1	39.9	37.2	2.7	435.9	322.4	1,219.5
1973	230.8	245.7	–14.9	184.7	200.0	–15.2	46.1	45.7	.3	466.3	340.9	1,356.0
1974	263.2	269.4	–6.1	209.3	216.5	–7.2	53.9	52.9	1.1	483.9	343.7	1,486.2
1975	279.1	332.3	–53.2	216.6	270.8	–54.1	62.5	61.6	.9	541.9	394.7	1,610.6
1976	298.1	371.8	–73.7	231.7	301.1	–69.4	66.4	70.7	–4.3	629.0	477.4	1,790.3
Transition quarter	81.2	96.0	–14.7	63.2	77.3	–14.1	18.0	18.7	–.7	643.6	495.5	472.6
1977	355.6	409.2	–53.7	278.7	328.7	–49.9	76.8	80.5	–3.7	706.4	549.1	2,028.4
1978	399.6	458.7	–59.2	314.2	369.6	–55.4	85.4	89.2	–3.8	776.6	607.1	2,278.2
1979	463.3	504.0	–40.7	365.3	404.9	–39.6	98.0	99.1	–1.1	829.5	640.3	2,570.0
1980	517.1	590.9	–73.8	403.9	477.0	–73.1	113.2	113.9	–.7	909.0	711.9	2,796.8
1981	599.3	678.2	–79.0	469.1	543.0	–73.9	130.2	135.3	–5.1	994.8	789.4	3,138.4
1982	617.8	745.7	–128.0	474.3	594.9	–120.6	143.5	150.9	–7.4	1,137.3	924.6	3,313.9
1983	600.6	808.4	–207.8	453.2	660.9	–207.7	147.3	147.4	–.1	1,371.7	1,137.3	3,541.1
1984	666.4	851.8	–185.4	500.4	685.6	–185.3	166.1	166.2	–.1	1,564.6	1,307.0	3,952.8
1985	734.0	946.3	–212.3	547.9	769.4	–221.5	186.2	176.9	9.2	1,817.4	1,507.3	4,270.4
1986	769.2	990.4	–221.2	568.9	806.8	–237.9	200.2	183.5	16.7	2,120.5	1,740.6	4,536.1
1987	854.3	1,004.0	–149.7	640.9	809.2	–168.4	213.4	194.8	18.6	2,346.0	1,889.8	4,781.9
1988	909.2	1,064.4	–155.2	667.7	860.0	–192.3	241.5	204.4	37.1	2,601.1	2,051.6	5,155.1
1989	991.1	1,143.7	–152.6	727.4	932.8	–205.4	263.7	210.9	52.8	2,867.8	2,190.7	5,570.0
1990	1,032.0	1,253.0	–221.0	750.3	1,027.9	–277.6	281.7	225.1	56.6	3,206.3	2,411.6	5,914.6
1991	1,055.0	1,324.2	–269.2	761.1	1,082.5	–321.4	293.9	241.7	52.2	3,598.2	2,689.0	6,110.1
1992	1,091.2	1,381.5	–290.3	788.8	1,129.2	–340.4	302.4	252.3	50.1	4,001.8	2,999.7	6,434.7
1993	1,154.3	1,409.4	–255.1	842.4	1,142.8	–300.4	311.9	266.6	45.3	4,351.0	3,248.4	6,794.9
1994	1,258.6	1,461.8	–203.2	923.5	1,182.4	–258.8	335.0	279.4	55.7	4,643.3	3,433.1	7,197.8
1995	1,351.8	1,515.7	–164.0	1,000.7	1,227.1	–226.4	351.1	288.7	62.4	4,920.6	3,604.4	7,583.4
1996	1,453.1	1,560.5	–107.4	1,085.6	1,259.6	–174.0	367.5	300.9	66.6	5,181.5	3,734.1	7,978.3
1997	1,579.2	1,601.1	–21.9	1,187.2	1,290.5	–103.2	392.0	310.6	81.4	5,369.2	3,772.3	8,483.2
1998	1,721.7	1,652.5	69.3	1,305.9	1,335.9	–29.9	415.8	316.6	99.2	5,478.2	3,721.1	8,954.8
1999	1,827.5	1,701.8	125.6	1,383.0	1,381.1	1.9	444.5	320.8	123.7	5,605.5	3,632.4	9,510.5
2000	2,025.2	1,789.0	236.2	1,544.6	1,458.2	86.4	480.6	330.8	149.8	5,628.7	3,409.8	10,148.2
2001	1,991.1	1,862.8	128.2	1,483.6	1,516.0	–32.4	507.5	346.8	160.7	5,769.9	3,319.6	10,564.6
2002	1,853.1	2,010.9	–157.8	1,337.8	1,655.2	–317.4	515.3	355.7	159.7	6,198.4	3,540.4	10,876.9
2003	1,782.3	2,159.9	–377.6	1,258.5	1,796.9	–538.4	523.8	363.0	160.8	6,760.0	3,913.4	11,332.4
2004	1,880.1	2,292.8	–412.7	1,345.4	1,913.3	–568.0	534.7	379.5	155.2	7,354.7	4,295.5	12,088.6
2005	2,153.6	2,472.0	–318.3	1,576.1	2,069.7	–493.6	577.5	402.2	175.3	7,905.3	4,592.2	12,888.9
2006	2,406.9	2,655.1	–248.2	1,798.5	2,233.0	–434.5	608.4	422.1	186.3	8,451.4	4,829.0	13,684.7
2007	2,568.0	2,728.7	–160.7	1,932.9	2,275.0	–342.2	635.1	453.6	181.5	8,950.7	5,035.1	14,322.9
2008	2,524.0	2,982.5	–458.6	1,865.9	2,507.8	–641.8	658.0	474.8	183.3	9,986.1	5,803.1	14,752.4
2009	2,105.0	3,517.7	–1,412.7	1,451.0	3,000.7	–1,549.7	654.0	517.0	137.0	11,875.9	7,544.7	14,414.6
2010	2,162.7	3,457.1	–1,294.4	1,531.0	2,902.4	–1,371.4	631.7	554.7	77.0	13,528.8	9,018.9	14,798.5
2011	2,303.5	3,603.1	–1,299.6	1,737.7	3,104.5	–1,366.8	565.8	498.6	67.2	14,764.2	10,128.2	15,379.2
2012	2,450.0	3,537.0	–1,087.0	1,880.5	3,029.4	–1,148.9	569.5	507.6	61.9	16,050.9	11,281.1	16,026.4
2013	2,775.1	3,454.6	–679.5	2,101.8	2,820.8	–719.0	673.3	633.8	39.5	16,719.4	11,982.7	16,581.6
2014	3,021.5	3,506.1	–484.6	2,285.9	2,800.0	–514.1	735.6	706.1	29.5	17,794.5	12,779.9	17,244.0
2015 (estimates)	3,176.1	3,758.6	–582.5	2,410.5	3,006.0	–595.5	765.6	752.6	13.0	18,627.6	13,506.3	17,985.0
2016 (estimates)	3,525.2	3,999.5	–474.3	2,724.2	3,201.1	–476.9	801.0	798.4	2.6	19,333.8	14,108.5	18,818.6

Note: Fiscal years through 1976 were on a July 1–June 30 basis; beginning with October 1976 (fiscal year 1977), the fiscal year is on an October 1–September 30 basis. The transition quarter is the three-month period from July 1, 1976 through September 30, 1976.
See *Budget of the United States Government, Fiscal Year 2016*, for additional information.

Sources: Department of Commerce (Bureau of Economic Analysis), Department of the Treasury, and Office of Management and Budget.

TABLE B–20. Federal receipts, outlays, surplus or deficit, and debt, as percent of gross domestic product, fiscal years 1943–2016

[Percent; fiscal years]

Fiscal year or period	Receipts	Outlays		Surplus or deficit (−)	Federal debt (end of period)	
		Total	National defense		Gross Federal	Held by public
1943	13.0	42.6	36.1	−29.6	77.3	69.2
1944	20.5	42.7	37.0	−22.2	95.5	86.4
1945	19.9	41.0	36.6	−21.0	114.9	103.9
1946	17.2	24.2	18.7	−7.0	118.9	106.1
1947	16.1	14.4	5.4	1.7	107.6	93.9
1948	15.8	11.3	3.5	4.5	96.0	82.4
1949	14.2	14.0	4.8	.2	91.3	77.4
1950	14.1	15.3	4.9	−1.1	92.1	78.5
1951	15.8	13.9	7.2	1.9	78.0	65.5
1952	18.5	18.9	12.9	−.4	72.5	60.1
1953	18.2	19.9	13.8	−1.7	69.5	57.1
1954	18.0	18.3	12.7	−.3	69.9	57.9
1955	16.1	16.8	10.5	−.7	67.4	55.7
1956	17.0	16.1	9.7	.9	62.1	50.6
1957	17.2	16.5	9.8	.7	58.6	47.2
1958	16.8	17.4	9.9	−.6	59.0	47.7
1959	15.7	18.2	9.7	−2.5	56.9	46.4
1960	17.3	17.2	9.0	.1	54.3	44.3
1961	17.2	17.8	9.1	−.6	53.4	43.5
1962	17.0	18.2	8.9	−1.2	51.6	42.3
1963	17.2	18.0	8.6	−.8	50.1	41.0
1964	17.0	17.9	8.3	−.9	47.7	38.7
1965	16.4	16.6	7.1	−.2	45.4	36.7
1966	16.7	17.2	7.4	−.5	42.0	33.7
1967	17.8	18.8	8.5	−1.0	40.6	31.8
1968	17.0	19.8	9.1	−2.8	41.0	32.2
1969	19.0	18.7	8.4	.3	37.2	28.3
1970	18.4	18.6	7.8	−.3	36.3	27.0
1971	16.7	18.8	7.0	−2.1	36.5	27.1
1972	17.0	18.9	6.5	−1.9	35.7	26.4
1973	17.0	18.1	5.7	−1.1	34.4	25.1
1974	17.7	18.1	5.3	−.4	32.6	23.1
1975	17.3	20.6	5.4	−3.3	33.6	24.5
1976	16.6	20.8	5.0	−4.1	35.1	26.7
Transition quarter	17.2	20.3	4.7	−3.1	34.0	26.2
1977	17.5	20.2	4.8	−2.6	34.8	27.1
1978	17.5	20.1	4.6	−2.6	34.1	26.6
1979	18.0	19.6	4.5	−1.6	32.3	24.9
1980	18.5	21.1	4.8	−2.6	32.5	25.5
1981	19.1	21.6	5.0	−2.5	31.7	25.2
1982	18.6	22.5	5.6	−3.9	34.3	27.9
1983	17.0	22.8	5.9	−5.9	38.7	32.1
1984	16.9	21.5	5.8	−4.7	39.6	33.1
1985	17.2	22.2	5.9	−5.0	42.6	35.3
1986	17.0	21.8	6.0	−4.9	46.7	38.4
1987	17.9	21.0	5.9	−3.1	49.1	39.5
1988	17.6	20.6	5.6	−3.0	50.5	39.8
1989	17.8	20.5	5.4	−2.7	51.5	39.3
1990	17.4	21.2	5.1	−3.7	54.2	40.8
1991	17.3	21.7	4.5	−4.4	58.9	44.0
1992	17.0	21.5	4.6	−4.5	62.2	46.6
1993	17.0	20.7	4.3	−3.8	64.0	47.8
1994	17.5	20.3	3.9	−2.8	64.5	47.7
1995	17.8	20.0	3.6	−2.2	64.9	47.5
1996	18.2	19.6	3.3	−1.3	64.9	46.8
1997	18.6	18.9	3.2	−.3	63.3	44.5
1998	19.2	18.5	3.0	.8	61.2	41.6
1999	19.2	17.9	2.9	1.3	58.9	38.2
2000	20.0	17.6	2.9	2.3	55.5	33.6
2001	18.8	17.6	2.9	1.2	54.6	31.4
2002	17.0	18.5	3.2	−1.5	57.0	32.5
2003	15.7	19.1	3.6	−3.3	59.7	34.5
2004	15.6	19.0	3.8	−3.4	60.8	35.5
2005	16.7	19.2	3.8	−2.5	61.3	35.6
2006	17.6	19.4	3.8	−1.8	61.8	35.3
2007	17.9	19.1	3.8	−1.1	62.5	35.2
2008	17.1	20.2	4.2	−3.1	67.7	39.3
2009	14.6	24.4	4.6	−9.8	82.4	52.3
2010	14.6	23.4	4.7	−8.7	91.4	60.9
2011	15.0	23.4	4.6	−8.5	96.0	65.9
2012	15.3	22.1	4.2	−6.8	100.2	70.4
2013	16.7	20.8	3.8	−4.1	100.8	72.3
2014	17.5	20.3	3.5	−2.8	103.2	74.1
2015 (estimates)	17.7	20.9	3.3	−3.2	103.6	75.1
2016 (estimates)	18.7	21.3	3.3	−2.5	102.7	75.0

Note: See Note, Table B–19.

Sources: Department of the Treasury and Office of Management and Budget.

[Billions of dollars; fiscal years]

Fiscal year or period	Receipts (on-budget and off-budget)					Outlays (on-budget and off-budget)										Surplus or deficit (−) (on-budget and off-budget)
	Total	Individual income taxes	Corporation income taxes	Social insurance and retirement receipts	Other	Total	National defense		International affairs	Health	Medicare	Income security	Social security	Net interest	Other	
							Total	Department of Defense, military								
1948	41.6	19.3	9.7	3.8	8.8	29.8	9.1	....	4.6	0.2	....	2.5	0.6	4:3	8.5	11.8
1949	39.4	15.6	11.2	3.8	8.9	38.8	13.2	....	6.1	.2	....	3.2	.7	4.5	11.1	.6
1950	39.4	15.8	10.4	4.3	8.9	42.6	13.7	....	4.7	.3	....	4.1	.8	4.8	14.2	−3.1
1951	51.6	21.6	14.1	5.7	10.2	45.5	23.6	....	3.6	.3	....	3.4	1.6	4.7	8.4	6.1
1952	66.2	27.9	21.2	6.4	10.6	67.7	46.1	....	2.7	.3	....	3.7	2.1	4.7	8.1	−1.5
1953	69.6	29.8	21.2	6.8	11.7	76.1	52.8	....	2.1	.3	....	3.8	2.7	5.2	9.1	−6.5
1954	69.7	29.5	21.1	7.2	11.9	70.9	49.3	....	1.6	.3	....	4.4	3.4	4.8	7.1	−1.2
1955	65.5	28.7	17.9	7.9	11.0	68.4	42.7	....	2.2	.3	....	5.1	4.4	4.9	8.9	−3.0
1956	74.6	32.2	20.9	9.3	12.2	70.6	42.5	....	2.4	.4	....	4.7	5.5	5.1	10.1	3.9
1957	80.0	35.6	21.2	10.0	13.2	76.6	45.4	....	3.1	.5	....	5.4	6.7	5.4	10.1	3.4
1958	79.6	34.7	20.1	11.2	13.6	82.4	46.8	....	3.4	.5	....	7.5	8.2	5.6	10.3	−2.8
1959	79.2	36.7	17.3	11.7	13.5	92.1	49.0	....	3.1	.7	....	8.2	9.7	5.8	15.5	−12.8
1960	92.5	40.7	21.5	14.7	15.6	92.2	48.1	....	3.0	.8	....	7.4	11.6	6.9	14.4	.3
1961	94.4	41.3	21.0	16.4	15.7	97.7	49.6	....	3.2	.9	....	9.7	12.5	6.7	15.2	−3.3
1962	99.7	45.6	20.5	17.0	16.5	106.8	52.3	50.1	5.6	1.2	....	9.2	14.4	6.9	17.2	−7.1
1963	106.6	47.6	21.6	19.8	17.6	111.3	53.4	51.1	5.3	1.5	....	9.3	15.8	7.7	18.3	−4.8
1964	112.6	48.7	23.5	22.0	18.5	118.5	54.8	52.6	4.9	1.8	....	9.7	16.6	8.2	22.6	−5.9
1965	116.8	48.8	25.5	22.2	20.3	118.2	50.6	48.8	5.3	1.8	....	9.5	17.5	8.6	25.0	−1.4
1966	130.8	55.4	30.1	25.5	19.8	134.5	58.1	56.6	5.6	2.5	0.1	9.7	20.7	9.4	28.5	−3.7
1967	148.8	61.5	34.0	32.6	20.7	157.5	71.4	70.1	5.6	3.4	2.7	10.3	21.7	10.3	32.1	−8.6
1968	153.0	68.7	28.7	33.9	21.7	178.1	81.9	80.4	5.3	4.4	4.6	11.8	23.9	11.1	35.1	−25.2
1969	186.9	87.2	36.7	39.0	23.9	183.6	82.5	80.8	4.6	5.2	5.7	13.1	27.3	12.7	32.6	3.2
1970	192.8	90.4	32.8	44.4	25.2	195.6	81.7	80.1	4.3	5.9	6.2	15.7	30.3	14.4	37.2	−2.8
1971	187.1	86.2	26.8	47.3	26.8	210.2	78.9	77.5	4.2	6.8	6.6	22.9	35.9	14.8	40.0	−23.0
1972	207.3	94.7	32.2	52.6	27.8	230.7	79.2	77.6	4.8	8.7	7.5	27.7	40.2	15.5	47.3	−23.4
1973	230.8	103.2	36.2	63.1	28.3	245.7	76.7	75.0	4.1	9.4	8.1	28.3	49.1	17.3	52.8	−14.9
1974	263.2	119.0	38.6	75.1	30.6	269.4	79.3	77.9	5.7	10.7	9.6	33.7	55.9	21.4	52.9	−6.1
1975	279.1	122.4	40.6	84.5	31.5	332.3	86.5	84.9	7.1	12.9	12.9	50.2	64.7	23.2	74.8	−53.2
1976	298.1	131.6	41.4	90.8	34.3	371.8	89.6	87.9	6.4	15.7	15.8	60.8	73.9	26.7	82.7	−73.7
Transition quarter ..	81.2	38.8	8.5	25.2	8.8	96.0	22.3	21.8	2.5	3.9	4.3	15.0	19.8	6.9	21.4	−14.7
1977	355.6	157.6	54.9	106.5	36.6	409.2	97.2	95.1	6.4	17.3	19.3	61.1	85.1	29.9	93.0	−53.7
1978	399.6	181.0	60.0	121.0	37.7	458.7	104.5	102.3	7.5	18.5	22.8	61.5	93.9	35.5	114.6	−59.2
1979	463.3	217.8	65.7	138.9	40.8	504.0	116.3	113.6	7.5	20.5	26.5	66.4	104.1	42.6	120.2	−40.7
1980	517.1	244.1	64.6	157.8	50.6	590.9	134.0	130.9	12.7	23.2	32.1	86.6	118.5	52.5	131.3	−73.8
1981	599.3	285.9	61.1	182.7	69.5	678.2	157.5	153.9	13.1	26.9	39.1	100.3	139.6	68.8	133.0	−79.0
1982	617.8	297.7	49.2	201.5	69.3	745.7	185.3	180.7	12.3	27.4	46.6	108.2	156.0	85.0	125.0	−128.0
1983	600.6	288.9	37.0	209.0	65.6	808.4	209.9	204.4	11.8	28.6	52.6	123.0	170.7	89.8	121.8	−207.8
1984	666.4	298.4	56.9	239.4	71.8	851.8	227.4	220.9	15.9	30.4	57.5	113.4	178.2	111.1	117.8	−185.4
1985	734.0	334.5	61.3	265.2	73.0	946.3	252.7	245.1	16.2	33.5	65.8	129.0	188.6	129.5	130.9	−212.3
1986	769.2	349.0	63.1	283.9	73.2	990.4	273.4	265.4	14.1	35.9	70.2	120.7	198.8	136.0	141.3	−221.2
1987	854.3	392.6	83.9	303.3	74.5	1,004.0	282.0	273.9	11.6	40.0	75.1	124.1	207.4	138.6	125.2	−149.7
1988	909.2	401.2	94.5	334.3	79.2	1,064.4	290.4	281.9	10.5	44.5	78.9	130.4	219.3	151.8	138.7	−155.2
1989	991.1	445.7	103.3	359.4	82.7	1,143.7	303.6	294.8	9.6	48.4	85.0	137.6	232.5	169.0	158.1	−152.6
1990	1,032.0	466.9	93.5	380.0	91.5	1,253.0	299.3	289.7	13.8	57.7	98.1	148.8	248.6	184.3	202.3	−221.0
1991	1,055.0	467.8	98.1	396.0	93.1	1,324.2	273.3	262.3	15.8	71.2	104.5	172.6	269.0	194.4	223.3	−269.2
1992	1,091.2	476.0	100.3	413.7	101.3	1,381.5	298.3	286.8	16.1	89.5	119.0	199.7	287.6	199.3	171.9	−290.3
1993	1,154.3	509.7	117.5	428.3	98.8	1,409.4	291.1	278.5	17.2	99.4	130.6	210.1	304.6	198.7	157.7	−255.1
1994	1,258.6	543.1	140.4	461.5	113.7	1,461.8	281.6	268.6	17.1	107.1	144.7	217.3	319.6	202.9	171.4	−203.2
1995	1,351.8	590.2	157.0	484.5	120.1	1,515.7	272.1	259.4	16.4	115.4	159.9	223.8	335.8	232.1	160.2	−164.0
1996	1,453.1	656.4	171.8	509.4	115.4	1,560.5	265.7	253.1	13.5	119.4	174.2	229.7	349.7	241.1	167.2	−107.4
1997	1,579.2	737.5	182.3	539.4	120.1	1,601.1	270.5	258.3	15.2	123.8	190.0	235.0	365.3	244.0	157.3	−21.9
1998	1,721.7	828.6	188.7	571.8	132.6	1,652.5	268.2	255.8	13.1	131.4	192.8	237.8	379.2	241.1	188.9	69.3
1999	1,827.5	879.5	184.7	611.8	151.5	1,701.8	274.8	261.2	15.2	141.0	190.4	242.5	390.0	229.8	218.1	125.6
2000	2,025.2	1,004.5	207.3	652.9	160.6	1,789.0	294.4	281.0	17.2	154.5	197.1	253.7	409.4	222.9	239.7	236.2
2001	1,991.1	994.3	151.1	694.0	151.7	1,862.8	304.7	290.2	16.5	172.2	217.4	269.8	433.0	206.2	243.1	128.2
2002	1,853.1	858.3	148.0	700.8	146.0	2,010.9	348.5	331.8	22.3	196.5	230.9	312.7	456.0	170.9	273.1	−157.8
2003	1,782.3	793.7	131.8	713.0	143.9	2,159.9	404.7	387.1	21.2	219.5	249.4	334.6	474.7	153.1	302.6	−377.6
2004	1,880.1	809.0	189.4	733.4	148.4	2,292.8	455.8	436.4	26.9	240.1	269.4	333.1	495.5	160.2	311.8	−412.7
2005	2,153.6	927.2	278.3	794.1	154.0	2,472.0	495.3	474.1	34.6	250.5	298.6	345.8	523.3	184.0	339.8	−318.3
2006	2,406.9	1,043.9	353.9	837.8	171.2	2,655.1	521.8	499.3	29.5	252.7	329.9	352.5	548.5	226.6	393.5	−248.2
2007	2,568.0	1,163.5	370.2	869.6	164.7	2,728.7	551.3	528.5	28.5	266.4	375.4	366.0	586.2	237.1	317.9	−160.7
2008	2,524.0	1,145.7	304.3	900.2	173.7	2,982.5	616.1	594.6	28.9	280.6	390.8	431.3	617.0	252.8	365.2	−458.6
2009	2,105.0	915.3	138.2	890.9	160.5	3,517.7	661.0	636.7	37.5	334.3	430.1	533.2	683.0	186.9	651.6	−1,412.7
2010	2,162.7	898.5	191.4	864.8	207.9	3,457.1	693.5	666.7	45.2	369.1	451.6	622.2	706.7	196.2	372.6	−1,294.4
2011	2,303.5	1,091.5	181.1	818.8	212.1	3,603.1	705.6	678.1	45.7	372.5	485.7	597.4	730.8	230.0	435.5	−1,299.6
2012	2,450.0	1,132.2	242.3	845.3	230.2	3,537.0	677.9	650.9	47.2	346.7	471.8	541.3	773.3	220.4	458.3	−1,087.0
2013	2,775.1	1,316.4	273.5	947.8	237.4	3,454.6	633.4	607.8	46.2	358.3	497.8	536.5	813.6	220.9	347.9	−679.5
2014	3,021.5	1,394.6	320.7	1,023.5	282.7	3,506.1	603.5	577.9	46.7	409.4	511.7	513.6	850.5	229.0	341.7	−484.6
2015 (estimates)	3,176.1	1,478.1	341.7	1,065.0	291.3	3,758.6	597.5	567.7	55.0	481.2	536.4	522.5	896.3	229.2	440.5	−582.5
2016 (estimates)	3,525.2	1,645.6	473.3	1,111.9	294.3	3,999.5	615.5	586.5	56.0	517.7	589.7	546.4	944.3	283.0	446.8	−474.3

Note: See Note, Table B–19.

Sources: Department of the Treasury and Office of Management and Budget.

Interest Rates, Money Stock, and Government Finance | 409

TABLE B–22. Federal receipts, outlays, surplus or deficit, and debt, fiscal years 2011–2016

[Millions of dollars; fiscal years]

Description	Actual				Estimates	
	2011	2012	2013	2014	2015	2016
RECEIPTS, OUTLAYS, AND SURPLUS OR DEFICIT						
Total:						
Receipts	2,303,466	2,449,988	2,775,103	3,021,487	3,176,072	3,525,179
Outlays	3,603,059	3,536,951	3,454,647	3,506,089	3,758,577	3,999,467
Surplus or deficit (–)	–1,299,593	–1,086,963	–679,544	–484,602	–582,505	–474,288
On-budget:						
Receipts	1,737,678	1,880,487	2,101,829	2,285,922	2,410,502	2,724,214
Outlays	3,104,453	3,029,363	2,820,836	2,800,036	3,005,957	3,201,064
Surplus or deficit (–)	–1,366,775	–1,148,876	–719,007	–514,114	–595,455	–476,850
Off-budget:						
Receipts	565,788	569,501	673,274	735,565	765,570	800,965
Outlays	498,606	507,588	633,811	706,053	752,620	798,403
Surplus or deficit (–)	67,182	61,913	39,463	29,512	12,950	2,562
OUTSTANDING DEBT, END OF PERIOD						
Gross Federal debt	14,764,222	16,050,921	16,719,434	17,794,483	18,627,577	19,333,800
Held by Federal Government accounts	4,636,035	4,769,790	4,736,721	5,014,605	5,121,246	5,225,309
Held by the public	10,128,187	11,281,131	11,982,713	12,779,877	13,506,331	14,108,492
Federal Reserve System	1,664,660	1,645,285	2,072,283	2,451,743	....	....
Other	8,463,527	9,635,846	9,910,430	10,328,134	....	....
RECEIPTS BY SOURCE						
Total: On-budget and off-budget	2,303,466	2,449,988	2,775,103	3,021,487	3,176,072	3,525,179
Individual income taxes	1,091,473	1,132,206	1,316,405	1,394,568	1,478,076	1,645,628
Corporation income taxes	181,085	242,289	273,506	320,731	341,688	473,304
Social insurance and retirement receipts	818,792	845,314	947,820	1,023,458	1,065,012	1,111,926
On-budget	253,004	275,813	274,546	287,893	299,442	310,961
Off-budget	565,788	569,501	673,274	735,565	765,570	800,965
Excise taxes	72,381	79,061	84,007	93,368	95,898	112,084
Estate and gift taxes	7,399	13,973	18,912	19,300	19,738	21,340
Customs duties and fees	29,519	30,307	31,815	33,926	36,762	38,374
Miscellaneous receipts	102,817	106,838	102,638	136,136	138,898	120,523
Deposits of earnings by Federal Reserve System	82,546	81,957	75,767	99,235	94,015	77,420
All other	20,271	24,881	26,871	36,901	44,883	43,103
Legislative proposals [1]	....	....	....	....	....	2,000
OUTLAYS BY FUNCTION						
Total: On-budget and off-budget	3,603,059	3,536,951	3,454,647	3,506,089	3,758,577	3,999,467
National defense	705,554	677,852	633,446	603,457	597,503	615,515
International affairs	45,685	47,184	46,231	46,684	54,970	55,951
General science, space, and technology	29,466	29,060	28,908	28,570	29,848	30,968
Energy	12,174	14,858	11,042	5,270	9,887	6,224
Natural resources and environment	45,473	41,631	38,145	36,171	41,743	44,311
Agriculture	20,662	17,791	29,678	24,386	21,797	22,288
Commerce and housing credit	–12,573	40,647	–83,199	–94,861	–28,617	–22,568
On-budget	–13,381	37,977	–81,286	–92,330	–28,059	–20,960
Off-budget	808	2,670	–1,913	–2,531	–558	–1,608
Transportation	92,966	93,019	91,673	91,915	92,893	98,742
Community and regional development	23,883	25,132	32,336	20,670	27,234	21,816
Education, training, employment, and social services	101,233	90,823	72,808	90,615	136,756	106,342
Health	372,504	346,742	358,315	409,449	481,232	517,726
Medicare	485,653	471,793	497,826	511,688	536,427	589,720
Income security	597,352	541,344	536,511	513,644	522,496	546,350
Social security	730,811	773,290	813,551	850,533	896,294	944,338
On-budget	101,933	140,387	56,009	25,946	31,094	36,234
Off-budget	628,878	632,903	757,542	824,587	865,200	908,104
Veterans benefits and services	127,189	124,595	138,938	149,616	161,424	180,324
Administration of justice	56,056	56,277	52,601	50,457	58,672	58,512
General government	27,476	28,041	27,737	26,913	22,810	26,983
Net interest	229,962	220,408	220,885	228,956	229,151	283,049
On-budget	345,943	332,801	326,535	329,222	325,160	374,728
Off-budget	–115,981	–112,393	–105,650	–100,266	–96,009	–91,679
Allowances	....	....	....	....	1,875	–24,100
Undistributed offsetting receipts	–88,467	–103,536	–92,785	–88,044	–135,818	–103,024
On-budget	–73,368	–87,944	–76,617	–72,307	–119,805	–86,610
Off-budget	–15,099	–15,592	–16,168	–15,737	–16,013	–16,414

[1] Includes Undistributed Allowance for Immigration Reform.

Note: See Note, Table B–19.

Sources: Department of the Treasury and Office of Management and Budget.

TABLE B–23. Federal and State and local government current receipts and expenditures, national income and product accounts (NIPA), 1965–2014

[Billions of dollars; quarterly data at seasonally adjusted annual rates]

Year or quarter	Total government			Federal Government			State and local government			Addendum: Grants-in-aid to State and local governments
	Current receipts	Current expenditures	Net government saving (NIPA)	Current receipts	Current expenditures	Net Federal Government saving (NIPA)	Current receipts	Current expenditures	Net State and local government saving (NIPA)	
1965	179.7	181.0	−1.4	120.4	125.9	−5.5	65.8	61.7	4.1	6.6
1966	202.1	203.9	−1.8	137.4	144.3	−7.0	74.1	68.9	5.2	9.4
1967	216.9	231.7	−14.8	146.3	165.7	−19.5	81.6	76.9	4.7	10.9
1968	251.2	260.7	−9.5	170.6	184.3	−13.7	92.5	88.2	4.3	11.8
1969	282.5	283.5	−1.0	191.8	196.9	−5.1	104.3	100.2	4.1	13.7
1970	285.7	317.5	−31.8	185.1	219.9	−34.8	118.9	115.9	3.0	18.3
1971	302.1	352.4	−50.2	190.7	241.5	−50.8	133.6	133.0	.6	22.1
1972	345.4	385.9	−40.5	219.0	267.9	−48.9	156.9	148.5	8.4	30.5
1973	388.5	416.6	−28.0	249.2	286.9	−37.7	172.8	163.1	9.6	33.5
1974	430.0	468.3	−38.3	278.5	319.1	−40.6	186.4	184.1	2.3	34.9
1975	440.9	543.5	−102.5	276.8	373.8	−97.0	207.7	213.3	−5.6	43.6
1976	505.0	582.1	−77.1	322.2	402.1	−79.9	231.9	229.1	2.8	49.1
1977	566.7	630.1	−63.5	363.5	435.4	−71.9	257.9	249.5	8.4	54.8
1978	645.4	691.8	−46.4	423.6	483.4	−59.8	285.3	271.9	13.4	63.5
1979	728.6	764.9	−36.3	486.8	531.3	−44.5	305.8	297.6	8.2	64.0
1980	798.7	879.5	−80.9	533.0	619.3	−86.3	335.3	329.9	5.4	69.7
1981	918.0	999.7	−81.7	620.4	706.3	−85.8	367.0	362.9	4.1	69.4
1982	939.9	1,109.6	−169.7	618.0	782.7	−164.6	388.1	393.2	−5.1	66.3
1983	1,001.1	1,204.9	−203.7	644.2	849.2	−205.0	424.8	423.6	1.3	67.9
1984	1,113.9	1,285.4	−171.4	710.7	903.0	−192.3	475.6	454.7	20.9	72.3
1985	1,216.0	1,391.4	−175.4	775.3	970.9	−195.6	516.9	496.7	20.3	76.2
1986	1,291.7	1,483.9	−192.2	817.3	1,030.0	−212.7	556.8	536.4	20.4	82.4
1987	1,405.5	1,556.6	−151.1	899.0	1,062.1	−163.2	585.0	572.9	12.1	78.4
1988	1,505.5	1,645.9	−140.4	961.4	1,118.8	−157.3	629.9	612.9	17.0	85.7
1989	1,629.8	1,779.0	−149.2	1,040.8	1,197.5	−156.6	680.8	673.4	7.4	91.8
1990	1,710.9	1,918.3	−207.4	1,085.7	1,286.6	−200.9	729.6	736.0	−6.5	104.4
1991	1,761.0	2,032.3	−271.3	1,105.6	1,351.8	−246.2	779.5	804.6	−25.1	124.0
1992	1,846.0	2,216.1	−370.2	1,152.1	1,484.7	−332.7	835.6	873.1	−37.5	141.7
1993	1,950.1	2,299.1	−349.0	1,228.8	1,540.6	−311.8	877.1	914.3	−37.2	155.7
1994	2,094.0	2,374.6	−280.7	1,326.7	1,580.4	−253.7	934.1	961.0	−27.0	166.8
1995	2,218.2	2,490.6	−272.4	1,412.9	1,653.7	−240.8	979.8	1,011.4	−31.5	174.5
1996	2,382.3	2,573.2	−191.0	1,531.2	1,709.7	−178.5	1,032.6	1,045.0	−12.5	181.5
1997	2,559.3	2,648.8	−89.5	1,661.6	1,752.8	−91.2	1,085.8	1,084.1	1.7	188.1
1998	2,731.7	2,713.6	18.1	1,783.8	1,781.0	2.7	1,148.7	1,133.3	15.4	200.8
1999	2,903.4	2,827.5	75.9	1,900.7	1,834.1	66.6	1,221.8	1,212.6	9.2	219.2
2000	3,133.1	2,966.7	166.4	2,063.2	1,906.6	156.5	1,303.1	1,293.2	9.9	233.1
2001	3,118.2	3,169.0	−50.8	2,026.8	2,012.4	14.5	1,352.6	1,417.9	−65.3	261.3
2002	2,967.0	3,358.4	−391.4	1,865.8	2,136.3	−270.5	1,388.4	1,509.4	−120.9	287.2
2003	3,042.8	3,567.1	−524.3	1,889.9	2,292.8	−402.9	1,474.6	1,596.0	−121.4	321.7
2004	3,265.1	3,772.7	−507.6	2,022.2	2,421.4	−399.2	1,575.1	1,683.4	−108.4	332.2
2005	3,663.5	4,034.9	−371.3	2,298.1	2,602.8	−304.7	1,708.8	1,775.4	−66.6	343.4
2006	4,001.8	4,268.3	−266.4	2,531.7	2,758.8	−227.0	1,810.9	1,850.3	−39.4	340.8
2007	4,202.4	4,540.8	−338.4	2,660.8	2,926.4	−265.6	1,900.6	1,973.3	−72.7	359.0
2008	4,041.8	4,840.8	−799.0	2,503.7	3,137.7	−634.0	1,909.1	2,074.1	−165.1	371.0
2009	3,689.0	5,209.7	−1,520.8	2,227.8	3,476.6	−1,248.8	1,919.2	2,191.2	−271.9	458.1
2010	3,885.0	5,451.0	−1,566.0	2,391.7	3,720.5	−1,328.7	1,998.5	2,235.8	−237.3	505.3
2011	4,077.6	5,537.6	−1,460.1	2,519.5	3,763.7	−1,244.1	2,030.5	2,246.4	−215.9	472.5
2012	4,301.0	5,612.7	−1,311.7	2,684.1	3,763.2	−1,079.1	2,061.2	2,293.8	−232.6	444.4
2013	4,788.6	5,662.9	−874.3	3,113.0	3,762.1	−649.1	2,125.6	2,350.8	−225.1	450.0
2014 p		5,813.1			3,884.5			2,431.5		502.9
2011: I	4,054.2	5,505.7	−1,451.5	2,514.6	3,751.0	−1,236.4	2,034.3	2,249.4	−215.1	494.7
II	4,071.5	5,585.1	−1,513.6	2,520.2	3,833.4	−1,313.2	2,052.1	2,252.5	−200.5	500.8
III	4,075.5	5,533.6	−1,458.1	2,512.2	3,743.5	−1,231.2	2,015.3	2,242.2	−226.9	452.1
IV	4,109.1	5,526.1	−1,417.0	2,531.0	3,726.8	−1,195.8	2,020.3	2,241.5	−221.2	442.2
2012: I	4,259.2	5,567.5	−1,308.3	2,664.0	3,737.2	−1,073.2	2,032.1	2,267.2	−235.1	436.9
II	4,292.0	5,628.1	−1,336.1	2,684.0	3,782.1	−1,098.0	2,050.6	2,288.6	−238.0	442.6
III	4,275.3	5,611.5	−1,336.2	2,657.4	3,759.6	−1,102.2	2,064.3	2,298.2	−234.0	446.3
IV	4,377.4	5,643.5	−1,266.2	2,730.9	3,773.9	−1,043.1	2,098.0	2,321.1	−223.1	451.5
2013: I	4,648.8	5,612.9	−964.2	2,974.9	3,721.0	−746.1	2,111.1	2,329.1	−218.0	437.2
II	4,896.0	5,678.4	−782.3	3,226.0	3,787.2	−561.2	2,121.2	2,342.3	−221.1	451.2
III	4,715.6	5,695.3	−979.7	3,043.9	3,793.7	−749.8	2,134.2	2,364.1	−229.9	462.5
IV	4,894.1	5,665.0	−770.9	3,207.1	3,746.4	−539.4	2,135.9	2,367.5	−231.6	448.9
2014: I	4,929.5	5,730.5	−801.0	3,242.6	3,802.7	−560.1	2,157.0	2,397.9	−240.9	470.1
II	4,965.6	5,791.3	−825.7	3,276.9	3,875.5	−598.6	2,193.8	2,420.9	−227.1	505.1
III	5,046.7	5,885.6	−838.9	3,331.1	3,953.2	−622.1	2,233.9	2,450.7	−216.8	518.3
IV p		5,845.0			3,906.5			2,456.5		518.0

Note: Federal grants-in-aid to State and local governments are reflected in Federal current expenditures and State and local current receipts. Total government current receipts and expenditures have been adjusted to eliminate this duplication.

Source: Department of Commerce (Bureau of Economic Analysis).

TABLE B–24. State and local government revenues and expenditures, fiscal years 1954–2012

[Millions of dollars]

Fiscal year [1]	General revenues by source [2]							General expenditures by function [2]				
	Total	Property taxes	Sales and gross receipts taxes	Individual income taxes	Corporation net income taxes	Revenue from Federal Government	All other [3]	Total [4]	Education	Highways	Public welfare [4]	All other [4,5]
1954	29,012	9,967	7,276	1,127	778	2,966	6,898	30,701	10,557	5,527	3,060	11,557
1955	31,073	10,735	7,643	1,237	744	3,131	7,583	33,724	11,907	6,452	3,168	12,197
1956	34,670	11,749	8,691	1,538	890	3,335	8,467	36,715	13,224	6,953	3,139	13,399
1957	38,164	12,864	9,467	1,754	984	3,843	9,252	40,375	14,134	7,816	3,485	14,940
1958	41,219	14,047	9,829	1,759	1,018	4,865	9,701	44,851	15,919	8,567	3,818	16,547
1959	45,306	14,983	10,437	1,994	1,001	6,377	10,514	48,887	17,283	9,592	4,136	17,876
1960	50,505	16,405	11,849	2,463	1,180	6,974	11,634	51,876	18,719	9,428	4,404	19,325
1961	54,037	18,002	12,463	2,613	1,266	7,131	12,562	56,201	20,574	9,844	4,720	21,063
1962	58,252	19,054	13,494	3,037	1,308	7,871	13,488	60,206	22,216	10,357	5,084	22,549
1963	62,891	20,089	14,456	3,269	1,505	8,722	14,850	64,815	23,776	11,135	5,481	24,423
1963–64	68,443	21,241	15,762	3,791	1,695	10,002	15,952	69,302	26,286	11,664	5,766	25,586
1964–65	74,000	22,583	17,118	4,090	1,929	11,029	17,251	74,678	28,563	12,221	6,315	27,579
1965–66	83,036	24,670	19,085	4,760	2,038	13,214	19,269	82,843	33,287	12,770	6,757	30,029
1966–67	91,197	26,047	20,530	5,825	2,227	15,370	21,198	93,350	37,919	13,932	8,218	33,281
1967–68	101,264	27,747	22,911	7,308	2,518	17,181	23,599	102,411	41,158	14,481	9,857	36,915
1968–69	114,550	30,673	26,519	8,908	3,180	19,153	26,117	116,728	47,238	15,417	12,110	41,963
1969–70	130,756	34,054	30,322	10,812	3,738	21,857	29,973	131,332	52,718	16,427	14,679	47,508
1970–71	144,927	37,852	33,233	11,900	3,424	26,146	32,372	150,674	59,413	18,095	18,226	54,940
1971–72	167,535	42,877	37,518	15,227	4,416	31,342	36,156	168,549	65,813	19,021	21,117	62,598
1972–73	190,222	45,283	42,047	17,994	5,425	39,264	40,210	181,357	69,713	18,615	23,582	69,447
1973–74	207,670	47,705	46,098	19,491	6,015	41,820	46,542	199,222	75,833	19,946	25,085	78,358
1974–75	228,171	51,491	49,815	21,454	6,642	47,034	51,735	230,722	87,858	22,528	28,156	92,180
1975–76	256,176	57,001	54,547	24,575	7,273	55,589	57,191	256,731	97,216	23,907	32,604	103,004
1976–77	285,157	62,527	60,641	29,246	9,174	62,444	61,125	274,215	102,780	23,058	35,906	112,472
1977–78	315,960	66,422	67,596	33,176	10,738	69,592	68,435	296,984	110,758	24,609	39,140	122,478
1978–79	343,236	64,944	74,247	36,932	12,128	75,164	79,822	327,517	119,448	28,440	41,898	137,731
1979–80	382,322	68,499	79,927	42,080	13,321	83,029	95,467	369,086	133,211	33,311	47,288	155,276
1980–81	423,404	74,969	85,971	46,426	14,143	90,294	111,599	407,449	145,784	34,603	54,105	172,957
1981–82	457,654	82,067	93,613	50,738	15,028	87,282	128,925	436,733	154,282	34,520	57,996	189,935
1982–83	486,753	89,105	100,247	55,129	14,258	90,007	138,008	466,516	163,876	36,655	60,906	205,080
1983–84	542,730	96,457	114,097	64,871	16,798	96,935	153,571	505,008	176,108	39,419	66,414	223,068
1984–85	598,121	103,757	126,376	70,361	19,152	106,158	172,317	553,899	192,686	44,989	71,479	244,745
1985–86	641,486	111,709	135,005	74,365	19,994	113,099	187,314	605,623	210,819	49,368	75,868	269,568
1986–87	686,860	121,203	144,091	83,935	22,425	114,857	200,350	657,134	226,619	52,355	82,650	295,510
1987–88	726,762	132,212	156,452	88,350	23,663	117,602	208,482	704,921	242,683	55,621	89,090	317,527
1988–89	786,129	142,400	166,336	97,806	25,926	125,824	227,838	762,360	263,898	58,105	97,879	342,479
1989–90	849,502	155,613	177,885	105,640	23,566	136,802	249,996	834,818	288,148	61,057	110,518	375,094
1990–91	902,207	167,999	185,570	109,341	22,242	154,099	262,955	908,108	309,302	64,937	130,402	403,467
1991–92	979,137	180,337	197,731	115,638	23,880	179,174	282,376	981,253	324,652	67,351	158,723	430,526
1992–93	1,041,643	189,744	209,649	123,235	26,417	198,663	293,935	1,030,434	342,287	68,370	170,705	449,072
1993–94	1,100,490	197,141	223,628	128,810	28,320	215,492	307,099	1,077,665	353,287	72,067	183,394	468,916
1994–95	1,169,505	203,451	237,268	137,931	31,406	228,771	330,677	1,149,863	378,273	77,109	196,703	497,779
1995–96	1,222,821	209,440	248,993	146,844	32,009	234,891	350,645	1,193,276	398,859	79,092	197,354	517,971
1996–97	1,289,237	218,877	261,418	159,042	33,820	244,847	371,233	1,249,984	418,416	82,062	203,779	545,727
1997–98	1,365,762	230,150	274,883	175,630	34,412	255,048	395,639	1,318,042	450,365	87,214	208,120	572,343
1998–99	1,434,029	239,672	290,993	189,309	33,922	270,628	409,505	1,402,369	483,259	93,018	218,957	607,134
1999–2000	1,541,322	249,178	309,290	211,661	36,059	291,950	443,186	1,506,797	521,612	101,336	237,336	646,512
2000–01	1,647,161	263,689	320,217	226,334	35,296	324,033	477,592	1,626,063	563,572	107,235	261,622	693,634
2001–02	1,684,879	279,191	324,123	202,832	28,152	360,546	490,035	1,736,866	594,694	115,295	285,464	741,413
2002–03	1,763,212	296,683	330,787	199,407	31,369	389,264	508,702	1,821,917	621,335	117,696	310,783	772,102
2003–04	1,887,397	317,941	361,027	215,215	33,716	423,112	536,386	1,908,543	655,182	117,215	340,523	795,622
2004–05	2,026,034	335,779	384,266	242,273	43,256	438,558	581,902	2,012,110	688,314	126,350	365,295	832,151
2005–06	2,197,475	364,559	417,735	268,667	53,081	452,975	640,458	2,123,663	728,917	136,502	373,846	884,398
2006–07	2,330,611	388,905	440,470	290,278	60,955	464,914	685,089	2,264,035	774,170	145,011	389,259	955,595
2007–08	2,421,977	409,540	449,945	304,902	57,231	477,441	722,919	2,406,183	826,061	153,831	408,920	1,017,372
2008–09	2,429,672	434,818	434,128	270,942	46,280	537,949	705,555	2,500,796	851,689	154,338	437,184	1,057,586
2009–10	2,510,846	443,947	435,571	261,510	44,108	623,801	701,909	2,542,231	860,118	155,912	460,230	1,065,971
2010–11	2,618,037	445,771	463,979	285,293	48,422	647,606	726,966	2,583,805	862,271	153,895	494,682	1,072,957
2011–12	2,598,043	446,099	476,447	307,335	49,031	584,499	734,632	2,591,475	869,196	158,562	489,505	1,074,212

[1] Fiscal years not the same for all governments. See Note.

[2] Excludes revenues or expenditures of publicly owned utilities and liquor stores and of insurance-trust activities. Intergovernmental receipts and payments between State and local governments are also excluded.

[3] Includes motor vehicle license taxes, other taxes, and charges and miscellaneous revenues.

[4] Includes intergovernmental payments to the Federal Government.

[5] Includes expenditures for libraries, hospitals, health, employment security administration, veterans' services, air transportation, sea and inland port facilities, parking facilities, police protection, fire protection, correction, protective inspection and regulation, sewerage, natural resources, parks and recreation, housing and community development, solid waste management, financial administration, judicial and legal, general public buildings, other government administration, interest on general debt, and other general expenditures, not elsewhere classified.

Note: Except for States listed, data for fiscal years listed from 1963–64 to 2011–12 are the aggregation of data for government fiscal years that ended in the 12-month period from July 1 to June 30 of those years; Texas used August and Alabama and Michigan used September as end dates. Data for 1963 and earlier years include data for government fiscal years ending during that particular calendar year.

Source: Department of Commerce (Bureau of the Census).

Table B–25. U.S. Treasury securities outstanding by kind of obligation, 1976–2014

[Billions of dollars]

End of fiscal year or month	Total Treasury securities outstanding [1]	Marketable							Nonmarketable				
		Total [2]	Treasury bills	Treasury notes	Treasury bonds	Treasury inflation-protected securities			Total	U.S. savings securities [3]	Foreign series [4]	Government account series	Other [5]
						Total	Notes	Bonds					
1976	609.2	392.6	161.2	191.8	39.6				216.7	69.7	21.5	120.6	4.9
1977	697.8	443.5	156.1	241.7	45.7				254.3	75.6	21.8	140.1	16.8
1978	767.2	485.2	160.9	267.9	56.4				282.0	79.9	21.7	153.3	27.1
1979	819.1	506.7	161.4	274.2	71.1				312.4	80.6	28.1	176.4	27.4
1980	906.8	594.5	199.8	310.9	83.8				312.3	73.0	25.2	189.8	24.2
1981	996.8	683.2	223.4	363.6	96.2				313.6	68.3	20.5	201.1	23.7
1982	1,141.2	824.4	277.9	442.9	103.6				316.8	67.6	14.6	210.5	24.1
1983	1,376.3	1,024.0	340.7	557.5	125.7				352.3	70.6	11.5	234.7	35.6
1984	1,560.4	1,176.6	356.8	661.7	158.1				383.8	73.7	8.8	259.5	41.8
1985	1,822.3	1,360.2	384.2	776.4	199.5				462.1	78.2	6.6	313.9	63.3
1986	2,124.9	1,564.3	410.7	896.9	241.7				560.5	87.8	4.1	365.9	102.8
1987	2,349.4	1,676.0	378.3	1,005.1	277.6				673.4	98.5	4.4	440.7	129.8
1988	2,601.4	1,802.9	398.5	1,089.6	299.9				798.5	107.8	6.3	536.5	148.0
1989	2,837.9	1,892.8	406.6	1,133.2	338.0				945.2	115.7	6.8	663.7	159.0
1990	3,212.7	2,092.8	482.5	1,218.1	377.2				1,119.9	123.9	36.0	779.4	180.6
1991	3,664.5	2,390.7	564.6	1,387.7	423.4				1,273.9	135.4	41.6	908.4	188.5
1992	4,063.8	2,677.5	634.3	1,566.3	461.8				1,386.3	150.3	37.0	1,011.0	188.0
1993	4,410.7	2,904.9	658.4	1,734.2	497.4				1,505.8	169.1	42.5	1,114.3	179.9
1994	4,691.7	3,091.6	697.3	1,867.5	511.8				1,600.1	178.6	42.0	1,211.7	167.8
1995	4,953.0	3,260.4	742.5	1,980.3	522.6				1,692.6	183.5	41.0	1,324.3	143.8
1996	5,220.8	3,418.4	761.2	2,098.7	543.5				1,802.4	184.1	37.5	1,454.7	126.1
1997	5,407.6	3,439.6	701.9	2,122.2	576.2	24.4	24.4		1,968.0	182.7	34.9	1,608.5	141.9
1998	5,518.7	3,331.0	637.6	2,009.1	610.4	58.8	41.9	17.0	2,187.6	180.8	35.1	1,777.3	194.4
1999	5,647.3	3,233.0	653.2	1,828.8	643.7	92.4	67.6	24.8	2,414.3	180.0	31.0	2,005.2	198.1
2000	5,622.1	2,992.8	616.2	1,611.3	635.3	115.0	81.6	33.4	2,629.4	177.7	25.4	2,242.9	183.3
2001 [1]	5,807.5	2,930.7	734.9	1,433.0	613.0	134.9	95.1	39.7	2,876.7	186.5	18.3	2,492.1	179.9
2002	6,228.2	3,136.7	868.3	1,521.6	593.0	138.9	93.7	45.1	3,091.5	193.3	12.5	2,707.3	178.4
2003	6,783.2	3,460.7	918.2	1,799.5	576.9	166.1	120.0	46.1	3,322.5	201.6	11.0	2,912.2	197.7
2004	7,379.1	3,846.1	961.5	2,109.6	552.0	223.0	164.5	58.5	3,533.0	204.2	5.9	3,130.0	192.9
2005	7,932.7	4,084.9	914.3	2,328.8	520.7	307.1	229.1	78.0	3,847.8	203.6	3.1	3,380.6	260.5
2006	8,507.0	4,303.0	911.5	2,447.2	534.7	395.6	293.9	101.7	4,203.9	203.7	3.0	3,722.7	274.5
2007	9,007.7	4,448.1	958.1	2,458.0	561.1	456.9	335.7	121.2	4,559.5	197.1	3.0	4,026.8	332.6
2008	10,024.7	5,236.0	1,489.8	2,624.8	582.9	524.5	380.2	144.3	4,788.7	194.3	3.0	4,297.7	293.8
2009	11,909.8	7,009.7	1,992.5	3,773.8	679.8	551.7	396.2	155.5	4,900.1	192.5	4.9	4,454.3	248.4
2010	13,561.6	8,498.3	1,788.5	5,255.9	849.9	593.8	421.1	172.7	5,063.3	188.7	4.2	4,645.3	225.1
2011	14,790.3	9,624.5	1,477.5	6,412.5	1,020.4	705.7	509.4	196.3	5,165.8	185.1	3.0	4,793.9	183.8
2012	16,066.2	10,749.7	1,616.0	7,120.7	1,198.2	807.7	584.7	223.0	5,316.5	183.8	3.0	4,939.3	190.4
2013	16,738.2	11,596.2	1,530.0	7,758.0	1,366.2	936.4	685.5	250.8	5,142.0	180.0	3.0	4,803.1	156.0
2014	17,824.1	12,294.2	1,411.0	8,167.8	1,534.1	1,044.7	765.2	279.5	5,529.9	176.7	3.0	5,212.5	137.7
2013: Jan	16,433.8	11,115.3	1,607.9	7,386.2	1,253.2	860.9	629.7	231.2	5,318.5	182.2	3.0	4,943.7	189.6
Feb	16,687.3	11,308.4	1,742.0	7,422.5	1,269.2	867.7	628.1	239.6	5,379.0	182.0	3.0	5,008.1	185.8
Mar	16,771.6	11,398.3	1,791.0	7,435.0	1,282.2	883.0	642.8	240.3	5,373.4	181.7	3.0	4,999.0	189.7
Apr	16,828.8	11,416.8	1,694.9	7,528.0	1,295.2	891.6	649.4	242.2	5,412.1	181.5	3.0	5,032.2	195.4
May	16,738.8	11,397.3	1,606.9	7,564.9	1,311.2	907.2	664.3	242.9	5,341.5	181.2	3.0	4,958.8	198.5
June	16,738.2	11,394.9	1,569.9	7,581.7	1,324.2	913.4	663.7	249.7	5,343.3	180.9	3.0	4,972.7	186.7
July	16,738.6	11,483.5	1,556.0	7,680.1	1,337.2	904.6	654.5	250.1	5,255.1	180.6	3.0	4,901.6	170.0
Aug	16,738.8	11,586.3	1,638.0	7,666.5	1,353.2	923.0	672.2	250.7	5,152.5	180.2	3.0	4,809.7	159.5
Sept	16,738.2	11,596.2	1,530.0	7,758.0	1,366.2	936.4	685.5	250.8	5,142.0	180.0	3.0	4,803.1	156.0
Oct	17,156.1	11,695.0	1,545.0	7,811.3	1,379.2	944.6	686.3	258.3	5,461.1	179.7	3.0	5,125.9	152.5
Nov	17,217.2	11,791.7	1,621.0	7,801.8	1,395.2	958.8	700.2	258.6	5,425.5	179.6	3.0	5,092.1	150.9
Dec	17,352.0	11,869.4	1,592.0	7,881.7	1,408.2	972.6	714.7	257.9	5,482.5	179.2	3.0	5,152.9	147.5
2014: Jan	17,293.0	11,825.3	1,486.0	7,929.1	1,421.2	959.1	701.7	257.4	5,467.7	178.8	3.0	5,143.6	142.3
Feb	17,463.2	12,011.4	1,614.0	7,949.3	1,437.2	968.0	701.6	266.4	5,451.8	178.6	3.0	5,131.1	139.1
Mar	17,601.2	12,135.5	1,652.0	7,992.9	1,450.2	984.5	717.1	267.3	5,465.7	178.3	3.0	5,144.0	140.4
Apr	17,508.4	12,016.5	1,459.0	8,034.2	1,463.2	989.2	720.9	268.3	5,491.9	178.1	3.0	5,166.5	144.3
May	17,517.2	12,048.6	1,449.0	8,027.9	1,479.1	1,008.6	738.6	270.0	5,468.5	178.0	3.0	5,143.4	144.2
June	17,632.6	12,084.2	1,388.0	8,089.3	1,492.1	1,019.2	741.1	278.1	5,548.3	177.8	3.0	5,223.9	143.8
July	17,687.1	12,162.9	1,410.0	8,123.3	1,505.1	1,013.8	734.8	279.0	5,524.3	177.3	3.0	5,203.1	140.8
Aug	17,749.2	12,245.3	1,452.0	8,116.6	1,521.1	1,031.9	752.4	279.6	5,503.9	177.0	3.0	5,186.5	137.4
Sept	17,824.1	12,294.2	1,411.0	8,167.8	1,534.1	1,044.7	765.2	279.5	5,529.9	176.7	3.0	5,212.5	137.7
Oct	17,937.2	12,362.6	1,413.9	8,199.7	1,547.1	1,050.2	764.0	286.2	5,574.6	176.6	.3	5,258.7	139.0
Nov	18,005.6	12,421.4	1,439.9	8,189.9	1,563.2	1,063.9	777.5	286.4	5,584.1	176.4	.3	5,263.1	144.4
Dec	18,141.4	12,518.4	1,457.9	8,229.2	1,576.2	1,077.6	791.9	285.7	5,623.0	175.9	.3	5,298.2	148.6

[1] Data beginning with January 2001 are interest-bearing and non-interest-bearing securities; prior data are interest-bearing securities only.

[2] Data from 1986 to 2002 and 2005 to 2014 include Federal Financing Bank securities, not shown separately. Beginning with data for January 2014, includes Floating Rate Notes, not shown separately.

[3] Through 1996, series is U.S. savings bonds. Beginning 1997, includes U.S. retirement plan bonds, U.S. individual retirement bonds, and U.S. savings notes previously included in "other" nonmarketable securities.

[4] Nonmarketable certificates of indebtedness, notes, bonds, and bills in the Treasury foreign series of dollar-denominated and foreign-currency-denominated issues.

[5] Includes depository bonds; retirement plan bonds through 1996; Rural Electrification Administration bonds; State and local bonds; special issues held only by U.S. Government agencies and trust funds and the Federal home loan banks; for the period July 2003 through February 2004, depositary compensation securities; and beginning August 2008, Hope bonds for the HOPE For Homeowners Program.

Note: In fiscal year 1976, the fiscal year was on a July 1–June 30 basis; beginning with October 1976 (fiscal year 1977), the fiscal year is on an October 1–September 30 basis.

Source: Department of the Treasury.

TABLE B–26. Estimated ownership of U.S. Treasury securities, 2001–2014

[Billions of dollars]

End of month	Total public debt [1]	Federal Reserve and Intra-govern-mental hold-ings [2]	Held by private investors									
			Total privately held	De-pository institu-tions [3]	U.S. savings bonds [4]	Pension funds		Insurance compa-nies	Mutual funds [6]	State and local govern-ments	Foreign and inter-national [7]	Other inves-tors [8]
						Private [5]	State and local govern-ments					
2001: Mar	5,773.7	2,880.9	2,892.8	196.0	184.8	153.4	177.3	113.3	225.5	316.9	1,012.5	513.1
June	5,726.8	3,004.2	2,722.6	195.5	185.5	148.5	183.1	112.1	221.2	324.8	983.3	368.5
Sept	5,807.5	3,027.8	2,779.7	195.7	186.5	149.9	166.8	111.5	235.2	321.2	992.2	420.7
Dec	5,943.4	3,123.9	2,819.5	192.8	190.4	145.8	155.1	115.4	261.2	328.4	1,040.1	390.2
2002: Mar	6,006.0	3,156.8	2,849.2	201.7	192.0	152.7	163.3	125.6	261.0	327.6	1,057.2	368.3
June	6,126.5	3,276.7	2,849.8	217.4	192.8	152.1	153.9	136.0	245.8	333.6	1,123.1	295.0
Sept	6,228.2	3,303.5	2,924.7	219.6	193.3	154.5	156.3	149.4	248.3	338.6	1,188.6	276.1
Dec	6,405.7	3,387.2	3,018.5	231.8	194.9	154.0	158.9	161.3	272.1	354.7	1,235.6	255.3
2003: Mar	6,460.8	3,390.8	3,070.0	162.6	196.9	166.0	162.1	163.5	282.7	350.0	1,275.2	310.9
June	6,670.1	3,505.4	3,164.7	155.0	199.2	170.5	161.3	166.0	285.4	347.9	1,371.9	307.7
Sept	6,783.2	3,515.3	3,267.9	158.0	201.6	168.2	155.5	168.5	271.0	356.2	1,443.3	345.8
Dec	6,998.0	3,620.1	3,377.9	165.3	203.9	172.4	148.6	166.4	271.2	361.8	1,523.1	365.2
2004: Mar	7,131.1	3,628.3	3,502.8	172.7	204.5	169.8	143.6	172.4	275.2	372.8	1,670.0	321.8
June	7,274.3	3,742.8	3,531.5	167.8	204.6	173.1	134.9	174.6	252.3	390.1	1,735.4	298.7
Sept	7,379.1	3,772.0	3,607.1	146.3	204.2	173.7	140.1	182.9	249.4	393.0	1,794.5	322.9
Dec	7,596.1	3,905.6	3,690.5	133.4	204.5	173.3	149.4	188.5	256.1	404.9	1,849.3	331.3
2005: Mar	7,776.9	3,921.6	3,855.3	149.4	204.2	176.8	157.2	193.3	264.3	429.3	1,952.2	328.7
June	7,836.5	4,033.5	3,803.0	135.9	204.2	180.4	165.9	195.0	248.6	461.1	1,877.5	334.4
Sept	7,932.7	4,067.8	3,864.9	134.0	203.6	183.6	161.1	200.7	246.6	493.6	1,929.6	312.0
Dec	8,170.4	4,199.8	3,970.6	129.4	205.2	184.4	154.2	202.3	254.1	512.2	2,033.9	294.8
2006: Mar	8,371.2	4,257.2	4,114.0	113.0	206.0	186.2	152.9	200.3	254.2	515.7	2,082.1	403.6
June	8,420.0	4,389.2	4,030.8	119.5	205.2	191.6	149.6	196.1	243.4	531.6	1,977.8	416.1
Sept	8,507.0	4,432.8	4,074.2	113.6	203.7	201.7	149.3	196.8	234.2	542.3	2,025.3	407.3
Dec	8,680.2	4,558.1	4,122.1	114.8	202.4	216.1	153.4	197.9	248.2	570.5	2,103.1	315.6
2007: Mar	8,849.7	4,576.6	4,273.1	119.8	200.3	219.6	156.3	185.4	263.2	608.3	2,194.8	325.3
June	8,867.7	4,715.1	4,152.6	110.4	198.6	220.6	162.3	168.9	257.6	637.8	2,192.0	204.4
Sept	9,007.7	4,738.0	4,269.7	119.7	197.1	225.4	153.2	155.1	292.7	643.1	2,235.3	248.0
Dec	9,229.2	4,833.5	4,395.7	129.8	196.5	228.7	144.2	141.9	343.5	647.8	2,353.2	210.1
2008: Mar	9,437.6	4,694.7	4,742.9	125.0	195.4	240.1	135.4	152.1	466.7	646.4	2,506.3	275.6
June	9,492.0	4,685.8	4,806.2	112.7	195.0	243.8	135.5	159.4	440.3	635.1	2,587.4	297.1
Sept	10,024.7	4,692.7	5,332.0	130.0	194.3	252.7	136.7	163.4	631.4	614.0	2,802.4	407.2
Dec	10,699.8	4,806.4	5,893.4	105.0	194.1	259.7	129.9	171.4	758.2	601.4	3,077.2	596.5
2009: Mar	11,126.9	4,785.2	6,341.7	125.7	194.0	272.5	137.0	191.0	721.1	588.2	3,265.7	846.6
June	11,545.3	5,026.8	6,518.5	140.8	193.6	281.6	144.6	200.0	711.8	588.5	3,460.8	796.7
Sept	11,909.8	5,127.1	6,782.7	198.2	192.5	285.5	145.6	210.2	668.5	583.6	3,570.6	928.0
Dec	12,311.3	5,276.9	7,034.4	202.5	191.3	295.6	151.4	222.0	668.8	585.6	3,685.1	1,032.2
2010: Mar	12,773.1	5,259.8	7,513.3	269.3	190.2	304.4	153.6	225.7	678.5	584.1	3,877.9	1,229.6
June	13,201.8	5,345.1	7,856.7	266.1	189.6	316.1	150.1	231.8	676.8	583.3	4,070.0	1,372.8
Sept	13,561.6	5,350.5	8,211.1	322.8	188.7	327.4	150.4	240.6	671.0	585.0	4,324.2	1,400.9
Dec	14,025.2	5,656.2	8,368.9	319.3	187.9	336.9	159.3	248.4	719.8	593.5	4,435.6	1,368.4
2011: Mar	14,270.0	5,958.9	8,311.1	321.0	186.7	346.3	163.8	253.5	755.5	582.4	4,481.4	1,220.4
June	14,343.1	6,220.4	8,122.7	279.4	186.0	251.7	164.1	254.8	775.8	569.4	4,690.6	950.8
Sept	14,790.3	6,328.0	8,462.4	293.8	185.1	371.5	162.0	259.6	818.7	558.0	4,912.1	901.4
Dec	15,222.8	6,439.6	8,783.3	279.7	185.2	387.3	168.5	271.8	902.4	561.7	5,006.9	1,019.8
2012: Mar	15,582.3	6,397.2	9,185.1	317.0	184.8	397.8	178.9	271.5	976.6	567.1	5,145.1	1,146.3
June	15,855.5	6,475.8	9,379.7	303.2	184.7	413.4	181.6	268.6	971.9	589.4	5,310.9	1,156.0
Sept	16,066.2	6,446.8	9,619.4	338.2	183.8	429.2	183.3	269.5	989.2	598.5	5,476.1	1,151.6
Dec	16,432.7	6,523.7	9,909.1	347.7	182.5	443.8	187.3	270.6	1,038.4	608.2	5,573.8	1,256.8
2013: Mar	16,771.6	6,656.8	10,114.8	338.9	181.7	453.3	191.6	266.6	1,108.0	617.3	5,725.0	1,232.3
June	16,738.2	6,773.3	9,964.9	300.2	180.9	456.1	199.3	262.6	1,086.0	620.2	5,595.0	1,264.5
Sept	16,738.2	6,834.2	9,904.0	293.2	180.0	366.8	202.4	262.3	1,098.8	591.7	5,652.8	1,256.1
Dec	17,352.0	7,205.3	10,146.6	321.1	179.2	492.3	203.4	264.3	1,125.8	593.6	5,792.6	1,174.3
2014: Mar	17,601.2	7,301.5	10,299.7	368.3	178.3	499.1	208.5	267.6	1,127.4	593.6	5,948.4	1,108.5
June	17,632.6	7,461.0	10,171.6	407.2	177.6	505.8	235.7	272.9	1,063.2	583.9	6,011.5	913.9
Sept	17,824.1	7,490.8	10,333.2	466.0	176.7	517.5	249.5	278.8	1,102.3	573.2	6,066.4	902.9
Dec	18,141.4	7,578.9	10,562.6	....	175.9	....	....	....	....	....	....	....

[1] Face value.
[2] Federal Reserve holdings exclude Treasury securities held under repurchase agreements.
[3] Includes U.S. chartered depository institutions, foreign banking offices in U.S., banks in U.S. affiliated areas, credit unions, and bank holding companies.
[4] Current accrual value includes myRA.
[5] Includes Treasury securities held by the Federal Employees Retirement System Thrift Savings Plan "G Fund."
[6] Includes money market mutual funds, mutual funds, and closed-end investment companies.
[7] Includes nonmarketable foreign series, Treasury securities, and Treasury deposit funds. Excludes Treasury securities held under repurchase agreements in custody accounts at the Federal Reserve Bank of New York. Estimates reflect benchmarks to this series at differing intervals; for further detail, see *Treasury Bulletin* and http://www.treasury.gov/resource-center/data-chart-center/tic/pages/index.aspx.
[8] Includes individuals, Government-sponsored enterprises, brokers and dealers, bank personal trusts and estates, corporate and noncorporate businesses, and other investors.

Note: Data shown in this table are as of January 22, 2015.

Source: Department of the Treasury.